A Reader in Canadian Planning

Linking Theory and Practice

A Reader in Canadian Planning

Linking Theory and Practice

Edited by

Jill Grant
Dalhousie University

THOMSON

™

NELSON

Australia   Canada   Mexico   Singapore   Spain   United Kingdom   United States

THOMSON

NELSON

A Reader in Canadian Planning:
Linking Theory and Practice
Edited by Jill Grant

Associate Vice President
Editorial Director:
Evelyn Veitch

Editor-in-Chief,
Higher Education:
Anne Williams

Executive Editor:
Paul Fam

Marketing Manager:
Sean Chamberland

Developmental Editor:
Katherine Goodes, MY EDITOR

Photo Researcher and
Permissions Coordinator:
Donna Dudinsky

Senior Content Production
Manager:
Tammy Scherer

Production Service:
International Typesetting
and Composition

Copy Editor:
Elaine Freedman

Proofreader:
Martha Ghent

Indexer:
Stephen Ingle

Manufacturing Coordinator:
Pauline Long

Design Director:
Ken Phipps

Interior Design:
Katherine Strain

Cover Design:
Glenn Toddun

Cover Image:
background image: Courtesy of Steffen
Käubler, CBCL Ltd. for Halifax Regional
Municipality; *front cover:* City of Vancouver

Compositor:
International Typesetting
and Composition

Printer:
Thomson/West

Library and Archives Canada
Cataloguing in Publication Data

A reader in Canadian planning: linking
theory and practice/edited by Jill Grant.

Articles first appeared in Plan Canada.
Includes bibliographical references
and index.

ISBN-13: 978-0-17-610357-6
ISBN-10: 0-17-610357-0

1. City planning—Canada—Textbooks.
I. Grant, Jill

HT395.C3R42 2007   307.1'20971
C2007-900108-4

To all the planners who offer visions of better futures while working tirelessly to resolve the problems they inherit.

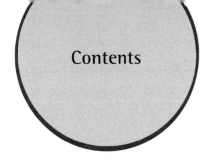

Contents

Section 1   *Background and Basics*

Section 2 *Philosophy and Practice* 135

Section 3   *Techniques and Tactics*

List of Figures

List of Tables

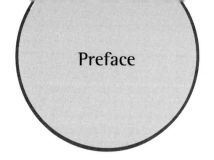

Preface

A Canadian Voice on Planning

In 1919, under the leadership of Thomas Adams, Canadian planners formed a professional organization, the Town Planning Institute of Canada. The institute soon established a publication, the *Journal of the Town Planning Institute of Canada*, which presented articles by such luminaries as Ebenezer Howard and such influential Canadian planners as Noulan Cauchon and Alfred Buckley. Although the national government saw town planning as a useful strategy for its rapidly expanding cities in the 1910s and early 1920s, it lost interest by the mid-1920s. After Kitchener, Ontario, adopted the first zoning bylaw in 1924, zoning swept the nation and effectively replaced planning. The institute and its journal ceased operation, and, in the wake of the Great Depression, planning disappeared from the national agenda.

After World War II, cities began looking to planning as a strategic device for managing growth. In 1959, the reconstituted Canadian Institute of Planners (CIP) reestablished a professional journal, calling it *Plan Canada*. This became the official voice of Canadian planning, publishing two or three times a year. In the early years, the journal included many scholarly articles, especially about the history of planning and on the fundamentals of land use planning and zoning. In 1968, Len Gertler, the first editor of *Plan Canada*, compiled a reader of materials from the journal, *Planning the Canadian Environment*. The 20 articles covered a range of themes and demonstrated the developing character of Canadian planning and its special interest in such issues as regional disparity.

Over the decades, *Plan Canada* went through a range of formats and several sets of editors (including me from January 2001 through December 2004). With the planning profession becoming increasingly well-established, the journal featured an eclectic mix of articles reporting on projects and trying to apply the latest planning theory to Canadian practice. By the 1980s, a clear Canadian voice about what planning could and should mean had emerged. The pages of *Plan Canada* offer a wealth of insights into the special features of Canadian practice. Practitioners and scholars from many communities and interests published their work in the journal, generating an ongoing debate about the character of Canadian settlements and the direction of the planning profession. Some high-profile international authors, including John Friedmann, John Forester, Leonie Sandercock, and Sir Peter Hall, also published in *Plan Canada*, thereby influencing Canadian discussions.

I have selected all of the articles for this reader from *Plan Canada*, except for my introductions to the chapters. Most papers were published after 1980. All make a useful contribution to an international understanding of planning practice and the application of planning theory. Most are by Canadian authors, although I have included several noteworthy pieces by others. The articles reveal and influence the particular historical and theoretical conception of planning from a Canadian perspective.

I used several criteria for selecting appropriate articles, mindful of space constraints that forced difficult choices. I wanted well-written and thoughtful articles that would interest students in studying planning and becoming planners. I hoped to create a compilation that would be useful for practitioners preparing to take the written exam for membership in the professional institute. I looked for pieces that have continuing relevance because of the questions they treat or the approaches they take. I selected applied cases from practice that might contribute to our thinking about the key theoretical questions in planning.

While I could have created a reader of articles on Canadian planning by selecting papers from various academic planning journals, I find coherence in the material from *Plan Canada*, grounded as it is in the nitty-gritty of practice. The journal reflects the continuing discussions within the profession about what it takes and what it means to plan communities in this vast and changing country. As a professional journal, *Plan Canada* brings the concerns of practitioners and academics together in a way that is rare in academic journals: It explicitly links practice with theory. Framing these articles in *A Reader in Canadian Planning* allows us to see how the profession presents itself to its members and to the wider community. Here we learn how planners define and situate their work and how they respond to the pressing issues of the times.

I have organized the book in three parts. Section I, Background and Basics, introduces Canadian planning and explores its history, context, ethics, and processes. Section II, Philosophy and Practice, explores the themes of uncertainty, diversity, beauty, health and safety, and sustainability as motivations for Canadian planning. Section III, Techniques and Tactics, examines issues in practice: land use, transportation, small and remote communities, the tools of the trade, and debates about growth. At the end of each chapter, I offer study questions to suggest ideas for further research or investigation.

Acknowledgements

Without the enormous contribution of generations of authors and editors of *Plan Canada*, I could never have contemplated putting this collection together. I thank the many authors whose work appears here and the Canadian Institute of Planners (CIP), holder of the copyright for the articles published in the journal, for granting permission for us to edit, abridge, and reproduce the papers. Although I tried to contact all the authors to let them view the edited versions of their articles, I could not find every one. I hope that those I could not reach would be pleased to see the book bring their work to a new generation of planners. I'm grateful that several authors updated their work and supplied photographs or illustrations for this edition.

I owe a special debt to Linda McFadyen, chair of the CIP publications committee, for believing in the project and for persuading the institute of its merit. CIP generously contributed funds for the research assistance that helped to make the book possible.

The staff of the publisher, Thomson Nelson, went beyond the call of duty. Anthony Rezek persuaded the press to provide financial support for research assistance. Maya Bahar and Katherine Goodes offered welcomed editorial guidance. Thanks also to Elaine Freedman for her inspired copy editing and general good humour through the final stages of the process.

I owe a special round of thanks to my excellent research assistants. Mary Ellen Wood helped locate, evaluate, and scan material: Hers was a sometimes thankless and all-consuming task, but she completed it with enthusiasm and careful attention to detail. Andrew Curran read through the articles on transportation. For producing elegant plans and charts and for tracking down photographs, I am indebted to Kevin Brooks. Leslie Tse drew the beautiful cartoons and illustrations. I am grateful to the many students, friends, and colleagues who shared their photographs.

As with everything I do, I treasure the support of my family. Thanks to Marty (my greatest fan), to Caleb (the family skeptic), and Sari (about to enter the working world).

Jill Grant, Halifax

Background and Basics

Chapter One
The Nature of Canadian Planning

Planning Canadian Communities

Jill Grant

Most people who know Canadian cities can list places they consider wonderful and places they think of as dismal. Cities like Vancouver enjoy an international reputation as vital, dynamic, diverse, and beautiful. Smaller cities like Ottawa, Kingston, and Victoria get good press as vibrant centres of government, education, and culture. Yet some Canadian towns and cities struggle to overcome the idea that they are ugly or in decline, places that young people abandon at the first opportunity. What factors make the difference in the character and destiny of our settlements? Can we apply the lessons we draw from successful cities to those with problems? As an optimistic society, we aren't ready to be fatalistic about our communities: Hence we look for tools to allow us to shape our own future and to make all of our settlements strong and beautiful.

Many of us take the communities we inhabit for granted. We know relatively little about the way they have come to take the form they present. We have a poor understanding of the infrastructure that makes them run effectively. We seldom think about what they may be like in our great-grandchildren's generation. Yet the health and sustainability of our communities depend on people who care about the past, present, and future of our settlements, and who help make decisions about how to organize and develop our communities. Most Canadian cities and towns employ community planners in this role.

Communities are shaped in part by natural processes but also by countless human choices, large and small. Decisions our ancestors made generations ago continue to influence our settlements. Early modern humans roamed the planet, developing technologies to open new niches for themselves. Some followed herds of game across the Bering land bridge and established settlements across the North American continent. Others sailed west from Europe, sending a second wave of immigrants to Canada. Military surveyors and generals, implementing a European political agenda, picked fine harbours and prominent locations for their new settlements, applying plans made in Europe to lands ill-suited to the rational geometry of the times. More than two centuries later, eastern cities like Halifax still struggle with rigid road grids running directly up dangerously steep slopes that make winter driving treacherous (Figures 1.1 and 1.2).

Settlers developed housing technologies and economic adaptations that affected where they chose to locate and what they built. Through the years, countless individual choices about the colour, size, and shape of houses contributed to the kaleidoscope of neighbourhoods we see in Canada today. The business decisions of entrepreneurs and innovations of inventors altered the fate of settlements,

Figure 1.1

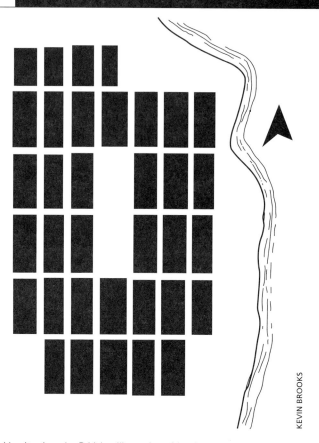

The 1749 Halifax grid epitomizes the British military plan of its day.

leading some to grow while others disappeared. Changing energy and transportation technologies gave some communities advantages that others lacked. In the late nineteenth and early twentieth centuries, settlements connected by railways boomed, while those off the network struggled to avoid decline. By the late twentieth century, road freight had replaced rail as the mode of choice, and some towns found themselves abandoned by failing railroads.

Throughout the development of Canada, government choices have affected the shape and trajectory of our settlements. In the early years, military surveyors set the dimensions of roads and blocks, and determined the locations of key civic facilities. Today governments decide requirements for infrastructure like piped water and sewers, and organize major projects like bridges, highways, port facilities, and airports. In the name of public safety, government policy guides choices about building materials and practices and the location of activities that may affect human health or well-being. Our cities reflect multiple layers of government rules and regulations applied through the decades and centuries.

When we look at our communities, we find that they reveal a range of choices: ancient and recent, individual and corporate. They tell a history influenced by the rigours of climate, the nature of building materials, and the exigencies of the economy. They describe changing popular tastes and trends, and an increasing interest by government in establishing rules for urban form. As the cities we inhabit today reveal the values and decisions made by our ancestors, the choices we make today inscribe the future of our settlements.

Figure 1.2

JILL GRANT

This entrance to a Halifax shopping centre illustrates the impracticality of a grid on steep hills.

Making choices involves planning: organizing current activities to achieve future objectives. People are always planning, whether in thinking about their day and the tasks they need to complete, in organizing a wedding, or in arranging to build a dream home. But communities also engage in planning: looking at possible futures and making choices about how to allocate land and resources in ways that can lead to desired ends. This book explores the Canadian way of planning communities as described by practitioners and scholars who have written about Canadian practice and planning theory over the past several decades in *Plan Canada*.

Planning on a municipal level is community-shaping behaviour. Community planning reveals the confluence of theory—ideas about what a good community is and how to achieve it—and practice—choices made in the context of particular people, resources, and properties. Planning involves the application of values that reflect a community's history and geography: In that sense, planning is a cultural practice. Canadian community planning has its own particular style which contrasts with practice in other nations and which reveals the values that Canadians hold dear.

Uniquely Canadian

Canadian planning has clearly been influenced by our colonial connections to Great Britain, as Jeanne Wolfe's article on our history (Chapter 2) makes evident. Early planners like Thomas Adams (described by David Stein, Chapter 2) came from England to establish town planning legislation and approaches that set the stage for Canadian practice. After World War II, another generation of British architect/planners arrived. Humphrey Carver, for instance, played an influential role in developing policies and programs through the work of the Central Mortgage and Housing Corporation, while other British planners took teaching and consulting positions.

We have also been influenced by the United States, our nearest neighbour. By the 1970s, widespread access to American mass media affected Canadian views of urban development. The popularity of writings by American planning academics shaped Canadian thinking about urban planning, and many Americans took teaching jobs at Canadian universities.

As Gerald Hodge suggests, though, Canadian planning retained its own flavour. While the British talk about "town planning," and the Americans practise "urban planning," the focus in Canada has been on "community planning." Settlements large and small matter, and local governments use planning tools to shape their fate.[1]

Where English town planning is highly centralized, Canadian planning is enabled by provincial planning laws but practised by local governments according to their own priorities. Canadian practice has not featured interventionist policies to provide housing and build complete new towns, as characterized town planning in the UK. While the British eagerly applied the garden city model of Ebenezer Howard,[2] less ambitious garden suburb ideas permeated Canadian practice.

Canadian planning differs from the American experience as well. Our cities are not challenged to the same extent as American ones, by racial segregation, inner-city abandonment, and the secession of the suburbs. A political context that makes Canadian cities subject to provincial policy has left them less independent than American cities, but has given them stronger planning powers. In the US, zoning is often more powerful than and separated from planning; in Canadian law, zoning serves as a tool for implementing planning.

Garden Cities and Garden Suburbs

In 1898, Ebenezer Howard published a small book articulating his idea of garden cities: a system of relatively self-contained satellite cities of 32,000 people linked by train, road, and canal with each other and with a central city. With land held in public ownership and public provision of abundant green space and facilities, garden cities would provide affordable housing with private gardens for working people in communities with clean air and water. The garden city would provide an answer to the misery of the industrial city, using town planning to achieve efficiency and quality in the urban environment.

With the immense appeal of garden city ideas, Howard formed a Garden Cities Association and began raising funds to demonstrate the viability of the concept. Letchworth Garden City in England began in 1903 and attracted a range of utopian socialists and freethinkers. In the process, though, many of Howard's original aspirations gave way to market realities: Someone has to pay for urban amenities. Given the challenge of financing such new towns, few complete garden cities were built until the British government adopted the strategy for rebuilding after World War II. Postwar new towns proved much larger than those Howard envisioned, and increasingly set aside the early principles of the garden city in favour of modernist thinking.

The designers of Letchworth, Raymond Unwin and Barry Parker, went on to plan some well-known garden suburbs and to influence planning practice in Canada as well. Hampstead Garden Suburb in London proved that some of the key design elements of the garden city, like abundant green space and attractive medium-density housing, could work, even in contexts where complete new towns were impossible. Design features like cul-de-sacs and winding streets became increasingly popular throughout the twentieth century, as garden city ideas became embedded within planning practice, typically within suburbs that featured single detached houses.

Thomas Adams planned some garden city towns during his tenure in Canada. Corner Brook, Newfoundland, and Temiscaming, Quebec, were new communities to serve resource industries (Figure 1.3). After World War II, another generation of planners laid out new towns like Don Mills in Toronto and Kitimat in British Columbia, following garden city ideas that had been adapted through the American development of Radburn, New Jersey.

While the early garden city projects represent some of the best aspects of the modern town planning movement and today remain beautiful settlements, as the ideas disseminated far and wide, they became increasingly diluted. By the late twentieth century, garden city ideas had degenerated into premises that seemed to support suburban sprawl. Vast swaths of housing surrounded by spacious gardens linked together with well-planned road networks had become a recipe for a new set of urban problems.

Figure 1.3

KEVIN BROOKS

The plan of Temiscaming, Quebec, by Thomas Adams.

Several features of Canadian planning theory and practice are distinct. We have only a few large cities in Canada but many mid-sized cities and small towns. Our landscape is sparsely populated, with a vast geography that presents special challenges for transportation and trade. Our cities generally have control of their suburbs, as cities readily annex their urban fringes to accommodate growth. The authority of urban centres has been consolidated with provincial decisions to amalgamate neighbouring municipalities and create regional municipalities in many jurisdictions. Such political control gives Canadian cities power over planning large urban regions, to the envy of American planners.

The largest Canadian cities are among the most ethnically diverse on the planet. The national government established a policy of multiculturalism over three decades ago, and it continues to encourage a public culture that embraces ethnic diversity. Our cities are generally seen as safe and healthy, although concerns about crime and environmental degradation are taken seriously. Canadians value our cities as good places to live and work.

Despite periodic scandals over corruption and dirty politics, Canadians generally accept the role of government in establishing peace and order, and in offering planning leadership. Although support for municipal planning has waxed and waned through the decades, planning has become firmly embedded as a function of local government. Planning is a tool we use to try to make our communities better places.

What Is Planning Theory?

Planners have been fretting about planning theory for decades. Some professions have clear and practical theory. For instance, doctors can turn to textbooks and journals to discover the latest theory on why Junior's head may hurt. Even social sciences have reliable theory: Political scientists develop theories to explain changing governance structures in the former Eastern bloc nations; anthropologists have theory that allows them to interpret kinship patterns. Why is it so difficult for planners to point to useful theory that explains practice and offers reliable strategies to deliver better futures?

Doctors seek to do no harm. Economists hope to offer strategies for growth. What motivates planners? Is it enough to say that planning seeks to promote the "public interest"? Does that give planners sufficient guidance to make choices in our everyday practice? Practitioners are looking for practical guidance for action. Do planning theory and philosophy texts offer sufficient clarity? As we look at planning literature and planning practice, we do find a framework of ideas that gives intellectual coherence to planning. We discover, however, that the breadth of the profession means that planners draw widely for ideas and for guidance.

The difficulty of pinning down planning theory is reflected in texts that go by that name. Campbell and Fainstein's theory reader contains chapters and articles from the late nineteenth century to the 1990s, on short-lived planning experiments and on eternal questions. Their introduction indicates their focus on political economy, but the text contains a host of concerns as variable as the decades in which they were written.[3] Alexander's brief text on planning approaches focuses on the planning process, reflecting the dominance of rational planning in planning procedures. He sees rationality as the underlying planning theory, despite the influence of other popular paradigms.[4]

Some practitioners don't believe that there is clearly defined "planning theory." Some describe a great gap between theory and practice. Those who attended planning schools took courses that purported to teach them "planning theory." So how is it that many practitioners find it hard to point to the theory that guides their professional activities? What is the role of planning theory and philosophy in planning practice? This key question for the profession is not easily answered.

Every discipline hopes to create a substantial body of theory to explain phenomena, to support practice, and to reduce guesswork. Planners want to be able to describe what happened, explain what happens, and predict what may happen. Theory helps us to justify our choices. In a profession as diverse and integrative as community planning, however, this proves challenging.

Theory provides a basis for understanding the world, for considering courses of action, and for developing skills. Alexander argues that theory is necessary to the practitioner, not just to academics.[5] Practitioners need to know what to do, yet they are often skeptical and out of touch with the latest developments in theory.

Martin, *et al.* surveyed Canadian planners to find out what practitioners identified as "important literature." They found that most planners identified classics from the 1960s and early 1970s, works they had studied in university.[6] Jane Jacobs's critique of planning was the text most commonly cited: If anything, her ideas have become more influential over the last four decades, as new urbanism and smart growth have become more popular. The fact that planners may continue to use theory developed by previous generations of thinkers might lead us to conclude that community planning does not move rapidly to adopt new theory.[7]

The Meaning of Planning

Ernest Alexander offers a useful definition of planning, which highlights the key components of a profession that can be difficult to describe:

> ...planning is the deliberate social or organizational activity of developing an optimal strategy for future action to achieve a desired set of goals, for solving novel problems in complex contexts, and attended by the power and intention to commit resources and to act as necessary to implement the chosen strategy.[8]

In some senses, planning is something people do everyday. It involves forethought—thinking ahead. Hence friends and family may give "planning students" quizzical looks, as if to say, "Why do you need to *study* to be a planner?" In a societal sense,

New Urbanism and Smart Growth

In the 1980s, a new design and planning movement began to gain steam in North America. Drawing on Jane Jacobs's ideas of vibrant, mixed-use, urban neighbourhoods, many planners and designers began experimenting with new developments based on traditional town-building principles. In Florida, Andres Duany and Elizabeth Plater-Zyberk worked with developer Robert Davis to build Seaside, an 80-acre site revealing the principles of neotraditional neighbourhoods. Homes with porches sat on small lots near the narrow streets arranged in a modified grid layout. Codes established high design standards for the public realm and created an incredibly beautiful settlement.

In California, Peter Calthorpe and colleagues were writing about pedestrian pockets and transit-oriented development. They argued that encouraging higher densities and compact form around public transportation nodes could create an urban structure that might provide alternatives to widespread car use while improving environmental and urban quality.

United by the mid-1990s through the Congress for the New Urbanism, the movement advocated pedestrian-friendly, mixed-use, affordable, and human-scale neighbourhoods organized into an effective regional network. Communities like Kentlands (Gaithersburg, Maryland), Celebration (Florida), and Orenco Station (Hillsboro, Oregon) illustrated the potential of new urbanism in the US. Projects like Cornell in Markham, Ontario, and McKenzie Towne in Calgary put new urbanism on the public agenda in Canada as well.

By the late 1990s, the smart growth movement was gaining ground in the US and Canada. Promoted first in the US by the National Governors Association and some states, smart growth built on new urbanism design concepts by adding theory and incentives. Where some communities had reacted against growth by imposing growth controls, smart growth treated growth as inevitable and potentially good, if properly channelled. Through government incentives and flexibility, developers might be enticed to engage more appropriate strategies in new development.

however, planning involves a process for making decisions about allocating resources and avoiding the externalities or negative effects that accompany action. It is a necessary process to facilitate decision making in difficult or competitive circumstances.

Planning is concerned with the interrelationships among key elements:

- people, physical objects, and ecological processes;
- problems, subject matters, and specializations;
- jurisdictions (federal, provincial, regional, and municipal);
- domains (social, economic, political, and physical).

It employs a rational or logical process and democratic community participation to achieve decisions and policies for future actions.

Let's examine the significant elements of Alexander's definition.

planning is the deliberate social or organizational activity of

Planning implies the desire to instill order, to choose a future (instead of merely inheriting one). Planning requires organized activity involving patterns of events and actions.

developing an optimal strategy

Planning seeks to find the best choices, ones that achieve the greatest good for the greatest number with the least possible costs or negative impacts.

for future action

Planning looks ahead to generations that will follow. As an activity, it reflects our ability to conceptualize a time beyond the present, to think of our heirs and successors.

to achieve a desired set of goals

Planning operates to achieve particular objectives. We seek a future where we can achieve our values. We look to a better situation ahead. Planning is purposeful.

Planning has no simple and consistent strategy for action. It has traditionally borrowed methods, techniques, and theories from other fields, such as ecology, urban sociology, and organizational development. Planners face complex choices, unintended consequences, and political uncertainty. Strategies that worked in 1970 would no longer be appropriate in 2007. Techniques that suited economic development in Iroquois Falls, Ontario, may not work in Montreal.

Planners have to deal with difficult questions:

- What action is necessary? Economic, social, and environmental values may differ and suggest alternatives. Planners have to deal with a range of scales: site, neighbourhood, local, regional, national, and global. Identifying the appropriate choice is a challenge.

Figure 1.4

Cornell in Markham, Ontario, exemplifies the principles of new urbanism.

- Who should act? Decisions of players of various kinds can affect outcomes: individuals, groups, corporations. Planners, politicians, and the public all play important roles in the process.
- How should we proceed? We have a variety of approaches and methods to choose from, but no clear criteria to guide us to one set of actions rather than another.

The Utility of Theory

Planners need conceptual guidelines to help answer the questions they face. So they look for useful theory and try to learn from the practice of others. Klosterman finds implicit consensus about four vital social functions of planning:

- It promotes the common or collective interests of the community.
- It considers the external effects of individual and group action.
- It improves the information base for public and private decision making.
- It considers the distributional effects of public and private action.

Because it fulfills these functions, planning is socially useful.[9]

The approach individual planners take depends on their theoretical bent, their values, or their local political situation. Then how can the planner know what to do? If historical precedents and examples from other communities cannot be used as direct models for action, how should planners use them? Learning from practice in other communities has to be the first step in trying to build theory that can offer guidance for practitioners facing complex choices. Accordingly, planners share their experiences in professional conferences and journals and begin to develop premises about what may work in particular situations.

Planning theories do not result in neat prescriptions or formulas. For instance, in transportation planning we can find a formula that tells us how to bank a road for a 80-km/h curve. An environmental planner can determine the optimal routing to protect important habitat areas from negative impacts. No theory, though, can answer the question: Do we need the road? That question entails values and choices. At their root, many planning questions are political.

No planning problem has a standard solution. A rational process gives an established method to use, but not a standard solution. Every problem is unique in form, context, character, and scope. Problems are, after all, social constructions defined by social interactions between community members. As a community, if we agree that something is "a problem," then it is. If we ignore it, we take no action to solve it: Thus in a societal sense, the problem does not exist. Defining problems involves some level of theorizing, if only implicitly. The range of possible solutions depends on how we define each problem.

For example, we may define the problem of Neighbourhood X in a variety of ways. Local police may say, "We need more surveillance to prevent crime." A social worker may say, "Residents need job skills and conflict management strategies." A resident may say, "We need jobs and respect." A designer may say, "This neighbourhood is poorly designed." Planners could choose any of those definitions or some combination of them. The definition people use in setting out the problem depends on their interest base, experience, social context, values, and theory. Values and theories change over time. Problem definitions that are popular in one era may seem preposterous in another.

Urban renewal is a clear example of a planning "solution" that generated new problems. In the immediate postwar period, Western society had a strong consensus about the problem of "blight"—many people defined the deterioration of urban neighbourhoods as a problem. The preferred solution, advocated in planning literature and in popular media sources, was "slum clearance." Rundown housing, experts said, caused health problems, fire risks, crime, suburban growth, and general unsightliness. Authorities agreed that saving cities required concerted action. Governments poured millions into tearing down impoverished districts. Only as the negative consequences of urban renewal (with the social dislocation it caused) became clear did authorities begin to redefine the problem of older city neighbourhoods and reconsider solutions.

The popularity of an idea is not a good indication of its potential for success. Good planning requires careful consideration of the possible redistributive effects of actions and the externalities generated by choices. Not everyone benefits from the choices we make about desirable futures. One role of the planner is to ensure that decision makers understand the implications of the choices they make.

People often define problems in terms of their preferred solutions. They say: "We need a park"; "We want low-rise housing"; "Zone this area for industry"; "Investment will bring back Main Street." Planners need to resist simple definitions or standard prescriptions if their mission is to find optimal solutions. The role of planning is to encourage people to start at the beginning: first defining their values and goals, then exploring various options for achieving their objectives. Planners help people expand their horizons in terms of the potential the future offers.

Planning theories can provide helpful ways of thinking about problems and selecting approaches to dealing with them. For example, if we believe that ecological theory makes sense, we are likely to approach problems with a particular perspective: We will value landscapes and use sensitive approaches to intervention. Our theoretical position can help us frame appropriate issues, select the methods, and prepare for implementation in a coherent way. In the absence of theory, we may be left with ad hoc approaches to problem solving, which are hard to explain and impossible to justify.

The Variety of Planning Approaches

A planning approach is the method used, or steps taken, in setting about a task. It indicates a particular way of thinking about a problem and tackling its solution. It implies a value set applied in making choices. Planners use the term "approach" in a particular way: We use it to suggest a conjunction between some kind of theoretical or philosophical basis and a method for tackling a task. The approach implies selecting some operating premises with related values and assumptions and applying appropriate tools for generating a solution.

For example, if the "problem" is that a developer has applied for permission to build a new shopping centre in Ourtown, then we can think of several ways of approaching the planning tasks involved in formulating positions on solutions.

- The developer's approach would be to do a market study of the area to determine demand and to assess the plan for the regulatory context. Do the plan policies foresee growth in this location? The developer will likely assume that the community will want the project and value its revenue potential. The developer will seek political support from council members. The developer's solution argues that development is good for Ourtown and should proceed. This represents a market approach.
- The citizens' committee's approach may be to do a community survey to look at traffic flow and safety concerns. Residents assume that the project will have an impact on their quality of life. The group will seek political support from its council member. It may argue that the project will disrupt the neighbourhood; therefore, the solution is to reject the proposal. We might call this a community interest approach.

- The municipal planner's approach will be to examine plan policies and any other regulations that may apply to consider whether the project meets the "intent of the plan." The planner will presume that developers will build to the maximum allowable and that the community may protest unwanted changes to the landscape. Planners will recommend that council approve projects that meet planning criteria, or reject those that do not: The solution will depend on the planner's interpretation of the project's ability to meet plan policies. Some would call this a technical approach.

No single approach is best for dealing with any particular problem or any class of problems. The approaches we select reflect our interest base and our values. Even "technical" approaches reflect value judgments. We cannot get away from the problem of choice.

For instance, an ecologist and a forest economist differ in the approaches they would use to decide the future of a stand of trees. They operate from divergent value sets: habitat conservation versus revenue generation. They would examine different factors, such as landscape connectivity versus lumber marketability. They will likely come to different conclusions and recommendations.

Should all perspectives be treated as legitimate? Can some approaches be defended more vigorously than others? This is a key question for planning. Such questions are at the heart of the debate about whether planners can be visionaries "speaking to power," or whether they are functionaries "speaking for power." To act as visionaries, planners have to demonstrate that planning can adopt a normative (value-based) framework that carries authority and can generate consensus. This would require technical expertise, good knowledge, and even better theory. Can planning meet that test? Planners may have technical expertise, but we recognize the limits to our knowledge and the weaknesses of contemporary theory. We lack consensus on our strategies, and so we experience contention over choices we must make. While many planners have visions of better futures, those visions may differ markedly from planner to planner.

Can we articulate a single set of ethics for the planning profession? Some planning theorists argue that we can, and must. For instance, the new urbanists and the proponents of smart growth advocate a specific set of premises that value traditional urban forms and patterns. The deep ecologists have equal visionary fervour, albeit around a different value set that puts nature ahead of people. Each group would argue that its approach should be *the* approach of the planning profession. But not everyone agrees. Planners can and do take many other approaches to problems, as practice reveals.

The Politics of Choice

Planning solutions are neither right nor wrong. Some options are better than others in the given circumstances; some are less costly; some last longer. The evaluation depends on the value base and the theoretical perspective of the assessor. A transportation planner evaluating the work of an environmental planner may well find fault with the assumptions made, methods used, or decisions taken; similarly, the environmental planner might criticize the choices made by the transportation planner. Choices reflect the values and interest base from which the planner operates. Unfortunately, we have no simple test of the "goodness" of a solution. An option that gains widespread support when it is made may seem wrong a generation later.

Do planners have the right to be wrong? Should communities hold planners liable for their advice? In the 1960s, Halifax Council brought in Dr. Albert Rose, a planning expert from Toronto. Rose had previously led the redevelopment of the poor Regent Park neighbourhood in Toronto. In Halifax, Rose supported the idea of relocating African-Canadian residents from their self-built housing in the community of Africville to public housing.[10]

Councils across the country followed the advice of the planning experts, with significant long-term social consequences. Thousands of poor households were forced from their neighbourhoods in favour of commercial and industrial uses. Some were moved into public housing, which developed its own pathologies. Should we blame the planners for these decisions and their consequences?

Planners operate in a political and cultural context where they frame their choices and their advice. As Pierre Filion argues (Chapter 5), the weight of the system can limit planners' options. In the 1950s and 1960s, every city across Canada was demolishing dilapidated housing as part of the monumental modernizing effort of urban renewal. The federal government financed the redevelopment, the provincial government encouraged it, the newspapers promoted it. The mass media ran frequent stories about abysmal living conditions in urban slums, calling for government to do something about the tragedy. The best planning theory of the 1950s advocated slum clearance. Planners willingly assisted in the great cultural project of cleaning up the city. They facilitated the transformation of areas of cities that had suffered disinvestment or municipal neglect. They absorbed and enabled the popular thinking of the time.

By the 1970s, though, planners were blamed for the problems of urban renewal: cultural dislocation, disempowerment of the poor, and brutal modernization of the city. Jane Jacobs led the charge that planning was destroying the city.[11] In response to the critique, planners redefined the problem of planning as the need for greater public participation in decision making. Their role changed from that of experts (telling councils what to do) to facilitators of public participation processes. Afraid of leading the charge for the "good city," they accepted the role of enablers of the visions of others. In the 1980s, planners became mediators and negotiators, helping communities develop strategic alliances with industry in search of growth. By the twenty-first century, some planners again operated as visionary leaders, steering new regional planning exercises that presented positive images of alternative futures achieved through better community design. Thus history and practice reveal a panoply of possible roles that planners can and have taken in Canadian communities.

If planners worry constantly about making mistakes, we risk paralysis. Planners operate within a democratic system, where political leaders have the ultimate responsibility to decide. We have the responsibility to be humble but vocal in articulating the values that may influence choices, thorough in our analyses, honest in our data collection, comprehensive in our presentation of options, and competent in our implementation of selected actions. Planners will not be right all the time; we will not be wrong all the time. The communities we work within will change their priorities through the years, rendering earlier choices an issue. As professionals, we have the responsibility to offer ideas, encourage deep thinking, and address significant social issues. Our work will not always be easy. Planners may not be popular, yet the work of planning is vitally important to human habitat. Planners shape the places where we live and the environments our grandchildren will inherit.

As long as we see planning as an ongoing process for making difficult decisions in a changing world, we can come to accept the possibility that while time may prove individual planners wrong, planners can sleep peacefully, knowing that when we had the opportunity to make a difference in the world, we did our best to help communities make reasonable and responsible choices.

Canadian Planning Issues

Issues facing Canadian planners have changed over time. In the 1920s, the profession tried to establish its credentials, urging governments to adopt planning as a municipal function, and explaining the economic and social benefits that scientific management could bring. In the 1960s, articles in professional journals focused on building the capacity of practitioners and exhorted governments to become serious about regional planning. By the 1980s, stories of community successes in planning initiatives offered examples for others to emulate and raised the profile of such issues as community engagement and environmental degradation.

The articles reprinted in the chapters that follow report on communities large and small, rural and urban, northern and Aboriginal. They describe efforts to use innovative strategies to achieve identified goals. They explain the bread and butter of planning: making choices that affect people's lives and futures. Canadian planning reveals a strong interest in finding ways to give communities tools and information to manage their futures.

A review of the pages of *Plan Canada* presents a history of the efforts of practitioners to implement the latest theories and ideas. In the 1960s, we find articles about urban renewal; in the 1970s and 1980s, attention shifts to issues like downtown revitalization; in the 1990s, new urbanism and smart growth became the preferred options. Beginning in the 1980s, the number of articles on diversity issues jumped sharply, as planners grew more attentive to issues of an aging and multicultural society. Through the years, some themes remained consistently important to planners: Recurrent discussions appear about the challenges of transportation systems, the role of regional planning, and the need for strong downtown areas.

Interestingly, we find relatively few reports of failures in the pages of *Plan Canada*. A profession optimistic about the future may hesitate somewhat to draw explicit negative lessons. The scholars who write in the journal have proven more likely to condemn past practices with detailed assessments; practitioners tend instead to move on to the next preferred approach. Of course, if we do not learn from our mistakes, we may be doomed to repeat them; so understanding why our strategies failed to deliver on their promises is an essential exercise in a profession like planning.

Despite a housing crisis that was well-recognized a century ago and that continues to haunt us in its changing incarnations, we see less discussion of issues of affordable housing or homelessness than we might expect in a professional planning journal. One might barely realize that poverty persists in Canada from reading *Plan Canada*, or that planners have a role in trying to ameliorate it. While progressive voices early in the town planning movement called for planning to generate greater equity and quality in housing, Canadian planning did not take that route. Housing issues and the state's role in resolving them featured front and centre in British planning in the postwar period, but not in Canadian planning. Goodman and Freund argued that American planning in the early twentieth century chose to ignore housing concerns, and instead focused on zoning, a path that led to the demise of planning.[12] While the American government dabbled in town planning as part of its New Deal strategy to end the Depression in the 1930s, Canadian governments chose to leave housing issues essentially to the market sector until after World War II. Canadian housing policy then concentrated on supporting the market and used planning as a process for managing land use and applying standards.[13] While planning has played a progressive role in resolving housing issues in some countries, Canadian planning has taken a different route. Planning can offer the tools to improve housing conditions, but without political will, the tools may achieve other ends.

The articles in this book reveal both the strengths and the weaknesses of Canadian planning. They reflect the propensity of Canadian governments to work with the market instead of taking a leadership role in shaping communities that may achieve such noble ambitions and values as equity, if that were our priority. They expose our pattern of often taking a regulatory role, trying to manage the externalities of growth and development, rather than engaging in vigorous proactive planning to shape our own destiny. Instead of using our planning tools to their fullest capacity, Canadian planning has often found its potential constrained by the priorities within which it must work.

The Character of Canadian Planning Practice and Theory

Over the years, the contents of *Plan Canada* illustrate patterns of continuity and change in Canadian planning practice and theory. Some topics retained strong interest through the decades, developing in theoretical sophistication and practical application. Other themes seemed popular at times, but disappeared from discussions after a few years.

One of the strongest continuing themes in Canadian planning has been the commitment to regional planning.[14] Early planners like Thomas Adams and Noulan Couchon advocated regional approaches. In the 1960s and 1970s, articulate voices like those of Hans Blumenfeld, Len Gertler, Reg Lang, Gerald Hodge, and Ira Robinson continued the call for regional planning. A vast and sparsely-populated country called for different approaches than might work in densely-inhabited Britain. Regional planning seemed to offer tools to reduce disparities: north versus south, rural versus urban, agricultural versus industrial, coastal versus inland. Although regional planning led to some colossal disasters, like the tragic relocation of outport communities in Newfoundland,[15] governments grew increasingly committed to regional approaches. In recent years, as the country became more urbanized and as global competition threatened Canada's economic position, provincial governments have sought to strengthen urban regions. By the early twenty-first century, most of the largest urban areas in Canada had some form of regional planning in place, which allowed them to govern land use over their peripheries.

Since the 1980s, several theories have been considerably elaborated through the initiatives of Canadians and have influenced Canadian planning practice extensively. First, the Canadian Institute of Planners (CIP) played a major role (along with the Federation of Canadian Municipalities, Health Canada, and the Canadian Public Health Association) in the development of the healthy communities movement: CIP served as its secretariat during the late 1980s. This theory, which captured imagination in the World Health Organization and sparked many initiatives in Europe, recognized that progressive community planning could help to improve individual health and well-being by creating environmentally and socially responsible environments.

By the late 1980s, following the report of the Brundtland Commission,[16] a wave of interest in the idea of sustainable development swept Canada. Sustainable development theory suggested that strategies must be found to ensure that future generations could enjoy the same quality of life as contemporary residents. Like the healthy communities approach, it took a holistic and integrative view of development; for the same reason, it appealed immensely to planning values. The national government supported sustainable development with its 1990 *Green Plan*, encouraging planners to encompass an environmental agenda into community planning. The language of sustainability made its way into the planning debates and has not disappeared, even as smart growth has become more popular.

Another noteworthy development of Canadian planning practice and theory is the widespread adoption of new urbanism principles and an interest in urban design. As early as the 1970s, Toronto and Vancouver planners began promoting higher-density and mixed-use projects in redeveloping their cities. Projects like the St. Lawrence district in Toronto and False Creek in Vancouver demonstrated viable alternatives to low-density suburban sprawl (Figure 1.5). As the new urbanism movement developed in the US during the 1980s and 1990s, many American new urbanists pointed to Canadian cities as living examples of what could be possible in the city of the future. New suburbs

Figure 1.5

JILL GRANT

The St. Lawrence market area in Toronto bustles on a pleasant day.

like McKenzie Towne in Calgary and Cornell in Markham represented the larger projects, but across the country, municipalities adapted their plans and regulations to encourage smaller lots, mixed use, and modified grid street patterns.[17] Many cities adopted urban design guidelines and hired urban design planners. Canadian planning demonstrated that once communities decided that they wanted options for the future planners could adapt land-planning tools to reshape the urban environment.

Several features of Canadian practice differentiate it from the British and American approaches. First, Canadian practice links planning and zoning together reasonably effectively. Each municipality adopts a plan following a public consultation process. The plan sets out policies that frame the future use of land in the community. Following the policies of the plan, a land use or zoning bylaw establishes zones that automatically permit listed uses. For instance, an R-1 zone might permit single detached houses on lots with a 15-metre frontage: A prospective builder need only apply for a building permit. Thus the application process is relatively straightforward if the project complies with what the plan and zone allows.

By contrast, in the UK, the government uses a system of development control to implement policy. The central government establishes planning policy guidance notes, which set the context within which planners in local communities frame plans and make decisions about applications for development. In England, the office of the deputy prime minister has in recent years issued guidance notes that advocate residential intensification, calling for 60 percent of new construction to occur in already developed areas. Local governments must find ways to enforce the targets. Each application is evaluated in light of the policies in a process that can sometimes seem cumbersome and lengthy.

Although each state in the US differs slightly, many jurisdictions have a weaker ability to achieve the objectives in their plans than is the case in Canadian cities. Some

Figure 1.6

JILL GRANT

Rembrandt Rosecliff Valley in London, Ontario, is a prime example of the new private community.

American cities have separate planning and zoning functions, with different organizations or components of government responsible for each. Zoning often becomes a way of managing the status quo and controlling land values rather than a tool to implement the plan. A large proportion of new development in the US occurs in private communities, which adopt extensive systems of codes and covenants to control uses and form. Private communities are also increasing in Canada (Figure 1.6).

Canadian cities are quite strong. Although Canadian cities are constitutionally creatures of the provinces, they have considerable scope to determine their own direction. Acts passed by provincial governments establish the authority and mandate of cities to engage in land planning. While the cities call constantly for greater economic resources from upper levels of government to meet the demands placed on them, they have managed to maintain high levels of public satisfaction with services. Canadian cities experience less segregation by race and class than is common in American cities, and less disinvestment in core areas. Urban densities are lower in Canada than in the UK but higher than in the US. Public transportation systems are reasonably good and well-used in many of the larger cities. The creation of regional governance has expanded the potential of Canadian cities for coordinated and comprehensive regional planning that has the potential to increase urban efficiency over the long term.

A unique feature of Canadian planning, as seen in the pages of *Plan Canada*, is the increasing attention given to issues of northern, remote, First Nations, and rural communities. While practitioners and scholars recognize that inequities persist between settlements of different sizes and in varying locales, they work to formulate strategies to engage a range of community members in improving their futures. By bringing these issues into the mainstream of professional discourse, Canadian planners ensure that every community has an opportunity to benefit from planning tools.

Like their colleagues in other countries, Canadian planners engage in debates about the role of the planner in communities and the role of planning in affecting the future of our settlements. They explore questions of ethics and values and try to determine what is in the public interest over the long term. We see in the articles reprinted here recurrent debates about what the planner should do in a context where the future is unclear and the choices complex. Canadian planners may not have all the answers to these enduring questions, but their practice reveals their willingness to engage the problems they face and work toward finding appropriate resolutions.

Canadian planning reveals a strong linkage between practice and theory. Planning is an applied discipline. It requires both the art of the possible and the politics of the important. While far from perfect, Canadian planning has a lot to make it proud. Planners have helped to shape cities that are seen worldwide as livable, clean, safe, attractive, diverse, and mixed. We have much to do to make them better, but we have built a good base for the future. Canadian planning reflects a legacy of caring about our communities and dedicating the resources to make futures happen. Although we recognize the shortcomings of community planning, Canadian planners refuse to give up faith in achieving better futures through good planning.

Study Questions

1. What are the social, economic, and environmental impacts of sprawl on Canadian settlements?

2. What are the major differences and the major similarities between Canadian cities and cities you have visited or studied in other countries? What key lessons can Canadian cities learn from others, and what can they offer to others?

3. In what ways does the practice of planning need to adapt to changing social, economic, and environmental issues in Canadian society?

4. How are smart growth and sustainable development ideas affecting development trends and patterns in Canada?

5. What is the role of planning in shaping our communities?

6. What is the appropriate balance between planning theory and practice in making good choices about community futures?

7. Interview your friends or family to discover what they know about zoning and planning, and whether they have ever become involved in community issues.

8. Examine your local news coverage to identify the key planning issues in your community.

Reference Notes

1. Hodge, G (2003) *Planning Canadian Communities: An Introduction to the Principles, Practices and Participants.* (4th ed). Toronto: Thomson Nelson.

2. Howard, E (1902) *Garden Cities of To-morrow.* Eastbourne, UK: Attic Books (New illustrated reprinted edition, 1985).

3. Campbell, S & S Fainstein (eds) (1996) *Readings in Planning Theory.* Oxford & New York: Blackwell Publishing.

4. Alexander, E (1992) *Approaches to Planning.* (2nd ed). New York: Gordon and Breach.

5. Ibid.

6. Martin, L, P Filion, & E Higgs (1988) A survey of the preferred literature of Canadian planners. *Plan Canada* 28(1): 6–11.

7. Jacobs, J (1961) *The Death and Life of Great American Cities.* New York: Vintage Books.

8. Alexander, E (1992) Op. cit.: 73.

9. Klosterman, R (1985) Arguments for and against planning. *Town Planning Review* 56 (1): 5–20.

10. Clairmont, DH & DW Magill (1987) *Africville: The Life and Death of a Canadian Black Community.* (Rev ed) Toronto: Canadian Scholar's Press.

11. Jacobs, J (1961) Op. cit.

12. Goodman, WM & EC Freund (1968) *Principles and Practice of Urban Planning.* Washington: International City Managers Association.

13. Hulchanski, JD (1986) General introduction to the issue. (Special issue on the history of Canadian housing policy.) *Urban History Review* 15(1): 1–2.

14. Hodge, G & I Robinson (2001) *Planning Canadian Regions.* Vancouver: UBC Press.

15. Matthews, R (1977) *There's No Better Place than Here: Social Change in Three Newfoundland Communities.* Toronto: Peter Martin Associates.

16. World Commission on the Environment and Development (WCED) (1987) *Our Common Future.* Brundtland Commission. New York: Oxford University Press.

17. Grant, J (2003) Exploring the influence of new urbanism. *Journal of Architectural and Planning Research* 20(3): 234–53.

Chapter Two

The History of Canadian Planning

A Canadian Perspective

Jill Grant

The character of planning practice reflects a nation's history and values. The articles here explore the development of planning in Canada and highlight some examples of the planners and projects that have made a difference in our practice and theory. Planning in this country drew extensively on a colonial legacy of town planning for military, trade, and economic purposes, while responding to the challenges of making a living in a northern landscape. A national commitment to peace, order, and good government created fertile ground for planning ideas and allowed planning to become established as a key function of local government in the twentieth century.

Industrialization in Canadian Cities

By the late nineteenth century, central Canadian cities were beginning to feel the effects of industrialization and rapid growth from immigration. As wealth became increasingly concentrated in large corporations, cities became centres of power and prosperity as well as dens of poverty.[1]

As Sanford illustrates, the changing patterns of settlement within cities like Toronto reflected both the centralization of industry and the social structure of inequality. New transportation technologies—the railroad and streetcar—facilitated segregation by class: The middle and upper classes had opportunities to distance themselves from the dirt, smoke, crime, vice, and social unrest of the central city. The first streetcars appeared in 1861 on three large arterials: Yonge, Queen, and King. In the 1870s, they expanded into the affluent northern enclaves. First, they allowed the wealthy to establish comfortable suburbs out of the city. Later, as the costs came down, the middle classes joined the exodus (Figure 2.1).

Engineering improvements began in earnest in Canadian cities in the 1870s. Toronto invested $2 million in waterworks, in what Rutherford called a "crusade to purify city life."[2] Governments and taxpayers were willing to spend on the physical plant of cities: railways, electric plants, telephone, waterworks, and gasworks. Cesspits, livestock care, and the disposal of animal carcasses in the urban environment came under increasing public regulation. The public health benefits of these improvements rapidly persuaded residents of the benefits of reform.

Figure 2.1

Streetcars allowed the city to begin its spread by facilitating commuting over longer distances.

The 1880s to the 1920s led to rapid urbanization. Canada's urban population jumped from 1.1 million (25 percent of the national total) to 4.3 million (50 percent of the total). Journalistic campaigns against crime, prostitution, and misery contributed to calls for reform. Crowding and inadequate sewer services and water supply fuelled epidemics.[3] Railways often cut off port cities from their waterfronts and redirected development patterns into linear corridors. Street railroads encouraged suburban and strip development radiating out from the core. Aging housing stock in early parts of the cities already faced decline.[4] Poor immigrants unable to make a living on the land flocked to the cities, creating an urban working class of meagre means and rough character. Slums had begun to appear. Racism and intolerance were growing. Women's groups, ministers, and businessmen joined the call for healthier and safer cities.

A survey of working class conditions in Montreal in 1897 illustrated the dismal life faced by many urban Canadians. The average worker faced a 60-hour work week with very low wages; 20 percent of the workforce was female, and 5 percent children. Only 27 of 178 miles of the streets had pavement. Over 5000 outdoor privies and few open spaces contributed to poor living conditions. The death rate was very high. Primary education was neither compulsory nor free. Reformers looked to planning to improve these dreadful living conditions.[5]

Housing conditions for workers were deplorable, with houses back-to-back on narrow alleys in urban districts. In 1889, Toronto passed a bylaw to regulate street widths (a minimum of 30 feet) and yard space (a minimum of 300 square feet). Sanford documents the relationship between infrastructure services and class. Wealthy neighbourhoods first received such services as water, sewer, and garbage collection: They could afford to pay for installation. Restrictions and covenants enforced high building standards in the new subdivisions appearing on the urban fringe.[6]

Cities in Atlantic Canada declined as capital and immigrants flowed west. Centralization of industry and wealth in the largest cities led to growth in some centres at the expense of others. The Maritime economy, once the backbone of the Canadian colonies, began to collapse as industries and capital sought richer markets. Montreal and Toronto became the economic hubs of the nation, the centres of industry and expansion.

Confederation in 1867 was good for central Canada, but proved the beginning of the end for the Maritimes. Atlantic cities were left on the periphery as fortunes were made in the West with the opening created by the railways. The rail lines led to greater functional separation within and between cities. The Maritimes industrialized in the early nineteenth century around ship building; but the need for sailing ships declined with technological change that resulted in steam ships. The early advantage of closer proximity to Europe diminished as the St. Lawrence River increased in importance, and declining shipping rates gave central Canada an additional advantage. Capital followed the lines west. The Maritimes had little to attract later settlers: Its good land had been given out a century earlier. Settlers flocked to central Canada for free land and ripe opportunities. Rapid deindustrialization hit Nova Scotia towns like Amherst, Truro, and Halifax. By the 1920s, the Maritime economy faced a depression, which lasted through the 1930s and undermined the region for decades to follow.

Reforming Canadian Cities

Reformers in the late nineteenth century drew attention to the many problems of the city. Their zeal resulted in several important urban initiatives, including public parks, sewer and water systems, and building code regulations. Aspects of urban life increasingly came under government regulation and public control. In this space, planning found its niche.

Municipal reform became a significant issue in the 1890s, a period seen as the beginning of the Progressive Era (1890–1920). Concerns about corruption and incompetence led to changes in the structure and function of municipal government. Many cities went to ward-based systems of representation, but retained a limited franchise; that is, only substantial landowners could vote. Larger cities hired civic administrators to manage the city, abandoning patronage politics for greater efficiency. Politicians and businesses put their faith in a bureaucratic model for the police, public health, utilities, parks, and social welfare administration. Provincial and federal governments supported the international movement urging reform in the industrial city.

The Union of Canadian Municipalities, formed in 1901, played a significant role in lobbying for municipal ownership of public utilities. Municipal politicians and reform-minded businessmen wanted efficiency and beauty in their communities; many of them campaigned for planning as a tool to achieve these ends.

Thus, we see that the interest in planning derived from a range of sources and enjoyed widespread support by the cultural values of the time. Government saw planning as a tool for managing expectations and opportunities in the urban environment. Business thought planning could improve efficiency and ensure that public infrastructure necessary to growth could be provided when required. Reformers hoped that planning could create a better society that might help transform poor immigrants and workers into good citizens and, in the process, make cities better for everyone. The history of planning in the twentieth century reflected those great hopes, but also a litany of challenges, as the articles that follow illustrate.

Jeanne Wolfe presents an overview of the development of planning in Canada. She begins by discussing the long-term implications of the early cadastral patterns, the surveying lines that set out land grants in the colonies and that continue to shape the form of contemporary development. She takes us through the key periods of the growth of the profession and considers some of the ways that planning shaped Canada in the twentieth century.

David Lewis Stein describes the contribution of Thomas Adams, the founder of the planning profession in Canada. Adams came to Ottawa from Britain in 1914 and, in less than a decade, prepared the country to shape its own future through planning. He found a nation eager to hear his message. After World War I ended, Canada went into a recession, and government interest in planning diminished. The reformist zeal that had characterized discussions of planning in the prewar period was repressed in the wake of growing fears of socialism. The Russian Revolution in 1917 created a backlash against ideas that smacked of radicalism or government intervention in free markets. Adams left government but remained in Canada until 1923, working as a private consultant doing plans for such communities as Jasper and Corner Brook. With other planners, he continued to advocate planning to facilitate growth and to protect property values, but in the booming 1920s, the cries fell on deaf ears. Frustrated with the turn in events, Adams left Canada to accept a position with the Regional Plan Association for New York.

Adams's pragmatic utilitarian philosophy remained dominant in Canadian approaches to planning throughout the twentieth century. While Adams made significant contributions to planning in three nations, only in Canada is he known as the "father of planning."[7]

Jeff Ward describes the planning of the only complete "garden city" in Canada, at Grand Falls-Windsor in Newfoundland. Many of the "master planned" communities of the twentieth century in Canada served resource industries in remote regions that lacked urban centres. The success of these communities has always depended on the health of the resource economy, making them especially vulnerable in times of change.

Challenges to Planning

The 1920s began with optimism, but brought high inflation and fiscal crisis in the wake of the war. Prime Minister Mackenzie King took a hard line against socialism and avoided any measure that could possibly be construed as left-leaning. Strikes and protests by workers for better wages were severely repressed, with the government sending in troops to keep the peace. As the Russians embraced planning and housing interventions, those ideas became anathema in Canada. However, one concept initiated by planners did catch on in Canada (as in the US), only to further undermine town planning efforts for the next three decades.

By the 1920s, zoning had become popular in American cities as a way of controlling land use (and land values) and increasing the predictability of development. During the mid-1920s through to the 1950s, zoning effectively replaced planning in many parts of the US. Instead of developing overall town planning schemes for cities, local politicians adopted zoning bylaws that confirmed the status quo while providing mechanisms to enable land use changes under appropriate conditions.

Moore argues that zoning worked well with patronage and populist politics in Canada and thus proved attractive to business interests, ratepayers, and councillors. By contrast, attempts to adopt plans in cities like Toronto during the 1920s were ignored or defeated.[8] As Wolfe explains, only after World War II did community planning really take off in Canada, using zoning as an implementation tool.

The major tool for municipal planning in the 1950s was the master plan. It used maps and text to lay out areas for such activities as development, subdivision, industry, shopping, water supply, parks, refuse facilities, and forest reserves. The plan provided a broad general strategy and guide to policy for 15 to 30 years. Often, it began with a detailed survey of the community and assumed a concentric pattern of growth (with high density in the centre, decreasing toward the periphery, and different functions in various areas). Many plans were prepared by consultants hired by the municipalities: Staff planning departments proved rare until the 1960s. While some of the work in this period set the stage for the modernization of Canadian cities, some of the decisions taken (for example, to destroy African-Canadian communities like Africville in Halifax), in hindsight, appear deeply flawed.

The mood of the times was one of optimism, belief in progress, and faith in science. Change was seen as necessary and good. Urban problems were viewed as amenable to intervention and solution. Planners played an increasingly important role in these times as facilitators of change, as experts who would apply scientific principles to an analysis of current problems and an exploration of future options. As Macklin Hancock describes in his article, by the 1950s, planners had a major impact on the shape of urban and sub-urban developments, for better or for worse.

Canadian cities began to develop their first modern suburbs in the 1950s, modelled loosely on the successful example of Don Mills. Located on the bank of the Don River (near the site of an old mill that contributed to its name), Don Mills constituted the first private-venture new town in a suburban location. (Earlier private new towns were typically associated with resource extraction in remote areas.) As Sewell notes, "Five concepts informed Hancock's remarkable plan: neighbourhoods, a discontinuous road system, a profusion of green space, new house forms and new lot configurations, and a separation of uses and activities."[9]

Two major routes, Lawrence Avenue and Don Mills Road, divided the site into quarters of about 7000 people. Each quarter accommodated neighbourhood units, with an elementary school at centre. Hancock and his team introduced new site planning elements at Don Mills. Wide lots of 60-foot frontage became common, allowing houses to be oriented either widthwise or lengthwise to the street. Homes with large picture windows facing the street rapidly became widely emulated. Varying setbacks from the street gave a sense of visual diversity to the streetscape. Interconnected green-belts wound through and around the community, protecting the ravines and stands of mature trees. Streets organized in a hierarchy limited through traffic in residential environments. T-junctions and cul-de-sacs represented a shift from the ubiquitous Toronto grid. Short curving roads gave the site a unique feel. An outsider driving through the community might find orientation difficult, but would be impressed with the greenery.

Don Mills provided a range of housing types. Of the more than 8000 dwellings built, over half were apartments (in three-storey walkups), with the rest a mix of single detached, semi-detached, and row housing. Both rental and freehold purchase were available to provide opportunities for a mixed income community. The success of Don Mills rapidly drove up the costs of housing and unfortunately put it out of the reach of lower-income households.

By the time that development was complete in 1963, the population had reached 29 000. Don Mills has proven a successful model through the years. Early on, it received a lot of media attention, won design awards, and hosted visits from developers and planners from across Canada and beyond. Its precepts were emulated time and again in the decades that followed. John Sewell called it an example of corporate suburbia, but it became the Canadian suburban ideal in many ways. A visitor to contemporary Don Mills finds a well-tended and diverse community of affluent means. Although some of the elementary schools have closed due to low enrollments, the structures have been retained as community facilities in the neighbourhood unit tradition. Unfortunately, the ideal of providing a self-contained community has not worked because the attractiveness of Don Mills drove up home prices: Those who work in local factories cannot afford to live in Don Mills, while those who live in Don Mills commute to work elsewhere.

Don Mills presents an example of successful collaboration between an innovative designer/planner and a prescient entrepreneur. Hancock's plan employed state-of-the-art concepts to create an attractive townscape and to protect the key features of the natural landscape. Taylor's marketing plan gave him the control he required, the time and resources to do things well, and the ability to reach out to prospective buyers. To facilitate implementation of municipal services, Taylor assumed most of the infrastructure costs, setting a new precedent in development that many municipalities across the country would soon emulate.

By making an excellent return on the project, Taylor demonstrated that Canadians were ready to embrace a new model of residential landscapes and that developers could prosper by following new principles. Thus the stage was set for the Don Mills example to replay itself across the country. As it did so, some of the model's key features fell by the wayside: Seldom did other developments protect natural features to the same extent or create reasonable densities or seek to provide a balance of different dwelling types. As the suburban ideal became entrenched during the 1960s and 1970s, it boiled down to a few simple principles: wide lots, detached houses, grassed lawns, winding streets, and cul-de-sacs. This is the legacy some attribute to Don Mills: good planning theories that led to less than ideal practice.

Our Common Past: An Interpretation of Canadian Planning History

Jeanne M Wolfe

1994, Plan Canada Special 75th Anniversary Issue: 12–34

Planning is about change, and the common belief of all planners, no matter their specialty, expertise, skill or area of endeavour, is that change can be managed for the betterment of the community. Planners argue endlessly about the public good—who is the public and what is good—but all share the sentiment that the human environment can be improved in some way. This essay traces the evolution of the profession of planning, its institutions, activities, underpinnings, and recurring debates (Table 2.1). It follows a chronological order, mirroring the major social currents of the times from early settlement to the mid-1990s.

The founding of the Institute in 1919 by Thomas Adams and a like-minded group of individuals marked the official beginning of the profession, but planning as an activity long predated this event. There are two strands to these preprofessional times: the active, represented in settlement history; and the reactive urban reform movements, which ultimately led to the establishment of the Town Planning Institute of Canada.

The Dominion Land Surveys

The European colonization activities wiped out the evidence of indigenous settlement patterns and conditioned the contemporary landscape. The positioning of forts and ports, the building of canals and railways, and, above all, the geometry of the original land surveys have shaped and still shape the form and morphology of Canadian settlements, whether rural or urban (Figure 2.2). The original division of lands—the long-lot in the French colonies, the township-concession systems of Upper Canada, and the square mile grid flung across the Prairies and draped over the Rocky Mountains—are all reflected in our contemporary communities. They influence the dimensions of urban blocks, patterns of land development, and siting of facilities, and they give each part of the country a distinct flavour.

Table 2.1	A Summary of Planning History		
	Images of the City	Social Currents	Major Planning Activities
1890–1914 Urban Reform Movements Progressive Era	Social disorder Congestion Unsanitary conditions Suburban speculation	Public health Parks and playgrounds Beautification Conservation Municipal reform	Provincial planning acts Voluntary and municipal initiatives City beautiful plans
1914–18 World War I	War production Inefficiency	Nationalism Scientific management	Thomas Adams, Commission of Conservation
1918–29 Boom Times	Growth Civic boosterism	Post-war unrest Social gospel	Zoning Town design Traffic planning Veterans' housing
1930–39 Depression	Congestion Poverty Unemployment	Social reform Conservatism	Unemployment relief projects (infrastructure, parks)
1940–45 World War II	War production	Nationalism	Wartime housing 1941–50
1945–55 Reconstruction	Crowding Slums	Modernization "Homes fit for heroes" Social housing Slum clearance	Neighbourhood design Public housing Central Mortgage and housing
1955–65 Great Expectations	Manageable, improving Urban area analysis	Prosperity, growth Industrial expansion Welfare state Technological innovation	Highways Suburban development Shopping malls Urban renewal Regional planning
1965–80 Consolidation and Confrontation	Pluralism Housing submarkets Interventionism	Heritage conservation Environmentalism Energy efficiency Participatory democracy	Neighbourhood improvement Regional development Cooperative housing Public participation
1980–90 Neoconservatism	Industrial restructuring Increasing homelessness User pay Over-regulated Global aspirations	Minority issues Deregulation, privatization Healthy cities Sustainable development	Large multi-use projects Reurbanization Light rapid transit Community development Third sector initiatives
1990s– New Urban Agenda	Over-taxed Crumbling infrastructure Unsafe, threatened Ugly, sprawling	Regionalism Empowerment of minority groups Professional ethics Global competition Regional urban amalgamations	New urban approaches Smart growth Urban design Regional planning Intensification

Figure 2.2

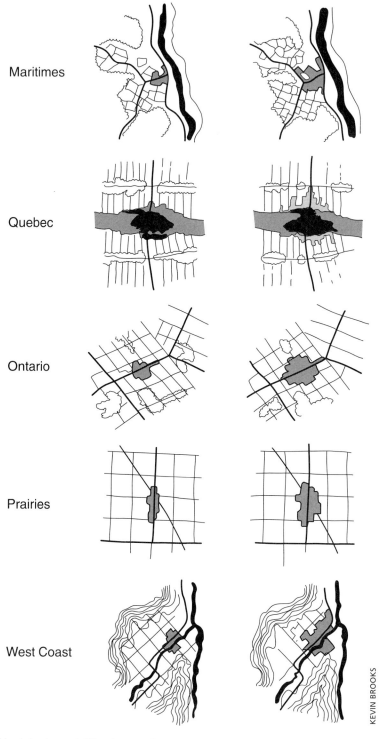

Maritimes

Quebec

Ontario

Prairies

West Coast

KEVIN BROOKS

Patterns of land development differed across the country.

Superimposed on this pattern were the early transportation routes, especially the railways, laid out in prodigious haste in the latter half of the nineteenth century. The original design of the Prairie railway town, devised by a CPR engineer, is well known from the Ontario-Manitoba border to Whitehorse.

Urban Reform Movements

The second preprofessional influence—reaction to the congestion and squalor of nineteenth-century industrial cities, reckless suburban speculative subdivision of land, corrupt municipal government, and wanton exploitation of natural resources—contributed to the foundation of the profession. The urban reform movements of the late nineteenth and early twentieth centuries sprang from these ills. Public health advocates, spurred on by the scientific development of the germ theory, pushed for clean water supplies, proper sanitation, fresh air and sunshine, and an end to the overcrowding of workers' dilapidated housing. Social surveys, such as that carried out by businessman Herbert Ames in Montreal in 1897, evocatively titled *The City below the Hill*, brought attention to the extent of poverty, overcrowding, and insalubrious conditions.

At the same time, the Parks and Playgrounds movement, largely spurred by the works of the various branches of the Council of Women, became established in most large cities. It lobbied for open space, playgrounds, and child welfare, and organized seasonal recreational activities in working-class districts.

Coupled with this was the development of landscape architecture as a profession, greatly spurred by the pioneering work of Frederick Law Olmsted in America. Inspired by democratic ideals and growing social concerns, his work reflected a quest for beauty and function combined with responsible land stewardship. The designation of the mountain of Montreal as a park in 1872 and the commissioning of Olmsted to oversee its design combined these two currents. Similar preoccupations led to his design commissions for parks in Niagara Falls, Stanley Park in Vancouver, and for private estates in several parts of the country. His Canadian protégé, Frederick Todd, continued his work, designing the Avon River parks in Stratford, Ontario, City Park in Kingston, and Assiniboine Park in Winnipeg.

Largely prompted by the Paris Exhibition of 1889 and the Chicago World's Fair of 1893, the fledgling architectural profession similarly began to look at the appalling conditions of cities through a critical lens. Inspired by these marvels of built form, the North American City Beautiful movement was born. Architects believed that the noble design of radial streets and the gracious siting of public buildings could bring dignity, order, beauty, and efficient traffic circulation to cities, while improving infrastructure and thus public well-being. Local associations of architects prepared City Beautiful plans for Toronto and Montreal between 1906 and 1909. The English landscape architect Thomas Mawson was retained to prepare a plan for Regina in 1913 and for Calgary in 1914, and that same year Charles W Leavitt Jr. of New York was brought to Berlin (Kitchener) by the Civic Association for a similar purpose. Meanwhile, Edmonton and Saskatoon retained Morell and Nichols of Minneapolis during the same decade. While, for the most part, such plans were not implemented, their wide circulation in local newspapers aroused great interest among reform groups.

At the same time, war was being waged on corrupt, inefficient municipal governments. Scandals abounded about voting improprieties and around the leasing of rights for public utilities, whether for electricity, gas, or streetcar routes. The advent of electric tramways meant that, for the first time, working-class people could live far from their place of work. But it also allowed entrepreneurs to simultaneously buy up all the land around their projected line and subdivide it, thus reaping benefit from both land sales and the transportation system.

Frenzied subdivision activity, often distant from the city centre, characterized most Canadian cities. Many municipalities faced bankruptcy, trying to provide infrastructure. The problem was held to be due to inefficient planning and management, and calls were made for city governance to be regulated and run on "businesslike lines." Later, many cities established planning commissions or boards made up of responsible citizens "to keep politics out of planning."

Commission of Conservation, 1909–1921

Many of the ideas of the various reform groups were brought together in the work of the Commission of Conservation. Established in 1909 by Clifford Sifton, then Canada's Minister of the Interior, it was originally intended to examine the squandering of the Dominion's natural resources. Government rapidly realized that the urban question was an integral part of the problem, as water resources, the demands for hydroelectricity, minerals, and lumber, agricultural difficulties, erosion, and the destruction of wilderness areas were all held up to scrutiny. Anticipating the *Brundtland Report* by over 70 years, the commission proclaimed that "each generation is entitled to the interest on the natural capital, but the principal should be handed on unimpaired."

The commission's medical officer, Dr. Charles Hodgetts, was largely responsible for shaping Canadian planning before 1914. A former public health officer and a fierce critic of the "army of land speculators and jerry builders," which he believed were ruining cities, Hodgetts lobbied for the appointment of a planning expert. He was not disappointed. In 1914, the commission retained the services of Thomas Adams as town planning consultant to the federal government.

By early 1915, Adams had visited all the provinces except Prince Edward Island. "The keynote of town planning," he said, is "the conservation of life and economy in the system of developing land [so as] to secure efficiency, convenience, health and amenity." He lobbied for and wrote planning legislation for many provinces, founded the commission's journal, *Town Planning and the Conservation of Life*, advised many municipalities on planning problems, often through the local Civic Improvement League, and designed several projects. Meanwhile, Adams wrote the first Canadian planning text, *Rural Planning and Development*, in which he railed against the rigidities of the grid, land speculation, the undercapitalization of farms, inadequate services, and declining rural populations. He proposed a wide-ranging and radical series of remedies, including an expanded role for government at all levels.

During the first decades of the century, planning legislation was prepared for most provinces, and many set up departments responsible for municipal affairs. The early planning acts were tame by today's standards. Planning and zoning were permitted, but planning was usually limited to the urban fringe for "town extensions" and not for replanning existing areas. Most acts included a clause allowing property owners to claim compensation if their land was adversely affected, and all mandated close provincial scrutiny of municipal activities, including plan approval.

Optimism and Despair: The First Decade, 1919–1929

During the 1920s, the major preoccupations of the profession were zoning, town design, and traffic. At first, the new professionals devoted their attention to campaigning for town planning. Journals such as *Canadian Engineer, Canadian Municipal Journal, Canadian Architect and Builder, Royal Architectural Institute of Canada Journal,* and, of course, the *Journal of the Town Planning Institute of Canada* extolled the virtues and economic necessity of planning and zoning, reported on planning progress all over the country, and described overseas achievements in glowing terms. The radical nature of some of these outpourings has seldom been matched.

Since so much land was subdivided on the outskirts of Canadian towns during the land-boom that peaked in 1913, little subdivision activity occurred in the 1920s. Planning often consisted of extending or publicizing the City Beautiful plans of the first part of the century. Many cities established planning commissions and started planning studies, although, for the most part, these were never adopted.

The first zoning bylaw in Canada was that of Kitchener in 1924, although nuisance acts preventing noxious industries such as tanneries, coal-gas plants, or liveries in residential areas date to the early public health initiatives of the nineteenth century. Restrictive covenants protected many residential areas such as Westmount (Montreal) and were in force not only against noxious uses but also to exclude various ethnic groups. Even Westdale, in working-class Hamilton, had such restrictions until 1944, the year Ontario passed its *Racial Discrimination Act.*

Meanwhile, traffic planning, or at least road widening, was becoming a major issue, which may explain the regular referral back to City Beautiful plans with their seductively wide boulevards. As early as 1920, the Pointe-aux-Trembles newspaper was complaining about "les maniaques de la vitesse" in east-end Montreal, as the automobile gained in popularity. None of the early planners seemed to complain about cars: In fact, quite a number were prominent in motoring clubs.

Depression, 1930–1940

The crash of the stock market in late 1929 left no facet of life in Canada untouched. As factories closed, unemployment multiplied. The failure of the grain harvests and the lack of demand for lumber and minerals led to enormous migrations of workers into the cities and towns. Almost no new housing was built, infrastructure was neglected, and urban conditions again became deplorably congested.

Some argue that planning came to an end during this era. And, in fact, the Town Planning Institute of Canada (formed in 1919) ceased operation in 1932, after funds provided by the Department of the Interior to publish the journal dried up.

Three sorts of things happened in this period, with lasting consequences. First were the unemployment relief projects, consisting of infrastructure construction (roads, bridges, waterworks, and parks). Their fine quality, a hand-built legacy, graces many cities and towns today. For instance, during this time in Montreal, Beaver Lake on Mount Royal was dredged and landscaped and the mountain-top chalet constructed; Ste. Helen's Island was completely redeveloped, and the riverside promenade in Verdun was built.

Second, the Prairie droughts, exacerbated by poor farming techniques, prompted the formation of the Prairie Farmers Rehabilitation Administration in 1935. Designed to promote soil and water conservation, good cropping practices, and scientific irrigation, its achievements in regional planning are as notable, although not as noticed, as those of the Tennessee Valley Authority.

A third thrust was the massive campaign for the introduction of social welfare, including the improvement of housing conditions. During the mid-1930s, many citizens' groups and social welfare agencies undertook surveys of living conditions, mapping overcrowding, low incomes, juvenile delinquency, accidents, and substandard housing in an effort to alert various governments to the ills of the cities. For instance, Humphrey Carver established the Housing Centre, a research and lobbying group in Toronto.

The most remarkable program for change was that of the League for Social Reconstruction. The league published an all-encompassing manifesto for a new social order. Titled *Social Planning for Canada*, it analyzed social conditions and proposed almost all of the benefits we came to enjoy: old age pensions, unemployment insurance, mothers' allowances, health care, town planning, and social housing.

While housing was always an issue during the Depression, and advocates for the poor and the withered construction industry lobbied for government intervention, it was not until 1935 that the *Dominion Housing Act* was passed. Then legislation seemed more a measure to stifle the protests of the unemployed than to alleviate housing. The act provided for loans for individuals who could make a 20 percent home down payment: Thus, it was essentially inoperative for low-income groups. In 1938, the first *National Housing Act* (*NHA*) made mortgage money more readily available, but its possible effects were soon overshadowed by the advent of war.

World War II, 1940–1945

The wartime years are rarely mentioned in planning histories, even though they significantly affected both the shape of cities and the profession. Notable, of course, were the tremendous surge in industry, the production of ships, planes, vehicles, and armaments, the great boost to the metal and energy industries, and full employment. Many large machinery plants were laid out, usually in then suburban locations, accompanied by worker housing. Wartime Housing Ltd., a Crown corporation, built 19 000 rental houses between 1941 and 1945 and, in the two immediate postwar years another 13 000. This incredibly successful program was then shut down and the houses gradually sold off to their occupants.

In 1941, looking toward the end of the war, the federal government struck an Advisory Committee on Post-War Reconstruction, chaired by Cyril James, a distinguished economist and principal of McGill. One of the volumes of the final report was *Housing and Community Planning*, published in 1943. Largely written by a Queen's economics professor, CA Curtis (for whom it is usually named), and Leonard Marsh, it urged the government to undertake a national program for social improvement, including housing, planning, and public education. It drew attention to the evils of slums and the wasteful uncoordinated suburbs, and proposed massive public intervention to make up for neglect in the Depression years and for shortages caused by the war.

Reconstruction, 1945–1955

With the end of the war in sight, sweeping changes were made to the *NHA* in 1944 to stimulate the construction of new houses, facilitate the repair and modernization of old, promote community planning, and provide employment. This was followed by the creation of the Central (now Canada) Mortgage and Housing Corporation (CMHC) to implement these policies.

CMHC's role in promoting housing and planning, planning education and research, and public awareness in these early years cannot be overemphasized. In the field of housing, direct lending to the public, and, later on, cost-sharing urban renewal with the provinces and municipalities, public housing (1949), and loans for sewage treatment (1960) did much to modernize our cities. From 1947 to 1986, 250 000 public housing units were built.

The first slum clearance project was Regent Park North in Toronto in 1948. Between then and 1964, over 50 redevelopment studies were undertaken from St. John's to Victoria, with 22 large projects completed. In the early days, slum clearance was seen as a direct solution to housing problems—raze the dilapidated sites and build good housing—as in the case of Regent Park South and Jeanne Mance, but gradually this was expanded to include mixed-use renewal and the provision of sites for other activities.

In the field of planning, CMHC recruited planners and architects, most often from Britain, promoted layout and design schemes, and promulgated and enforced subdivision design and construction standards. Examples include Cité Jardin (Montreal), Crawford Park (Verdun), and Westmount (Halifax) laid out in a Radburn-like pattern. CMHC was able to push municipalities into planning and zoning by threatening not to approve mortgage lending.

To publicize planning, for many years, CMHC published its own journals, *Habitat* and *Living Places*, which were sources of lively information. In 1946, CMHC founded the Community Planning Association of Canada (CPAC), an organization to promote planning ideas, provide a forum for citizens, politicians, developers, and planners to debate issues, run short courses, and publish the now-defunct *Community Planning Review*.

CMHC also made money available for research and education, aiding the first university planning programs at McGill (1947), Manitoba (1949), UBC (1950), and Toronto (1951) through direct grants and student scholarships. It produced useful brochures, such as one on how to do planning studies, and its popular book, *Choosing a House Design*.

The provinces also took up the challenge. For instance, Ontario established the Department of Planning and Development in 1944, revised its planning act in 1946 to establish the "official plan" to include not only cities and towns but also townships, and set up subdivision and zoning rules, which laid the basic elements for practice to this day.

In 1952, the moribund Institute was revived as the Canadian Institute of Planners (CIP), largely by a group of Toronto planners. *Plan Canada* started publishing in 1959.

Great Expectations, 1955–1965

In the decade following the immediate postwar years, Canadian planning became truly institutionalized and assumed many of its present characteristics. This was a decade of prosperity and expansion. Jobs were readily available in all sectors of the economy. Many of the social programs, which have since come under such severe scrutiny, were being adopted or designed. Optimism prevailed.

Population growth was vigorous, and building highways and suburbs were major preoccupations. Don Mills, designed by Macklin Hancock, was built in this period (1952–1962). It became the complete corporate suburb, built on 800 hectares of land by a single private developer. Both admirers and critics agree that Don Mills set the subsequent pattern of urban expansion by use of the neighbourhood concept.

Another example from this time is the nine-square-mile suburb of Mill Woods, Edmonton. Its form was evidently conditioned by the Prairie grid; it consists of eight "communities," each more or less one square mile and each made up of three neighbourhoods, with the central section occupied by the town centre (Figure 2.3).

Highway construction, "roads to resources," was rampant. The St. Lawrence Seaway was built, the first suburban shopping centres started to appear, and provincial planning regulations and procedures became more sophisticated.

During this period, the planning process became systematized. Through scientific analysis and the application of objective judgment, many believed, planning problems could be solved. The rational model was codified and the planning professional, bolstered by the quantitative revolution in the social sciences, was portrayed as a value-neutral and efficient technocrat.

To cope with rapid urbanization and resource management, metropolitan and regional planning was widely advocated. Metro Toronto was created in 1953, as was the Lower Mainland Regional Planning Board in British Columbia in 1954; and in the later 1950s, Alberta put regional planning districts in place. Urban renewal expanded to

Figure 2.3

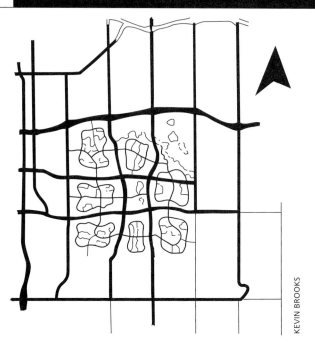

KEVIN BROOKS

Mill Woods in Edmonton reveals the loops and crescents of postwar suburban development.

become urban redevelopment. In 1964, the *NHA* was revised to include redevelopment of nonresidential areas and the rehabilitation (rather than razing) of substandard housing.

Consolidation and Confrontation, 1965–1980

The 1964 amendments to the *National Housing Act* had an extraordinary effect. They resulted in a frenzy of planning activities, as municipal governments read them as an opportunity for economic revitalization. Between 1964 and 1972, more than 300 renewal studies were made with CMHC aid. About 90 renewal projects were authorized, many aimed at redevelopment for central-area purposes, whether commercial or public. Examples include the CBC site in Montreal and Hamilton's Civic Square.

Meanwhile, the provinces were becoming more conscious of federal dominance in the housing field and its direct influence on municipalities. Uncomfortable with being bypassed in policy matters, most set up provincial housing agencies in the mid-1960s, through which CMHC monies were channelled.

The paradox of progress or of urban redevelopment began to be felt toward the end of the 1960s. The earliest slum clearance schemes were fairly well received, but when massive demolition for transportation facilities or for new private-sector offices and apartments threatened functioning neighbourhoods, preservationist and conservation movements sprang up all over the country. Some of these drew national attention: the Stop Spadina movement in Toronto, Milton Park in Montreal, Portage and Main in Winnipeg, Strathcona in Vancouver. Similar struggles were conducted with varying degrees of success in many urban centres. Coupled with the disruption of residential neighbourhoods was the loss of some fine architecture: Thus the historic conservation movement was born, and quickly embraced by planners.

Urban unrest led to the election of populist civic governments in the early 1970s in cities like Toronto and Vancouver. The fact was driven home to planners that planning is a political process: It is not objective and value free. The idea of advocacy planning began to take hold, as some municipalities set up storefront offices to respond to citizen demands for transparency. Public participation became institutionalized in most jurisdictions.

The late 1960s were marked by an extraordinary proliferation of studies and reports on planning and housing issues, culminating in the establishment of the federal Ministry of State for Urban Affairs in 1970. The ministry had a short life—a single decade from 1970 to 1979—but its influence, through the research it undertook, the projects it implemented, and the materials it disseminated, proved widespread. Peter Oberlander of UBC was one of the deputy ministers, as was André Saumier. Len Gertler took leave from Waterloo for a time to be head of policy and research. These staff members later had considerable impact on planning education.

At the same time, the environmental movement, popularized by the counterculture flower-power generation, was gaining ground worldwide. By 1972, Canada had passed its first environmental act, with the provinces following suit quickly. The idea of judging the impact of a project before development was then novel. Planning practice changed to accommodate this new concern.

In the field of regional and rural planning, attitudes were also changing. The Agricultural Rehabilitation and Development Administration had been set up in 1961 to combat rural poverty. It undertook remarkable pilot projects, for example, in the Interlake area of Manitoba and in Prince Edward Island. In Eastern Quebec, pioneering efforts in *animation sociale* came to influence the future techniques of public participation. Before long, authorities realized that rural areas could not be planned without reference to the urban centres that provide services. Consequently, in 1969, government formed the Department of Regional Economic Expansion to promote diversified development in poorer regions of the country.

The oil crisis of 1973 was also a learning experience. With Canada's doubtful distinction of having the highest per capita energy consumption in the world, planners started to think about energy efficiency.

In 1973, sensing the winds of change, CMHC revised its urban renewal policies. By this time, large-scale public housing had fallen into disrepute, so housing programs were refocused on rehabilitation through the Residential Rehabilitation Assistance Program (RRAP) and the Neighbourhood Improvement Program (NIP). Homeowners in designated areas were eligible for RRAP grants and low-interest loans for renovation, while municipalities received grants to repair infrastructure and upgrade amenities. Between 1974 and 1983, when NIP ended, 125 towns and cities across Canada had participated, with 270 neighbourhoods improved and over 310 000 houses rehabilitated.

At the same time, CMHC started up its first major cooperative housing program, which was viewed as a way to provide secure housing for low- and modest-income groups while avoiding the stigma of public housing projects. In the period 1973–1978, 7000 units were built or renovated. Revisions to the program in 1978 led to 40 000 units being completed between 1979 and 1985, when fiscal restraint set in. A revised program, catering only to the core needy, provided 12 000 units between 1986 and 1991.

With the cooperative housing program, the third sector (nongovernmental organizations) received a tremendous boost. Funding was made available for the formation of community resource organizations to furnish technical aid to groups wishing to build co-ops. At the same time, many municipalities created nonprofit housing corporations to take advantage of the various federal and provincial programs available. Much of the energy generated in the third sector during the late 1970s reemerged in the community development arena in the 1980s.

In the 1970s, the other aspect of housing to become an issue was gentrification. Several factors including downzoning of inner-city areas, neighbourhood improvement, weariness with the suburbs, and a rediscovery of the delights of city living contributed to the displacement of working-class residents from inner-city areas by "yuppies" (young urban professionals).

Neoconservatism, 1980–1990

The conservative decade was one of accelerating industrial restructuring, a loss of jobs, increasing criminality in the cities, fiscal crises, and globalization of the economy. Planning, like postmodern society, has been pulled in many directions. At the beginning of the decade, the real-estate boom led many planners into supporting such projects as the IBM building in Montreal, Scotia Plaza in Toronto, and Pacific Place in Vancouver, along with numerous condominium projects, all of which continued the relentless transformation of central areas. Public-private partnerships were touted as a solution to diminishing public funds, and planning took an entrepreneurial turn: Wheeling and dealing became a *modus operandi* for many professionals.

The 1980s also saw a great surge in what is now known as reurbanization, the reuse of worn-out industrial districts (brownfields), railyards, and former harbour lands for residential and other uses. Some of these involved the ingenious redesign of industrial buildings for use as condos, offices, and shops, such as the Stelco buildings on the Lachine Canal in Montreal, Queen's Quay in Toronto, and the waterfront at Trois-Rivières. The demand for urban design skills accelerated.

In the face of intractable unemployment, many local agencies turned to community development work. The emphasis for many planners changed to economic and social development in a desperate attempt to create jobs.

The way planners think was affected by the changing nature of society: changing family structures; increasing proportions of elderly, single-parent families, and two working parents; the special problems of immigrants and visible minorities; requirements of native communities; working at home; implications of gender differences. Cities faced challenges to restrictive bylaws, such as those banning a daycare centre in a residential zone because it is a commercial operation or limiting the number of unrelated persons occupying a single detached house. Neotraditional planning, or new urbanism, that is mixed-use communities as first promoted by Andres Duany and Elizabeth Plater-Zyberk, became increasingly popular with planners.

Healthy Communities, 1986

Toward the end of the decade, two new movements appeared. The healthy cities movement, first conceived by Leonard Duhl, was brought to Canada in 1986, adopted as policy by the World Health Organization in Europe, and, thus endorsed, was vigorously embraced by Canada. The healthy communities movement recognizes that a good physical environment and a supportive community do more for people's health and well-being than most technological advances in medicine. A healthy community goes beyond the health of its individual residents to encompass a healthy environment and a healthy society that promotes social cohesion and helps enable individuals to realize their full physical, social, and intellectual potential.

By 1994, 10 provincial networks with over 250 municipalities adopted healthy community programs. Initiatives ranged from such large-scale ventures as Healthy Toronto's *State of the City Report* and its yearly health promotion week to such single-action initiatives as improving river banks, eliminating the domestic use of herbicides, curbing dogs, building bike paths, setting up teenage recreational programs, and initiating toxic waste disposal programs.

The three challenges set out by healthy communities involve reducing inequities, increasing prevention, and enhancing coping. The promotion strategies of self-care and mutual aid made this a grassroots movement. The process is bottom up, guided by local committees. People saw something in it for themselves: The dangers of toxic wastes, sick buildings, alienated youth, and poisonous pesticides are tangible fears. While there are evident parallels between the healthy communities movement and the turn-of-the-century public health advocates, the main differences were in approach.

Sustainable Development, 1987

Just as the healthy communities movement was getting under way, the *Brundtland Report* from the World Commission on the Environment and Development was published, bringing new perspectives to notions of environmental planning. How are cities and nations to resolve the contradictions between environmental protection and economic development? Sustainable development is a broad idea, nudged along by alarming research on global warming, climatic change, holes in the atmosphere, and other threats to planetary survival. Many nations rapidly adopted it as public policy. Canada established a National Round Table on the Environment and the Economy. It recommended setting up focus groups to bring together industry, government, and environmentalists to develop sustainable economic policies. Provincial round tables quickly followed. Environmental reporting by all levels of government, whether federal, provincial, or local, became a growth industry.

For a while, it seemed as though the healthy communities movement would be eclipsed by the newer buzzword of "sustainability." But as research progressed into what sustainable development means and how it can be achieved, the two streams of thought increasingly converged (and by the late 1990s were incorporated within ideas of smart growth). Many planners now advocate an ecosystems approach, which endeavours to embrace both.

The 1990s

The neoconservative decade raised some fundamental questions for planners. In a context of deregulation, privatization, cost recovery, attempts to shrink government, and the profit motive being given priority over public service and equality of opportunity, what should a planner do? In retrospect, it is not surprising that professional ethics became a major issue in the mid-1980s, not only in planning but in all professions.

The sparkling images of the new downtowns and redeveloped industrial sites were increasingly marred by the homeless, soup kitchens, and rising crime. Municipal governments, strapped for funds, complained of crumbling infrastructure and worried about tax revolts.

Although one of the tenets of postmodernism is to dispute the idea of the master-narrative, many of the largest Canadian cities produced new general plans in the 1990s. For instance, Montreal, Ottawa, Toronto, Hamilton, Calgary, and Vancouver all engaged in that pursuit during the early 1990s. Vision statements, in line with Daniel Burnham's axiom "make no little plans," became the mode.

Meanwhile, entrepreneurial planning and community development—planning by negotiation—continued to be important. Unfortunately, the foundering of the property development industry in the recessionary 1980s (except in British Columbia), the retreat of the federal government from the social housing field in the late 1980s, and provincial and municipal government retrenchment reduced opportunities in these areas. At the same time, the bureaucratic-regulatory function of planning came under scrutiny. Many jurisdictions looked at ways to fast-track the approval of development proposals.

What of the future? Agenda 21, the declaration of the UN Environment Summit in Rio de Janeiro in 1992, demonstrated that the technical capacity to achieve appropriate sustainable development is easier to imagine than the political processes required for implementation. We can only hope that our heightened awareness and new negotiating skills will lead us in better directions.[10]

Thomas Adams: The Father of Canadian Planning

David Lewis Stein

1994, Plan Canada Special 75th Anniversary Issue: 14–5

It may be some comfort to remember that Thomas Adams (1871–1940), the godfather of Canadian planning, was an international figure who suffered because of the public mood swings that still affect the planning profession.

Adams was born in 1871 on a dairy farm just outside of Edinburgh, Scotland, and in his early twenties he even operated a farm himself. From these agrarian roots, he went on to become a founding member of the British Town Planning Institute, founder of the Town Planning Institute of Canada, and a founding member of the American City Planning Institute, forerunner of the American Institute of Planners.

Adams accomplished this institutional hat trick—as well as becoming one of the most important early private practitioners—not so much because of the originality of his ideas, but because he was a vigorous individual fortunate enough to be in the right place at the right time.

While a farmer on the outskirts of Edinburgh at the end of the nineteenth century, Adams became a local councillor. He later moved to London to pursue a career in journalism and got caught up in the excitement of the garden city movement. He qualified as a surveyor and became the first person in England to make his living entirely from planning and designing garden suburbs, doing no less than seven of them. By 1910, Adams was so widely recognized in his new profession that he became the first president of the British Town Planning Institute.

He believed that Britain's *Housing and Town Planning Act* of 1909 would help to establish a planning process throughout the country. Following passage of the act, he became an advisor to councils but found little will in the formidable British bureaucracy to advance the cause of urban planning. However, it took three invitations before Adams agreed to come to Canada in 1914: Charles Hodgetts, the medical officer of Canada's Commission of Conservation, who had been impressed by Adams at a conference, pressed Clifford Sifton to invite Adams to this country to work for the commission.

The commission was headed by Sifton, a Manitoba businessman and politician, whose wide-open immigration policies had led to the populating of the Prairies. Sifton was trying to deal with the impact of close to one million immigrants—many non-British—who had come to Canada between 1896 and 1914. By 1911, with half of Canada's population settled in urban centres, the commission was seeking ways to cope with a wildly speculative housing market and the lack of regulation for land development. Adams's contribution to the commission was to bring the garden city ideas of environmental standards and England's ideas about local government control. He became an advocate for provincial municipal affairs departments and local planning boards.

As a private practitioner, Adams undertook plans for a number of new communities, including Corner Brook in Newfoundland, Temiscaming in western Quebec and, most notably, the Richmond district of Halifax. Adams was given the job of replanning Richmond, which had been devastated by the explosion of a munitions ship in Halifax harbour in 1917, one of the great disasters of World War I. Because of the emergency situation and war pressures, Adams was able to acquire extraordinary powers for a bureaucrat. Overruling local interests, he drew up a plan for Richmond that respected the district's hilly nature and put in diagonals to break up the street's grid pattern, a Canadian tradition that Adams particularly disliked.

Philosophically, Adams was a late-Victorian liberal who believed in a sturdy, property-owning yeomanry rather than placing people in "socialistic," government-owned housing. In 1919, he helped found the Town Planning Institute of Canada, primarily to promote the new discipline of planning. He also wrote extensively in *Town Planning and Conservation of Life* and published *Rural Planning and Development*, the first Canadian planning book.

In the early 1920s, many of the functions for which the Commission of Conservation had been created were taken over by federal and provincial ministries, and so Adams moved to the United States in 1923. There he distinguished himself by producing the first regional plan for New York. In his final years, he divided his time as a private practitioner between Great Britain and the US.

Although Adams's idea that planning is a technocratic, value-free, scientific endeavour has been shown to be untrue, his ideas about the wasteful use of natural resources, the follies of premature subdivision, and the need to plan roads concordant with topography are as true today as they were then.

White Coal: The Birth of a Company Town

Jeffrey P Ward

2005, Plan Canada 45(3): 32–5

Ask a student of planning what was the first planned community of the modern era in Canada. She is not likely to name Grand Falls, Newfoundland, but it was the first fully realized garden city experiment in Canada.

The story of how the community originated begins in Fleet Street, London, the centre of the newspaper district. Alfred Harmsworth (Lord Northcliffe, 1865–1922) and his brother Harold (Lord Rothermere, 1868–1940) ran the *Daily Mail*, a morning paper still publishing. Alfred and Harold were two of several children in an over-achieving family. In 1906, Alfred became the youngest-ever peer of the realm for his efforts to support the Conservative government. Like Grand Falls, the barony "Northcliffe" would be his invention.[11]

Northcliffe found inspiration in the garden city. In 1898, Ebenezer Howard advocated separating work and home in an environment that blended the best of the city with the best of the country. For better or worse, his work became the foundation of modern land use planning and helped shaped the suburbs.

Northcliffe is quoted as saying to Howard, "Yours is the most concrete example of the force of an idea that has ever come within my knowledge."[12] Northcliffe publicized Howard's ideas in his newspapers and offered to carry free advertising for the Letchworth project.[13] In 1903, he contributed £1000 to the founding of Letchworth, the first garden city in England. Two years later, he began investments in his own project in Newfoundland, which would dwarf this trifling donation.

What motivated Northcliffe and Rothermere to invest in Newfoundland were rumours of war. They decided to establish a secure supply of newsprint away from the uncertainty of Europe. The railway, completed in 1898, opened the interior of the island for the first time. Several locations were considered in Newfoundland, including Grand Lake (now the source of power for the mill at Corner Brook) and Grand Falls. After a period of deliberation that included a rare dispute between the brothers, Northcliffe selected Grand Falls. Detailed surveys of the lands were commissioned to a firm from St. John's. With the help of British bankers, in 1905, Northcliffe initiated construction of Grand Falls through his new enterprise, the Anglo-Newfoundland Development (AND) Company. The persons who planned the townsite are not known. Nonetheless, the concept fully reflects the intents and ideals of the garden city movement.

Townsite and Architecture

The original plan consists of five parts: the mill, town centre, two residential districts, and a recreational area. The mill sits on a bend of the Exploits River, where a constriction forces water over a short, narrow gorge: As Northcliffe remarked, this was "white coal."[14] To the east of the mill lies High Street, the commercial and administrative centre of the community. Further east is a residential area with a distinctive circular road around the district (Figure 2.4). Two pairs of intersecting streets form a grid within the circle (Figure 2.5). Houses are arranged on spacious lots, with front and rear "gardens" as per the dictates of Howard's garden city model. How radical this design must have appeared to Englishmen and Newfoundlanders alike! In contrast to the brick row houses of Victorian England, the scattered fishing houses of coastal Newfoundland, or the densely packed homes on the hills of St. John's, the regular and spacious design was a striking departure.

Figure 2.4

TOWN OF GRAND FALLS-WINDSOR. COURTESY OF JEFF SAUNDERS

Cottages housed workers in Grand Falls.

Figure 2.5

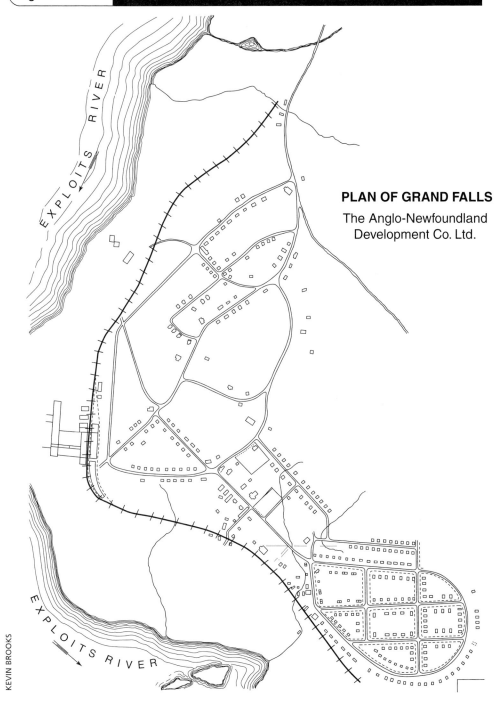

PLAN OF GRAND FALLS

The Anglo-Newfoundland
Development Co. Ltd.

KEVIN BROOKS

The Grand Falls site plan, circa 1907, shows garden city influences.

North of the mill, another residential area featured an irregular curvilinear street network dictated by the hilly terrain. Spacious lots prevailed. To the east of this neighbourhood lay a recreational area with a race park and grandstand. (It now boasts a civic park and playground.)

True to Howard's vision, the initial structures on the townsite used local materials, chiefly wood. The work force employed to build the structures were familiar with abundant local materials. Later, imported Scottish brick decorated several large structures, including the town hall and a hotel (the Carmelite House).

The design and substance of the domestic architecture varied depending on the intended occupant. Thus, Northcliffe's home, Grand Falls House, was a large, traditional Tudor-style dwelling, which seems lifted from the English countryside.[15] The Tudor style, in vogue at the time, often appears in garden city projects.[16] Down the management ladder, dwellings rapidly became more modest. Drawings of the most common dwelling types survive.

The building program lasted from 1906 until 1912, with a later brief development thrust after World War I. A total of 485 houses were constructed. More than 50 other buildings were also erected, ranging from stables to a hospital, and from schoolhouses to churches. The company paid for all construction. The contractor (at least in the early period) appears to have been the Horwood Lumber Company of St. John's.

Thus, Northcliffe completed the first modern planned community of twentieth-century Canada, and the second garden city after Letchworth. In 1909, a year after he acquired *The Times*, Northcliffe visited Grand Falls with his wife to officially open the mill. At the opening banquet on the floor of the mill, he said, "We hope to make Grand Falls a garden city, and I am pleased that in a humble way, we are beginning to do so."[17]

A Study in Contrasts

These facts about Grand Falls seem so obscure that they do not even warrant a footnote in most histories of the garden city movement. Most significantly, Thomas Adams ignored it; in his 1917 survey of recent planning trends, for example, he made no mention of Grand Falls, although he wrote at length about the garden city concept. It might be argued that the omission was because Newfoundland was not then part of Canada. This may be accurate, as he did not discuss the state of planning in the United States either.

But there may be other reasons. In 1930, a biographer described Rothermere's disappointment with the grand experiment: "This may not grow to the size and importance once imagined."[18] By 1910, the brothers had spent more than six million dollars on the mill, the townsite, and a railway to Botwood, but Grand Falls had not reached Howard's mythical 32 000 and was not utopian.

Part of the reason lay with Northcliffe. He was, quite frankly, a xenophobe and anti-Zionist. While he ensured that Church Street—a wonderful ecclesiastical panorama—offered space for nearly all of the Christian religions of the time, he would not permit other races or competing religions. Thus, many who came to the community from the coast or St. John's or farther afield—those people who knew the new town would need dry goods stores, laundry services, theatres, and furniture stores—could not live in the town. Even lumberjacks could not buy their way in. Only mill employees could become leaseholders within the town.

Therefore, the neighbouring community of Grand Falls Station grew in parallel with Grand Falls. Its growth was nowhere near as orderly. When the Government of Newfoundland granted a four-mile by eight-mile allotment to the AND Company, just behind the train station, it neglected to foresee the demand for land outside the townsite borders. It did not expect the exclusivity that Northcliffe would impose, and the rapid settlement that would occur outside the town.

Grand Falls Station (renamed Windsor in honour of the Royal Family in 1939) became the place for action. Just north of the train station, a main street quickly developed as a service district for Grand Falls. Near the mill, on High Street, a sedate downtown had been established with company club, haberdashery, restaurant, and blacksmith. But the real economy lay across the tracks, four miles away. Private jitney services ferried people between the two downtowns: The service operated until the 1960s.

By the time the government answered applications for land grants near the station, residents had already set down roots in a haphazard manner. Grants were made to match the land claims; in the tumult, roads were not reserved. By 1945, the lanes showed little sense of order. Many of the streets had no continuity due to topography and landowners, neither of which proved cooperative.

Even today, after more than a decade of remedial efforts by the town engineering staff following amalgamation of Grand Falls-Windsor in 1991, the community layout north of the train station may be characterized as disorderly. For example, several streets end at fences or in somebody's driveway. Other streets and lanes stop short of their natural intersections. And a common feature of the community is backlot development, that is, more than one dwelling on a lot. This reflects a traditional Newfoundland pattern of dividing property among offspring—a practice tolerated until recently.

Historic Lessons

For its 15 000 residents, Grand Falls-Windsor is a wonderful place to live, on either side of the tracks. But the lesson of Grand Falls and Windsor provides a cautionary tale for planners. While the planning intent of the original townsite was fully realized, its impact was not anticipated. The planners, investors, and government failed to understand the full effects of their undertaking, and neglected the need to accommodate all those who wished to share in their initiative. The garden city model worked, but like so many idealized planning models, its merits were not recognized beyond the original townsite. As a result, Grand Falls-Windsor offers a flawed example of Ebenezer Howard's vision.

Don Mills: Paradigm of Community Design

Macklin Hancock

1994, Plan Canada Special 75th Anniversary Issue: 87–90

One consequence of the population explosion after World War II was the rapid expansion of urban development, especially in the areas adjacent to Toronto. By July 1952, enlightened industrialist EP Taylor (chairman of Argus Corporation) and his corporate strategist, Karl Fraser (first president of Don Mills Developments Ltd.), had assembled a 2000-acre tract of rolling terrain in what was then rural North York. This land was to be the location for a "new town," a modern industrial locus away from Toronto's traditional manufacturing hub. It was separated from the Toronto suburbs of Leaside and East York by the deep, wide, and heavily vegetated Don River Valley, and bifurcated by the narrow and winding Don Mills Road. Financed, planned, and implemented with private resources, this manufacturing initiative was to accommodate anticipated new businesses and housing that would inject postwar life and energy into the southern Ontario hub, a conurbation with a population of less than one million.

The timing of the initiative (as well as its marked difference from previous edge communities) triggered considerable public analysis, which pushed it to the forefront of modern planning practice as a distinctive pattern or paradigm. The numerous developers and city builders who later attempted to emulate this community failed to recognize that its unique characteristics and configuration were, at least in part, the result of the area's social, ecological, and geographical features. Location not only made it possible to address the ballooning challenge of the automobile and society's growing fascination with the elevator, but also the importance of preserving irreplaceable valley and watershed systems.

My involvement in the project began early on, when, during the initial assembly period, Karl Fraser became interested in my work at Harvard's Graduate School of Design. At that time, I was using simulated planning models to study urbanization in the new towns of England and Sweden. Decentralization was at the heart of these new towns and was considered an important principle for the creation of economical, meaningful, and satisfying future human settlements, in the face of a swelling global population and the need for more equitable regional distribution. Based on this work, Fraser hired me to plan and design the new community of Don Mills (Figure 2.6).

Figure 2.6

KEVIN BROOKS

The site plan for Don Mills shows its neighbourhoods grouped around the town centre.

What we visualized was an integrated community that would house 35 000 people and employ 20 000. In harmony with the natural resources and ecological systems of the Don Valley, 450 acres were set aside for housing and ancillaries, and in the two polar locations adjoining this, 450 acres for industry. In close coordination with the municipality, its neighbours, and the Province of Ontario, the Don Mills new town would produce affordable housing, jobs, and all the necessary and accompanying urban functions and infrastructure. Residential, commercial, and transportation land uses would occupy 1100 acres.

For the North York Planning Board, which had already determined that it could not cope successfully with undifferentiated urbanization rippling outwards from Toronto, the Don Mills initiative represented an excellent opportunity for controlled urban development. Here was a chance to press forward, innovatively and with private capital, in the creation of a model community. Don Mills would be an exemplar, a fine urban community with a balanced tax base; with amenities for the young and the old, for families and their extensions; and of lasting socioeconomic benefit for residents, for employees and employers, for developers and builders, and for the municipality itself.

In 1952, a small planning team comprising myself, Marjorie and Donald Hancock, and Noboru Koyama prepared plans and models of the new town. The team's educational and experiential bias toward landscape, civic art, and agrology ensured that the community would be designed with the preservation of the priceless natural resources of the Don Valley, its related streams, and aquifers in mind, and with as little humanization of the landscape as possible. In the meantime, capital investors assembled more land in anticipation of the future expansion of the Don Mills community. More critical mass would mean not only increased employment and housing opportunities, but also greater control of circulation, transportation, and watershed expression at stream confluences.

One of the essential features of the new community was its higher-than-normal density. Using a more compact development form than had been previously regarded as necessary for peripheral city expansion in North America allowed us to optimize land capability and preserve the most ecologically sustainable open spaces. With a density of almost 90 persons per hectare on the 1000 gross acres of housing land, we would have to integrate town and cluster housing and low-cost horizontal and vertical apartment developments with single family and semi-detached dwellings in a market-oriented community that was both desirable and affordable.

At the outset, most dwellings were inexpensive and small (between 900 and 1300 square feet) to reflect the means and needs of Don Mills residents (Figure 2.7). These were primarily families whose heads would find work opportunities with such companies as IBM, Upjohn, and other industrial and commercial employers attracted to the townsite and environs. Appropriate lands were designated for libraries and high schools; churches and elementary schools were positioned to be the focal points of each neighbourhood, their grounds ample to provide, ultimately, for church-operated seniors' housing. Plans were laid for police and fire protection facilities and leisure, civic, and sports clubs. We selected young architects and teamed them with responsive new builders to pioneer innovative dwelling types and housing, building, and layout systems.

Planners and designers (who became implementers) organized tree planting, landscape, and colour schemes for each lot and apartment site to enhance the built environment visually and ecologically. Taking planted space into consideration, precipitation was handled with ditch, swale, and original water course drainage, which allowed for water retention and, in some cases, aquifer recharge. A sewage treatment plant on the Don River would deal with effluent in advance of a Don River–aligned outfall to an expanded lakeside system. The fundamental and unique feature of the new town was

Chapter 2 / The History of Canadian Planning

Figure 2.7

Don Mills homes set a suburban standard widely emulated across the country.

its vascular, internal, open-space pedestrian and bike system, separated from traffic and embracing educational facilities.

Automobile use in advance of metropolitan mass- and rapid-transit and commuter rail was an important consideration, and provisions were made for future arterials. With the imminent construction of Highway 401 across Toronto's northern metropolitan limits, we saw the need for an umbilical roadway that would connect the new town with the mother city. A conceptual layout of the Don Valley Parkway, including a future Highway 404 extension, was put forward to the then Toronto and York Roads Commission. In 1954, under a new name, the Metropolitan Toronto Corporation quickly proceeded with the design, development, and construction of the parkway, which was scheduled to open in seven years.

Under the name "Project Planning Associates," the original team members completed the final stages of development planning for Don Mills between 1957 and 1959. The result of our efforts was a truly unique North American community. Its topographically organized, hub-oriented road system (constrained only by the encircling and bifurcating railroads) and 500-acre linked, open-space system of pedestrian walkways and greenways, parks, and school and church grounds allow each of the community's neighbourhoods access to green areas, a core of shopping, leisure and community facilities, and the greater regional valley system established with the voluntary transfer of valley lands to the Metropolitan Toronto Corporation.

To this day, with its unmistakable new town community structure, Don Mills remains a viable, stable, and thriving feature of the southern Ontario region. Although the area is undergoing some evolutionary changes (the result of an over-widening of Don Mills Road), it is to be hoped that future alterations will be tempered with the kind of good judgment and planned enhancement that will ensure, not jeopardize, the community's long-term environmental sustainability, growth, and prosperity.

1. What national and international factors contributed to the acceptance of community planning by governments in the 1940s through 1960s?

2. What role has the technology of construction and transportation, and the regulations imposed upon the use of those technologies, played in the changing shape and character of the city during the last century?

3. If we look back in history, we can point to ancient cities that epitomize the best of planning for their times (e.g., Chang'an in the first millennium, Paris in the nineteenth century). Make a case for which city "represents" Canadian planning in the twentieth century. (You could make the case for the "best" city of the century, or the "typical," or the city most likely to be remembered in 2000 years.) How does this city epitomize the nature of planning practice in the twentieth century?

4. Why did the period of the Progressive Era (1890–1920) prove so "ripe" for the origin of modern town planning?

5. Why did so much suburban development since the 1950s fail to deliver on the promise of the garden city and Don Mills?

6. Many would argue that new urbanism is the direct descendant of City Beautiful ideas inspired by baroque precepts informed by classical Greco-Roman concepts. Why do beautification themes keep returning to the practice of planning and community design?

7. Study maps of your community. Based on the patterns of the streets and what you know about when particular patterns were in vogue, estimate the dates when areas were built. Do you see areas that draw on colonial history or others inspired by the legacy of Don Mills? Identify the economic factors, transportation modes, and planning theories that affected the urban form of your community through its history.

8. Identify a "menu" that characterizes the differences in types of Canadian communities, for example, postwar suburbs, turn-of-the-century railway towns, fishing communities of Newfoundland. Pick the ones that interest you, and try to determine the physical and social features that set them apart as cultural landscapes.

1. Sanford [Rahder], B (1987) The political economy of land development in nineteenth century Toronto. *Urban History Review* 16(1): 17–33.

2. Rutherford, P (1984) Tomorrow's metropolis revisited: A critical assessment of urban reform in Canada, 1890–1920. In GA Stelter & AFJ Artibise (eds) *The Canadian City: Essays in Urban and Social History*. Ottawa: Carleton University Press: 437.

3. Bliss, M (1991) *Plague: A Story of Smallpox in Montreal*. Toronto: HarperCollins.

4. Lewis, R (2002) The industrial suburb is dead, long live the industrial slum: Suburbs and slums in Chicago and Montreal, 1850–1950. *Planning Perspectives* 17: 123–44.

5. Copp, JT (1974) The condition of the working class in Montreal, 1897–1920. In M Horn & R Sabourin (eds) *Studies in Canadian Social History*. Toronto: McClelland and Stewart: 189–212.

6. Sanford [Rahder], B (1987) Op. cit.: 17–33.

7. Simpson, M (1985) *Thomas Adams and the Modern Planning Movement: Britain, Canada and the United States, 1900–1940*. London: Alexandrine Press Book, Mansell.

8. Moore, PW (1979) Zoning and planning: The Toronto experience, 1904–1970. In A Artibise & GA Stelter (eds) *The Usable Urban Past*. Toronto: Macmillan Canada: 316–41.

9. Sewell, J (1993) *The Shape of the City: Toronto Struggles with Modern Town Planning*. Toronto: University of Toronto Press: 82.

10. An update on the arguments here is presented in J Wolfe (2002) Reinventing planning: Canada. *Progress in Planning* 57: 207–35.

11. Ferris, P (1972) *The House of Northcliffe: A Biography of an Empire*. New York: World Publishing.

12. Meacham, S (1999) *Regaining Paradise: Englishness and the Early Garden City Movement*. New Haven: Yale University Press.

13. Purdom, CB (1963) *The Letchworth Achievement*. London: JM Dent & Sons: 10.

14. Fyfe, H (1930) *Northcliffe: An Intimate Biography*. New York: Macmillan: 139.

15. Macfarlane, D (2000 [1991]) *The Danger Tree: Memory, War, and the Search for a Family's Past*. Toronto: Vintage Canada.

16. Symonds, R (2001) *The Architecture and Planning of the Townsite Development, Corner Brook 1923–5*. St. John's: Heritage Foundation of Newfoundland and Labrador.

17. Tucker, WB (chairman) (1986) *The Forest Beckoned: Reminiscences and Historical Data of the Town of Grand Falls Newfoundland from 1905 to 1960*. Grand Falls: Exploits Valley Senior Citizens Club: 3.

18. Fyfe, H (1930) Op. cit.: 134.

Chapter Three

The Context of Planning

The Culture and Theory of Canadian Planning

Jill Grant

Community planning occurs not in a vacuum but in a particular context. Some factors that affect outcomes and processes are purely local: Communities differ in the issues that occupy attention and in their ways of doing business. But planning also occurs within larger contexts that apply more generally. In this chapter, we get a sense of how the larger cultural context and the professional development of theory may contribute to shaping planning practice in Canada.

Culture

Cultural values and priorities change over time. Prosperity waxes and wanes, affecting the viability of communities and the choices they must make. While tradition in city building meant continuity over centuries in some cultures, the contemporary era in Canada involves trendiness in built form as in clothing. For instance, grid street patterns dominated development in the late nineteenth and early twentieth centuries before serpentine patterns became popular; by the late twentieth century, the grid became fashionable again for new development in some regions. Our cities reflect continual adaptations to innovation in technologies (Figure 3.1). Accommodations for new transportation technologies clearly had major effects in the nineteenth and twentieth centuries. What innovations (or disasters) will shape the twenty-first?

The trajectory of planning reflects the changing concerns of government about growth. Growth is a key concept in our economic system. Capitalism sees expansion as positive and economic contraction as negative. A fear of great depressions, and even of minor recessions, has had a major impact on thinking about the role and nature of planning in Canada.

Marxist geographers and planners have pointed to the tensions and contradictions that planning helps to mediate in our society.[1] The dilemma of capitalism is that although it advocates open markets, it actually needs government mechanisms to regulate the land market to ensure that conditions are good for the growth of capital. Even the most pro-market advocate is unlikely to want to allow a tannery to build next to a valuable commercial project and thereby undermine land values. Planning and zoning help to safeguard the predictability or profitable conversion of land values. Yet, because planning and zoning constrain the choices of capital, they may be resisted. Planning is needed but resented.

As several authors in this chapter note, Canadian planning tends to be reactive. Thomas Gunton argues that it responds cyclically to crises, getting ready to address problems that are already subsiding

Figure 3.1

The standard mass-produced suburb reflects a car-dependent society.

by the time policies take effect. We might see planning as a coping mechanism by which we try to manage problems and improve conditions. If so, it is always catching up to a moving target. Many planners would prefer to be visionaries, idealistic gazers and future makers who proactively engage the future. The literature on planning reflects an unending and perhaps irresolvable tension about the role of the planner. Should the planner respond to the people (helping them to achieve the aspirations they define), or should the planner lead people to a better future? Is the planner ideally a civil servant (some may say "technocrat") or a visionary expert or facilitator? This debate continually permeates discussions about planning. As Michael Dear and Glenda Laws suggest in their article, whichever role planners choose, they have the obligation to reflect on their practice and to learn from their own successes and failures.

How good are planners at predicting the future? We return to that question in Chapter 6, when we discuss planning for uncertainty. But in these commentaries on the context of planning, we see what planners a decade or more ago thought was coming. Did their predictions come true? Did these authors recognize the potential impact of the deindustrialization of cities in the late twentieth century? How could they have anticipated the decision of provincial governments to create amalgamated regional cities? What other concerns did they miss because they could not easily escape the context of their own times?

Since the nineteenth century, planners have recognized some persistent unsolved problems: Adequate, affordable housing immediately comes to mind. Housing was a major focus of postwar planning in the UK. It led to satellite new towns and a major program of public housing, but it did not trigger comparable action in Canada. How can we explain this difference? Political context clearly plays a role. British cultural and political values (likely engendered by the wartime experience) supported greater government intervention in the built environment. In Canada, constitutional issues have served as an excuse for not dealing with housing problems. Housing comes under a provincial mandate in our distribution of powers, but only the federal government has the funds to potentially address it. The provinces readily download the problem to municipalities, which lack the finances to cope. Only a few provinces and cities have a reasonable record in addressing the desperate need for housing. In recent decades, we have seen homelessness become a national tragedy. If we can't plan to meet basic shelter needs, what does that say about our society?

Planning is necessary but not beloved in Canadian society. It has not been able to address some essential problems that plague us: the impact of inequality and poverty; the effects of uneven growth in regions of the country. But planning persists because it keeps the land development process manageable and predictable. It provides mechanisms for managing conflict over land and resources. It provides a process for accommodating debate about community choices and futures. Thus, it has found a place in Canadian culture.

Theory in Planning

Canadian planning is overwhelmingly rational.[2] Rational planning (also called synoptic planning) has been the dominant paradigm in contemporary town planning since the early twentieth century.[3] It operates from many of the same premises as the scientific method. It presumes objective experts, who can process information without being biased by their own values. It assumes that the universe operates according to orderly rules that can be determined and employed for prediction. It requires that the experts use predefined and logical sets of operations to accomplish defined tasks. The significance of rationality in planning also reflects the significance of capitalist logic in our culture. The principles of the market—maximization of pleasure/profit, avoidance of risk, supply and demand—also drive rational planning.

Rational planning assumes that society can define and achieve its goals. In this model, planners seek the "public interest," the choices that reflect the wishes and common good of the community. The simplest models assume a unitary public interest: that one choice is undeniably best for the community. Other models may recognize some dispute about the public interest, but assume that the planner can determine which choices best approximate that goal. The planner then strives to achieve a level of consensus on the public interest. Jill Grant's article explores the complex issues around this notion of the public interest.

The role of the planner in a rational planning model is as technical expert, drawing together the strands of information required for decision making, analyzing all the factors relevant to the situation, and offering advice on the best choice for the community.

Through the years, many varieties of rational planning have come and, in some cases, gone. In the early years of town planning, planners talked about "town planning schemes." These were partial plans, often for beautification of the civic centre of the community. By the postwar period, these gave way to the concept of master plans. Master plans attempted to cover the key elements of urban planning: transportation, housing, industry, economy, future land use. They typically looked 20 to 50 years into the future to set out where highways would be needed, where industry may locate, where housing should be built (Figure 3.2). The master plan attempted to be comprehensive in its scope.

Challenges to the approach and demands for public participation in the planning process in the late 1960s and early 1970s led to redefinition of municipal plans. Comprehensive plans and development plans often replaced the master plans. Planners remained committed to a rational planning process but increasingly provided opportunities for the public to participate in the process. Relabelling the process as "comprehensive" helped to accommodate this change.

Developers working on new large-scale community projects continued to use the language of "master plan." This reflects the kind of conceptualization required for

Figure 3.2

JILL GRANT

A "future bus zone" reveals rational planning at work: Implementation remains an aspiration.

designing new communities: It is essential to take a long-range perspective and endeavour to consider all the variables that may come to play in making a successful town.

In the 1960s and 1970s, many countries—but not Canada—participated in national planning or societal planning exercises. For instance, Britain had a series of national plans with development targets. Since international lending and aid agencies required developing countries to prepare such plans as a condition of aid, most Third World countries adopted national plans. These development plans set out targets for transforming the economy from agricultural bases to industry or tourism. Planning was being used to modernize nations. Methods that had succeeded in creating growth in the West or in the Soviet Union were often emulated in an attempt to use rational methods to create change. For the most part, these efforts were not successful: Planning could not overcome gross inequities and market disadvantages.

The 1960s and 1970s brought another rational model to the forefront: systems planning.[4] The ability of computers to process large amounts of data in complex ways appealed to planners eager to integrate volumes of information. Computer models were designed to churn out options for a variety of purposes. Demographic projection models found an important place in planning, as they simplified the calculation of population forecasting. In the baby boom era, these models had a persuasive effect in driving home the need to plan for continued population growth. They also raised public concern about the future of the planet, with the publication of documents like the Club of Rome's *Limits to Growth*.[5]

As many discovered, the models are only as good as the presuppositions used by the designers. Birth rates plummeted in the 1980s, proving most of the population models inaccurate.

Systems planning featured extensively in transportation planning. Sophisticated transportation models deal with a wide range of variables, including population, car ownership, and transit use. The models proved a "scientific" way to justify demand for new highway construction. Again, the veracity of the models depended on the accuracy of the programming premises. As computer programmers say, "Garbage in garbage out."

Systems models declined as planners realized that computers didn't necessarily make decision making easier or transparent. Public demands for participation and openness in planning rendered efforts to use such models impossible. Computer modelling remained important for population projection, transportation planning, economic modelling, and geographic information analysis, but it could not expand beyond these kinds of activities.

During the 1980s, Western societies took a giant step to the political right. The fiscal concern initiated by the 1973 energy crisis, compounded by the end of the baby boom era, drove economies into recession. The days of big spending in the welfare state gave way to government retraction in the name of fiscal responsibility. Economists often criticized planning as stifling the market through unnecessary regulation. Postwar societies assumed that growth was a natural condition: They certainly craved it. When growth disappeared, planners searched for factors to account for its absence. Planning became a target. Many planners lost their jobs in the 1980s and into the 1990s, as "downsizing" became a passion of government.

The profession's response to this challenge to its legitimacy was to develop a new rational model that "spoke to power." Strategic planning drew on the language and the premises of corporate planning.[6] Strategic planning encouraged planners to analyze the strengths, weaknesses, opportunities, and threats (SWOT) to their communities. The SWOT analysis would provide guidance to a community to determine where its competitive advantage may lie. Community stakeholders, those with identified interests in issues, would be engaged in the planning process. The resulting action plans would identify priorities for the community.

Strategic planning had a major impact on the language and the practice of the profession in the 1980s.[7] Planners committed to strategic planning often found themselves seconded to the task of helping their municipal corporations develop strategic plans. In Winnipeg, for example, the strategic planners were transferred to the mayor's office to lead the planning process. *Plan Winnipeg: Vision 2020* resulted. Developed out of a visioning process, the plan identifies general goals for the city. This is not a land use plan of the kind developed in the 1970s. Instead, the plans result from a participation process that Michael Seelig and Julie Seelig criticize as planning by polling. In many communities in the late 1990s and early 2000s, "vision plans" became commonplace. Although strategic planning started off as a new type of rationalism, in practice it led to partial plans. Many municipalities in the late 1990s generated a series of plans on different themes, such as open space, transportation, and housing: Coordinating their content and objectives presented a significant challenge.

Regional Planning: A Perennial Favourite

As a form of rational planning, regional planning has experienced many incarnations through the years.[8] Figure 3.3 illustrates several approaches. Patrick Geddes initiated the interest by drawing together the insights of German and French regional geographers with his own ideas of planning cities. He presented the concept of the valley section, the idea that cities exist in a natural region of watershed units.[9] This kind of regional

Figure 3.3

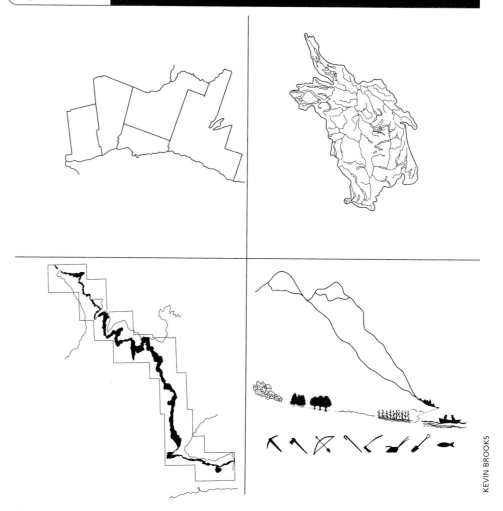

Regional planning comes in many versions: (clockwise from upper left) urban-centred region (as in the GTA), watershed unit (as in the Fraser River), the valley section (à la Patrick Geddes), or geographic feature–based region (as in the Niagara Escarpment).

planning remains popular in environmental planning models and gained popularity in the Toronto region in recent years.

In the 1920s, many planners built on the idea of regional planning. For instance, Noulan Cauchon, a planner in Ottawa, proposed a regional plan for the Hamilton area. These early planners recognized that urban problems existed in a wider region and urged a comprehensive approach to planning. Their arguments fell on deaf ears in Canada at the time.

Regional planning flourished under the American New Deal in the 1930s, as Franklin Roosevelt established the Tennessee Valley Authority. The TVA had regional planning powers to manage the river basin to control flooding, harness power, and promote development.[10] The TVA reflected the success of the Regional Planning Association of America's efforts to promote regional planning as a rational strategy for land management.

Ontario also adopted regional planning in identifying conservation authorities to manage river systems draining into the Great Lakes to prevent flooding and to establish recreational areas. In the 1970s, Ontario established the Niagara Escarpment

Commission to manage land use conflicts along the escarpment and to conserve a valued environmental resource.[11] Provinces engaged regional planning to manage agricultural and hydroelectric resources as well.[12]

In the 1960s, though, a new form of regional planning appeared: regional economic development planning. In this incarnation, regional planning meant harnessing local, provincial, and federal resources to stimulate economic development in disadvantaged regions. In some areas, that meant agricultural development; most often, it meant industrial expansion. Regional planning promised tools to encourage growth in areas where there was none. The planners were to determine the formula to apply techniques successful elsewhere. Investment decisions in the 1960s and 1970s reflect these efforts to promote regional planning. Government investments improved infrastructure in many economically distressed areas, but achieving economic success through planning proved challenging.

In the 1990s, yet another form of regional planning became popular. Jane Jacobs and others floated ideas about "city states," which needed the authority to manage themselves in a new international context.[13] Nations began to worry about how to make their cities competitive in an increasingly global economy. And new urbanists wondered how to manage growth effectively to maintain urban quality of life.[14] These trends and forces inspired new interest in regional planning for more powerful urban regions.

Provincial governments in Canada also reexamined regional planning in the late twentieth century. In the 1990s, Alberta and British Columbia weakened regional planning in their legislation and municipal structures; but Nova Scotia, Ontario, and Quebec strengthened regional planning. Provincial governments passed legislation to amalgamate municipalities to create larger regional cities in Halifax, Toronto, Ottawa-Carleton, and Montreal. The changes reflect provincial desires to make their major cities more effective players in the global economy. While regional cities may create the potential for more effective regional planning, they do not guarantee it. The political furor that followed amalgamation in some provinces led to changes in political leadership, and a "de-merger" referendum in Montreal.[15] On the whole, though, we can argue that Canada has taken a leading role in reshaping local governments to enhance the potential for effective regional planning.

Although they have assumed many forms through the years, rational planning approaches have retained their appeal in Canadian planning. The particular shape they take reflects the economic themes and political priorities of the time. As a function of government, planning must respond to its cultural milieu. Thus, its shape and articulation remains dynamic. Nonetheless, we find the driving values of order, rationality, and efficiency remaining paramount in planning practice even though contemporary planning theory pays greater attention to issues of communication, collaboration, and diversity.[16]

The Social Theory of Planning

Michael Dear and Glenda Laws

1986, Plan Canada 26(9): 246–51

What is meant by a "social theory of planning"? It is a deceptively simple phrase, but few agree on the meaning of "planning," and perhaps even fewer agree on the concept of "social theory." In the space available, we can provide only an abbreviated account of this rich but complex realm of analysis. First, we review the major issues in contemporary social theory, focusing on those with direct relevance to planning. Second, using the insights developed in these prefatory remarks, the social history of planning is unravelled. Finally, we explore the implications of our analysis for theory, practice, and education.

Contemporary Social Theory

(a) Precepts
According to Giddens, the "main concern of social theory is the ... illumination of the concrete processes of social life."[17] Within this very general charge, one core concern of social theory during the past decade has been the structure and evolution of society over time and space. This focus has placed a new prominence on history and geography, the two disciplines with special claims to time and space.

Similar concerns, however, are strongly rooted in sociology and (to a lesser extent) other social sciences. A common problem in these disciplines is to understand how social, political, and economic processes are constituted over space and time.[18] Human organizations are necessarily mediated and constrained by the complex interdependencies between these processes and the time-space dimensions, but how can we begin to explain the production and reproduction of human organization in time-space?

(b) Theory
Social theory encompasses a large number of potential explanations. Marx and Weber provided the foundations for two of the more popular bases for social inquiry. Marxian theory has tended to emphasize the broader structural features of society, including class and mode of production.[19] Weberian theory, on the other hand, has emphasized the role of bureaucracy. This theory is expressed through scholarly interest in corporatism and managerialism.[20] In addition, "pluralist" views of society have dominated American scholarship (a "hermeneutic" school, etc.).

All these versions of social theory have, directly or indirectly, influenced contemporary planning thought. Indeed, this variety of theories is one of the strengths of the contextual approach. It does not aim to resolve the conflicts between the various theories in favour of one grand theory. Rather, it maintains the creative tensions between theories.[21] From openness to different interpretations, we hope to gain an accelerated insight and understanding, but how do we begin to discriminate between the claims made by the advocates of conflicting theories?

(c) Method
A prerequisite for comparative analysis is the availability of a language for intertheory discourse. This is perhaps the most difficult task in modern social theory. How can we make comparative judgments about diverse theoretical presuppositions and then persuade each other of the validity of our respective critiques? One approach is to begin by rejecting all claims of privilege by a single theoretical domain. Any case for privileged status must be scrutinized and defended. Assessors must be alert to their own and others' views about the object being examined, together with their place in and with respect to that object. Simply stated, this position underlines that we are part of the world that we are trying to explain and that it is impossible to separate ourselves from it.

Contemporary social theory is reaching, of necessity, toward a methodology which enables us to interpret various views of our "situatedness" or contextuality. We need to systematically account for the contingent nature of human society, and to incorporate the reflexive relationship between ourselves and the object(s) of our analysis. As Sayer puts it, "In order to understand and explain social phenomena, we cannot avoid evaluating and criticizing societies' own self-understanding."[22]

(d) Substantive Focus

To understand how the foregoing remarks tie into planning, let us begin with some simple propositions. Planning has always been preoccupied with the construction of a built environment. This was true of the nineteenth century utopian thinkers, and for their technocratic counterparts concerned with unsanitary conditions of expanding industrial towns. In the twentieth century, the absorption of planning into the apparatus of the state meant that urbanization increasingly resulted from interaction between the state and civil society, especially the planning apparatus of the state and the civil decisions of private firms and households.[23]

The wider logic of the built environment's social construction lies in the dual notions of *society and space* and *structure and agency*.[24] The city has been created by skilled and knowledgeable actors (or agents) operating within a social context (or structure) which both limits and enables their actions. It is impossible to predict the exact geographical outcome of the interaction between structure and agency because, while individual activities are framed within a particular structural context, they can also transform the context itself. Any narrative about landscapes, regions, or locales is necessarily an account of the reciprocal relationship between relatively long-term structural forces and the shorter-term routine practices of individual human agents. Economic, political, and social history is therefore time specific, in the sense that these relationships evolve at different temporal rates; it is also place specific, in that these relationships unfold in recognizable locales according to some particular logic of spatial diffusion. Geographical patterns, such as the city, are evolving manifestations of a complex social process (Figure 3.4).

As society evolves, so does its spatial expression. By the same token, the geographical form will have repercussions on the social forces themselves. This reflexive impact of space on society can be achieved in many different ways. In the simplest terms, social relations are constituted through space (e.g., the organization of production in

Figure 3.4

Multistorey factories that served the needs of industry a century ago today find new uses as residential lofts or office buildings.

resource-based activities and environments), constrained by space (such as the inertia imposed by obsolete built environments), or mediated through space (including the development of ideology and beliefs within geographically-confined regions or locales).

A Social History of Planning, 1945–1985

Any account of planning is necessarily contextual in nature (i.e., time and place specific). In this section, we provide an abbreviated social history of planning. There are two purposes behind this history: first, to provide the necessary context for understanding a contemporary social theory of planning; and second, to summarize what is conventionally called "planning theory" (to avoid privileging any particular viewpoint on planning discourse).

The period following World War II was one of massive physical and social reconstruction. In Western Europe, extensive war damage meant that nations were preoccupied with the rebuilding efforts. This period spawned, for example, the British new town legislation, which was to provide an important model for the next four decades of controlled urban growth in Western Europe. In Canada, cities such as Toronto (which had not suffered significant physical destruction through war) tentatively moved toward large-scale comprehensive metropolitan plans. In the United States, new federal initiatives were undertaken, especially in the field of housing. In short, the early postwar years were a period in which an extensive (renewed) mandate was granted for state intervention in the land and property development process. In North America, it was a time when the incipient planning profession consolidated its physical land use planning identity.

The decade of the 1960s was a time of remarkable ferment in planning. Two major philosophies were to impact the discipline. The first was a new scientism, which suggested that planning could and should take on the methodologies of the natural sciences; the second was a new concern with populism in planning, which arose largely out of a worldwide surge in participatory democratic politics and the consequent crisis in the profession's sense of legitimacy.

The new scientism, which shook most social sciences, was represented in planning as a commitment to systems theory.[25] It provoked a fundamental shift toward rationality, and it was the initial impetus toward the substantive-procedural rift in planning. The substantive focus (on the objects being planned) served to propel the existing practice of land use planning toward a more scientific approach (akin to the rationality of engineering or architectural building methods). The rational-substantive approach received a strong reinforcement and consolidation through the advent of mathematical model building in planning.[26] The use of quantitative methods in computer-based, large-scale land use and transportation models was particularly prominent in the US. It provided a considerable legitimacy for believers in the scientific method of planning. This was further reinforced by the spillover from computer-assisted methods of architectural design.

The movement toward scientific planning was accelerated by what was initially perceived as a competing theoretical domain. Procedural theories of planning also derived from rational systems models. However, as applied to planning, they laid emphasis on the administrative and managerial context of planning decisions.[27] They sought to establish rules of rational decision making and to pursue the reasons for irrationality in the practice of planning. Although many writers later pointed to the damaging effects of the procedural-substantive dichotomy and the ultimate need for both in planning, the dichotomy had a strong appeal for protagonists in each camp. Its legacy persists.

As well as being a period of scientific optimism, the 1960s was a highly charged political decade. In planning, this took the form of growing citizens' involvement in planning decisions within the general context of an increasingly participatory democratic politics. Importantly, at the same time, professional planners began a deep search for their sources of legitimacy. A loose coalition of essentially liberal-minded planners rallied under the banner of a choice theory of planning. This somewhat ill-defined theory emphasized the significance of citizen choice in, and control over, planning decisions. As it became obvious that citizen participation did not significantly alter the balance of power in development decisions, advocacy planning enjoyed a relatively brief vogue as a means of enfranchising citizen groups. The net effect of 1960s populism was to place planning irrevocably on the political agenda. In no period has the structure of political power been so rawly exposed as in these early community battles.

Optimism and prosperity spilled over into the early years of the next decade. Two overtly ideological concepts of planning emerged. The first was the movement toward transactive (or creative) planning. The second was a more radical critique: a firestorm of criticism ignited by a rejection of both the transactive philosophy and the studied apoliticism of the rationalists. The transactive-creative approach in planning emphasized "mutual learning," a creative use of a community's intelligence and planners' skills to invent the urban future.[28] The lineage of this approach can be directly traced to an underlying belief in rationality and a commitment to involving communities in planning their futures. Transactive-creative planning was ultimately an atheoretical view of planning, and, as such, it lacked any attraction for those who did not share its essentially liberal-democratic ideology.

The radical critique, which resurfaced in the mid-1970s after being largely quiescent since the 1930s in Canada, was provoked by the perceived inadequacy of the theoretical bases of planning.[29] Critics argued for a social theory of planning that would specifically incorporate its political economic setting. Deriving impetus initially from a neo-Marxist or materialist philosophy, they emphasized planning's fundamentally subordinate role in the context of capitalist urbanization. The radical critique provided a new way of thinking about planning; however, the debate was generally conducted at such a high level of abstraction that practitioners and theoreticians alike had difficulty in linking it to everyday practice.

Then, in the late 1970s, a potential resolution of the liberal-radical split was plucked from the social theory of the Frankfurt School and of Jürgen Habermas in particular.[30] The phenomenological and hermeneutic schools of thought became influential for two reasons. First, hermeneutics (the discipline concerned with the interpretation of meaning) offered a firm theoretical basis for the essentially dialectical or interpretive method which was implicit in transactive-creative planning. Second, because the origins of hermeneutics are to be found in Marxism, it provided the opportunity for a new alliance with the radical left. Liberal theorists, however, quickly managed to separate hermeneutics from a Marxist political agenda. In short, hermeneutics provided a new theoretical and practical legitimacy where it was urgently needed.

The recession-ridden 1980s were accompanied by an increasing frenzy of discourse on planning. Doubts and uncertainties began to assail the left, and a centre-right coalition began to reassert itself. The net effects were a selective retreat from context and a rediscovery of function in planning. In the first place, the sparkling promise of hermeneutics did not translate readily into practice, nor was its theoretical promise realized. Second, radical critics became quiescent. For some, the increasingly strident political conservatism was cause enough for retreat; others were absorbed in the search for a wider social theory of planning. The political commitment of others may have become diluted. Kiernan's "politics of positive discrimination," for instance, builds a new planning from the social context of Marx, with Weberian notions of key bureaucrats, and guides the systems with Rawlsian notions of justice.[31]

In the vacuum left by the apparent retreat of the social theorists, and in a conservative economic and political culture, a new attempt developed to recapture the centre ground in planning. Planning was again defined as land use planning. This retreat to the traditional core of the discipline is undoubtedly an effort to reaffirm planning's identity and to clearly demarcate its professional "turf." The core movement reveals itself in many ways, for instance, in direct attacks on social theories of planning (which are perceived as harming planning's professional credibility) and in the emphasis on public-private partnerships in the land development process.

The strongest evidence for a revitalization of traditional land use planning lies in the rejection of what is perceived to be "practice-irrelevant" theory, and in the rebirth of physical planning theory. This trend is well-represented in Breheny's revealingly-entitled article "A practical view of planning theory." He identified with those "who are concerned to pin down the essential features of planning before proceeding with the task of theory building."Not surprisingly, Breheny concludes that:

> Land-use . . . planning is concerned with government intervention in the private land-development process. . . . The role of planners is to assist in the administration of this activity and in helping governments make and implement decisions.[32]

Implications: Theory, Practice, Education

Planning today adds up to little more than a "pastiche"—an unordered, unsystematic discourse. Planning "theory" has been isolated as a Babel of languages, most of which are voluntarily ignored by practitioners. Planning "practice" has evolved into a ritualized choreography of routines. One dimension of practice has been deeply embedded in the apparatus of the state. In essence, planning serves to legitimize the actions of the state. The second dimension of practice is part of land and property development interests. Planning is a passive tool capable of only the most muted social criticism. In this case, planning serves to legitimize the actions of capital.

Because every approach in planning has its own advocate, pastiche is in the ascendancy. Paradoxically, however, the dominant focus of all discourse is increasingly restricted. For instance, the long heritage of utopian concerns was all but excised from our vocabulary in the 1980s, and the ideological commitment of the 1960s and 1970s apparently lost much of its power of persuasion.

But what of the future of planning? Two scenarios might be drawn. First, assume that we have entered a long period of recession or no-growth. Under such circumstances, the retrenchment experienced in planning in the 1980s is likely to accelerate. Planning will survive as a subordinate technocracy in which a substantive theory of planning will predominate. The development planner will be the most common species. Second, assume economic recovery. A long, but slow, period of expansion would witness a chastened profession seeking to regain its credibility and its roots. The planning discourse is likely to be one in which pastiche is tolerated. We would essentially relive the expansionary experiences of the 1960s and 1970s. By the year 2000, we should be in the same spot as we were in 1986.

Is there no way out of this impasse? Our contextual analysis of the social history of planning has suggested a somewhat sterile future, with planning acting as little more than a fig leaf to cover the actions of state and capital. But another future is possible. A social theory of planning implies a future in which context-aware planners self-consciously analyze the limits and potential of their roles in theory and practice. It seems to us that this task is the responsibility of all planners, irrespective of ideological persuasion. This self-reflexive social theory of planning should enable us to transcend the apparent limitations on the future development of planning.

Hence, a social theory of planning is fundamentally based on three levels of analysis in space and time: *structures*—including such divisions as class and state; *institutions*—the phenomenal forms of structures, including the planning apparatus; and *human agency*—including the planner's role in design and mediation. Not all levels of analysis will be necessary in every situation.

A social theory of planning requires a methodology that has the capacity to operate at all three levels of analysis. It will need to move from the abstract to the concrete, and vice versa. Finally, it will (when necessary) link zoning outcomes to class struggle, and planning law to multinational capital. The methodology of such planning necessarily implies an interpretive discourse. It rejects the privileging of any single theory of planning. The need for discourse at several levels of analysis and the contingent, reflexive nature of theory imply a level of sophistication that currently seems to be beyond our grasp. Hence, partial analysis (at any single level) must continue and, indeed, is likely to remain necessary.

A social theoretic viewpoint defines planning as a set of contingently-situated practices concerned with manipulating the production of the built environment. Such practices include design, evaluation, and political mediation. Given this contextualized reading of planning, it makes no sense to maintain the distinction between "theory" and "practice" in planning. A context-based planning is firmly rooted in real-world social relations (Figure 3.5). Theory and practice are intimately related, and the distinction between them should be collapsed.

The role of planners is to inform decision making in the built environment. The precise criteria used in providing information depend upon planners' political beliefs and their situation in the practice matrix. They may, for example, advise governments on costs and benefits to minimize social harm, or they may assess political feasibility and profitability.

The practice of pedagogy in planning includes instruction on necessary professional skills. In a self-consciously contextual view of planning, however, it makes little sense to teach rational decision procedures that have no reference to any known decision situation, nor to teach analytical techniques divorced from the politics of everyday practice. Certain planners may have a special responsibility (although not an exclusive claim) to dream of utopian schemes, but all planners have a pedagogical responsibility to evaluate their practice critically and contextually.

Figure 3.5

CITY OF VANCOUVER. COURTESY OF ANN McAFEE

Planners work with community members to inform decision processes, as in this workshop in Vancouver.

Chapter 3 / The Context of Planning

A further implication of a contextual view of planning is that the discipline must be firmly aligned with other social sciences and humanities to provide the necessary theoretical input into our constructs of planning. We cannot ignore this input unless we choose to remain detached observers as the world changes. The social theory of planning has recently achieved a new prominence in the academic literature. Its lessons have been slow to percolate through to the practical world of land use planning; they have been more readily absorbed in social planning, especially by those social planning councils that operate independently of state and capital through voluntary contributions. Such academic- and practice-based efforts reveal how it is possible to transcend the context in which one is situated. If these efforts are pursued systematically and carefully, then a totally new basis for planning theory and practice should be revealed.

Acknowledgment: The authors are grateful to Jennifer Wolch for critical comments on an early draft of the paper.

A Theory of the Planning Cycle

Thomas I Gunton

1985, Plan Canada 25(2): 40–4

In the 1980s, planning came under considerable attack. Those on the left of the political spectrum attacked planners as supporters of the status quo and the property industry.[33] The neoconservatives, meanwhile, challenged some of the basic assumptions of public planning.[34] As the weakening of planning efforts attest, these criticisms combined with slower economic growth had a negative effect on planning activity.

To respond to such challenges, Canadian planners must understand the broader forces that shape planning activity in Canada. This paper presents a brief interpretation of these broader forces. I will argue that the current state of planning is part of a normal cycle, which Canadian planning practice has followed for decades. Further, if planners understand the dynamics of this cycle, they will be able to be more effective practitioners. By way of background, I begin with a brief review of the evolution of Canadian planning.

Evolution of Canadian Planning

The first period of formal planning activity commenced just after 1900, when Canada experienced a rapid and somewhat unexpected surge in urban growth. In response to this growth, Canadian governments launched a series of major planning initiatives, including passage of planning legislation, preparation of plans for most major cities, formation of planning agencies, publication of planning journals, and creation of a new professional planning organization.

But, just as Canadian planners were laying these theoretical and legislative foundations for comprehensive planning, the rapid growth that had inspired their efforts was subsiding (Figure 3.6). Consequently, support for planning dissipated, and some of the new planning apparatus such as the Commission of Conservation was dismantled as the economy entered a postwar recession.

Ironically, while these planning initiatives were being weakened in the early 1920s, a postwar building boom, which peaked in 1928, created new urban problems. Authorities were again forced to launch new planning initiatives. However, these initiatives were implemented only after the problems began to subside and were replaced with the challenges of an economic depression for which the planning proposals were conspicuously irrelevant. For example, Vancouver completed the Bartholomew plan,

Figure 3.6

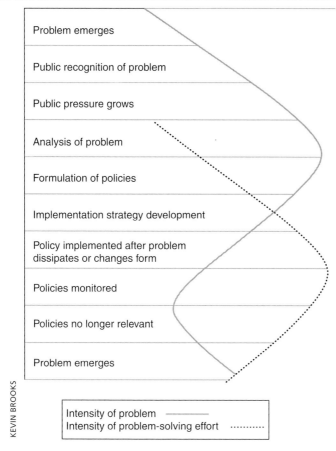

Problem emerges

Public recognition of problem

Public pressure grows

Analysis of problem

Formulation of policies

Implementation strategy development

Policy implemented after problem dissipates or changes form

Policies monitored

Policies no longer relevant

Problem emerges

KEVIN BROOKS

Intensity of problem ——————
Intensity of problem-solving effort ···········

The planning cycle: By the time planning ramps up, the crisis has passed.

designed to manage rapid growth, just as the economy collapsed.[35] Consequently, the growth management strategies developed during the 1928 to 1930 period were largely abandoned, and the capability of the planning system returned almost to the level it had been at the turn of the century.

Interest in planning did not fully revive until the later stages of World War II, when urban expansion, combined with an anticipation of postwar problems, convinced governments that some action was necessary. The resulting initiatives implemented from 1944 to about 1950 included preparation of a comprehensive framework for postwar planning, major amendments to provincial planning legislation, passage of new housing legislation, formation of new institutions such as the Central Mortgage and Housing Corporation, re-creation of the professional planning organization, and preparation of comprehensive master plans for most major cities. The first comprehensive urban renewal project at Regent Park and the first integrated new town at Don Mills appeared. But despite these important achievements, the new postwar planning system was not fundamentally different from the system existing in 1930.

From 1950 to the mid-1960s, few major initiatives were launched. In contrast to the comprehensive planning systems envisaged earlier, postwar planning practice consisted largely of ad hoc zoning and urban renewal projects. Absence of significant urban stress eliminated any motivation for major advances or implementation of comprehensive urban and regional plans.

By the mid-1960s, the situation had changed again. The sustained period of postwar growth created new problems. As the Economic Council of Canada noted in its fourth annual review, issues of urban congestion, scattered sprawl, land speculation, loss of resource lands, inadequate housing, and dislocation of residents by freeways and urban renewal required immediate attention.[36] The federal government responded by forming the Hellyer Task Force, which published its report in 1969. Highly critical of the rather ad hoc system of planning which had guided urban development for the previous decades, the report urged a complete overhaul. "To put it simply," concluded the report, "the present system for assembling and servicing land in much of urban Canada is irrational in concept and inefficient in practice."[37]

The call for reform was repeated in another federal report on urban problems by Lithwick, who concluded that urban regions were characterized by complex interdependent problems that could be mitigated only by comprehensive public planning. In words reminiscent of Thomas Adams, Lithwick argued that congestion in central areas and sprawl in suburban and rural areas were interdependent problems that could be solved best by broad regional strategies to decentralize growth from the congested zones to integrated satellite communities or new towns within the urban region. Like Adams, Lithwick maintained that this decentralization could be accomplished only by combining negative controls such as zoning to prevent development in undesirable locations with positive measures involving public land development and public initiation of new towns.[38]

Beginning in the early 1970s, Canadian governments began to implement some of the recommendations of these reports. The federal government created the Ministry of State for Urban Affairs and introduced major amendments to the *National Housing Act*, which allowed for substantial funding for new town construction, public land development, comprehensive neighbourhood planning, and cooperative housing. Most provincial governments enacted legislation to protect agricultural land, amended planning acts, and fostered formulation of regional plans. Municipal and regional governments, meanwhile, got on with the task of producing comprehensive plans.[39] However, by the time most of these initiatives were operational, the urban crisis had begun to subside as the economy entered another recession in the 1980s. Consequently, support for planning dissipated, and many of these programs were weakened.

The Planning Cycle

Through the period described, planning appears to have followed a cyclical pattern related to the economic cycle, with periods of heightened planning occurring in response to building booms. The only major exception is the period of heightened planning activity during World War II undertaken in anticipation of rapid postwar urban growth.

The initiation of major planning activity in response to rapid growth has rather ironic implications. Because of the lag between the emergence of problems caused by the growth and responsive planning activity, the planning initiatives did not have significant effects until well after the problems that inspired them had begun to subside or changed form. Consequently, support for the initiatives dissipated, and the programs were either weakened or withdrawn until building activity accelerated again. The result, then, is that planning capability has been strongest when the need for planning is weakest.

The second interesting aspect of the trends is that planners from several periods have proposed remarkably similar solutions to the problems of urban growth. From Adams to Lithwick, Canadian planners have maintained that planning must be done at several spatial levels, from the broad regional plan, which sets out the framework for guiding growth, down to the detailed site plan. They have recognized the interdependency between congestion in the urban core and scattered sprawl development on the periphery. Planners have consistently advocated the decentralization of growth to integrated satellite communities as a means of mitigating both problems. They have called for the protection of valuable resource lands and the prohibiting of development on hazard lands. They have emphasized that planning should be a flexible ongoing process instead of a rigid blueprint. As Adams stated more than 50 years ago:

> The plan must not be too rigid or attempt to deal with smaller matters of detail that cannot be determined in advance; it must be elastic and capable of variation as circumstances and conditions alter.[40]

More specifically, planners cautioned that urban renewal should be undertaken only if provisions were made to find alternative accommodation for those displaced. Insisting on a comprehensive approach, planners throughout the century maintained that, because all components of the urban system are interdependent, planning must deal with all facets of the system. And they have consistently recommended that planning would work only if negative regulations were complemented by positive actions, such as public land banking and public development corporations. As Adams put it, planning and development must be integrated. Yet, despite this consistency in theory, planners have been unable to fully implement their proposals because of the dynamics of the planning cycle.

A Case Study

A case study of planning activities may help to illustrate the nature of the planning cycle. During the late 1960s, Metropolitan Vancouver grew at the rapid rate of about 3.2 percent per annum. The resulting stress forced both the provincial and regional government to respond. Despite strong pressure, the provincial government finally passed the much-heralded *Land Commission Act* to preserve disappearing agricultural land only in 1973. In 1975, the government took further action by assembling a large tract of land for an integrated satellite development, along the lines recommended in the Lithwick report. At the regional level, the Greater Vancouver Regional District (GVRD) began its Livable Region Program in 1969 and, in 1975, published a new regional planning strategy.[41] The strategy—which called for the decentralization of employment from the downtown to outlying regional town centres to achieve a better job to population balance in each sub-region—was remarkably similar to policies proposed by planners more than four decades before and to strategies implemented in European cities during the postwar period (Figure 3.7).

Despite valiant efforts to cultivate broad support and understanding through public participation processes and despite emphasis on an ongoing action-oriented program, planners were again defeated by changing events. The rate of growth declined from 1970 to 1980, and the anticipated expansion that the strategy was supposed to manage never materialized. Consequently, support for the plan declined, and many of its recommendations were ignored. In the 1980s, the provincial government curtailed the powers of the Greater Vancouver Regional Planning Department and substantially weakened the British Columbia Land Commission. Plans for the proposed satellite town were abandoned.

The case shows that the long lag between the emergence of the problem and the preparation and implementation of programs and policies meant that action was not taken until after the problem had changed form. Consequently the program was largely withdrawn or not fully implemented. Further, the policies advocated were remarkably similar to policies proposed during previous building booms. Planners seemed to be spending valuable time reinventing the wheel.

Figure 3.7

CITY OF VANCOUVER. COURTESY OF ANN McAFEE

Rapid growth in the Vancouver region placed considerable pressure on valuable farmland.

Implications for Planning

The planning cycle obviously impedes the ability of planners to mitigate urban problems. Therefore, if planning is to be effective, planners must learn how to overcome the impediments imposed by the cycle. First, considerable effort must be made to convince decision makers of the need for anticipatory versus reactive planning. The best time to prepare growth management strategies is during a period of slow growth. Unfortunately this is inconsistent with basic liberal democratic tendencies of undertaking new government initiatives only in response to political pressure generated by an existing problem. However, extensive documentation of the increased difficulty of mitigating problems after they have arisen compared to preventing them from developing in the first place should help build support for a more anticipatory planning environment.

Second, planners should undertake preparatory work in anticipation of future problems instead of waiting for formal requests from politicians and the public. For example, planners should begin preparing policies to manage future urban growth during recessions instead of waiting for the recession to end. In this way, planners can be ready to respond when the pressures arise.

Third, lags in the policy-making process must be reduced so that planning policies are implemented before the problem they were supposed to solve changes form or subsides. One way of doing this is for planners to use less analytical and more action-oriented approaches to policy making. For example, planners should abandon the comprehensive style of planning in favour of short-term problem-oriented planning or a more flexible approach. For instance, strategic planning involves several iterations beginning with a quick-and-dirty overview of the problem and becoming increasingly comprehensive on subsequent rounds on only those aspects of the problem requiring additional analysis. Planners should not be apprehensive about the reduced level of analysis in these action-oriented approaches, for, as this analysis of Canadian planning indicates, planners can draw on a comprehensive body of theory and experience built up over the last decades. Indeed, despite lengthy analysis, planners from different periods have come up with remarkably similar proposals for solving problems. Therefore, by drawing from past experience instead of attempting to "reinvent the wheel," planners can shorten the plan formulation process without sacrificing analytical rigor.

Finally, planners must shift from being passive regulators to active entrepreneurs capable of implementing their programs through positive means. As the experience with regulatory behaviour reveals, passive regulators have insufficient first-hand knowledge of how the industry works to provide good regulation. They remain highly vulnerable to shifts in public opinion as well as to the demands of the parties they are supposed to regulate. The untimely withdrawal of many Canadian planning initiatives has been due to opposition from those being regulated and capricious shifts in public opinion. Consequently, during those brief periods of strong broad support, planners must lobby for strategic reforms such as public-land banking that may strengthen their powers enough to allow them to continue their activities independently of the "planning cycle."

Ending the Cycle

While it is difficult to identify broad trends in Canadian planning, this brief review lends support to two propositions. First, planning theories and proposals were remarkably consistent throughout the twentieth century. Second, planning practice appears to have followed a counterproductive cyclical process, with planning being strongest when the need for planning is weakest.

If planning is to escape from this irrational cycle, planners must become more action oriented and seize opportunities as they arise. They must resist the urge to do more studies and concentrate, instead, on implementing their proposals before the opportunity disappears. They must adopt such alternative planning styles as incremental and strategic planning and must devote more energy to achieving such institutional reforms as increased entrepreneurial powers that will allow them to initiate anticipatory planning when the intensity of the problem and public concern is at a low point in the cycle. If they don't, the cyclical nature of planning will continue, and planners will be doomed to spend tomorrow solving yesterday's problems.

Can Planners Be Leaders?

Michael Seelig and Julie Seelig

1996, Plan Canada 36(5): 3–4

"The world is full of people whose notion of a satisfactory future is, in fact, a return to an idealized past," said the late Robertson Davies, a keen observer of human nature in general and of Canadian mores in particular. This essentially nostalgic and conservative nature of most of the population leaves planning in a bind. How do we plan for the future if people just want the past?

As planners, are we now left to be leaders of the "don't worry, be happy" generation? Are we merely the creators of comfort terminology, coining such phrases as "sustainability," "traffic calming," "livability," "take part—make a difference" (the motto of Vancouver's *CityPlan*)? Are we mimicking the advertising trade as purveyors of pleasant slogans to lull our clients to sleep and avoid controversy?

Planners were once experts. Their expertise lay in their understanding of the social, economic, environmental, and demographic matters affecting a community. They had vision. They also developed a secondary expertise in the art of the possible: in articulating what we must give up to achieve our goals.

Planners today are singularly without vision and without authority or ability to lead, to develop concepts, and to articulate long-range goals. "Professionalism" has become a hollow term. The distrust with which planning is viewed is similar to the cynicism with which lawyers, architects, and doctors are viewed in today's doubting age.

The lack of leadership and of a clear-cut vision has its origins in the very nature of North American planning. Planners, unlike lawyers or doctors, require input from the general public to develop their plans. But public consultation has gone too far and become an albatross around the neck of sound public planning. Lately, it seems impossible to move beyond the consultative phase.

Planners are very familiar with public consultation. They pioneered the concept of participatory democracy in the 1960s in response to insensitive schemes of urban renewal and freeway construction. Those planners were right 30 years ago. However, now we are left only with the legacy of consultation and are bereft of planning. For example, Vancouver's major planning effort *CityPlan* involved the participation of 20 000 residents in the 1990s. The idea—or non-idea—behind this exercise was that assembling what hundreds of people say will lead to a plan. It is not a plan. As Mayor Philip Owen put it, it is a "general, flexible blueprint." Planners view it merely as round one in a dialogue with the public.

Planners have left the day-to-day business of planning and have become polltakers on behalf of elected politicians who may not wish to make decisions without a guarantee of public support. Politicians send the planners out to face angry neighbours to sample their opinions. The planners hear the shrieks of "Not in my backyard" and "Make it into a park" and "Don't increase density" and "Don't tear anything down," and head back to the office unable to move.

It is time for the pendulum to swing back in the other direction and for planners to show leadership and to make suggestions for the future they envision. This does not mean returning to the autocratic planning era of the 1950s; it does mean an end to the passivity displayed by many planning departments as they try to fathom the public will, calling a distillation of opinions a "plan." It is time to recognize the unbreachable gap that exists between finding out what people want, giving them a confusing variety of choices and the ultimate aim of a sound plan that is to offer some recommended directions for the future.

As Alice Munro said, "When you live in a small town you hear more things, about all sorts of people. In a city you mainly hear stories about your own sort of people." The planner's job is to hear many voices and many opinions and to create an overall plan that accommodates all. By becoming mired in the citizen participation quagmire, they run the risk of hearing one neighbourhood at a time and one set of parochial concerns at a time. This isn't planning or looking toward the future: It is brokering among fragmented short-term points of view. It just isn't good enough for our profession. It is time for us to renew our leadership and visionary skills and lead from in front by conceptualizing and presenting our version of plans. This essential step will educate citizens, give them a focal point to which they can respond and move us forward.

Rethinking the Public Interest as a Planning Concept

Jill Grant

2005, Plan Canada 45(2): 48–50

Our professional *Code of Practice* says that planners "acknowledge the inter-related nature of planning decisions and their consequences for individuals, the natural and built environment, and the broader public interest."[42] When prospective members of

CIP take the oral entrance exam, they often face questions about the public interest. As planners, how do we understand and use the concept?

While the question is fundamental to our profession, the answer is far from simple. In the early years of modern town planning, we enjoyed considerable consensus about the common good. We no longer find such certainty. Today we recognize and embrace diversity. The realities of contemporary practice make us rethink our understanding of the concept of the public interest. We increasingly see the public good as an abstraction: necessarily fluid, tenuous, and context sensitive. Our conceptualization of the public interest is inevitably framed by a particular space and time. It reflects cultural, professional, and personal values. What one generation defines as "the common good" may disgust subsequent generations.

The Public Interest in History

Formal definitions describe the public interest as the objective of duly authorized governments carrying out activities necessary to the welfare of the community. Closely associated with the professionalization of the civil service, the term gives those working for government an ideal to serve. Although critics argue that government aims too often reflect the interests of capital or social elites, the machinery of the nation state alleges that decisions reflect the common good of all classes.[43] The public interest means more than the sum of competing interests, or even some way of "balancing" competing interests. It provides the ultimate ethical justification for the demands of the state on the individual. The public interest becomes a unifying symbol and social myth.

By the 1960s, the profession faced challenges to particular definitions of the public interest. In recent years, we ask questions about the merits of the concept itself. Yet, in practice, the public interest remains rhetorically significant. Used in discourse and debate as a way to explain and justify recommendations and outcomes, the concept provides a theorem for expert advice, and a calculus for the distribution of benefits and costs. Unfortunately we cannot demonstrate the public interest through any straightforward formula.

The public interest is an essentially contested concept: People agree on its significance, but dispute its meaning and content.[44] Some argue about how to identify the public interest, while others claim it does not exist.

The Public Interest as Myth

Conceptualizations of the public interest appear within a particular constellation of values in time and space. In the 1950s, a broad popular consensus saw the public interest as growth and progress. Planners helped to redesign cities to accommodate rising affluence. We advised governments to tear down blighted neighbourhoods, rebuild civic centres, and accommodate the poor in upgraded public housing. We separated pedestrian and vehicular traffic. Our profession praised the resulting projects. Today we recognize that those solutions spawned new problems: urban sprawl, traffic gridlock, sterile landscapes. The failure of urban renewal and public housing projects exposed the fallacy of the postwar conceptualization of the public interest. Values change.

Since Paul Davidoff[45] introduced the idea of advocacy planning, planners have acknowledged multiple interests.[46] The civil rights and feminist movements helped planners recognize the political context of our work. Advocacy planning involves the radical assertion of difference. It denies a single "public" interest while illuminating political choices. Each decade brings new players with their own views about what serves the public.

Although at one level, planners accept competing interests as equally valid, we continue to appeal to the public interest when we need to offer advice or make decisions.

As conventional conceptions of the public interest floundered, planning theory turned increasingly to examining the planning process. Mainstream planning theory worked toward developing a framework for articulating options that could serve the common good. If planners could no longer claim to have the skills to ferret out the public interest, then we would focus on helping community members to define it.

The Public Interest as Process

John Friedmann shifted attention to planning as a form of mutual learning where the process is as important as the outcome.[47] Others have extensively developed and refined these ideas through the last three decades. Forester argues that planners serve the public interest by open, honest, and transparent communication in their dealings with the public and decision makers.[48] Planners have the responsibility to inform, illuminate, and listen—to help people achieve their own ambitions and to speak truth to power.

In recent years, collaborative planning theory has gained adherents.[49] It suggests that stakeholders work together to define the public interest. Planning involves finding open and productive ways to resolve difference and find win-win scenarios. In this view, the consensus outcome represents the public interest.

Process views of the public interest define the role of the planner as facilitator. Strategic planning initiatives built on the concept as governments redefined their approach. However, in recent years, we have seen concerns raised: If planners are merely facilitators, then what is our independent professional expertise? The desire of planners to strengthen professional standing through title restriction and licensing has brought renewed concern about clarifying the public interest.

The Public Interest as Substance

Substantive theories assume that the public interest exists and that trained experts can recognize it. Such theories expound planning principles that promise good communities or healthier futures. As experts, planners define the public interest through applying the preferred planning principles.

The most popular of these normative planning theories are new urbanism and smart growth.[50] They define good urban form as a common benefit. They see the public interest as served by designs that include mixed use, compact form, reduced concentrations of poverty, transit orientation, and pedestrian-friendly and connected streets. Such principles currently dominate new planning documents in Canada.

A competing normative theory of environmental responsibility argues that sustainability requires that humans reduce energy and material demands and protect ecosystem health. A healthy environment is in the planet's interest. Such approaches may employ ecological footprint analysis and advocate simple living.[51]

Substantive normative theories are popular with planners because they offer clear formulae for professional expertise and authority. As history has proven, however, they are subject to debate and displacement. Even where consensus makes them popular at one point, as times change, they lose favour. Unexamined normative theories promote particular values as if they were universal values. In so doing, they elevate some interests while demonizing other views.

The Public Interest as Process and Substance

Planning has had a small radical theory movement within it for decades. Radical planning defines the public interest as overcoming the hegemony of the powerful by putting the needs of the most disadvantaged to the forefront. Creating a just society, some say, serves the public interest.[52] Good communication and good form are not enough to overcome unequal power. The radical planner's role is a controversial one: a guerrilla in the bureaucracy, fighting oppression. Not surprisingly, few practitioners select this option.

The Public Interest in Practice

The public interest is a slippery concept. It encapsulates hidden assumptions and unstated values. While it seems to provide a convenient justification for planning decisions, it cannot withstand close scrutiny.

What lessons does theory offer planners who want to operate in the public interest?

- Respect and accommodate difference in interests, values, and means.
- Enable and respect participation.
- Offer and explain options, alternatives, benefits, and costs.
- Communicate effectively, openly, honestly, humbly, and transparently.
- Stay current in the field to understand where the discipline and our communities have been and are going.

Can planners serve the public interest? As community advisors, we must make our values explicit and illuminate the ethical choices embedded within planning outcomes. Planning involves political choices about the disposition of land, facilities, and resources. The outcomes are not necessarily win-win. Consensus is not always possible. Resources are increasingly limited. Our role involves exposing issues and options for those who make decisions and to those affected by the decisions. Our professional credibility depends on openness about our assumptions and transparency in process. We do not serve anyone's long-term interest by presuming that we know the formula for the good community.

Does this mean that planners cannot be leaders or visionaries, that we are stuck being process technicians? Not necessarily. But if we seek to implement a personal or professional agenda, then we are ethically obliged to do so explicitly, not behind a cloak of imputed "public interest." We must be clear about why we believe particular strategies are timely to achieve explicit community aims. And we must prepare to have history prove us wrong.

Players in the planning process often advocate their own normative positions as the public interest. Ultimately, though, outcomes are political choices. Tearing down poor neighbourhoods for redevelopment seemed a popular political choice in nineteenth-century Europe and again in twentieth-century North America. Planning organizations have recently awarded prizes to those who designed new urbanist schemes to rejuvenate public housing projects by mixing in market housing. In the US, new urbanist planning principles have created beautiful new districts while facilitating the net loss of some 60 000 public housing units.[53] Clearly, neighbourhood renewal serves some interests, while hurting others. Planners who define the public interest in physical terms without considering the social repercussions of actions reap the whirlwind.

Feel free to debate the public interest with community members and colleagues, but recognize the challenges inherent in using it to defend any particular position.

1. How does the role of the planner change in response to the changing context of planning in Canadian society? How would you define the appropriate role of the planner in society?

2. How does competition and conflict between varying levels of governments affect planning efforts to address such social concerns as the availability of adequate affordable housing?

3. What are the commonalities and differences in the varying approaches to regional planning employed in Canada?

4. To what extent did the predictions made by some of these commentators in the 1980s come true by the end of the twentieth century? What changes and issues did planners in the mid-twentieth century fail to predict?

5. Papers written in the 1980s often reveal an underlying pessimism about the effectiveness and purpose of planning. Critiques from recent years challenge planning to be visionary. Describe the competing positions on what the primary purpose of planning should be and discuss the way these positions have changed since the 1980s.

6. How do the values of popular culture affect planning traditions in different countries? What factors account for different planning approaches in the US, UK, and Canada?

7. Nigel Richardson [Are planners irrelevant? *Plan Canada* 27(10): 277–8] wrote in 1988: "Ultimately, planning is not about statistics, subdivisions and street furniture, but about a way of looking at things: a way that is synoptic, or holistic if you prefer, as opposed to the specialized expertise of most other professions." Hans Blumenfeld in 1987 [Ain't no such animal as a planner. *Plan Canada* 27(2): 37–8] concurred: "A planner is a specialist with a generality. The generality is synopsis." What challenges do you see to establishing planning as a profession if its practitioners are generalists?

8. Look for examples in recent debates about planning decisions to see what appeals are made to the "public interest" or "common good." (Most newspapers frequently feature land use or planning disputes and quote those active in the discussions.) What assumptions and values do you see behind the appeals?

Reference Notes

1. Foglesong, R (1986) *Planning the Capitalist City. The Colonial Era to the 1920s* Princeton, NJ: Princeton University Press.

   Harvey, D (1982) *The Limits to Capital*. Oxford: Blackwell Publishing.

2. Kiernan, MJ (1990) Urban planning in Canada: A synopsis and some future directions. *Plan Canada* 30(1): 11–22.

3. Alexander, E (1992) *Approaches to Planning*. (2nd ed) New York: Gordon and Breach.

   Branch, MC (1983) *Comprehensive Planning: General Theory and Principles*. Pacific Pallisades: Pallisades Publishers.

4. Chadwick, G (1971) *A Systems View of Planning*. Oxford: Pergamon Press.

5. Meadows, D (1974) *Limits to Growth: A Report on the Club of Rome's Project on the Predicament of Mankind*. New York: Universe Books.

6. Seasons, M (1989) Strategic planning in the public sector environment: Addressing the realities. *Plan Canada* 29(6): 19–27.

7. Kaufman, J & HM Jacobs (1987) A public planning perspective on strategic planning. *Journal of the American Planning Association* 53(1): 23–33.

8. Hodge, CL (1968) *The Tennessee Valley Authority: A National Experiment in Regionalism*. New York: Russell and Russell.

9. Geddes, P (1949) *Cities in Evolution*. London: Williams and Norgate.

10. Hodge, G & I Robinson (2001) *Planning Canadian Regions*. Vancouver: UBC Press.

11. Lewis, C & L Pim (1995) The Niagara escarpment: Planning for environmental protection. *Plan Canada* 35(6): 39–40.

12. Robinson, IM & G Hodge (1998) Canadian regional planning at 50: Growing pains. *Plan Canada* 38(3): 10–4.

13. Jacobs, J (1985) *Cities and the Wealth of Nations: Principles of Economic Life*. New York: Random House.

14. Calthorpe, P & W Fulton (2001) *The Regional City: Planning for the End of Sprawl*. Washington: Island Press.

15. Brown, D (2003) Mergers and de-mergers: Implications for environmental planning and management in Montreal. *Plan Canada* 43(3): 24–6.

16. Friedmann, J (2002) *The Prospect of Cities*. Minneapolis: University of Minnesota Press.

    Sandercock, L (1998) *Towards Cosmopolis: Planning for Multicultural Cities*. Toronto: John Wiley & Sons.

17. Giddens, A (1984) *The Constitution of Society*. Berkeley: University of California Press.

18. Gregory, D & J Urry (eds) (1985) *Social Relations and Spatial Structures*. London: Macmillan.

19. Harvey, D (1982) *The Limits to Capital*. Chicago: University of Chicago Press.

20. Grant, W (ed) (1985) *The Political Economy of Corporatism*. London: Macmillan.

    Saunders, P (1981) *Social Theory and the Urban Question*. London: Hutchinson.

21. Alford, RA & R Friedland (1985) *Powers of Theory: Capitalism, the State and Democracy.* Cambridge: Cambridge University Press.

    Cooke, P (1983) *Theories of Planning and Spatial Development.* London: Hutchinson.

22. Sayer, A (1984) *Method in Social Science: A Realist Approach.* London: Hutchinson: 41.

23. Dear, M & AJ Scott (eds) (1981) *Urbanization and Urban Planning in Capitalist Society.* London: Methuen.

24. Dear, M & J Wolch (1987) *Landscapes of Despair: From Deinstitutionalization to Homelessness.* Princeton: Princeton University Press.

    Thrift, N (1983) On the determination of social action in space and time. *Society and Space* I: 23–57.

25. McLoughlin, JB (1969) *Urban and Regional Planning: A Systems Approach.* London: Faber and Faber.

26. Webber, MJ (1984) *Explanation, Prediction and Planning: The Lowry Model.* London: Pion.

    Wilson, AG (1974) *Urban and Regional Models in Geography and Planning.* New York: John Wiley & Sons.

27. Faludi, A (1973) *Planning Theory.* Oxford: Pergamon Press.

28. Friedmann, J (1973) *Retracking America: A Theory of Transactive Planning.* New York: Doubleday.

29. Scott, AJ & S Roweis (1977) Urban planning in theory and practice: A reappraisal. *Environment and Planning A* 9: 1097–119.

30. Forester, J (1980) Critical theory and planning practice. *Journal of the American Planning Association,* 46: 275–86.

31. Kiernan, MJ (1983) Ideology, politics and planning: Reflections on the theory and practice of urban planning. *Environment & Planning B: Planning & Design* 10: 71–87.

32. Breheny, MJ (1983) A practical view of planning theory. *Environment & Planning B: Planning & Design* 10: 101–15.

33. Gerecke, K (1977) The history of city planning. In J Lorimer & E Ross (eds) *Studies of Urban and Suburban Canada. The Second City Book.* Toronto: James Lorimer: 150–62.

34. Goldberg, M & P Horwood (1980) *Zoning: Its Cost and Relevance to 1980.* Vancouver: Fraser Institute.

35. Vancouver, City of (1928) *A Plan for the City of Vancouver.* Vancouver: Vancouver Town Planning Commission.

36. Economic Council of Canada (1965) *Fourth Annual Review.* Ottawa: Supply and Services.

    Lithwick, NH (1970) *Urban Canada: Problems and Prospects.* Ottawa: CMHC.

37. Hellyer, P (1969) *Task Force on Urban Development and Housing, Report.* Ottawa: Queen's Printer: 165.

38. Lithwick, NH (1970) Op. cit.

39. Gunton, T (1983) Theory and practice of Canadian planning. *City Magazine* (Spring): 19–29.

40. Adams, T (1914) Town planning. *Canadian Club of Vancouver, Addresses and Proceedings, 1914-1917,* December 15: 5.

41. Greater Vancouver Regional District (1975) *The Livable Region, 1976/1986.* Vancouver: GVRD.

    Lash, H (1976) *Planning in a Human Way.* Ottawa: Ministry of State for Urban Affairs.

42. Canadian Institute of Planners (2004) *Statement of Values and Code of Practice,* point 1.3, http://www.cip-icu.ca/English/members/practice.htm (accessed 3 December 2004).

43. Foucault, M (1977) *Discipline and Punish: The Birth of the Prison.* (Translated by A Sheridan) New York: Vintage Books, Random House.

44. Gallie, W (1956) Essentially contested concepts. *Proceedings of the Aristotelian Society* 56: 167–98.

45. Davidoff, P (1965) Advocacy and pluralism in planning. *Journal of the American Institute of Planners* 31(4): 331–8.

46. Sandercock, L (1998) Op. cit.

47. Friedmann, J (1973) Op. cit.

48. Forester, J (1989) *Planning in the Face of Power.* Berkeley: University of California Press.

49. Healey, P (1997) *Collaborative Planning: Shaping Places in Fragmented Societies.* Vancouver: UBC Press.

50. Duany, A, E Plater-Zyberk, & J Speck (2000) *Suburban Nation: The Rise of Sprawl and the Decline of the American Dream.* New York: North Point Press.

    Talen, E & C Ellis (2002) Beyond relativism: Reclaiming the search for good city form. *Journal of Planning Education and Research* 22: 36–49.

51. Wackernagel, M & W Rees (1995) *Our Ecological Footprint: Reducing Human Impact on the Earth.* Gabriola Island: New Society Publishers.

52. Fainstein, S (2000) New directions in planning theory. *Urban Affairs Review* 35(4): 451–78.

    Sandercock, L (1998) Op. cit.

53. Goetz, EG (2003) *Clearing the Way: Deconcentrating the Poor in Urban America.* Washington DC: Urban Institute Press.

Chapter Four

Ethics and Values in Planning

Understanding Ethics and Values

Jill Grant

The early years of *Plan Canada* contain relatively little discussion of ethics, as planners operated according to the principles of the rational (modernist) paradigm. By the 1960s, though, debates about proper behaviour for planners began appearing. In the 1980s, ethics became a prominent concern in the profession, as it continued to be in subsequent decades. While the search for the good community constituted a technical quest in the early years of planning, through time, we have come to recognize it as significantly more complicated. The planning profession is involved in politics, whether we like it or not. Planning choices involve values, and the debate about what values to privilege is at the heart of ethics. Deciding what is "good" and "right" is never easy.

Ethics offers guidance for action. The dictionary defines ethics as a system of moral principles that help us understand right and wrong. As developed in recent decades, planning ethics involves a code of values and conduct to inform and guide professional behaviour. Professional bodies representing planners have adopted and refined such codes to reflect national and international concerns. The Canadian Institute of Planners revised its code in 2004, adding several clauses to its earlier version and adjusting the wording to update the statement of values and its code of professional practice.

Canadian Institute of Planners: Statement of Values

1. To respect and integrate the needs of future generations. CIP members recognize that their work has cumulative and long-term implications. When addressing short-term needs, CIP members acknowledge the future needs of people, other species and their environments, and avoid committing resources that are irretrievable or irreplaceable.

2. To overcome or compensate for jurisdictional limitations. CIP members understand that their work has a potential impact on many jurisdictions and interests. They must therefore practise in a holistic manner, recognizing the need to overcome the limitations of administrative boundaries.

3. To value the natural and cultural environment. CIP members believe that both natural and cultural environments must be valued. They assume roles as stewards of these environments, balancing preservation with sustainable development.

4. To recognize and react positively to uncertainty. CIP members believe that the long-term future is unpredictable and that adaptable and flexible responses to deal positively with this uncertainty must be developed.

5. To respect diversity. CIP members respect and protect diversity in values, cultures, economies, ecosystems, built environments and distinct places.

6. To balance the needs of communities and individuals. CIP members seek to balance the interests of communities with the interests of individuals, and recognize that communities include both geographic communities and communities of interest.

7. To foster public participation. CIP members believe in meaningful public participation by all individuals and groups and seek to articulate the needs of those whose interests have not been represented.

8. To articulate and communicate values. CIP members believe in applying these values explicitly to their work and communicating their importance to clients, employers, colleagues and the public.

Source: Available online at http://www.cip-icu.ca/English/members/practice.htm

The interest in ethics has not resolved debates about what the planner should do. In fact, we see a range of ethical approaches informing theory and practice in recent years and competing for adherents. For instance, environmental ethicists and ecologists have raised questions about the aims and methods of planning and the faith the profession has had in growth.[1] Advocacy planning put the client's interests and values forward, challenging the idea that planners can define a single public interest.[2] Radical and equity planning advance the interest of the most disadvantaged. New urbanism praises the values of beauty and order in the city.[3] As articles by Nigel Richardson and by Mark Wexler and Judy Oberlander explain in this chapter, planners face an array of choices in ethical positions to take and values to promote.

Values are things that matter most to people. They reflect core beliefs and understandings about the way the world works and what is important in it. In any society, values that affect planning may differ between individuals, yet we see evidence that particular values permeate a culture and are reflected in landscapes and townscapes.

Through the decades, some values have remained central to Canadian planning. Efficiency and health are clearly core planning values: They give a public purpose to planning and are common in mainstream theories and in Canadian practice. Other values may be important at times and neglected at others. Here we might cite amenity and equity: Some planning theories and practitioners advocate these values, while others minimize them. Amenity had high priority in the City Beautiful movement of the early twentieth century and does once again in the new urbanism paradigm that is influencing development patterns. Equity is a key value in radical and equity planning, but it has had little impact on planning practice in Canada.

What other values are included in the many that guide planning in our society? As we try to answer that question, we can point to a range of value sets that influence practice. Scientific values such as rationality, objectivity, and quantification affect the way we

Figure 4.1

Signature high-rise buildings in urban cores reflect the valuesof our economic system.

approach planning and the methods we use. Social values around such themes as family, privacy, individualism, and cooperation may affect the processes we use and the decisions we make about residential landscapes. Political values such as democracy, order, and freedom affect decision-making processes. Economic values such as prosperity, competition, and thrift play a key role in debates about growth and choices about investments. Religious values such as obedience, charity, and humility may affect the way people think about their communities and their approach to government. Aesthetic values such as beauty, convenience, and harmony influence the way we envision the city and our own place in it. As we can see, some of these values have a significant impact on townscapes and landscapes. For example, suburban landscapes reflect values attached to family, privacy, individualism, and nature. Urban-core townscapes may reflect values associated with affluence, competition, technology and convenience: the values of capitalism (Figure 4.1).

Values inform the goals we set. Community goal setting involves a participatory process, whereby community residents offer their input into the goals that will direct choices for the future. Goal setting requires a level of consensus building. Consensus is generally fairly easy to achieve when people share values. As any negotiator will admit, however, when people have divergent values, they cannot easily reach consensus. Value conflict involves the most basic level of disagreement. Unfortunately for planners, planning disputes often reveal divergent values.

For example, in a dispute over the future use of a piece of farmland, different parties hold contrasting opinions. Agricultural experts may urge that land remain in agricultural

Chapter 4 / Ethics and Values in Planning

Figure 4.2

Community members might debate the best options for land, but here its future as a road is clear.

use to protect long-term food supplies. Environmentalists may recommend that woods, ravines, and streams on the farm be designated as environmentally sensitive habitat zones protected from development. Neighbours may protest the potential for increased traffic and disrupted views from urban expansion. Developers may welcome the jobs and taxes generated and the affordable homes to result. In each case, the participants' values influence the options they favour (Figure 4.2).

When planners seek consensus in goal setting, we risk ending up with low-order agreement. We can agree that we want clean, safe, vibrant, and caring communities. Hence, vision statements from dozens of Canadian cities include those words or some variation on them.[4] Such "motherhood" statements offer little precision or clarity, however. To create workable land use plans that will generate the kinds of communities we seek, we need greater specificity in our goals.

Do Canadian values differ from those driving planning in the US or UK? We do find some unique characteristics of Canadian planning practice. Peace, order, and good government have always had high priority in Canada. Therefore, we see acceptance of the authority of the state to limit ownership rights to meet community needs or concerns. The resistance to planning that sometimes hinders practice in the US is less common in Canada. At the same time, though, Canadians expect that the loss of such rights should generate compensation. The kind of nationalization of development rights that occurred in the UK would likely encounter resistance in Canada. Canadian planning may also reflect a unique position on diversity, as we will discuss in Chapter 7.

Politics and Practice

This chapter includes five articles that present a range of perspectives on ethics and values in planning. In the mid-1980s, John Forester saw the planning profession as changing, as becoming more concerned about ethics and politics and coming to understand planning in a different light. His paper reflects his desire to develop a practical ethics of planning, an interest he pursued in several books in the last two decades. Reg Lang argues that planners need to put equity issues forward. He suggests that it is not always ethical to use a strictly rational process. In some cases, planners should privilege disadvantaged groups to ensure fairness. This represents a radical shift from the rational principle of the greatest benefit for the greatest number, but it constitutes a position commonly heard in recent years. Leonie Sandercock expands on Lang's theme by arguing that a growing cultural diversity complicates planning choices and requires new knowledge, skills, and "literacies" from planners. Planning, she says, must be value sensitive and work on behalf of vulnerable populations. Nigel Richardson proves more cautious. He notes that it is not so easy for the planner to decide what is right and ethical. Planners should hesitate to impose their own values. He suggests that planners are responsible to four constituencies with different expectations. Mark Wexler and Judy Oberlander present four profiles of how planners operate. They see types of planners varying in values and ethics.

Readers interested in ethics should read Alterman and Page for an understanding of the immense influence of values in planning.[5] Udy argued that key eternal values propel planning.[6] Gerecke and Reid contributed to the discussion about politics and ethics,[7] while Harper and Stein argued for a normative approach to planning.[8] Hendler has written often about planning ethics and edited both a book and a 1990 issue of *Plan Canada* on ethics. Another theme issue on ethics and values in 2002 brought the debate up to date.[9]

Debates about ethical behaviour will continue as long as planning remains a function of government. Decision making must be informed by debates about what is right to do. And, of course, what people see as ethical behaviour will continue to depend on their value base.

Politics, Power, Ethics and Practice: Abiding Problems for the Future of Planning

John Forester

1986, Plan Canada 26(9): 224–7

Can we speak of the future of planning without being condemned to repeat the same old homilies of the past? We all know this future of planning by heart: Surely public and private will have to work together; academics will have to understand the world of practice; theory will have to improve and become more relevant; the lion will have to lie down with the lamb. This view of planning may be the most certain—if also probably the least useful—thing that we know about the future of the planning profession.

So let's consider the problem differently. How might the internal thinking of the profession be changing and developing? To address this question, we can review four clusters of problems—old problems to which our conventional answers might finally be changing: i) the place of politics in planning; ii) planning in the face of power; iii) the undiscussability of ethics in real terms; and iv) the recognition that planning practice embraces far more than formal techniques.

Toward a New Politics of Planning?

Soon, "politics" may no longer be a dirty word in planning. As it has often been used in our profession, politics has implied "compromising professionalism." Politics has meant conflict; conflict has meant irrationality; irrationality certainly has meant loss of control. Politics has meant, as one planner put it, "people yelling at each other," when he wanted to work on the reports, the impact analyses, instead.

This image of politics has had its costs. Shunning the politics of planning, some planners tried to be detached, "objective" professionals, but this identity has always been problematic. Planning problems are not only uncertain and often poorly defined, they are ambiguous, too. We often have to interpret what a goal, policy, regulation, or bylaw means. Once we do that, knowing that multiple and conflicting interpretations are always possible (some favouring some people, others favouring others), we're right back to politics.

After the fall of large-scale modelling, discovering the dilemmas of systems analysis, and recognizing the limits of cost-benefit analysis, the ideal of the detached objective professional may be weakening. If this is half right, planners will feel more pressure than ever to develop a professional identity that can take the necessarily political character of planning seriously.

In the schools, however, the analysis of politics has not done terribly well. Many analyses seem to end where they might better have begun: by recognizing, of course, that planning is political. Fine, we should say, so what? What do we now need to know, to think about differently, to be able to do? To note that planning is political should not be the last word of an analysis, but the first!

The very unpredictability of planning practice may now lead us to a different image of the politics of planning. Politics will still mean conflict, and people will still yell, but it will mean much more than that. The new image of politics in planning is likely to focus less upon counting votes and more on the questions: "Why those votes at this time on those issues?" Decisions will remain central, but more attention may now be given to agendas and to institutions—to the stages on which the key participants in the planning process act. This meaning of politics will then require renewed attention to the many *relationships* that planners have with others as they do their work, because the character and quality of those relationships shape project outcomes.

Politics, then, will mean not just covert bargaining, but relationship building. The politics of planning will not present puzzles to be solved, but patterns of practical relationships—each with histories, investments, multiple goals, and precarious relations of trust—to be anticipated. Politics will thus also mean coming to terms with the unique and particular identities of the planned-with and the planned-for (i.e., being able to listen and speak across differences of race and gender). We should remember: "Whether or not all people are created equal, when they walk into the planning office, they're just not all the same." And most people, of course, never walk in.

The wholehearted confession and recognition that planners act politically—affecting the intricate balance of relationships around them—will lead to an increasing appreciation of the role of negotiation and mediation in planning practice. Renewed attention to conflict, then, will lead planners to learn essential theories and strategies of negotiation and mediation, for these are activities that many planners are already involved with in relatively ad hoc and arbitrary ways. The limits of these skills, in turn, are likely to lead us to examine issues of power and empowerment in a more serious way than we have so far. Negotiations always depend on the "walk away" options of the parties. If one party is so poor, so hungry, or so desperate for housing that it has no options and so makes a deal, we ought to be at least as concerned about its prenegotiation lack of options as we are about the so-called consensual quality of any outcome it has achieved via negotiation.

Focusing on relationships rather than decisions will bring us face to face with inequalities of access, information, wealth, and political power. It will be hard, then, not to ask, How do planners serve to reproduce such inequalities, or, alternatively, to resist reproducing them? What might planners do here?" These questions will lead directly to concerns with the power and influence of planning staff themselves.

Planning in the Face of Power

Far too little is known about the power and influence of planning practitioners. The conventional wisdom, which is less wisdom than doctrine, goes like this: Planners have skills; politicians have power. Planners do analyses and present options; politicians, or someone else, make the decisions. This doctrine is partially correct, but deeply misleading. It hides from our view—and from our debates in the profession—what discretion and influence planners might actually have. Can this doctrine communicate the excitement of planning to anyone else? If our basic posture is to take refuge or to be above it all, can we attract innovative and imaginative people to the profession?

Research about power and influence in the planning process raises many more questions than it answers. The results are puzzling. Studies show that planners can be quite reticent to talk about power, even while some 75 percent of the profession recognizes a significant political dimension of their work.

Why might this be so? Because the dominant culture of the profession celebrated ideals of detachment and rationality, planners had few acceptable ways to examine and evaluate their own power and influence. Because "politics" was a dirty word, the actual exercise of power and influence by planners has been a "guilty little secret" in the profession. Even in the most traditional local permitting processes, though, planners provide inside advice about processes and politics: They broker information, they affect timing, they encourage or discourage participation, they shape agendas of project reviews, and so on. Planners have such discretion and influence because power is rarely monolithic—wholly in the mayor's or in the developer's office. Planners weren't supposed to be exerting influence (the conventional doctrine says), yet they had to, as a practical matter, because no process is simply what the flowchart says it is.

Even today, planners have no acceptable way of admitting that they have such political influence. This is still difficult because the culture and ideology of the profession focus more on the analysis of projects—impacts, costs and benefits, alternatives—and less on the institutional processes that planners have to deal with all the time and that call for inevitably political judgments about desirable or undesirable participation, openness, levels of expertise available to affected parties, representation, interpretation of goals, and so on.

The rub is this: If planners do have multiple sources of influence but feel perpetually at risk in admitting this, they doom themselves to walking on a lumpy rug. Undiscussable in the profession, power and influence will remain difficult to learn about in anything other than wholly idiosyncratic ways. This situation promises professional tragedy. The very ideal of the detached professional threatens to undermine planners' influence by making such day-to-day issues of making a difference difficult—even dangerous to subject to careful and explicit scrutiny, criticism, and study.

Toward a Practical Ethics of Planning

If thinking about politics differently will lead us to think more clearly about power and influence, then facing those issues might well press us all to change the ways we think about ethics. Here, again, our conventional, deeply cultural, and ideological views of ethics may change. We now understand "ethics" as hardly practical, even though that's exactly what the field of ethics is supposed to be. We ordinarily think about ethical theory as if it were a kind of mental pasta machine: In go the ingredients of the situation; out comes the "right" thing to do. What happens usually, though, is quite different: In go the ingredients; out comes mush.

There are, however, other ways to think about and so embrace and use ethics. We can understand ethical theories as ways of arguing about what ought to be done in messy, conflictual, uncertain, and threatening situations. How much of a serious profession can we have if we treat ethics simply as window dressing? This does not imply that we should now all march to the tune of certain principles; that is likely to be not ethical, but simply doctrinaire.

Figure 4.3

Development issues often pitch conservation and heritage values against economic values, as in this Halifax construction site.

Ethics need not be equated with calculating what's right in an abstracted world.[10] Ethics, we may come to see, is all about what we should do when things are messy, when loyalties and obligations conflict, when rules aren't clear, when our jobs are threatened, and when what's important, good, or right is anything but clear. Again, recognizing questions of discretion and influence (i.e., how much and what information to give to whom and when) is likely to prompt us to trade in the calculating (or pasta) machine theory of ethics and to begin to take the character of arguments over conflicting values seriously (Figure 4.3).

Notice, again, the historical, cultural, and ideological currents against which a rethinking of ethics cuts. Social scientists have taught us to think that we can be rational about facts but not about values, yet few people writing about ethics today believe that (which should be welcome news to us in the planning profession). This is because planners are called upon to be rational about value judgments all the time, to defend such judgments with arguments, and to make such arguments with reasons, evidence, precedents, and so on.[11]

Notice the directions that Carol Gilligan has pointed toward in her work on moral development and gender: the delineation of an ethics of care to complement an ethics of rules and a focus on concrete relationships as well as upon abstract rights.[12] These developments run parallel to the directions in which the planning profession (without any traditional commitment to feminist theory) seems to be moving. Gilligan's work challenges not only the traditionally male-dominated field of psychology, but the similarly dominated—and now, let us hope, changing—field of planning, as well. So, if necessity sometimes spurs invention, the increasing recognition of politics, power, and influence in planning may force a long overdue reexamination of ethics (and of all evaluation) in the planning profession.

Coming to See Practice Anew

Finally, our attitudes toward practice and learning from practice are likely to change. We are likely to shift from the attempt to discover recipes for what works to the attempt to understand and develop repertoires of strategies appropriate to varying situations.

We are now a bit like cooks trying to learn just one or two complicated recipes, even as the available ingredients and the dinner guests keep changing. We need, however, not one best recipe (or an inventory of recipes) for the soufflé we call economic development or zoning appeals, but to learn how to cook. We need to learn about various strategies allowing us, perhaps informally, to adapt or change any basic recipe to fit a particular problem (the particular ingredients that we have at hand). So we might begin to look to studies of practice and the stories we tell one another not only for what worked, but also for the range of skills, judgments, interpretations, and strategies that practitioners have devised in their unique situations.[13]

This means, too, that we may come to look at planning history in new ways. We are likely, soon, to drop the view of history captured so wonderfully in a simple cartoon: One school child says excitedly to another, "I love history! It's all about dead celebrities!"

We will always be interested in the practice of exemplary practitioners. Now, however, instead of looking at what worked, we will try to learn from the sorts of judgments that such skilled practitioners made: the complex ways they responded, practically, to the challenges, difficulties, and uncertainties of their day.

Finally, then, we may also develop a more nuanced idea of planning traditions. We are likely—the attention to politics, power, and ethics will force us—to recognize planning traditions as complex, always problematic, yet rich legacies with which we work. Rejecting such traditions altogether as egalitarian, utopian, or liberal or even sexist is no longer likely to do (it misses the point), because traditions are not just unitary recipes writ large. Traditions (like comprehensive planning) are, instead, enormously varied and complex families of practices; we may invite one cousin to dinner without assembling the whole multigenerational clan. So, we may face the problems of "appropriating traditions critically." Recognizing, too, that traditions live and change, we will do our parts both to carry forward and to change the planning traditions that we inherit.

A Hasidic tale might make the point best. The disciples of Rabbi Noah's deceased father took the son, their new teacher, to task: "Why do you not conduct yourself like your father?" "I do conduct myself like him," replied Rabbi Noah. "He did not imitate anybody, and I likewise do not imitate anybody."

In the planning profession, too, we are likely to learn from contemporary practice, from planning history, and from our evolving traditions, not through the limitation of strategies but through study. We must not just repeat other planners' words, but we must understand their promise in our time, in the messy, uncertain, data-poor, and highly politicized situations we now face.

Equity in Siting Solid Waste Management Facilities

Reg Lang

1990, Plan Canada 30(2): 5–13

The siting of solid waste management facilities—sanitary landfills, incinerators, transfer stations, and the like—presents municipalities and their planners with an urgent and confounding problem: Everyone benefits from these facilities, but no one seems to want them nearby. The problem is often characterized as NIMBY, implying that the position taken by those upon whom this label is conferred is an expression of narrow self-interest. Yet "Not in my backyard" can also be heard as "Why us, why here?" This may be a cry for fair treatment.[14] Accepting the latter interpretation offers promise for finding waste management sites that are not only technically feasible, but also politically and publicly acceptable and more equitable for those directly affected.

This paper begins by exploring the concept of equity and the nature of the waste management crisis. Drawing mainly on the Ontario context and the author's experience, it presents evidence of inequity in the siting of solid waste management facilities and offers an alternative framework for employing principles of equity. Since such an approach would be a significant departure from current practice, there is a discussion of the implications of introducing it up front, when policies and siting guidelines are being established, rather than leaving equity to be determined at environmental assessment hearings when it may be too late.[15]

Equity

Equity here refers to the fairness of siting a facility at a particular location and the fairness of the process for reaching that decision: "a just distribution, justly arrived at" in the words of David Harvey.[16] Equity, therefore, is a matter of distributive justice and procedural fairness. It calls for equal treatment of equals and, conversely, for unequals to be treated unequally.

How can we decide what is equitable, fair, just? Lucy suggests consideration of five conceptions of equity: equality (everyone should receive the same service, within reason); need (those requiring a service should get more of it); demand (those showing an active interest in a service should be rewarded); preference (to include those whose interest in a service is not exposed through its use); and willingness to pay (people who use a service should pay for it, non-users should not have to pay). This typology usefully exposes not only the various dimensions of equity, but also how complex it can be.[17] Lucy's conceptions of equity are often in conflict. Some have thresholds, others are difficult to measure, and all are subject to varying interpretations.

In practice, it is not possible to distribute society's goods and "bads" equally, to the satisfaction of all. Likewise, it is often difficult to sort out competing claims between efficiency and equity—maximizing total benefit to the community versus distributing benefits fairly amongst its members. Small wonder that practitioners are inclined to consign confusing equity issues to the larger mess called "politics."

Recent years have shown a dramatic upsurge of interest in ethics across the board, from business and the professions to politics and everyday life. Because the costs and benefits of waste disposal are distributed unequally, siting of waste management facilities is at the forefront of ethical concerns. The fact that these facilities are usually unwanted adds to the controversy, and the urgent need for them makes for a crisis.

The Waste Crisis

Crisis, that overworked word, certainly applies to waste. In Ontario, landfill sites are rapidly running out of capacity.[18] Each year, Canadians produce on average more than a tonne of garbage, residential and industrial included, half again as much as 25 years ago (Figure 4.4). If new waste disposal facilities were being sited and constructed at an appropriate rate, there would be no crisis. But they are not—far from it. Metro Toronto is a case in point. Environmental pressures forced the closing in 1988 of its aging incinerator and abandonment of a new landfill which was to have been located in a nearby municipality. In concert with neighbouring municipalities, Metro began searching for a new landfill site, but without success.[19]

This is the crisis then: an increasing volume of waste; rapidly decreasing capacity in existing waste management facilities; new facilities not coming on stream fast enough; and formidable barriers to speeding up the process. The problem is deeply rooted.

Figure 4.4

STEPHANIE BOHDANOW

Such urban activities as construction and renovation generate large volumes of waste that require disposal.

Waste is something we no longer want, need, or have a use for. It is culturally determined, and its definition has changed over time. From the mid-1940s, Canadians began consuming more resources per capita and substituting goods that are more difficult to dispose of, such as plastics for wood, detergents for soap, and synthetics for natural fibres. These trends combined with population growth to create rapid increases in the amount of waste accompanied by wasteful behaviour that endures. Our society grows ever-more wasteful and is only beginning to face the consequences.

The approach used to site waste facilities has not helped. Technical rationality dominates waste planning and management. This mindset stresses scientific methods as an objective means of providing information to decision makers, relies on facts separated from values as the basis of knowledge, favours quantified data and models as means of inquiry, emphasizes analysis over interaction, and searches for the "best" solution to problems.[20] While the technical approach has valuable applications, especially in science, it also has significant limitations. It is especially unsuited to such complex situations as waste management, in which conflicts are often about values, and where a multiplicity of perspectives must be respected. Then, a technical/analytic approach needs to be combined with an interactive/political approach.[21] Unfortunately, this happens all too rarely. Engineers, planners, and others do their studies, prepare their reports, and typically tack public participation onto the process. Affected interests are informed and perhaps consulted, but reality for decision makers and their advisors remains grounded in technical rationality. For example, environmental assessments routinely treat noise solely as an objective measure of sound determined by arbitrary standards without acknowledging something obvious to the ordinary person—that it is the meaning we attach to sound that makes it pleasant and desired, or stressful and "noisy." This technical bias carries over into environmental hearings, which occur in quasi-judicial and frequently adversarial settings monopolized by lawyers, where "hard" data and objective testimony by experts receive the most attention.

A related root cause of the crisis is moral and philosophical. Timmerman sees this as a clash between a means-oriented managerial approach based on bureaucratic rationality and an ends-oriented "mutualistic community" perspective that refuses to see people as a means to an end.[22] When a local government proposes that residents of a smaller community bear the brunt of the costs, inconvenience, and risk associated with a waste management facility so that the larger community of which they are part may benefit, then trouble is sure to follow. Because of the competing moral perspectives involved, the ensuing controversy is especially difficult to handle and particularly dangerous to the stability of the social order and the legitimacy of "the system." Perhaps that is why governments are loath to impose such facilities, no matter how strong the objective argument, and why they prefer to keep waste management issues in the technical realm.

Because these are root causes, they will not be quickly or easily addressed. Equity is one promising point of entry. Some parts of our society generate much more waste than others, and some members of society benefit more from the economic growth that produces this waste, yet these individuals and groups rarely bear a proportionate share of the costs represented by waste. A technical approach to waste planning and management distorts this distributional injustice;[23] it favours certain kinds of information inputs to decision makers while discriminating against other kinds, often to the disadvantage of those adversely affected by proposed facilities. Finally, the clash of moral universes and the renegotiation of the social contract that it implies calls for choices that are fundamentally about ethics and about equity.

Inequity in Waste Management

Specific evidence of inequity in waste management is not hard to find. Moreover, attempts to deal with the waste management crisis as often as not aggravate inequity rather than alleviate it. The problem is occurring at all levels. At the global scale, developing countries are attempting to unload their worst wastes on less-developed countries. In Ontario, as regional municipalities scramble for solutions to the waste crisis, equity appears to be low on the list of concerns. For instance, in looking for options for its crisis, Metro Toronto considered creating an "interim landfill" in the Rouge River valley, an environmentally significant area that was to have become a provincial park; paying a neighbouring municipality to accept Metro's waste and expanding a huge existing dump in another; and transporting waste 240 kilometres northeast to the Town of Kapuskasing. While critics strenuously opposed the landfill proposals on environmental and equity grounds, the province indicated that, in light of the urgency of the situation, it would exempt interim landfill proposals from environmental assessment, thereby closing the main avenue for public participation. It seems that governments sometimes allow situations to become a crisis so that equity and environmental considerations can be "trumped" by urgency, and local interests can be subordinated to "the larger good."

Landfills alone seldom yield benefits to people who live beside them. Instead, such waste management facilities are likely to result in increased hazards and reduced environmental quality (pollution, heavy truck traffic, noise, odour, and other nuisance effects) along with the fear of reduced property values, stress, and an assortment of other ills. On equity grounds, it is reasonable to argue that a community or local area that has had to live with a landfill or incinerator for decades has done its share for the larger good; now, it's someone else's turn. But this argument seems not to impress those responsible for facility siting. A study done in 1988 showed that three-quarters of the municipalities engaged in waste management planning favoured "the proximity option": locating new landfills next to existing ones. The reasons, seldom articulated officially, include:

"The existing site has proved to be reasonably satisfactory, and therefore we can expect another one beside it to be equally so. Besides, a landfill next to another landfill is a compatible land use." "We already have a monitoring system in place at the existing landfill. This will save us having to install another." "The environment at the existing landfill (e.g., groundwater) is already degraded. Why spoil another part of the municipality?" "The people who live beside the existing landfill and along the haul routes have gotten used to it." "It's much easier to get government approval for an expansion than for a new facility."

These arguments convey a disturbing impression: Municipalities and their advisors perceive that it will be easier to locate new facilities alongside existing ones. Facing urgent requirements to get these facilities sited (often because they waited so long to begin planning or misjudged the amount of time it would take), and afraid that ruling out an adjoining site on equity grounds could deprive them of an excellent location or even the best one for the facility, they feel the proximity option is justified.

Residents who have lived with a landfill or other such facility for many years are infuriated by these arguments, not just because they promote inequity but also because they are seriously flawed. Whether it is fair to locate a new landfill beside one that has been there for a long time is a question that is both procedural and substantive. Procedurally, it may be fair to consider a site adjoining an existing landfill if affected communities and residents are fully included in the study. Substantively, however, it is manifestly unfair to require that the environmental and social impacts of garbage disposal be borne over a long period of time by a single community or part thereof. The political principle of equality provides that people have a right to equal treatment, that is, to the same distribution of goods or opportunities as anyone else has or is given.[24] While there cannot be a totally fair distribution, to deliberately place the burden of waste disposal on one segment of the community generation after generation is undeniably unfair. "Deliberately" is a key word, because random inequity is much more bearable than inequity that is or appears to be intentional.

How to be fairer to those living in close proximity to a waste management facility is therefore an exceedingly complex and difficult problem. Its solution requires, among other things, that equity considerations be explicit in the policy guidance given to appointed officials and consultants when they begin the facility-siting process.

An Equity-Based Approach to Waste Management

A facility-siting approach based on equity is unlikely to be eagerly embraced by decision makers. Politicians know that such an approach, besides reducing the pool of available sites, would require tough decisions sure to displease one or another interest group. Crisis decisions are easier to justify. It is also less controversial to go along with staff proposals that appear to be logical, scientific, unbiased, and inevitable. In any case, if the technical approach produces a politically undesirable recommendation, politicians feel they can always overrule it. They may also hope that when a site is finally designated, the support of the many that benefit (relieved that the garbage problem is being taken care of, and not in their backyard) will greatly outweigh and overshadow the complaints of the directly impacted few. The problem with this approach is that it often does not work, either in producing acceptable sites or in avoiding controversy. Furthermore, claims of unfair treatment persist far beyond the final decision, as does broader public uneasiness about the precedent of trampling on individual rights.

Clearly, equity is a matter of politics; for politics is about the allocation of resources. Leaving equity to be dealt with at the end of the siting process is tantamount to giving it no consideration at all. By the time a long and costly selection process has designated a site, it is quite difficult for elected decision makers to reject it on equity grounds.

To accept political responsibility for equity means debating equity principles openly at the outset and then providing guidelines for the site selection process. Ten such principles are proposed. Note that they are an interrelated set, and therefore the list ought not to be sampled at random. Also, the principles are not cast in stone but are intended to be adapted, through public consultation, to each locality.

Principles

1. All elements of society share responsibility for the generation of waste and its disposal.
2. Each region has a responsibility to take care of its own waste. One region should not export its waste problem to another without previously agreed-on reciprocal arrangements.
3. Adverse impacts should not be imposed on people and their environments, or on future generations, if these impacts can be avoided. Every effort should be made, prior to facility siting, to reduce the amount of waste that requires disposal.
4. Waste creates social and environmental costs that are not borne equally. Within the region, all efforts must be made to distribute waste management facilities equitably, in terms of both space and time. Each area must bear its share of this responsibility in proportion to its share of the region's waste stream.
5. Regional and inter-regional strategies are necessary to provide the context within which waste management facilities may be equitably sited. Multiple siting—identifying all facilities required in the future rather than siting one facility at a time—would require each community and each region to consider its ultimate future, integrate its waste production with its land development process, and establish a pattern of facilities that is as equitable as possible. Achieving this may necessitate constructing more, smaller facilities instead of a few large ones.
6. It is inevitable that some individuals, groups, and communities will be called upon to assume a disproportionate amount of the impacts and risks associated with waste disposal. Every effort must be made to render the imposition of such facilities as voluntary as possible, to minimize adverse impacts, to share unavoidable risks, to mitigate the impacts that remain, and to compensate fully those who bear the burden of these residual impacts.
7. Individuals and interest groups who are affected by a proposed facility can reasonably expect that an analytically sound and politically fair process will be followed in site selection.
8. A community that is selected for a waste management facility can expect, and should receive, firm assurance that it will not be selected for further facilities of this nature in the future.
9. After the facility is in place, there should be ongoing opportunities for those directly affected to be kept informed about and involved in its operation. Their involvement should include a measure of control (e.g., shutdown of the facility when it exceeds operating guidelines) to ensure conformity, and the appearance of same, to requirements and promises of performance set out when the facility was assessed and approved.
10. Imposing unwanted risks and impacts upon the few for the benefit of the many is fundamentally an ethical problem. It therefore deserves open consideration at the beginning of a facility siting process. That process, and the planning that precedes it, must have sufficient lead time so that site selection will not occur in an atmosphere of crisis, which may cause other equity principles, such as provision for full environmental assessment, to be set aside.

Front-end guidance on equity would still need to be complemented by back-end assessment of a designated proposal's equity impacts as part of environmental and social impact assessment.

Equity impact assessment could take this form:

- Establish criteria for considering equity, making these explicit rather than leaving them hidden, as impact assessments tend to do. This requires interaction with the various stakeholders, the effecting and affected interests.

- Examine the history of solid waste disposal in the region served by the proposed facility, including to what extent, over time, each area had assumed responsibility for its waste and that of other areas.

- Identify and analyze the equity concerns of residents at each site, recognizing that equity is both "objective" and perceptual.

- Use techniques such as the focus group to provide a further analytic base for identifying and evaluating equity-related impacts.

- Summarize and compare the equity-related social impacts at each site, as the basis for further discussions with stakeholders.

Applying equity principles would have certain implications. For instance, Principle 3 calls for full adoption of the 4 Rs—reduction, recycling, reuse, and recovery of waste— and in the appropriate sequence. It is unfair to impose a landfill or incinerator on a community before all possible efforts have been made by the larger community to reduce the waste load. And Principle 7 goes beyond equity to the issue of public distrust of institutions, a major part of the siting problem. It is essential that siting processes be perceived as legitimate. No waste management program can succeed unless people have confidence in the proponents in government and industry, first, to give health, safety, and environmental concerns top priority (not to sacrifice them for political popularity or profit), and second, to treat all parties with respect and scrupulous fairness. In the absence of such trust, governments have recourse only to imposition—overriding local interests to site-needed facilities. For nonhazardous solid waste management, the justification for that approach is questionable, and the political price can be high. Several of the principles go against conventional wisdom and practice.

An equity-based approach has a further implication for land use planners. Kasperson makes it clear that the problem involves more than finding sites for waste management facilities: It requires a waste generation, processing, movement, and disposal system integrated with land use planning.[25] Integration is a trendy term, capable of disguising needed action of a more controversial nature.[26] In this case, it is not merely a matter of coordinating planning for waste management with planning for economic and physical development. What happens when a municipality or region can no longer handle the waste generated by its development? Until now, solid waste has not been one of the "growth shapers." The main infrastructure investments influencing the amount, type, and timing of development have been sewage capacity, water supply, and transportation facilities. The assumption has been that somewhere, either in the municipality or beyond, solid waste will be disposed of. Equity principles and environmental considerations bring this assumption sharply into question. They raise the spectre of having to limit development to a level consistent with the municipality's ability and willingness to dispose of the waste it generates.

That taking account of ability to deal with outputs (waste) when admitting inputs (new development) seems radical says something about how superficially the ecological paradigm has penetrated the growth mindset. The same principle underlies "sustainable development," another fashionable concept whose full implications are as yet unrecognized. Unless humankind shoots its garbage into space, limits to growth (at least of the current kind) must be confronted eventually. The longer we ignore this, the more difficult it will be, and the more unfair to generations to come.

Waste as a limit to growth need not mean a halt to development. Countries like Japan have demonstrated the vast scope of the 4 Rs, and there are forms of development that are less waste intensive than others. Taking waste as a growth limit seriously, however, constitutes a major challenge for planners, especially in areas where development pressures are strong and development interests are well-entrenched in the political system: in other words, in the very areas that produce the most waste and therefore need this limit most.

Planning and Equity Issues

Benefits derived from waste management are widely dispersed, whereas costs are concentrated in specific local areas. This imbalance makes the planning and management of facilities fundamentally an equity issue. Indications are that this issue has not been handled well, to the point where some areas are facing a waste crisis. Efforts are being made to find solutions that minimize inequity, but governments and industries have often preferred a technical approach that gives equity minimal consideration. As that approach fails, there is a tendency to pursue courses of action that are less, rather than more, equitable. Even if these approaches work in the short run, they are doomed sooner or later to be counterproductive, especially if they further erode public trust in institutions. The prospect is greater challenges to the siting of much-needed facilities and a worsening of the waste management crisis. That will create inequity of another sort—intergenerational. We owe future generations a legacy that is at least as good as the one we received.

A fairer and politically difficult, but potentially more effective, approach is to create, in each community and region, a sound ethical base that can guide site selection processes and help rebuild public trust. The set of equity-based principles outlined herein could provide the foundation for such an approach. They are grounded in a systems perspective that reframes the waste problem from a siting of facilities to formulation of regional strategies that address both the disposal and generation of waste. Integration of planning for waste management with planning for economic and physical development as part of this equity-based approach acknowledges, as a limit to growth, the ability and willingness of a region to handle the wastes it generates. The challenge this presents to planners is to find new forms of development that are sustainable and fair, and to take a stand against development that is not.

Equity is now part of the waste management problem. Somehow, it must also become part of the solution.

A Portrait of Postmodern Planning: Anti-Hero and/or Passionate Pilgrim?

Leonie Sandercock

1999, Plan Canada 39(2): 12–5

A dozen years before the fall of the Berlin Wall signalled the symbolic end of the hopes that had been invested in socialism, and the system of central planning that was its core, the anti-hero of Hungarian George Konrad's novel endures his own crisis of conscience. In a harrowing monologue that runs the length of the novel, this unnamed anti-hero, this twentieth-century architect/city planner in an unnamed East European city, considers his life, his work, and the many-layered history of the city he and his family—architect/planners all—have helped to mould. In his mind, the narrator/anti-hero carries on an impassioned dialogue with the city, cursing and praising, excusing and lamenting. This city builder's ruthless honesty and intelligence, his expanding awareness of having "got it wrong" in a myriad ways, make him, in a sense, the battleground where modernist ideas (and idealism) are locked in confrontation with an ambiguous present and an even more uncertain future. His is a journey from hubris to humility.

For as long as there have been cities, there have been women and men seeking to define and then perfect the art and science of city building. Artists and designers, inventors and theologians, feminists and socialists are among the many who have turned their thoughts to perfecting the pattern of human settlement. From architectural to political, technical to religious, social to spiritual to environmental solutions, we have juggled with the elements of the city—its political economy, its built, social and natural environments—dreaming its perfection many times over, but never bringing the dream to fruition. Around the beginning of the twentieth century, a new profession emerged, staking out a claim for itself in relation to city building. The profession of town and country planning, these days usually referred to as urban and regional planning, emerged at that time in response to the perceived ills of the industrial city, and among its founding ideas, although always contested, was a distinct stream of utopian thinking. Perhaps the most powerful expression of this utopian stream was the paradigm that came to dominate planning in the twentieth century: the so-called modernist paradigm.

I want to take the fictional journey of George Konrad's anti-hero as a reflection of the journey of the planning profession in the twentieth century. I want to suggest that the profession is now "between paradigms," wandering between two worlds, one of them lost, the other yet to be found. For the past 30 years, the modernist paradigm has been under attack from within planning and architecture as well as from outside these professions. It may be crucial at this moment to remind ourselves that the modernist vision was indeed a vision, both profoundly idealistic and profoundly technocratic. It was faith in the powers of scientific and technical reason that underpinned the vision, and undermined it.

If the modernist project has crumbled, as many have argued, how might it be reconstructed in such a way that its idealism, its ethical underpinning, is not lost? What can we learn from the anti-hero's journey? What might inspire and reinvigorate us for the twenty-first century? And what qualities will we need, as a profession, to face the challenges ahead?

The Anti-Hero's Journey

Many have written at length about the fatal flaws of the modernist planning project. Here I can only summarize, acknowledging the risk of caricature. The dream of the modernist project was the dream of the Rational City.[27] The hubris of the city-building professions was their faith in the liberating potential of their technical knowledge, and their corresponding belief in their ability to transcend the interests of capital, labour, and the state to arrive at an objective assessment of the public interest. Consider the following five pillars of modernist planning wisdom, along with some ways of thinking beyond their limitations.

In the old model, planning was concerned with making public decisions more rational. The focus was predominantly on advance decision making, on developing blueprints for the future, and on an instrumental rationality that closely considered and evaluated options and alternatives. While means-ends rationality may still be a useful concept—especially for tasks like building bridges and dams—we also need a different kind of rationality that focuses on the formulation of goals. Rather than being technically based, this rationality is communicative, with a greater and more explicit reliance on practical wisdom. Ignorance of the future is not a solvable problem; it is rather an inescapable part of the human condition. We cannot comprehend a world continually in flux, and thus our ability to project the future consequences of alternative actions with any degree of certainty is severely limited.

In the old model, planning was regarded as most effective when it was comprehensive. Comprehensiveness was written into planning legislation, and referred to multifunctional and multisectoral spatial plans as well as to the intersections of economic, social, environmental, and physical planning. Planning's task was understood as one of coordinating and integrating, and was regarded as necessarily hierarchical. Today, planning is no longer seen as being exclusively concerned with integrative, comprehensive, and coordinating action, and is increasingly identified with negotiated, political, and focused planning,[28] a planning oriented less to the production of documents and more to interactive processes and to people.

In the old model, planning emerged out of the engineering mindset of the late nineteenth century, and drew its authority from a mastery of the theory and methods of the social and natural sciences. Planning knowledge and expertise was thus grounded in positivist science, with its propensity for quantitative modelling and analysis. Today, there is growing acknowledgment that there are many kinds of appropriate knowledge in planning. New epistemologies—among them hermeneutics, action research, feminist, and other ways of knowing and social learning—are displacing the sole reliance on the powers of positivist social science as a basis for action. Local communities have grounded, experiential, intuitive, and contextual knowledge manifested more often in stories, songs, visual images, and speech than in the typical planning sources. Planners need to learn and practise these other ways of knowing.

In the old model, planning was a project of state-directed futures, part of a two-hundred-year modernization project that began with the industrial revolution. There is now a thriving, community-based planning practice in which planners link their skills to the campaigns of mobilized communities, working as enablers and facilitators. Rather than speaking for communities, as in the older advocacy model, this new style of planning is geared to community empowerment. Planners bring to the table skills in research and critical thinking, knowledge of legislation and the workings of state agencies, specific skills in fields like housing and local economic development, organizing and financial skills, and a commitment to social and environmental justice.

This is not, however, meant to be an argument for rejecting state-directed planning. There are transformative and oppressive possibilities in state planning, just as in community-based planning. And victories at the community level almost always need to be consolidated in some way through the state, through legislation, and/or through the allocation of resources.

In the old model, as it existed until at least the late 1960s, planning was held to operate in the public interest, and it was assumed that planners' education enabled them to identify that public interest. In the wake of Marxist, feminist, and poststructuralist dismantling of this concept, it seems more useful to talk about planning for multiple publics or for a heterogeneous public. Planning has never been value neutral. It ought now to be explicitly value sensitive, working on behalf of the most vulnerable groups in multicultural cities and regions, accommodating rather than eradicating difference. This, in turn, means deconstructing a myth of "community" often held to be the radical "other" to the public interest, acknowledging that the dominant notion has typically been an ideal of homogeneous and exclusionary groups, and replacing this notion with a concept that is more inclusionary and democratic. In this new arena of planning for multiple publics in multicultural societies, new kinds of multi- or crosscultural literacies are essential.

These are the bare bones of a shifting paradigm. The old planning served modernist cities in a project that was, in part, dedicated to the eradication of difference: to the erasure of history, context, and culture. Its dominant images are of identical Levittowns sprawling across the landscape, and of identical high-rise towers planted in windswept wastelands, each of them "machines for living" in the modern age (Figure 4.5). The new planning emphasizes communicative rather than instrumental rationality, is less document-oriented and more people-centred, practises many ways of knowing rather than relying exclusively on technical knowledge, works through community-based

Figure 4.5

High-rise housing, like this Kitchener apartment building, originated in modernist ideals of equality but left a mixed legacy.

organizations as well as through state agencies, questions the notion of the public interest, and affirms the existence of multiple publics. A "politics of cultural recognition"[29] is fundamental to the new planning. But what are its embodied inspirations?

Inspirations for Twenty-first-Century Planning

The inspiration for and legitimation of this postmodern planning project comes from the wide variety of social movements that have emerged across the planet in recent decades, each demanding that its voice be heard in decisions affecting neighbourhoods, cities, and regions. I am thinking of three broad sociocultural forces that have been and will continue to reshape our cities: migration and an accompanying new politics of multicultural citizenship; postcolonialism and a corresponding politics of reclaiming urban and regional space by indigenous and formerly colonized peoples; and the rise of civil society in the form of multiple urban and environmental movements, all seeking to expand our vocabulary of justice (from economic to social, cultural, and environmental) and to expand our democratic practices. These struggles, in their failures as well as their successes, are managing to transform values and institutions, and the stories of these struggles constitute an emerging planning paradigm, which requires a very different style of planning, a familiarity with the lifeways of different communities, and new kinds of cultural, political, economic, and environmental literacies.

Necessary Qualities

When students sign up for a planning course, they usually assume that they are going to be acquiring "the skills of the profession." And indeed, planning schools teach them many skills that could be described as technical, among them basic statistics and computing, economic and demographic data collection and analysis, the use of GIS and other computer packages, report writing and basic graphics, and, of course, the ability to read plans and understand planning legislation. Not all planners need all of these skills. Some of them can be picked up or refined in the workplace. Some technical skills become quickly outdated as technologies advance. It is important to be cautionary in how we teach these techniques. Technical skills come with embedded assumptions, are used in highly ideological ways, and always depend on certain values that inform their use. How does a transportation planner decide what data to feed into her model? Why is the model privileged over other forms of analysis? The politics of statistics, beautifully articulated by Alonso and Starr,[30] needs to be taught within a statistics course. Being technically literate, then, ought to imply a whole lot more than familiarity with a range of technical skills and subjects.

It goes without saying that the kinds of technical skill listed above are an essential part of any planner's basic toolkit and need continual refreshing and upgrading. What is problematic is an educational and political climate in which both practising and trainee planners/students think that this is all there is to planning. What further qualities are required of a planning profession that is committed to a larger project of positive social change? For that, we need a whole other set of knowledges, or literacies, about context, about history and culture, about human and organizational behaviour, about politics and power. We need not only analytical and critical thinking, but substantive as well as process-oriented knowledge concerning such challenging issues as local economic development, cultural diversity, environmental degradation, and the relationship between design and behaviour. Let me expand on this, then, by talking about the multicultural, ecological, and design literacies that ought to be part of planning curricula as well as subjects for a continuing professional education program.

a) Multicultural Literacy

When people with different histories and cultures arrive in our cities, their presence inevitably disrupts the normative categories of social life and urban space. The same is true when existing residents, hitherto invisible, begin to assert their difference, make claims on urban space and services, and challenge accepted social norms. Women, gays, and indigenous peoples may claim and contest urban space and try to make a place for themselves. Their urban experiences, the focus of their struggle to redefine the conditions of belonging to society, are not only reshaping cities today, but are of necessity reshaping the way we think about planning.

As new and more complex kinds of ethnic, racial, and cultural diversity come to dominate the city, these multiple experiences increasingly demand a new basis for understanding and defining planning. There is a new cultural politics of difference in the air, and planning needs to come to terms with it. Historically universalist ideals of community and citizenship have operated to construct a homogeneous society. Planners have encouraged the ideal of towns and neighbourhoods in which people all know one another and have the same values and lifestyles. The current popularity of both the "new urbanism" and gated communities is the latest manifestation of this denial of diversity and fear of difference.

Given that we are living in what Canadian philosopher James Tully has described as "an age of diversity," in which the desire for cultural recognition, for voice and space, has forcefully emerged, it seems essential that planners find ways to respond.[31] One way is to think about how the built environment affects, and is affected by, cultural diversity. Another is to ask whose cultural norms are embedded in planning legislation, and whether it is appropriate, in multicultural societies, that the norms of one particular culture should be dominant. Yet another response is to learn new languages, both literally and metaphorically:

new ways of knowing, being, and acting, ways that are more humble, more collaborative, more respectful of the value of difference and cultural diversity. Planning's core concepts of rationality, comprehensiveness, and the public interest need rethinking in the light of new concepts of empowerment, alternative ways of knowing, and multiple publics.

This is what I mean by multicultural or intercultural literacy. It involves valuing alternative forms of knowledge and methods of knowing, including traditional ethnic or culturally specific modes: from talk to storytelling, as well as a wide range of nonverbal forms of expression, such as music and painting. It involves listening and interpreting, developing skills that are sensitive to everyday ways of knowing. It suggests a different practice in which communication skills, including openness, empathy, and skillful and attentive listening, are crucial; in which we are alert to and respect class, gender, and ethnic differences in ways of knowing, and actively try to learn and practise those ways in order to foster a more democratic and inclusive planning. It involves learning to work with diverse communities, rather than speaking for them.

b) Ecological Literacy

American environmental educator David Orr has described an ecologically literate person as someone who is engaged and informed, has local knowledge and a sense of place, experiences kinship with all forms of life, and seeks to assert and practise civic competence. Such a person will appreciate "something of how social structures, religion, science, politics, technology, patriarchy, culture, agriculture, and human cussedness combine as causes of our predicament."[32] This is a very different approach from that which prevails in most of our planning schools, in which there might be one subject devoted to "the environment," or in which only those students who are enrolled in the "environmental stream" or take the "environment elective" get any exposure to environmental thinking. Orr's approach is essentially ethical.

Wendy Sarkissian, one of Australia's leading social planning practitioners, endorses Orr's premise that the environmental crisis cannot be solved by the same kind of education that helped create the problems: a modernist education that privileges scientific and technical knowledge. Sarkissian has developed a five-dimensional model of ecological literacy for planners, with the overarching goal of nurturing an ethic of care for nature. She emphasizes teamwork, experiencing nature directly, a grounding in community (including community struggles for social and environmental justice), and the study of environmental ethics.[33] While skills workshops can be run for practising planners on such topics as environmental impact assessment, what is really needed is a kind of re-visioning of planning through an ecological lens, as exemplified in the work of Timothy Beatley.[34]

c) Design Literacy

In the US from the 1950s onwards, the case was made that urban planning is fundamentally a social or policy science, and that questions of design belong in architecture schools. This separation of design from planning, of the built environment from the social and political environment, has impoverished our understanding of the urban field and the arts of city building. The retreat from design was a reaction against simplistic cause-effect notions of how the physical environment determines human behaviour. It was also a rejection of the aesthetic emphasis of design programs in favour of a social and political-economic emphasis. Much has been lost as a result of this separation. First, there is the ability to "read" the built environment and understand what makes it work or why it doesn't work; to look at a streetscape or park or square or ensemble of buildings and analyze the qualities of good public space. Second, there's the ability to read the "maps" and blueprints of the design profession and comment on them intelligently, to be able to translate visual renderings into a completed three-dimensional scheme and speculate about its likely impact. Third, there's the ability to engage in site planning as part of a team whose other members are trained in the design professions. And finally, there's a more general wisdom, an understanding of and feel for the city of memory, of desire, and of spirit without which the planning professional is rendered one-dimensional, devoid of passion for or any understanding of the magic of the city (as opposed to its social structure or political economy).

In the end, we cannot ignore the inescapable connections between the built environment and human well-being, both individual and collective. We can't deny the power of design in daily life, for good and bad. This power can be as simple and obvious as the transformative effect of trees in a residential street, the qualities of natural light in a dwelling or workspace, the sounds of water created by a fountain in a busy downtown development. Or it can be as complex as the workings of patriarchy in and upon space, through design. Feminist architects, urban designers, and planners have been interested in these connections, specifically as they affect the lives of women in cities and suburbs. Hayden, Weisman, and Spain offer insights on the powers of design to express and enforce relations of subordination.[35] Other writers on urban design have noted the architectural tropes that send messages about who belongs in a space and who does not, referring to shopping malls and other public/private places where only certain kinds of people are wanted.[36]

Understanding the social and psychological aspects and impacts of design does not reduce planning to mere physical determinism (as many of us believed in the 1970s), but rather enriches its capacity to create meaning. We need to connect the history of struggles over urban space with the poetics of occupying particular places. Some urban planners are now working with artists, anthropologists, landscape architects, and communities to do just that, in public history and public art, in community mapping and urban landscape projects that seek a more culturally inclusive approach to planning. This can be done only by designing with culture, as well as designing with nature.

Restoring design literacy to the profession requires teamwork among planners, landscape architects, urban designers, artists, and communities. This needs to begin in planning schools, and involves the blurring of jealously guarded boundaries between the different factions of the "city-building professions."

Planning as an Ethical Inquiry and Practice

There are, and will continue to be, multiple roles for planners, including that of facilitating global economic integration through spatial planning. But the normative position, which this essay has taken, is for a consciously ethical and political profession, one prepared to address issues of social, cultural, and environmental justice in cities and regions whose contours are shaped by larger forces of economic and demographic mobility and technological change. Such a stance amounts to a paradigm shift and demands new planning literacies. This (possibly heroic) call for an ethical planning, which is inclusive of technical matters but which goes beyond them in the way it poses questions and the way it seeks answers, is an explicit assertion of planning's ongoing moral relevance in addressing and redressing the problems of cities and regions.

Passionate pilgrim that I am, my personal vision is for a planning profession that embraces concerns for social and environmental justice, for human community, for cultural diversity, and for the spirit. In modernist planning's pursuit of the rational city, some of its capacity to address these concerns was lost. We must return to those age-old questions of values, of meaning, of the good city. But in attempting to answer those questions, we must look for guidance from those hitherto excluded or marginalized; we must listen to all voices. We must respect the city of memory (the past) as it jostles with the city of desire (the present and future). We must rediscover the city of spirit and invent new forms of enchantment of the built environment. The goal of planning education is not how to stuff the most facts, techniques, and methods into students' minds, but how to raise these most basic questions of values: How might we

Figure 4.6

Base before Development   Base after Development

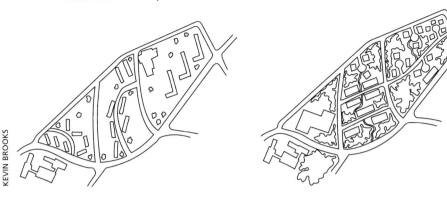

KEVIN BROOKS

With many military bases closing, proposals for reuse are engaging many communities.

manage our coexistence in shared space? How might we live with each other in active acceptance of all of our differences, in the multicultural cities and regions of the next century? And how might we live lightly and sustainably on the earth?

My hope is to inspire coming generations to want to answer these questions, and to shine some light for them.

Four Constituencies Revisited: Some Thoughts on Planners, Politicians and Principles

Nigel H Richardson

1990, Plan Canada 30(2): 14–7

Let's pretend that you are the planning director of a medium-size town whose economy was heavily dependent on a military base which has just been closed. National Defence is, however, willing to sell the land and buildings to the town for a dollar (remember, this is let's pretend). A developer has moved in quickly with a proposal to purchase the site and build a regional shopping centre plus office and condominium towers, with the rest to be leased for industrial use (Figure 4.6).

You have been instructed to prepare a report on this proposal. You already know very well where the mayor and most of the council stand: As far as they are concerned, it is a great deal. They claim that it will add substantially to the tax base; create badly needed jobs; attract shoppers from out of town; and help to put your town on the map, to the benefit of every citizen.

But after pecking at your computer for awhile and looking at the cost of servicing the proposed development, you are not so sure of the fiscal benefits. The jobs created immediately will be few and poorly paid. You cannot figure out who is going to buy the new condos, rent the office space, or lease the industrial sites. But you are pretty sure that the shopping centre will eventually turn the old downtown, which you have been working hard with the chamber of commerce to improve, into a wasteland of empty stores and rundown buildings.

And there's more to it than that. The former base includes abandoned married quarters that would provide badly needed low-cost family housing. Other buildings could easily be converted to accommodation for the aged, also urgently needed. There are excellent recreation facilities in a town in which lack of occupation for young people is becoming a problem. Furthermore, a pleasant creek valley fortuitously preserved within the boundaries of the former base provides habitat for a butterfly that may soon be entered on the endangered species list.

So you are faced with an ethical problem, turning on the question of what is the "right" or "proper" course to pursue. Do you, as a dutiful municipal employee, give your council the report you know it wants and expects? Or, as a planning professional, do you choose a different course, and, if so, which one, and how do you justify it?

Ethical problems are like planning problems in that when faced with one, it is always wise to analyze it carefully and identify its different aspects. I once suggested that the planner is ethically responsible to four constituencies: conscience, moral values, or personal integrity; professional standards; employer or client; and the "public interest."[37] Let us try to apply this paradigm to the dilemma to see if it helps to sort it out.

As a socially and environmentally aware person, you believe that your town should provide low-cost housing for the needy, accommodation for the aged, and recreation facilities for the young, and that the creek valley should be preserved and its wildlife protected. Fair enough: But can you represent these aims as in some sense "good planning"? Perhaps you can; but if they are expressions of your personal convictions and no more, are you entitled to allow your report to be influenced by such convictions? (As a perhaps more graphic and contemporary illustration of the issue, consider the responsibilities of a planner of strong convictions asked to report on the amendment of a zoning bylaw to provide for abortion clinics.)

With regard to professional standards, you feel that you stand on somewhat firmer ground. As a good planner, you have carried out a fiscal cost-benefit analysis, looked at the traffic and transportation implications of the proposed development, compared proposed floor space with foreseeable demand, and so on. You do not feel that your conclusions favour the proposal, but you are confident that you cannot be faulted either on the grounds of technical competence or of objectivity.

But professional standards are a matter of more than just technical competence, you realize. As a member of a professional institute, you are subject to a code of conduct governing your relations with your employer, your staff, and your professional colleagues. But there is little that seems to have any particular application to the dilemma with which you are confronted, so in that area, at least, your problems are not compounded. On the other hand, you are not given any help, either, and somehow you feel that you should be; should not a code of planning ethics give guidance to the planner confronting an ethical problem peculiar to the practice of planning?

Bypassing, for the moment, your third ethical constituency, your council, let us consider the fourth—the public interest, the community, the general good. Here, you decide with a sigh of relief, is where you justify your personal concern for the homeless, the old, young people, and the environment: Protecting all of these is in the interest of the community. But how do you know? By what criteria? Which community, anyway? After all, your council, elected by "the community," obviously does not agree, or at least apparently believes that the net general benefit from the developer's scheme will be greater. What entitles you, as a municipal official, to substitute your judgment for theirs? As I pointed out in the earlier paper, planners "should be very cautious about assuming that they are gifted with special virtue to know the public good, or special wisdom to do the public will."

And so, back to the remaining constituency—your council. It goes without saying that you owe a certain loyalty to the council that hired you and pays your salary. On this point, furthermore, such diverse authorities as the CIP's *Code of Practice and Statement of Values*[38] and the New Testament ("Render unto Caesar") seem to support the provisions of your province's *Municipal Act*. You accept the principle, but you wonder how much that loyalty demands of you. After all, you are only too well aware that some members of council are not exactly intellectual heavyweights, and the majority (elected by less than 30 percent of the eligible voters) has an unmistakable bias toward the interests of a particular socioeconomic sector of the town's population. You know that there is evidence that the mayor is on notably friendly terms with the developer. Nevertheless, in addition to being your employer, the council has been duly and democratically elected to represent the people of the town and is accountable to them. You are accountable to the council, even though you feel that the term "public servant" ought to be taken seriously.

You seem, in fact, to be back where you started, with the problem of deciding your course of action when the wishes of your council conflict with your own judgment. But, in fact, the issue has been somewhat clarified. You have concluded that where your personal values cannot be translated into objectively defensible planning criteria, you have three options: to set them aside altogether, to identify them clearly for what they are, or, if you feel strongly enough about them, to disqualify yourself from advising on the issue. You do not feel that the third course is called for, and suspect that the second might only weaken your submission by appearing both gratuitous and pretentious; so you decide not to refer to your personal views at all. You have rejected the idea of employing generalities about "the public interest" or even "the needs of the community," although you consider that it is quite within your professional competence and responsibility to document the present inadequacies in the availability of certain kinds of facility in the town, and the extent to which these inadequacies could be remedied by the use of facilities existing on the former base. You even feel comfortable about quoting the views of various provincial, federal, and even international bodies with regard to protecting endangered species.

You have, in short, defined to your own satisfaction your professional responsibility to your council. You can now report, as objectively as a human being ever can, on the range of pros and cons attaching to the proposed development. You can, and indeed should, conclude by offering your best professional judgment—which ultimately is the most important thing you are paid to provide—as to whether, on balance, the proposed development scheme, reuse of the existing buildings and facilities, or perhaps some third option would be in the best interests of the town. But if so, you must explain what you mean by "best interests," and you should probably point out that to some extent your judgment (and anyone else's) depends on the weighting attached to the value of particular factors.

Having done all this to the best of your ability, you believe that you have carried out your responsibilities conscientiously and ethically both as a public servant and as a professional person. In return, you believe that your council has certain responsibilities to you and, perhaps more to the point, to the public. It should not penalize you for doing your job, even if it does not like the results, unless it really does want a planning director who will simply give it the reports it wants. It is not entitled to suppress or misrepresent your report, and it is not entitled to expect you to misrepresent your own analysis or conclusions.

Well, despite the complaints of a couple of councillors about officials who do not do what council wants, you do not get fired. Your report is covered (inaccurately) by the local paper and radio station, and is available in full to be read by anyone who cares to visit the town clerk's office. As you expected, the proposed development has been approved by council, and you now have some more ethical dilemmas to confront. The necessary amendment to your general plan has to go before a public meeting, which will certainly be attended by some vociferous opponents quoting your report. It will then have to be reviewed by the province's municipal board. And after it is approved (as you are sure it will be), you will have to work with the developer in refining and implementing the scheme.

The second and third hurdles do not give you too much concern. The provincial board is quite accustomed to distinguishing between the case presented by municipal officials on behalf of their councils and those officials' own professional opinion; and your mayor understands that you will be under oath and bound to give your professional opinion if asked to do so. As to subsequently working with the developer, the final decision having been made by those politically responsible for doing so, you foresee no ethical problem in implementing that decision while doing what you can to gain some of the ends for which you argued in your report.

No, what worries you is that public hearing, which is unlikely to be as sensitive as the board to subtle role distinctions. You will be grilled hard, and you will have to tread a very fine line to avoid betraying either your duty to your council or your professional integrity. All you can do, you decide, is to stick firmly to the facts: the proposal, the content of your report to council, and council's decision. You must not be led or bullied into giving an opinion on that decision. But is it ethical for you, a public servant, to refuse to do so, when, of course, you have such an opinion?

The Ethics of Practice

While the particular case I have described may be fictitious, it encapsulates several real ethical dilemmas that planners are very likely to encounter, some of them often, in their professional careers. I believe that the principles adopted by our imaginary planning director in dealing with the council are sound.

In general, planners should set aside their purely personal views (biases, as they would be called by those who disagree with them) and unfocused notions like "the public interest" and similar concepts, unless they can be translated into specific (which does not necessarily mean quantified) and defensible planning criteria. The principal exception arises where the case involves strong moral or religious convictions, which planners cannot (and should not) ignore; in such circumstances the proper course is to make their position known and suggest that they be relieved of the responsibility.

As both public servants and professional persons, planners are responsible for giving their employers the full benefit of their professional training, experience, and judgment, even where those lead to a position different from that favoured by the employer. A political decision having been made, it is also the planners' responsibility to work conscientiously and in good faith to carry it out, even if they believe it to have been the wrong decision.

These (or any) guidelines do not provide a solution to every potential ethical problem, and sooner or later any conscientious planner may have to fall back on personal judgment as to the "right" course of action. But in such a situation, it may be helpful for the planner to analyze the ethical responsibilities relative to the four constituencies with which we started out: conscience, profession, employer, and the community at large.

This discussion suggests, however, that the blanket use of the term "professional standards" to identify one of the four constituencies seriously oversimplifies what is, in fact, a group of related but distinct kinds of obligation. In the words of Jennings, "Professionalism should be more than technical expertise... In ethical terms, to be a professional is to be dedicated to a distinctive set of ideals and standards of conduct."[39] Newton elaborates on the theme:

> The professional must begin with a sense of who and what he [sic] is, as a professional, of which the first derivation is a powerful sense of responsibility for the conduct of his own professional life, the conduct of the profession as a whole, the protection of the client and the protection of the society of which it forms a part, with respect to the area of his profession's expertise.[40]

Thus, the term "professional standards" as applied to planners arguably embraces at least three distinct kinds of obligation. First, there is, simply, fair and honest dealing, an aspect which should not need to be elaborated and which is the main concern of the CIP's Code.

Second is what might be called the integrity of the good artisan to do your work as well as your knowledge, skill, and experience allow, and to present it without bias and without concealing its deficiencies.

And finally, there is the aspect of professional ethics that deserves much more attention from Canadian planners than it has so far received: our particular responsibility, as planners, to Canadian society. Fair dealing and technical integrity, after all, should characterize any profession, but some professions rightly undertake a commitment to something more, to the furtherance of some broad social goal; as Jennings would put it, to a positive contribution to "the common good" as distinct from mere respect for "the public interest."[41]

Given the social, environmental, and economic implications of urban and regional planning, our profession has a greater obligation than most to assume an explicit responsibility to the common good. While a detailed elaboration might be out of place here, I would propose that the fundamental guiding principle and rule of professional conduct of the planning profession should be a commitment, in essence, to the creation of a socially, biologically, and physically healthy environment for everyone.

Would the adoption of this third ethical criterion help you as our imaginary planning director to resolve your dilemmas? In practice, it would be unlikely to make life any easier for you and might well have the reverse effect (no one ever said that true professional responsibility is a light burden). But at least, if justifiable, it might sometimes provide you with professional resources in the struggle for causes that would otherwise have to rely on those professionally flimsy arguments, personal conviction, and the public interest.

More to the point, it might help the planning profession to gain and deserve the collective sense of purpose, self-confidence, and public credibility that it now rather notably lacks. And that would be to the advantage of our planning director and all the rest of us.

The Four Faces of Planning Ethics: A Value Profile

Mark N Wexler and Judy Oberlander

2002, Plan Canada 42(2): 19–21

In theory and practice, the values of the planning community vary, based on both the context in which planning is done and the personal dispositions of the planners within the firm or the project. We offer a basic blueprint of the four faces of the planning community (Figure 4.7). Along the vertical axis, we distinguish planners and planning contexts that emphasize control from those that emphasize flexibility. On the horizontal axis, we distinguish planners and planning contexts that stress competition and external forces from those that are inward-looking and lean heavily upon systems maintenance. In crossing the vertical (control versus flexibility) with the horizontal axis (competition versus systems maintenance), we arrive at four value profiles: the planning community as a competitive business (control-competition), as a regulatory self-governing system (control-systems maintenance), as a communitarian call to grassroots inclusion (flexibility-systems maintenance), and as a visionary call to generate innovation and change (competition-flexibility). Let's turn to each profile.

"Buccaneer" planning culture places emphasis on planning as a series of activities and documents rooted in pragmatic, instrumental values transacted in a pay-for-service,

Figure 4.7

The four faces of planning ethics: What role does the planner choose?

profit-oriented market. The planner is an entrepreneur. Customers must be satisfied. Control goes to the planner as a director competing with other planners for power, influence, and fortune. Plans are strategic opportunities. Good plans reap profits and are widely disseminated and emulated. Poor plans fail in the marketplace and do not confer power, influence, and fortune. This world of control and competition emphasizes comfort and freedom for those who can create and/or pay for a good plan. The "good" world is one of freedom and individuality for winners. Losers do not fare nearly so well in buccaneer capitalism. In this entrepreneurial context, inequities are seen as essential to market-dependent planning. Without markets, plans stagnate. Planners with no ability to meet a client's needs rise to the top; and planning, buccaneers argue, becomes strictly a government function.

Regulatory planning culture emphasizes the governance structure as the essence of the planning profession. Rather than manifesting the values of the pragmatic, instrumentally-oriented buccaneer, regulatory planners stress the standards, codes, and technical rationality of the profession. Procedural values are preeminent, a state of affairs that applies to contexts of both the public and the private sectors. The planner in this value quadrant is an analyst adhering to principles, tradition, and the evidence required to meet technical, even scientific standards. Here peer-based evidence and not the market is central. In practice, the "just do it" value of the buccaneer planner gives way to the more careful, risk-averse, "research it" value of the regulatory planner. Systems require care. Planning in this context is not a form of profit maximization but a deliberate effort at uncertainty reduction. The values of stability, prudence, and due diligence prevail.

By contrast, communitarian planning culture enhances the social-contract values of sharing, trust, empowerment, and community inclusion. The shift toward flexibility in communitarian planning emphasizes the use of community norms as opposed to the rules and markets of regulatory and buccaneer planning. Community norms require interpretation and the close involvement of the planner and the community. The planner functions neither as the credentialed expert of regulatory planning culture nor as the freewheeling producer of buccaneer culture, but rather as a mentor or facilitator. Values in practice in communitarian planning focus on "dialogue" through consensus, participation, and inclusion. The winner-take-all disposition of the buccaneer in competitive markets is relegated to the periphery, and, in its place, communitarian planning stresses egalitarianism in which win-win solutions are the ideal.

In the final profile, visionary planning culture crosses flexibility with competition. Here, planning is understood as a vehicle for change and innovation. Planners work in loose coalitions of communities of practice seeking to push the envelope. Unlike the stability-seeking practitioners of regulatory planning culture, the innovators and brokers in visionary planning attempt to establish new techniques and outcomes. And unlike buccaneer planners, visionary planners try not only to satisfy clients' existing needs but to create platforms where new ones can be met. Whereas communitarian planning culture is rooted in a notion of stable community, visionary planning is project based. People who have high international reputations in a problem area come together for short periods to work on key planning issues and high-profile projects and, in so doing, thrive on the prestige conferred upon those who consistently deliver. The values here are extremely competitive and yet flexible. The "good" world is one that is loosely networked, agile, quick, and thus able to readily adapt to change. Visionary planning may be practised locally, but its impact is global. The work, in so far as it establishes novelty, is emulated by others.

In practice, all of our occupational cultures are rooted in elements of each of these four value profiles. The ideal types illustrated in the figure help us to identify characteristics. The unique character of a planner or planning firm is influenced by the four values, which, in turn, both divide and generate creative tensions in the planning community. Each quadrant has much to contribute to planning, and those who insist that their quadrant become the centre are not advancing the field. We all need to recognize the importance of diverse viewpoints and seek consensus-based solutions in our work. Planners will readily see that the four value profiles, each of which are necessary to do planning, are stressed differently by different planners, planning firms, government agencies, and communities.

We must, after all, remain economically solvent. However, only the buccaneer planner takes this aspect of value profile to heart. We must all rely on standards, codes, and reliable regulatory criteria. It is, however, only the regulatory planner who places this at the centre of the enterprise. The buccaneer seeks to alter or bend the rules to meet and satisfy client needs. The regulatory planner seeks to enhance the rules to create a stable system with reliable measures and sound criteria by which plans can be assessed. The market, regulatory planners insist, is no platform for planning because it is too fickle, too shortsighted, and too dependent upon the ephemeral winds of fad and fashion.

If we seek to plan, we must serve and act as agents for the community. Recognizing that plans are contextually rooted, communitarian planners invest a great deal of time, energy, and capital in developing techniques that tie planning to community development. Theirs is a world of trust, sharing, and empowerment, in which plans give voice to community concerns and, once articulated, give life to positions that require more dialogue.

We must develop new ideas, techniques and models if we are to plan. With their call to planning as a form of exploration, visionary planners devote most of their time to such developments. This approach is not grounded solely in market, rules, or communities, but in the creative abilities of the best planners to earn the right to work on high-profile, breakthrough projects in the public limelight.

In practice, the four faces of planning intersect, as individuals express their different viewpoints. Since each of these value profiles is drawn from diverse contexts, controversies and tensions may arise when they coexist in a private firm, a public-sector agency, a community consultation process, or a small committee of planners. The conflicts result in ethical controversies; the tensions lead to problems of implementation. Conflicts tend to impede communication between participants from different planning cultures, and tensions raise the probability of difficulties. A workable solution can be found through effective communication and dialogue.

One must recognize that inclusion of different values comes to an occupational community at the price of value tensions and ethical or moral controversies. There is a tendency in many planning communities to attempt to lower the costs of value pluralism by privileging one of the four faces—buccaneer, regulatory, communitarian, or visionary—as the most important. We do not recommend this, for value pluralism generates a form of constructive dialogue within the profession. It requires us to deal with potentially irksome "others" inside the profession and to avoid perceiving them as outsiders or interlopers.

Ethical controversy is necessary if we seek to develop an occupational culture with a conscience. The existence of competing values requires us to attend to our values and our colleagues. The tensions that emerge from dialogue can help us to shape our views and ultimately our conduct as professional planners. Striking a delicate balance forces us to consider different viewpoints, respect the "other," and, in each circumstance, seek a creative solution for the task at hand.

1. How and why have the values that influence Canadian planning practice changed through the decades?

2. What connections and incongruities do you note between the four constituencies that Richardson identifies the planner as responsible to and the four planner profiles that Wexler and Oberlander postulate?

3. What challenges do you see to implementing equity principles in land-use decision making in contemporary planning practice?

4. Contrast and compare the values and ethical principles guiding the Canadian Institute of Planners with those adopted by the American Planning Association and those used by the Royal Town Planning Institute (UK). (All are available online by searching the Web sites.) Identify the priorities, strengths, and weaknesses of the CIP *Code of Practice*.

5. Many authors and professionals believe that the public interest must be the core ethical paradigm of planning. Explain why you agree or disagree.

6. Based on your own experience and knowledge of Canadian communities, consider how values associated with the family and privacy affect the form and development of residential areas.

7. Examine the documentation from a planning dispute in your community to identify the ethical positions taken and the values promoted by the various participants in the dispute.

8. Given that planners can serve many constituencies, how should they order their priorities to facilitate decision making?

Reference Notes

1. Botzler, RG & SJ Armstrong (eds) (1998) *Environmental Ethics: Divergence and Convergence*. (2nd ed). New York: McGraw-Hill.

   Wackernagel, M & W Rees (1995) *Our Ecological Footprint: Reducing Human Impact on the Earth*. Gabriola Island: New Society Publishers.

2. Davidoff, P (1965) Advocacy and pluralism in planning. *Journal of the American Institute of Planners* 32(4): 332–8.

3. Forester, J & N Krumholz (1990) *Making Equity Planning Work: Leadership in the Public Sector*. Philadelphia: Temple University Press.

   Sandercock, L (1998) *Towards Cosmopolis: Planning for Multicultural Cities*. Chichester: John Wiley & Sons.

4. Grant, J & J Orser Smith (2006) Visions of a common future. *Plan Canada* 46(2): 16–8.

5. Alterman, R & J Page (1973) The ubiquity of values and the planning process. *Plan Canada* 13(1): 13–26.

6. Udy, J (1980) Why plan? Planning and the eternal values. *Plan Canada* 20(3/4): 176–83.

7. Gerecke, K & B Reid (1991) Planning, power and ethics. *Plan Canada* 31(6): 59–74.

8. Harper, T & S Stein (1993) Normative ethical theory: Is it relevant to contemporary planning practice? *Plan Canada* 33(5): 6–12.

9. Hendler, S (2002) It's the right thing to do—or is it? Contemporary issues in planning ethics. *Plan Canada* 42(2): 9–11.

10. Forester, J (1989) *Planning in the Face of Power*. Berkeley: University of California Press.

11. Johnson, RH & JA Blair (1985) Informal logic: The past five years, 1978–1983. *American Philosophical Quarterly* 22: 181–96.

12. Gilligan, C (1982) *In a Different Voice*. Cambridge: Harvard University Press.

13. Krumholz, N & J Forester (1990) *Making Equity Planning Work*. Philadelphia: Temple University Press.

14. Simmons, J (1985) Rights and wrongs in hazardous waste disposal. In *Not-In-My-Backyard*. Charlottesville: Institute for Environmental Negotiation, University of Virginia: 11–9.

15. Lang, R (1988a) *Potential Social Impacts of Halton's Landfill Proposal on Communities at Site F in Burlington*. Toronto: Canadian Environmental Law Association.

16. Harvey, D (1973) *Social Justice and the City*. Baltimore: Johns Hopkins University Press.

17. Lucy, W (1981) Equity and planning for local services. *Journal of the American Planning Association* 47: 447–57.

18. Martin, T (1989) Up to our ears. *Globe and Mail Report on Business*, August.

19. Lang, R (1988a) Op. cit.

20. In 2005, the amalgamated Toronto with a population of 2.5 million, shipped 120 truckloads of waste to Michigan daily. An ambitious recycling program hopes to reduce the volume by 60 percent by 2006, but that still leaves 40 percent looking for a landfill.

21. Lang, R (1988b) Planning for integrated development. In FW Dykeman (ed) *Integrated Rural Planning and Development*. Sackville: Mount Allison University, Department of Geography: 81–104.

22. Timmerman, P (1984) *Ethics and Waste Facility Siting*. Toronto: Institute for Environmental Studies, University of Toronto.

23. Kemp, R (1982) Critical planning theory—review and critique. In P Healey, G McDougall, & M Thomas (eds) *Planning Theory: Prospects for the 1980s*. Oxford: Pergamon Press: 55–67.

24. Beehler, R (1983) The concept of fairness. In ES Case, *et al.* (eds) *Fairness in*

Environmental and Social Assessment. Proceedings of a Seminar. Calgary: University of Calgary, Faculty of Law: 1–14.

25. Kasperson, RE (1986) *Hazardous Waste Facility Siting: Community, Firm and Governmental Perspectives.* Worcester: Clark University, Center for Technology, Environment and Development.

26. Lang, R (1988b) Op. cit.: 81–104.

27. Boyer, C (1983) *Dreaming the Rational City.* Cambridge: MIT Press.

28. Christensen, KS (1993) Teaching savvy. *Journal of Planning Education and Research* 12: 202–12.

29. Tully, J (1995) *Strange Multiplicity: Constitutionalism in an age of diversity.* Cambridge: Cambridge University Press.

30. Alonso, W & P Starr (eds) (1987) *The Politics of Numbers.* New York: Russell Sage Foundation.

31. Tully, J (1995) Op. cit.

32. Orr, D (1992) *Ecological Literacy: Education and the Transition to a Postmodern World.* Albany: State University of NY Press: 85–6.

33. Sarkissian, W (1996) With a whole heart: Nurturing an ethic of caring for nature in the education of Australian planners. Unpublished PhD thesis, Murdoch University, Perth.

34. Beatley, T & K Manning (1997) *The Ecology of Place.* Washington: Island Press.

35. Hayden, D (1984) *Redesigning the American Dream.* New York: WW Norton.
    Weisman, L (1992) *Discrimination by Design.* Urbana: University of Illinois Press.
    Spain, D (1992) *Gendered Spaces.* Chapel Hill: University of North Carolina Press.

36. Davis, M (1990) *City of Quartz.* London: Verso.
    Sorkin, M (ed) (1992) *Variations on a Theme Park.* New York: Noonday Press.

37. Richardson, NH (1980) *Four Constituencies: Dilemmas of the Planner as Public Servant.* Toronto: Department of Urban and Regional Planning, Ryerson Polytechnical Institute.

38. Canadian Institute of Planners (2004) *CIP Statement of Values and Code of Professional Practice* (adopted June 30, 2004) Available online at http://www.cip-icu.ca/English/members/practice.htm.

39. Jennings, B (1987) The professions: public interest and common good. *The Public Duties of the Professions.* Hastings Center Report, Special Supplement, 17(1): 8–20.

40. Newton, L (1981) The origin of professionalism: Sociological conclusions and ethical implications. *Business and Professional Ethics Journal,* (Summer): 33–44.

41. Jennings, B (1987) Op. cit.

5

Chapter Five
The Process of Planning

The Planning Process

Jill Grant

Patrick Geddes, the great Scottish biologist, sociologist, and environmental planner of the late nineteenth century, first articulated the steps of the planning process that remain at the core of contemporary planning when he said: "Survey before plan" (Figure 5.1).[1]

The planning survey involves collecting necessary information about the land and the people so that we begin with a good knowledge base. We collect data about bedrock, soils, drainage, vegetation, land use, and ownership as background for making decisions about land capability and potential for development. We profile the population characteristics (e.g., age, education, income, household composition, and size) to make judgments about demand for housing, infrastructure, and local services. Part of the survey requires that we define the study area. Geddes preferred to create planning units that were natural regions: usually a watershed or what he illustrated with "the valley section." Because all of the land in a watershed drains into a common river system, managing land use effectively in the watershed can protect water quality and quantity and ensure that those making a living lower in the watershed can continue to prosper. In Canada, we more commonly plan along political boundaries that pay little attention to natural regions. In recent years, the amalgamation of major cities with their suburbs has created powerful urban regions with the tools to generate regional plans.

Analysis involves examining and interpreting the information we collect to understand the issues. Making meaning of a vast array of facts is an essential component of planning. While some may argue that "the facts speak for themselves," we can rarely say that in planning. Someone has to interpret the facts along with the values of the community to answer the most important question, "So what?" If our analysis reveals this information, what do we need to do to achieve the kind of future we want in our community?

The plan we generate lays out the strategies that must be taken to achieve good development. It clearly articulates the goals we set, the policy we will follow, the tools we may use to implement our ambitions. It outlines the directions for our future.

Over the years, planning theorists and practitioners have expanded on this elementary model of the planning process to include additional steps. They recognized that communities need clear goals before they begin to collect information. They established that analysis typically identifies a series of alternatives, not a single option. And those alternatives must be evaluated before a choice is made.

By the 1960s and 1970s, the model was significantly elaborated. Setting objectives had been added to the early stages. Monitoring and evaluation extended the process beyond the development of a

Figure 5.1

Patrick Geddes established a simple rational process: first a survey of conditions, followed by analysis, and ending with a plan.

plan. Feedback loops acknowledged that the process is not linear, but iterative. Public participation increasingly made its way into the various steps of the process.

As typically described, the planning process is a rational or logical process. It involves empirical analysis, complete consideration of all possible options, and selection of the best possible option. In general, the steps are: Define the problem, define the goals and objectives, collect data, analyze data, describe alternatives, evaluate and select alternatives, implement action, monitor results, evaluate progress, redefine the problem, and begin again (Figure 5.2). Public participation may occur at any step. Reconsideration of previous steps may occur after any step.

The Role of the Public

How have the issues and approaches to public participation changed through time? In the early years of planning, legislation typically required authorities to notify those who would be affected by planning decisions; and local government usually placed an advertisement or notice in the newspaper or posted a sign on the property to be developed (Figure 5.3). Aside from political influence with decision makers, citizens had few opportunities to express their views about development or to shape planning policy.

By the late 1960s, legislation in most provinces changed to require public meetings and hearings to allow people to express diverse views; the laws also set out mechanisms

Figure 5.2

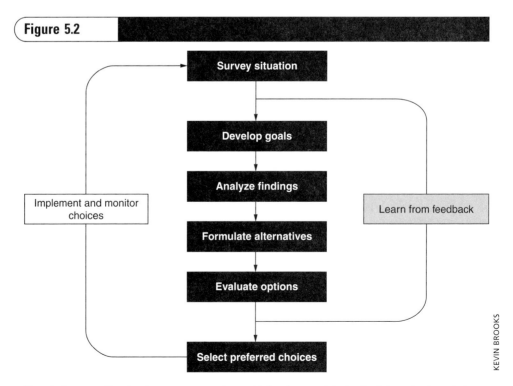

Through the years, the planning process saw steps added and appropriate feedback loops implemented.

Figure 5.3

Many cities post signs on property to alert residents to the owner's intention to redevelop or rezone property.

for citizens to appeal decisions. Some characterized the process as involving three elements: Decide, announce, and defend. Decision makers told the people what they had decided and left planners to defend and explain the choices.

In the 1970s, many communities experimented with citizen action programs that actively engaged residents in preparing neighbourhood plans. For example, the Neighbourhood Improvement Program supported by Canada Mortgage and Housing Corporation provided funds to older urban neighbourhoods to plan for and invest in basic infrastructure. Citizens became active partners in the planning process, working with planners to advise decision makers on policy directions. Harry Lash called the approach taken in Vancouver in this period "planning in a human way."[2] His triangle of participation described an equal partnership between planners, politicians, and the public (Figure 5.4).

By the 1980s, fiscal crisis led governments away from active citizen-based planning. Planners began talking about stakeholder engagement in planning processes and searching for ways to manage conflict. The change in terminology reflected the growing interest in strategic planning in the halls of power. Citizens had gone from being full partners to being perceived as having "interests" that had to be managed. Dispute resolution and conflict management provided ways of dealing with tensions that erupted between stakeholders. In the 1990s, consensus building also became popular, developing out of healthy communities and sustainable development approaches and supported by communicative theory in planning.

Recent years have brought greater interest in design charrettes, a technique popularized by new urbanism advocates. Visioning processes that involve community residents in long-term projection of urban futures became a popular means of goal setting by the year 2000. Almost every city in the country has adopted a vision statement and is using it to build community commitment to collective action (Table 5.1).

Figure 5.4

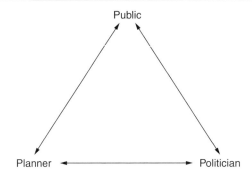

Planning involves a partnership between planners, politicians, and the public, what Harry Lash called the triangle of participation.

A postcard distributed by *imagineCALGARY* in summer 2005

Shaping our city's future

- What do you value about Calgary?
- What is it like for you to live here?
- What changes would you most like to see?
- What are your hopes and dreams for Calgary in 100 years?
- How could you help make this happen?

Tell us at imagineCALGARY.ca or 403.537.7006 and enter to win cool prizes
(see also http://www.imaginecalgary.ca)

With each new development in participation methods, many of the earlier techniques persisted in use, and new strategies were added to the planner's toolkit. Participation has become well-entrenched within community planning practice. At the same time, though, it remains a challenge for planners. The development of a range of new methods has not changed the fundamental reality: Planning often involves processes for managing disagreements about the future of community resources. Efforts to improve or to streamline the process cannot avert the tensions, but effective participatory approaches can help planners manage the exercise.

The articles in this chapter reflect on the planning process and the role of citizens in it. Ann McAfee describes the successes of *CityPlan* in Vancouver, a visioning process that put Vancouver at the forefront of participatory planning not only in Canada but beyond. Michael and Julie Seelig offer a different perspective on the process, arguing that too much unfocused participation leads to wishful thinking, which cannot direct significant

Table 5.1	Changing Participation Methods
pre-1960s	announcements to the public through newspapers, signs, letters
late 1960s–1970s	public meetings, hearings, and appeals of decisions, neighbourhood planning
1980s	stakeholder engagement, conflict management
1990s–	consensus building, collaborative action, charrettes, visioning

community action. Nancy Marshall and Richard Roberts explain the differences between public involvement and consultation and describe some issues planners have to consider in using participatory processes. John Blakney describes methods for mediation and conflict resolution that have become vital to contemporary planning. Stanley Makuch forces us to ask how far planners should push developers to offer communities benefits in return for development permissions. Pierre Filion reminds us that planners don't act independently in carrying out their duties: They operate within a system with its own processes and expectations that narrow choices and options for planners. Planning is a complicated game played on a shifting field, with the ground rules constantly changing.

When Theory Meets Practice—Citizen Participation in Planning

POINT

Ann McAfee

1997, Plan Canada 37(3): 18–22

> APPLAUSE...*CityPlan* wins awards from CIP and PIBC for innovation in public participation.
> APPROVED...Vancouver City Council adopts *CityPlan*.
> ACCUSED...Academic berates planners as powerless poll takers.

The changing nature of planning practice is being played out in newspaper headlines. Proponents of the planner as the "guru of societal values" criticize others in the profession for asking citizens to plan their future. Often, the former are academics who teach plan making; the latter are municipal planners faced with the challenge of implementing plans.

In the "guru" process, the planner assesses trends, identifies a preferred future, and prepares a draft plan. The planner then seeks public comment. The objective of the process is to give the public "a focal point to which they can respond." This process presupposes that there is a "right" answer for how a city should develop. The process relies on the power of analysis and the wisdom of the planner to identify the right answer. This is the process often taught in planning schools.

Many graduates, confident in their newly acquired wisdom, get jobs with municipalities. We prepare our first plans. When we unveil our plans for public comment what we get is criticism. "It's our neighbourhood. Why didn't you involve us?"

The planners are successful in creating a "focal point" for discussion. Indeed, planners become the focus of citizen outrage. Any attempts to discuss the merits of the plan are overwhelmed by public suspicion. Since the planner, not the public, considered the issues and consequences of alternate actions, there is no basis for the public to assess the merits of the plan. The era of "Trust me, I'm the planner," if it ever existed, is long gone.

In 1992, the Vancouver City Council, faced with opposition to plans prepared by staff, asked the Planning Department to develop a process for people to talk to people about future directions for Vancouver. *CityPlan* illustrates a "citizen as planner" public process.

Between 1993 and 1995, over 100 000 people identified ideas for Vancouver's strategic plan, considered the consequences of these ideas, and proposed directions to Council. City Council adopted the directions that emerged from this broad public process.

CityPlan involved citizens throughout the process. This addressed the citizens' concerns with regard to being invited to participate after significant choices have been made.

CityPlan addressed concerns from politicians with regard to "raised expectations" and "hijacking." To ensure the process did not result in unrealistic expectations,

Figure 5.5

CityPlan involved thousands of Vancouver residents.

"ideas" and "solutions" travelled together. Ideas for the plan had to be accompanied by suggestions for how they would be accomplished. Information with regard to city revenues and expenditures informed people about available resources. As a result, *CityPlan* did not become an unrealistic wish list.

To ensure the process was not hijacked by special interest groups, participation techniques facilitated wide involvement. Those with time attended workshops. Busy folks read about the choices and responded to questionnaires. The planning tools, whether surveys, polls, or workshops, were designed to facilitate broad public input (Figure 5.5). The voices of many, not just a few special interest groups, were heard.

The test of a process is the product. Does the plan make difficult choices and set supportable directions? *CityPlan* does both. Public discussion focused on major choices. Should growth be limited and, if not, where should growth occur? What services should the city provide, how, to whom, and who pays?

Difficult choices were made. For example, prior to *CityPlan*, policies preserved 70 percent of Vancouver's residential areas for low-density housing. Jobs were downtown. New housing displaced industrial uses, sending city-serving businesses out of town. These policies increased travel. Roads were the preserve of the car.

The *CityPlan* directions promote sustainability. New policy directions were adopted for the low-density neighbourhoods to provide more choice of housing, jobs, and services. This will make more efficient use of land and existing services and reduce travel. Some lands are kept for city-serving activities. Greenways for walking and biking reduce pollution and make multiple use of city streets.

So who criticized *CityPlan*? Some citizens criticized the product. Twenty percent of the participating public did not support the plan's directions. Most concerns were about growth. Astonishingly, 80 percent of participants supported adding more housing in lower-density single-family areas to increase housing choice and reduce regional sprawl.

Some academics criticized the process. They expressed concerns that in turning planning over to the public, the wisdom planners bring to the table is lost. This is not true. Planners bring the same expertise to the process. Trends are analyzed. Consequences of options are identified. The difference is that this information informs the public process. Citizens wrestle with the consequences of choices that will affect their city and neighbourhood. The planner's tools have not changed: Their application has.

Those who suggest that the planner's job is to hear many voices and many opinions and create an overall plan that accommodates all display a remarkable naiveté about the reality of planning in the context of a diverse society and limited resources. No plan can meet the needs of many voices. Choices must be made. Planners bring these many voices to the table to face the difficult choices. As density increases, those who will live in closer proximity identify ways to coexist. As funds are limited, users design services to meet their needs. Many of the problems cities face today are the legacy of yesterday's plan makers. Low-density suburbs do not support transit services. Suburban malls leave distressed downtowns in their wake. Big-box retail puts the customer on the road.

Experience suggests planners do not have all the "right" answers. What planners have are techniques to analyze information and assess consequences. Planners have a responsibility to suggest new ways to meet new challenges. What planners do not have is the right to choose and thereby limit the options society considers when difficult choices must be made.

Charging citizens with the responsibility for decisions that affect their lives is not a new idea. In the words of Thomas Jefferson:

> I know no safe depository of the ultimate powers of the society but the people themselves; and if we think them not enlightened enough to exercise their control with a wholesome discretion, the remedy is not to take it from them, but to inform their discretion.

CityPlan: Participation or Abdication?   COUNTERPOINT

Michael Seelig and Julie Seelig

1997 Plan Canada 37(3): 18–22

The time has come to examine Vancouver's *CityPlan* and other citizen participation efforts to establish when, where, and how participation can be most effective. A brief review of Vancouver's *CityPlan* indicates what happens when a good concept is pursued to the level of absurdity. When citizen participation becomes an end rather than a means, cities run the risk of losing all sense of purposefulness in their urban planning endeavours. In this counterpoint article, our aim is to show the pitfalls of citizen participation and to make a plea for some sense of proportion.

What is *CityPlan*?

The first part of Vancouver's *CityPlan* process spanned three years from 1992 to 1995 and "involved" over 20 000 people. "Involvement" in the *CityPlan* context means everything from viewing a display, visiting the Futures Tour, participating in a phone survey, to attending meetings. Many of the same people participated in more than one activity and, therefore, have been counted twice. More active participation, such as suggesting ideas or completing a questionnaire, yielded much smaller numbers of between 2000 and 3000 participants, or one-half of one percent of Vancouver's population.

Quibbling over numbers aside, what is the actual result of this tremendous effort? We learn that citizens eventually chose Future Number One, "A City of Neighbourhood Centres." *CityPlan* Future Number One yields the startling conclusion that Vanouverites want a city of neighbourhoods with distinctive and affordable housing, good jobs close to home, better health and social services, more parks, clean air and water, more arts and culture, money, and all of this delivered by a financially-sound government. Five years of intense effort and millions of dollars delivered a mouse. We need that brave young boy who yelled out that the emperor was stark naked.

The first round of *CityPlan*, which yielded the "City of Neighbourhoods" concept, cost $4 million. The next round, which gets us somewhat closer to some sort of ultimate vision, will be carried out on an extremely labour-intensive neighbourhood-by-neighbourhood basis and will cost $11.5 million. Communities are "to explore their needs and aspirations, and to generate visions which move in *CityPlan* directions." January to September of 1997 will engender a pilot project in two neighbourhoods of the city.

Someday, this visioning business will be complete in roughly two dozen neighbourhood areas of the city. By that time, an enormous amount of money, time, effort, and patience will have been expended, but we will still be very, very short on specifics. We are expressly told that "A vision will generally not include new zoning bylaws, design specifications for community greenways, or the locations of bus stops, traffic circles or speed bumps. It will set directions, guide decisions, lead to actions, and identify priorities for further work." Zoning and other bylaws to create and develop processes such as densification will not be in place yet.

Why is Any Process like *CityPlan* Destined to Fail?

What is wrong with this $15 million extravaganza of fairs, Futures Tours, surveys, kitchen-table discussions, neighbourhood portraits, neighbourhood mapping, school programs, and newspaper contests? Why doesn't it work?

One of the major pitfalls in most citizen participation programs is the assumption that everyone is interested. A cartoon portraying the average New Yorker's view of the world shows a detailed map of New England and New York State, then a vague blur to the west of that area, ending at the Pacific with a small square representing California. Such egocentrism is common to every walk of life, and, of course, planners think the world is interested primarily in planning. But the truth is that most Canadians are struggling to get through the day, to make ends meet, and to look after themselves and their families. Their attention span for "visioning" the future of their metropolis is limited. So the broad basis for citizen participation is a chimera—the more we pursue it, the more we find only a select few people who turn out evening after evening.

As the geographic scale of the planning exercise broadens, interest inevitably wanes: People who may care passionately about their neighbourhoods care far less about the overarching abstractions that describe the city as a whole. NIMBYism has been so widespread and effective, simply because it deals with people's backyards. *CityPlan* tries to buck this human trait by telling us that "Vancouver has a strong tradition of community participation in the review of major projects, and the preparation of local area plans. The *CityPlan* process extended this participation into the development of a city-wide plan."[3] We maintain that such an extension of participation is impossible.

Another difficulty with the *CityPlan* process is the choices, which we characterize as: "Would you rather be rich and happy, or poor and unhappy?" What emerges from the open-ended *CityPlan*-style process is a wish list, with no analysis of costs, benefits, or tradeoffs. There is no distinction between trivial and significant wishes. The *CityPlan* document begs people to consider the cross-impacts of their choices: "When you've finished making your choices, it will be important to review them to make sure they fit together."[4] If only people would do as they are told.

It takes so long to produce the wish list—a matter of years—that the final product may well be out of sync with the times. For example, in Vancouver, now that citizens have spent several years visioning and are poised to embark on a year of minivisioning at the neighbourhood level, they have been given a major slap in the face by the

Province of British Columbia, which has cut $17 million from its grants to the city. The city now finds itself with a total $27.5 million budget shortfall.

The timing is unfortunate: As *CityPlan* winds up several years of asking everyone what they want, the mayor of Vancouver has been forced to engage in his own citizen participation blitz to ask citizens to "choose" whether to cut the deficit by means of tax increases or through service reductions. Now that's "visioning"! In fact, the mayor's exercise is an example of participation that works. People were asked about something very specific which affects them directly and were given a limited amount of time in which to respond. They participated, they made choices, and they made a difference.

Once the citizens have placed their orders, for example, an order for "a City of Neighbourhood Centres," planners and politicians find themselves woefully unable to deliver the goods. The tools available to planners are blunt and essentially conservative, consisting of such techniques as zoning and other land use regulations, which are mainly effective in maintaining the status quo. These methods do not enable planners to respond to the citizens' wish list, which includes such desires as job security and increased cultural opportunities at the neighbourhood level. When planners and politicians cannot deliver the wish list, those who participated are left feeling cynical and bitter.

A final reason why the extensive citizen participation exemplified by *CityPlan* does not work is that our municipalities can never have enough money to finance such an all-encompassing public participation program. Vancouver, a relatively wealthy city, is a case in point. After $15 million of expenditures and years of effort, the city will have many visions but little reality. In the dawning era of slashed budgets, municipalities are tied up in knots with these visioning exercises and are unable to answer such basic and pressing questions as what the city's skyline should look like. In a moment of panic, because time might run out on a $500 000 grant linked to the preservation of a heritage theatre, Vancouver City Council approved a controversial 137-metre tower in the downtown area without waiting for the results of a much needed skyline study. It is unfortunate that a process like *CityPlan* deprives a city of the time and money needed to address some basic planning issues. These issues should have been given priority.

What Is the Planner's Role?

Addressing the topic of *CityPlan* leads us to the fundamental question of concern to the profession: What is the role of the planner? This question has been debated in the professional literature for decades. We have been through many iterations, and we have viewed the planner's role as that of technocrat, bureaucrat, advocate, and subversive. But common to all of these roles was a notion of a goal or end result, and processes were developed which served to achieve them.

Today, it seems that planners are making it their particular expertise to produce wish lists. So we have the new notion of the planner as a department-store Santa to replace earlier roles. In this notion of planning, the end is not defined and the goal is to have a successful process without regard to substance. *CityPlan* started with the notion that a process of asking people what they want would produce something at the end. Planners and politicians may call the end result a "general, flexible blueprint" or a "first round in the dialogue with the public," but what is it really? It is nothing more than a wish list prepared by some interested citizens that provides no insight into how to shape the future of the city. The kids may want a toy train and bicycles. Whether the city-parent can deliver is for the credit department to decide—not Santa.

There is only so much energy, so much passion, and so much planning that can be done. It is time to look comprehensively at the citizen participation phenomenon to make sure that our efforts are commensurate with our city budgets, with our other priorities, with our patience, and, most importantly, with the results achieved. Citizen

Chapter 5 / The Process of Planning

participation has taken on a life of its own. It is time to rethink the constructive role planners must play in shaping the future of our cities.

An Update on *CityPlan*

Ann McAfee

While the Seeligs are entitled to their opinions about the value of public participation, a few of their statements about *CityPlan* process are incorrect. Since we asked people if they had engaged in previous *CityPlan* activities, we were able to avoid double-counting participants. Interestingly, in annual budget surveys, over 20 percent of households (reflecting 100 000 people) responded that they had participated in *CityPlan* activities.

The net cost of *CityPlan* was in the order of $3 million, not $4 million: $1.5 million for staff costs, and $1.5 million for public processes, including translation to engage Chinese, Indian, and other recent immigrants. The Seeligs' estimates of the follow-up community visions costs are also high: The city has spent about $3.8 million on eight Community Visions (area plans) by 2006, with one left to complete.

CityPlan was a process to generate choices: Ideas and solutions "travelled together" to ensure realistic expectations. While some of the choices were weak (especially in the environment areas), other choices on land use (e.g., to add new housing to lower-density neighbourhoods) and budget allocations addressed difficult decisions.

Ten years after adoption of *CityPlan*, we see its success in successful rezonings for new housing in neighbourhood centres. So far the *CityPlan* "City of Neighbourhoods" direction has generated capacity for 17 000 new dwelling units in previously singlefamily areas. Other new capacity has been approved on brownfield sites. At a typical public hearing, we have seen upwards of 80 people attending to cheer Council's approval of new housing opportunities in their neighbourhood. The direction to increase transit, walking, and biking has resulted in new transportation plans and redirecting City expenditures to bikeways and transit.

After ten years, the results from *CityPlan* exceed the results of previous planning processes. Having participated in developing the plan, residents are "holding the City's feet to the fire" to implement it.

That Thing Called Public Involvement

Nancy Marshall and Richard Roberts

1997, Plan Canada 37(3): 8–11

Populist ideas, the information revolution, and disenchantment with corporate and elected officials who fail to act in the public interest have spurred the public toward greater involvement in the decisions that affect their lives. To avoid conflict, decision makers are often forced to take public opinion into account, or suffer the consequences.[5]

Many planners first became aware of the issues related to public involvement through a landmark article by Sherry Arnstein, in which she described a "typology of citizen participation" used in urban renewal, antipoverty, and model cities programs in the United States.[6] These gave citizens varying degrees of power along a "ladder" of public decision making (Figure 5.6). The *Town and Country Planning Act* of 1968 included public involvement in planning procedures in England and Wales. The US *National Environmental Policy Act* of 1969 started the trend toward public consultation in environmental decision making. In 1972, Canada followed with the Environmental Assessment and Review Process, which required public involvement as an integral part of any assessment process.[7]

Figure 5.6

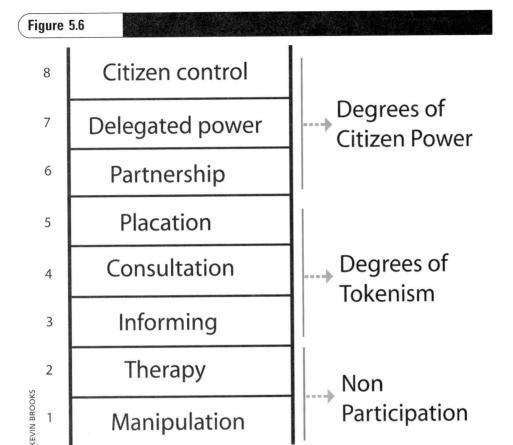

8	Citizen control	
7	Delegated power	Degrees of Citizen Power
6	Partnership	
5	Placation	
4	Consultation	Degrees of Tokenism
3	Informing	
2	Therapy	Non Participation
1	Manipulation	

KEVIN BROOKS

Sherry Arnstein's famous ladder of participation illustrates the range of involvement in public processes.

Today, public involvement in land use planning occurs in Canadian municipalities through a variety of procedures required by provincial planning acts. In Alberta, for example, public involvement is required during the drafting of statutory plans, for amendments to land use bylaws, in the application of land use redesignation, and for publication of notices about development permit approvals. Although not mandated by legislation, public input is also often sought through the circulation and posting of notices about development permit approvals. Broader public involvement in land use planning has primarily occurred informally or on an ad hoc basis in Canadian cities for several years. In contrast, public involvement is often an integral part of social policy planning.

A Definition of Public Involvement

The terms "public involvement," "public consultation," and "public participation" are often used interchangeably without recognition of the subtle and not-so-subtle differences between them. Public involvement is the process for involving the public in the decision-making procedures of a municipality or corporation. This can be brought about through a series of approaches or techniques that range from consultation to participation. The key difference hinges on the degree to which those involved in the process are able to influence, share, or control the decision making.[8] Consultation includes education and information sharing, with the goal being better decision making by the organization through consulting the public. Participation brings the public directly into the decision-making process.

Degrees of Public Involvement

When an organization begins to think about how to develop a public involvement process, it often starts with a public relations exercise. However, there is a continuum of degrees of possible involvement:

- *persuasion:* the use of techniques to change public attitudes without raising expectations of involvement.
- *education:* the distribution of information to the public to create awareness about an organization's project and/or issues.
- *information sharing and feedback:* the distribution of information by an organization concerning its position, with the intent of receiving and considering public comments on the stated position.
- *consultation:* two-way communication between an organization and the public based on established, mutually-accepted objectives.
- *joint planning or shared decision making:* public representation in the decision-making process through voting and decision-making authority.
- *delegated authority:* the transfer to the public of responsibilities normally associated with the organization.
- *self-determination:* the undertaking of a process initiated by the public, with the organization accepting the outcome.

Any public involvement program may involve a number of these steps, including education, consultation, and possibly joint planning, depending on the stage of the process the organization is in at the time.

When Will the Public Be Involved?

The public will be concerned when something new, large, or different is proposed in or near their own community. Concerns will be even greater if the project or activity is located close to their place of residence. Given the high profile of environmental issues and public concerns for health, safety, and quality of life, if developments are located near people or near environmentally sensitive or ecologically significant areas, concerns will almost certainly follow.

Who Is the Public?

The "public" is a constantly changing group of affiliates and alliances that shift and regroup according to projects and processes. There is no single public. The entire community or population will not likely become involved in every process. People do not have the time, energy, or inclination to participate in every project. They prioritize what is most important to them and participate when they believe they will be affected by a certain decision. An individual or group might be more or less involved over the life of a project, either as the consequences of proposed actions become clear or in relation to the proximity of critical decision points. Thus, a number of "publics" may emerge during a process, depending on their particular concerns and the issues involved.

The public may have local, regional, provincial, national, or international interests. Ethnic, cultural, and geographic diversity often requires special consideration. Issues may have no geographic boundaries, making it difficult to define the stakeholders. People are often linked by causes rather than by easily identified factors or communities.

Participants can also be experienced or inexperienced with public processes; informed or uninformed about the specific issues; hostile or apathetic in the ways they become involved; and united or divided on issues and implications. Each of these factors may require a different approach to the public involvement process used.

Current Issues in Public Involvement

Planners need to consult internal publics. In the rush to "go public," staff and management working in an organization are often left in the dark about the organization's true intent regarding public involvement. Staff members may be uninformed and consequently lack buy-in. There is a need to involve them in any process.

Planners must beware of unrealistic expectations. Although some processes are straightforward, many can be time and resource intensive and involve complicated political issues. Public involvement should not be regarded as a panacea for problems that result from decisions made within an organization. The public may also have unrealistic expectations about the relative weight their input will hold with decision makers. Be clear about what issues are, and are not, on the table for discussion.

Paying the public to participate has become more common. In some formal processes and jurisdictions, there has been a demand for "intervenor funding" to assist with the research or participation costs incurred by those directly affected by a project. Also, an increasing number of government agencies are establishing advisory committees, boards, and stakeholder committees to negotiate issues and agreements. Often, these committee members are reimbursed for expenses and given honoraria.

The public is becoming increasingly skeptical about "public involvement" because people do not always see organizations using the results of their input. They ask, "Why should we bother participating this time when you didn't use our input last time?"

The growing trend toward requiring public involvement in decision making is overloading the public and its ability to respond. Due to the required commitment of time and resources, the public is increasingly "shutting down" and withdrawing. However, a negative reaction to a request to participate should not be interpreted as a lack of interest in the process.

Staff, decision maker, and data overload are also a risk. If public involvement processes are added to an already heavy workload, staff may skim the surface of issues and miss valuable public input. Organizers may experience data or information overload. Many do not effectively manage large volumes of written and verbal public input, since most organizations are more familiar with managing quantitative rather than qualitative or open-ended information. Decision makers may also be overloaded with information gathered from one or many concurrent processes and, thereby, become unable to manage the content of the input. As a result, they do not use it effectively.

Technical and scientific "facts" may not match public perceptions. The public gathers information from a multitude of sources and may base its opinions on biased or incorrect information. Technical experts at odds with each other over apparently factual evidence, as well as the tendency of some organizations to discount inherited, traditional, or local knowledge, complicate this issue and isolate the participants.

Consultation with indigenous and ethnic groups is expanding. With greater diversity in many jurisdictions and the internationalization of public involvement, planners increasingly emphasize the development of approaches and techniques appropriate to different cultures, communities, and individuals. Planners must rethink their approaches to consultation and participation given the rise of influence and power in First Nations, indigenous, and aboriginal communities around the world.

A recent trend in public processes is to focus on stakeholder representation or multistakeholder consultation processes. In some cases, the process works exceptionally well. In other cases, it is unclear whether stakeholders represent their organization, several organizations, or only themselves. Of even greater concern is whether participants effectively communicate the results of their discussions and negotiations back to their membership(s). Organizations undertaking public involvement processes need to realize that stakeholder processes are only one technique in the broad spectrum of public involvement.

The Future of Public Involvement

The evolution of the role of the general public, special interest groups, and corporate institutions in society has created a lasting place for public involvement in decision making. Ongoing debate over the extent of participation should be encouraged for different projects and processes. Although public involvement does not guarantee that democracy is served, or that citizens are well represented, it brings people closer to driving the democratic machine than does simply casting a ballot.

An informed and active public has growing opportunities to influence or block corporate decisions that were once made behind closed doors. With corporations becoming more accountable to the public and to their stockholders, the public will be increasingly involved, taking ownership in decisions and understanding their implications. The greatest guarantee of the continuing growth of public involvement, however, is the public itself. If the public is not invited to participate, history shows that people will demand it. Community residents live with the consequences of decisions and thus expect to share in and be responsible for their making.

Citizens' Bane: Consensus Building in Planning

John L Blakney

1997, Plan Canada 37(3): 12-7

The involvement of the public in community planning decisions is well accepted. The observations I make in this article are both personal and professional, based on my experiences in the urban and rural planning profession and my related work with an appellant tribunal deciding planning issues. Over the years, I often came away from public consultation processes believing planners did what the legislation required, but we lacked the tools to deal with the real hopes, fears, concerns, and desires of the interest groups that responded to public policy or development proposals with positions that created impasses. Those of us involved in planning issues are well aware that not dealing with the real concerns of individuals and groups often results in protracted debates before municipal councils, planning boards, and committees, and hearings before tribunals and the courts.

My objective is to explore alternate approaches to building planning policy, dealing with disputes over development proposals, and "cultivating consensus" to enhance the approach to such traditional rights-based and authoritative approaches as "Decide, Announce, and Defend."[9]

Many situations that involve the intervention of planning principles end in destruction of relations, even long-term friendships, that are often difficult to repair. One particular instance comes to mind. A situation arose in a developing suburban community where many residents were drawn into a family dispute as a result of the issuance of a permit for a mobile home. Because the planning process could not deal with the interests, in fact did not even recognize them, a historical dispute between two family members resulted in the polarization of positions held by the municipal council and residents on the issue of locating mobile homes in the community. The numerous public and private meetings held between the two people and their family members, individuals, and resident groups (all of whom had chosen positions around the issue) served only to promote anger. The increased emotion resulted in the breakdown of a dedicated and hard-working municipal council and planning board, a further separation of families and members of neighbourhoods, and the eventual relocation of some to another community. A well-meaning municipal council and an administrative tribunal legislatively designed to settle such disputes did not have the tools to deal with a situation that damaged what was otherwise a tightly knit, hard-working, and proud community. The tribunal issued an order to deal with the mobile home issue, but it was unable to mend the broken community. Even those who wanted to see the community get back to normal lacked the energy and enthusiasm to take on the task.

Planning exercises often do not identify the quality of incompatible interests that underpin a situation: When they do, they avoid conflict by explaining that the municipality does not have the authority to deal with the situation. Nor are the systems designed to repair damaged relationships when one person or stakeholder wins and the other loses. The social, economic, and human costs are too high for communities. Consequently, we need to develop and use methods that will improve existing planning systems and reduce social and economic costs. We need to recognize conflict situations as an opportunity to develop effective and enduring policy, rule-making, and development decisions.[10]

The minimum requirements for public participation and consultation are set out under planning legislation. Traditionally, public participation and consultation follow the options that have been developed by professionals, planning or policy development committees, and politicians. Public hearings, meetings, and workshops are usually designed to inform and exchange positions, but they do not effectively deal with issues and interests raised by residents and groups that underpin positions. Do conventional processes for public participation go far enough in dealing with the varied and competing interests of the various groups that must be involved in cultivating consensus (Figure 5.7)?

I have some observations on the conventional approach to public participation and consultation. While we do our homework on the technical side, our methods of dealing with the interests of people affected by a proposal fall short. Developers, politicians, and professionals often contend: "There is too much process; let's just make a decision and get on with it. This is good for the economy and in the public interest." They may fail to take into account the one opposing group with enough energy and resources to create a barrier.

The traditional approach is ineffective with regard to dispute resolution where positions are firm. The existing system that involves exercising legal rights before an administrative tribunal (e.g., the Ontario Municipal Board, The Island Regulatory and Appeals Commission, and the court system), while adhering to the rules of natural justice—the right to be heard and principles of fairness, can normally not address or deal with the real interests of stakeholders. Some issues can be decided only by the legal system, such as the legal right to a development permit under the regulatory regime. However, some interests such as stakeholder needs, hopes, fears, desires, and concerns cannot be dealt with because of legal requirements.

An adversarial approach to settling a dispute creates winners and losers, but it has difficulty dealing with the interests that underlie the situation. After going through traditional participatory processes, instead of being neutralized, interest groups end up expressing their influence and creating serious consequences if their interests are not satisfied. The interaction between groups with competing interests results in win-lose decisions and a breakdown in relations.

Clearly, we need a better forum and process to offer a range of approaches to develop effective working relations between interest groups: from educating and informing, to increasing dialogue, to actually building a consensus on a solution to a problem. We

Figure 5.7

WAYNE CALDWELL

Cattle are endearing to many rural residents, but the odour and effluents they generate can sometimes lead to conflict.

need methods in which local politicians have confidence that the outcome will reflect the public interest: the interests of those affected and not just a single interest group.

Conflict Management

Conflict management is an important consideration for urban planners.[11] Principles of dispute resolution systems design suggest that we need a forum and process to enhance rights-based and conventional methods of involving interest groups with complex objectives in developing planning policy and resolving disputes. The system is based on the concept of principled negotiation[12] and consensus building.[13] A consensus-building process will involve information sharing, education, facilitation, and mediation. The underlying principle is that cultivating consensus on incompatible interests in planning improves outcomes. A mediation process enables the formation of stakeholder constituencies, which become effective work groups by taking an integrated bargaining approach to resolving issues in dispute. The deliverables are short- and long-term negotiated urban policy and plans that include acceptable options and realistic solutions.

A mediation process involves a preparation stage for negotiations, an introductory stage, an issues identification stage, an interest identification stage, and a solutions stage.[14] Mediation provides a process to identify not only disputing parties' positions and issues, but also the "quality of the interests"[15] that underpins those positions and issues. The mediation process offers the assistance of a neutral party, the trained mediator, to hear the positions and issues. The mediator frames issues in such a way as to gain participants' agreement. A mediator can assist in revealing certain underlying feelings and emotions of the participating parties and understanding their relevance to the positions held. Through a process of active questioning, the mediator can help transfer the issues into interests to determine what is important to the parties.

We need to transform the conventional structure and process of public participation to one characterized by shared vision, empowerment and recognition, and a consensus-building process.[16] Instead of avoiding urban and rural conflict situations, we can use them to channel the resources and energy of special-interest groups toward consensus-building processes that construct acceptable and deliverable planning outcomes.[17] In general, the objective is to develop consensus-based approaches to improve governance.

The Principles

To deal with competing community interests, we need to establish a forum and process for cultivating consensus based on increased information sharing, dialogue, and interest-based negotiation guided by key principles. Most approaches to solving planning issues involve people exercising their legal rights. The process must respect those rights.

We can approach pressing urban and rural issues with the view that conflict between interest groups arising as a result of varied objectives and associated incompatible interests presents an opportunity for change while contributing to the resolution of disputes. We should emphasize creating a forum for information exchange and dialogue at the early stages of planning, using common language and common definitions while increasing awareness and motivation and establishing a shared perception of the issues.[18]

The process should be characterized by participant voluntarism, empowerment, and recognition of the disputing parties. It should consider education, understanding, and the maintenance of social relationships and partnerships as more important than just making a decision.[19] The approach should involve a dispute resolution system that identifies sources of conflict and allows conflicting interest groups to help solve problems. It will be designed to deal with disputes as they occur, with a focus on problem solving that is based on interest, not on position.[20]

The options for solution should draw on the collective wisdom of the parties at the negotiating table. They should allow a large number of individuals who represent a particular view to form one constituency represented at the dialogue table by one speaker, instead of stacking a meeting with members of a single interest group and creating an imbalance to influence the consensus of the public meeting or hearing.

Finally, political commitment and openness of government are essential.[21] Over the long term, the rewards of consensus-building methods will be a reduction in the real community costs of planning disputes.

Eight Principles of Consensus Building

To commit to a consensus-building process, a municipal government should adopt the following principles to guide council, the planning advisory committee, municipal staff, and participants to deal with situations that are potentially confrontational.

Principle #1: Focus the planning process on early consultation with interest groups.

Principle #2: Decide whether to host a consensus-building event, and do not preclude any other stakeholder from hosting such an event. In cases where the municipality is invited to participate, the council should determine its role and the role of staff (whether as full participant or observer).

Principle #3: In cases where the developer proposes a development concept that requires a change to policy or a bylaw, or—in the opinion of the council—that causes change to an area and results in resistance or confrontation, the developer should be required to host a multiparty process with the objective to satisfy stakeholder interests. (Council should attach the resolution to the application for development.)

(continued)

Principle #4: Ensure that discussions between stakeholders focus on interests (values and concerns) and not on positions (favoured solutions).

Principle #5: Ensure the process emphasizes multiparty participation incorporating a broad, representative view of the situation.

Principle #6: Ensure that any policy resolutions are acceptable to all stakeholders affected, including the municipal government, and that they can be implemented.

Principle #7: Begin with procedures that encourage reaching a consensus among the participants, such as facilitation. Then move to procedures that require the independent decision of a third party, such as arbitration. Procedures should be used in order of priority: facilitated dialogue, mediation, advisory-mediation, mediation-arbitration, and then arbitration.

Principle #8: If during an independent third-party arbitration process the situation becomes favourable for negotiation, the procedures should allow the parties to reenter an interest-based process.

The Solution

Planners are in a strategic position to disseminate information; educate community members, groups, and organizations; and contribute to establishing an environment for preventing conflict in a community. Significant efforts have been made to introduce consensus-building processes into municipal planning systems; and these efforts appear to be making a positive contribution to the development process.[22] The task is to expand the use and application of the principles to deal with situations at all stages of the plan-making process: from what information we need to collect, to policy creation and implementation. These suggestions are put forward with the caveat that they merely offer a simple framework to be debated, modified, and adapted to specific situations. The purpose is not to substitute for but to enhance existing approaches.

Municipal councils must implement a consensus-building process to enhance the planning process in dealing with conflict situations. A municipality or regional authority can adopt general policy, guiding principles, and procedures to establish the necessary forum and process. A consensus-building process to resolve a planning situation should be based on an integrated bargaining approach and use principled negotiation to allow participants to collectively find solutions that satisfy their interests, probably with the assistance of a skilled and trained neutral facilitator or mediator.

Building Consensus Step by Step

Step #1: Initiating process. When a planning issue is identified, planning staff will analyze the merits of having a consensus-building event with the assistance of a trained facilitator or mediator. Staff will report to the advisory planning committee (if one exists), which will, in turn, report and make a recommendation to the council. Council will determine whether or not such an event is to be hosted by the municipal government.

Step #2: Hosting. If council determines that a consensus-building event is necessary then it will take the lead to establish an event, inviting participants relevant to the situation.

Step #3: *Preparing.* The council engages the services of a convenor to work with the host to broadly define what the problem is and identify those who should be initially involved in the event.

Step #4: Involving participants. The convenor meets with each participant individually to explain the proposed process and determine interest and willingness to participate. Also, the convenor determines the potential participant's commitment to the process and willingness to participate, and reports back to the host. At this step, with the assistance of the convenor, constituencies can be formed and structured to promote full participation through the formation of appropriate work groups and subgroups.

Step #5: Scheduling and holding the event. Once the participants and the host have agreed, then an event can be scheduled and held.

Step #6: Structuring the discussions. The physical layout of the room has the table as the centre of discussion. A convenor (facilitator/mediator) and a spokesperson for each constituency sit at the table. For multiparty events, constituency members select a spokesperson and appoint a steering committee to represent and provide feedback to members.

Step #7: Determining other potential participants. During the process, if the group of participants or the negotiating group finds it necessary to expand the list of participants to ensure everyone is involved, then it may do so. Participants may be full negotiating partners or observers with the flexibility to change their role either as the process evolves or depending on the issue being discussed. The objective is to develop a positive environment for those who are at first reluctant to participate, but later change their view and find it necessary and worthwhile to fully participate in the negotiations.

Step #8: Producing outcome and deliverables. A resolution can include a written report comprising the identified agenda and issues to be discussed, the identified preferred set of options, and the actions necessary to implement the options. For the long- and short-term planning function, the outcome can be a "negotiated plan" or "negotiated policy"[23] and rules. For an event that deals with a site plan redesign, the outcome could be a negotiated site plan and new bylaw standards. The outcome should provide, at the very least, options to address participants' interests and give greater assurances that they will be dealt with in future. If a consensus-building event does not solve a complex situation, the outcome should be the formation of a partnership between normally disputing stakeholders and the establishment of a structure and process focused on consensus building.

Challenges

Using consensus building to enhance public involvement in planning processes requires investment of substantial resources (time and money) at an early stage. In times of cuts to municipal budgets affecting services, municipal governments may be reluctant to make such an investment. However, when we examine conventional approaches to public participation and consultation, which result in protracted debates before council, administrative tribunals, and the courts, the situation is really one of pay now or pay later.

The real benefits are those achieved when consensus-building processes involve everyone who should be involved, produce practical and enduring solutions, improve the public involvement processes we are all acquainted with, and strengthen and maintain social relationships. Politicians will continue to face the challenges of influential groups with competing interests. It is the responsibility of the politician to open government and commit to strategic use of information to properly inform interest groups and to build a political climate for interest-based negotiation that will achieve enriched policy while settling disputes. Political awareness of the role of consensus building is essential.

Planners can perform at least four roles in the consensus-building process: technical expert, principled negotiator, interventionist, and third-party neutral facilitator/mediator. Planners should become aware of how consensus-building processes work to reach resolutions on planning issues. Consequently, one immediate challenge is education and training to establish the foundation for cultivating consensus. Education will increase awareness by politicians, municipal officials, planners, and citizens about what the consensus-building process is and what it can do. Training is necessary to increase the specific skills and tools of those who want to assist parties to build consensus. The nature of the planning work with public processes often means that planners find themselves in facilitator, negotiator, and mediator roles. Formal training in the skills used in conflict management, principled negotiation, and multiparty negotiation will equip planners with the tools they need.

Although there are many challenges inherent in trying to achieve consensus, one that is fundamental is the need to increase community awareness of conflict situations and recognition that such states of uncertainty can contribute to bringing about positive urban change for the public good. With this in mind, we must continue to explore approaches to conflict management and recognize the contributions that can be made through planning. Our exploration must focus on how we can be more imaginative and more innovative in our efforts to brainstorm for solutions.

Planning or Blackmail?

Stanley Makuch

1985, Plan Canada 25(1): 8–9

In the City of Toronto in the mid-1980s, a group known as Downtown Action agreed to withdraw an appeal respecting an approval of a 68-storey $400 million development known as Scotia Plaza if the developer, Campeau Corporation, paid $2 million to the Cooperative Housing Federation of Toronto for building low-income housing. There was no authority in legislation for demanding the payment of the money. Prior to its approval of the same development, the City of Toronto secured an agreement from Campeau to build a daycare centre in the Scotia Plaza. There is no provision in the *Ontario Planning Act* for the imposition of such a condition upon the approval of a development. Have we reached the situation where planning has become blackmail? The payment of the money and the building of the daycare centre were both for the same purpose—to secure a speedy approval of the project. Are we in a situation where developers have to buy planning permission? Should developments not be accepted or rejected on their merits, and not on the extra legislative concessions forced out of a developer?

These questions raise fundamental issues regarding rule of law values, fairness, and equity in planning. One goal of the legal system is to ensure those persons subject to legal rules—be they zoning bylaws, tax legislation, or contract law—have an opportunity to know what the rules are and to have the rules apply uniformly. If this happens, then individuals will not be granted favours nor have inordinate burdens placed on them. This value is clearly at the basis of zoning. Zones are supposed to be set out in advance. Regulations are to apply uniformly to all property owners in a zone, and development occurs not because of blackmail or favouritism but because of the uniform application of zoning laws. The imposition of requirements on a case-by-case or negotiated basis for the payment of money or the construction of nonauthorized facilities runs sharply against this value.

However, it is also clear that negotiations dealing with developments on a case-by-case basis are an important part of planning today. All provinces have subdivision control procedures, which allow the imposition of conditions that may vary from subdivision to subdivision. Indeed, the Ontario Municipal Board, in reviewing the imposition of lot levies pursuant to the process of subdivision approval, has stated that levies must be reasonably related to development. This is an attempt to individualize the levies and not require a levy of uniform application.

Moreover, virtually all provinces have provisions for development control. This technique enables conditions to be imposed, not on a uniform basis, but rather on a case-by-case basis. Agreements containing the conditions that vary from development to development can be entered into by municipalities and developers. Development control powers found in the *City of Winnipeg Act*, the *Ontario Planning Act*, the *Alberta Planning Act*, the *Nova Scotia Planning Act*, or the *Vancouver Charter*, for example, all anticipate, to varying degrees, the discretionary negotiation of conditions that will be imposed on development on a case-by-case basis and that uniform rules or standards for approving developments are inappropriate.

Such an approach is not "bad," even though it runs counter to the rule of law value mentioned earlier. It provides and encourages flexibility and variety in development that zoning would not allow. Moreover, it enables individualized discretion. The demands placed on different developers should not necessarily be the same. To impose the same conditions on all developments (e.g., the requirement to build a daycare centre or to widen roads in all cases, even when not needed) would be foolish. Different developments create different demands. The conditions imposed should, therefore, be individualized and not uniform. This is why the Ontario Municipal Board requires that levies be reasonably related to a development, and not simply imposed on a uniform basis.

In this light, we should not be so concerned about conditions being imposed for the payment of money or the construction of a daycare centre in the Scotia Plaza situation. Moreover, the agreement in Toronto between Campeau and Downtown Action, by which the group abandoned its appeal of the city's original decision approving the Scotia Plaza in return for a payment, was no different from a payment in a settlement regarding litigation. It can be seen, therefore, as being very similar to an agreement to settle a lawsuit between the Ford Motor Company and the Rusty Ford Owners Association.

Yet there are some serious concerns about the Toronto situation in particular and the imposition of conditions generally. First, it is important that where publicly elected bodies such as municipal councils are exercising authority, they do so within the legislative power given. They should not consciously attempt to exceed their powers and impose conditions not authorized by legislation. If no authority is granted to impose levies, for example, they should not be imposed. If daycare centres cannot be required under the law, they should not be required.

Second, because a system of discretionary control is open to abuse, the imposition of conditions should be done only in accordance with the provisions of an official or municipal plan, and as much information as possible should be made public before and after a deal is made. This would ensure that public information, especially after the negotiations are completed, will not jeopardize negotiations when they occur, and yet ensure that decision makers justify the conditions they impose to the public and to other developers. Moreover, the availability of information about conditions being imposed will encourage the imposition of similar conditions in similar situations and help rule of law values.

In conclusion, negotiations, the imposition of conditions, and the treating of different developers and developments differently is not in itself wrong. These powers are important aspects of discretionary planning control, although they do not reflect rule of law values. There is great benefit from the $2 million payment and the daycare centre extracted from Campeau. It is important, however, that these controls, since they are open to abuse, be exercised within the scope and purpose of planning legislation and adopted plans and in an open and accountable manner.

The Weight of the System: The Effects of Institutional Structures on Planners' Creativity and Flexibility

Pierre Filion

1997, Plan Canada 37(1): 11–5

A few years ago, Jane Jacobs launched a vitriolic attack in the *OPPI Journal* against "brain-dead" municipal planners, lamenting an absence of vision.[24] Frequently, members of the press have portrayed planners as rigid bureaucrats. In my opinion, it is unfair to lay the brunt of the blame for planning's current shortcomings at the door of municipal planners, since much of their behaviour is dictated by the agencies in which they work, by planning legislation, and by the nature of existing processes. Planners are themselves frustrated by their work environment, in particular by insufficient understanding on the part of their political masters.[25] Planners should not be faulted without our acknowledging the weight of the system on their actions. Criticism is more deservedly targeted at planning's institutional framework than at some intrinsic creativity and flexibility deficiency on the part of planners.

A cursory glance at municipal governments' organizational features reveals a number of restrictions on municipal planners' activities. First, there are the effects of the hierarchical structure of municipal government, which assures that major decisions (including those concerning municipal planning) are taken or ratified by elected representatives and that the civil service is submitted to orientations set by council, and thus to interests represented by council members (hence the clout of the development industry in many growing municipalities). In this context, if it is true that planners can use their expertise to influence their political leaders, experience shows that, when serious disagreements arise, planners' heads often roll. Is it then fair to criticize planners for not being sufficiently critical of prevailing planning practices that are popular with both political leaders and the public? For example, planners face dire consequences if they promote residential intensification in an established suburban neighbourhood in the face of residents' and politicians' forceful opposition (Figure 5.8). This hierarchical form of decision making has other repercussions on planning practice. It slows the planning process and reduces planners' capacity to make commitments. Electoral legitimacy requirements are not unrelated to the adoption by government agencies of elaborate decision-making procedures that bring major issues to council after a foray through the bureaucracy: hence the red tape reputation of municipal planning.

At a more general level, all organizations can be perceived as conditioning environments using elaborate systems of rewards and penalties to control their members' behaviour and to assure concordance with organizational objectives.[26] Core objectives of the civic service, including planning departments, are to provide services according to the established mandate and to assure the implementation of policies adopted by council. Actions conforming to these designs, including efforts to improve the fulfillment of the mandate and the implementation of policy, are rewarded. But municipal employees open themselves to penalties when they depart from the mandate and from council's stands.

Decisions emanating from the municipal hierarchical structure bear the mark of two determining factors: the electoral and fiscal imperatives.[27] The electoral imperative, which is channelled through the representative system, emanates from the need for politicians to heed public opinion as well as demands with a high mobilization potential to be elected or reelected. Given low turnout at municipal elections and a concentration of participation among wealthier residents, municipal politicians tend to favour the

Figure 5.8

JILL GRANT

Building at higher densities, as in the St. Lawrence area of Toronto, makes better use of infrastructure, but it can raise community concerns about crowding and traffic.

concerns of owner/occupiers over those of tenants (as evidenced in Ontario by higher tax rates on a square-foot basis for rental apartments than for single-family houses). Overall, the electoral imperative requires local politicians to accommodate occasionally contradictory preferences held by voters. This forces representatives to assure simultaneously the delivery of good-quality services, the upkeep of infrastructures, low tax rates, neighbourhood preservation, and so on. By contrast, the fiscal imperative pertains to the need by municipalities to secure a healthy fiscal base to be able to satisfy the electorate by delivering abundant and good-quality services while keeping taxes low.

The effect of these two imperatives is to seriously narrow the planner's possible range of action. On the one hand, the electoral imperative makes it difficult for planners to run against public opinion and implement new formulas that have yet to secure a broad constituency. Little wonder then that municipal planning has a tendency to stay the course and to be perceived as lacking creativity. On the other hand, the fiscal imperative translates into an accommodating attitude toward fiscally lucrative land uses, which results in an oversupply of land zoned for industrial and commercial purposes. Hence, the form municipal planning takes is, in part, tributary to fiscal considerations, which is obvious in the tendency to zone high-accessibility sites to the maximum of their market potential. Related to these constraints are the effects of another factor of influence on municipal planning: the dependence on private development to achieve planning objectives, which forces planners to adjust their objectives to market laws. A final point of relevance is the risk-averse nature of public-sector agencies. These tend to avoid unproven development formulas because of their potential negative fiscal impacts, such as the waste of a given site's tax revenue potential due to a failed development, with resulting blight and infrastructure underuse. Many municipal officials find it unwise to take risks with the public purse, particularly in difficult economic times.

Still, this is not to suggest that creativity and flexibility are fully eradicated by constraints inherent in municipal governance. Quite to the contrary, municipal planners can derive significant benefits from being creative and flexible in the daily operation of their department, as long as this does not clash with the constraints noted. For example, successful use of creativity has resulted in striking technical improvements in the practice of planning, and increased flexibility has brought about more effective ways of dealing with the public.[28] There is also some room within planning departments to conceive alternative futures and use this to alter the thrust of municipal planning. But for this to happen, planners must rely on alliances with interest groups that are electorally or fiscally powerful and thus apt to sway local politicians. Such alliances can then promote the transformation of municipal institutional structures as well as of planning processes and objectives.[29] In the 1960s and 1970s, some planners sided with neighbourhood activists to open the process to public participation, and, since the 1980s, a group of planners has joined efforts with environmentalists to promote urban intensification. More recently, planners have attempted to bring economic interests on board by stressing the positive financial implications of more concentrated forms of development. Yet, despite these possibilities, municipal planning departments remain less conducive to the denunciation of prevailing practice and to the championing of alternative forms of development than are other types of environments: hence the tendency for critical perspectives to emerge from outside the departments.

Some individuals assume the role of critics of current practices and envision alternative forms of planning as well as their possible outcomes. They mostly express themselves in books and through the media. Their public profile and, in some cases, livelihood hinges on their critical and visioning capacities. The conditioning environment of these individuals is thus entirely different from that of municipal planners. Theirs is not an unbridled creativity, however, since it is submitted to the rules of the media. As the planning models that have left their mark over the century demonstrate, the message must be easily understandable and apt to capture the imagination (this is the case of Howard's garden city, Le Corbusier's towers in a park, Jacobs's return to traditional neighbourhoods, and, lately, new urbanism and smart growth). As amply demonstrated by experience, the implementation of these models has turned out to be more complex and their consequences rather less enticing than anticipated. Critical thinkers pioneered the development of the planning system and of the models that have transformed our urban landscapes.

Interest in planning, which led to the adoption of planning legislation and the creation of planning departments, was stimulated by visions put forth by this category of thinkers.[30] There is, indeed, a great deal of persuasive power in the capacity to picture—often with the help of illustrations—the alternative future that would ensue from changes in planning practice.

Consultants, too, are better positioned to come up with innovations than are municipal planners, as Jacobs observed in her *OPPI Journal* article. To survive, consulting firms are forced to engage in an ongoing search for formulas that accord with emerging realities (the economy, the political reality, and consumer preference patterns). Unlike their municipal counterparts, who must be cautious when handling the public purse, planning consultants operate in an entrepreneurial mode, which entails taking the risk of developing and championing new development models with the hope that they will be widely adopted. For example, many firms that were early in embracing the "new urbanism" model were financially rewarded. In this regard, consulting firms are not that different from any private enterprise experimenting with new products and expecting that some will generate profits.

This short article has addressed reasons for the observed concentration of planning's visioning and creative activity outside municipal planning departments. I attribute this situation not to the personal characteristics of planners employed by municipalities, but rather to the nature of their working environment. The argument stressed the influence of organizations on the behaviour of their members. After all, organizations are essentially devices controlling their members' behaviour to permit the attainment of organizational goals. Municipal planning departments are poorly suited to the generation of critiques susceptible to open the formulation of new planning models. This accounts for the view that planning creativity emerges more readily from outside than from inside these departments.

Study Questions

1. What factors may alter the ability of citizens to affect planning outcomes? How do these factors change through time?

2. To what extent is consensus building possible in a complex and diverse society? What can planners do to facilitate it?

3. How do the characteristics of the planning process act to constrain the choices that planners and communities have? How do planning processes differ in practice from what theory suggests?

4. Why are municipal employees likely to be cautious in their efforts to change the planning process? What would be required to generate greater innovation?

5. What risks arise when planners negotiate deals with developers? What kinds of benefits are reasonable for communities to require of developers?

6. Look at the City of Vancouver's website to see how far *CityPlan* has progressed in its process of envisioning for neighbourhoods. Consider whether you agree with McAfee's assessment or with the Seeligs' skepticism.

7. Compare the vision statements of three Canadian cities (available online) to identify the kind of future we hope to enjoy. What differences and similarities do you find between the visions?

8. How well do planning departments explain the planning process to their citizens? Pick a city and examine its planning website to analyze how well it describes the process and the rights and responsibilities of citizens in the process.

Reference Notes

1. Geddes, P (1968) *Cities in Evolution: An Introduction to the Town Planning Movement and to the Study of Civics*. New York: H Fertig.

2. Lash, H (1977) *Planning in a Human Way: Personal Reflections on the Regional Planning Experience in Greater Vancouver*. Urban Prospects Series. Ottawa: Ministry of State for Urban Affairs.

3. Vancouver, City of (1994) *CityPlan*. Vancouver: Department of Planning and Development: 43.

4. Vancouver, City of (1994) Ibid: 2.

5. Roberts, R (1995) Public involvement: From consultation to participation. In F Vanclay & DA Bronstein (eds) *Environmental and Social Impact Assessment*. New York: John Wiley & Sons: 221–45.

6. Arnstein, SR (1969) A ladder of citizen participation. *Journal of the American Institute of Planners* 35(4): 216–24.

7. Federal Environmental Assessment and Review Office (FEARO) (1973) *Environmental Assessment and Review Process*. Ottawa: Federal Environmental Assessment and Review Office, Government of Canada.

8. World Bank, Environment Department (1993) Public involvement in environmental assessment: Requirements, opportunities and issues. *Environmental Assessment Sourcebook* Update, No.5: 1–8.

9. Raab, J (1994) *Using Consensus Building to Improve Utility Regulation*. Berkeley, CA: CEEE Books on Energy Policy and Energy Efficiency: 222.

10. Sherman, L & J Livey (1992) The positive power of conflict. *Plan Canada* 32(2): 12–6.

    Sloan, G (1996) Discussion of "quality of the interest" in the Mediation II course. Ottawa: Canadian International Institute of Applied Negotiation.

11. Minnery, JR (1985) *Conflict Management in Urban Planning*. Brookfield: Gower Publishing.

12. Fisher, R & W Ury (1991) *Getting to Yes*. (2nd ed) New York: Penguin Books.

13. Abbott, J (1996) *Sharing the City*. London: Earthscan Publication.

14. Moore, CW (1996) *The Mediation Process*. (2nd ed) San Francisco: Jossey-Bass.

15. Rosell, SA et al. (1992) *Governing in an Information Society*. Montreal: Institute for Research on Public Policy.

16. Bush, RAB & J Folger (1994) *The Promise of Mediation*. San Francisco: Jossey-Bass.

17. Hoffman, B (1993) *Win-Win Competitiveness Made in Canada*. North York: Captus Press.

18. Convening Partners (1995) *Sustainability: It's Time for Action*. Conference Summary Report. Vancouver.

19. Bush, RAB & J Folger (1994) Op. cit.

20. Fisher, R & W Ury (1991) Op. cit.

21. Abbott, J (1996) Op. cit.

22. Diehl, R (1995) Resolving community development disputes: The Kamloops experience. *Plan Canada*, 35(5): 30–4.

    Willmer, J (1996) Personal communication, Planning and Development Department, Kitchener.

23. Sherman, L & J Livey (1992) Op. cit.

    Sloan, G (1996) Op. cit.

24. Jacobs, J (1993) Are planning departments useful? *OPPI Journal*, July-August: 4–5.

25. Witty, D (1994) Taking the pulse of Canadian planners: A snapshot of the profession. *Plan Canada*, July, Special 75th Anniversary Edition: 153–9.

26. Mintzberg, H (1979) *The Structure of Organizations: A Synthesis for Research*. Englewood Cliffs: Prentice Hall.

    Mintzberg, H (1983) *Power in and around Organizations*. Englewood Cliffs: Prentice Hall.

Perrow, C (1972) *Complex Organizations: A Critical Essay.* Glenview IL: Scott Foresman.

27. Filion, P (1987) Core redevelopment, neighbourhood revitalization and municipal government motivation: Twenty years of urban renewal in Quebec City. *Canadian Journal of Political Science* 20(1): 131–47.

28. Forester, J (1989) *Planning in the Face of Power.* Berkeley: University of California Press.

Healey, P (1992) A planner's day: Knowledge and action in communicative practice. *Journal of the American Planning Association* 58: 9–20.

29. Filion, P (1993) Factors of evolution in the content of planning documents: Downtown planning in a Canadian city, 1962-1992. *Environment and Planning B, Planning and Design* 20: 459–78.

30. Hodge, G (2003) *Planning Canadian Communities: An Introduction to the Principles, Practice and Participants.* (3rd ed) Scarborough: Thomson Nelson.

Philosophy and Practice

Chapter Six

Preparing for an Uncertain Future

Plans for the Future

Jill Grant

If we had no thought about the future, we wouldn't need to plan. We engage community planners because we know that the decisions we make today will affect future generations. We plan because we want a good future for our descendants.

What does the future hold (Figure 6.1)? Can we expect endless economic expansion or catastrophic environmental decline? Soothsayers for both options fill the media. The cheerleaders of better times ahead promise growth in income, lifespan, and technological improvement. The skeptics warn about the risks of war, terrorism, growing inequality, and pandemics. Books about Armageddon, cultural collapse, and potential plagues become best sellers.

The early town planning movement found its inspiration in two late nineteenth-century utopian novels about the future. Edward Bellamy's *Looking Backward* and William Morris's *News from Nowhere* encouraged positive images of what planning could achieve. By contrast, today's popular novels about the future prove less optimistic. Margaret Atwood's *Oryx and Crake* envisions genocide. Movies like *Blade Runner* and *Mad Max* present dystopian futures. Have we lost the ability to imagine a better tomorrow, or do these representations of potential failure overtly challenge us to plan harder to achieve our ambitions?

Most people seem to agree that we live in uncertain times. The last decades and centuries have spawned remarkable changes. Change and even turbulence have become constants. In his article in this chapter, Gary Paget suggests that we cannot hope for equilibrium and continuity. William Rees argues that much of what we plan for the future will turn out to be wrong, so we have to adapt to survive.

How far ahead should we plan? Provincial planning acts often mandate five- or seven-year reviews of plans, suggesting a fairly short time horizon. In practice, local governments make fiscal decisions through an annual budgeting process, often resulting in a shorter time line. In his paper on long-range planning, though, Mark Seasons suggests that, in some cases, we should gaze into the distant future, especially when we are investing in substantial cultural infrastructure like parks and public buildings.

Figure 6.1

Some foresee utopian futures, while others fear dystopian disasters.

Forecasts offer projections, often quantified, about changes in variables over time. Communities rely on population forecasts to predict demand for housing, schools, hospitals, and other services. Forecasts are at the heart of land use planning.

Scenarios are alternative stories about the future, which communities may use to consider possible reactions to external changes or to identify preferences for alternative choices. Planners develop scenarios that take contrasting assumptions about what the future may hold to generate discussion on important choices. Preferred alternatives may then be used to generate planning policy.

Visions articulate desired futures. They are often created through a public process that brings people together to share their values, aspirations, and hopes for better communities. Visions may then direct planning goals and objectives.

Ideas about the future are inevitably bound up in contemporary concerns. We create images of futures to resolve the problems we face today. Those predicting future concerns in the 1980s and early 1990s got many things right, but they missed some issues that we now need to address. They said little about globalization, the impact of free trade leading to deindustrialization of our communities, the transformation of our economy through threats to primary industries (fisheries, coal mining, forestry, agriculture). Since the 1960s, planners have tended to presume that growth would continue. Population projections forecast high growth in the postwar era. Although population growth has slowed, forecasts of population expansion, especially in urban areas, continue to drive planning scenarios. The risks presented by communicable diseases, like the SARS outbreak that hit Toronto in 2003 or the potential of a global pandemic influenza, rarely seem to influence population projections and planning decisions. History tells us, though, that we may expect, at some point, to need to plan for decline as well as for growth.

The ideal places of our dreams are ephemeral: Like a mirage, they disappear from our reach as we approach them. Planning suffers from a persistent tension between the present and future, the practical and the ideal. If planners deal with the present and the practical, we may find ourselves accused of being reactionary and technocratic. If we turn to focus on the future and the ideal, we may be called naive and unrealistic. Yet planning is both present and future oriented. It is grounded in the present as we try in practical ways to resolve the issues that face our communities. At the same time, planning looks always to the future to think about how the policy and regulations we adopt today may move us steps closer to (or away from) the ideal community of our dreams.

Turbulence: How Do Planners Respond?
1981, Plan Canada 21(1): 24

"Planning starts out, as a rule, with the trends of yesterday and projects them into the future—using a different 'mix' perhaps, but with much the same elements and configuration. This is no longer going to work....A time of turbulence is a dangerous time, but its greatest danger is a temptation to deny reality....A time of turbulence is also one of great opportunity for those who understand, accept and exploit the new realities."[1]

In 1981, Henry Hightower and Ted Rashleigh, the editors of Plan Canada, sent several questions to planners across Canada:

- Is turbulence affecting the work of planning agencies?
- How are they responding? How should they respond?
- What in your opinion are the elements of an appropriate planning strategy when changes to our society, its communities, and economies are imminent, if not under way, and while uncertainties remain more clear-cut than actual prospects?
- Should planners be working differently with the public and decision makers?
- Has your planning program developed new orientations and emphases?
- Do you still hold to Burnham's dictum "Make no little plans"?
- Are planning offices best run on a hierarchical or collegial basis?
- If you do not agree with his assessment of current times, how do you view conditions as they affect planning?
  Some of the responses follow.

A Responsibility to Understand, to Engage in Dialogue, and to be Creative
Gary Paget

1981, Plan Canada 21 (1): 25–6

The concept of turbulence invokes images of a society that is disturbed, unruly, boisterous, agitated, and tumultuous. In planning, it has become jargon: to reflect, to tame contradiction, and to tackle uncertainty and lack of consensus. It is ironic that turbulence has become such a stable concept.

Turbulence describes the everyday reality of so many working in public-sector environments. While we may be reaching consensus that "yes, our work is turbulent," we certainly are far from realizing what it means for professional practice, or theory for that matter. Schön and Nutt described five possible responses to turbulence.[2]

- *Denial*: Nothing is different, everything is stable, and our methods and techniques are sufficient.
- *Flight*: There is an answer to turbulence, and it can be found in another discipline or technique.

- *Research*: Turbulence can be tamed if only we could find the right theory or technique. In the meantime we forgo action.
- *Forecasting*: If we can forecast possible futures, then we will be prepared.
- *Learning*: If we rethink the relationship between theory and practice, between what we do and what we think we do, then we can effectively deal with turbulence.

Research and forecasting are valid responses, provided they do not represent flight and denial: an excuse for inaction. I would argue, however, that the most appropriate response is learning. To me, that means accepting the inevitability, desirability, and freedom inherent in turbulence. It requires developing our understanding of that reality and humbly searching for responsible ways to act, to manage, and to create under conditions of turbulence.

Turbulence is often contrasted with stability. Some argue that, in the past, "things were under control." Society was firm, fixed, steady, and manageable. I am not too sure that "stability" described the 1930s, 1940s, or 1950s. Regardless, society then was seen to be in equilibrium. Consensus prevailed. What is, was good. The major questions were not: "What do we want to do?" or "Why are we going to do it?" They were: "How?" and, in particular, "How do we keep what we have?" Hence, there was an emphasis on method, technique, and, more recently, process. Under conditions of equilibrium, the planner was able to separate and to isolate himself from the subject of his work (the who) and the purpose of his efforts (the what) and concentrate on method (the how). One result of this attitude, on an everyday basis, was the destruction of the urban environment: for example, the kind of urban renewal that Jane Jacobs castigated. At the same time, this detached attitude provided strong individuals full scope to shape our physical environment and to act irresponsibly, without concern for human needs and social impact. This generated a particular attitude in designers. In Christopher Alexander's words, the designer "feels he must be in control, that he must inject the creative impulse, that he must supply the image which controls the design."[3]

In my view, equilibrium is a false hope for these turbulent times. It is neither feasible nor desirable. An appropriate approach to planning for this decade must accept the uncertainty, the complexity, and the freedom of turbulence, while emphasizing the responsibility to understand, to engage in dialogue, and to be creative. In terms of my current experience in planning for resource community development, I see several key needs.

- *A need to understand*: We must explore problems, search for their causes, and, as Rittel and Webber argue, discover the range of resolutions rather than solutions. We need to recognize that for every problem, there is a different expression or way of resolving it. Understanding implies and requires "design from the inside out" rather than "design from the top down."[4]
- *An overall social purpose, principle, or ethic of planning for people*: Planning must be undertaken with a concern for equity, justice, human needs, and participation.
- *An ecological ethic of "enlightened self interest"*: Rights must be assigned to nonhuman nature and limits placed on our actions so as to maintain the self-renewing capability of our environment.
- *"Planning by invitation"*: We need to reject insular corporate planning approaches that rely on compulsion and accept instead the social realities of communities, organizations, and governments. We need to accept that by working with the people who will ultimately "own" the problems and developing/articulating organizations, we will make it happen, but in a socially sensitive manner.
- *The freedom to dream:* We must go beyond irresponsible infatuation with technique or process and accept the responsibility to actively engage ourselves with the problems of our communities. This implies conscious design, which causes the right things to happen. We also need a flexibility, openness, and receptiveness to modify or change our actions based on experience.

By accepting these features, we confirm the importance of responsibility, understanding, dialogue, and freedom. At the same time, we give up the pursuit of power, accept humility, and possibly achieve anonymity. In this way, we can learn to live and to thrive under turbulence.

> "The notion of the Paradise Lost of a stable and predictable past is an optical illusion. Uncertainty and turbulence have been part of the human condition since Adam and Eve." (Hans Blumenfeld, 1981, *Plan Canada* 21(1): 27)

Institutional Mutagenics

William E Rees

1981, Plan Canada 21(1): 28

Evolution is Nature's way of turning out "the latest model," and it has worked rather well for billions of years. The diversity and abundance of natural creations is enough to humble the most imaginative and prolific of human designers and artisans. However, appearances to the contrary, there is no grand design behind Nature's obviously abundant success. Evolution proceeds by random mutation: minor tinkering with existing models. If the new version works better than the old, it survives to change some more. If it doesn't—and it usually doesn't— it expires unnoticed on the evolutionary scrap heap. In short, those entities best thrive whose mutations, randomly served, equip them better than their contemporaries for current environmental realities. If so haphazard a process seems improbable, remember that, in an environment that changes unpredictably, purposeful adaptation or design is pointless.

What has all this to do with "planning under change"?

First, it should be obvious that planning agencies—or any other social institutions that cannot adapt to changing conditions—are doomed to extinction or, even worse, irrelevance. Moreover, we all recognize that change is the only constancy in life. The important question then is what, other than our own arrogance, distinguishes today's "turbulent field" from the mere "changing conditions" of a few decades ago? Perhaps the difference can be summed up in the single word "unpredictability." It used to be that shifting socioeconomic indicators could be counted on to show a definite trend over time. The bulk of social planning and government programs is based on the assumption of an ever-increasing economic pie. Even Nature seemed to respond mechanically and predictably to human demands. For 25 years after World War II, launching more fishing boats meant catching more fish. No more. Today, there are those who fear that even stock-enhancement programs are more likely to endanger than benefit the fishery. It seems we can no longer be sure how either sociological or ecological systems will respond to even the best planned of human interventions.

How can the planning profession adapt for survival in this age of uncertainty? To begin, Burnham's dictum might better be restated: Make not big but little plans, but make several (Figure 6.2). If there are many roads to your version of Rome, take several at once in the hope that one actually gets there. In short, planners, don't put all your egos in one stochastic basket.

In fact, in an unpredictable world, much of what we choose to do will turn out to be wrong! We therefore need multiple solutions to many planning problems and more in reserve. If such "redundancy by design" seems inefficient, just think of the resources that today serve only to prop up whole museums full of institutional dinosaurs. It goes without saying that, like mutants in the natural world, only those ideas and institutions that continue to work in some corner of the contemporary environment should be permitted to survive.

Figure 6.2

MAKE NO LITTLE PLANS . . . MAKE LOTS OF SMALL ONES

LESLIE TSE

Daniel Burnham admonished planners to "make no little plans," but Bill Rees advocates that planners make several smaller and more sustainable ones.

Fortunately, human self-awareness confers a real advantage on cultural over organic evolution. We can consciously benefit from our mistakes. To take full advantage of this, however, society must develop new attitudes toward "failure" and a new measure of success. Planners should therefore adopt the attitude that each plan is a hypothesis and each implementation an experiment. When failure is evident, it is best to admit and study our blunders rather than fearfully attempt to cover them up. We always learn more from the cold chill of failure than the complacency of success. If we openly monitor our plans and projects even as they fizzle, perhaps we can avoid repeating the same errors quite so often. This means that planners and others engaged in the implementation of policy should not develop undue loyalty to a particular project or approach. As circumstances change, we must respond with adjustments or even wholesale alternatives rather than defend the no-longer defensible. In short, conceptual agility, combined with deliberate institutional mutagenesis, is essential to ensure our social survival and evolution. To quote one wallboard graffitist: "The situation demands mutation: deviate, deviate, deviate." Some of those deviations may just pull us through (Figure 6.3).

Planning for Uncertain Futures: Thoughts for Practice

Mark Seasons

1991, Plan Canada 31(6): 31–7

Long-range planning is an exercise often characterized by good intentions, best guesses, and sometimes stubborn determination. In an environment of increasing uncertainty

Figure 6.3

Calgary took a risk planning its light rail system, but it has proven extremely popular.

and complexity, long-range planning is needed more than ever, yet is much more difficult to practise. This paper explores the confusing context within which long-range planning occurs, and describes the kinds of attitudes, skills, and techniques that planners need to understand, anticipate, and plan for uncertain futures.

Turbulence, Uncertainty, and Long-Range Planning

Those of us involved in long-range planning face significant challenges. Life in general and planning in particular are clearly more problematic in this period of rapid change, increasing turbulence, and considerable uncertainty. In a continuing situation of constraint, we face changes that in the past might have been resolved by growth[5] or by traditional solutions.

In the absence of a clearly defined and predictable future, planners must prepare for a range of possible futures. As Perks and Jamieson say: "If Canadian planners have learned anything in the past several decades, it is that there are multiple futures, multiple possibilities and multiple choices."[6] This begs the question: What kind of future are we planning for?

Clearly, the future will be considerably different from the past. We can expect continual and widespread change. Ramirez offers a useful definition of change as the process that makes outcomes mismatch expectations. Communities—their character, physical layout, and quality of life—are now, and will be, affected by the local impacts of multiple macrolevel forces of change.[7]

In planning practice, we need to consider the individual and combined effects on communities of changes in demography, society, culture, values, economy, politics, institutions, environment, and technology. We are all familiar with the high-profile issues: environmental stress, a multicultural and aging society, and the regional impacts of possible constitutional arrangements.

Of course, many other forces demand attention. For example, Gregg and Posner tracked trends that are generic, ubiquitous, and seem to have longevity:

- increasing uncertainty and discomfort about rapid change;
- increasing scrutiny of traditional institutions, leading to the development of alternative nontraditional organizations;
- clear and widespread desire for decisive leadership;
- increasing emphasis on personal and community-based empowerment;
- severe fiscal restraint by government;
- increasing concern and focused actions on the environment;
- increasing concern for the quality of life in our communities; and
- mixture of anxiety, bewilderment, and optimism as we witness continued geopolitical and economic changes.[8]

In essence, our communities are experiencing a shift from the stable state described by Schön to a state of increasing uncertainty, rapid change, and chronic instability.[9] Community residents share what Littrell calls a "queasiness" about managing organizations (and, by extension, planning communities) in this and future decades.[10] There is a compelling need to minimize risk and uncertainty in the interests of continued community stability.

Planners have to deal with "wicked problems":[11] a host of complex, interconnected problems that defy easy solutions. The more complex the planning environment, the more perceptive, adaptive, and responsive our planning techniques must be. This means that the traditional bureaucratic planning that characterizes so much practice will be necessary but not sufficient. We need long-range planning more than ever, if we do it properly. What makes long-range planning especially exciting is that the problems seem to change faster than the time allowed for solutions; we often face moving targets.[12] We therefore have greater trouble identifying what constitutes a problem to be managed or, conversely, potential opportunity to be realized; the usual points of reference often seem irrelevant.

One dominant theme in the literature concerns environmental change or turbulence. According to Friedmann,[13] an environment is turbulent when the impact of any action will yield an unpredictable outcome that threatens the organization. As Morley[14] notes, planners have to act under circumstances in which belief in the ability of the existing analytical techniques to meet these challenges has been undermined. Morley describes the symptoms of turbulence as accelerating rates of change, increasing scales of perturbations or shifts in conditions, increasing unpredictability of events, a continuing sense of crisis, frequent confrontation with problems that are too complex to be resolved through normal intervention strategies, and increasing amounts of time spent on responding to the unintended effects of previous actions.

Morley's point is not so much that the concept of change is particularly new, but that planners operating in an increasingly integrated decision-making environment must understand the nature of change to plan for and manage change. The concept of "chaos theory" has gained a certain currency. In simple terms, chaos is order without predictability. As Cartwright notes, this has significant implications for planning practice because:

> Most planners assume that, given enough information, they can anticipate what is going to happen in a particular situation and thus can determine how best to act so as to promote, defer, deflect, or divert . . . Chaos theory suggests, on the contrary, some systems are inherently unpredictable and can never be understood, no matter how much effort or expense is devoted to trying.[15]

Clearly, caution is necessary when interpreting this literature. Morley acknowledges that proponents of turbulence and uncertainty theories may exaggerate the nature of change and its effects on communities, and underestimate the adaptive capacities of communities to cope with change.[16]

Mintzberg argues that environments seldom undergo continuous dramatic change. Instead, most change is minor and temporary. Occasionally, we may experience a "gestalt shift" in the environment, when truly momentous change does take place. Such significant changes are relatively easy to detect and therefore manage. The real challenge lies in detecting the subtle discontinuities in a community's environment.[17]

Planning and Policy

Planning for the future is clearly fundamental to planning theory and practice. This future orientation is reflected in Alexander's[18] definition of planning as the deliberate activity of developing a strategy of future action to achieve desired goals. Ackoff also defines planning as something we do in advance of action: anticipatory decision making. In other words, long-range planning is supposed to show where we should go and how to get there. It leads from the present to the future.[19]

Political leaders and community managers demand pragmatic assistance with policy formulation and implementation from planners.[20] And planners have always been expected to deliver operationally meaningful assistance to decision makers by systematically collecting, interpreting, and presenting judgments on the future.

Long-Range Planning

Long-range planning is a tricky business, fraught with uncertainty. The reason is readily apparent: The future is yet to be experienced. The future is intangible. We are therefore operating in the realm of ideas, none of which can be proven right or wrong (at the moment). Our ideas of the future develop from our perceptions of how the world works and how it is changed.

How long is long-range? In practice, few people feel comfortable with looking beyond 20 years. Helmer argues that long-range refers to the period 5 to 30 years ahead.[21] Most official plans or general municipal plans are prepared on the basis of a 20-year time horizon. Yet many would argue that we need to rally around a grand vision that sets out the future 100 years hence (Figure 6.4). Indeed, some plans (e.g., park master plans such as those prepared for the Meewasin Valley Authority, the Niagara Parks Commission, or the National Capital Commission) provide this century vision. Such plans are the exception to the norm, usually in cases where large-scale public land ownership affords the luxury of long-term planning.

Typically, long-range planning has assumed continued (positive) trends and has constructed "elegant abstract conceptualizations" of the planning environment.[22] Our tradition, according to Sherman, is to forecast the future with great certainty, describe the appropriate future by systematically eliminating alternatives, and then present this view of the future to our clients.[23]

To plan for the long term, planners have used such empirical methods as simulation, optimization, and multivariate statistical modelling, all of which, as Goldberg puts it, represent simplifications of and abstractions from the "normal reality most of us would agree upon."[24]

As Perks and Jamieson note, many of these quantitative models assume relative stability and predictability of the future: patterns of behaviours that do not change significantly over time.[25] This assumption of relative stability seems to fly in the face of our recent experience of uncertainty. Why, then, should we rely on attitudes and methods that suggest that the future is generally predictable, that forecasts and projections provide reliable insights into the future? Why should our analyses assume that the future will be more of the same, only better?

Figure 6.4

What is it like for you to live here?

IMAGINECALGARY POSTCARD COURTESY OF CITY OF CALGARY. USED WITH PERMISSION

ImagineCalgary circulated postcards like this one to seek input for its 100-year vision.

Part of the answer is provided by Gimpl and Dakin, who identify a fundamental paradox in human behaviour: The more unpredictable the world becomes, the more we rely upon forecasts and predictions.[26] Christensen notes that "planners hate uncertainty as much as most other people do, and they spend their working lives trying to reduce it."[27]

We should be honest: There is something comforting and credible about visions of the future based on numbers generated from quantitative models, often relying on historical precedent. And there are other incentives: Long-range planners are hired to provide answers and certainty of results, not soft conjecture.

The Challenge for Practice

Change seems to be occurring at ever faster rates, and its implications are discernible more rapidly in our society generally and in our communities specifically. The pace and extent of change should be of particular concern to those who conduct planning exercises that assume a steady state or the continuation of past trends.

We clearly need planning practices that respond to the rapidity, complexity, and interrelatedness of change. As Michael explains, increasing awareness of these phenomena places considerable pressure on planners to confront, comprehend, and adapt to change, and upon planners who must work with communities to peer into a decidedly uncertain future.[28]

Nelson states the challenge nicely:

> It is obvious that, in a turbulent setting, marked by both speed and complexity, you need to have a wider sense of the "moment" you are in rather than in a placid and little-changing situation. In the midst of change and uncertainty, you must (a) look further ahead; (b) look wider around; and (c) understand the dynamics of change in which you are caught.[29]

Planning for change demands special skills of individuals and organizations. This may involve new attitudes and ways of thinking, different types of education and training, and different technical skills. Many of the obstacles to effective long-range planning are situational; others are clearly attitudinal. Isserman refers to planners' neglect of the future, caused by budget cuts and a climate that makes idealism, vision, and inspiration seem anachronistic; the press of daily job requirements; and the skepticism and lack of confidence in planners' ability to act meaningfully about the future.[30]

Instead of relying on conventional analytic models in organizational planning and management practice, Schön argues that organizations require a variety of skills to acknowledge, anticipate, and adapt to change.[31] Management guru Peter Drucker says that:

> ... a period of rapid change makes obsolete a good many of the old concerns or at least makes ineffectual a good many of the ways in which they have been addressed. At the same time, such a period creates opportunities for tackling new tasks, for experimentation, and for social innovation.[32]

Goldberg argues that by acknowledging that "uncertainty is itself a virtual certainty," we can begin to devise means for planning and acting adequately in the face of the unknown and unknowable.[33] Wicked problems exist in a dynamic and largely uncertain environment, which creates the need to accept risk, ambiguity stemming from different perceptions of issues, and conflicting values.[34] Accordingly, both contingency planning and the flexibility to respond to unimagined and possibly unimaginable events are necessary. A new approach to planning must therefore make both ignorance and uncertainty explicit and part of the knowledge base.

For Schön, the challenge is: first, to recognize that our society and all its institutions are in a continuing process of instability; second, to learn to understand, influence, and guide these transformations; and third, to become "learning systems" capable of managing their future evolution.[35] Michael acknowledges the need to accept great uncertainty, evaluate the present in light of anticipated futures, and be open to changes in commitments and direction.[36]

Urban and regional planning theoreticians have long followed similar lines on this issue of fostering planned change. Dyckman believes that organizations and the strategies they develop must be adaptive and fluid.[37] Friedmann calls for improved understanding about both internal and external environments, a general attitude of openness toward the future, and a quickening of response times to new learning opportunities.[38] Friedmann's work on transactive planning, with its focus on shared learning through improved communications between planner and audience, indicates movement in this interactive, integrative direction.[39]

Read sees wisdom as the act of combining the knowledge of complex interactions with careful value judgments and, on the basis of considering both of these elements, deciding the appropriate action.[40] Good judgment is defined as the mature, integrative ability to draw efficiently upon scientific knowledge, intuition, creativity, and skill. Ackoff adds that wisdom represents the ability to control what is controllable and "not to fret over what is not."[41] Wisdom implies a specialized application of these abilities in addressing important issues. Facts are available to anyone, but wisdom is not.

Preparing for the Long Term

Common themes emerge from the public administration, urban and regional planning, management, organization, and policy studies literature. Long-range planners operating in an increasingly turbulent environment need to:

- adapt and be responsive to change;
- learn from experience;
- balance creativity and accountability;
- understand multiple operating environments;

- question conventional wisdom;
- balance the short term and the long term;
- shift from mechanistic problem-solving to intuitive approaches; and
- integrate qualitative and quantitative analysis.

The degree of uncertainty and increasing complexity with which planners must contend demands new and different modes of thinking and analysis. Instead of rigidity in planning, we need flexibility and adaptability. Instead of stifling bureaucracy, we need organizational environments conducive to creativity and innovation. This challenge faces all professions. Instead of formulaic approaches to problem solving, we need wisdom. Instead of uncritical reliance on the conventional wisdom and habit, we need constant evaluation of planning attitudes and practice. We need the constant and clear communication of ideas, issues, perspectives, information, and interests within the organization (or community) and among organizations (or communities) to deal with complex problems.[42] Finally, we need to consider Isserman's criticism:

> [Planners] do not know how to study the future. Our training in the social sciences makes us too cautious, too unwilling to speculate about the future. Although we often proclaim that we are living in a period of rapid change, we have very short memories and an atrocious knowledge of history.[43]

We need an enhanced awareness of context to understand the nature of the multifaceted environments in which communities and planners function.

As Richardson and Baldwin note, no single analytical technique, organizational development model, professional training, or decision-making technology can attain all these objectives. Nor, for that matter, do planners adopt a prescribed model and follow it religiously in their daily routines. Rather, planners must adapt and apply combinations of models and theories to meet evolving circumstances and to cope with organizational realities.[44]

To be successful and perceived as such, long-range planning must be presented as a process that provides an improved context for decision making through the incorporation of qualitative and quantitative information, the explicit acknowledgment of context, the integration of policy with action, and the enhancement of creativity and innovation. Pal tells us that "insight and fresh perspectives seem to be among the main contributors to policy analysis. Rational techniques help in developing these insights and perspectives, but a more essential ingredient is imagination."[45]

Suggestions for Long-Range Planning Practice

The long-range planner's ability to function adequately in future practice will be a function of (a) the complexity of the planning environment, and (b) the planner's ability to "read" that environment. Clearly, the more stable the planning environment and the shorter the time horizon, the greater the ease with which conventional long-range planning techniques, such as population projections, might be used. In such environments, the past may very well shape the future. The future—in fact, a "preferred" future—may be easier to identify.

Given turbulence and uncertainty, however, we can assume that the stable environment will be the exception to the rule in most communities. Instead of relative stability, we can expect more complicated planning environments featuring complex dynamics of change. These phenomena will be difficult to interpret correctly. In this situation, long-range planners will need to concentrate on a planning process that constantly scans and evaluates the implications of the community's evolving environment. The product should be a continual process of planning rather than a static plan for the future.

In planning environments of increasing uncertainty, long-range planners need to:

1. Constantly (and critically) examine our perceptual framework. Our interpretation of problems or crises in our operating environments reflects personal world views, values, and training. Planning is never value free; the values that underlie analyses must be explicitly stated and reflect a process of vigorous community discussion.

2. Think in terms of multiple, rather than single, futures that evolve rapidly. We must avoid determinism and prepare instead for a variety of plausible futures, as well as the unexpected. We need a clearly defined set of fall-back positions; contingency planning is clearly an appropriate model to apply as uncertainty increases.

3. Integrate qualitative and quantitative analysis. Qualitative techniques should include scenario building[46] and creative visioning to stimulate creative thinking and to put the future(s) in clear perspective. Quantitative techniques, such as population forecasts derived from cohort survival models, are useful when linked to scenarios of possible futures.

4. Discuss, listen, and communicate effectively. Long-range planning should be a shared responsibility and community based: a process that encourages broad consultation leading to a shared vision of the future, and the delegation of responsibilities to achieve that vision. The opinions, advice, expertise, and information of community stakeholders are essential to long-range planning exercises to complement staff analysis by providing different perspectives, to build a broadly-based constituency of support for action. Citizen-run futures committees have considerable credibility. Such techniques as the Delphi model can introduce expert opinion to long-range planning research. Other techniques such as focus groups, opinion polling, or nominal group techniques can complement the research program.

5. Constantly scan the operating environments, following the strategic planning process.[47] Long-range planners should regularly review leading periodicals and related studies, and participate in networks of futurists, long-range planners, or related professions. Environmental scanning should be a shared responsibility; long-range planners need to tap into networks of organizations and individuals within the community to help read the evolving environment.

6. Develop policies, programs, and projects that are sufficiently adaptable to evolving futures. This is particularly true of community investment in "hard" services, such as transportation systems or school construction. Whenever possible, the "soft" solution (e.g., attitudes) or making better use of existing facilities is preferable to inflexible commitments.

7. Ensure credibility by designing long-range visions that include basic building blocks: the short-term, tangible, and "doable" actions that generate support for the vision and bring the vision to life. Lee's advice to avoid grandiose, complicated plans,[48] and Cartwright's support for incremental steps in long-range planning are especially appropriate in a period of uncertainty.[49]

8. Avoid the temptation to extrapolate current habits, traditions, or practices into the future. Given the pace and diffusion of change in the past, why should we assume that today's behaviour or technologies will be appropriate or desired in the future? Planners need to understand that solutions as well as issues change with time.

9. Reach beyond analysis to the synthesis of information. In other words, learn to understand the combined effect of various phenomena on communities, to see the interconnectedness of forces of change.

10. Finally, avoid the limited role of planner as technocratic or bureaucratic expert, and become more comfortable with the multiple roles of planner as facilitator and communicator. Our communities need planning professionals with the confidence

and courage to admit incomplete knowledge; the maturity to work with the community as partners in planning; and a desire to explore futures yet to arrive.

Carpe diem.

Visions of the Future

Jill Grant

1994, Plan Canada, (July) Special 75th Anniversary Issue: 99–103

In the early 1990s, I participated in a visioning session with a group of senior planning students. "Put yourself in the future. It's the year 2020, and you're hovering 500 metres above your ideal healthy community." To the melodic questions of the facilitator, each of us created an image of the future. Or was it the past? As I floated through my vision, I couldn't help thinking that I must have read too many LM Montgomery (of *Anne of Green Gables* fame) books to my children. To my surprise, though, the other participants shared basic elements of my fantasy: They too visited small, safe, agricultural-based communities with cottage industries, trees, and animals. The facilitator explained that across Canada the visioning exercise produces similar results: Everyone pictures the medieval village; no one sees cars in the future.

Nostalgia may shape the community we desire; but what is the future we expect? How can we possibly explain a dream so different from the reality we know? Perhaps the fairy tales and novels we loved as children led us to idealize the convivial communities of myth and legend. While we recognize that we cannot create this vision, nonetheless we find elements of it cropping up time and again in planning models. The garden city movement, which played such an important role in the early development of our profession, attempted to link urban areas with a countryside devoted to agricultural production; it fused an industrial infrastructure onto the traditional village. More recently, we note that the neotraditional towns and suburbs springing up across the continent pay homage to themes from the vision in their pedestrian-oriented designs. Yet, in the years that professional planners have been advising Canadians, the world has changed significantly. I suspect that a visioning exercise conducted in 1970 would have produced a vigorously modern future for discussion: Then, we expected technology would solve all our problems. Perhaps the environmental and economic crises we currently face make us skeptical and therefore nostalgic for simpler days.

Time for a reality check here. Transport mode of choice: automobile. Economy: megacorporations, international trade, unemployment, environmental crisis. We may have passed 1984 without "big brother" taking over, but technology and power constrain the future for us all. Technology simultaneously lures and frightens us. We live in an age of genetic engineering, cellular telephones, and PCB incinerators.

In our early years in Canada, town planners faced tough problems. Public health issues focused energies on planning water, sewer, and garbage collection systems. Of the 112 or so hearty souls who convened the Town Planning Institute of Canada in 1919, 68 listed themselves as engineers or surveyors. Those early planners believed that they could make healthier, safer, more prosperous communities by applying scientific principles to urban management. By and large, history has proven them correct. With the most severe problems corrected by the mid-1920s, however, planning entered a hiatus. Municipal politicians quickly adopted zoning to control land development and land values, but dismissed planning as unrealistic and unnecessary. After World War II, though, the government of Canada again sought the vision of planners to spur the nation into recovery. Social scientists flooded into the profession. Planners settled

Figure 6.5

JILL GRANT

Neotraditional communities play on our nostalgia for the past, as in this development in Windsor, Ontario.

into comfortable routines with challenging, if predictable, tasks at hand. We planned suburbs, renewed downtowns, and drafted policies. Gradually, we moved away from the grand visions. Some would say we became technocrats.

However we see ourselves, we approached the end of the millennium with our eyes veiled. What does the future hold for our communities, and for us? It's time for us to think seriously about the difficulties our communities could face in the years leading toward the centenary of our professional organization. Time to seek visions for the future.

On the economic front, most of us hope for a society of full employment, quality of life, and democratic local control. The trends make me worry, though. Unemployment and underemployment are systemic: Was the leisure society supposed to mean no work? What can we do as planners to give people hope? Corporate mergers continue apace, undermining community viability as factories downsize or close. Can planners find ways to help communities replace lost employers? Certainly, many planners promote community economic development as an option for development based on local skills and resources. Will the postindustrial society bring an information age or a new era of primary production? Some futurists suggest that social and economic stratification may increase as the few take advantage of high-tech jobs while most scrounge for subsistence. Can we ensure that Canadians will find skilled jobs? Planners have a role to play in identifying educational needs, designing skills programs, and conserving natural resources. With effective management and careful attention to priorities, communities can plan to meet the challenges they face.

On the environmental front, many of us feel especially nervous. With the certainty that graces only adolescents, my daughter described humans as a blight on the planet. What is our professional opinion on what used to be called "the population problem"? Can planners continue to accept the premise that "growth is good" without comment? Can we watch species expire, farmland urbanize, and ancient forests fall without participating forcefully in the debate about sustainable development? If planners cannot help communities resolve their problems in the next 25 years, we may find ourselves designing biodomes to keep the affluent safe from global warming and ozone depletion. Ecosystems could collapse if the worst predictions come true. To ensure the viability of our communities and our profession, planners should observe the motto of the environmental movement: Think globally, act locally. We can begin, for example, by protecting environmentally sensitive areas, encouraging energy conservation, limiting urban sprawl, and promoting community health.

On the political front, we can expect several more decades of uncertainty as we watch to see if the experiment "Canada" succeeds. Will our nation still link three seas by 2020? Will the Canadian Institute of Planners have a historic ring to it, as does the name of its predecessor, the Town Planning Institute of Canada? Today we worry about portability of CIP membership; by then, we may have shifted our concerns to portability of citizenship. As planners, we need not sit on the sidelines for these debates. For the past two decades, we have described ourselves as facilitators and communicators. We can offer our listening and negotiating skills to our communities to encourage dialogue and mutual understanding.

On the social front, we foresee many potential hazards. We may, for example, encounter continued growth in crime: Poverty breeds hopelessness. What can planners do to promote safety and reduce alienation? Few of us want to end our days designing fortified enclaves for the rich. As an organization, we could participate in debates about violence in the media and in our communities. Perhaps we should become "proactive," as our jargon advocates. What planning actions can reduce crime or improve social relationships? Crime prevention through environmental design has grown in popularity during the past 20 years; unfortunately, it only controls the symptoms of crime, not the causes. If planning cannot solve all of the problems of modern society, and clearly it cannot, then what roles should planners play in promoting community well-being? Do we have a vision of the "good society," or has the very notion grown outmoded?

Increasing rates of environment-linked illnesses and cancers are already sending us early warnings that we have to make our communities healthier places. Planning truly healthy communities takes more than signing on to well-meaning programs: It requires that we transform the way we live. Can planners offer Canadians better means for dealing with the problems of an industrial society? What are the real options? Should we stop planning roads because people see no cars in their future? Obviously, people do not intend to abandon the mobility or the sense of freedom they derive from their cars. Planners have a role to play in helping people understand the implications of the choices they make today for achieving their aspirations for tomorrow. At the same time as we keep planning roads, though, we need to divine the important messages latent in the carless vision.

Planning faces an uncertain future. Some Canadians see planning as a luxury communities can afford only in good times. We may expect to hear calls for less planning. Demands for market control have increased during the last decades, with the move to the political right. Does planning impede economic prosperity? Is it a leftover from the welfare state apparatus? Our viability as a profession may be sorely tested by the combined economic, environmental, political, and social pressures our communities will experience. If planners are to retain some utility and significance, then we must have something to offer our employers and our communities. We must believe that we offer tools to promote cooperation, prosperity, and health.

And here I return to the darkened room where I found my vision of the ideal community. My image may not be the one to push. I admit that it's hopelessly nostalgic. Nevertheless, take note of the lesson of visioning: Canadians crave a sense of community and of place. As planners, we want to provide people with good communities. No, we should not stop planning roads, but we should continue to encourage more environmentally benign options for our communities. As a profession, do we have alternative visions that can inspire us and others to sustain or create healthy communities for the next millennium? If we do not, then maybe we should begin a process to generate visions and hope for the future.

Telling Stories to the Future: Approaches to Planning for the New Millennium

Doug Aberley

2000, Plan Canada 40(1): 24–5

As I begin, I would like to make it clear that I believe planning a unique and often wonderful discipline. In a Western civilization that is all too often determined to treat the social and physical worlds simply as machines, we occupy a special intellectual and practical territory. Our fundamental purpose is to "see" the whole of a place, a region, a culture.

We perceive patterns where others are concerned only with texture. Our task is to synthesize what has been dispersed and to connect what has been divided. We work at the intersection of art and science, attempting to balance intuition, emotion, and imagination with the careful application of problem-solving techniques and complex technology. It is a profound privilege to do what we do. That said, many aspects of current planning theory and practice should be phased out, and many others deserve to become part of our day-to-day practice, and thus to be considered candidates for our new millennium resolutions.

What We Must Get Beyond: In Theory

As a neophyte of planning theory, I dedicated many weeks to searching through shelves of dusty planning journals from Canada, the United States, and Great Britain. I copied nearly 100 of these offerings and arranged them according to year and topic in a score of binders. A close reading of this potential treasure trove ultimately delivered a rather paltry reward. It is not difficult to identify some of the deepest causes of my disappointment.

The mythical tenets of rationalism continue to straitjacket our collective professional personality. Although many of the empirical tools associated with the rational planning model should be preserved, it is high time that we symbolically bury the theoretical structure in which they are arrayed. Perhaps the tenets of comprehensive planning should be carved on a stone placed on the top of a tall mountain somewhere. Every student planner should have to walk towards, and up, this mountain, making stops at a women's shelter and a First Nation community, at council meetings in villages and metropolitan centres, and at the boardroom of a transnational corporation. A single simple conclusion would be more than evident at the conclusion of this odyssey: While rational planning may be admired as a mythic goal, it does not describe how we act in the real world (Figure 6.6).

Traditionally, a tension has been cultivated between normative theorists who propose planning as it ought to be and equally persuasive advocates of descriptive theories based on planning as it is practised. Theorists from each school tend either to ignore the work of the other or to engage in slyly impolite slugging matches in the pages of planning journals. As a result, we are rarely presented with the view that all of the major theories of planning have developed through a series of reactive coevolutions. Normative rational planning begat descriptive incremental planning; descriptive advocacy planning begat normative transactive planning; and so on. We have been poorly served by theorists who do not explain continuity and connection, but rather amplify artificial differences.

Figure 6.6

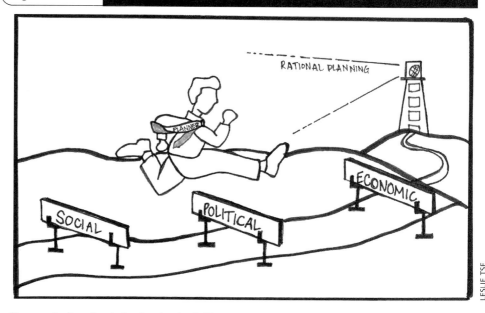

Planners aim for rational planning, but inevitably encounter

It is by now well chronicled that there are too few approaches, promulgated by too few theorists, to the problems that planners are asked to conceptualize and solve. This situation is exacerbated by the use of difficult language and styles of exposition, the repetition of tired themes, and the dominance of a few, largely male, voices. Inspirational pieces have been written, but in the eyes of a working planner the overall impression is one of obscurity and indulgence. The relatively few women, nonprofessionals, and persons of indigenous origin who do write planning theory often offer criticism instead of alternative prescription. This does not mean that planning theory should be "dumbed down"; it only means that we have to increase the size, diversity, and clarity of the chorus that we trust to sing our intellectual orientations to life.

In Practice

Almost all practising planners complain that academic planners in general and planning theorists in particular have their collective head in the clouds. As valid as this opinion may be, practising planners are open to the same metalevel of criticism. Despite good intentions, working planners often do not consistently employ the processes on which our profession is founded. In this case, our critics originate not from within our own ranks, but from the many publics that we fail to serve. Again, the factors that contribute to this crisis are not difficult to identify.

(a) *Planners as de facto police:* The highest cost of institutionalizing our profession has been that we have accepted the placement of very strict boundaries around the definition of what we do. Although we periodically venture into creative territory, most of our collective work involves making and enforcing rules. In this mode, success involves crafting legislation whose goal is to subvert any form of variation. That we benignly accept the direction to be so concerned with preserving order must colour, to our very core, the way we feel and act, both professionally and as individuals.

(b) *Planners as technicians:* Great pressure continues to be exerted on planning schools to turn out graduates who can hit the ground running with quantitative and technical skills. This kind of training is expected to take precedence over a more interdisciplinary approach to education, one that emphasizes skills involving listening, research, and many forms of communication. While no one will argue that technical skills are not critically important to learn, the teaching of GIS or decision analysis too often ignores the qualitative sensibilities that must ultimately guide their use.

(c) *Planners as mercenaries:* Many planners appear to have divided their personal systems of value from the professional tasks they perform. Perhaps this separation emanates from the simple need to work, or from a sincere belief that it is possible to turn one part of our consciousness off so that another value structure can take its place. The danger of this type of professional behaviour is that our employers see us merely as loyal soldiers, always ready to take a public participation process only so far or to put tough decisions about sustainability off for just a while longer. We readily sell our skills, but we do not persist in communicating that the stated goals of our profession go far beyond merely maintaining the status quo.

(d) *Planners as cynics...or worse*: Arguably, our worst collective fault is cynicism. We are left dangling by one too many politician or get manipulated by one too many developer who does not live up to her or his word. We get excluded from the decision-making loop by administration or engineering departments, or go too long without giving or receiving praise. The stress of this situation can culminate in a cynicism that will poison the atmosphere of any planning office. The final stage of cynicism is "group-think," a delusional condition exhibited by any cadre that feels besieged. Serious mistakes in judgment multiply, as clients, interest groups, or colleagues who would normally be served with respect are treated as enemies.

What We Must Head Toward

In the new millennium, planning theory will not be considered the exclusive responsibility of theorists. It will be widely accepted that philosophical discourse involves the intertwining of normative and descriptive elements. The process of successfully adopting these new approaches to the evolution and use of planning theory will require the completion of several related tasks.

We will have agreed that it is essential to review the existing body of planning theory and to model—in a variety of ways—the relationships that exist between them. The goal of this cooperative exercise will not be to come up with a single typology that "speaks" to every planner. Instead, many typologies will be developed, including those that show to what degree a planning theory is sensitive to gender issues, different cultural settings, or decentralized decision-making processes. Successive generations of planning students will be encouraged to survey this body of work and to add to it, as their needs or sensibilities change over time.

It will also have been accepted that, if there can be no single, uniform theory of planning that allows us to act objectively in the world, it is of paramount importance for us to be thoroughly conversant with issues related to ethics. As planners begin to operate from more transparent value frameworks, we will be healthier collectively and more honest in the professional relationships we seek to nurture.

Planning theories will increasingly invoke the philosophical concepts and vocabulary of a much wider range of academic disciplines. Dewey's "pragmatism," Habermas's "communicative action," Gramsci's "hegemony," and Melucci's "new social movements" will be familiar to all of us. While it will be a daunting task to gain this wider orientation, it will be deemed essential that we become better at the art of philosophical discourse. The resulting expression of true interdisciplinarity, made with confidence, will help to provide the "special knowledge" that our discipline has so long sought to offer.

Reforming Practice

Reforming the practice of planning in this new millennium will pose a far greater challenge than reforming the theories of the discipline. In fundamentally changing the way in which we conceptualize our purpose and act in the world, we must meet a number of challenges.

We will learn to step back from the "busyness" of our day-to-day jobs so that we can regularly appraise the larger agenda that we set for ourselves as professionals and individuals. This larger agenda will be inspired as much by our hearts as by our minds. We will also learn to share these feelings and aspirations easily with other planners, as well as with constituents of the institutions and communities in which we are employed. We will become valued as much for our clear expressions of issues related to beliefs and values as we are for the application of our technical expertise.

The idea that our professional success should be judged solely on how well we serve the mandates of our employers will be successfully challenged. In nurturing a new tradition of service we will work more regularly for "free," choosing a prudent amount of personal or consultancy time to dedicate to causes beyond the bounds of the status quo. In addition to broadening the constituency for planning in general, we will promote the spread of innovative demonstration projects that help define how ecological sustainability and social justice can actually be achieved.

Planners will reorient our practice to the central consideration that human activity is best organized within relatively small territories called "bioregions." Issues related to self-reliance in staples production, watershed restoration, efficient movement of goods, and creation of bottom-up structures of governance and development will evolve within this regional context. Planners will lead the way in explaining processes by which colonial "straight-line" boundaries will be replaced by new administrative limits that have greater respect for biophysical and cultural continuities.

Telling Stories

In my work with First Nation communities, I have often heard that the purpose of one's life and work should be the collection of stories that will someday make you a respected Elder. At this stage, you will have passed through experiences of a type and variety that engender the celebration of your worth as a repository of knowledge, humour and insight. It is my guess that stories of bylaw enforcement or official community plan revision, or tales of how you worked to maintain late capitalism, would not cut the mustard. To be valued, our stories will have to be based on a different range of experiences. How did you help bring social justice to governance? How was biodiversity reestablished as local watersheds were restored? What bravery did you attain—either purposefully or unwittingly—as old ways of doing things were confronted and replaced?

If you are unfortunate, you see planning only as a career. If you have somehow managed to keep your "private heart" alive, and have helped individuals and communities realize aspirations for social justice and ecological sustainability in whatever form, you have made your life something more. It is this joining of service to a spectrum of generally-accepted purpose that I hope will define planning in the new millennium. In this way, we will be able to participate more fully in the many processes that weave strong connections between humans and the ecosphere, between neighbours, and between cultures. We will be better able to balance what we "do" with what we "believe." Simple as that.

1. Go online to find vision statements and vision plans from Canadian communities. What commonalities and differences do you find? How realistic are the visions? What kind of a future do they represent?

2. Examine images of the future in popular media (film, TV, literature) and consider what directions they may offer planners in trying to plan for better communities.

3. Examine population forecasts from Canadian cities to identify what trends they predict and what assumptions they make. (How do forecasts reveal cultural values and expectations?)

4. Explain your thoughts on the following statement: We should plan for the future we expect to happen because the future we desire is mere fantasy.

5. In what ways does the cultural need for planning reflect perceptions about the rate and nature of social, economic, and environmental change?

6. What are the key trends that futurists today would suggest that Canadian communities should be following and preparing for?

7. What arguments can be made for planning at 5-year, 20-year, or 100-year time horizons? What challenges face communities that are working to those deadlines?

8. If people living in 1800 could scarcely have imagined how the railroad would change their world, and people living in 1900 had no idea of the potential impact of the automobile, then what techniques can we use to help imagine how technological innovation may affect our communities over the next century?

Reference Notes

1. Drucker, P (1980) *Managing Turbulent Times*. New York: Harper and Row.
2. Schön, D & T Nutt (1974) Endemic turbulence: The future for planning education. In DR Godschalk (ed) *Planning in America: Learning from Turbulence*. Washington: American Institute of Planners.
3. Alexander, C (1979) *The Timeless Way of Building*. New York: Oxford University Press.
4. Rittel, H & M Webber (1973) Dilemmas in a general theory of planning. *Policy Sciences* 4: 155–69.
5. Stewart, J (1986) *The New Management of Local Government*. London: Allen and Unwin: 3.
6. Perks, WI & W Jamieson (1991) Planning and development in Canadian cities. In T Bunting & P Filion (eds) *Canadian Cities in Transition*. (1st ed) Toronto: Oxford: 514.
7. Ramirez, R (1983) Action learning: A strategic approach for organizations facing turbulent conditions. *Human Relations* 36(8).
8. Gregg, A & M Posner (1990) *The Big Picture*. Toronto: Macfarlane, Walter and Ross.
9. Schön, D (1971) *Beyond the Stable State*. New York: WW Norton.
10. Littrell, WB (1980) Introduction. *Journal of Applied Behavioural Science* 16(3).
11. Rittel, HW & MM Webber (1973) Op. cit.
12. Ramirez, R (1983) Op. cit.
13. Friedmann, J (1987) *Planning in the Public Domain: From Knowledge to Action*. Princeton: Princeton University Press.
14. Morley, O (1986) Approaches to planning in turbulent environments. In O Morley & A Shachar (eds) *Planning in Turbulence*. Jerusalem: Magnes Press.
15. Cartwright, TJ (1973) Problems, solutions, and strategies. *Journal of the American Institute of Planners* 39: 53.
16. Morley, O (1986) Op. cit.
17. Mintzberg, H (1987) Crafting strategy. *Harvard Business Review* 65(4).
18. Alexander, ER (1986) *Approaches to Planning: Introducing Current Planning Theories, Concepts and Issues*. New York: Gordon and Breach.
19. Ackoff, R (1970) *A Concept of Corporate Planning*. Toronto: Wiley-Interscience.
20. Rondinelli, D (1976) Public planning and political strategy. *Long-range Planning* 9(2).
21. Helmer, O (1983) *Looking Forward: A Guide to Futures Research*. Beverly Hills: Sage.
22. Ackoff, R (1970) Op. cit.
23. Sherman, L (1989) Negotiated plan making and design: The importance of being uncertain. *Ontario Planning Journal* 4(1).
24. Goldberg, M (1986) Rational planning and uncertainty: Moving beyond the narrowly analytic to cope with the unforeseen and unforeseeable. In D Morley & A Shachar (eds) *Planning in Turbulence*. Jerusalem: Magnes Press: 43.
25. Perks, WI & W Jamieson (1991) Op. cit.
26. Gimpl, ML & SR Dakin (1984) Management and magic. *California Management Review* 27(1).
27. Christensen, KS (1985) Coping with uncertainty in planning. *Journal of the American Planning Association* 51: 63.
28. Michael, DN (1973) *On Learning to Plan and Planning to Learn*. San Francisco: Jossey-Bass.
29. Nelson, R (1988) *Sport, Recreation, and Fitness in the Year 2000* (Canoeing in Changing Waters): Ministerial Theme Paper. Ottawa: Square One Management: 5.
30. Isserman, A (1985) Dare to plan. *Town Planning Review* 56(4).
31. Schön, D (1987) Towards a new epistemology of practice. In B Checkoway (ed) *Strategic Perspectives on Planning Practice*. Toronto: Lexington Books.
32. Drucker, P (1986) *The Frontiers of Management*. New York: EP Dutton: 145.

33. Goldberg, M (1986) Op. cit: 47.

34. Mason, RO & I Mitroff (1981) *Challenging Strategic Planning Assumptions.* Toronto: John Wiley & Sons.

35. Schön, D (1971) Op. cit.

36. Michael, DN (1973) Op. cit.

37. Dyckman, J (1971) New normative styles in urban studies. *Public Administration Review* 31(3).

38. Friedmann, J (1971) The future of comprehensive urban planning: A critique. *Public Administration Review* 31(3).

39. Friedmann, J (1976) Retracking America: A theory of transactive planning. In WD Bennis (ed) *The Planning of Change.* (3rd ed) Toronto: Holt, Rinehart and Winston.

40. Reade, E (1985) An analysis of the use of the concept of rationality in the literature of planning. In M Breheny & A Hooper (eds) *Rationality in Planning: Critical Essays on the Role of Rationality in Urban and Regional Planning.* London: Pion.

41. Ackoff, R (1970) Op. cit.: 1.

42. Pal, L (1987) *Public Policy Analysis: An Introduction.* Toronto: Methuen.

43. Isserman, A (1985) Dare to plan. *Town Planning Review* 56: 490.

44. Richardson, IK and S Baldwin (1982) Decision-making. In K Kernaghan (ed) *Public Administration in Canada: Selected Readings.* (4th ed) Toronto: Methuen.

45. Pal, L (1987) Op. cit.: 63.

46. Godet, M (1987) *Scenarios and Strategic Management.* Toronto: Butterworths.

47. Sorkin, D, N Ferris, & J Hudak (1984) *Strategies for Cities and Counties: A Strategic Planning Guide.* Washington: Public Technology.

48. Lee, D (1973) Requiem for large-scale plans. *Journal of the American Institute of Planners* 39(3).

49. Cartwright, TJ (1991) Planning and chaos theory. *Journal of the American Planning Association* 57(1).

Chapter Seven

Planning for a Diverse Society

Embracing Diversity

Jill Grant

Diversity is a recognized and valued feature of the Canadian landscape. We expect differences between rural and urban, west and east, north and south, French and English parts of the country. Within our cities, we also see variations in ethnic origins, religion, and household types. Moreover, we expect different needs according to gender, age, income, and ability. In sum, we know that diversity defines contemporary societies, and planning must recognize and accommodate widely divergent populations.

Since the 1960s, with the backlash against urban renewal and the development of the civil rights and feminist movements, planners have recognized the imperative to accommodate diversity. Reacting to criticisms that rich, white men dominated planning, we have come a long way in trying to expand our vision of who we plan with and for. Despite the accomplishments, however, we continue to face challenges to planning good communities for all.

The articles profiled in this chapter reflect the growing interest among Canadian planners in the key themes of planning for an aging society and for increasingly multicultural cities. In their paper, Lynda Hayward and Michael Lazarowich remind us that while some active seniors enjoy comfortable incomes and can choose varied options for their golden years, others may be poor and disabled, finding life challenging in cities designed for active young people (Figure 7.1). Accommodating greater numbers of seniors means making changes in our cities to ensure good transit, mixed use, and adequate support facilities. Those interested in further reading about planning for seniors can find several other articles in *Plan Canada*.[1]

The popularity of retirement communities like Elliot Lake, described here by Glenn Tunnock, reveals the possible impact of seniors as a consumer group. Attracting seniors may offer salvation for communities losing traditional employers, such as resource industries or military bases. Taking advantage of such amenities as climate, mountains, beaches, or inexpensive housing has become a marketing option for some places.[2] A concentration of seniors can, however, coincide with land use changes that some communities find troubling: For instance, the parts of Canada with high concentrations of gated enclaves are also those with high numbers of seniors.[3]

Canada is a land of immigrants. David Ley and Annick Germain offer a portrait of the shifting composition of immigrants in our largest cities. Newcomers now arrive from different parts of the world than did immigrants a generation ago. Mohammad Qadeer shows that over time, these immigrants become more like other Canadians in their rates of home ownership and housing conditions.

Figure 7.1

JILL GRANT

Homes with front steps, like these in Garrison Woods in Calgary, may limit access for those with impaired mobility.

In recent years, we have seen that many choose to retain vital features of the culture they bring with them. Although space could not accommodate their paper, Kumar and Leung explain that Chinese immigrants in Toronto choose to congregate in ethnic enclaves in the suburbs to locate near services they want.[4] This kind of self-selected segregation reveals the development of strong social networks and communities based on language, religion, or other motivations in our multicultural society.

The pages of *Plan Canada* reflect divergent views on whether high rates of immigration are good or bad for our cities. This chapter ends with contrasting opinions: Meyer Burstein argues that immigration is essential to maintaining the competitiveness and dynamic character of Canadian cities; Grant Moore suggests that allowing most immigrants to settle in our major cities undermines urban livability.

Planning for diversity is not easy, in Canada or elsewhere.[5] Over the past decades, the *Charter of Rights and Freedoms* and provincial acts limiting discrimination have clarified rights and reduced grounds for discrimination in many ways, with significant implications for land use planning. For instance, municipalities may no longer discriminate against students in university towns by limiting the number of unrelated people living in homes in particular zones: Nonfamily households have rights, too. At the same time, though, we are learning that planning processes set up to ensure fairness of the application of the law may lack the subtlety to deal with conflicting cultural values over land uses. Laws and rules created in times when cities were dominated by immigrants from parts of Europe may create problems for recent immigrants whose sensibilities and expectations differ.

Diversity in values may lead to conflict. Canadian communities have their share of frustrating efforts to providing housing for special-needs populations. Such projects often run into community opposition, sometimes characterized as NIMBY: not-in-my-backyard syndrome.[6] Negotiating solutions that address such conflicts has become an important part of planning work.

We need cities that better accommodate seniors and persons with disabilities,[7] that are safe and functional for women and children, and that can overcome economic inequities and lack of opportunity.[8] The job of planners is, in large measure, trying to find ways to make the dream of accommodating diversity possible.[9]

A Resting Development

Lynda Hayward and Michael Lazarowich

1998, Plan Canada 38(4): 15–8

When planning for an aging population, especially for the large baby-boom cohorts, one cannot assume that it is simply a question of greater numbers. Too often, projections of future demand are based on the estimated number of older people that will be in the population. Assuming that current use patterns will continue, they pay little attention to the changing characteristics of older people and their communities. But with an increasingly diverse older population cohort, survival analysis is not enough.

With the recent shift to a community-based approach to meet the needs of seniors,[10] local planners are challenged to find ways to integrate an aging population into communities that have not been designed for this purpose.[11] Many of the ways this goal can be achieved depend on whether older residents will decide to age-in-place in their preretirement homes, make a local move within the community, or migrate into or away from the community. Planners need to know more about seniors' residential mobility choices because of the different policy implications.

Aging-in-Place

The trend in policy development for aging-in-place is to emphasize the role of formal community support services, with some acknowledgment of family and friends as caregivers, but little recognition of the related housing and land use issues. Although the community care model has gained acceptance, issues about how it will be implemented, the relationship between formal services and support from family and friends, privatization of services, and the coordination of service delivery remain contentious.[12]

The affordability and suitability of homes for aging-in-place are also important considerations.[13] Sources of supplementary income (such as home occupations, home sharing, or accessory apartments) can be issues. An additional dilemma that planners face when trying to facilitate aging-in-place is the extent to which private housing can or should be regulated to be barrier free or adaptable, as compared with a continuing policy to subsidize the rehabilitation of housing or to compensate for unsuitable accommodation with community support services.

Community composition and the availability of physical and social supports for aging-in-place within neighbourhoods are also concerns.[14] In particular, as single land use postwar suburbs mature, planners are becoming increasingly aware of the lack of enabling physical environments for the elderly in these neighbourhoods.[15]

Moreover, regional disparities in the demand for social services have developed as a result of the homogeneous age structure of such neighbourhoods.[16]

The local environment can also represent familiar surroundings, with family and friends as sources of support for seniors aging-in-place. However, an increasing social and spatial separation of the elderly from relatives and friends suggests that planners need to rethink the meaning of community for the elderly and the potential role of community building as a policy alternative.[17]

Local Mobility

Most moves made by the elderly are local. Local movers tend to have a relatively low resource level, particularly low-income, poor-health, and widowed movers.[18] The policy implications for planners wishing to facilitate local mobility vary. Since local movers remain in their greater community or neighbourhood and in the same service delivery system, their needs often appear synonymous with those who are aging-in-place. Although local moves are often thought to be primarily housing adjustments,[19] a move to a more manageable home near kin can influence the balance of the informal and formal support services used. Even a desired move can, however, be mentally and physically demanding for the elderly. More attention needs to be focused on relocation services that would help with the housing search, the move itself (financially and physically), and settling into the new residential situation.

With local mobility, housing and/or neighbourhood specialization issues become important, and the policy focus shifts to providing housing options for seniors (Figure 7.2). For example, some municipalities have encouraged the development of medium- or high-density alternatives (especially condominiums) for older homeowners, to make more low-density housing available to young families.[20] However, debate continues concerning the distribution and condition of housing stock, the "overhousing" of seniors, and their place in the housing market.[21]

Figure 7.2

JILL GRANT

Condominium housing has become popular in retirement destinations like Kelowna.

A related issue is whether housing designed specifically for seniors should be age integrated or segregated at the building level and/or at the neighbourhood scale. While some local planners emphasize the physical and social integration of older people into the community at all levels, relying heavily on age-integrated housing policies and inclusionary wording in planning documents,[22] others encourage retirement communities designed specifically to meet the needs of older people.

Although land use regulation is often a barrier to the development of housing options for seniors, it can be used to facilitate or encourage the provision of housing options for older people through, for example, as-of-right zoning.[23]

Migration

The elderly who make long-distance moves, usually just after retirement, tend to be younger, wealthier, healthier, and married.[24] With migration, policy concerns focus on issues associated with the distribution of the elderly population. Concentrations of the elderly can appear either through migration to communities rich in amenities that attract older people or through aging-in-place coupled with the out-migration of younger age groups, creating communities with very different policy implications.

The economic development potential of the in-migration of healthier and wealthier older people has gained the attention of local planners.[25] However, little is known concerning the long-term economic impact of migrants as they age.[26] There is some evidence that elderly migrants can become more dependent on formal community services, possibly because of a lack of local family and friends to provide support.[27] The growing trend of amenity moves to less accessible communities could exacerbate long-standing problems of service provision in rural communities with few financial resources.[28]

Less attention has been given to the consequences that communities may face because they are losing their younger, relatively well-off elderly through amenity migration and may be gaining older, more dependent elderly through return migration.[29] Some communities may be carrying the bulk of the burden of caring for the dependent elderly population.

Communities with elderly concentrations due to aging-in-place, coupled with the out-migration of younger age groups, would have similar concerns. However, since the out-migration of younger people is sensitive to economic conditions, these communities have an added problem: a population that ages in fits and starts. As a result, the differential residential migration of the elderly can lead to localized service demand variations. Often resource allocation is based on numbers; however, the actual requirements reflect the characteristics of the local population.[30] Communities with similar concentrations of the elderly may have very different needs. Hence, an understanding of the characteristics of the local older population can be more important to planners than a simple estimate of raw numbers.

Directions

Integrating an aging population into local communities presents complex issues that planners need to understand. Local planners need to get past the numbers and recognize that the aging population challenges both the substance and style of planning. Moreover, impacts will vary considerably with local context, in terms of both the issues that arise and their timing. Planners need to start thinking about where senior cohorts are concentrating, the local policy implications of different residential mobility choices, and how to build upon local resources (financial, physical, and social) to facilitate the integration of an aging population.

Elliot Lake: More than a Retirement Community

Glenn Tunnock

1998, Plan Canada 38(4): 23–6

"I can still recall the proliferation of trailer parks in the rough and tumble days that marked the genesis of Elliot Lake as a mining community, little realizing as a young lad that someday I would write the community's Official Plan. This "jewel in the wilderness" has evolved since the mid-1950s to become a modern, urban-centred community whose willingness to survive has transcended the demise of uranium mining as its economic mainstay."

Planner, Glenn Tunnock

When the uranium industry vanished in Elliot Lake, Ontario, the community's lifeline did, too. The population dwindled, leaving vacancies everywhere. By establishing itself as a retirement destination, Elliot Lake's economy went from being untouchable to desirable.

Elliot Lake is located in northern Ontario, 160 kilometres west of Sudbury, 200 kilometres east of Sault Ste. Marie, and 30 kilometres north of Highway 17. It consists of an urban centre surrounded by nine townships. The economic transformation of Elliot Lake stemmed from the implementation of its 1990 mission statement and concomitant eight-point goal statement. The national, and indeed international, profile of this city of 14 000 in 1997 (down to 12 000 by the 2001 census) is linked to one of those goals: "to establish Elliot Lake as a centre of excellence for retirement living." Just over 4000 seniors migrated to the city over the period from 1991 to 1996, following an aggressive campaign to market an excess supply of housing vacated by mining families. Here is the story of how it worked.

City of Elliot Lake Mission Statement

To establish Elliot Lake as a balanced and diversified community in terms of population and employment serving as a provincial or regional centre in a number of fields by building upon the present strengths of the community.

To serve and enhance the quality of life for residents through the provision of high quality and affordable public services, health and social services and educational opportunities and through the preservation and enhancement of the natural environment.

Elliot Lake was built around the uranium mining industry, with the first mine beginning operation in 1955. After 12 mines came into production, Elliot Lake became the uranium mining capital of the world, with the population swelling to 25 000 in 1960. This was followed by the first bust in 1966, when the population declined to 6600; a subsequent revitalization in the late 1970s; and a second bust in the late 1980s, when a number of contracts expired or were terminated by Ontario Hydro. Since 1990, 3500 mining jobs have been lost, along with an estimated 2800 support and secondary jobs. The final mine closed in 1996. With the population exodus, upwards of 2000 units of the 6300-unit housing stock became vacant. High vacancy rates depressed the housing market, resulting in townhouse units being sold for as little as $19 000.

The Elliot Lake of 1990 was a desolate community with a significant component of its housing stock vacant and with companies like Ontario Hydro allowing infrastructure to deteriorate. Elliot Lake had no other employer base to substitute for mining, and its relative isolation made it an unattractive setting for new economic ventures. The vacated housing supply, however, became the silver lining for the city's new economic development strategy. Although built for the mining industry, the mix and price structure of the housing stock was a "good fit" for retirement living.

A New Strategy

The retirement living concept was experimented with as early as 1987 by Denison Mines. Between 1987 and 1989, a test case was initiated through a triparty agreement between Denison, Rio Algom, and the city, whereby each party contributed $10 000 toward marketing excess housing to seniors. A market feasibility study, undertaken by the Province of Ontario in 1990, suggested that the variety of housing types and price made the housing stock a very saleable commodity to seniors. Most of the original stock had, in fact, been built by Rio Algom and Denison Mines for moderate-income families. Even today, there is very limited upscale housing in the community. Of the supply, 46 percent is singles, 35 percent is multiples (townhouses or apartments), and the balance is two-unit dwellings and mobile homes.

In 1991, Retirement Living Inc. was incorporated as a nonprofit housing corporation to market Elliot Lake as a retirement community. Start-up funds from the Province of Ontario provided $7 million, half of which was spent on acquiring 1414 units (853 apartment units, 142 townhouses, and 419 two- and three-bedroom singles and semis). The balance was used to rehabilitate the housing stock and to administer the housing program. The board of directors was intended to be broadly based, with representation from city council, the hospital board, the chamber of commerce, the mining companies, the community at large, Huron Lodge seniors' residence, and the customer base.

Marketing was carried out on a national basis, emphasizing the natural environment lifestyle of northern Ontario and the most affordable retirement program in the country. In 1997, the average price of a single detached dwelling in Elliot Lake was $51 000: an attractive feature to outsiders considering relocating to the city. Other features of the

Figure 7.3

JILL GRANT

Clair Creek Village in Waterloo is among dozens of retirement communities that appeal to seniors who choose to move for their golden years.

marketing campaign included a "community commitment" to the retirement concept and an "integrated community," featuring modern amenities including a hospital, airport, community college campus, theatre, shopping centre, and recreational facilities.

The objectives of the retirement living strategy were to:

- increase the number of seniors living in Elliot Lake;
- decrease the number of seniors leaving Elliot Lake;
- increase the level of expenditure of seniors in Elliot Lake;
- increase the number of senior-related visits to Elliot Lake; and
- increase the level of senior-related investment.

Prospective buyers or renters were invited to Elliot Lake, taken on tours of the community, and accommodated during their stay by the housing corporation. Visits quickly increased from 160 in 1990 to 2600 in 1991, and have averaged 2750 a year since. The corporation achieved close to full occupancy of its units and acquired an additional 96 units. Since Retirement Living Inc. does not regard its role as housing all of the seniors who decide to retire in Elliot Lake, the corporation has acted as a catalyst for private-sector involvement as well.

The corporation's success was enhanced through a separate private sector initiative in which outdoor recreational sports enthusiasts Wayne and Bob Izumi purchased 170 townhouse units and marketed them on a television sports program. The linkage to tourism promotion was a goal of the city's mission statement: "to establish Elliot Lake as a four-season destination for outdoor recreation." The technique worked well, and the units sold quickly. Absentee investors also snapped up units in the artificial real estate market, where a townhouse could be purchased for $19 000 and a single detached dwelling for as little as $40 000. In some circumstances, purchasers could afford to maintain a dwelling in Toronto as well as a second unit in Elliot Lake. This spawned another facet of the marketing program—selling units to "sunbirds" (e.g., Floridians) as summer homes.

By 1998, seniors (aged 50 and over) constituted 30 percent of the population of Elliot Lake and contributed $42.5 million in annual expenditures (including food, shelter, household and personal goods, travel and recreation, and income taxes). Of these seniors, some 77 percent were retired. It is estimated that every two retiree tenants represent the equivalent of one manufacturing job in purchasing power. Positive benefits included a surge in the renovation industry, with expenditures averaging better than $2 million annually.

The retirement living concept has been the signature anchor in a program for economic recovery, which has included other features, some of which are complementary to the concept. Tourism has been bolstered with the addition of infrastructure (including hiking, skiing, and snowmobile trails; boating and docking facilities; and a fire tower lookout). An art, culture, and education program saw the creation of a 359-seat theatre, the establishment of an active arts council, and a commitment to a local university degree program in fine arts. A hotel in the city has been converted to a provincial centre for drug and alcohol addiction treatment, with residents coming from all parts of the province. Elliot Lake is now an acknowledged centre for research and commercial development of environmental goods and services, and technologies linked to the decommissioning of uranium mines. The stability of the economic base is not a given, but serious interest is being shown in proposals for light industrial and office commercial development in the community—the first such interest in a decade. This complements the mission statement objective of providing for economic diversification.

The Consequences of Change

The retirement living concept was built around existing community resources: a surplus supply and diverse mix of affordable housing; infrastructure capable of supporting a population of up to 28 000; a pristine outdoor environment; a mature commercial core; a transit system; a safe living environment; and an active cultural milieu brought about by a proactive arts council. The integration of an influx of people has not been without its impacts or concerns, however. A subcommittee of the Economic Development Office tracked the impact of the retirement living concept, ostensibly to sensitize municipal authorities to the needs of seniors and to enable them to respond to needs or issues.

An issue not uncommon to retirement communities is turnover of the retirement-aged population. In Elliot Lake, Retirement Living Inc. loses about 10 percent (100–150) of its tenants annually as a result of deaths or relocations. Consequently, maintaining a critical mass of seniors in the community is part of the marketing program. Also, while isolation is a benefit to providing for a safe community, it remains a negative factor because of the distance to larger urban centres and to families. Elliot Lake is not on the main Highway 17 corridor and, consequently, operates more or less as a destination community.

Tension between new and old citizens has also been cited as a concern since long-time residents feel that there is too great a focus on seniors' needs. Youth are also caught up in this syndrome as concerts have been cancelled in deference to seniors' concerns about noise. The sense that Elliot Lake is still a one industry town—now seniors instead of mining—is also mentioned as a weakness.

While the community is endowed with medical and other community facilities, it lacks facilities to meet the needs of the "very old" and does not have the critical mass to warrant the gerontology services found in larger city communities. Interestingly, the adjustment to providing medical services for an older population has resulted in regular visits by specialists in internal medicine from larger centres: Some consider this level of service to be superior to that found in larger communities.

A current issue in the community is the lack of any long-term care units for seniors. The mission statement of the community hospital was to build 50 long-term care units in a few years, although demand from the retirement population is forecast to be more than double this target. Adjusting to the community's health-care needs will continue to be a challenge.

From a land use planning perspective, the official plan is sensitive to some of the new impacts of a community with a large seniors' population. Residential and winter city design principles are incorporated into the plan to make the community more livable for seniors, as is recognition of the necessity to redesign active park spaces for more passive recreational uses or uses that balance the needs of all ages. Mixed-use concepts are encouraged to revitalize the central commercial core and make it more of a "people place." Policies for public service facilities also recognize the institutional needs of an aging population.

The economic transformation of Elliot Lake is well in hand, largely because of the success of the retirement living concept. This has provided a degree of stability and new economic wealth for the community. It has enabled city officials to shift their focus to furthering the program for economic diversification in other directions. Seniors have been the saving grace, but Elliot Lake remains a one-industry community in which seniors have been substituted for mining. There is no illusion that this is a realistic, long-term solution. In fact, there is local reticence to refer to the community as a retirement destination. It seems fair to say that the community has reached a "seniors" saturation level. Seniors are an asset, inasmuch as they provide a building block for the broader objectives indicated in the mission statement. No direct reference is made to seniors in the statement; rather, the context is set to foster a lifestyle based on the principles of diversification.

Elliot Lake will continue to experience adjustments while harmonizing the needs and aspirations of its seniors. An example was the hiring of a seniors issues officer by the local police service to assist seniors with security concerns. Other considerations include extending the hours of the transit service, creating walking trails, providing more bilingual services, improving intercity transportation services, building a fitness and whirlpool centre, and ensuring barrier-free access to buildings and facilities. Response to these needs will depend on the resources of the community. Through implementing a retirement living concept, Elliot Lake has once again rebounded from the economic doldrums. Its long-term economic health, however, will be measured by how well the community can parlay this achievement into its objectives of economic diversification.[31]

Immigration and the Changing Social Geography of Large Canadian Cities

David Ley and Annick Germain

2000, Plan Canada 40(4): 29–32

The 1967 *Immigration Act* redrafted the social geography of immigration in large Canadian cities. In the 1960s, most immigrants came from Europe. Today, half of the immigrants who arrive each year come from Asia, and large numbers come from Africa, the Caribbean, and South America. This change has implications for the work of physical and social planners, social workers, architects, landscape architects, and other professionals in metropolitan areas such as Toronto, Montreal, Vancouver, and Ottawa-Hull.[32] Thanks to research associated with the federally-funded Metropolis Project, a great deal has been learned recently about immigrants, refugees, and their relationship with the built environment of Canadian cities.

Immigrants in Urban Areas

Recent immigration settlement has been far more focused in major cities than in the past. The 1996 census reported that 17.4 percent of Canadians were immigrants, but this group was heavily concentrated in a few locations: Immigrants make up 42 percent of the population of Toronto's Census Metropolitan Area (CMA), the highest proportion in any major centre in North America, closely followed by Vancouver at 35 percent. In Montreal, the proportion is 18 percent; in Ottawa-Hull, it is 16 percent. During 1998, three out of four newcomers landing in Canada identified one of these four cities as their destination, with Toronto cited by 42 percent (Figure 7.4).

Variations in Immigrant Class

There is also a notable variation between cities in their share of immigration categories, which affects requirements for public and private settlement services and housing. Vancouver typically receives the highest share of the economic class (65 percent of the city's arrivals in 1998 and 70 percent in 1997). In the late 1990s, these immigrants were often members of millionaire households arriving through the business immigration program. Vancouver receives the smallest proportion of refugees (5 percent in 1998).

In contrast, a much higher proportion of refugees settles in Ottawa-Hull (28 percent of all arrivals in 1998) and Montreal (20 percent), with proportionately fewer who qualify as skilled workers. Although Montreal receives its share of business immigrants, the wealthiest of the entry categories, many of these immigrants subsequently move to Toronto or Vancouver.

Toronto receives a smaller share of economic immigrants than Vancouver (58 percent of arrivals in 1998) and a smaller share of refugees (11 percent) than Ottawa-Hull or Montreal. The remaining major entry group, the family class, where family

Figure 7.4

Businesses catering to and employing immigrants add to the diversity of our major cities, as here in Toronto.

sponsorship and a welcoming social network offset some initial settlement needs, is distributed more evenly (25 to 30 percent in 1998) among the four CMAs.

Changing Immigrant Origins

The geographical origins of immigrants display further diversity between metropolitan areas. Country of origin affects the ease with which newcomers can integrate and the types of services they need. The ability to speak English or French, for example, has been shown to correlate significantly with economic achievement.

Toronto has the most diverse immigrant origins. Its overall profile shows the effects of long-term European immigration, particularly from the United Kingdom and Italy, and more recent immigration from the rest of the world that includes large numbers from Hong Kong, India, and China (Table 7.1). Among more recent arrivals, the top five countries of origin are in Asia; the next five include one European country, three Caribbean nations, and a sixth Asian country.

Table 7.1	**Toronto: Total and Recent Immigrants (1991–96) by Place of Origin**			
	Total Immigrants		Recent Immigrants	
	(n= 1,772,905)	100%	(n= 441,035)	100%
1	UK	8.9%	Hong Kong	11.0%
2	Italy	8.3%	Sri Lanka	8.3%
3	Hong Kong	6.3%	China	8.0%
4	India	5.6%	Philippines	7.5%
5	China	4.9%	India	7.5%

Table 7.2	Vancouver: Total and Recent Immigrants (1991–96) by Place of Origin			
	Total Immigrants		Recent Immigrants	
	(n= 633,745)	100%	(n= 189,660)	100%
1	Hong Kong	13.6%	Hong Kong	23.6%
2	UK	11.9%	China	14.2%
3	China	11.5%	Taiwan	11.8%
4	India	8.4%	India	8.5%
5	Philippines	5.5%	Philippines	7.2%

Data on 1998 arrivals indicate an increase in the number of Asian immigrants: Asian nations make up eight of the top ten countries of origin. Only Jamaica has English as the mother tongue, and the only European nation is Russia. A distinctive feature of the Toronto CMA is the high level of suburbanization of immigration. The concentration of immigrants is higher in a number of inner suburbs than in the old City of Toronto.

Vancouver, with its Pacific Rim location, developed an Asian profile earlier (Table 7.2). The 1996 census found that the top six countries of origin for immigrants arriving in the 1990s were Asian, and that Asians made up 80 percent of all immigrants, with only the UK and US representing significant earlier sources of immigration. The mix of old and new source countries shows up in the overall enumeration of immigrants, where the UK remained in second position as of 1996, even though immigrants from the UK, like some other European populations, are aging and declining in number.

The 1998 update showed little change in these trends, although China has replaced Hong Kong in the first rank, just as it has in Toronto. During the 1990s, immigrant districts expanded into suburban communities. There is a concentration of Chinese, mainly from Hong Kong, in Richmond, and of immigrants from India, principally Sikhs, in North Surrey.

Quebec has one of the highest rates of immigrant concentration, with almost 90 percent of the provincial total located in the Montreal CMA. And unlike Toronto, immigrants are largely concentrated in the city itself and its older suburbs. Although the overall immigrant share of 18 percent is lower than those of Toronto and Vancouver, the countries of origin are distinctive, with a clear francophone and Latin emphasis among the total immigrant population in 1996, when the leading immigrant sources included Haiti, France, Lebanon, and Vietnam, as well as the southern European nations of Italy, Greece, and Portugal (Table 7.3).

Table 7.3	Montreal: Total and Recent Immigrants (1991–96) by Place of Origin			
	Total Immigrants		Recent Immigrants	
	(n= 586,470)	100%	(n= 134,535)	100%
1	Italy	12.3%	Haiti	7.4%
2	Haiti	7.3%	Lebanon	7.1%
3	France	5.5%	France	5.6%
4	Lebanon	4.5%	China	4.9%
5	Greece	3.9%	Romania	3.9%

Table 7.4	Ottawa-Hull: Total and Recent Immigrants (1991– 96) by Place of Origin			
	Total Immigrants		**Recent Immigrants**	
	(n= 161,885)	100%	(n= 38,045)	100%
1	UK	14.1%	Somalia	8.7%
2	Lebanon	6.2%	China	8.4%
3	US	4.9%	Lebanon	7.7%
4	Italy	4.7%	Vietnam	3.9%
5	China	4.2%	India	3.8%

To a lesser extent, this trend is also noticeable among those who arrived in the 1990s, although Asians have become well established and now make up five of the top ten sending countries. But the linguistic and cultural uniqueness of Montreal has been maintained: In 1998, Algeria and Morocco, nations with few representatives in other cities, emerged in second and seventh ranks (with France in first position).

Ottawa-Hull has the lowest immigrant population among the four CMAs, lower even than the national average. Nonetheless, in 1996, the Ottawa-Hull CMA was home to more than 160,000 immigrants (Table 7.4). The important role of refugees in the metropolitan profile is highlighted by the ranking of arrivals in the 1991–96 period, led by Somalia, and including Yugoslavia, Iran, and Ethiopia in the top ten list. This gives Ottawa-Hull a singular configuration among Canadian cities.

Aside from those who live in the traditional settlement area in the inner-city district west of Bronson Avenue, immigrants are dispersed in a number of nodes throughout the Ontario part of the region. Immigrant numbers are much smaller on the Hull side of the Ottawa River.

Immigrant Segregation and Multiethnic Neighbourhoods

Residential segregation has always been a feature of Canadian cities. Segregation not only creates poorer areas like Vancouver's Downtown Eastside and immigrant areas like a Little Italy or a Chinatown, but it also affects established, wealthier groups in districts such as Rockcliffe or Westmount. The expansion of new immigrant communities in Canadian cities in the past generation has contributed to a new round of discussion. Should we be concerned that many immigrants tend to settle in ethnocultural clusters?

First, although segregation does occur in Canadian cities,[33] it seldom approaches the high concentrations noted in black-white studies in the US. Second, we should remember, as Peach has noted, that there is both "good" and "bad" segregation.[34]

Good segregation is the concentration of ethnocultural groups characterized by close social ties and networks of support provided by the extended family, clubs, and places of worship. These institutions provide a nurturing and welcoming community by helping newcomers find shelter and employment within the ethnic economy, offering advice and experience for successful settlement, and sustaining homeland culture through language, religion, and diet. Usually, these communities provide a transitional home, leading after some years, at most a generation, to some degree of integration.

A few groups, including Jews and Italians, continue patterns of segregation in second-generation suburban districts. For some groups, continued residential segregation exacts a penalty. Studies in Vancouver have shown that residential concentration of ethnic groups may be associated with other forms of separation, including occupational segmentation, in-group marriage, and mother tongue retention, and that all of these forms of separation correlate negatively with personal income.[35] In other words, there is a "bad" consequence of segregation: Prolonged spatial segregation can impair economic success.

Because segregation levels in Canadian cities are typically moderate, many immigrants share residential space with others of different national origins. Immigrant settlement is not so much a mosaic of "little homelands" as a subtle model of ethnic diversity.[36] The diversification of recent immigration has created more cosmopolitan landscapes and widespread multiethnic neighbourhoods.

Thirty years ago, for example, Parc Extension, a district of 30 000 people in the middle of the Island of Montreal, was two-thirds Greek. Today, Greeks make up only a third of its population, which includes Indians, Haitians, Sri Lankans, and Latin Americans, among others. Chinatown remains near Old Montreal, but the proportion of Chinese people in the area has declined. The proximity of others of diverse origins is now the daily experience of many inhabitants of both central neighbourhoods and the suburbs. In such districts, the real minorities may be the so-called "charter" groups: Canadians of French or British ancestry.

Cohabitation in common spaces, defined both physically and symbolically, has become a dominant feature of Canadian urban multiculturalism, whether the contacts are positive or conflictual. Contemporary urban planning needs to accommodate this changing social geography of our major cities.

Urban Planning and Multiculturalism: Beyond Sensitivity

Mohammad A Qadeer

2000, Plan Canada 40(4): 16–8

Put yourself in the shoes of a senior planner in a Canadian municipality and imagine how you and your department have responded to the needs of ethnic minorities, immigrants, and other culturally distinct groups. Furthermore, ask yourself what approaches you could have followed to be more responsive to their needs. You will probably acknowledge the need for more culturally sensitive planning, but chances are you have no specific ideas about how to achieve this goal. You may say: "Here and there, we could have been more accommodating, but we can do only what the planning and municipal acts allow and what our political bosses approve."

Planners feel that they are sensitive to cultural and social differences and that planning policies are, by and large, unbiased. Yet the literature on multiculturalism and urban planning is full of admonitions about sensitizing planners to differences between cultures, lifestyles, and genders.[37] The perceptions of theorists about urban planning's response to cultural differences are distant from planners' feelings about their work. Much of the current academic debate is driven by the assumption that urban planning is characterized by systematic bias, dominated by the culture of the majority, and based on a belief in universal norms and rational decision models. Is this assumption valid? What can be done within the scope of the institutionalized mandate of urban planning to (further) tailor planning policies and processes to cultural differences?

What Is Multiculturalism?

Multiculturalism is more than the tolerance of people with different beliefs, behaviours, and lifestyles. It is a vision of nation-state and society in which different cultural groups and communities coexist as equals, entitled to their ways of life in their private realms but bound to common institutions in the public sphere. Cultural diversity within the private sphere also implies a reconstructed public sphere based on common institutions that incorporate the values and ideals of all citizens; in other words, a new social contract.[38]

A multicultural society (and state) is a community of communities. Its many cultures may be more evident among immigrants and ethnic groups, particularly those from different racial groups, but that multiplicity is not limited to these communities. Canada's *Multiculturalism Act* acknowledges "the freedom of all members of Canadian society to preserve, enhance and shape their cultural heritage." In urban planning, multiculturalism means creating urban forms, functions, and services that promote a plurality of lifestyles and sustain diverse ways of satisfying common needs. Have Canadian planning systems fulfilled the demands of multiculturalism?

Multiculturalism and Urban Development

In the growth and development of cities, citizens' needs are met through market processes, backed and regulated by institutionalized urban planning and other public policies and programs. Culturally determined differences in people's needs come into play in two ways: in the provision of health, education, employment, and recreational services; and in the delivery of sites and community services through the urban planning system.

The Canadian urban planning system's effectiveness in meeting diverse needs for housing, locations, sites, and services can be seen in the outcomes. The urban landscape is a tapestry of Chinatowns, Italian villages, Indian bazaars, and Asian malls. Community facilities also reflect diversity: soccer fields, cricket pitches, Korean retirement homes, South Asian housing cooperatives, mosques, *gurdwaras*, and Chinese churches are all part of Canadian cities (Figure 7.5). The market may have delivered these multiple forms of development, but the planning systems certainly facilitated and approved them.

Noteworthy is the development of varied communities in suburbs rather than in inner-city ghettos. Richmond in the Vancouver Region and Markham in the Greater Toronto Area (GTA) are two examples of the cultural change that has swept through

Figure 7.5

Planning to accommodate mosques, like this one in Scarborough, presents new challenges.

Table 7.5	Housing Conditions of Immigrants				
Non-immigrants		Immigrants who arrived:			
	Total	Before 1976	1976–85	1986–90	1991–96
% At or above housing standard	71	70	53	40	31
% Owners	67	76	66	50	31

suburban municipalities. Both have been transformed from prosperous but stolid suburbs to thriving multicultural communities within the past 15 years. Even the high-tech information economy has been affected by multiculturalism. Silicon Valley North (Kanata and Nepean in the Ottawa-Carleton Region) thrives on the labours of new Canadians from Russia, India, and China, and on the investments of immigrant entrepreneurs. Some 27 mosques have been developed in the GTA, many after a rough ride through local councils and citizen meetings.[39]

Even evidence of the housing conditions of immigrants indicates integration. Table 7.5 shows that, as immigrants settle, their housing conditions become more like those of Canadian-born residents. The housing conditions of new immigrants are generally poorer than those of established Canadians, but major improvements are attained with each decade after arrival.

This evidence suggests that the planning system has been successful in accommodating cultural differences in its typical incremental, procedural, and reactive ways, not through comprehensive policy initiatives. Yet, for many minorities, success has come only after difficult public hearings, political battles, and intercommunity confrontations characteristic of the Canadian planning system.

Because the planning process has evolved as the arena for the battle of interests, minorities are left feeling discriminated against, even when they succeed in getting approval for developments of their choice. The paradox of multicultural developments is that the achievements are more positive than the social, financial, and emotional costs of the process of getting them.

Institutionalizing Pluralistic Planning

Three critical issues need to be addressed to institutionalize the practice of pluralistic planning:

a) Planning by persons, or by functions and use

At the heart of culturally sensitive planning is the issue of whether urban planning should be based on persons or on use and functions. For example, should funeral homes not be allowed near Chinese residential areas, but approved if the neighbours come from a different ethnic group? This question highlights the dilemma of attempting to create different policies for different people. The Ontario Municipal Board has ruled in one case that "Personal preconceptions are matters that cannot be addressed in a planning context."[40] The board interprets the compatibility of land uses in terms of impacts on uses, functions, and forms of buildings. The way to accommodate cultural differences is to design policies, criteria, and norms that take diverse needs into account. There would be more inequities, to the disadvantage of minorities, if planning were applied selectively.

b) Reconstruction of planning principles and common institutions

The key to accommodating the cultural and social diversity of citizens lies in comprehensive planning and policy development. For example, our current notions and norms regarding such things as parking requirements, traffic impacts, compatibility of land uses, and service provisions are embedded in the social patterns of the dominant culture. They should be thoroughly reviewed. Should planning policies define the size and structure of households? Are funeral homes compatible with residential neighbourhoods? Do Asian malls generate more traffic because they have restaurants as anchors? Such questions need to be researched and examined from a multicultural perspective to formulate policies and norms that serve the common interests of all. (For example, funeral homes could be dealt with by reevaluating their compatibility as a land use and by revising zoning and site standards to reflect diverse interests concerning their locations.) Pluralistic planning can best be promoted in this way, and not by tailoring policies to clients' cultural backgrounds at the project level.

c) Reforming the planning process

The planning process (particularly project reviews and approvals) largely proceeds in an adversarial way. It brings different interests into conflict, causing public controversies and costly delays and often leaving all involved dissatisfied and dazed. The process is particularly harsh on the politically weak or unorganized and on minorities, as it tends to be driven by the politics of local power structures and vote banks. To accommodate cultural differences, the planning review process should be redesigned. Implementing a code of ethics for public discussions and entrenching the provisions of procedural nondiscrimination and human rights in planning acts may help ensure a fair hearing for all interests, powerful as well as not so powerful. Civility and cultural sensitivity need to be instituted in the public discourse about planning matters. The planning approval process is already under review because of its costly delays, complexity, and uncertainty as a part of the regulatory reform programs. It should also be reviewed for procedures and rules regarding public discussions, including what can and cannot be brought up in public hearings.

Reconstructing Common Institutions

Multicultural urban forms are common in Canadian metropolitan areas. They have emerged one by one, mostly through market transactions that have been accepted or approved by planning systems. Canada's national multiculturalism policy and *Charter of Rights and Freedoms* have helped ethnic groups carve out distinct private spaces. The planning system has supported the expression of cultural differences in the private realm. Yet the success of multiculturalism comes slowly for immigrants. Many new arrivals, particularly those whose poverty impedes their integration, have to wait a long time to enjoy material and social equality.

The challenge of multiculturalism lies in restructuring common institutions, rethinking planning principles, and realigning planning models, assumptions, and criteria. A multicultural approach to planning has yet to evolve. It entails reconstructing common institutions, not merely ensuring that planners or planning bodies respond sympathetically to differences in needs on a case-by-case basis.

Managing Multicultural Issues in Cities　　POINT

Meyer Burstein

2000, Plan Canada 40(4): 14–5

Canada leads the world in its efforts to recruit immigrants to build a diverse, pluralistic society. For this bold national "experiment" to succeed, governments at all levels will need to demonstrate leadership, creativity, and the courage to work together to address issues that cross jurisdictional boundaries.

Nowhere is this task more evident than in our cities: in urban neighbourhoods, in schools, in the workplace, in hospitals, in playgrounds, and on sports fields. How we manage growing diversity in our cities (themselves undergoing rapid economic and structural change), the balance we strike between the needs of newcomers and those of the host population, and the ways in which we create access and opportunity will be crucial to the success of our society and to Canada's place in the global economy.

Growing and Nourishing Global Cities

Many analysts hold that the economic prospects of countries will depend on the ability of major cities to compete in the global marketplace. To be competitive, these cities will need the capacity to assemble and retain financial and human capital. For Canadians, this means that our future will likely depend on the ability of Montreal, Toronto, Vancouver, Calgary, and Ottawa to attract both investment and skilled knowledge workers, including the highly educated and skilled immigrants in demand throughout the world.

Recruiting and retaining these workers, along with other highly skilled entrants, will require the cooperation of federal, provincial, and municipal policy makers. Ministries of finance, industry, human resources, citizenship and immigration, education, municipal planning, and municipal development need to collaborate to create a fiscal, social, and physical environment that makes Canadian cities more appealing than cities in other countries to the best and brightest immigrants and their families.

Managing the Gap

As Canada and other countries seek to offset demographic decline by admitting larger numbers of immigrants, the gap will grow between cities that are home to a polyglot, multiracial, multiethnic citizenry and smaller urban centres that are more homogeneous (Figure 7.6). This divide will express itself in virtually every aspect of private and public life.

Canada can expect to face increasingly differentiated demands for government services and programs. Everything from how to use public space, through health care, education, and the projection of Canada's commercial and political interests abroad may be affected. Governments will be challenged to manage the "large city versus rest of country" gap to build support for diversity policies and the potential benefits they yield.

Enhancing Civic Engagement and Participation

The ability of countries to invest in public infrastructure and national endeavours depends on trust, shared values, and common expectations. Improved communications, cheaper transport, and relaxed access to citizenship benefits may, however, produce transnational communities whose allegiance to the particular nation-state is weaker than it was when mobility was more circumscribed. The result may be diminished interest in public investment that does not clearly benefit the community in question. The challenge for governments is to promote civic engagement and shared citizenship, a task that requires national, regional, and local institutions to change rules and behaviours to foster belonging and improve access to services by new entrants and members of diverse communities.

Ending Transgenerational Poverty

There is evidence of spatially concentrated, transgenerational poverty among ethnic, religious, and racial minorities in our cities. This departs from historic patterns that saw new groups arrive, struggle, and find success, if not in the first generation, then through their children. If these problems persist, all levels of government need to collaborate to

Figure 7.6

With a large Asian population, cities like Vancouver have come to take on a truly international feel.

reverse such development. At all costs, Canada must prevent the development of urban ghettos and the formation of a visible underclass. In particular, educational and housing policies need revamping.

Combating Racism and Intolerance

Public willingness to invest in the programs and services that contribute to successful integration will determine the extent to which we end up living together or living apart. Surveys tracking public attitudes and empirical studies of economic and social integration among immigrant and visible minority populations suggest that Canadians should not be complacent.

Government plays an important role in creating acceptance, providing access to opportunities, and educating newcomers and host populations alike to appreciate cultural, racial, and religious differences. This has implications for federal, provincial, and urban agencies.

Increasing the Capacity of Municipalities to Integrate Minorities

The growing importance of cities has created new challenges for local government. Cities will need to improve their capacity to think strategically and to plan effectively around immigration issues. Meetings between municipal planners and developers, including the urban forum workshops, suggest that this process has already begun.

Changing the Focus

Until recently, only the federal government and Quebec played substantial roles in producing diversity through control over immigrant admissions and managing diversity. Yet such decisions have significant and far-reaching consequences for the pattern of services and for the fiscal position of provinces and cities. To get a better handle on these impacts, provinces have taken a greater interest in immigration management since the early 1990s. It would not be surprising to see Canadian cities follow suit.

Cities in some jurisdictions have been outspoken on immigration issues. New York City has been a vocal proponent of immigration, crediting it with renewal of the urban core. Some California cities have taken a different position, arguing that the negative effects of immigration outweigh the positive ones. Many European cities have participated in migration-related issues, often because the cities have sole or primary responsibility for service delivery.

Although Canadian cities have been absent from deliberations on immigrant admissions, they have been vocal advocates of immigration and diversity. They have responded to changing population structures with, among other things, programs aimed at promoting equity, nondiscrimination, and social justice. Adaptive measures have also begun to affect mainstream city functions like transport, public health, zoning, and economic development.

The growing interest by all levels of government in better managing migration and diversity, coupled with growing competency at the municipal and provincial levels, is a necessary but not sufficient condition for cooperation. What is needed is consensus on the critical issues confronting Canadian cities, and recognition that successful management requires a strategic response that transcends jurisdictions.

Immigration: The Missing Issue in the Smart Growth Deliberations   `COUNTERPOINT`

Grant Moore

2004, Plan Canada 44(1): 32–5

In the Greater Toronto Area (GTA), managing growth and planning for the region-wide transportation, water, and sewage infrastructure is a prime concern of urban planners and elected officials. And the main reason for the rapid growth in the GTA is that fully one-half of Canada's yearly intake of immigrants settles there. Immigration is responsible for 75 percent of the population growth in Greater Toronto, with natural increase and internal migration accounting for 25 percent. This could have a significant impact on urban form, since Canada Mortgage and Housing Corporation analysis indicates that immigrants will drive the future demand for housing in the GTA, and that single-detached housing is the preferred type.

The Province of Ontario has taken two initiatives to deal with growth in the GTA. The Greater Toronto Services Board was established in 1999 with membership from 41 municipalities. The board's mandate was to coordinate action on issues confronting the GTA. In 2002, the government established the Central Ontario Smart Growth Panel, one of five such panels in the province. Much of the work of the smart growth panel builds on that of the services board.

Dealing with Growth: What Are the Options?

Three options for dealing with the forecast population growth in the GTA can be readily identified: maintaining the status quo, reducing immigration levels, or leaving immigration levels unchanged while attempting to direct immigrants away from the GTA. Maintaining the status quo is the option implicit in the work of both the services board and the smart growth panel. It accepts a forecast population increase of 2.3 million in the GTA by 2026 and the related need for infrastructure upgrades. Also required are transit-supportive land use policies to integrate compact mixed-use development. The nature of the population growth is not an issue addressed in either the services board or the smart growth reports.

Reducing immigration levels is an option that distinguishes between natural growth (births among existing residents) plus internal migration and growth through immigration. Since natural growth and migration cannot be controlled, reducing immigration levels is identified by some as a means of relieving growth pressures.

Maintaining immigration levels but attempting to direct immigrants away from the GTA was a proposal made in 2002 by the federal Ministry of Immigration to "fast track" applicants who agree to locate outside of Canada's major cities. The previous Ontario government attempted to seek a made-for-Ontario agreement with the federal government to ensure that more immigrants to Ontario settle outside of the GTA.

What to Do?

The status quo option is reasonable under current circumstances. Immigration is a federal responsibility, and Ottawa has given no indication of plans to reduce Canada's yearly intake. Neither is there, at present, any organized movement clamouring for change. And many of the initiatives emerging from the smart growth deliberations such as denser forms of residential development and restrictions on the expansion of suburban infrastructure at public cost should be considered anyway. The glaring weakness of this option is a lack of any discussion of whether continued rapid growth in the GTA is good public policy. The brochure *Ontario Smart Growth: A New Vision* cheerfully asserts that "growth is good," since it "generates new businesses, new jobs and the revenue we need to support . . . the programs we equate with a high quality of life." Nothing more is said on this issue as though growth-is-good is a truism requiring no further elaboration.

However, it is not at all clear that the recent population growth (an annual average of almost two percent from 1992–2002) and economic growth in the GTA (the TD Bank estimates real annual gross domestic product growth of four percent) have had any meaningful payoff for the average citizen. This same period witnessed $10 billion provincial budget deficits, unprecedented confrontation between government and public sector unions, congested highways, and longer commuting distances for workers. The City of Toronto exists in a state of financial exhaustion, and, in 2002, the provincial government suspended the trustees and forced the Toronto District School Board to adopt a balanced budget. In the hinterland, the school boards in Durham, Peel, and York regions struggle with millions of dollars of unfunded capital projects and acres of portable classrooms. Those looking for good news in income data will not find any. Despite all the talk about government efforts to boost the standard of living of Canada's poorest, the gap is actually increasing.

Other Options

Reducing immigration levels is the most obvious way of controlling growth in the GTA. Certainly, the rationale for a large-scale Canadian immigration program has come under increased scrutiny (some would say attack) in recent years. Such authors as Daniel Stoffman, Martin Collacott, and Diane Francis have argued that much of the existing justification for current immigration levels is unfounded. Stoffman, the coauthor of *Boom, Bust, and Echo*, argues that economic growth does not depend on immigration, and that a mass influx of young immigrants is not required to support retired baby boomers.

Most residents of the GTA are familiar with highly educated but unemployed/underemployed immigrants, their situation usually explained by a lack of Canadian work experience, language difficulties, or professional qualifications not recognized here. But a logical and obvious explanation, in many cases, may be that their services are not required. Similarly, although proponents of employment equity policies claim that immigrants, particularly visible minorities, suffer from individual and systemic bias related to race, colour, ethnicity, and place of origin, it is equally plausible that less insidious and conspiratorial reasons account for the difficulties immigrants and visible minorities experience in the labour force; that is, jobs and promotions are hard to come by for just about everyone.

Certainly, some highly skilled immigrants are required to fill jobs in sectors of the economy where specific shortfalls exist, but the record here is weak. After having received almost two million newcomers in the past decade, shortages of family physicians and nurses in rural areas persist, and the automotive and construction sectors continue to report shortages of young apprentices in the skilled trades. If immigration were the solution, these problems should have been resolved years ago.

Two significant obstacles prevent governments from reducing immigration levels, even if that may be warranted on the basis of objective analysis. The first obstacle is the emotional dynamic. In Canada's largest cities, immigration policy and multiculturalism are sensitive issues, with charges of racism and prejudice always lurking, ready to pounce on unwary commentators. Municipal officials and journalists question the status quo at their peril: most never do. Federal political leaders may be reluctant to scale back immigration levels for fear of the backlash here and abroad.

The second obstacle involves Canada's stature in the world community. Lacking an exportable popular mass culture or the military and economic clout to assert itself as a key player on the world stage, Canada has contributed to the community of nations by taking in refugees fleeing wars or persecution and providing immigrants with the opportunity for a better life. In this way, immigration functions as a component of Canada's foreign aid activities. No doubt, Canada's reputation for tolerance and fairness owes, in part, to liberal and welcoming immigration policies.

Leaving immigration levels unchanged but directing immigrants away from the GTA may have the potential to be an attractive win-win option. For the federal government, this option avoids the political difficulties encountered in making wrenching, wholesale changes to existing immigration policy. Similar to the recent shift away from family reunification applicants toward those who score high on education, job skills, and fluency in English or French, this option can be seen simply as a fine-tuning of existing policy. For the Ontario government and GTA municipalities, the capital investment in new infrastructure otherwise required could be scaled back or implemented over a longer time frame.

The City of Toronto, in particular, would benefit from a reduced intake of immigrants. High immigration levels have been, indisputably, a significant contributor to poverty in the city and to the never-ending shortage of affordable housing. With almost 40 000 people on the waiting lists for subsidized units, there will never be enough low-cost accommodation if Toronto continues to receive thousands of immigrants each year.

New immigrants themselves may benefit in locating to smaller communities, where rental accommodation is cheaper and housing far less expensive. In simple economic terms, it makes no sense for immigrants, particularly those who are poor or unskilled, to take up residence in areas where the cost of living is the highest in the nation.

Finally, Canada's smaller cities and towns could benefit handsomely from an influx of younger, skilled, and energetic newcomers. The business activities of entrepreneur-class immigrants that do not, of necessity, require a GTA location could enhance smaller centres by providing new jobs and economic stimulation.

Is Growth Good?

Several things are clear with respect to development in the GTA, smart growth, and Canadian immigration policy. The first is that a much better public debate is needed about the notion that growth is good. Is it the quantity or the quality of growth that matters? Where will smart growth lead in terms of quality of life if, over the next 25 years, a population equivalent to the existing city is added to the GTA?

Immigration trends and immigration policy must be discussed. How can public support for smart growth develop if the cause of rapid growth in the GTA (and the cost) is scarcely mentioned and options for dealing with it are not explored?

"Immigrant dispersal" has a theoretical attractiveness, but the key issue is implementation. Dispersal will not be easy: The unimpeded growth of the major immigrant groups in the GTA over the past 30 years has created strong incentives for future newcomers to locate there. Coercive measures are not available. Section 6(2) of the *Canadian Charter of Rights and Freedoms* dealing with mobility rights states, "Every citizen of Canada and every person who has the status of a permanent resident of Canada has the right: a) to move and take up residence in any province; and b) to pursue the gaining of a livelihood in any province." Still, it is worth pursuing strategies to encourage immigrants to choose smaller communities.

If current trends continue, the rapid growth and ethnocultural diversity in the country's three or four largest cities will only accelerate. Canada will truly become, in the words of Diane Francis, "a handful of city-states." Meanwhile, other regions will experience, in varying degrees, slow growth/stagnation/decline and be characterized by an aging, less diverse population, while suffering out-migration of younger residents to larger centres. The lifestyle, experiences, and rhythm of everyday life in these areas will become increasingly disconnected from that of the largest cities.

Planners with an interest in regional development will want to follow these issues closely. Confederation has historically been a tenuous, fragile arrangement in Canada. The most notable threat to the country's unity has been the ebb and flow of separatism in Quebec; but there are many other strains—Western alienation, vast geographic distance separating major population settlements, and the historic economic challenges faced by the Maritime provinces, to name a few. If democracy in Canada becomes simply a "numbers game," existing regional grievances may potentially deepen as the agendas of the largest rapidly growing urban conglomerations increasingly marginalize the rest of the country. Dealing with this challenge requires a full and unfettered public debate of all relevant issues, and the energy and creativity of Canadians in the search for solutions.

Study Questions

1. Concerns about addressing diverse needs began with the civil rights movement and feminist movements of the mid-twentieth century. Consider whether contemporary urban planning does an adequate job of meeting the needs of the widest range of community members. Frame your response in terms of the requirements of a particular group, such as those with impaired mobility or impaired vision, or who are psychiatric survivors, frail and elderly, or homeless.

2. Burstein argues that immigration is essential to the long-term competitiveness and success of Canadian cities internationally, while Moore suggests that immigration policies undermine the livability of rapidly growing urban regions like Toronto. Discuss their contrasting views on immigration to our largest cities, and consider the role urban planning may play in managing immigration issues.

3. By looking at examples of land use disputes adjudicated at municipal or appeal boards, consider how the *Canadian Charter of Rights and Freedoms* and provincial nondiscrimination legislation may be affecting land use planning principles and practices.

4. If a particular ethnic group's spiritual values prohibit placing cemeteries near residential areas, is that appropriate grounds for changing land use designations? Discuss the pros and the cons of the arguments.

5. Do Canadian communities adequately address the mobility needs of persons with disabilities? How could we plan better inclusive communities where people can age in place through the range of their abilities?

6. Should planners be accommodating requests for specialized communities for senior citizens, or should we seek to build inclusive communities for all ages? What factors make older residents consider segregated lifestyle communities?

7. Examine your home community to find evidence of the way that its immigration history and pattern of diversity is reflected in the built form and organization of the place.

8. How do the differing immigration patterns in our major cities affect the kinds of planning issues that those communities need to address?

Reference Notes

1. Mehak, MC (2002) New urbanism and aging in place. *Plan Canada* 42(1): 21–3.

    Mish, J & B Rice (1998) Senior partners: Regina's work in progress, planning for a senior-friendly city. *Plan Canada* 38(4): 30–4.

2. Chipeniuk, R (2005) Planning for rural amenity migration. *Plan Canada* 45(1): 15–17

3. Grant, J, K Greene, & K Maxwell (2004) The planning and policy implications of gated communities. *Canadian Journal of Urban Research: Canadian Planning and Policy* 13(1): 70–88.

4. Kumar, S & B Leung (2005) Formation of an ethnic enclave: Process and motivations. *Plan Canada* 45(2): 43–5.

5. Yiftachel, O & I Aharonovitz (2005) Urban planning and ethnic diversity: Toronto and Tel Aviv. *Plan Canada* 45(2): 40–2.

6. Finkler, L (2006) Re-placing (in)justice: Disability-related facilities at the Ontario Municipal Board. In Law Commission of Canada, *The "Place" of Justice.* Winnipeg: Fernwood Publishing: 95–123.

7. Mish, J & B Rice (1998) Op. cit.

8. Modlich, R (1988) Planning implications of Women Plan Toronto. *Plan Canada* 28(4): 120–31.

    Kiernan, M (1982) Ideology and precarious future of the Canadian planning profession. *Plan Canada* 22(1): 14–24.

9. Sandercock, L (1998) *Toward Cosmopolis: Planning for Multicultural Cities.* Chichester: John Wiley & Sons.

10. Gee, EM & SA McDaniel (1994) Social policy for an aging society. In VW Marshall & BD McPherson (eds) *Aging: Canadian Perspectives.* Peterborough ON: Broadview Press: 219–31.

11. Yeates, M (1978) The future urban requirements of Canada's elderly. *Plan Canada* 18(2): 88–104.

12. Gee, EM & SA McDaniel (1994) Op. cit.

13. Golant, SM (1992a) *Housing America's Elderly: Many Possibilities/Few Choices.* Newbury Park: Sage.

    Howe, DA, NJ Chapman, & SA Baggett (1994) *Planning for an Aging Society.* Planning Advisory Service Report Number 451. Chicago: American Planning Association.

    Pollak, PB & AN Gorman (1989) *Community-Based Housing for the Elderly: A Zoning Guide for Planners and Municipal Officials.* Planning Advisory Service Report Number 420. Chicago: American Planning Association.

14. Greenberg, L (1982) The implications of an ageing population for land-use planning. In AM Warnes (ed) *Geographical Perspectives on the Elderly.* Chichester: John Wiley & Sons: 401–25.

    Hodge, G (1990) Op. cit.

15. Golant, SM (1992b) The suburbanization of the American elderly. In A Rogers, WH Frey, P Rees, A Spear Jr, & A Warnes (eds) *Elderly Migration and Population Redistribution: A Comparative Study.* London: Belhaven Press: 163–80.

16. Moore, EG & MW Rosenberg (1994) Residential mobility and migration among Canada's elderly. In VW Marshall & BD McPherson (eds) *Aging: Canadian Perspectives.* Peterborough: Broadview Press: 51–69.

17. Hodge, G (1990) Op. cit.

18. Wiseman, RE (1980) Op. cit.

19. Joseph, AE & DS Cloutier (1991) Elderly migration and its implications for service provision in rural communities: An Ontario perspective. *Journal of Rural Studies* 7(4): 433–44.

    Wiseman, RE (1980) Op. cit.

20. Municipality of Metropolitan Toronto (1996) *Housing Patterns and Prospects in Metro*. Toronto: Municipality of Metropolitan Toronto, Metro Planning, Research and Information Services Division.

21. Golant, SM (1992a) Op. cit.

    Greenberg, L (1982) Op. cit.

22. City of Toronto (1991) Planning to grow old in Toronto. *Report #19*, City plan '91. Toronto: City of Toronto, Planning and Development Department.

    Golant, SM (1992a) Op. cit.

    Hodge, G (1990) Op. cit.

    Laws, G (1994) Implications of demographic changes for urban policy and planning. *Urban Geography* 15(1): 90–100.

23. Pollak, PB & AN Gorman (1989) Op. cit.

    Shifman, CR (1983) *Increasing Housing Opportunities for the Elderly*. Planning Advisory Service Report Number 381. Chicago: American Planning Association.

24. Biggar, JC (1980) Who moved among the elderly, 1965 to 1970: A comparison of types of older movers. *Research on Aging* 2(1): 73–91.

25. Hodge, G (1991) The economic impact of retirees on smaller communities. *Research on Aging* 13(1): 39–54.

    Laws, G (1994) Op. cit.

26. Northcott, HC (1988) *Changing Residence: The Geographic Mobility of Elderly Canadians*. Toronto: Butterworths.

27. Joseph, AE & DS Cloutier (1991) Op. cit.

28. Ibid.

29. Northcott, HC (1988) Op. cit.

30. Rosenberg, MW, EG Moore, & SB Ball (1989) Components of change in the spatial distribution of the elderly population in Ontario, 1976–1986. *The Canadian Geographer* 33(3): 218–29.

31. In another effort to encourage economic diversification, the city recently acquired land from the province for waterfront residential development on its lakes. Lake-management plans will protect water quality and shoreline conditions. The initiative may attract retirees who want summer residences in a wilderness setting at reasonable cost.

32. The authors acknowledge the contribution of Dan Hiebert, who provided some of the information for Ottawa-Hull.

33. Bourne, L (2000) *People and Places: A Portrait of the Evolving Social Character of the Greater Toronto Region*. Report to the Neptis Foundation. Toronto: Department of Geography, University of Toronto.

    Hiebert, D (1999) Immigration and the changing social geography of Greater Vancouver. *BC Studies, The British Columbian Quarterly* 121: 35–81.

34. Peach, C (1996) Good segregation, bad segregation. *Planning Perspectives* 11: 379–98.

35. Ley, D (1999) Myths and meanings of immigration and the metropolis. *The Canadian Geographer* 43: 2–19.

36. Germain, A (1999) Les quartiers multiethniques montréalais: une lecture urbaine, *Recherches sociographiques* 40(2): 9–32.

37. Burayidi, MA (2000) Urban planning as multicultural canon. In M. Burayidi (ed) *Urban Planning in a Multicultural Society*. Westport: Praeger.

    Sandercock, L (1999) A portrait of postmodern planning: Anti-hero and/or passionate pilgrim? *Plan Canada* 39(2): 12–5.

38. Kymlicka, W (1998) *Finding Our Way*. Toronto: Oxford University Press.

39. Qadeer, M and M Chaudhry (2000) The planning system and the development of mosques in the Greater Toronto Area. *Plan Canada* 40(2.): 17–21.

40. Ontario Municipal Board. (1998) Tilzen Holdings vs. Town of Markham (PL956623): 13.

Chapter Eight

Aiming for Well-Designed and Beautiful Cities

In Search of Good Design

Jill Grant

In the opening commentary in this chapter, Joe Berridge argues that making cities beautiful constitutes the mandate of planning. His views reflect the ascendance of urban design influences in planning in recent years, as cities and towns across the country work to revitalize and improve their public spaces in town centres, waterfronts, and historic districts. The global city competes with others at least partly on the basis of its aesthetic appeal to consumers and industries with mobile capital. Hence, creating communities with character and a sense of place has become a planning mantra.

While Canadians may agree that planning to achieve efficiency, health, and safety is a well-established function of government, do they share the same level of consensus on urban aesthetic values? What makes urban spaces beautiful? Is beauty in the eye of the beholder? While Ian Wight argues that we should search for humane visions to replace the "sub"urban landscapes many inhabit, Hok-Lin Leung suggests that recent efforts to find design solutions have produced places that exclude many urban residents.

How do we generate meaningful public spaces—the "streets full of life" that Bev Sandalack and Andrei Nicolai advocate in their article? Do projects like the new urbanism communities of McKenzie Towne, described by Doug MacDonald, and Bois Franc, discussed by Louis Sauer, offer answers for our future? For much of the 1990s, planners seemed to agree that neotraditional developments and new urbanism presented responses to bland and inefficient suburban landscapes. Cities like Calgary and Markham (north of Toronto) became strong advocates of new urbanism principles: compact form, urban infill and intensification, mixed use, mixed housing types, pedestrian-friendly streets, transit accessibility, open-space networks, heritage conservation, and quality urban design. As a result, they have some beautiful neighbourhoods that others might emulate.

A trip through most Canadian communities, though, reveals a variety of approaches to urban design. Town centres often celebrate local history with heritage-inspired lamp standards and street furniture. Waterfronts have become festival marketplaces with themed activities programmed throughout the summer months to entertain tourists and a leisure class. At the same time, suburban areas reflect a mix of choices made by urban developers and housing consumers with varying means and tastes:

While designers may think the resulting melange is ugly, the average home buyer finds it perfectly attractive. Our cities offer a range of images of the beautiful urban environment.

What are the features of good design? In the 1950s and 1960s, suburban Don Mills won design awards. Spacious suburban landscapes met the fantasies of the time: big picture windows, expanses of lawns, a car in every driveway. With each copy made, though, the results proved a little less classy, and the model was reduced to sterile and monotonous pabulum. Few planners in the twenty-first century seem ready to call conventional suburbs attractive. Most argue for a different image of the city: an urban but vaguely traditional picture.

Since the early 1990s, Canadian planning has increasingly adopted new urbanism principles. The pages of *Plan Canada* reveal the growing interest in new urbanism and urban design throughout the period. Duany Plater-Zyberk Associates of Florida participated in the design process for both McKenzie Towne (Calgary) and Cornell (Markham) and advised other cities on urban design questions. Carma Developers built projects implementing neotraditional development forms in Edmonton (Terwilligar Towne) and Calgary (McKenzie Towne). The Province of Ontario supported new urban approaches by sponsoring design competitions and publication series. Canada Mortgage and Housing Corporation funded research and demonstration projects to promote the new principles. Whether in small cities like Kelowna, British Columbia, or large cities like Vancouver and Montreal, new urbanism provided design guidelines to enable more compact development forms. The principles also influenced approaches to urban infill and encouraged intensification of development in many parts of the country.

Although we may agree that new urbanism has contributed to making our communities more beautiful, some may ask whether the historic models used have always been appropriate. At some point, heritage conservation and appreciation may become a formula, just as modernism did. Is the eighteenth-century plan for Savannah, Georgia, an appropriate form to emulate in contemporary Quebec urban developments? Are New England–style brownstones well-suited to an Alberta prairie suburb? Does building farm-style homes in Ontario remind us of a proud farming heritage or mock the spread of urban development over farm fields? Can we develop a Canadian urban aesthetic that celebrates our past effectively while making a space for everyone in our diverse communities?

We can find some good examples of the potential for new urban approaches. Garrison Woods (Figure 8.1) and Garrison Green are rising on the lands of the former Canadian Armed Forces base in Calgary. A mix of rehabilitated base housing and new units at medium density in an inner suburban area meets many of the goals of the new urbanism movement, including mixed use and transit accessibility. Although a strong housing market has driven up prices, Canada Lands Company has otherwise produced an exemplary model of the potential for urban intensification with new urbanism principles.

Despite the interest of the planning profession in new urbanism, development practice reveals the challenge of making new urbanism work. Both Bois Franc and McKenzie Towne were only partly built as traditional revival developments: Later phases changed as the market proved weak for the product. Cornell is also developing more slowly than expected. Of all the projects, Garrison Woods seems to have done best, building out ahead of schedule.

The conventional development market has avidly adopted some of the design features of new urbanism, like front porches and pitched roofs. Some might call this picturesque sprawl. At the same time, the conventional appeal of attached garage homes remains strong. The suburbs still attract those who are not ready to abandon their cars or to sacrifice space and privacy for more convenient access to the city.

Figure 8.1

Housing around the square in Garrison Woods in Calgary reveals high design standards associated with new urbanism development.

Planners and developers have found it hard to achieve a workable mix of uses in new urbanism projects. Stores in McKenzie Towne and Cornell took years to fill, reducing returns for the developers who made major investments in the public infrastructure. Providing affordability by mixing housing types has seldom worked. Project success drives up housing prices, while a soft market may protect affordability but usually undermines the long-term viability of the concept for the developer.

Other distressing trends in the suburbs reflect the challenge of achieving social objectives while creating beautiful living environments. Many of the beautiful new suburban projects involve private communities or even gated enclaves. Our planning principles promote connectivity and diversity, but the market facilitates separation, fragmentation, and isolation.

Norman Pressman reminds us that Canadian cities are winter cities. Good design in a cold climate requires that we consider the nature of public spaces in December as well as July. We have the technology and know-how to plan for four seasons, but too often we have focused our investments on an urban infrastructure that pays little attention to the environment.

Fortunately, several communities offer rays of hope that public initiatives can make a real difference. Sonny Tomic describes the City of Hamilton's efforts to design public spaces for greater legibility for visually-impaired members of the community. Sandy James describes projects in Vancouver that let urban residents reclaim their streets and make them uniquely beautiful. People care about their neighbourhoods, wherever they may live. They want well-designed spaces to meet their needs. Planning offers tools we can use to improve the urban and suburban environment to address the priorities we identify as important.

Beauty, Truth, and Order, or Something Like That

Joe Berridge

2000, Plan Canada 40(1): 14

At the beginning of the twentieth century, Daniel Burnham, the great Chicago city planner, provided his prescription for the practice of city building: "Let your watchword be order and your beacon beauty." What exactly did he mean? We've had lots of order in twentieth-century planning. Probably far too much. But beauty? There's a word that got lost. Beauty could well be the commodity in shortest supply in the next numbered set of years, just as it was in the last. What if workers in the planning factories of the world had but one responsibility: the production of beauty?

I have just returned from a millennial pilgrimage, to pay homage to a masterpiece, Frank Gehry's new Guggenheim Museum in Bilbao, Spain, undoubtedly one of the most beautiful objects of the twentieth century, yet placed so close to the transition to the next century that it may legitimately claim this status for another 100 years. To visit the Guggenheim is to be both enriched and chastened: enriched because the creation of beauty is the only truly human act, chastened in the presence of the magnificent inequality of genius.

City planners have been many things: social workers, bureaucrats, approvers of a world of which they privately disapprove. They have been dogged improvers, dreamers, cranks, purveyors of prose. What planners have rarely been are city planners, doing the one and the only thing they are legally and professionally empowered to do: Make beautiful cities.

We have all accepted that beauty is relative, skin deep, expensive, in the eye of the beholder: that it is elitist, arrogant, and not universally available. For these reasons, planning acts never mention the word. Beauty is all of those things. It is also absolute, unchanging, instantly recognizable, and profoundly humble. The planners of Bilbao appreciated that the tide of the twentieth century was flowing against them, but they anticipated the flow of the next 100 years. Gehry's building is not there by accident. Bilbao actively sought out the Guggenheim and, through an aggressive commitment to architectural excellence, won the prize of the museum, despite competition from other, far more prepossessing cities. The strategy for economic regeneration envisaged urban beauty as the essential added value. Can we do better?

In Search of Grander Humane Visions   `POINT`

Ian Wight

1996, Plan Canada 36(4): 3–4

Does anyone know what "urban" means anymore? Does anyone care? In the context of retrofitting the suburbs, how far back should we go to find the model for our refit? What kind of truly urban notions might we want to reintroduce? Or, will we be content to realize a postmodern form of our hard-to-shake antiurban bias?

I offer this commentary with certain personal biases. I am a reformed suburbanite, now living in an old suburb of the old inner city of Winnipeg. I am a renter and a public-transit user. I teach in an urban planning school, after years of rural and regional planning practice. I am living an urban life for the first time since my student days, and I find this "neat."

How do you like your "urban"? At a distance? Surb'd? Ex'd? Or Neat? I have come to view suburban life as just that, a subform of urban life. We do ourselves no credit in continuing to be seduced by this lesser lifeform; no wonder our civilization is regressing and our cities deteriorating. The "sub-urban" dimension now dominates as a manifestation of urbanization in North America, though it is increasingly eclipsed in planning significance by the new kid on the urban block: exurbia. For those who like their urban "neat," exurbia is an X-rated form of urban life, a scary mutation with cancerous qualities.

Apparently we are on the verge of the suburban century.[1] So it looks as if we are going to have more of the same social and environmental madness that caused us, out of abhorrence, to value instead "livability" as a planning mantra: What had gone before clearly did not meet this amazingly basic standard. Not that we seem to have realized livability by our planning since. In fact, we are now moved by a more fundamental concern with sustainability. Will survivability come next?

The multifaceted urban cocktail image I am retailing has been bottled in a much more scholarly fashion by Robert Fishman.[2] In the *Wilson Quarterly*, Fishman elucidates the notion of a new city in terms of "megalopolis unbound." This is edge-city country on a gross scale—exurbia personified. Characterized as a new city of time instead of space, it is also a time-space of self-serving impersonal networks, deficient in terms of the diversity and community of a classic urban blend. It is also beginning to experience troubling landscape degradation, paving the way for concerns about long-term environmental sustainability. Interestingly, Fishman concludes with the observation that "preserving and enhancing the common landscape might become the issue on which the people of the new cities finally come together as communities."

This brings me back to my opening questions. I would urge a more conscious and caring consideration for what "urban" might mean, if only to be clear about the unurban essence of suburbia and exurbia. We will neither be complete as a civilization nor as a planning profession until we shake our antiurban bias. We need grander humane visions for our refit models: Livability and sustainability are appallingly minimalist. These qualities should go without saying. Let's reach for much more challenging standards such as conviviality, "eco-logicality," and a heightened civic consciousness. From my own experience, a good place to start would be to take the bus more often and get to know, and possibly enjoy, your fellow citizens just a tad better.

A New Kind of Sprawl

COUNTERPOINT

Hok-Lin Leung

1995, Plan Canada 35(5): 4–5

In the last 30 years or so, the image of good living for the social and economic elite has changed. At first, there was resentment of the invasion of the suburbs by the lower classes. Then there was a reevaluation of the suburban ideal. Suburb became "suburbia": a twilight zone, a sprawl of look-alike, single detached houses, aesthetically displeasing, environmentally destructive, and socially blasé.

New environmental ideals for the elite have begun to emerge. The rage now is "new urbanism": neotraditional designs that seek to recreate the ambience of the nineteenth-century American small town. This new urbanism represents a radical departure from the conventional suburb. As an ideology, it sees the private plot with deep setbacks and large yards as a symbol of social disengagement and environmental irresponsibility. It affirms the urban street and communal open space as the glue that binds the good society. As a design approach, it advocates smaller lots and closer houses (Figure 8.2), forsaking the conventions of privacy through separation distances and using site layout, building orientation, fenestrations, and materials to achieve visual and auditory privacy.

Figure 8.2

New urbanism development — like these units in Angus Glen — has become commonplace in Markham.

Governments are placing great hopes on these "higher-density" approaches as models of affordable housing for the growing number of citizens who can never hope to own a conventional suburban single detached home because of rising prices and dwindling incomes. Environmental interests see compact development as the basis of sustainable communities. But is this new urbanism affordable and sustainable?

The "higher" densities of these designer suburbs do not necessarily translate into lower housing costs. The dwelling types (more attached houses and smaller lots) and layouts (narrower streets and smaller setbacks) may suggest compactness. But we should not confuse built form with density. The built-up part is often surrounded by or interspersed with generous open spaces. This makes the actual land consumption much higher than the look of the development suggests. The overall density (number of dwellings divided by total acreage) is often comparable to that of a conventional subdivision. With no savings on land, housing prices will not come down. Designer suburbs are not meant to be affordable.

In a way, new urbanism can be interpreted as an effort by the elite to reclaim its earlier suburban ideals of democracy and community, lost through the invasion of the masses. Nowhere is this more clearly illustrated than in the conception and treatment of open space. There is a shift from yards to parks, from individual private open space to communal open space. This is aimed at catering to the life cycle of the old and the lifestyle of the young. Fewer kids and fewer parents stay at home. The emphasis is on larger open spaces rather than "fragmented" ones: spaces that celebrate community spirit and protect natural habitats. If this new urbanism catches on in a big way, there may be significant regional consequences.

Imagine all the new developments having compact buildings in the centre and generous open spaces around them. Development sizes will vary according to site sizes, which, in turn, vary according to the pattern of private land ownership. And the pattern of private land ownership bears no necessary relation to either ecology or community.

There will be clusters of compact housing, from a few units to a few hundred, separated by open spaces, the shapes and sizes of which are governed more by property lines than by the dictates of natural or social relations. These clusters will also be linked by roads and other infrastructure. Thus, instead of Le Corbusier's "towers in the park," we will now have "horizontal towers in a sea of green": picturesque sprawl that will take up just as much land and use up as much energy as the conventional suburban sprawl of old.

New urbanism introduces a different set of assumptions about how dwellings should be designed, and how they should relate to one another and to the land and nature around them. More significantly, it suggests how people should live. It is the "unspoiled nature" on the outside and "modern comfort" on the inside that make new urbanism attractive to the elite. It will be to our peril to see only the "communal" facilities and "humble" building forms without seeing the intention of exclusivity and status behind them.

Whatever Happened to the Public Realm?

Beverly A Sandalack and Andrei Nicolai

2002, Plan Canada 42(2): 24–7

Much of our everyday urban existence occurs within the shared city spaces defined by both public and private buildings and made up of streets, sidewalks, parks, and squares. These elements, known collectively as the public realm, are spaces that all citizens have a right to occupy. They primarily provide access to homes, offices, public buildings, and places of entertainment and culture. They also offer space for the many other functions traditionally associated with urban life, such as markets, public festivals, and, importantly, the ad hoc meetings and happenings that make urban life "urban." Within this context, the public realm is the receptacle that contains and facilitates urbanity, and our experience of the city is mostly of it.

The urban experience is partly formed by the character and shape of the public realm's built edges, made up of both public and private components. Private buildings usually form the edges and act to define and articulate public space. The public components (sidewalks, streets, and public open spaces) are part of the same composition. The street is a major component of the public realm.

In Calgary, most people can list those streets where the heart of public life seems to beat at its fullest, where one can find what Sennett calls "streets full of life" and "places full of time."[3] It is almost a mantra that urbanites chant: "Fourth Street, Seventeenth Avenue, Eleventh Street, Kensington, Inglewood." These areas, which emerged independently and over time, are popular with local residents and have become destinations for all Calgarians (Figure 8.3). However, they represent a relatively small sample in a rapidly growing city, recently noted for some of the worst streets on the continent. Planetizen, an association of urban planners, criticized Calgary for having "stripmallish development every bit as dispiriting as every sun belt city" in the urban United States.[4]

Critics of the placelessness of contemporary urban form and the decline of the public realm have effectively drawn attention to the general qualitative decline of public space in North America. Jane Jacobs and Kevin Lynch focus their criticism on urban form, specifically the unsatisfying products of modern development and the lack of proper public urban spaces.[5] Michael Hough and Edward Relph have eloquently pointed out the lack of sense of place of much of modern development, and have joined those who protest the increasing standardization of the appearance and function of cities.[6] Roger Trancik brought into our vocabulary the term "lost space," a new category made necessary by the proliferation of surface parking, empty lots, and traffic interchanges.[7]

Figure 8.3

Calgary's downtown streets provide venues for many activities.

Manuel Iniquez summarized the concern about the loss of the public realm:

> The city, ancient or modern, has some characteristics that define it forever: The street, the square, the public buildings, the residences have established between them, through a slow and uninterrupted process, laws of composition. If such compositional laws are forgotten, as in recent years, the City, deprived of measurement and proportion, corrupts the architectural components within it, creating a monstrous medley which can never be called a true City.[8]

The degradation of public space directly affects public life. A 1990 feature article in *Harper's* titled "Whatever became of the public square" convened several prominent architects, town planners, sociologists, and artists to debate this issue. The group concluded that the problems included the lack of civic engagement in today's society and the loss of appropriate public spaces. That this issue found its way into the popular press is significant.

Clearly, all is not well. While the loss of public life is an extremely complex issue, as planners and urban designers, we need to address the decline of public space.

How Did We Get Here?

Most cities and towns in North America are less than 200 years old—many barely a century—and have been rapidly transformed from primitive conditions to total modernity. Most of these cities were planned around a central public space, with a hierarchy of streets and public open spaces extending from it. For example, Halifax was built around the Grand Parade (Figure 8.4), early Regina included Victoria Park, Winnipeg centred on the legislative grounds, and countless Prairie railway towns included a public garden adjacent to the railway station.

Figure 8.4

MARK NENER

Originally a military yard, the Grand Parade in Halifax now provides public space in the centre of the city.

The original plan for Calgary featured a grid network of streets, typical of towns and cities built on the western railway. Thomas Mawson prepared the first commissioned city plan in 1914. Mawson envisioned a system of streets, civic spaces, and squares, focused on the rivers and modelled after the City Beautiful movement. The plan was clearly based on a strong vision of the public realm and its importance: Owing to the combination of an economic downturn, World War I, and the inappropriateness of some of Mawson's architectural ideas, it was never carried out.

Town planning during the second half of the twentieth century departed from the tradition of designing around the public realm. History, tradition, and local and regional identity were thought old-fashioned; economic development generated by private enterprise took precedence over concerns for the provision of public amenities; and huge areas of cities, towns, and landscapes were destroyed to make way for new developments. The lifestyles that go along with the spatial forms produced—the housing projects, suburbs, shopping centres, and strip malls—are now taken for granted. They contribute to several contemporary urban problems, including suburban sprawl, decline of the central business district, and neglect of the traditional public realm: that is, the street and the public square.

Public space is largely shaped by the buildings around its edges. When buildings are designed with attention only to the building envelope and the interior, then the space outside the building—the public realm—is usually lost space.

Where Do We Go from Here?

Two important influences on the decline of the public realm are the privatization of the urban development process, and the growing separation of city planning and the design professions. The proactive, visionary urban planning and development that produced our early civic centres, especially in the capital cities, was replaced by a hands-off (from the civic side) development process, in which urban councils and planners assume the roles of private development facilitators and regulators. In a related process, the various design disciplines involved in the development of urban form have been pre-occupied with staking out their individual jurisdictions: Architects too often focus on individual buildings and rarely consider the spaces in between, and landscape architects deal largely with site-specific and market-driven projects.

Currently, as a society we devote more of our design attention to individual buildings, to programming, and especially to trends and fashions than to the most permanent elements: the public realm and the landscape. The less permanent elements come and go, but the public infrastructure, the integrated system of public spaces, persists and can give a sense of continuity and quality to a place. What has been neglected is design at the city scale and a focus on the public realm.

A renewed vision of public and civic life would require the answer to some fundamental questions: Who do we want to be, or what does our community aspire to become? What kind of society do we value? If the answers include a stated desire for civic engagement, then the public realm, the space now created mostly by default, would become the focus of the municipal planning departments, the specialists, and, above all, the community.

Ideals need to be translated into appropriate form, and city planning should again be concerned with building and protecting the public realm. Ideally, urbanism can be one of the highest forms of environmentalism, one of the best expressions of good conservation practices. A return to the best traditions of city building, combined with a renewed vision of public and civic life, may provide the means of developing a high-quality public realm.

McKenzie Towne: What Is It?

Doug MacDonald

1995 Plan Canada 35(1): 20

Based on a neotraditional concept plan designed by Andres Duany and Elizabeth Plater-Zyberk and commissioned by Carma Developments, McKenzie Towne is located in the southeast corner of Calgary, about 20 kilometres from the city centre. It comprises some 2400 acres and will accommodate 12 000 units (30 000 people) in 13 residential neighbourhoods. The first phase, approved late in 1993, consists of one residential neighbourhood and the Town Centre a large commercial area that will be developed along a traditional Main Street theme (Figure 8.5), reminiscent of small-town Alberta.

All of the principal neotraditional design elements occur in McKenzie Towne: a strong central focus, transit-supportive size, a concentrated housing pattern, a pedestrian-oriented environment, and prominent public spaces. A central square serves as the social focus of each neighbourhood. McKenzie Towne neighbourhoods are predicated on a five-minute walking distance to the bus stop. A transit stop will serve each neighbourhood, in association with a convenience store and heated waiting facilities.

McKenzie Towne will have a mixture of housing types in varying concentrations, particularly around the neighbourhood square. The first ring of blocks will contain street-oriented townhouses and apartments, with a three-storey maximum height and a one-metre setback from the street. The next ring will comprise single-family homes with the ability to construct a studio suite or granny flat above the rear garage, and the outer blocks will contain a variety of single-family homes on lots of different sizes.

Figure 8.5

High Street in McKenzie Towne, Calgary, provides neighbourhood commercial uses.

JILL GRANT

McKenzie Towne includes simple inner-city design features that have all but disappeared in the suburbs. The grid layout itself, with the absence of collector streets, is intended to slow and dispense traffic flows within the neighbourhood. The road rights-of-way will accommodate sidewalks, boulevards, and trees on both sides. Laneways have eliminated the need for front-drive garages. McKenzie Towne places a high priority on public spaces. It contains a series of sites suitable for churches, community buildings, a library, a firehall, an elaborate system of parks, and linear linkages within the neighbourhood itself and between neighbourhoods. The Town Centre is located off the arterial grid in the centre of the community and is adjacent to a proposed future light rail station.

The neotraditional movement poses two challenges for local government. At the macro level, local governments must create realistic, workable, market-sensitive policies that will accommodate a number of solutions and receive the endorsement of the private and public sectors. Calgary is currently confronting this challenge head-on through the formulation of a new transportation plan and a suburban growth study. McKenzie Towne will be a pilot project.

The microlevel challenge is the inevitable conflict between neighbourhood design innovation and existing zoning controls, engineering standards, and other suburban design criteria. These are entrenched in the planning system and reflect conventional ways of doing things. In its simplest terms, innovation means nonconformity with existing rules. In response to this reality, Calgary has developed a special review process that stresses consultation between the administration and the developer, negotiation in the development of creative solutions, and acceptance and commitment by the various civic departments on agreement. And, since experimental areas such as McKenzie Towne are not bound by the normal rules, the city can deal with innovation in a limited manner without setting precedents for other developers.

Creating a "Signature" Town: The Urban Design of Bois Franc

Louis Sauer

1994, Plan Canada 35(5): 22–7

On 589 acres in the City of Saint-Laurent in Montreal lie Canadair's manufacturing (air- and spacecraft) facilities, including the Cartierville Airport. Bombardier Real Estate Inc. wanted to redevelop this site for a new residential community, called Bois Franc. This "signature" town would include up to 10 000 housing units (for 20 000 to 25 000 people) and retail space, offices, and recreation facilities. Bombardier was willing to pay for the construction of street and utility infrastructure, oversee and pay for the design of public parks, sell land to accommodate private facilities to developers/builders, and coordinate an overall advertising plan and a marketing office.

From the client's perspective, the Bois Franc master plan would have to achieve several objectives: accommodate a wide range of market segments and building types; accommodate a flexible construction program; create a distinct visual image; and develop a clear communal identity. Townhouses, rather than detached single-family units, were to be the dominant building type, and at least 60 percent of the total property area had to be earmarked for private development.

From the city's standpoint, the master plan (created by Daniel Arbour and Associates in Montreal) had to relate strongly to the city's proposed Nouveau Saint-Laurent neighbourhood plan, designed by Montreal's Cardinal and Hardy, Architects and Planners. Public community buildings could not be considered, because existing public institutions located elsewhere in the city were sufficient to service the needs of the residents. Twelve contiguous acres would accommodate an outdoor swimming pool, tennis courts, and soccer and baseball fields. The city agreed to pay for the construction of all public parks.

In addition to these constraints placed on the development of the new community, the urban designer had to heed specific regulations that would not permit corner stores, buildings over 12 storeys, habitable areas below ground level, garage doors visible from public streets, and surface water drainage to offsite properties. Also, a cluster of Bombardier's existing main buildings on 93 acres would remain in use and direct parking lot access for the anticipated 3000 cars an hour, which would be arriving from the northwest, would be required. All other manufacturing buildings and the airport on the remaining 496 acres would be demolished for the redevelopment.

There were other constraints as well. Arterials with extremely heavy traffic run along the site's north and east sides. Industry, strip commercial, and poorly maintained residential development adjacent to the site on its east and north sides are not conducive to a middle-class residential development. And the flat site (with only a one percent slope northwest to southeast) does not provide for appealing design qualities.

The urban designer faced having to invent a new context for the site's interior layout. The saving grace was that a portion of the site adjacent to Nouveau Saint-Laurent would lend itself to a strong formal public open-space relationship to the Nouveau Saint-Laurent central park axis.

Creating an Identity

To create a unique "signature" town, the designer opted to employ natural elements, with water as the principal thread. Water would not only capture people's imagination but would enhance also the contrast found in a Nordic climate between summer and winter city landscapes.

Figure 8.6

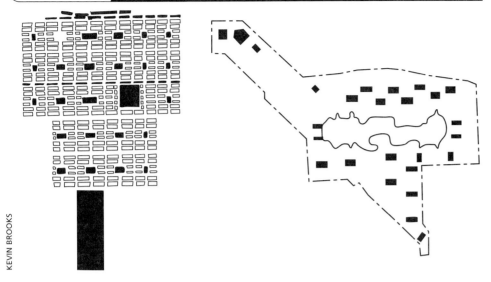

KEVIN BROOKS

Like the Savannah plan (left), Bois Franc (right) uses public squares, shown in black in the diagram, as an organizing feature.

The vision stemmed principally from a desire to inject new life into the existing city. Therefore, rather than diffuse the design qualities of old and Nouveau Saint-Laurent and the new community of Bois Franc, the designer enhanced the existing qualities by creating a large urban neighbourhood with its own strong identity. The new community would not look foreign or be easily confused with a typical suburb found in Montreal or the US. Such a plan was to provide, at once, a singular image as well as to allow flexible land sales and construction phasing and the integration through time of various economic groups, building types, and architectural styles.

The design approach involves creating small-scaled neighbourhoods focused on squares and short streets, based on the idea that people are more receptive to neighbourliness when their homes are arranged in spatially defined public territories. Public open spaces and a central park with major water features were incorporated into the plan's design to heighten community identity and place legibility.

Proven planning design precedents were used to develop the design concept. In particular, the designer used the Savannah Historic District's pattern as the model for the Bois Franc plan (Figure 8.6). A new pattern was developed for Bois Franc's central park—the Lake District—as no precedent existed for this type of function.

Designing Bois Franc's Open Spaces

The design approach involved three phases: analyzing the client's, city's, and designer's objectives to determine the key physical elements, such as green spaces, streets, houses, shops and community facilities, and water areas, and where they should be situated; combining the physical elements into a spatial vocabulary obtained from precedent to create a new form pattern (six urban design typologies were developed); and testing concepts to determine the strategic and sequential steps needed to achieve the desired overall design qualities.

Functions and Form Precedents

The designer and client visited various sites to help them arrive at relevant precedents, such as the following:

- *Local streets*: to define short and narrow linear neighbourhoods and to provide vehicular access to other neighbourhoods via green corridors.
- *Boulevards*: to make linear neighbourhoods longer and wider, and to provide interconnections between interior and exterior neighbourhoods and the internal (central) Lake District.
- *Esplanades*: to make larger-scaled linear neighbourhoods; to provide dominant linear green connections between large parks bordering the site and the central Lake District; to define larger-scaled neighbourhoods with a linear park focus; and to provide recreational activities for adjacent and more distant residents.
- *Squares*: to make centric neighbourhoods; to provide strong local green landmarks containing recreational activities; and to promote socialization opportunities between neighbourhoods.
- *Placettes (small squares)*: to make narrow, small-scale neighbourhoods; to provide passive recreational amenities; to create incremental green landmarks along boulevards; and to extend the boundaries of the central Lake District.
- *The Lake District*: to develop a central neighbourhood with a strong water focus; to accommodate a mix of public- and private-sector uses, a main street centrally located with a mixed-use neighbourhood, special places for socialization opportunities, and discrete residential territories interwoven among surrounding neighbourhoods; and to create unique landmarks.

The Strategy

Cavendish Boulevard is extended through the site, effectively splitting the site into a narrow section adjacent to Nouveau Saint-Laurent and a broader section to the east. To the south, Cavendish Boulevard directly connects to an expressway. The western section has an extension of the semicircular Nouveau Saint-Laurent Park and a water basin centred on its axis. The eastern section has a wide and long park at the centre of the site. At the south edge, a smaller lake will extend the regional park system into the site, thereby creating not only a transition between the larger and the smaller public open space, but also a contrast between the natural world and the urban ambience.

Six of the nine streets connecting the site with the surrounding areas will be boulevards and esplanades that allow one-way traffic (one lane with parking on one side) on both sides of the planted medians (24 to 35 feet for boulevards and 100 to 150 feet for esplanades). A one-way street to the south provides direct access for vehicles travelling from Henri Bourassa Boulevard to Canadair's parking lot.

Six of Bois Franc's connecting streets were designed with continuous green medians to create linear residential neighbourhoods for passive recreational areas. Buildings range from three to six storeys, and have a mandatory continuous frontage setback of 10 feet. Zoning provides opportunities on boulevards and esplanades for cultural facilities, such as churches and schools.

As an existing edge street, Laurentien Boulevard is the only one with no green median. New Bois Franc zoning provides for commercial office service uses in three- to nine-storey buildings. Bois Franc's main street extends only three blocks and is designed to accommodate commercial retail, offices, and residential uses (Figure 8.7). A canal with linear pedestrian plazas will run along its north side. At its west end, a park, boat-house island, and a semi-circular Village Plaza will face south. At its east end will be a view of 12-storey buildings clustered along the lakeshore. Zoning allows parking lots for the interior of several of the main street's adjacent blocks.

Squares form neighbourhoods, referred to in Bois Franc as urban blocks, each with a distinct identity. To maintain their use as quality destination places and to provide a framework for social interchanges, the neighbourhoods are connected by a network

Figure 8.7

JENNIFER MEURER

Homes in Bois Franc in Saint-Laurent front on squares, greens, and parks.

of local streets converging on the squares. In contrast, the smaller squares are conceived as supplementary places—discrete small neighbourhoods—and either provide green landmarks to local collector streets or function as "ports" along longer streets. This approach effectively extends the range of the Lake District area and provides a pedestrian-scaled spatial modularity.

Twenty-five larger urban block squares (typically 120 by 240 feet) and 10 smaller squares or *placettes* (50 feet wide by 100 to 150 feet long) are located within two blocks of each other: a five-minute walk. All squares and *placettes* allow for one-way (one-lane) traffic with parking restricted to the side adjacent to the two- to four-storey residential buildings with a mandatory frontage setback of 5 feet.

Neighbourhoods feature local streets of short lengths. These neighbourhoods form linear "rooms" spatially terminated with buildings or Lake District views. Setbacks vary from 5 to 24 feet. The north-to-south local streets connect neighbourhoods to the Lake District or to the Nouveau Saint-Laurent Park via squares or esplanades. In the eastern section where squares predominate, east-to-west local streets connect neighbourhoods via the squares.

The design of the Lake District area seeks to create an image that conforms to society's cultural mixing of public and private initiatives, services and institutions, both to blur the distinctions and to create dynamic interchanges between public and private domains. To achieve this objective, a new asymmetric, geometric pattern was conceived that involved intertwining the public areas like lakes, canals, and parks with the islands and edges of private development. As well, the close proximity between public and private development will provide increased defence against undesirable activities that might take place in the public open spaces.

The Urban Design Achievement

Bois Franc achieves the goals of heightened community identity and place legibility, and quality design. A formal public open space network, consisting of wide esplanades, boulevards, parks, and lakes, will provide strong place images, visual continuity, and legibility at the overall community scale. Short streets effectively create a variety of small-scaled neighbourhoods. Small parks are organized into squares for individual neighbourhood social landmarks. The parks are surrounded by narrow streets to provide pedestrians an intimate walking environment and to allow easy surveillance from adjoining residences.

The land's market value was increased by a very strong open-space structure with clear and imaginable hierarchies of large- and small-scale places. This organization provides the developer with a range of densities and building types, important in light of unpredictable future social conditions and market conditions. In one year, during a recession in the 1990s, close to 300 of the 1000 dwellings being developed during the initial construction phase were sold. Bombardier has initiated developer/builder designs for the second phase. The developer targeted 2003 as the anticipated completion date.[9]

Urban Form for Stressful Climates

Norman Pressman

1996, Plan Canada 36(2): 30–2

Climate, with all its extremes, shapes national character and common identities. Given its impact on human behaviour, climate constitutes a modifying or determining force in architectural and urban design. Urban form, particularly in its vernacular expression, often bears testimony to cultural and climatic influences. Applying local materials and building techniques to topography and climate, the essence of the vernacular approach to design, usually results in a composition that balances unity and diversity.

Even under the most stressful conditions, people have managed to survive and create permanent settlements by linking lifestyles and built forms to local and regional biophysical imperatives. And, even where conditions are severe and life out-of-doors is carried out in a calculated, determined manner, a quality of life has evolved beyond the simple need for shelter, nourishment and clothing.

Anticlimatic Development

While urban settlements have survived in the northern hemisphere for centuries, human endeavours to generate climate-responsive urban form are a relatively recent phenomenon. The winter cities movement has firmly established the need for explicit, systematic inquiry and strategic action to improve the comfort and lifestyles of northern dwellers.

With the industrial revolution, once-vital climatic concerns gradually lost their importance as design determinants of livable urban spaces. Rapid economic development emerged as the major force behind the planning and design of urban settlements. The art and science of creating harmonious forms of shelter, so meticulously adapted to climatic demands over the centuries, began to disappear.

At the turn of the twentieth century, with the birth of sociology, theories linking climate and behaviour were criticized and even rejected. New paradigms based on economic determinism replaced climatic and geophysical concerns in discussions about human nature and urban form. International standardization neutralized climatic considerations.

Vernacular Architecture

The art of conceiving and organizing shelter reflects the perception and understanding of universal phenomena: of existing constraints imposed by site and climate and of time-tested solutions derived from memory and experience. Influenced by the needs and desires of people living in various climatic conditions, vernacular architecture offers a specific response to climatic elements. A kind of secular "science" that has withstood the test of time, it springs from a symbiosis with nature and is strengthened by powerful feelings of "belonging to place."

Industrialization and standardization tend to ignore ancestral tradition and impose innovative solutions that almost entirely reject vernacular experience. The seasons cease to exist in the organization of space. As standardization rejects accustomed ways of life, its impact on traditional societies can be brutal. The authentic art of city building, though, is rooted in cultural tradition: It stems from the interdependence of relationships among actors who shape, use, and enjoy the urban environment.

The quality of urban and architectural design, and its adaptation to physical localities and cultural values, is deteriorating. Hence the rise of neotraditionalism as a popular design: People look back in order to move ahead. Standardized models fail to respond to fundamental human requirements. Applying modern building regulations results in similar designs in Reykjavik and Phoenix, Toronto and Tampa.

With the global tendency to "atrium-ize," "galleria-ize," and "privatize" urban space, life has become sterile. Thermally-neutral environments, where temperature and humidity are constant, provide little meaningful relationship between outdoor and indoor spaces. Isolated from prevailing cultural and landscape factors, buildings and spaces epitomize "placelessness."

Accelerated urbanistic and architectural homogeneity requires a special effort to produce a regionally-anchored and culturally-based urban vocabulary that offers symbolic meaning and a real sense of place. No longer focused on cultural exchange, city centres are about making money. Climate-controlled shopping malls, skywalks, and underground pedestrian concourses have emerged in every type of climate as a means of corralling purchasing power. Especially in North America (where such projects proliferate), international underground design is justified on the pretence of climatic well-being. These underground malls, though, eliminate sensory delight in favour of a vulgar materialism. This anticlimatic planning for the sole benefit of profit robs human beings of any sense of place or identity. The extent to which these developments are privatized, albeit used by and accessible to the public, raises a serious question about the loss of the public realm in the effort to obliterate climate.

Climate-Sensitive Urban Vision

Given our easy access to resources and sophisticated technologies, the fundamental need for shelter from the rigours of nature has diminished. Postindustrial information and communication technology has accelerated the acceptance and proliferation of anticlimatic urban form on a global scale. With the advent of such climatic equalizers as artificial light, superheating, air conditioning, and artificial snow, hot and cold regions now possess nearly identical built forms often bereft of meaning.

In taking a narrow view of the complexity of the city and its essential biodiversity, we are stunting the growth of urban places traditionally characterized by a rich blend of interaction and interdependence. The delicate urban grain—the ingredient of the historic city—is quickly becoming a coarse tissue determined to erase the human scale.

Climatic changes and emerging global economic imperatives confront urban society with enormous challenges to achieve an ecologically sustainable balance on earth. An essential weapon will be the integration of specialized knowledge in a wide spectrum of disciplines. A thorough understanding of vernacular building theory and cultural tradition, coupled with political determination and will, are necessary instruments to preserve our fragile human habitats. New development standards and urban design criteria will be required as urban form continues to evolve.

With the proper supports in place, cities will gradually abandon their automobile-dominated spatial patterns in favour of more healthy, humane, equitable, and efficient ones. Every human being has the basic right to a balanced life: to economic prosperity, mobility, and accessibility in an environment that is sensitive to nature and human health; to community participation and a sense of belonging, or "place"; and to a full and satisfying lifestyle at every level of human experience.

Planning for the Winter City

The city's public realm—its streets, squares, parks, open spaces, lanes, boulevards, alleys, arcades, passages, and skywalks—is a critical determinant of the quality of urban life. Under severe conditions, the establishment of climatic comfort in urban space can help to preserve human well-being. With thermal comfort and safety comes respect and beautification of public spaces.

The physical environment of the winter city can either further or hinder social activities in outdoor public spaces. Social activities are particularly important in the cold, dark months, when isolation and other winter stresses adversely affect mental health.

Public urban spaces in winter cities should reflect microclimatic principles that block winter winds and allow sunlight to penetrate between buildings. Inhospitable surroundings should be "walled-out" by clustering buildings and using vegetation, windscreens, snow fences, shelterbelts, and a relatively compact spatial configuration. Shadow, wind, and snowdrift impact statements are essential. Using such tools and techniques, designers can create a favourable microclimate that can be improved through appropriate and skillful fitting of buildings to the natural terrain. The summer and marginal seasons can then be extended to the point where summer-type activities, such as sitting in the sun, can take place on midwinter days.

Swedish architect and planner Ralph Erskine suggests that microclimatic planning and design concepts can extend the outdoor season by up to six weeks. To improve quality of life in winter cities, it is necessary to reduce inconvenience, offer protection from the excessive negative stressors associated with winter, and optimize exposure to its beneficial aspects. This calls for developing highly creative and innovative approaches with a positive attitude toward winter. Designers can play on the characteristics that make northern communities unique.

The main principles for designing cities, especially northern cities, are year-round usability, contact with nature, user participation, cultural continuity, and a pedestrian- and transit-friendly environment. The shapes, volumes, textures, colours, materials, and urban spaces that appear between buildings should reflect the landscape and cultural heritage of the environs. By considering these elements, planners can design multi-season cities that celebrate human life in all seasons.

It is not only the broader theoretical tendencies of international planning and design that will influence a new urban "grammar" of the north but also principles that have evolved over centuries of town-building and human life. Vernacular urban design and folk architecture have much to teach, even today. The search continues for innovative built forms that are more sensitive to northern requirements than those expressed in the current conventional vocabulary (which is largely predicated on formal, classical elements of architectural composition and urban imagery). The yield should be a wide variety of approaches rooted in ideology and influenced by practicality, playfulness, folk tradition, classical design concepts, and, most importantly, climate.

To improve the quality of urban life in city centres around the globe, community consciousness and individual awareness and understanding must be elevated to the point where urban dwellers can play an active role in making the decisions that influence their lives. Adopting a climate-sensitive approach to urban design will allow planners to make a significant and environmentally responsible contribution to creating sustainable living spaces. Fashioning built environments that celebrate geophysical and climatic diversity, rather than negate it, makes perfect sense for Canadian planning.

Hamilton Urban Braille System: Urban Design for an Aging Society

Sinisa (Sonny) Tomic

2003, Plan Canada 43(1): 41–3

The City of Hamilton, one of North America's most accessible cities, is well known for its efforts to improve accessibility for all citizens. Its urban Braille system is a user-driven approach to planning and designing sidewalks and public spaces. The system is primarily designed for the severely visually impaired, the elderly, the infirm, and users of a variety of such mobility devices as wheelchairs and scooters. The system allows physically challenged users to "navigate" through the complex urban environment as easily and conveniently as the rest of the population. The system addresses sidewalk and ramp design, curbs and road crossings, and street signage.

The urban Braille system is intended for urban areas with higher pedestrian traffic, such as downtown districts, waterfronts, special public spaces, and special character areas where seasonal events may attract large numbers of pedestrians. The quality of horizontal surfaces and their maintenance play an important role in meeting the system's objectives.

A Collaborative Effort

The "made in Hamilton" urban Braille system was developed collaboratively by the City of Hamilton (Planning and Public Works Departments and the former City's Pathways Committee), McMaster University, and the Canadian National Institute for the Blind. The city's urban designers worked with citizens, politicians, transportation engineers, and social and health experts to create a simple and effective system for accessible sidewalks and other public spaces.

The concept, introduced with the *Hamilton GO Area Urban Design Study*, was physically implemented during the 1996 reconstruction of Hamilton's Parkdale Street. The principles were further supported by the *Pathways Committee's Pedestrian Pathways Obstruction Report*. A revised and simplified version of the design was constructed on King Street East/Gore Park and part of King Street West in Hamilton Downtown (1997–2002), and during the implementation of the new Stoney Creek Town Square in 2001.

Performance Standards

To make public spaces truly accessible, the city introduced performance standards.

- Sidewalks and other urban open spaces should be planned and designed in harmony with the local climate, that is, a four-season design that takes into account dramatic annual weather variations and uses such strategies as direct and reflected sun, shade control, wind control, windscreens, protection against weather elements, and construction of sun pits.
- Design must ensure that public spaces are safe and inviting both day and night.
- Sidewalks and other surfaces in public places must ensure freedom of movement for those who are infirm or permanently or temporarily physically challenged.

Tactile Communication and Navigation through Public Space

Canadian society is aging. More people are experiencing health problems, and a significant percentage of the population is experiencing difficulties with their eyesight. The visual channel is severely blocked for the blind and significantly blocked for the visually impaired. For that segment of the population, an alternate sensory channel that can be used is the tactile (sense of touch) channel. Tactile information can be located within a wheelchair path 1.5 metres wide (Figure 8.8).

The blind and visually impaired can be trained to distinguish four or five materials and a variety of textures with their hands or canes. Only two textures (smooth and grooved) on sidewalks and other horizontal surfaces can produce up to 10 distinct clues or "letters of urban Braille."

The urban Braille system communicates information that users can read: directional change (compass N-S-E-W); hierarchy of pathways (major path versus minor path); entrances to buildings; sidewalk and road boundaries; ramps versus raised pedestrian crossings/intersections; signage/way-finding; and other information (e.g., underpasses, social activities, building information, addresses, business information).

System Elements

Main pathways offer unobstructed paths for wheelchair and scooter users to bypass each other and other sidewalk users. All obstructions (including light poles, hydrants, tree grates, flower beds, benches, and temporary signage) must be outside the limits of the main pathway. The wheelchair path must be a minimum of 1.5 metres wide when measured inside the shorelines. *Minor pathways* act as alternate routes to the main pathway,

Figure 8.8

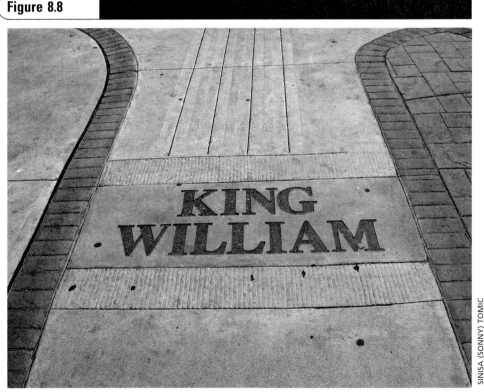

The Hamilton urban Braille system uses textures and markings along a wheelchair path to aid the visually impaired.

where parking "bump-outs" provide an opportunity for accent areas containing obstacles such as restaurant patios and flower beds.

Textured bands provide clear "tactile" direction on intersections. Textured bands should be located perpendicular to and between the shore lines of a wheelchair path in areas such as at the start and end of driveway approaches; at corners, parallel to and behind the curb within the limit of wheelchair ramps; perpendicular to roadways on either side of the grey portion of the nameplate; and perpendicular to the roadway in front of decision-node symbols.

Bus-stop detection strips help blind users to recognize the proximity of a bus stop/ shelter. Location is subject to the design of a bus stop area and must be approved by a public transportation agency prior to installation. *Decision-node symbols* indicate locations in "clear-way" areas that offer more than one possible route of travel.

Shore lines are highly contrasting lines marking wheelchair paths. They are 0.23 metre (9 inches) wide and are constructed of dark grey, stamped concrete, granite, or other suitable material. *Corner curbs/ramps* must meet current Hamilton standards for accessibility.

Street name sidewalk plates, located at all corners to indicate intersecting streets, show the name of the street that is perpendicular to the path of travel. The lettering on the plates is oriented to be read while facing the intersecting street. *Street name signage* is located on traffic and streetlight poles. Larger plates allow for greater traffic safety and easier way-finding.

Intersection/crosswalk visual and audio timers are located at dangerous intersections adjacent to hospitals and to other land uses where seniors use the public spaces. Audio and visual timers are installed in conjunction with pedestrian traffic lights.

An Ongoing Need

As part of the *Mobility Street Master Plan*, the City of Hamilton Planning Department continues working on a comprehensive way-finding system in the downtown area to provide additional destination, commercial, and cultural information through Braille lettering. Although great progress has been achieved with respect to accessibility in the barrier-free design of buildings, sidewalks and open spaces between buildings are still not designed, constructed, and maintained to ensure free movement, safety, and comfort for people with special needs. Unfortunately, most public open spaces are still left to ad hoc initiatives.

Public spaces are the living rooms of our communities. They are expensive to design, construct, and maintain. Most Canadian cities may be considered "winter cities" because of the long, harsh winter season. Current design practices are based on one season (summer) and predominantly focus on the young and healthy. This unsustainable practice should be replaced with pedestrian-friendly urban design strategies and public space designs that meet the wider needs in our communities.

Blooming Boulevards

Sandy James

2003 Plan Canada 43(4): 37–8

Kensington-Cedar Cottage is a neighbourhood of about 45 000 located on the east side of Vancouver. In 1998, after two years of intensive community involvement, Vancouver City Council approved the *Kensington-Cedar Cottage Community Vision*. The Vision is the community plan for the neighbourhood for the next 25 years, covering such topics as housing, transportation, parks and public places, environment, and shopping areas. The Vision helps guide the delivery of city services and programs to the community, and focuses neighbourhood volunteer efforts.

The Vision staff team then moved on to deliver the program in another community. The Vision-implementation staff team came in to work with the neighbourhood to make the Vision a reality. The city's commitment to Visions implementation has paid rich dividends in building bridges with and within the community.

The Blooming Boulevards Demonstration Project on Windsor Street is a striking example of the positive impact that visions implementation has had on the community. The vision identified a 25-block stretch of Windsor Street for enhanced walking and biking opportunities. From a planning perspective, Windsor Street is a natural pedestrian spine in the community. From a neighbourhood perspective, it offered little community character. While Windsor Street linked several parks and schools along its length, it suffered from traffic shortcutting, prostitution, and poor pedestrian safety and amenity.

A Green Vision

In 2000, residents began to discuss how they could make Windsor Street friendlier for walking and biking. Windsor was endowed with wide boulevards, providing some respite from the street. This boulevard space was largely neglected, but provided an opportunity for residents to brand the street in a special way. Could these boulevards be gardened? Would planting contravene city policy? Some informal gardens line boulevards in other parts of the city, but could residents plant boulevard gardens under a formal, city-supported program?

The project began when a resident of Windsor Street put a bench on the boulevard in front of his home. The resident invited community members to use the bench. They did. An elderly couple sat there when returning from their shopping. Grandparents dropping their grandchildren at the school across the street waited on the bench for the children to return. The bench was the catalyst that encouraged people to use the street and think about how it could be designed to better reflect community aspirations and needs.

The city was reticent about permitting gardens on public boulevards because of liability and maintenance concerns. Gardens could pose a trip hazard; someone could fall in the garden and sue the city. Or a child might run onto the street from behind an overgrown garden and not be seen by a driver. Grassy boulevards permit easy access to underground utilities and also allow the city to trim street trees without fear of damaging garden beds.

With these concerns in mind, the group approached the city to partner on a demonstration project for boulevard gardens along Windsor Street. Residents worked with city engineering and planning staff to develop the following standards:

- All plant material would be less than one metre high to provide for sightlines to and from the street.
- Some plants must provide structure for winter interest.
- Gardens were to be "mounded" 20 to 30 centimetres to allow for root development, and to maximize separation from any city utilities under the boulevard.
- Parks Board arborists would be consulted for specific advice for planting around the street trees and roots.

With these simple guidelines, the residents applied for several grants through the provincial Ministry of Municipal Affairs and through the Parks Board Neighbourhood Matching Grants. Successful in receiving $10 000 of initial funding, they immediately contacted residents on the street to gain interest.

The City of Vancouver Engineering Department runs the city's landfill site and collects green waste. The green waste generates fabulous compost that is pH-balanced and weed tested. Residents participating in the Blooming Boulevards program were offered free compost for their gardens, as well as grants from the funding sources for plants.

Windsor Way Blooms

By 2002, residents had formed the Windsor Way Blooming Boulevard committee. The group recognized the importance of connections with the schools. Hence, boulevard gardens near schools were eligible for grants up to $500 for plant purchases. Gardens on corner lots and next to lanes were eligible for up to $300. Midblock boulevard gardens could obtain grants for plant material to a maximum of $200.

The Windsor Way committee established blooming boulevard primary contacts: residents who were prepared to offer advice on establishing and maintaining gardens on the street. Once a garden plan was completed, it was sent to the city for approval. Engineering staff reviewed the plan to ensure that the plants were perennial, hardy, and appropriate. As part of the approval, resident contacts signed a good neighbour agreement, promising to maintain their boulevard garden, and understanding that the city reserved the right to disturb the gardens to access city services or to trim street trees. The city also reserved the right to returf a garden if it was not maintained.

As the gardens were planted, they took distinct forms, reflecting the individuals who tended them (Figure 8.9). Neighbours started to talk to each other, and to walk along the street to look at the gardens. Residents of an adjoining portion of Windsor Street, not included in the demonstration project, asked to participate. Calling themselves the Windsor Way Gateway, this group also received $3500 in funding for plant purchase. In one season, it created 10 gardens. The Gateway group painted a mural on the side of a neighbourhood store, installed bike racks at the store, did several neighbourhood cleanups, and organized a huge street party, which has now become an annual event.

Figure 8.9

Digging the blooming boulevards became a passion in Vancouver.

Creating a Special Place

In two years, over 35 boulevard gardens were built on Windsor Street. A master gardener and a landscape architect living near the street volunteered their services to help with garden design. "Dig in" street parties were held to dig up soil and pile it for composting. So much community enthusiasm was generated that residents created a boulevard garden for a neighbourhood elementary school. Students in grades six and seven painted designs on the picket fence bordering the garden, and created special signage advising that students maintain the garden.

Windsor Street has become a special place where local people walk, enjoy the seasonal change in the gardens, and talk to their neighbours. Prostitution has moved off the street. Windsor Street residents have twice been runners-up for the Most Beautiful Block in Vancouver competition run by the Vancouver Garden Club. And the British Columbia Society of Landscape Architects presented a Community Involvement Award to the residents.

In 2003, Windsor Street was declared a city bikeway. Traffic-calming measures including traffic circles will be installed. Windsor Street residents are also involved in the Windsor Way Art Way, a community project to create public art to hang from light fixtures. The theme is "Petal to Pedal," an allusion to the blooming boulevards and Windsor Street's designation and development as a city bikeway.

The Windsor Street Blooming Boulevard Demonstration Project illustrates the power of gardening to transform green space through community development. Other initiatives to improve the neighbourhood have benefited as residents partnered with the city. Community development, the foundation of Visions implementation work, has given the community new tools to work with to build trust and confidence in cooperation and local initiative. By gardening the city boulevards, residents defined their perceptions of community and began community building, literally from the grassroots up.

The Blooming Boulevard program has gone citywide and attracted international attention. Similar projects are being developed in Great Britain and the United States.

1. How have new urbanism ideas influenced suburban development in your community?

2. What design trends and values do you see in new development patterns in the suburbs? What appeals do developers make to consumers in their advertising?

3. Where would you place beauty in a hierarchy of planning values that might include equity, amenity, efficiency, health, and safety?

4. What is the appropriate place for heritage conservation in contemporary urban design? Study buildings constructed in different eras in your community to analyze how ideas of beauty and design have changed through time.

5. How does the mass media contribute to interpretations of "good design" standards? (Examine magazines in the grocery store racks for the latest ideas.)

6. How have the uses of and perceived need for the public realm and public open space changed through time?

7. Wight suggests that nonurban living options are subordinate and lesser options. Leung argues that some of the forms that claim to be urban are merely a new kind of sprawl. Articulate your view in this debate.

8. What are the key requirements in planning and designing winter cities?

Reference Notes

1. Schneider, W (1992) The suburban century begins. *Atlantic Monthly* (July) 33–44.

2. Fishman, R (1990) Megalopolis unbound: America's new city. *Wilson Quarterly* 14(1): 24–5.

3. Sennett, R (1990) *The Conscience of the Eye: The Design and Social Life of Cities.* New York: WW Norton.

4. Reid, M (2001) Alberta roads earn 'ugly' reviews. *Calgary Herald*, 13 March B1.

5. Jacobs, J (1961) *The Death and Life of Great American Cities.* New York: Random House.

6. Relph, E (1987) *The Modern Urban Landscape.* London: Croom Helm.

7. Hough, M (1990) *Out of Place: Restoring Identity to the Regional Landscape.* New Haven: Yale University Press.

8. Trancik, R (1986) *Finding Lost Space: Theories of Urban Design.* New York: Van Nostrand Reinhold.

9. Ellin, N (1996) *Postmodern Urbanism.* Oxford: Blackwell Publishing.

10. Due to slower-than-expected sales, in 1999, Bombardier Immobilier received permission from the municipality to build a golf course over 40 percent of the site, http://saintlaurent.ville.montreal.qc.ca/en/intro/histvsl/terri/quartdev/boisfranc/boisfranc.asp (accessed 18 October 2005).

Chapter Nine

Designing Healthy and Safe Communities

Planning's Prime Directives

Jill Grant

Since the early days of the modern town planning movement, health and safety have topped the urban agenda. Protecting the community constitutes the primary justification for state intervention in limiting private property rights. Providing safe water, eliminating communicable diseases, and improving housing conditions dominated planners' concerns in the early decades of planning. With those issues largely resolved, new health and safety concerns began to draw attention: managing traffic for pedestrian safety, developing spacious and healthy residential areas, and removing swaths of "blighted" slum housing. Many young Canadians cannot remember a time when officials believed that building highways and tearing down tenements would improve public health and safety, but the pages of planning journals from the 1950s and 1960s expose that history.

Direct discussions of health and safety reappeared in the planning literature in the 1980s and have become underlying themes in recent approaches like sustainable development and smart growth. This chapter presents two articles on the healthy communities movement and several articles suggesting strategies to respond to concerns about safety in the city.

Figure 9.1

Are the suburbs getting fat?

Do the Suburbs Make Us Fat?

Recent studies suggest that people living in the suburbs are less physically active and weigh more than people living in denser, mixed-use communities.[1] People who have to drive everywhere—the argument goes—suffer additional stress and anxiety and have few opportunities to work off the pounds. Organizations like the David Suzuki Foundation link fighting sprawl to promoting community health.[2] They suggest that compact communities with transportation alternatives allow people to walk or cycle more often. Active transportation supports active lifestyles and improved individual and community health.

While few seem ready to defend car-dependent lifestyles, some say that it is not fair to blame the suburbs for growing obesity levels. Critics of our fast-food culture suggest that poor eating habits contribute most significantly to our growing waistlines. Not everyone in the suburbs is fat, after all, and many suburbanites walk or cycle for exercise.

Healthy Communities

The public health movement got a boost in the 1980s.[3] Rising health-care costs encouraged government to consider strategies for preventing illness, rather than managing it. Planning could play an important role and gain a "renewed sense of purpose to the profession" by helping to create communities that promote health.[4] In the same issue of *Plan Canada,* Lane described a model of how to develop a healthy communities project, with Winnipeg as the test case. Experiments with promoting health through planning activities were going on across the country. Planners worked with public health advocates and municipal officials to envision a new mission and agenda for planning: health for all.[5]

Canada played a key role in the international movement for healthy communities. The founding charter bears the name of Ottawa, where the ideas took root and inspired the World Health Organization. Susan Berlin, the director of the Canadian Healthy Communities Project, describes the mission and promise of the Canadian project in this chapter. Sue Hendler raises a prescient caution in response, wondering whether the project would flourish or die a swift death, as so many planning fads have before. Indeed, after only a few years of providing funding, the national government withdrew support for the Canadian project, leaving communities to plot their own routes to better futures. Although the movement continued in several provinces, its overall influence in community planning suffered from a lack of support for special initiatives.[6] A later issue of *Plan Canada* considered the legacy of the movement, suggesting that, despite its fragmentation, it had a lasting impact on planning discourse and on community concerns.[7]

Fearful Communities

While Canadian communities enjoy a high standard of living and commonly top international ratings for livability, we also see signs that people have grown increasingly fearful in the city. Paradoxically, as crime rates decline, the fear of crime remains strong, enhanced at every turn by television programs and films that turn crime and punishment into entertainment.

What is the contemporary planning response to enhance safety? Planners' interest in the principles of new urbanism means that "eyes on the street" have become the watchword in community design. Jacobs held that streets full of people with windows close to the sidewalk are safe streets.[8] The principle of natural surveillance has been embedded in many community plans across the country.

In this chapter, Gerda Wekerle describes Safe City programs, a concept developed more fully in Wekerle and Whitzman.[9] The Safe City strategy suggests that instead of taking a strong law-and-order approach communities can accomplish more through local initiatives to manage and control space to reduce the fear of crime. Mayja Embleton discusses safety audits, a tool that community members can use to evaluate their spaces and to develop strategies to improve safety.

Tom McKay's article reviews crime-prevention strategies used by police services in collaboration with community groups: These programs regularly use natural surveillance along with concepts related to territorial defence to improve community control over spaces (like vacant lots) where crime may occur. Crime Prevention Through Environmental Design, or CPTED, has become an integral tool for community policing in Canada.[10] CPTED principles have been used in many planning exercises, including evaluations of proposals to intensify urban areas.[11]

The market reveals that some Canadians are making other responses to perceptions that cities are unsafe. The affluent in some parts of the country employ guards and gates to control space, as Jill Grant notes in her article. Fears of dealing with others lead some to seek privacy and separation; rather than enhancing perceptions of safety, such strategies may reinforce fear.

Since 9/11, the threat of terrorism has led officials to reconsider the design and planning of civic buildings and public spaces. While the effects are most notable in cities like Washington or London, our own larger cities are not immune to the response. A focus on target hardening encourages the barricading of entries to significant public buildings. Closed-circuit cameras are popping up in many public and private places. Security has become a top priority.

Healthy and Safe Futures

Each generation defines its health and safety issues differently. In the contemporary era, we focus on livability and sustainability. We hope to plan communities that empower and enable people to achieve their full potential.[12] We envision healthy environments and healthy neighbourhoods that protect options for the future and that provide places for everyone. We promote active living and critique car-dependent suburbs that undermine opportunities for walking. We look for quality of life.

Protecting health and safety are ongoing concerns for planning, even as the nature of the threats changes. Climate change, sealevel rise, tsunamis, hurricanes, and earthquakes present real risks whose consequences require anticipatory planning. Another concern the media has flagged is the risk of potential pandemics. Ancient and medieval cities were often hit hard by plagues. With our dense and large urban systems, well connected and integrated in global networks, how do we plan to manage infectious diseases that may emerge and sweep the planet? What kinds of cities offer the promise of greatest resilience for these and other threats to public health and safety? Planning requires that we constantly sweep the horizon to anticipate the dangers ahead.

The Canadian Healthy Communities Project: Shapes of the Reality

Susan Berlin

1989, Plan Canada 29(4): 13–5

> "The necessary preconditions of health are peace, shelter, education, adequate income, a sustainable environment..." *Ottawa Charter for Health Promotion*

Words set the limits of our thinking; shifts in the meaning of words can powerfully affect what we see as possible. The meaning of the word "health" has changed several times in the last century, as medical knowledge has made mere survival less problematic. With the virtual elimination of early death from childhood infectious diseases, the extension of life expectancy, a growing awareness of environmental impacts on health, and a greater sense of the social elements of health, new questions are being asked, a new paradigm created within which to think about health.

For example, if we know that people at the bottom end of the economic scale can expect six to seven fewer years of life than those at the upper end—and 14 fewer years of disability-free life—where is the boundary between economics and health? If we also know that people with low literacy levels are likely to have limited incomes, where is the divide between education and health? If the chief cause of "illness" in the elderly is depression, fuelled by isolation, is access to public transportation a health issue?

Health for All

In 1986, responding to questions like these, Health and Welfare Canada published *Achieving Health for All*, a policy document outlining a health framework for the country. The document outlined three major health promotion strategies:

1. fostering public participation in processes and decisions that affect health;
2. strengthening community health services by improving links between services and the communities they serve, particularly the disadvantaged;
3. coordinating healthy public policy, so that professionals in all public policy areas become aware of their interest in and responsibility toward health in their communities.

Following publication of the document, Health and Welfare Canada provided three-year contribution agreement funding for the Canadian Healthy Communities Project (jointly sponsored by the Canadian Institute of Planners, the Canadian Public Health Association, and the Federation of Canadian Municipalities), under which community-based programs could put the strategies into practice.

This project recognizes that most of the health issues that ordinary people are concerned about today—the environment, community violence, the future of work, the aging of our population—are actually dealt with at the municipal level through the delivery of government and private agency services. However, none of these issues is "owned" by any one municipal department, so they cannot be successfully dealt with in the usual way. For example, dealing with family violence involves the police department, social services department, board of education, and health department. Similarly, the situation of the elderly in communities requires the resources of housing, social services, health, transportation, and education departments. Effective responses to environmental issues entail the cooperation of parks, public works, purchasing, and education departments.

In addition to municipal involvement, an adequate response to health issues requires community participation in identifying local needs and designing responses to them. Community members are the "experts" on living in their community: The absence of their participation in any aspect of the process produces apathy, lack of support for solutions, and the NIMBY (not-in-my-backyard) syndrome, not to mention cynicism and erosion of the idea of democracy. Moreover, many health issues in the environment and the workplace require action from the private sector, so it is essential to have people from that sector taking part in the Healthy Communities process.

Project Design

How does the project work? First and foremost, it operates at the local level, providing a model that allows communities to integrate their resources so as to take effective action on health. The project design envisages that a municipality that wants to participate will pass a resolution in council indicating its political will. A decision-making body—including representatives from all departments, community members, and representatives of the private sector—will work together to identify and address a few health issues facing the community. Any "screen" may be used to select these issues. For example, at the outset of the process, criteria such as urgency, quick returns, and low cost might let the community see how well the process works before making major financial commitments to it. The program must include an evaluation component to identify what does and does not work in the approach.

Because all the groups sitting around the table are already providing services that affect health, they can accomplish a great deal to improve health without significant additional expenditures. Most municipal departments and a wide range of private-sector agencies spend money on programs dealing with housing, employment, youth, the environment, and the elderly. Rarely is this money spent under a coordinated policy developed with the participation of the people affected and delivered in an integrated fashion.

Local healthy community projects are supported by a national Healthy Communities office, which provides resource material, contacts with experts, workshops and communication with other communities.[13] A quarterly newsletter reports on the work of projects across Canada, offering rapid transfer of ideas.

Sample Projects

Perhaps the single most interesting fact to report is that every community has done it differently; the Canadian refusal to take direction from the centre has proved fruitful. In Dartmouth, Nova Scotia, for example, leadership toward a healthy community was provided neither by staff nor by community volunteers, but by the mayor and his city manager. They decided that they first must put the city's house in order. As part of a five-year strategic plan, they required department heads to generate health impact statements for their departments. Managers were asked to review departmental plans and priorities in view of these impact statements. These are some of the results. The Public Works Department discovered that accident rates in the community would decline if highest priority was given to paving

Chapter 9 / Designing Healthy and Safe Communities

roads and clearing snow in areas with large populations of elderly people, disabled residents, and small children. The Purchasing Department reviewed its orders to eliminate environmentally harmful items, like styrofoam cups, and to encourage recycling. Later a community consultation initiative was developed to create the full Healthy Communities process.

In Toronto initiatives already under way united within the Healthy Communities Project. A community consultation process within the Toronto Public Health Department led to the publication of a policy document *Healthy Toronto 2000*, a statement on how the city can implement the World Health Organization goals of *Health for All* by the year 2000. The Public Works Department set up a recycling program, which garnered enormous public support. An interdepartmental steering committee reported to the committee of heads on the effectiveness of a formal commitment to participating in the Healthy Communities Network.

In Edmonton, where the Public Health Department is entirely a provincial responsibility and where health staff has no links with municipal government, setting up a Healthy Communities project presented obvious challenges. Nevertheless, Board of Health personnel used a model developed in Seattle to create a "KidsPlace" project. Children in three inner-city schools were asked to "map" their neighbourhoods by assigning to various familiar places a prepared list of adjectives, both positive and negative. They then developed a set of issues of concern: too many stray dogs, bigger kids chasing littler ones out of parks, absence of the kinds of recreation programs they wanted, and so on. A roster of departmental staff—community police, social services, the recreation department, board of education—participated in responding to the children's requests.

Figure 9.2

Early Healthy Communities projects often spearheaded community recycling drives, helping to make recycling a Canadian institution.

In Quebec, a provincial Healthy Communities network was established: *Villes et villages en santé*. Many small communities developed strong healthy communities projects. Some had children produce designs for the projects and then used them internally and as part of community economic development packages.

Growth and Change

As the project develops, shifts in the overall design will respond to lessons from experience. The Canadian project steering committee designed the project to be inclusive, rather than exclusive, unlike the WHO Healthy Cities Project, where cities compete for recognition as having achieved healthy cities status. The project seeks to support member communities in reaching their health goals. The rewards of membership in the Healthy Communities project will be the intrinsic value of participation and knowing that each community has made a commitment to improving health.

The Canadian Healthy Communities Project: Relevant or Redundant?

Sue Hendler

1989, Plan Canada 24(4): 32–4

> When asked what is a healthy community, people respond by talking about a clean environment, clean air, safe and clean water, lots of trees and green space; basic needs such as food, shelter and housing for everyone; work for all that is health enhancing, flexible and satisfying; neighbourhoods that are people oriented, where the streets are safe and where there is a good mix of housing, people, services and facilities; good health and social services accessible to all; local government that is accessible and responsible and that involves people in making decisions about their lives; and so on.[14]

The Idea of a Healthy Community[15]

It is difficult to argue with the tenets underlying the idea of a healthy community. A clean environment, an equitable distribution of resources, and free, creative individuals reflect the foundations of a moral society. The principles represent empowerment, fairness, and the ubiquitous "quality of life." However, my experience is that such broadly-based premises appear too broad for many people to accept as workable and useful. In other words, and with apologies to Aaron Wildavsky: "If a healthy community is everything, maybe it's nothing."[16] This level of generality often leads to skepticism regarding the viability of the project. Some voice concern that the premises grounding a healthy community are, at best, redundant with established planning principles.

In a conceptual context, whether the image evoked by healthy community literature is *the* good society remains to be seen. Theorists have long been struggling with the question of what constitutes a good city,[17] with little consensus emerging. Thus, the idea and justification of a healthy community may require further analysis to ascertain its conceptual legitimacy.

The Practice of Healthy Communities

There are a number of pragmatic difficulties associated with the development of healthy communities. First, a healthy community must be part of a healthy environment. This is not to spout the usual rhetoric of a "stable ecosystem" and so on. Rather, it means that we need to know what a healthy ecosystem or landscape or environment is, and how to get one. The problem is that ecological theorists have thus far been unable to tell us what constitutes a healthy environment, and, while work continues in the area of ecological health and integrity,[18] operational guidelines for environmental planning have proved elusive.

A second difficulty has to do with developing appropriate goals and objectives for communities. Toronto, for example, adopted the following mission statement in its program for attaining a healthy city by the year 2000: "The mission of the City of Toronto Department of Public Health is to make Toronto the healthiest city in North America."[19] While the intent of such a principle was a good one, it seems clear that it could easily lead to competition rather than cooperation between communities. It could, for instance, result in discarding untreated wastes in an effort to develop a healthy local economy without concern for the environmental health of whoever (and whatever) lives downstream. A truly healthy community should, it seems, follow the popular maxim "Think globally, act locally," rather than concentrate on making any community "better" than another. Thus, arriving at suitable goals and objectives that pique citizens' curiosity and interest, but that also may be analytically legitimated, is not a simple task.

Third is the issue of developing suitable indicators for individual communities. This problem is particularly tenacious in terms of reaching a consensus as to what constitutes appropriate measures of the movement of a society toward the ideal of a healthy community. Reasons for this pertain, I believe, to the difficulties inherent in quantifying social and environmental phenomena in any reasonable or meaningful way and, further, reaching agreement as to what does and does not count. Is a measure of aquatic phosphates more important than an evaluation of people's self-esteem? Is one conceivably contingent on the other? Such questions remain; they should be a focus of work in the area of indicator development and research.

Fourth is the ever-present problem of harnessing political will. A healthy community properly conceived functions as an integrated multisectoral unit. Limited resources, overworked staff, and a continuous need for crisis management and firefighting dominate the public agenda. Any municipal or regional body must be convinced that the long-term benefits of a healthy community approach will outweigh the short-term costs.

A fifth issue pertains to the methods used in constructing and running the community workshops typically used for assessing needs, developing goals and objectives, and devising implementation scenarios. My experience is that such events are often rushed, frantic, and possibly superficial. Carefully conceived methods must be used in structuring community workshops, particularly since their outcome will often represent the health "plan" for the area in question and thus be regarded (consciously or subconsciously) with some authority.

Finally, the vision of the Healthy Communities Project is sometimes perceived as yet another fad, which the planning profession has decided to adopt as its own. The profession has bounced from one normative commitment to another, including advocacy planning, ecological planning, and negotiation/mediation. While healthy communities appear to represent an intuitively appropriate direction for the renewal and revitalization of the profession, the perception that the project will die a quick death is widespread and must be dealt with constructively for the project to have an air of continuity and accountability.

It seems to me that students, practitioners, and academics are pretty evenly split as to whether the Canadian Healthy Communities Project will have staying power. Problems like those listed, along with others involving basic issues of implementation and monitoring/ evaluation, must be recognized and accommodated so that the optimists among us may succeed in our quest to make Canadian communities healthier. However, to make us feel that our efforts are worthwhile, we should assess the theoretical and practical potential of the project.

The Theoretical Potential of the Project

As a teacher of planning theory, I have been interested in the theoretical bases of the Healthy Communities Project and their relationship with current trends and directions in planning theory. First, a Healthy Communities project uses many of the processes and perspectives of strategic planning doctrine: environmental scans, an interactive and dynamic model of the planning process, a general outlook on strategies, and accompanying programs. The recent emphasis placed on strategic planning in many schools and much of the planning literature indicates that the healthy community focus may be an appropriate one.

Second, the grassroots or bottom-up approach inherent in the national Healthy Communities Project is part of a growing emphasis on empowerment and emancipation as evidenced in normative planning theory. We see an increasing focus on, in Friedmann's terms,[20] social learning and mobilization (transformative process) over policy analysis and social reform (processes that maintain the status quo). This provides a theoretical base for the project also manifested in recent policy documents.[21]

The link, or discontinuity, between planning theory and practice has long been a thorn in the sides of both teachers and practitioners. While such integration does not in itself spell success for a project, it can only assist in attaining the goals of the endeavour.

The Practical Potential of the Project

I was originally attracted to the discipline and profession of planning because it offered a structured, interdisciplinary area of inquiry. Here, I thought, was a way to integrate my concerns for environmental and ethical issues and perhaps to have an impact on the explication or resolution of some of them. To me, the Healthy Communities Project represents a means of meshing the disparate strands of the profession and provides a contemporary connection with its historical roots in public health. In linking theory and practice, the project bridges planning in its current form with its historical purpose and with the many disciplines that contribute to the profession.

Second, a key aspect of the project is its attempt to demonstrate to stakeholders the value of their participation: In initiating a local healthy community endeavour, one must derive convincing reasons why specific individuals and groups should be involved. Again, a lack of resources (time, money, and so on) can easily dissuade actors from contributing to the project; its leader must convince people it is in their best interest to participate. A healthy communities project can increase the effectiveness of existing organizations, an added dimension of its practical potential.

Relevant or Redundant?

Difficulties abound with the Healthy Communities Project and underlying concepts. Nevertheless, the national project has already met with some success. The amount of critical thinking and discussion it has generated has inherent value. Indeed, this sort of activity enables societies to grow and develop; it politicizes members to want to contribute to the planning of their communities. And this is what the planning profession is, or perhaps should be, all about.

The Canadian Healthy Communities Project is off and running. Whether it is a real contender in the race to deal with our pressing environmental and social problems remains to be seen. Here, I have voiced my concerns, as well as my optimism, about both the conceptual and the practical aspects of the project. In the light of further discussion with other interested parties, the national office should focus on strengthening its assets and attending to its apparent liabilities. This will facilitate the planning of

Canadian healthy communities. What could be a more appropriate means to combat the perception that the planning profession is potentially irrelevant?[22]

Planning for Safety in Cities

Gerda R Wekerle

1996, Plan Canada 36(2): 3–5

Annual ratings of the livability and competitiveness of major world cities place urban safety as second only to the economy in the views of urban residents. Yet, how cities respond to demands for increased urban safety varies substantially. One solution—the neoliberal solution—is becoming more popular in American cities. Typically, it has been to hire more police, arrest more criminals, and toughen sentences, which leads to an increase in the prison population. Target-hardening solutions, such as gated and walled communities for suburban residents, are a popular variation. This, along with private security forces that patrol and control access, reduces reliance on urban police forces. The American model has made inroads into Canada, most notably in Kelowna, where gated communities have become the new suburban development prototype (Figure 9.3).

These solutions threaten Canadian cities. In this period of social safety net cutbacks, privatized "solutions" to urban crime are tempting. To some, they suggest a solution to burgeoning urban police budgets and to the painful tradeoffs that politicians are forced to make between budget cuts to policing or to welfare and other essential social services. Yet, the impact of these private market solutions to urban crime is devastating: Only communities that are affluent, powerful, and organized can afford the high cost of 24-hour private security. Others are left to their own devices, competing for scarce public

Figure 9.3

JILL GRANT

In some British Columbia communities like Kelowna, gated communities attract retirees to the good life.

Copyright © Canadian Institute of Planners, 1996. Used with permission.

infrastructure dollars. As urban safety becomes defined as limiting access and increasing control over space, at home and at the workplace, the public realm—open equally to all citizens—is the loser.

Paradoxically, at a time when fear of crime is increasing in urban areas, statistics show that reported crime rates are actually decreasing. Understanding why people respond to crime with fear, especially in urban public spaces, is the key to planning for urban safety. Managers of such urban spaces as parks and transit systems have noted over the years that urban residents respond to signs of incivility with fear and avoidance. Yet these signs of incivility—graffiti, garbage, poor maintenance, boarded buildings, bad lighting, and limited sightlines—are visual social cues that the environment is not well tended. Ill-considered urban design, which creates blank walls, isolated public spaces, and limited outdoor seating, is also a signal that nobody cares.

Paying attention to some of these small details of daily life may seem like an insignificant gesture in the context of the massive social and economic problems facing cities, but it conveys the message that caring for public spaces may be something that extends to the city's residents.

Safe City Approaches

Canadian cities are celebrated for their civility. They have been attracted to the Safe City approach to crime prevention, an approach initially pioneered by the City of Toronto. Safe City initiatives are rooted in the experience and priorities of each locality, and typically include multiple stakeholders: community residents, politicians, municipal staff, the police, and the business community.

Planners play a key role in these initiatives. In Toronto, the right to a safe city has been enshrined in the official plan, and council has adopted design guidelines for safer cities, which are used in the process of design review and development approvals; new bylaws have been passed to improve security in underground parking garages in both residential and commercial buildings; new pedestrian-oriented lighting has been installed on city streets; and the parks department has developed a security plan for High Park and design guidelines to improve park safety. Many of these initiatives were developed through joint citizen-planner working groups and are grounded in detailed, site-specific safety audits conducted by users, who have made recommendations based on their own experience to improve urban safety.

The Safe City approach has the potential to expand the notions of citizenship and the boundaries of civil society. Traditionally, urban safety has been left to the police and private security experts. A Safe City program aims to make urban safety the concern of all citizens. Safe City initiatives harness the resources and legitimacy of city government and combine them with the experience of residents committed to improving urban safety. By becoming involved in defining their own needs and local solutions, ordinary citizens take ownership of urban safety problems in their parks, neighbourhoods, and workplaces. Obtaining a positive response from local government and experiencing success in implementing new policies or amending existing ones demonstrates to citizens that government can respond positively.

In Canadian cities, the Safe City approach has provided a framework for the emergence of a mix of initiatives, including community development, social programs, urban design solutions, and regulatory changes. The high public priority placed on urban safety is often only a starting point in dealing with such wider community issues as urban civility, connection to place, the sense of community, and the exercise of citizenship in the local polity. By involving the community in both the definition and solution of potential and real problems, Safe City initiatives respond to local conditions and have taken positive steps to address the widespread fear of crime in urban areas. The Safe City concept offers the best planning alternative to the threat of neoliberal solutions.

Table 9.1	Approaches to Controlling Urban Crime

1. **Law and order**
   Focuses on:
   - Increasing police and security
   - Imposing tougher laws
   - Ensuring stiffer sentencing

   Assumes that crime and the fear of crime results from too many criminals and a lax criminal justice system.

   Leads to fortress mentality, private security, withdrawal from city, gated enclaves, and "cocooning."

2. **Root causes**
   Focuses on:
   - Training and educating
   - Creating jobs
   - Encouraging economic development
   - Resocializing youth

   Assumes that crime results from poverty, marginality, and social breakdown.

   Leads to outreach work, education, and long-range community development work.

3. **Safe cities**
   Focuses on:
   - Developing partnerships between government and citizens, especially marginalized groups
   - Preventing criminal behaviour through environmental design and community development education
   - Combining social prevention and physical changes
   - Promoting urban safety as a catalyst for change

   Assumes that fear of crime is as important as crime itself; citizens are experts on urban violence.

   Leads to immediate solutions to improve safety in housing estates, transportation systems, city centres, and parks. Looks for long-term solutions relating to youth crime, education, community development, and prevention of violence against women.

Source: Table adapted from: G Wekerle & C Whitzman (1996) Controlling Urban Crime: What Can Cities Do? *Plan Canada* 36(2): 9. Copyright © Canadian Institute of Planners, 1996. Used with permission.

Community Safety Audits

Mayja Embleton

1996, Plan Canada 36(2): 18–9

Imagine being apprehensive about leaving your house after dark. Imagine feeling afraid to walk through your neighbourhood park or nervous about walking home from the bus stop. Many people living in urban areas have these fears. In fact, fear is increasing—which probably has some relation to police statistics that indicate more and more citizens perceive criminal activity to be on the rise, even though such is not the case.

The media and changing demographics must share the blame for this misunderstanding. The media sensationalizes crime by focusing on violent events, while the general population tends to become more fearful as it ages. In an effort to minimize the harmful effects of this escalating fear of crime, municipalities across the country are introducing their citizens to the concept of safety audits.

Safety audits were first introduced by Toronto's Metro Action Committee on Public Violence Against Women and Children. The guide and checklist developed by this committee laid the foundation for a safety audit process since adopted by Vancouver, Winnipeg, Edmonton, and Calgary.

The Safety Audit

Safety audits are based on the principles of Crime Prevention Through Environmental Design (CPTED)—to create safer and more hospitable living environments—and have been practised by humans for thousands of years. Europeans chose the highest hills on which to build their castles and fortresses; Louis XIV of France installed 7000 lights in 1701 to prevent vandalism and increase security in Paris. In one way or another, all of these strategies aim at preventing crime and maintaining social order.

More recently, Oscar Newman advocated creating a sense of territoriality or ownership as a means of improving safety, especially in public-housing schemes. His design features include using real or symbolic boundaries, clustering residential units, mixing facilities, and locating windows and lighting to enhance natural surveillance.[23] Timothy Crowe, an American criminologist with 25 years of experience in law enforcement and crime prevention and a strong background in architecture and behaviour management through design, has become a leading advocate of safety audit principles. Crowe believes that a pleasing, quality living environment can be created using the three design approaches fundamental to CPTED: natural access control, natural surveillance, and territorial behaviour. These design elements are often absent in places where criminal activity occurs.[24]

Research on sexual assaults indicates that five environmental factors are usually present when an assault takes place:

- predictability of time and path;
- an ambush site;
- an attack site (enclosed on three sides);
- a minimum of two escape routes for the offender; and
- conditions that make the offender unidentifiable from a distance of 25 metres.

Removing even one factor may be a significant crime deterrent.

By conducting either a CPTED evaluation or a safety audit, citizens may be able to understand the potential for criminal activity in their community and then go about creating better design solutions. A safety audit is a tool to help reduce the opportunity for attack. An audit is easy to accomplish in six steps.

1. Gather volunteers, preferably from a cross-section of the population.
2. Determine the areas that are going to be audited by using focus groups or arranging discussions with the volunteers and other interested parties.
3. Hold a "walk around" or audit, with the volunteers visiting the areas to be audited and closely evaluating each area's strengths and weakness. (A checklist that examines visibility, audibility, sightlines, escape routes, and maintenance is a useful tool.)
4. Examine the answers received and compile recommendations to improve the area.
5. Communicate these recommendations to the appropriate person, landowner, agency, or city department that has the power to make the improvements.
6. Ensure the audit team takes responsibility for checking that changes are implemented, as much as possible, and for monitoring the area to ascertain whether the improvements have made a difference.

The Calgary Experience

In Calgary, the Action Committee Against Violence was charged with implementing 66 recommendations identified by the mayor's 1991 Task Force Against Family and Community Violence. One recommendation was to create a *Calgary Safety Audit Handbook*. The handbook,

Figure 9.4

Many cities have adopted neighbourhood watch or block watch programs to reduce crime.

which describes a safety audit and explains how to conduct an audit, was designed primarily to guide community residents in their auditing efforts. A safety audit coordinator was hired to assist this process in a number of ways: be available to make presentations to communities; help in soliciting volunteers and organizing community audits; provide advice when final reports were being compiled; and help to get the recommendations implemented.

Calgary's success has been quite remarkable. Over 30 communities expressed interest in the audit process. Many have finished conducting audits with the focus on such public areas as playgrounds, light rail transit stops, schoolyards, and community halls. In most cases, the communities asked to increase lighting in areas and trim hedges and bushes. The response by city departments to meeting with community representatives to work out solutions to identified problems has also been positive.

Communities are also encouraged to come up with their own solutions, including establishing block watch and citizen watch programs (Figure 9.4). Individual landowners are approached if problems are occurring on their land. As well, neighbours are informed about light rental agreements that are available through the city Electrical Department if there is a requirement to light up dark alleys and lanes.

An Ongoing Concern

Although several municipalities across Canada have encouraged community safety audits by providing information and handbooks, there does not seem to be an efficient mechanism for introducing recommendations for improvement at the city level. Each city involved in the safety audit process seems to have its own way of handling recommendations. For example, through its Safer Cities Initiative, the City of Edmonton invites residents to submit their audit results to the Citizen Action Centre, which passes on the recommendations to the appropriate city department. Calgary used the safety audit coordinator as a liaison between the community and the city: The coordinator directs the community to the correct person in each department who can help to implement a recommendation, offers advice when it comes time to putting the results in final form, and suggests workable designs or programs.

Toronto's Metro Action Committee model for safety audits gives responsibility for ensuring that improvements are implemented to the original audit team. While this approach has its merits, the method may not be the most effective. Communities need to remain involved throughout the entire process, but individual community members often find it frustrating and time consuming to deal with city departments.

Municipalities that actively encourage their citizens to become involved in safety audits, or similar CPTED evaluations, must ensure that an effective process for implementing the results is conceived. Safety is an ongoing concern.

Empty Spaces, Dangerous Places

Tom McKay

1998, Plan Canada 38(1): 35–6

As a Crime Prevention Through Environmental Design (CPTED) specialist with Peel Regional Police, my attention is most often directed toward the built (or soon-to-be-built) environment. The body of knowledge, literature, and case studies detailing the relationship between crime and the built environment in the Peel Region continues to grow. Missing from this focus, as a review of almost any index on the subject will show, is sufficient attention to underutilized or vacant space. This article documents the impact of these spaces on a southern Ontario community and shares its success in addressing the concern.

Reactions to Empty Spaces

Criminals consciously scan the environment for criminal opportunities. A public place that lacks significant ownership interest is often perceived by prostitutes, drug dealers, and others as an environment that may tolerate and support their activities (Figure 9.5). These and other underutilized and empty spaces are readily recognized and exploited by criminals. Often referred to by environmental criminologists as "good" (for the criminal) environmental cues, they draw the offender's attention with their apparent lack of activity, ownership, maintenance, or care.

Equally important is the fear empty spaces generate in the average resident or normal user. Frequently seen as intimidating, these spaces are avoided by normal users, thereby exacerbating the problem and encouraging the criminal element. Vacant lands can be exceptionally problematic since many absentee landlords pay little attention to them. The Victoria Hills community of Kitchener provides a fairly representative example of the difficulties encountered with vacant lands.

Victoria Hills

Consisting of a vacant lot surrounded by a school and three high-density, low-rent apartment buildings, the Victoria Hills site had become an overgrown, garbage-strewn, and intimidating place to the more than 1200 residents of the area. Illegal activity in the area closest to Mooregate Crescent resulted in police constantly being called to this locale. Many residents simply avoided the place, considered "an unsafe and negative presence in the community."[25]

Figure 9.5

KEVIN BROOKS

Areas with extensive graffiti may appear to invite crime.

Recognizing this problem, Constable Rob Davis, a CPTED-trained Waterloo Regional Police Officer, spearheaded a successful transformation of the area by applying the standard CPTED strategy of placing a safe activity in an unsafe or vulnerable area. Constable Davis introduced the idea of a community garden, effectively assigning a purpose to the space and compensating for its lack of legitimate activity and overt signs of ownership.

The results were tremendous. In the first summer of activity, police incidents at the three apartment buildings surrounding the site dropped by 30 percent. The results continued to improve in 1995 and 1996, with reported police incidents dropping by 48.8 and 55.7 percent, respectively. Plus, local residents now had their own fresh vegetables to eat! Nowhere has the crime rate changed more dramatically than at 80 Mooregate Crescent, a previous trouble spot. Crimes reported at this location decreased 75.4 percent in 1996, from a pre-garden high of 187 to a post-garden low of 46.

As impressive as these results are, a qualitative measure of safety showed that participants also experienced a decrease in their concerns about property vandalism and walking in their community at night. Indeed, residents cited many factors contributing to a safer feeling in their community. Most prevalent among these were "the physical presence of people in the garden late into the evening"; the fact that they "knew more people in their neighbourhood"; and the feeling that "neighbours were also watching out for them, their children, and property."

These increased feelings of trust and friendship translated into more interaction between ethnic groups and increased cohesion in the community. A boost in community pride was also evident: Qualitative survey responses showed that people now feel "good about the fact that they are involved in their community" and are "more attracted to living in their community." Other positive developments included a feeling of empowerment by the residents and a general physical improvement of the area. Even outside observers saw benefits to the community.

Lessons Learned

The introduction and development of a community garden is a classic example of the CPTED strategy of placing a safe activity in an unsafe area. In Victoria Hills and other communities, such as Selby-Dale in St. Paul, Minnesota, the garden transformed an unsafe vacant lot into a positive and safe community space.

It is the challenge of planners, city officials, and police officers to recognize the deleterious effect empty spaces have on a community, to guard against their presence, and, where empty spaces are unavoidable, to mitigate their impact. By encouraging the sale of undevelopable parcels of land to adjacent landowners, empty spaces can be eliminated. Where they are unavoidable, creative partnerships and solutions must be sought to make these spaces part of, and not apart from, the communities in which they are found.

Open Society or Cloistered Enclaves? Urban Form in the Information Age

Jill Grant

2004, Plan Canada, 44(2): 42–4

While some may argue that early twenty-first-century Canada can boast an open society with human rights and civil liberties that are the envy of other nations, we must also acknowledge the evidence of some troubling trends in our communities. Access to the technology of the communication age is not evenly distributed. Moreover, we see growing indications that privilege is spatially concentrated in our cities. This paper reviews some contemporary trends in built form in Canada and argues that they raise significant questions for planners committed to supporting democratic urban environments in the information age.

Contemporary Trends in Urban Form

Over the last few decades, our cities have invested extensive public resources in urban regeneration. We have improved central areas through promoting heritage conservation, facilitating waterfront revitalization, and encouraging economic development (especially through tourism). Many cities now boast condominium projects and commercial enterprises on former brownfield or greyfield sites, and thereby attract urban professionals and affluent retirees to the inner city. Thus, we find the city cores increasingly populated by a "leisure class," there to enjoy the views and shops and to walk to work and market. They populate the trendy sidewalk cafés, stepping carefully past the panhandlers and homeless youth congregating nearby.

Certainly, a high proportion of these new urbanites carry cell phones and laptop computers. While they may not understand the intricacies of wireless networks and data management, they are nonetheless full-fledged citizens of the information age. The rejuvenated cityscape provides an attractive backdrop in which they enjoy fast-paced and cultured lives.

In the 1990s, the desire for a return to the small town or urban village popularized new urbanism as a movement. Many expected that adopting new urbanist principles would generate compact city living for economic vibrancy, sociability, and integration. Urban villages for a communication age would produce attractive spaces accommodating high technology in livable and walkable environments where everyone would find a niche. In practice, new urbanism often produced big houses with gingerbread trim on small lots in the suburbs, but with relatively little mixing of classes.[26] In these affluent neighbourhoods, residents generally have access to the latest technology: Victorian touches mask twenty-first-century innards. Some of the infill new urbanist projects, like Garrison Woods in Calgary, seem quite successful: In inner-city sites, they enjoy ready access to

Figure 9.6

New urbanism communities, like Garrison Woods in Calgary,

transit and nearby destinations. In the far-flung suburbs, though, new urbanist forms have not reduced car dependency, commuting rates, or housing costs. They prove no more open and inclusive than the garage-fronted neighbourhoods they replaced (Figure 9.6).

Among the noteworthy trends in Canadian communities today is the increase in gated enclaves. These developments are walled, fenced, or bordered by fine hedges or ravines. They are closed to the world, with gates that limit entry to residents and their guests. Turned inward, gated enclaves often have attractive amenities: pools, golf courses, club houses, fountains. They represent pockets of homogeneity, generally by age, class, and interests. They reflect a need for privacy, a search for identity, and a flight from fear.[27] As relatively new and affluent developments, most are well connected to the Internet: open to the world. Some residents do work from home, although we lack sufficient information to know whether they are more likely than others to telecommute. These private spaces do, however, offer a stark challenge to the rhetoric of an open society.

In the US, four million households live in enclosed communities.[28] Our ongoing inventory of gated communities in Canada identified 314 gated projects, a figure we estimate to be less than half of the true total (Table 9.2).[29] This form is especially common in British Columbia, but also appears in other provinces (Alberta, Ontario, Nova Scotia, Saskatchewan, and Manitoba). Most Canadian enclaves have fewer than 100 units, with only 14 of those catalogued having more than 500 households. The built form is proving popular in the market. A growing number of people are choosing to wall themselves off from the world, safe in their domestic cocoons.

Diverse Forms, Common Trends

The diversity in contemporary urban forms cannot deny some common trends. Paramount among these is the growing gap between the "haves" and "have-nots." Our social

Table 9.2	Documented Gated Projects in Canada (March 2004)			
Province surveillance	Total gated projects	500 units or more	with guards	with video
British Columbia	228	3	5	5
Alberta	21	3	1	2
Saskatchewan	8			
Manitoba	1			1
Ontario	49	8	9	5
Nova Scotia	7			2
Canada total	314	14	15	15

safety net fails to address the needs of the poorest amongst us. The cost of housing continues to rise, while the most popular trends in the market do little to ameliorate the problem. Homelessness and personal debt continue to escalate. Planning has done little to improve this situation, despite decades of good intentions.

The haves are wired and connected. They can access the latest information, participate in international dialogues, advance their interests, and control their spaces. Some even employ closed-circuit TV to monitor the activities of others: Video cameras are proliferating in the urban environment, watching for unacceptable behaviour. The open society has many spies.

Meanwhile, the have-nots fall further behind: disconnected, disadvantaged, disengaged. Many drop out of school, face poor job prospects, do not participate in the political process, have limited access to adequate health care, and face a chronic search for affordable housing. The contemporary city fails to address their needs or to provide spaces that improve their life chances.

Some may argue that our cities have lost their commitment to provide public spaces to serve community functions. We no longer create much new public space, aside from zones designated to fulfill commercial purposes in areas like our waterfronts or heritage districts. Many municipalities today prefer cash in lieu of parkland in new development areas: Do we no longer think it important to provide neighbourhood play spaces for children? In many cases we lack sufficient resources to maintain or improve common urban infrastructure; instead, our transit systems and other public systems age in place. Are we abandoning the public realm?

In the contemporary environment we find stark contrasts. In theory, we enjoy an open society with opportunity never seen before in history. New technologies allow us to reach out to the world, to exchange information and experience across the broadest spectrum. At the same time, though, we recognize evidence of privileging of small segments of society, as witnessed in the increasing incidence of cloistered and controlled enclaves. The privileged urban forms of the contemporary city are more likely to be wired and equipped for the communication age than are other districts. Those who belong reap the benefits, while those who do not are excluded.

The affluent are increasingly moving to private systems of governance, setting up homeowner or condominium associations to manage their attractive residential spaces and maintain community values.[30] Private communities restrict amenities to those who live within, closing off part of the city as exclusive "club realms."[31] Is this kind of enclosure simply a sign of the times, the logical outcome of a society trapped in fear and committed to a consumer lifestyle (Figure 9.7)?

Figure 9.7

Developments on private roads are common features in resort communities like Port Stanley, Ontario.

Planning the Good City

As planners, do we accept that residents should be able to gather their families safely within privileged private realms where they may participate in a global society without facing the discomfiting realities of a local society racked by the manifestations of inequality? Certainly the technologies of the information age facilitate that kind of spatial segregation by making it possible for people to isolate themselves from their local environment while participating in global networks with friends and coworkers. Contemporary development practices are increasing segregation and separation. But I would suggest that this is not the kind of urban environment that planners have traditionally seen as a manifestation of the good city. Perhaps it is time for a renewed debate about the future of our cities? How can we plan communities that reflect democratic principles while adapting to the information age? Are the trends we currently facilitate the choices we wish to make?

1. Although the Healthy Communities Project is no longer a national program, what evidence do you find that healthy community concerns continue to affect planning policy and practice in major Canadian cities?

2. Crime Prevention Through Environmental Design has become a key element of police practice in Canada. What are its essential principles, and how can planners use them to design safer spaces?

3. The concept of "livability" has been gaining in influence as an umbrella concept that includes issues like community health and urban beauty. What priority should health, safety, and social inclusiveness have in planning our cities?

4. What role can community members play in ensuring that they inhabit safe cities?

5. Do gated communities reduce fear of crime? Should municipalities restrict or permit the development of enclave communities?

6. New urbanism advocates "eyes on the streets": natural surveillance by those living in a community and watching over spaces outside their windows. Gated communities reduce access to private space. Security cameras increasingly watch over public spaces. What are the strengths and weaknesses of these differing approaches to promoting safety?

7. How are threats of terrorism affecting the design and planning of Canadian cities?

8. Are vacant lots always a "problem" that planning should try to fix? Should authorities implement programs to remove graffiti and fix broken windows immediately?

Reference Notes

1. Frank, LD, MA Andresen, & TL Schmid (2004) Obesity relationships with community design, physical activity, and time spent in cars. *American Journal of Preventive Medicine* 27(2): 87–96.

2. David Suzuki Foundation (2003) Stopping urban sprawl must be a priority for provincial governments, http://www.davidsuzuki.org/Campaigns_and_Programs/Climate_Change/News_Releases/newsclimatechange10140301.asp (accessed 23 December 2005).

3. Mathur, B (1989) Community planning and the new public health. *Plan Canada* 29(4): 35–44.

4. Ibid: 35.

5. Lane, BJ (1989) Healthy Winnipeg: A proposed model. *Plan Canada* 29(4): 28–31.

6. Healthy community initiatives continued through voluntary networks and project grants. The Quebec government funded Villes et villages en santé, continuing the Ottawa charter principles (http://www.rqvvs.qc.ca/anglais/reseau/intro.htm). The directory of healthy communities projects at http://www.fsi.ulaval.ca/oms/p2En.html lists current activities, but few achieve the original charter aims.

7. Sherwood, D (2002) The state of the healthy communities movement in Canada. *Plan Canada* 42(4): 11–2.
   Witty, DR (2002) Healthy communities, what have we learned? *Plan Canada* 42(4): 9–10.

8. Jacobs, J (1961) *The Death and Life of Great American Cities.* New York: Random House: 5.

9. Wekerle, GR & C Whitzman (1996) Controlling Urban Crime: What Can Cities Do? *Plan Canada* 36(2): 7–11.
   Wekerle, GR & C Whitzman (1995) *Safe Cities: Guidelines for Planning, Design and Management.* New York: Van Nostrand Reinhold.

10. McKay, T (1996) A CPTED case study. *Plan Canada* 36(5): 39–40.

11. McIlroy, A & RMM Bryan (1996) Creating safer communities: Is intensification the answer? *Plan Canada* 36(2): 20–4.

12. Weiler, J (1992) Making places livable: A collaborative, consensual approach. *Plan Canada* 32(1): 30–6.

13. Health Canada funded a national office only until 1991.

14. Hancock, T (1987) *An Introduction to the Healthy Communities Project.* Mimeo: 3.

15. The author wishes to acknowledge Alice Ormiston who contributed to the collection and analysis of the literature related to Healthy Communities/Healthy Landscapes. Financial support for the work was provided by the Advisory Research Committee, Queen's University.

16. Wildavsky, A (1973) If planning is everything, maybe it is nothing. *Policy Sciences* 7(3): 127–53.

17. Haworth, L (1963) *The Good City.* Bloomington: Indiana University Press.

18. Schaeffer, D, E Herricks, & H Kerster (1988) Ecosystem health: 1. Measuring ecosystem health. *Environmental Management* 24(4): 445–55.

19. Hancock, T (1986) Public health planning in the City of Toronto. Part 1: Conceptual planning. *Canadian Journal of Public Health,* 77: 181.

20. Friedmann, J (1987) *Planning in the Public Domain.* Princeton: Princeton University Press.

21. Spasoff, R, P Cole, F Dale, et al. (1987) *Health for All Ontario.* Report of the Panel on Health Goals for Ontario, Toronto.

22. Richardson, N (1988) Are planners irrelevant? *Plan Canada* 27(10): 277–8.

23. Newman, O (1973) *Defensible Space: Crime Prevention Through Environmental Design.* New York: Macmillan.

24. Crowe, T (1991) *Crime Prevention Through Environmental Design.* Oxford: Butterworth Heinemann.

25. The details about the case and quotes cited are available in the *Victoria Hills Community Garden Project Program Evaluation* (1994) John Howard Society of Waterloo.

26. Grant, J (2002) From 'sugar cookies' to 'gingerbread men': Conformity in suburban design. *Planners Network Journal*, 151 (Spring): 10–3. (Also available online at http://www.plannersnetwork.org/htm/pub/archives/152/grant.htm)

27. Blakely, EJ & MG Snyder (1997) *Fortress America: Gated Communities in the United States*. Washington: Brookings Institution Press.

  Low, S (2003) *Behind the Gates: Life, Security, and the Pursuit of Happiness in Fortress America*. New York: Routledge.

28. Sanchez, TW & RE Lang (2002) *Security versus Status: The Two Worlds of Gated Communities*. Draft Census Note 02:02 (November). Alexandria: Metropolitan Institute at Virginia Tech.

29. The table updates data presented in the original paper. Since the inventory process was completed, the researchers learned of other gated enclaves in Newfoundland & Labrador and Quebec.

30. McKenzie, E (1994) *Privatopia: Homeowner Associations and the Rise of Residential Private Government*. New Haven: Yale University Press.

31. Webster, C (2002) Property rights and the public realm: Gates, green belts, and Gemeinschaft. *Environment and Planning B: Planning and Design* 29: 397–412.

Chapter Ten

Working for Sustainable Cities

Environmental Planning for a Sustainable Future

Jill Grant

Canadian planning has long expressed concern about maintaining and ensuring environmental quality. As I searched through old issues of *Plan Canada*, I rediscovered many articles dealing with important environmental themes. The quality and diversity of the work made it challenging to select articles for this chapter.

Some of the most useful contributions within the journal come from papers dealing with water-related issues. For instance, Smith discusses floodplain management, while Mathur describes planning for conserving urban river corridors in Saskatchewan.[1] Pedersen links planning for open space and conservation in a paper on Garrison Creek.[2] The December 2000 issue presented several papers and talks from the Canadian Institute of Planners conference in Charlottetown with water as its theme. Taking place just after the disaster in Walkerton, Ontario, that took several lives because of *E. coli* in the drinking water, the conference drew attention to the links between land use and human health that have long concerned planners.

The literature on environmental and sustainability themes in Canada is well established beyond the pages of the journal. Robert Dorney, Paul Eagles, and other faculty members from the University of Waterloo developed strategies for environmental management and trained generations of planners in the techniques.[3] Calgary professor Bill Perks and colleagues published on integrating environmental assessment in municipal planning. Bill Rees and his colleagues at UBC developed such influential concepts as the "ecological footprint" (Figure 10.1).[4] Mark Roseland at Simon Fraser published several books and reports promoting sustainable development.[5] Ray Tomalty worked to encourage communities to take ecological approaches to planning.[6]

Canadian Approaches

Effective planning can protect environmental quality. Some areas in Canada, like the Waterloo region in Ontario, established a reputation for safeguarding environmentally sensitive lands through planning processes. *Plan Canada* carried several articles on efforts to conserve especially sensitive areas like the Oak Ridges Moraine and the Niagara Escarpment.[7] Despite the initiatives, though, few planners would suggest that we can rest on our laurels. Environmental degradation and threats from development remain significant concerns in many communities. As Cox and Witty noted, for instance, planning has made insufficient progress in reducing wetlands loss in urban areas.[8]

Figure 10.1

Wackernagel and Rees pioneered the concept of the ecological footprint.

Those committed to environmental protection and conservation in Canada found the new approach of sustainable development an especially persuasive paradigm in the late 1980s. The World Commission on Environment and Development suggested that a sustainable approach to development would mean protecting the environment while ensuring that people meet their economic and social needs.[9] Sustainability requires considering the needs of future generations as well as our own as we make decisions about what we do today. Sustainable development clearly entailed integrated comprehensive planning that would focus on creating healthy communities within healthy environments. Within a short period, the rhetoric of sustainable development permeated Canadian planning: Putting it into practice in light of the pressures for development presented many obstacles.[10]

A search of the online consolidated index for *Plan Canada* retrieves over 50 articles on sustainable development. Ideas of sustainability have become intricately connected to Canadian urban planning: hence the focus of this chapter.

The first paper, by Nigel Richardson, asks what a sustainable city might mean.[11] Judith Maxwell considers the same question, but from a different perspective. These two papers reflect something of the range of issues that authors raise in the sustainability debate: The field is far from unified in its concerns.

Ken Tamminga describes Markham's efforts to apply ecological sustainability principles. Ecological planning has been an important theme through the years: Tamminga effectively demonstrates what it takes to make a commitment not just to protect what we have but to actively restore elements of the environment that we have degraded.[12]

Fern Hietkamp profiles a major environmental initiative in the Fraser Valley in British Columbia: sustainable development in action. The Fraser River ecosystem is vital to the economic health of the region. Government has been working for the past decade in engaging the community to actively conserve and rehabilitate the river: community environmental stewardship, a key theme of contemporary planning.[13]

Space precludes covering other significant contributions of Canadian planning. Interest in measuring progress toward sustainability led to the development of various indicators, such as those for quality of life and sustainable community.[14] Many of the sustainability measures are also indicators of healthy communities. Increasingly, principles of ecological integrity, social equity, meaningful livelihood, and participatory democracy have become central to what a range of planning approaches define as important for our communities.

Despite the long-term interest in planning for environmental quality and sustainable communities, the environmental threats remain real for Canadians. Global warming and resulting climate change pose significant threats. Melting Arctic zones endanger northern adaptations.[15] Habitat destruction, deforestation, and environmental degradation represent opportunities lost for future generations. Although Canadian planning has made sustainable development a dominant theme in its theory, community planning practice remains far from having set the standard internationally.

What is a "Sustainable City"?

Nigel H Richardson

1996, Plan Canada 36(5): 34–8

Since the publication of the *Brundtland Report*, the terms "sustainable development" and "sustainability" have become common currency in political and academic discourse and have even entered the broader public vocabulary.[16] As a perhaps inevitable consequence, they have come to be used in different ways, and often their intended meanings are unclear or ambiguous. A brief historical review may therefore be helpful.

Although the idea can be traced back at least to the UN's 1972 Stockholm Conference on the Human Environment, the term sustainable development was first used explicitly and defined in the *World Conservation Strategy*:

> Development is defined here as: the modification of the biosphere and the application of human, financial, living and non-living resources to satisfy human needs and improve the quality of human life. For development to be sustainable it must take account of social and ecological factors, as well as economic ones; of the living and non-living resource base; and of the long-term as well as the short-term advantages and disadvantages of alternative actions.[17]

The best-known and most commonly quoted, though much less precise, definition of sustainable development, however, is that used by the Brundtland Commission seven years later: "development that meets the needs of the present without compromising the ability of future generations to meet their own needs."[18] The fact that both "development" and "needs" can be understood in materially different ways has permitted a wide range of interpretations of the Brundtland definition (which may partly account for its popularity).

Typically, perhaps, Canadians have generally overlooked the fact that Canada had its own counterpart of the Brundtland Commission, the contemporaneous National Task Force on Environment and Economy. The task force produced its own definition of

Figure 10.2

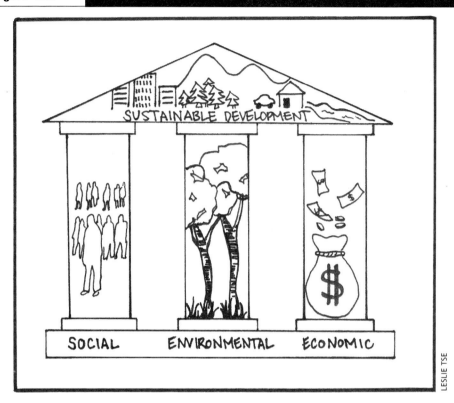

Sustainable development depends on three pillars for support: environmental, social, and economic.

sustainable development, interpreted explicitly as sustainable economic development, "which we generally define as development that ensures that the utilization of resources and the environment today does not damage prospects for their use by future generations."[19] Thus the task force saw sustainable development specifically in terms of the relationship between human activities on the one hand and natural systems and natural resources on the other. Whether or not one agrees with this interpretation, it has the merit of being fairly unambiguous.

Nevertheless, the task force view of sustainable development has not prevailed in Canada (Figure 10.2). According to the proceedings of a national workshop on urban sustainability indicators held in 1995:

> While there are many variations on how sustainable development should be defined, a consensus has emerged that there must be progress on three fronts— economic development, social development and preservation of the environment— to move toward a sustainable state, and that strong linkages exist between these dimensions.[20]

Sustainable Urban Development and Urban Sustainability

The World Conservation Strategy gave no special attention to the increasing urbanisation of the globe's rapidly rising population, or to the growth of "megacities." The *Brundtland Report* corrected the omission, but it dealt mainly with the urban crisis in developing countries and only rather cursorily with the cities of what it called the industrial world. Canada's National Task Force on Environment and Economy entirely ignored cities as such, which is rather curious considering that, to a large extent, cities are the medium through which economic activity affects the Canadian environment.

The rather scanty attention to cities and urbanization in the early stages of the debate over sustainability and sustainable development has been amply corrected in recent years: "The last decades have witnessed the emergence of 'urban sustainability' as a leading concept in the debate over urban issues."[21] This passage is quoted from a paper that argues that the concept of urban sustainability should include a human or social dimension. This was not, in fact, a novel idea. For example, Crerar clearly assumed that the "sustainable city" had to be defined partly in human terms.[22] In keeping with the *World Conservation Strategy's* definition of sustainable development, a human dimension has been incorporated in the concept of sustainable urban development from the first. A definition attempted by the present writer, described sustainable urban development as "foster[ing] economic development while conserving resources and promoting the health of the individual, the community and the ecosystem."[23]

"Sustainable urban development must consider the relationship among four rather than two [economic development and the natural environment] basic elements:

- the natural environment and natural resources…
- economic activity…
- the built environment…
- the human environment: the totality of these, considered as a setting for human life."[24]

Mitlin and Satterthwaite adapt and elaborate on Brundtland to assert that sustainable urban development means meeting the economic, social, cultural, health, and political needs of urban populations without compromising the ability of future generations to meet their own needs, by "minimizing use or waste of non-renewable resources…sustainable use of renewable resources…wastes from cities keeping within absorptive capacity of local and global sinks."[25]

The common theme here is that, as cities are created to serve human needs, sustainable urban development cannot be thought of in any meaningful way without reference to the extent to which it meets those needs, as well as to its environmental and resource-use impacts. This is, however, a limited argument that merely qualifies the term "sustainable urban development." It does not imply any particular set of criteria or "performance standards."

Recently, the terminology of the debate has shifted almost entirely from sustainable urban development to urban sustainability and the sustainable city. According to Maclaren, "the term urban sustainability has gained popularity because of potential misunderstandings over the meaning of the word 'development' and its confusion with 'growth.'"[26] However, while the three terms have come to be used more or less interchangeably, they are actually quite distinct in meaning. Urban development, sustainable or otherwise, is a process; urban sustainability, however defined, is a state or condition; and the sustainable city, to whatever extent it may exist, is a tangible, concrete artifact. The distinction is important because it makes a difference to the substantive terms of the debate. To employ the terms urban sustainability and, still more, sustainable city is to imply the existence of some particular level, standard, or set of characteristics required to achieve the condition of sustainability.

What Is a Sustainable City?

The currently prevalent interpretation of urban sustainability is that it simply consists of a basket of desirable characteristics—physical, social, economic, and perhaps others—assumed to be linked in some way. Nozick comprehensively and coherently argued this position: Her work is as much concerned with such issues as the ability of urban communities to govern their own affairs, including their economic development, as with what the author calls "harmonizing with nature."[27] However, she deals expressly with sustainable communities, not necessarily the same thing as sustainable cities.

But this view of urban sustainability raises several questions. Who decides what should be in the basket and the appropriate level or standard of adequacy for each component of its contents? The most obvious answer is the people of the city; each urban population decides on its own definition of sustainability. But disregarding the practical difficulties, this deprives urban sustainability of any generic meaning and eliminates any basis for systematic evaluation and comparison. Is a city with, for example, a high average income level but little social cohesion and a serious air quality problem more or less sustainable than one with much poverty but a strong sense of community and clean air? Is it, in fact, meaningful to assert that the one city is more or less sustainable than the other? And if not, in what way is the term "sustainable" useful? What differentiates a sustainable city from a "healthy" city or a "good" city? Would it not be more practical to set aside the notion of a "basket" and simply evaluate and compare individual characteristics: water quality, prosperity, literacy, and so forth? Or perhaps, as suggested earlier, just to accept urban sustainability as a useful slogan and no more?

These questions may be summed up in one: Does sustainability, as a concept, have a definable meaning transcending, or at least clearly distinct from, a mere collection of individual characteristics? The entire debate over sustainability, urban and other, rests on the premise, stated or implicit, that it does; and indeed if urban sustainability is to be a concept with real descriptive and analytical utility and not a mere flavour-of-the-month catch phrase, it must have such a meaning.

That there are linkages between the various elements in the urban sustainability "basket" is not in question. Some of those linkages may be clearly identifiable and even quantifiable: The relationship between the levels of certain atmospheric pollutants and human physical health is an obvious example. But the definition of urban sustainability has to go beyond identifiable connections between individual elements: It must lie in a particular relationship among factors, or a particular combination of factors (perhaps not precisely the same combination in every case) that interact to produce something more than the sum of the various parts, as (to employ a rather rough analogy) a Black Forest cake is more than just a random mixture of ingredients. The difficulty is that currently we are still a long way even from being sure we know what all the components are, let alone just how they interact to produce something distinctive we can identify specifically as urban sustainability.

The City as Ecosystem

Perhaps we can achieve a clearer perception of urban sustainability, if not a definition, by using the analogy of ecosystem health. "An ecosystem consists of a community of different species (including humans) interacting with one another and with the physical and chemical factors making up its non-living environment."[28] The fundamental principle underlying an ecosystem is that "everything is connected to everything else": Change in one component, or the introduction of a new component, will affect all the others. A healthy ecosystem has at least two essential features: It is not degrading (diminishing in diversity and complexity); and it is capable of adjusting successfully to new conditions, including the intrusion of new components.

On this analogy, a sustainable city would be one characterized by: either a continuing stable balance among its human/social, its economic, and its biophysical aspects, or growth in the diversity of such elements and in the complexity of interconnections, without any one element expanding at the cost of others; and resilience, or the ability to adapt successfully to changing conditions, internal and external, even to the extent of surviving physical destruction or loss of economic base.

Balance, stability, diversity, resilience, and so forth are, however, only outcomes or descriptors: They tell us what the characteristics of urban sustainability are, but little or nothing about how they come about. Again, it may be helpful to consider the ecosystem analogy. An aquatic ecosystem, for example, coheres because all its living components share a common matrix of sunlight, water, and solid materials within which they all exist and on which all are dependent, but they are also dependent on each other (mainly as links in the food chain). We can find an approximate societal equivalent in the concept of *community*, defined as:

> a form of social organization that is both territorial and cultural in nature. The territory involved is determined therefore by solidarity, neighbourhood ties and by community members' sense of belonging [including] the perception of community members...that, if they support the community, it will support them in turn.[29]

If an ecosystem is a biological community, a community can equally be considered a social ecosystem.

On this basis, we can argue that the essence of urban sustainability is the existence of community in the sense described, or at least that community, in this sense, is an indispensable element. The difficulty this presents is that while the strength of community depends in part on shared history, language, culture, and traditions, it also depends very much on more intimate factors, such as informal personal acquaintance, common institutions, and shared home-related interests. A strong sense of community therefore necessarily relates to a geographical entity that is rather small in size and population; it will inevitably become increasingly attenuated as the scale of the area and population in question increase. The Greater Toronto Area may be defined as a community in certain terms, but clearly it is not a community in the same sense as is a neighbourhood in one of its municipalities, and still less than (say) the tiny, isolated Yukon hamlet of Old Crow: There, 200 people live in the most intimate relationship with nature in their historic dependence on the annual migration of the Porcupine caribou herd, so that there is a pattern of immediate, strong, and evident connections both among community members and between them and their biophysical environment.

This argument does not lead to the absurd conclusion that Greater Toronto is somehow less sustainable than Old Crow. Literally hundreds, if not thousands, of small communities have disappeared from the map of Canada as their economic base was lost in one way or another; these could hardly be considered sustainable by any reasonable definition. The argument is only that while a comprehensive concept of sustainability may be applicable to Old Crow because the community can be analysed quite readily in ecosystem terms, it does not necessarily follow that the same concept is equally applicable to Greater Toronto, a vastly larger and more complex system of systems that is correspondingly vastly more difficult to analyze in those terms.

Research toward Sustainability

This discussion has not produced a definition of urban sustainability, nor was that the intention. What it has done is to raise some questions about the present utility and indeed the conceptual validity of the interpretation of urban sustainability simply as a diverse mix of social, economic, environmental, and perhaps other values. This would certainly be legitimate if we could devise a general theory of urban sustainability that would enable us not just to recognize but with confidence to identify the precise linkages and interrelatedness between, say, air quality and educational level, or per capita water consumption and economic diversification.

Perhaps continuing research, conducted within the framework of an ecosystem approach, will one day make this possible. Meanwhile, to adapt an observation made a number of years ago about planning: If urban sustainability is everything, maybe it's nothing; and it may be both more conceptually defensible and more practically useful to adopt the more modest position of considering urban sustainability as being about the relationship between urban populations, their needs and activities, on the one hand, and the productive, life support, and absorptive capacities of the ecosphere on the other. Between the sustainable city (or perhaps "ecological city") and the healthy city ("humane city"?) concepts, with the health of the natural ecosystem and the "wellness" of the person as their respective basic criteria, a fruitful theoretical dialectic could then complement effective practical collaboration.

Sustainable Cities

Judith Maxwell

2003, Plan Canada 43(4): 13–5

Cities, large and small, must now have their turn as the centre of policy attention in Canada, for at least three reasons. First, cities are facing economic challenges flowing from the industrial restructuring driven by globalization and new technologies. Second, they have inherited major new responsibilities, as both provinces and the federal government have adjusted the scope of their activities. Third, they have welcomed an influx of new and diverse residents from rural areas and outside of Canada. As they search for options, city leaders find themselves handicapped by constitutional constraints and limited taxing powers. These are both challenging issues, but in this presentation, I want to focus on issues that are more directly relevant to two themes: building capacity and building connections.

The first issue is to explore the forces working against the sustainability of our cities. The second is to summarize insights from Canadian Policy Research Networks' research on how innovative cities solve problems.[30]

What Is Sustainability?

To begin, however, let me define what I mean by sustainable cities. To me, it means striving for harmony in the development of civil society, economy, environment, culture, and political institutions.[31] The principal challenge facing leaders in cities and communities is how to weave together progress on all these fronts. It takes a breadth of thinking and citizen involvement that far surpasses traditional approaches to urban issues in this country. I regret to say that the evidence from our case studies shows that Canadian communities are only now getting started along this road.

To build the necessary connections, civil society organizations, business, educational institutions, and governments require a sense of shared responsibility for what happens in their community and a shared commitment to solving problems.

The Productivity Dimension

It is important to emphasize that this notion of sustainability is not soft and fuzzy. It has a direct productivity connection. Everything we now know about the new economy points to the success of economic clusters, and we know that successful clusters depend on a complex web of informal relationships. We know, for example, that:

- a high quality of life attracts and retains a highly skilled work force;
- informal networks among businesses, research and educational institutions, and governments are important drivers of innovation;[32]

- cost competitiveness is deeply affected by the efficiency of transportation within and between cities so that both people and goods can move quickly and at reasonable cost;
- informal networks strengthen neighbourhoods and communities, helping people to find jobs and obtain the training opportunities they need; and
- strong public education and effective community health services are an essential underpinning for working people and employers.

Out of these basic facts, it is possible to visualize the kind of cities (large and small) we want: cities where quality of life is part of the overall planning process. The trouble is that powerful market and policy forces stand in the way. I want to highlight three trends that are taking us in the wrong direction: spatial segregation, a new wage structure, and a new social policy structure.

Spatial Segregation

In the postwar years, Canadian cities were noted for their lack of spatial segregation compared to that in other countries, especially the United States. In fact, we bragged about our lack of inner-city problems. However, since 1980, poverty has tended to concentrate in our cities (the average rate of low income in all cities was 22 percent in 1995 versus 16 percent for people living in rural areas) in particular neighbourhoods or census tracts.[33] Myles and colleagues have also documented the extreme polarization of income by neighbourhood.[34] Our cities demonstrate far greater disparity between high- and low-income groups than we see in either the provincial or national data. The other important dimension to this "ghettoization" is the tendency for visible minorities, Aboriginals, lone-parent families, and disabled people to cluster in these poor areas.

Needless to say, this segregation of poor people goes against the whole notion of inclusive societies and will create a new Canadian underclass if it continues: not what we are aiming for in sustainable cities. The way to prevent this social exclusion is to create well-paid jobs, affordable housing, good public transit, access to child care and adult training, excellent education and health services, and so on.

A New Wage Structure

The new economy has produced a new wage structure, which explains the income polarization just mentioned. The new economy has created opportunities for many and generated a lot of wealth. For example, it produces more millionaires: A newspaper report in 2002 suggested we have 160 000 of them. However, real minimum wages have fallen by 15 to 20 percent since 1975, depending on the province. Furthermore, one in six adult Canadians works for less than $10 per hour.[35] Even if these people work full time, all year, they can earn a maximum of only $21 000, which falls well short of the income required to support a family.

These working Canadians are extremely vulnerable, but they look remarkably like the rest of the population. One-third of them have postsecondary education, and another third have completed high school. About 35 percent of them are the only earners in their families. Two-thirds are women. They are the working poor, and their biggest challenges are to find affordable housing, reliable transportation, access to child care, recreation, and so on; yet, as a society, we assume that anyone who has a job can be self-reliant.

A New Social Policy Structure

Compounding the problem of low wages are the changes that have taken place in federal, provincial, and municipal social programs over the past 15 years, which have affected both income transfers and social services. Most of them are now aimed expressly at poor people, families, or, in the case of health services, specific health conditions.

Thus, qualifying for social supports becomes much more difficult, and, once people do qualify, it becomes very easy to lose them. For example, a person earning $25 000 a year who is offered a promotion may face a marginal effective tax rate of 80 or 90 percent, because the income and every social benefit they receive will be "taxed." When we add to this the fact that federal and provincial governments stopped investing in social housing in the early 1990s, we begin to see that the cards are stacked against these vulnerable people. In effect, there is a poverty trap for the working poor.

Sustainability Matters to Everyone

These three trends are creating a new Canadian divide between poor people and everyone else. This matters because it means that a large number of Canadians are being left behind, and growing swaths of our urban space are becoming "distressed" communities. It becomes increasingly difficult for these people to participate in work and civic life. So there are two kinds of cost: The first is the loss of human capital in an economy where brains really matter; and the second are the costs of policing, social transfers, and health care for a segment of the population that is so vulnerable.

The sustainability of our cities matters enormously to these people. If they have the good fortune to live in a community that offers efficient public transit, affordable housing, high-quality and affordable child care, recreation and sport without user fees, and other essential services, their quality of life will be far higher than their low incomes would suggest. Of course, sustainability also matters enormously to the middle class, still the largest segment of our population. Good transit, a diverse housing stock, good child care, and recreation mean a lot to these people as well. It makes them value their community; it enables them to feel like real citizens and encourages them to engage in sustaining that community. These are the foundations for the sustainable community described earlier.

Planners Can Mobilize for Sustainability

How do planners make our cities and communities become sustainable in the face of perverse trends? The main challenge is that the problems are broad, while the perspectives of all the key players in the community are narrow. No one working alone has the leverage to make change. Planners are in touch with all these domains—governments, business, developers, educational institutions, civil society organizations, and others. Planners have the opportunity to propose new ideas and to help bridge the gaps across these "solitudes":

- Senior governments have a mandate to serve all citizens, urban and rural. As a result, they are not comfortable serving local needs and cannot provide local leadership.
- Municipal governments are often fragmented because special purpose agencies or geographic boundaries give them only half of the problem. In addition, most have weak policy capacity to cope with their expanding mandates.
- Businesses are preoccupied with costs of doing business and the quality of infrastructure, especially for transportation. They also worry about attracting skilled workers and ensuring amenities for their staff.
- Educational institutions in Canada are underresourced and tend to be focused inwardly, although some colleges and universities already see themselves as major players in urban progress.
- Civil society institutions, like the United Way, can often bridge solitudes in pursuit of their goals to promote social equity and social inclusion.

Each of these sectors has important strengths, but they do not naturally collaborate with each other to create shared problems. As Neil Bradford says, a community that knows how to engage all these actors in planning for the future is a learning community.[36] In addition, if they are going to collaborate, then they must be prepared to think in three dimensions:

- regionally—to see the full scope of the economic, environmental, and infrastructure needs and possibilities;
- inclusively—to see that people from different walks of life and socioeconomic status are all part of the solution; and
- from the bottom up—to ensure that needs are defined locally, based on neighbourhood and family needs.

Whether we wish to reverse economic decline, improve competitiveness, or deal with social blight, the higher-order goal is to make the community a better place for the people who will live there tomorrow. How then do we get started?

Ingredients for Success

Communities are rising to this challenge across the industrialized world: from Denmark, to Spain, to the United States, and, more recently, here in Canada.[37] Bradford's list of the ingredients for success, based on 11 case studies, include:

- a local champion to provide the leadership;
- institutional intermediaries to connect with senior governments;
- equitable participation to engage local stakeholders;
- a civic culture of creativity (doing things differently and better);
- adequate financial and technical resources (money, land, regulatory skills, etc.); and
- strong accountability mechanisms, including an agreed set of indicators to track progress.

Overall, however, what Bradford finds in these innovative cities is connectedness in two directions: horizontally, involving the sectors in society, and vertically, engaging senior governments. Many Canadian communities are now launched on this voyage of collaboration: big ones like Toronto and lots of smaller ones like Kelowna, Kitchener-Waterloo, Halifax, Saskatoon, and the Beauce. The initiative invariably comes from the community itself, but it cannot succeed without responsive participation from provincial and federal governments. Unfortunately, the Organization for Economic Cooperation and Development tells us, senior governments in Canada have been slow to get their act together.[38]

The voyage to sustainability is not easy. There are many roadblocks. Innovative cities begin with a single project. Agreeing on a common goal and how to achieve it together is the first important step. Typically, the experience of working together begins to build a sense of mutual trust. Cities can then build on their success to set even more ambitious goals for the future. In the new economy, a city achieves economic success by meeting the social and economic needs of all its citizens, rich and poor. That is sustainability.

Restoring Biodiversity in the Urbanizing Region: Towards Preemptive Ecosystems Planning

Ken Tamminga

1996, Plan Canada 36(4): 10–5

Postindustrial forces are presenting new and dynamic challenges for planners of urbanizing Canadian landscapes. Related processes of redemocratization and "green" land use legislation are providing opportunities for planners to put some flesh on the still-skeletal paradigm of ecosystems planning.[39] As the city's influence expands haltingly outward in suburban and exurban forms, calls for ecosystem health and integrity tax the most integrative of planners and policy makers.

Ecological health is a capacity of the land (and all its organisms) for self-renewal.[40] Ecological integrity is the capability of an area to support and maintain assemblages of organisms that have a composition and functional organization comparable to that of the region's natural habitat.[41]

Although it is in the urban and near-urban realm that landscape degradation and ecological fragmentation have their clearest expressions, relatively little systematic ecological planning has been devoted to urban bioregions. In examining some compelling ecological logic, this paper raises several questions for planning practitioners: Have we conceded, perhaps through naiveté or avoidance, that urban bioregional health is unachievable? Are we practising ecological nihilism, accomplices to accelerating processes of ecological dysfunction? By focusing on the ecological variable of the ecosystems planning "equation,"[42] it is possible to argue that until the planning community is more clearly informed of biodiversity values, the principles of applied ecology, and the realities of denatured urban regions, key goals inherent in ecosystems planning will be unattainable.[43]

Preservation: The Partial Imperative

From the 1950s through to recent times, planning policy in Canadian urbanizing regions and locales contributed to a 200-year-long process of resource extraction and settlement that left spindly, isolated, and commodified natural communities in their wake. A degraded ecology remains, severed from large, healthy ecosystems and drained of genetic resilience and interactive indigenous species and processes. These "ecological simulacra" and their surrounding urban matrices tend to house invasive and cosmopolitan species fed on urban form, energy, and other social artifacts—further anathema to indigenous biodiversity.

Confronting the environmental legacy of human populated and stress-adapted landscapes requires more than the glorification of preserved natural remnants. It requires reciprocity. A vital missing ingredient in applied ecosystems planning in North America is a systematic approach to ecological restoration. Strategies for the recovery of natural habitat and flows of genetic material, energy, and nutrients require the combined efforts of applied ecologists and planners. Ecological principles, combined with bioregionally and watershed-based restoration planning criteria, can inform planning policy in providing a framework that may enhance biodiversity through time.

Many sources distinguish between ecological restoration and rehabilitation, with inconsistencies evident across the spectrum. As used in this paper, restoration entails human interventions that lead to near-pristine and self-perpetuating natural conditions. Restoration may contribute to a more general environmental rehabilitation or regeneration when woven systematically into the landscape mosaic.

Practising ecologists can contribute to the urban sustainability discussion. By turning their sights to the late modern/postmodern landscape, they can promote a concept of sustainability that acknowledges an ethical, compensatory obligation to reverse ubiquitous states of environmental damage. In calling for more than neutrality, they can posit a sobering reality: Most urban and suburban ecological preserves are too small to support healthy, indigenous plant and animal assemblages in perpetuity; links made to achieve natural area integrity are too tenuous; fragmented habitats, interrupted riparian corridors, and crenellated vegetative patterns serve to reduce regional biodiversity.[44] Clearly defined and scientifically defensible goals and objectives are integral to ecosystems planning.

Linking Biodiversity and Restoration

Several applied ecologies offer timely direction for ecosystems planning. Landscape ecology, conservation biology, and restoration ecology are three synthetic ecologies, or "synecologies," involved in bringing together component parts of an ecosystem at various spatial levels.[45] They are undergirded by other sciences, including biogeography, wildlife biology, and those concerned with genetic resources, species diversity and ecosystems diversity.

The synecologies work in favour of the most prominent and, what should be to planners, the most relevant of ecological concepts: biodiversity. Wilson submits that biodiversity is the key to global world health, contributing to "holding the world steady."[46] Biodiversity matters chiefly in its underpinning of ecological function under varying environmental conditions.[47] It is also increasingly considered an ingredient of sustainability in cultural landscapes; ultimately, it implies a diversity of regions themselves.[48]

Primary local and regional threats to biodiversity include habitat fragmentation, simplification of ecosystems and gene pools, the spread of exotic plants and animals, and human intrusion.[49] Each of these threats can be introduced or exacerbated through even well-intentioned planning decisions, among other more direct forms of human intervention. For example, as Katz concluded, "protection" and "conservation" of urban natural areas could serve to sustain the integrity of urbanizing natural areas.[50] While a pragmatic reiteration of a common theme, this restoration-exclusive approach subverts a growing body of ecological research that suggests that most such areas are experiencing steady declines in species richness and diversity, as well as other indexes of ecological integrity.[51] Increasingly, ecological preservation and restoration is perceived as the only effective means to redress urban regional degradation. This more holistic perspective is driven by a quickly expanding body of literature on the values of biological diversity (Table 10.1).

Biodiversity has been virtually ignored in North American planning periodicals. *Plan Canada* has largely published extrapolations on classic environmental preservation and management models. For example, Thompson focuses on environmental management and resource conservation; Katz on landscape ecology in informing ecological protection and *in situ* conservation; Robinson on preservation of vestigial ecosystems and greenway corridors for human access.[52] Only Hostovsky and colleagues make passing reference to restoration as a step yet to be examined in Ottawa-Carleton's natural environment systems strategy.[53]

In the early 1990s, the *Journal of the American Planning Association* and *Planning* each published one article referencing concepts of biodiversity and restoration: Soulé's offers a landscape ecology primer for urban regions; Steiner refers to Tucson's Wildlands Project and its promotion of near-urban grey wolf recovery.[54]

Table 10.1	Values of Biodiversity and Restoration

Anthropocentric Values

Consumptive/Utilitarian: value in genetic resources of direct use to humans

Transformative: values that enhance or ennoble the human condition (aesthetic, recreational, educational, and so on)

Biocentric Values

Intrinsic: value apart from human use, as an inherent right

Instrumental: value relative to ecosystem itself

A crucial missing element of the few comprehensive plans completed for Canadian urban regions is a visionary layer of restoration-designated lands. When withdrawn from the mill of land speculation and urban fringe development, they can be either actively restored or permitted to undergo natural succession. For ecosystems planning, a challenging logic unfolds. If regional urban planning espouses an ecosystems approach (i.e., it values ecosystems integrity), and if the urbanizing region this approach addresses is ecologically fragmented, and if undersized and fractured wildlife habitats are primary causes of genetic depletion and dwindling biological diversity, and if indigenous biodiversity is a primary component of healthy ecosystems, then the forces of undue stress must be reversed and reparations made at a scale sufficient to rehabilitate the system affected.

In 1986, Noss and Harris, rejected in good part, the prevailing heterogeneous landscape model that promoted "edge effect" as an ecologically benign condition of the cultural landscape mosaic. For settled regions they proposed a contrasting biocentric model while retaining the structures drawn from landscape ecology. They suggested patterning naturalistic ecosystems in cultural landscapes along "multiple-use modules" that could still accommodate dynamic natural fluxes of energy, nutrients, and genetic material.[55] These modules would contain inviolable core ecological areas linked by wide wildlife travel corridors and surrounded by graduated buffer lands. This model has particular applicability in such settings as southern Ontario, where the paucity of indigenous habitats—an interrelated system of tableland deciduous forest, incised riparian corridors, and aquatic regimes—strongly suggest native revegetation as the kingpin of any ecological network.

Every landscape system has its own indelible natural patterns and processes. Just as the notion of landscape as "palimpsest"—a word of Greek origin used to describe the faintly visible rubbings on an old parchment that has been reused many times—has facilitated an understanding of cultural landscape history, so the landscape may reveal layers of dynamic natural heritage. Each urban bioregion must reveal its own story and thresholds as a prelude to recovery.

Beyond the Hypothetical: The Markham Study

A case in point is the *Town of Markham Natural Features Study*. It presents a prototypical and, in its rigorous approach to ecological restoration, unparalleled precedent in a Canadian context. Markham is a large municipality near the centre of the Greater Toronto bioregion. Its southerly land base has the old villages of Markham and Unionville as its twin cores, flanked by corporate centres, strip commercial development, and suburbs spreading northward over cropped tablelands (Figure 10.3). Exurban nodes punctuate the rural landscape.

Spurred by grassroots activists, municipal council hired a multidisciplinary consortium, spearheaded by Gore and Storrie Limited with Hough Stansbury Woodland Limited, to prepare a comprehensive environmental planning study. The synthesis of background information and the preparation of the culminating *Plan for the Environment* was a joint effort of ecologists, planners, and landscape architects. The consultants examined current and historic information on ecological disturbance and human stresses on natural systems to determine whether key abiotic or biotic structures had been lost or crippled. The first phase of the study reported 13.6 percent of Markham's land area as naturally vegetative communities, of which eight percent is anthropogenic in origin. As predicted, plants and animals generally indicated a fragmented and disturbed natural environment (Figure 10.4).

The final report expressed "a vision for the community that provides a framework for protecting, restoring and linking up natural features in Markham to achieve a high quality environment, ecological diversity and numerous outdoor recreation opportunities."[56] Riley and Mohr note that Markham is one of the most denuded municipalities in the province, approaching the five percent forest cover of Kent and Essex Counties in the

Figure 10.3

KEN TAMMINGA

Markham's urban–rural interface.

grain belts of the extreme southwest corner of the province.[57] It is beyond the "preventive treatment" stage, in need of "emergency room" reconstructive surgery.[58]

Significantly, the report's biodiversity objectives were informed by theory, extensive field inventory and observation, precedent, and localized knowledge amassed by the consulting team.[59] The report adapted the multiple-use module model to accomplish these objectives. However, it grounded published empirical findings by building a site-specific, opportunistic, and bottom-up rationale for the extensive ecological network. Foreshadowing Rapport and Regier's call for a minimum of 10 percent of any Great Lakes watershed to be preserved in a representative and near-pristine state to help achieve ecosystem integrity, the plan laid out a systematic network of preserved and restored natural areas.[60] Importantly, it worked within the constraints of the landscape matrix, as interpreted by the team's planners.

Markham's *Plan for the Environment* prescribed a bold series of plus-100-hectare ecological blocks, spaced at roughly 2.5 kilometres and connected by wide corridors supporting interior forest habitat. The plan also proposed reconnecting disjointed riparian habitat, thus initiating a multilayered strategy responsive to both upland and lowland complexes. Three overlay schedules formed the plan's strategic hierarchy:

- environmental protection areas;
- ecological restoration areas; and
- greenway system.

Ecological Nodes

Nodes were devised as existing natural preserves, augmented by restoration infilling and fringing to enlarge the core area, reintegrate isolated fragments and reduce edge effect. Seven cohesive blocks were delineated, totalling well over 700 hectares. This major initiative—singular in Canadian urban bioregions—would help to achieve an aggregated target (existing forest and successional vegetation plus proposed vegetative infill and buffer areas) of 11 percent upland woodlot cover.

The recommended plus-100-hectare size for major nodes was a result of a combination of inputs, largely from published sources, but also from local and regional data amassed before and during the two-year study. The Markham study identified

Figure 10.4

Ecologically fragmenting forces at work in Markham: suburban expansion, exurban development, and agricultural production.

empirically-based minimum dimensions for ecological nodes and corridors, focusing on the needs of neotropical migrants (e.g., warblers), neotemperate migrants (e.g., red-shouldered hawk), and resident species (e.g., pileated woodpecker). For example, parasitism from cowbirds is often noted as the major impact on interior-breeding neotropical migrants in fragmented landscapes. Wilcove found that circular woodlots smaller than 100 hectares contain no interior secure from significant predation and parasitism.[61] Riley and Mohr later confirmed the consultants' recommendation, citing published articles suggesting a minimum forest interior habitat (threshold) size in the order of 100 hectares as desirable for important bird species in the Great Lakes basin.[62]

The shape of the large nodes was as nearly circular as possible to reduce the edge-to-area ratio and to minimize edge effect. Because of landownership, agronomic, and infrastructural patterns, enlarged and restored nodes tended to be blocky and conformed to the original land survey grid and lot alignments, a reasonable compromise reflecting a creative team synergy.

A 2.5-kilometre spacing of major, connected natural nodes was recommended as comparable to the spacing between nests of interior-forest bird species with large home ranges. Each node would function as a linked but discrete ecosystem with minimal territorial disputes. This reserve spacing is also roughly modeled on the natural territorial spacing of the Cooper's hawk, sharp-shinned hawk, northern goshawk, and great horned owl.[63] The reality of field conditions also played an important role in reserve location. Field inventory revealed that concentrations of regionally rare and significant species tended to congregate near stream confluences—biodiversity "hot spots"—where dendritic hydrological patterns coincided with remnant areas of lowland and upland vegetation (Figure 10.5). Perhaps coincidentally, these major existing natural areas were spaced quite consistently at about 2.5 kilometres.

Ecological Corridors

Corridors reflected the landscape ecology principle that species dispersal between patches is crucial to preventing genetic isolation or stagnation in small breeding populations, and to recolonizing after periods of environmental stress.[64] Harris and Callagher found that corridors bolster the small natural reserves to which they were attached, effectively enabling populations to occur in urban-agronomic landscapes that might not otherwise support them.[65] If consistent with bioregionally-specific conditions and substantial in width, the potential costs of corridors (such as the transmission of fire, disease, and invasive species) could be outweighed by their benefits.[66] As with ecological nodes, substantial corridors may themselves provide a modicum of interior habitat for specialists, such as neotropical migrant birds, reptiles and amphibians, and some small mammals.

The study team chose a 100-metre corridor width as a size marginally able to accommodate some interior habitat. It is also the suggested width required to maintain forest-interior tree species, including beech.[67] As preliminary GIS-based greenway mapping was field checked and tested in workshop settings, many opportunities arose to establish corridors as wide as several hundred metres, attaining the greater minimum-width criteria for southern Ontario suggested by Riley and Mohr.[68] Hedgerows that had been haven to predatory or parasitic generalist species, such as the pernicious cowbird, were reconsidered as framing elements for to-be-forested corridors linking isolated woodlots and forming lateral ecological conduits between watersheds. Long-denuded stream verges also provided an essential framework for restoring riparian corridors associated with the Rouge and Little Rouge rivers.

Integrating with Cultural Patterns

Although the plan for Markham's environment focused on naturalistic ecology, human artifacts and activities were explored during the planning process. An extensive greenway system, for example, was conceived as a constituency-building ally in the larger task of ecological renewal.

Planners and ecologists worked together to synthesize an ecological pattern that responded to both contemporary barriers and edges (infrastructure and landownership patterns) and historic features (Mennonite farmsteads and hedgerow plantings). Plan making thus became an interactive and iterative process of concept development and measurement against ecological, recreational, and cultural criteria and opportunities. The result was a substantial but sensitive ecological network that fit its cultural landscape

Figure 10.5

KEN TAMMINGA

A major ecological node in the making. This upland–lowland complex along the Little Rouge River is ripe for ecological enhancement and buffering.

context. If implemented preemptively, the network may serve to frame and inspire a plurality of sustainable development forms.

For Southern Ontario and many Canadian urban bioregions, preservation-inclusive restoration will be the key means of reintegrating anything more than token biodiversity. Restored ecological networks (nodes, linkages, and buffers) in urbanizing bioregions can never be a complete panacea for the biodiversity problem. For example, restored ecological networks in most urban bioregions would likely not accommodate the complete assemblage of genetic diversity of rare species necessary to avoid interbreeding. Nor will they usually be able to support top predators that often control invasive or overabundant species, but they can counteract environmental stresses in the urban-rural gradient.[69] The primary role of planners, then, is to ensure a land base for these renewed ecological patterns and processes.

Ecological networks are payment on urban Canada's massive ecological debt and an investment in a flourishing, sustainable future. This normative concept should be greeted with a belated measure of professional humility. Only when cohesive substantial recovery of natural habitats and functions is evident can planners lay some claim as co-purveyors (with ecologists and others) of an emerging ecoregional paradigm for the twenty-first century.

Writing on open spaces, urbanist William Whyte noted that "the land that is still to be saved will have to be saved within the next few years. We have no luxury of choice. We must . . . look to this landscape as the last one."[70] Had Whyte been able to anticipate the continuing depletion of biological diversity and natural functions, his "last landscape" would have called for systematic ecological recovery with a similar sense of urgency.

Using Stewardship as a Guide for Planning

Fern Hietkamp

1996, Plan Canada 36(4): 28–32

In the rapidly urbanizing Lower Mainland of British Columbia, where the Fraser River flows into the sea through a delta historically rich in habitat for fish and wildlife, stewardship initiatives are at work to protect the remaining salmon habitat and to restore past damage, primarily caused by escalating development. Through the Fraser River Action Plan, funded by the federal Green Plan, the initiative was carried out jointly by Fisheries and Oceans Canada and Environment Canada. The focus of the program was principally habitat protection for those species of fish that use streams for spawning, rearing and migrating to and from the ocean. The Fraser River Action Plan offered important lessons about stewardship in planning.

Fish Habitat and Human Settlements: Making the Connection

The Lower Mainland stretching from Vancouver to Hope is part of the rapidly developing Georgia Basin bioregion. Its urban and rural settlements, spreading over a large valley bordered by mountains, are home to over two million people. Between 1961 and 1991, the Lower Mainland population doubled and is projected to grow to three million by 2021. Development to meet the needs of this escalating population has already affected sensitive habitats in valley bottoms and steeper slopes where many streams originate. The result: a significant loss in habitat for the five species of salmon—chinook, sockeye, pink, chum, and coho—that use these streams and wetlands. Lower Mainland coho are particularly threatened since they spend a considerable time in the delta's many small freshwater streams; indeed, 65 percent of the entire Fraser River coho production occurs in these streams. Is it possible to plan for human settlements and sustain a fisheries resource within the same ecosystem?

Since settlement began in the Lower Mainland a century ago, much of the estuary and wetlands area has been lost due to dyking, farming, and urban development. The amount of stream habitat available to fish has been halved in urban areas. Of the 3216 kilometres of streams in the delta area, 1140 kilometres (44 percent) flow through land that has been urbanized. Of this, 588 kilometres (42 percent) of streams have been lost: built on, culverted, or paved over. In addition, the cumulative impacts of development have damaged riparian areas, eliminated forests, polluted water, channelized streams, dyked watercourses, led to water extracted for irrigation, and increased flooding due to an increase in impervious area. In an attempt to navigate a path through the complex interactions between fish and humans trying to survive in the same ecosystem, through the Fraser River Action Plan, Fisheries and Oceans Canada has adopted a stewardship approach, with the ultimate goal of sustaining the productive capacity of fish habitat.

What Is Stewardship?

Government agencies and community groups concerned with habitat protection developed this working definition of stewardship, which Fisheries and Oceans used to guide program planning:

"Stewardship refers to co-operative forms of planning and management of environmental resources in which all users and managers share the responsibility for management and conservation. Stewardship embodies a new ethic of caring for local ecosystems in the interests of long-term sustainability.

Stewardship includes but goes beyond voluntary efforts by community groups. Stewardship requires sharing of decision-making authority, of responsibility for ecosystem protection and of the benefits of a given resource. Stewardship provides priorities for the management of local ecosystems for sustainability."[71]

Using a Stewardship Approach

The work involved in implementing a stewardship approach has yielded valuable lessons.

Lesson 1: Stewardship Involves a Commitment to Cooperation and Partnership

Fish and streams know no legal boundaries; they are affected by events that occur locally and at a watershed level. Planning on a watershed basis enables protecting an intact riparian system—an essential part of fish habitat because it provides fish with food, shade, and the large organic debris needed to create complex watercourses.

To make cross-boundary initiatives work, several partnership initiatives have been implemented. One of these, Partners in Protecting Aquatic and Riparian Resources, is a joint endeavour of Fisheries and Oceans Canada and BC Environment, where all three levels of government and community representatives work together to develop proactive mechanisms to protect fish habitat. Initiatives include streamlining development approval processes to protect fish habitat through memoranda of understanding and putting existing planning tools to better use. The development community, a key partner for this endeavour, is exploring the implications of proactive planning for protecting fish habitat. A survey of the development community identified stream stewardship as a key issue of concern. The Urban Development Institute, BC chapter, established a stream stewardship committee to examine the connections between fish habitat and development.

Building these partnerships meant establishing trust, developing communication links, harmonizing procedures, setting goals together, and taking the steps to achieve these goals. Although it takes time and energy to forge new partnerships, the effort is necessary to halt the current trend: the continued loss and degradation of fish habitat.

Lesson 2: Stewardship Is Essential for the Health of Humans and Fish

A viable fish habitat contributes to a healthy ecosystem. As conservationist Roderick Haig-Brown noted in the *Vancouver Sun* on 17 May 1996: "The health of the salmon and the abundance of that fish on the spawning beds is a harbinger of our health and well-being; our well-being is an extension, and extends to the well-being of other lifeforms."

Since salmon habitat is a product of the hydrologic, geologic, and aquatic processes of the entire watershed, salmon production quickly reflects changes in the environment. Ergo, the salmon is a true indicator of the health of the Lower Mainland ecosystem.

There are obvious economic and social benefits to having healthy fish populations and fish habitat. Many small coastal communities depend on fishing for their economic well-being. As well, protecting the riparian system and floodplains and managing storm water help to prevent flooding by detaining spring runoff and maintaining groundwater supplies.

Good planning for fish habitat is good planning for human settlements, a lesson reinforced by recent flooding in North America and beyond. Despite the benefits, however, poor planning and mounting development pressures continue to threaten fish habitat. Stream setbacks may be reduced to the minimum amount possible to maximize development yield. Restrictive covenants, which legally bind a landowner to prevent alteration to the riparian portion of a property covered by the covenant, and other like measures have a poor record in protecting the riparian area. A 1995 study commissioned by the Fraser River Action Plan of Fisheries and Oceans Canada and a local municipality found that voluntary compliance for restrictive covenants applied to setbacks is abysmal: 86 percent noncompliance.

Lesson 3: Stewardship Involves Comprehensive Planning for Human Settlements

Through the stewardship initiatives implemented in Lower Mainland communities, it has become very clear that planning at the local level is crucial for protecting fish habitat. While such legislation as the federal *Fisheries Act* and the provincial *Waste Management Act* allows senior governments to penalize habitat destruction, local governments have the capacity to plan proactively to protect aquatic and riparian areas.

The provincial *Municipal Act* provides local governments with a mandate for land use and development control. Fundamental to protecting environmentally sensitive areas is a municipality's official plan, which can include environmental policies along with an environmentally sensitive area inventory to reflect the tools that local government is willing to use in encouraging proactive planning for stream stewardship. Environmental protection bylaws or zoning that reflects the sensitivity of a lot adjacent to a watercourse or wetland can also protect aquatic and riparian habitat. (An inventory of measures adopted by local governments, however, found that only one-third of municipalities in the Lower Mainland had substantial procedures to consider fish habitat issues in their development application review and inspection processes.) At the regional level, planning provisions under the *Growth Strategies Act* (amending the *Municipal Act*) should benefit fish habitat through regional coordination of planning and greater consistency between local official plans.

The use of local planning tools to implement stewardship goals adds another dimension to the working definition of stewardship. Land use and development planning are an integral part of planning for the environment; if the two are kept separate, neither will meet their long-term objectives.

Lesson 4: Community Groups and Nongovernment Organizations Are Essential to Realizing Stewardship Goals

Residents in the Lower Mainland care about fish and their habitat. From such hands-on efforts such as stream rehabilitation, fish restocking, habitat restoration, and fish and stream health monitoring, to such political work as ensuring that municipal councils put "fish" on the agenda, community groups are key to making fish a local priority. Through its focus on stream stewardship, Fisheries and Oceans Canada has been able to support some of these efforts.

- The Township of Langley, through the Langley Environmental Partners Society, involves volunteers and young people in training, projects such as tree planting to restore riparian habitat in the Salmon River watershed and updating municipal watercourse maps;
- Land for Nature (of the Federation of BC Naturalists) uses stream stewardship materials from the Fraser River Action Plan in community workshops and direct landowner contact to raise awareness about fish and wildlife habitat.

Chapter 10 / Working for Sustainable Cities

Figure 10.6

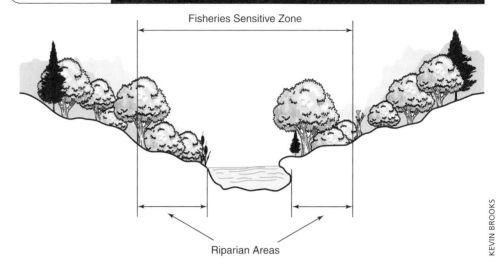

Fisheries Sensitive Zone

Riparian Areas

KEVIN BROOKS

With appropriate technical information about river systems, community residents can participate in restoration projects.

Lesson 5: Stewardship Requires Strategic Planning

The strategy for stewardship initiatives embedded in the Fraser River Action Plan is based on areas of greatest need and of greatest potential effectiveness. With fish habitat in the Lower Mainland in a vulnerable state, it has been a difficult task to balance the need for good program planning with the need for emergency response measures.

A major project has involved raising awareness of fish habitat protection measures. The *Stewardship Series* of booklets produced as part of the Fraser River Action Plan illustrate how fish habitat can be planned for and protected. Another priority has been to produce accurate and accessible technical information to enhance habitat management (Figure 10.6). Orthophotos overlaid with maps identifying watercourses where there is information on fish presence/absence, for example, are now available in hard copy or electronically. Accompanied by written summaries, these maps help Lower Mainland municipalities make early decisions about the suitability of lands for development. They can also help community groups planning habitat enhancement projects.

The zoning bylaw and other land use regulations can protect environmentally sensitive areas (ESA) in their natural state. For example, avoid putting polluting uses near ESAs; when planning for future subdivisions, develop lot configurations in a way that conserves ESAs; ensure that setbacks at streams meet land development guidelines provided by the Department of Fisheries and Oceans; require fencing to control public access at extremely sensitive habitats through land use regulations; and implement landscape provisions to promote use of native plants. Stream stewardship involves protecting sensitive areas in their natural state.

Protecting Habitat

In the Lower Mainland, fish and their habitat are receiving increasing attention. From the provincial government's Urban Salmon Habitat Program to schoolchildren growing and releasing fry and to habitat reconstruction work, stream stewardship initiatives are multiplying. The provincial Minister of Environment made riparian areas and clean air top environmental issues in the mid-1990s. These activities signal an increase in a stewardship approach toward a rich and sensitive resource.

Now more than ever, fish need all the help they can get. But fish will only realize the benefits of these efforts if remaining habitat is protected and priority is placed on restoring damaged habitat so that numbers have a chance to increase. Such progress will involve coordination, strategic planning, and community action. The Fraser River Action Plan provides useful lessons for those adopting a stewardship approach to habitat protection.

1. What are the key attributes and requirements of urban sustainability? How do the definitions of sustainability offered by authors in this chapter differ?

2. What variables or indicators suggest that Canadian cities are making progress toward sustainable communities? What indicators suggest we are losing ground?

3. Under what conditions should communities make ecological restoration a high priority in planning policy?

4. What strategies can communities use to protect riparian (riverside) habitat from destruction or to restore it to health?

5. In what situations might stewardship be the best alternative for environmental protection? What is required for an effective community stewardship program?

6. Examine environmental policy in your local community plan. In what way do those policies promote sustainability? How could they be strengthened?

7. How do sustainability issues differ in rural and urban settings; and in inland and coastal settings?

8. What unsustainable land development practices persist in the communities that you know, and why?

Reference Notes

1. Mathur, B (1989) Conserving the urban river corridor: Experience from Saskatoon. *Plan Canada* 29(5): 43–9.

   Smith, D (1989) Towards a policy for floodplain management: A case study of the experience in Moose Jaw, Saskatchewan. *Plan Canada* 29(1): 52–62.

2. Pedersen, E (1999) The Garrison Creek linkage plan: A model for developing an open-space system. *Plan Canada* 39(5): 20–1.

3. Dorney, R (1989) *The Professional Practice of Environmental Management*. New York: Springer-Verlag.

   Eagles, P (1984) *The Planning and Management of Environmentally Sensitive Areas*. New York: Longman.

4. Rees, WE (1989) *Planning for Sustainable Development: A Resource Book*. Vancouver: UBC Centre for Human Settlements.

   Wackernagel, M & WE Rees (1996) *Our Ecological Footprint: Reducing Human Impact on the Earth*. Gabriola Island: New Society Publishers.

5. Roseland, M (1992) *Toward Sustainable Communities: A Resource Book for Municipal and Local Governments*. Ottawa: National Round Table on the Environment and the Economy.

   Roseland, M (ed) (1997) *Eco-city Dimensions: Healthy Communities, Healthy Planet*. Gabriola Island: New Society Publishers.

   Roseland, M (2005) *Toward Sustainable Communities: Resources for Citizens and Their Governments*. Gabriola Island: New Society Publishers.

6. Tomalty, R (1994) *Ecosystem Planning for Canadian Urban Regions*. Toronto: ICURR Publications.

7. Louis, C & L Pim (1995) The Niagara Escarpment: Planning for environmental protection. *Plan Canada* 35(6): 39–40.

   Van Patter M & S Hilts (1990) Natural heritage protection: Voluntary stewardship or planning control? *Plan Canada* 30(5): 20–8.

   Yip, S (1994) Applying sustainable development principles to residential community planning. *Plan Canada* 34(2): 31–4.

8. Cox, K & D Witty (1993) Wetlands conservation: Is planning enough? *Plan Canada* 33(6): 7–10.

9. World Commission on Environment and Development (1987) *Our Common Future*. Oxford: Oxford University Press.

10. Grant, J (1994) Rhetoric and response: Sustainable development in residential environments. *Environments* 22(3): 3–12.

11. Richardson, NH (1989) Land use planning and sustainable development in the Canadian north. *Plan Canada* 29(2): 56–62.

    Richardson, NH (1994) Canada in the twentieth century: Planning for conservation and the environment. *Plan Canada* (Anniversary edition, July): 52–69.

12. Horton, KW (1976) Of trees, natural ecosystems and community design. *Plan Canada* 16(3/4): 208–12.

    Tyler, ME (2000) Ecological planning in an age of myth-information. *Plan Canada* 40(1): 20–1.

13. Beavis, MA (1991) Stewardship, planning and public policy. *Plan Canada* 31(6): 75–82.

14. Bond, W, D O' Farrell, & J Engeland (1999) Sustainable community indicators program. *Plan Canada* 39(5): 24-6.

    Keogh, N (2003) Calgary's citizen-led community sustainability indicators project. *Plan Canada* 43(1): 35–6.

    Sherwood, D & D Parish (1993) Identifying the quality of life in your community: Quality of life indicators. *Plan Canada* 33(6): 11–4.

15. Johnson, K (2001) Community planning and climate change in the Canadian North. *Plan Canada* 41(1): 16–17.

16. World Commission on Environment and Development (WCED) (1987) *Our Common Future*. (*The Brundtland Report*) New York: Oxford University Press.

17. International Union for Conservation of Nature and Natural Resources (IUCN; now World Conservation Union) (1980) *World Conservation Strategy: Living Resource Conservation for Sustainable Development*. Section 1, paragraph 3. Gland, Switzerland: IUCN.

18. WCED (1987) Op. cit.: 8.

19. National Task Force on Environment and Economy (1987) *Report to the Canadian Council of Resource and Environment Ministers*. Ottawa: The Council: 3.

20. Dilks, D (1996) Measuring urban sustainability. *Proceedings, Canadian Indicators Workshop*, June 19–21, 1995, State of the Environment Directorate, Environment Canada: 1.

21. Yiftachel, O & D Hedgcock (1993) Urban social sustainability: The planning of an Australian city. *Cities* 11(2): 139–57.

22. Crerar, AD (1989) The sustainable city. *Policy Options*, March: 3–5.

23. Richardson, N (1989) *Land Use Planning and Sustainable Development in Canada*. Ottawa: Canadian Environmental Advisory Council: 14.

24. Richardson, N (1992) Canada. In *Sustainable Cities: Urbanization and the Environment in International Perspective*. Boulder: Westview Press: 48.

25. Mitlin, D & D Satterthwaite. (1994) *Cities and Sustainable Development*. Background paper prepared for Global Forum '94. London: Human Settlements Program: 5.

26. Maclaren, VW (1995) *Developing Indicators of Urban Sustainability: The Canadian Experience*. Interim report for Measuring Urban Sustainability: Canadian Indicators Workshop, prepared for the State of the Environment Directorate, Environment Canada: 2.

27. Nozick, M (1992) *No Place Like Home: Building Sustainable Communities*. Ottawa: Canadian Council on Social Development.

28. United States Environmental Protection Agency & Canada Department of the Environment (1995) *Practical Steps to Implement an Ecosystem Approach in Great Lakes Management* (workshop report): 7.

29. Masse, S (1995) *Community Forestry: Concept, Applications and Issues*. Ottawa: Canadian Forest Service, Quebec Region: 3.

30. Bradford, N (2003) Cities and communities that work: Innovative practices, enabling policies. *Canadian Policy Research Networks*, http://www.cprn.com/en/doc.cfm?doc=318 (accessed 10 May 2006).

31. Polese, M & R Stren (2000) *The Social Sustainability of Cities*. Toronto: University of Toronto Press.

32. Maxwell, J (2003) *Innovation is a Social Process*, http://www.statcan.ca/english/research/88F0006XIE/88F0006XIE2003006.pdf.

33. Hatfield, M (1997) Concentrations of poverty and distressed neighbourhoods in Canada. *Social Development Canada*, http://www.sdc.gc.ca/en/cs/sp/sdc/pkrf/publications/1997-002563/page01.shtml (accessed 10 May 2006).

    Lee, K (2000) *Urban Poverty in Canada*. Canadian Council on Social Development, http://www.ccsd.org.

34. Myles, J, G Picot, & W Pyper (2000) *Neighbourhood Inequality in Canadian Cities*, http://www.statcan.ca/bsolc/english/bsolc?catno=11F0019MIE2000160 (accessed 10 May 2006).

35. Maxwell, J (2002) *Smart Social Policy: Making Work Pay*, http://www.cprn.com/en/doc.cfm?doc=199 (accessed 10 May 2006).

36. Bradford, N (2003) Cities and communities that work: Innovative practices, enabling policies. *Canadian Policy Research Networks*, http://www.cprn.com/en/doc.cfm?doc=318 (accessed 10 May 2006).

37. Ibid.

38. Organization for Economic Cooperation and Development (2002) *Territorial Review: Canada*. Paris: OECD.

39. Rapport, DJ & H Regier (1995) Disturbance and stress effects on ecological systems. In B Patten & S Jargensen (eds) *Complex Ecology: The Part-Whole Relation in Ecosystems*. Englewood Cliffs: Prentice Hall: 397–414.

    RCFTW (Royal Commission on the Future of the Toronto Waterfront) (1992) *Regeneration: Toronto's Waterfront and the Sustainable City*. Final report. Toronto: Queen's Printer of Ontario.

40. Leopold, A (1949) *A Sand County Almanac and Sketches Here and There*. New York: Oxford University Press.

41. Riley, JL & P Mohr (1994) *The Natural Heritage of Southern Ontario's Settled Landscape*. Toronto: Queen's Printer of Ontario.

42. RCFTW (1992) Op. cit.

43. This work was supported by a grant from the College of Arts and Architecture, Penn State University. Thanks to Michael Hough and Derek Coleman for their helpful insights.

44. Luymes, D, D Nadenicek, & K Tamminga (1995) Across the Great Divide: Landscape architecture, ecology and the city. *Proceedings of the 1995 Annual Meeting of the American Society of Landscape Architects*. Cleveland: 187–196.

    Noss, R (1983) A regional landscape approach to maintain diversity. *BioScience* 33(11): 700–6.

    Reese, KP & JT Ratti (1988) Reconsideration of the edge effect. *Transactions of the 53rd North American Wildlife and Natural Resources Conference*: 127–36.

    Soulé, M (1991) Land use planning and wildlife maintenance: Guidelines for conserving wildlife in an urban landscape. *Journal of the American Planning Association* 57(3): 313–23.

45. Jordon, WR (1995) Good restoration. *Restoration & Management Notes* 13(1): 3–4.

46. Wilson, EO (1992) *The Diversity of Life*. Cambridge: Harvard University Press.

47. Perrings, C, KG Maler, C Folke, CS Holling, & B Jansson (eds) (1995) Introduction: Framing the problem of biodiversity loss. *Biodiversity Loss: Economic and Ecological Issues*. New York: Cambridge University Press: 1–17.

48. Van der Ryn, S & S Cowan (1996) *Ecological Design*. Washington: Island Press.

49. Salwasser, H (1991) Roles for land and resource managers in conserving biological diversity. In DJ Decker, ME Krasny, GR Golt, CR Smith, & DW Gross (eds) *Challenges in the Conservation of Biological Resources: A Practitioner's Guide*. Boulder: Westview Press: 11–31.

    Soulé, M (1994) What is conservation biology? In RE Grumbine (ed) *Environmental Policy and Biodiversity*. Washington: Island Press: 35–53.

50. Katz, GE (1995) Natural areas in city, suburb and town and the practical application of landscape ecology. *Plan Canada* 35(6): 18–21.

51. Gilpin, ME & M Soulé (1986) Minimum viable populations: Processes of species extinction. In M Soulé (ed) *Conservation Biology*. Sunderland: Sinauer Associates: 19–34.

    Riley, JL & P Mohr (1994) Op. cit.

    Soulé, M (1991) Land use planning and wildlife maintenance: Guidelines for conserving wildlife in an urban landscape. *Journal of the American Planning Association* 57(3): 313–23.

52. Katz, GE (1995) Op. cit.

    Robinson, PA (1995) Protecting the environment in a rapidly urbanizing community. *Plan Canada* 35(6): 22–5.

    Thompson, D (1995) Curing institutional Alzheimer's: Tools for more effective and efficient environmental planning. *Plan Canada* 35(6): 14–7.

53. Hostovsky, C, D Miller, & C Keddy (1995) The natural environment systems strategy: Protecting Ottawa-Carleton's ecological areas. *Plan Canada* 35(6): 26–9.

54. Steiner, F (1994) Sprawl can be good. *Planning* 60(7): 14–7.

    Soulé, M (1991) Op. cit.

55. Noss , R & L Harris (1986) Nodes, networks and MUMS: Preserving diversity at all scales. *Environmental Management* 10(3): 299–309.

56. GSHSW (Gore & Storrie Limited and Hough Stansbury Woodland Limited) (1992, 1993) *Markham Natural Features Study, Phases 1 and 2*. Markham: Town of Markham, ES1–ES2.

57. Riley, JL & P Mohr (1994) Op. cit.

58. McCaull, J (1994) The natural community conservation planning program and the coastal sage scrub ecosystem of Southern California. In RE Crumbine (ed) *Environmental Policy and Biodiversity*. Washington: Island Press: 287.

59. GSHSW (1992, 1993) Op. cit.

60. Rapport, DJ & H Regier (1995) Op. cit.

61. Wilcove, DS (1987) From fragmentation to extinction. *Natural Areas Journal* 7: 23–9.

62. Riley, JL & P Mohr (1994) Op. cit.

63. Harris, L & PB Gallagher (1989) New initiatives for wildlife conservation: The need for movement corridors. In G. Mackintosh (ed) *Preserving Communities and Corridors*. Washington: Preservers of Wildlife: 11–34.

64. Noss, R (1983) A regional landscape approach to maintain diversity. *BioScience* 33(11): 700–6.

    Noss, R (1987) Protecting natural areas in fragmented landscapes. *Natural Areas Journal* 7: 2–13.

    Noss, R (1992) *Conserving Oregon's Coast Range Biodiversity: A Conservation and Restoration Plan*. Newport OR: Coast Range Association.

    Soulé, M (1991) Op. cit.

65. Harris, L & PB Gallagher (1989) Op. cit.

66. Mann, CC & ML Plummer (1995) Are wildlife corridors the right path? *Science* 270: 1428–30.

67. Simberloff, D & J Cox (1987) Consequences and costs of conservation corridors. *Conservation Biology* 1(1): 63–71.

68. Ranney, JW, MC Bruner, & JB Levenson (1981) The importance of edge in the structure and dynamics of forest islands. In RL Burgess & DM Sharpe (eds) *Forest Island Dynamics in Man-Dominated Landscapes*. New York: Springer-Verlag: 67–95.

69. Riley, JL & P Mohr (1994) Op. cit.

70. Middleton, B (1995) Ecology of greenways. *Restoration Ecology* 3(4): 319–20.

71. Whyte, WH (1968) *The Last Landscape*. Garden City: Doubleday: 354.

72. Quadra Planning Consultants (1995) *Protection of Aquatic and Riparian Habitat by Local Governments: Measures Adopted in the Lower Fraser Valley,* http://www.dfo-mpo.gc.ca/Library/224986.pdf (accessed 10 May 2006).

Techniques and Tactics

Chapter Eleven

Land Use Issues

Municipal Planning and Managing Land Issues

Jill Grant

The primary duty of the municipal planner is regulating land use and managing the issues that arise in the process. Some land use issues change through time, as we have discussed in earlier chapters, while others remain high priority.[1] Wherever they live, people need shelter, clean water, waste removal, transportation systems, job opportunities, and access to goods and services. Municipal plans look to the future in an effort to address these concerns and to ensure that communities can continue to thrive, even as circumstances change.

The challenges of managing land use, in part, reflect changing demands and problems associated with transforming technologies of transportation, production, and communication. Early in the twentieth century, planners worried about getting basic services in place and accommodating new technologies like electricity, the telephone, and the automobile. In the early twenty-first century, we try to accommodate wireless transmitters and find financing for rapid transit services.

We can also see that changing demographics and economies can alter the context for land use planning. The last century has brought several shifts in household size and dynamics, thus altering housing demand and service needs (Figure 11.1). The postindustrial economy is forcing municipalities to adapt to new needs and interests from workers and consumers. Greater attention to human rights and cultural diversity has redrafted the planning rules and is reshaping the urban landscape. Public participation in the planning process generates abundant opportunities for contention to arise over land use decisions.

In this chapter, we profile some land use issues not previously discussed in the book. Keith Nicol draws attention to the potential to reduce energy demands by carefully siting buildings to take advantage of solar gain. Since the energy crisis of the 1970s, we understand the potential of planning for energy efficiency. As our cities show, however, we still have a long way to go to manage the ecological footprint that our avaricious consumption of fossil fuels entails. (We will return to this issue next chapter, when we discuss transportation planning.)

We considered environmental issues in earlier sections, such as Chapter 10 on sustainable cities. *Plan Canada* includes many articles on key themes, like finding locations for land fill sites or effectively managing storm water.[2] Rural planners understand the need to manage agricultural uses effectively to avoid contaminating surface and groundwater supplies.[3] Here we focus on managing demand for water, with an article by John Bianchin: He suggests that planners can and should use several tools to reduce water consumption.

Figure 11.1

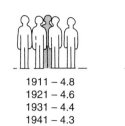

1891 – 5.3	1911 – 4.8	1961 – 3.9
1901 – 5.0	1921 – 4.6	1971 – 3.5
	1931 – 4.4	1981 – 3.3
	1941 – 4.3	1991 – 3.1
	1951 – 4.0	2001 – 3.0

Through the last century, the average household size in Canada has dropped steadily from five people or more to three.

Marc Denhez's article highlights the growing significance of heritage as a factor in planning Canadian communities. Since the 1970s, most cities have adopted strategies for protecting their cultural heritage. Many have used heritage resources as the basis for developing a stronger tourism industry.[4]

Communities have to accommodate a mix of uses: housing, retail, industrial, and institutional. Planners have long recognized the need for adequate and affordable housing.[5] While the pages of *Plan Canada* include many articles on housing, the profession has struggled with meeting its lofty objectives. By and large, Canadians are well-housed, but finding affordable housing in suitable locations remains a challenge for many low-income households. In recent years, planners have seen increasing the proportion of land zoned for multifamily housing and encouraging urban strategies like intensification (permitting more units in existing neighbourhoods) as "sustainable" techniques for improving housing supply. In this chapter, Stanley Yip reports on an attempt to design a sustainable subdivision in the Oak Ridges Moraine.

To ensure the vitality of the local economy, municipalities often find themselves preoccupied with local economic development.[6] Providing adequate land for industrial and employment activities is always a high priority. Here, Rowan Faludi writes about the changing character of commercial development and its effects on land use. Consumption increasingly shapes our urban landscape, and changing shopping patterns have immense effects on our cities. Big-box retail drives urban sprawl, contributing to the decline of urban centres and older shopping malls.[7] Maintaining the vibrancy of declining downtown areas has generated considerable investment as well as debates about how best to achieve planning objectives.[8]

Pamela Blais challenges planners to consider how the information age may shape the city of the future.[9] With increasing numbers of people working at home or telecommuting,[10] Blais argues that planners need to consider the kinds of services available throughout the urban fabric and the impact the changing economy may have on land uses in suburban areas.

Effective land use planning is arguably a necessary condition for creating more livable communities, but alone it may not be sufficient to ensure we meet all of our objectives. Making better places is a continuing challenge for all community residents.

Building Orientation and Heating Requirements in Canada

Keith Nicol

1987, Plan Canada 27(6): 154–61

Urban planners are primarily responsible for designing and regulating development in the urban areas of Canada. Since the early 1970s, when energy prices began to increase rapidly, land use planners have focused more attention on how they might reduce overall urban energy consumption through careful planning and design.

The largest potential for planners attempting to conserve energy in urban areas is in reducing energy use in transportation and within buildings. Transportation accounts for roughly 25 percent, while building energy consumption accounts for about 35 percent of Canada's total energy budget.[11] Specific policies that might reduce building energy consumption include promoting the solar orientation of streets and buildings, encouraging landscaping and energy efficient building standards, and protecting solar access.

The focus of this paper is on one aspect of this series of planning measures: the influence of orientation on residential energy consumption. The advantages of influencing orientation is that it is relatively inexpensive, calculated to make active solar collection more effective in the future, and controllable by planners.

To determine the influence of building orientation (the direction in which most of the windows in a dwelling face) on building heating requirements, a computer model (Hotcan) was used.[12] The Hotcan model was tested in a variety of broad climatic types across Southern Canada, where most Canadian cities are located. The results are displayed in percentage savings as well as actual dollar savings per dwelling, so that the overall effects of building orientation can be more quantitatively assessed.

Orienting Design

Long before building design starts, decisions are made that will affect the final orientation of a building. Subdivision designers, surveyors, and urban planners control the final street layout of a residential neighbourhood, typically basing their decisions on the location of connecting roads, drainage conditions, views, and economic factors. They normally do not consider the energy required by future dwellings constructed along the streets.

Street layout largely dictates lot orientation, which greatly controls building orientation.[13] Furthermore, residential buildings, regardless of their specific shape, have most of their windows facing either toward or directly away from the street.[14] Since studies show a strong relationship between building energy use and window distribution, it is likely that building orientation in concert with site planning and building design will have a major influence on the final energy requirements of Canadian buildings.[15]

Energy-Efficient Subdivision Design

With the advent of higher energy costs, planners at all levels of government began to investigate methods by which energy use might be diminished. By the late 1970s and the early 1980s, Canadian municipalities had started to introduce various energy conservation measures. In 1978, the first Canadian bylaw protecting solar access passed in Millet, Alberta. In 1979, Brampton, Ontario, introduced a bylaw requiring that building and street orientation favour passive solar collection for the proposed Alliance subdivision. To facilitate this, it encouraged grid patterns with the majority of streets oriented east-west (Figure 11.2). Bylaw 139-79 stipulated that buildings be constructed so that the main wall facing north should not vary from the east-west axis by more than 12 to 20 degrees.[16]

Other municipalities began to follow Brampton's lead in energy-conscious planning. For example, Champlain Heights, a new subdivision in Vancouver, was built on south-facing slopes utilizing a majority of east-west streets to ensure maximum solar access.[17] Saskatchewan's Bill 106 contained regulations that allow the minister responsible to set standards for energy efficiency in subdivisions: This includes requirements about the orientation of lots and roads for maximum solar benefit.[18] The Regional Municipality of Hamilton-Wentworth also promoted energy-efficient neighbourhood planning.[19]

Figure 11.2

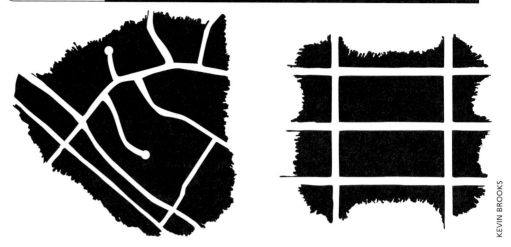

KEVIN BROOKS

Streets running east-west can facilitate situating homes for passive solar gain. Other route orientations provide a challenge for solar design.

Numerous other reports have encouraged an energy-efficient east-west street orientation.[20] It would appear, then, that a prime technique that municipalities can use to reduce residential energy consumption is control over street alignment. A subdivision with mostly east-west streets favours passive and active solar collection since shading is minimized and south-facing windows can be maximized. Most studies, however, do not actually quantify the energy savings that might be associated with a particular street and building layout. Because of the relative permanence of street patterns, it is imperative that planners have access to information that will allow them to make decisions based on the actual costs or savings of energy related to building and street orientation. Two studies that addressed this particular problem point to some interesting conclusions.

In Lethbridge, a modern bungalow facing north used 22 percent more energy than the same dwelling oriented south. The most important factors in improving neighbourhood energy efficiency are related to increased densities and a more efficient transportation network. A study of energy-efficient subdivision design prepared for Guelph concluded that total energy savings varied greatly with the type of building being constructed.[21] Clearly, a building with equal amounts of glazing on each wall will not be sensitive to orientation. As window area begins to vary significantly from wall to wall, however, orientation effects become more important. In the Guelph study, orientation alone reduced energy use by up to 10 percent depending on initial building design.

Testing the Effects

The heating loads for a "standard" building were determined for 12 locations across Canada for the four cardinal directions. In all cases, the houses oriented toward the south produced the lowest heating loads. The magnitude of the energy savings, however, varied considerably between the locations tested. Generally, east or west orientations had similar heating requirements and would produce intermediate energy savings compared to the worst case: a north orientation.

Within any of the building standards tested, the variation in heating costs across Canada was a function of the severity of the winter (producing a heating demand) and availability of solar radiation (which acts to reduce heating demand). Because of a higher heating load induced by a severe but sunny winter climate, the Prairie provinces show the largest impact of orientation. For instance, a north-facing house in Suffield, Alberta, was calculated to pay 17 percent more for heating than the identical south-facing sample house. The effect of orientation is least influential in overcast environments, where the heating season extends throughout much of the year. For example, in St. John's, Newfoundland & Labrador, the effect of north versus south orientation was calculated to be just seven percent.

At locations between these climate types (cold, sunny winters or extended heating seasons in the overcast conditions), the influence of orientation produces intermediate energy savings. In Southern Ontario, Southern Quebec, and the Maritimes, orientation (south facing versus north facing) produces calculated savings of 10 to 13 percent.

As insulation standards are increased and building air-tightness improved, the percentage savings related to orientation increase. Again, the same pattern across the country is apparent with maximum impacts felt in Western Canada, with generally lesser impacts in Eastern Canada and with St. John's showing the least energy reductions. The percentage savings are true regardless of the fuel type used, although actual dollar savings will depend on the cost of the fuel.

To assess the overall impact of street orientation on building energy use, one must consider other factors. Although energy costs stabilized or in some cases diminished in the late 1980s, longer-term forecasts indicate that energy costs will again escalate. These increases will accentuate the influence of orientation, in spite of the construction of better-insulated houses. For instance, with a doubling of electrical costs, a north-facing house constructed to superinsulated standards would pay at least 25 percent (generally 30 to 40 percent) more than its south-facing counterpart. As well, since houses and subdivisions are built with a lifespan of at least 25 years, these savings accumulate. Also, if street orientation (and thus building orientation) is appropriate in the first place, then the future addition of active solar collectors for space heating and hot water is much easier than attempting to retrofit a poorly-designed subdivision with solar collectors at some future date.

Designing for Efficiency

In the past, our communities have been shaped and controlled by many factors. Because it was relatively inexpensive, energy was not one of these. Consequently our settlements are better suited to a situation of cheap energy rather than the situation predicted for the future. Local governments, however, through their control of city plans and subdivision and zoning bylaws, can produce urban patterns that are more conducive to energy efficiency.

Controlling favourable street orientation is an increasingly common technique whereby Canadian municipalities can attempt to reduce residential heating costs. A dominant grid or semigrid pattern of east-west streets produces a lot type suitable for passively solar-heated buildings. This road layout, similar to residential street design prior to 1945 when cul-de-sacs and crescents began to be used in Canadian cities, minimizes shading and allows large amounts of south-facing glass to be used. Once optimum street patterns are in place, the energy conscious planner should encourage builders and developers to take advantage of these patterns and construct energy efficient dwellings.

Don't Be a Drip: Planning for Water Efficiency

John Bianchin

1999, Plan Canada 39(4): 10–1

In Canada, the use of water and the cost of providing it are both increasing, but the funds for building new facilities are drying up. So the government is stressing conservation rather than construction. Here's how planners can help in getting the public to turn on to turning off.

Water is expensive. Despite our perception of Canada as a water-rich nation, the process of providing this resource is a costly one, considering that 75 percent of the population relies on municipal systems for safe and secure drinking water. The costs include those related to physical infrastructure, energy required for pumping, and labour for operation, administration, and maintenance.

More important, per capita water use is increasing, as are the costs associated with replacing old facilities or constructing new ones. At the same time, government's financial support for such large capital projects is either disappearing or is contingent on meeting strict conservation goals.

Compounding this situation, the current water-supply rates do not take into account the accumulation of sufficient funds for infrastructure replacement. For example, $1 billion worth of infrastructure with a 50-year life cycle requires $20 million per year in replacement costs. With many Canadian municipalities possessing several billion dollars worth of infrastructure, the burden of replacing or expanding these systems is enormous and may prove unbearable for many. Therefore, water efficiency is beginning to attract attention as an important, viable, and relatively inexpensive solution to water supply concerns.

In general, strategies based on efficiency are faster, easier, and cheaper to bring online than traditional water-supply capital projects. Moreover, since the tremendous, irreversible commitment of money required to build large supply, storage, and treatment projects is not required, the financial risk of miscalculating water demand is reduced.

The Planner's Role

Traditionally, planners have not played a direct role in water-efficiency planning even though they are in a strong position to promote water efficiency. Planners' responsibilities, which include the determination of lot size, the placement of structures, and the design of common and open space, are important to the process of improving water-use efficiency in residential areas. Furthermore, a major impetus for water efficiency is accommodating future urban growth. Since the relationship between urban growth policies and policies that control the provision of drinking water are deeply interconnected the planner's role becomes increasingly important.

Five Steps to a Water-Efficiency Strategy

Most communities should have a least-cost planning mandate. They should also promote coordination between entities (particularly the works and planning departments) and establish a mix of initiatives that have target efficiency levels as their primary goal.

Step 1. *Designate a coordinator.* In almost all successful strategies, one individual is responsible for coordinating and developing the strategy and implementing the resulting action plan.

Step 2. *Convene a water-efficiency committee.* Chaired by the coordinator or perhaps by an enthusiastic local politician, a committee formed by the community can focus on water-efficiency goals and options. Although the planning department should be an integral part of this committee, input is also required from community members, such as home builders, works and utility representatives, plumbers, environmentalists, and citizens who may be affected by new policies or initiatives.

Step 3. *Discuss community growth targets in relation to water supply.* The committee can then discuss key questions: Does the existing system have the capacity to satisfy projected growth? What capacity will be needed, when will it be needed, and what are the costs of obtaining it if efficiency is not encouraged? Following this discussion, defined goals and a stronger sense of purpose (or urgency) will emerge.

Step 4. *Decide on the types of initiatives to pursue.* Depending on community needs, initiatives may target overall demand or summer peak demand. Likewise, they may concentrate on indoor or outdoor water use and focus on one or more sectors of the community.

Step 5. *Fine-tune the strategy.* An integrated, properly coordinated, but modestly budgeted strategy will have far more success than a single-purpose, large-budget strategy. Therefore, the process of choosing initiatives is crucial. These questions must be considered: Can the initiative be implemented? Is it cost effective? Is its success measurable? Will the initiative result in substantial and sustainable improvements in water efficiency, and does it consider and respond to community goals and water needs? Although the list of considerations is long, exploring them will lead to a final group of viable, cost-effective initiatives.

The Planner's Toolkit

The qualifying principle in considering the types and magnitude of water-efficiency initiatives is that a viable efficiency initiative is both cost effective and capable of maintaining an acceptable level of service. Table 11.1 shows four categories of water conservation: regulation, education/promotion, technology, and pricing. Although all four are important elements of a successful strategy, the first two are most relevant to planners. Some specific examples follow.

Land development codes introduce a procedure to determine the appropriate design of new residential developments in relation to water efficiency. Variables include

Table 11.1	Water Efficiency Initiatives

Regulation

- land development codes
- tap fees for development hookups
- turf limitation bylaw
- efficient land development patterns
- subdivision agreement modifications
- water permits
- plumbing code changes
- lawn watering restrictions
- landscape water assessments
- once-through cooling system bans
- industrial, commercial, and institutional water use inspections
- limited-use contracts

Technology

- retrofitting or replacing fixtures in existing homes
- rain barrel and lawn sprinkler timer installations
- downspout disconnection from combined sewer systems
- automatic irrigation systems
- centralized, automatic meter reading
- system leak detection and repair
- water pressure reduction

Education/Promotion

- demonstration gardens
- "environment" days
- educational videos or booklets
- conservation hotlines
- water facility tours
- product giveaways
- radio and television spots
- bill inserts

Pricing

- full-cost pricing
- seasonal pricing
- increasing block rates
- lifeline base price with inclining pricing
- excessive use charges

infrastructure capacity, the amount of groundwater in storage, groundwater recharge rates, the annual amount of water demand based on population projections, and historical water use data. If the proposal is not acceptable in light of these variables, the developer and planner must implement an appropriate plan of action to improve design efficiency before final approval is granted.

With tap fees for development hookups, a point system for each proposed development adds points for inefficient elements of construction and subtracts them for efficient ones. The fee is based on the total points that each development generates. Motivated developers will design efficiency into their proposals, focusing on the most efficient fixtures and landscaping techniques.

Some jurisdictions in the US have adopted ordinances which, depending on lot size, limit the size of turf areas on properties. Lawn size thus increases much more slowly than lot size, while the excessive use of turf is prevented and water-efficient landscaping is encouraged. This type of initiative is especially effective in existing subdivisions, where development policies are not applicable. Water-efficient landscaping bylaws can regulate the types of plantings used in a development as well as the location of certain plants. They can also ensure that the overall landscaping of the proposed development is done with consideration for water efficiency (Figure 11.3).

A demonstration garden featuring water-efficient plants and landscaping techniques will increase public awareness of the importance of water efficiency. The garden can promote and support other initiatives and regulatory measures related to water efficiency, while doubling as a recreational and educational resource. Examples include the Queen's Park Xeriscape Garden in Toronto, the Xeriscape Demonstration Garden in Kamloops, British Columbia, and Durham Region's Water Efficient Garden in Whitby, Ontario.

The recent trend toward smaller, denser housing, although partly motivated by high costs, also promotes efficiency by replacing private open space with common open space, where increased design control exists. The Seaton Design Competition, sponsored by the Ontario government in the 1990s, yielded a number of excellent designs. One based the magnitude of development on the amount of water that fell on the land and included a proposal for "living machine" sewage treatment for residential dwellings.

Figure 11.3

PHOTO COURTESY GREEN ROOFS FOR HEALTHY CITIES (WWW. GREENROOFS.ORG) AND SHIM-SUTCLIFFE ARCHITECTS. USED WITH PERMISSION.

This green roof project in the Thousand Islands won a 2004 award for its designers.

Monitoring and Evaluation

Unfortunately, the implementation of efficiency initiatives is, by itself, not enough. Because the results derived from each initiative become an important element of development and water supply planning, one must know how well the overall strategy is working. A program of continual monitoring and evaluation should include the following:

- Review what each initiative is expected to contribute to water efficiency and what its specific goal is. Concentrate on measurable benefits.
- Define the information necessary for measuring costs and benefits of each initiative and its contribution to overall efficiency. Identify sources where this information can be found and design tools for gathering it.
- Gather information in a timely manner and maintain functional and durable databases.
- Analyze periodically the success, cost, and other relevant characteristics of each initiative, such as the effect on customers' lifestyles or the natural environment.
- Report on progress made, costs incurred, customer participation and response, and other effects, both expected and unforeseen.

Although planners should play a vital role in the process, it is clear that no one person or agency can change the way Canadians use water. Only an integrated and well-coordinated strategy that supports systematic and gradual changes in behaviour will result in substantial and sustainable improvements in efficient water use. Water efficiency should become second nature to Canadians, so that current water supplies and infrastructure are extended, the construction of new facilities is delayed, and our water resources are protected.

Applying Sustainable Development Principles to Residential Planning

Stanley Yip

1994, Plan Canada 34(2): 31–4

To interpret the concept of sustainable development in terms of policies, local governments must address the issues of ecological conservation, landscape enhancement, energy efficiency, resource preservation, and efficient land management. While public and political support has been growing for the development of appropriate land use policies in pursuit of a sustainable society, the application of the concept to specific sites is relatively new to Canada's development industry and planning profession. In the 1990s, the Province of Ontario began to prepare land use policies to protect the Oak Ridges Moraine in the Greater Toronto Area (GTA). A 200-unit community in the Oak Ridges Moraine illustrates the application of sustainable development principles to a specific site.

The Oak Ridges Moraine

An environmentally sensitive area, the 160-kilometre-long moraine extends from Trenton to the Niagara Escarpment. Within the GTA, it is about 90 kilometres long and up to 13 kilometres wide. It rises up to 230 metres above the surrounding area and stretches across the regions of Durham, York, and Peel. An important headwater ecosystem, the moraine plays a critical role in maintaining safe water resources and natural heritage for Canada's largest metropolitan area.

Figure 11.4

Urban uses increasingly threaten forest and farmland in the Oak Ridges Moraine in King City.

One of the most significant physiographic features in Southern Ontario, the moraine formed as a band of glacial deposits between two opposing ice sheets during glaciation. The moraine has an important hydrogeological function, acting as both a groundwater recharge and discharge area. Prior to major settlement, the moraine was characterized by a native vegetation cover of mixed deciduous and coniferous woodland. Throughout the past 200 years, massive forest clearance for agriculture and the establishment of communities have shaped the rural land use pattern within the moraine (Figure 11.4). This rural landscape has been characterized by natural vegetation remnants, regenerated woodlots, farm activities, a grid of concession roads, small towns and hamlets.

Today, the moraine is subject to intense development pressures, which have started to change the rural landscape dramatically and degrade its environmental qualities. Typical developments include suburban residential subdivisions around communities, aggregate extraction, golf courses, and commercial strips along the old concession roads. Having declared the moraine an area of provincial interest, the Province of Ontario issued interim guidelines to protect the area while it developed a conservation plan.[22] To assess any proposed development activities in the moraine area, the interim guidelines established eight basic principles: growth and settlement, ecological integrity, landform conservation, significant natural areas, woodlands, watercourses and lakes, highly permeable soils, and groundwater resources.

To promote a sustainable development approach in land use planning for the moraine, the Oak Ridges Moraine Implementation Guidelines were applied to a site proposed for residential development.

Interpreting Sustainable Development in Aurora

Most residential developments within the outlying suburban areas of the GTA are typically subdivisions with single-detached freeholds with large frontages. Because this form of development normally requires large areas of land, it has a significant impact on the landscape. Such projects are serviced with standard municipal roads (with a minimum 20-metre- or 66-foot-wide right-of-way) and have restrictive grading requirements and conventional storm water management facilities. While developers, builders, market consultants, politicians, municipal planners, and engineers are familiar with this form of development—and most, if not all, have developed an established level of comfort in approving and delivering these residential projects—this development form is not efficient from an environmental perspective. Applying the principle of sustainable development to the planning of residential community demands a rethinking of the way development should happen within a site.

A 200-unit residential development proposal in Aurora within the Oak Ridges Moraine area attempts to interpret the implementation guidelines and the principles of sustainable development on a site-specific basis. The 45-hectare site is situated at the southwest corner of Bayview Avenue and Vandorf Sideroad. Part of the site falls within an environmentally significant area designated by the Lake Simcoe Region Conservation Authority. The project would be serviced with full municipal water supply and sewage systems. The proposal demonstrates how environmentally responsible planning ideas are applied to the site by the landowners and consultants. The fundamental principle in this approach is recognizing at the outset that the environment comes first in the decision-making process.

Putting the Environment First

A full understanding of the ecosystem and environmental issues comes through preparing a series of technical studies, including documenting all the natural resources information collected from available sources and directly from the field: a hydrogeological study; surface-water management study; fisheries, woodland, and natural area management studies; and municipal servicing report. The planning process that led to the development concept can be summarized in three steps: understanding the ecosystem and the interrelationship among the different environmental components; establishing an environmental enhancement strategy for the site; and formulating a sensible development approach, built forms, and densities.

The 45-hectare site includes a continuous wooded valley along the central part of the property, extending from north to south. Strategically, it links the White Rose West Forest life sciences area of natural and scientific interest (defined by the Ministry of Natural Resources) south of the property with the wooded valley to the north. The valley bisects the site. A branch of the Holland River headwater flows from south to north along the valley. The areas on both sides of the woodland are abandoned farmland with rolling relief and varied topography. The undulating landscape on the valley's western side has created two distinct ridges running in a north-south direction. The Lake Simcoe Region Conservation Authority has designated part of the site as an environmentally significant area due to its function as an aquifer and stream recharge zone.

Past farming activities had disturbed the natural environment significantly. Many of the existing features within the site reflect the impact of these agricultural activities on the natural environment: straight, geometrically shaped woodland edges with restricted biodiversity; cleared woodlands and vegetation along streams and watercourses; disturbed fish habitat; fragmented clusters of regenerated vegetation with no connecting corridors; exposed watercourses and warming of the surface water; high level of nitrate concentration in the ground; and an old farm access lane cutting across the wooded valley and obstructing fish passage.

An environmental enhancement strategy was developed to help nature reclaim the site. By adopting a sensible and responsible development form within the site, along

Chapter 11/Land Use Issues

with developing corrective measures to restore areas and features of environmental degradation, the project could improve and enhance the environmental quality and diversity of the ecosystem.

The sustainable planning principles followed depart from the conventional residential subdivision planning approach:

- Take development projects as opportunities to enhance the environmental qualities of the land by incorporating positive measures to encourage natural regeneration and habitat restoration, promote habitat connectivity, and assist nature to reclaim.
- Adopt cluster housing forms, nonfreehold tenure, and responsible site planning criteria to achieve a high level of environmental efficiency. A development density similar to conventional freehold subdivisions is attainable, while existing landform and natural areas are conserved.
- Employ an environmentally-friendly stormwater management approach that encourages infiltration and enhancement of runoff quality. Incorporate innovative stormwater management practices to replace conventional runoff collection and concentration facilities.
- Include design elements that promote environmental education and interpretation. Design neighbourhoods to maximize opportunities to appreciate the interrelationship between the human and natural environments.

Tests for Sustainable Residential Development

The proposed residential community in Aurora received support from the Ministry of Natural Resources and the Lake Simcoe Region Conservation Authority because of its perceived compatibility with the fundamental principles outlined in the implementation guidelines. The proposal established site-specific planning and design criteria in accordance with sustainable development principles (Table 11.2). In contrast to the widespread misconception that no development will ever be "approvable" in the moraine area under the guidelines, the development plan demonstrated that an alternative exists to the conventional suburban single-detached freehold subdivision. Nevertheless, there are three further tests beyond the ministry endorsement: municipal land use policies, development control/design performance standards, and the market.

The development industry commonly adopts cluster housing forms (townhouses, courts, walk-up apartments) and nonfreehold (condominium or leasehold) ownership for urban projects. However, these are not traditional land uses commonly found in suburban fringe areas within the GTA. An environmentally efficient development form can be achieved without sacrificing development densities based on nonconventional land uses and built forms. Interpreting this approach on a broader regional planning perspective suggests a way to achieve a balance between the public objective to promote sustainable development and the accommodation of settlement growth in urban fringes.

On the other hand, cluster housing and condominium ownership on a significant scale are generally the least understood by residents, municipal politicians, and municipal staff. Most local official plans include specific policies for estate and suburban freehold residential developments, which specify densities, scale, minimum lot sizes, and frontages. But they seldom include specific enabling policies to encourage alternative built forms and ownership as the means to promote sustainable development.

Developers are familiar with the notion that the typical suburban residential product is a two-storey, single-detached home with double garage sited on a freehold lot. Is there a market for innovative condominium cluster housing in urban fringe areas? Market

Table 11.2   Site-Specific Planning Criteria

Protect ecological integrity

- protect existing woodland as part of a greenway system
- respect existing natural topography and features

Create new habitats and encourage natural regeneration

- assist natural woodland edge regeneration
- create woodland corridors and enhance habitat connectivity
- enhance riparian vegetation along watercourses
- enhance existing wetlands
- protect fish passage
- revegetate environmentally degraded areas
- encourage natural rejuvenation of disturbed watercourses

Conserve landform and natural significant areas

- identify major ridgelines and slopes for protection
- adopt cluster housing, condominium ownership, and creative site planning standards
- retain existing rural character

Preserve and enhance groundwater resources

- adopt site-specific stormwater drainage approaches to reflect local soil conditions
- promote infiltration and replace curbs and gutters with roadside infiltration ditches and check dams
- incorporate infiltration trenches within rear yards
- respect natural topography in overflow design

Promote environmental education and interpretation

- provide direct trail connection to the town-wide trail network
- develop the local park as a nature park based on ecological principles
- plant native species along streets and in amenity areas

research indicates a strong demand by empty nesters and young families for reasonably-priced dwellings that are maintenance free, close to small towns, and located in an attractive environment. While some projects currently planned to capture this specific market will turn out to be successful, the depth of the market remains untested.

The proposed residential development encompasses site-specific site planning criteria, innovative stormwater management practices, private-access road standards, flexible site grading, and nonconventional municipal road cross-sections. The design would require the town to accept several modifications to municipal design standards, including replacement of the curbs and gutters with roadside ditches.

The project proposes nonfreehold tenure because this is currently the only way to achieve a higher level of flexibility in the planning and design of the site. An ownership arrangement like leasehold or condominium development allows the project to free itself from established municipal public right-of-way and grading design requirements. This flexibility, in turn, permits the project to achieve its environmental objectives. A flexible engineering design approach and creative site planning criteria are necessary to accommodate settlement growth while protecting the natural environment. However, adopting alternative landownership approaches as the only means to achieve sustainable development objectives is restrictive. Municipalities need to incorporate flexible site engineering, grading, and road design criteria for areas of environmental significance, irrespective of the type of land ownership.

Save What Needs to Be Saved

The proposed residential community in Aurora illustrates how a specific development proposal practises the principles of sustainable development. The project demonstrates that confrontational situations between town officials, developers, and conservationists can be averted by a balanced approach that saves what needs to be saved and builds what needs to be built.

Why Bother with Heritage Anyway?

Marc Denhez

2003, Plan Canada 43(2): 13–6

Is there life after bungalows or high-rises? Not according to most planning departments engulfed in greenfield sprawl and downtown redevelopment issues, although they make the occasional bow toward "intensification" of existing neighbourhoods. However, fertile ground can be found in another kind of development: improving the existing built environment, with the highest profiles being in heritage properties and districts.

Pre-World War II buildings account for one-seventh of Canada's built environment. Although legally designated heritage properties represent only a tiny fraction of these, their catalytic effect on development patterns is dramatically disproportionate to their numbers.

Existing Buildings: Views of the Past

Since the overwhelming majority of the buildings that Canadians will occupy in 2020 have already been built, the fundamental planning question is how will they be used and maintained? That question has been swept under the carpet for decades because of thinking dating from the 1930s when old buildings were broadly despised. Opinion leaders, including most architecture professors, adopted Walter Gropius's view that Victorian and Edwardian buildings were a "source of shame,"[23] what one editorial called "architecture at its worst."[24] According to McGill Principal Cyril James, it was "a comparative misfortune, in that none of the Canadian cities have yet been levelled by the war, but . . . as soon as war has finished [Canadians will] wipe [them] out from one end of this Dominion to the other, in order that you may rebuild effectively."[25]

Government then intervened to make this vision of "progress" a reality. Since the Great Depression, many economists believed that our consumer economy depended on planned obsolescence: Everything, including buildings and cities, should be thrown away. Accordingly, buildings were presumed to depreciate at breakneck speed, repairs were marginalized, and the best tax treatment given to structures was for demolition— even better than for donation of the building to charity (a situation that prevailed for more than 30 years and helped to fuel the demolition binge of 1960s urban renewal).

The United States did likewise, subsidizing the "doughnut effect" in American downtowns. A backlash began in the mid-1960s, when the US Conference of Mayors recommended a dramatic demonstration to prove that even the oldest, most deteriorated neighbourhoods could be returned to splendour.[26] Their tactical choice was as high profile as possible: historic districts. Their report was successful beyond the mayors' dreams. Areas like Boston's Beacon Hill and Washington's Georgetown spawned so many imitators that they launched a multibillion-dollar building rehabilitation industry (with tour-

Figure 11.5

KEVIN BROOKS

St. John's has used its heritage to its advantage in stimulating investment and tourism.

ism spinoffs). The scale of the demonstration effect surprised everybody: By the 1970s, every self-respecting yuppie was busy fixing something.

The spillover into Canada was equally dramatic. In 1982, residential renovation's share of gross domestic product overtook new home building (and has stayed on top almost continuously since), even in the total absence of a national strategy to do so. The experience in the cities that actually made an effort to use heritage strategically was startling: St. John's, which had one of the country's most distressed downtowns when it embarked on a heritage rehabilitation policy in 1978, effected such a turn-around that in 2000, Construct Canada named its revitalization one of the top Canadian construction achievements of the twentieth century (at about the same time as the city's first million-dollar condominium, in a heritage building, was coming on the market). The impact on the tax base has been huge.

Some people did not care about the economics: They were what modernist Adolf Loos called the "criminals and pathological cases" who simply liked ornamented old buildings.[27] Together, with what some planners affectionately label "hysterical societies," they wanted selected older buildings preserved on cultural grounds. Like many, they assumed that the economic threat to these buildings was inherent rather than contrived, and the resulting debate was often construed as being for or against "development."

The Development Debate

Heritage is not an alternative to development: It is an alternative form of development. Instead of the 1960s pattern of flattening buildings to start over (or disguising them through remodelling), heritage-type work makes exteriors look as they were intended, while upgrading interior systems and livability to contemporary standards. Making a building look "as intended" may be for historic authenticity or, more often, simply because things usually look better when they do not look "designed by a committee." Most of this multibillion-dollar market centres on buildings from before 1945.

This trend received a boost from the sustainable development debate, which called for extending the economic life expectancy of everything we produce. In Canada, where almost one-third of landfill deposits comprise used construction material, a society intent on recycling items as small as pop bottles and tin cans began to consider reusing buildings and cities. However, neither the planning theory nor the tools kept pace. Despite some worthwhile ventures into neighbourhood revitalization (often in struggling commercial districts, like Ontario's business improvement areas and Quebec's *Rues principales* areas), tools to assist heritage reuse were mired in misconceptions.

Those tools mostly derive from the century-old treatment of historic monuments in Europe (where "Canadian heritage" is sometimes seen as an oxymoron, heritage-type development is seldom discussed as an economic force, except in terms of tourism, and Old Town Yellowknife, founded 1934, has them rolling in the aisles). Unlike North America, where heritage programs originated for planning/economic/tactical reasons and culture was a bonus, the European experience was the other way around: The programs originated for cultural reasons, and economics was considered a bonus. European planning for heritage focused on three pillars: triage, regulation, and subsidy. First, a government would identify a representative sampling of historic buildings; second, these would be subjected to special protective regulations; and third, an economic package would offset the so-called economic burdens invariably associated with heritage.

This approach, adopted by Canada in the 1960s, effectively placed its architectural icons "under a glass case." Pursuant to special laws, planners drew lines on maps around selected areas like Peggy's Cove, Vieux-Montréal, Vieux-Québec, and Vancouver's Gastown, along with a collection of individual sites from every province. Outside the lines was open season; inside the lines was a regulatory package, with a veto on alterations to these legally designated properties and (everywhere but in Ontario) on their demolition. The third pillar (money) was harder to find. On the assumption that heritage designation intruded on property rights and that subsequent work on those buildings would be both museological and exorbitant, it was seldom used. After three decades of effort, designated heritage properties today account for less than one-quarter of one percent of the building stock, thus marginalizing them in the daily work of most planners right off the political radar screen.

But was this the last word? By the 1980s, some heritage activists themselves were challenging the premise that heritage was about setting aside an infinitesimal percentage of the building stock to be frozen in time, to save it from normal economics (by either threatening the owners with legal sanctions or buying them off). Furthermore, organizations like the Canadian Home Builders' Association (parent of the Canadian Renovators' Council) argued that many supposedly uncompetitive rehabilitation projects would be feasible if people knew how. In other words, the primary obstacle was not normal economics, but a shortage of rehabilitation skills among entrepreneurs and trades (along with a web of hidden regulatory and tax disincentives left over from the 1940s and 1950s). Although an aggressive training program would not deliver museological expertise to the typical renovation contractor, it could produce enough know-how to deal with older buildings on an attractive economic basis, thereby reducing the need for government intervention.

Augmenting the Rehabilitation "Wave"

Today, the heritage file in Canada is at a crossroads. The federal government and several provinces are discussing ambitious new programs. These may be ignored by people who are content to focus on the 1.5 percent of Canadian buildings under construction in any given year, rather than think about the 98.5 percent already built. At the other extreme, new initiatives may cause horror among those who like the existing system, where heritage is a statistical aberration: If heritage development increased exponentially, such "dilution" might threaten the pillars of heritage planning (triage, regulation, and subsidy) with overload and logistical collapse.

Unfortunately, aside from the three pillars, few planning tools are at Canada's disposal (yet), so we must make the best of them for now. But for the longer term, these facts remain:

- The rationale for heritage programs in North America has always been much bigger than protecting isolated pockets of cute buildings. It should be part of a wider campaign to reverse the declining condition of the building stock as a whole.
- Heritage is not just about little collections of properties. It is about a specific kind of development process.
- Each heritage project could spawn dozens of imitators in buildings that are old (or not so old). The strategy apparently works. Not only has it reversed conventional wisdom about expendability of the building stock, but it also spawned the renovation boom of the last generation. In cases like St. John's, it performed beyond all expectations. If all this could occur in the absence of any clear national policy, systematic training, or coordinated effort, then what is Canada capable of if it gets serious about this subject?
- The largest obstacle, according to many voices in industry, is neither antipathy nor economics. During the last two generations, while treating its older buildings with disdain, Canada lost much of the managerial, professional, and technical expertise to deal with them. Developers doing conventional projects have easy access to know-how; but for heritage developers it is hit-and-miss.

The public and private sectors are both increasingly demanding that the problem be corrected, and that Canada's current wave of rehabilitation activity be turned into a tsunami. Are Canada's planners positioned to ride that wave?

Emerging Retail Development Trends in Canada

Rowan Faludi

1992, Plan Canada 32(6): 30–4

Changing demographic and economic patterns are having significant implications on the evolution of the Canadian retail structure. New development forms, such as warehouse clubs, power centres, and outlet malls in the 1990s, began to force planners to rethink the traditional commercial hierarchy. In addition, many older shopping centres no longer able to serve their markets effectively have to be remerchandised and often redeveloped to regain their competitiveness. These projects can take on different forms: Smaller centres can be upgraded to regional malls; specialty themes introduced; new uses added; the retail function significantly downscaled or eliminated all together; and enclosed malls converted into strip centres. Older shopping centres also represent excellent sites for much needed residential and commercial intensification. With a thorough understanding of these emerging trends, planners can reevaluate existing official plan and zoning designations to take advantage of the new opportunities available to their municipalities. This article reviews some of the trends facing the development industry, while commenting on how commercial planning policies may be influenced.

Membership Warehouse Clubs

In the early 1990s, warehouse clubs gained momentum across the United States, British Columbia, and Alberta. While many retailers suffered severe recessionary setbacks, such warehouse giants Costco and Price Club, with their bulk discount prices, experienced tremendous market share growth.

Most warehouse clubs offer a wide variety of merchandise. Price Club's product mix includes fresh meat and produce departments, scratch bakeries, pharmacies, optical dispensaries, photo finishing, home improvement areas, and prenegotiated vehicle purchase programs. They carry between 2500 and 3500 stock-keeping units. This represents only a small fraction of the number carried by supermarkets or traditional full-line department stores but usually includes the fastest-selling merchandise items.

Small businesses account for a significant number of warehouse club members. The rest are "group" members: employees of large firms, associations, government agencies, and other organizations. Members pay a nominal annual fee. Membership requirements are loose to accommodate a large number of potential customers.

The successful warehouse operation relies on several factors:

- rapid inventory turnover (18 times/year);
- low working capital requirements;
- low-cost warehouse operations;
- direct purchasing;
- minimizing inventory losses;
- limited advertising expenses; and
- low labour costs.

A typical outlet varies between 100 000 and 150 000 square feet of gross leasable area and requires a parcel of about 10 to 15 acres. A common strategy by warehouse clubs is to locate in industrial zones. In this way, they can minimize both land costs and property taxes. They typically occupy highly-visible, free-standing buildings easily accessible from a major highway.

Other retailers have recognized the drawing power of warehouse clubs and often locate nearby. These may include furniture/appliance dealers, fast-food outlets, automotive dealers, discount stores, and other common highway commercial uses. In mature US markets, warehouse clubs may locate across the street from each other. Warehouse clubs also benefit by locating near to other retailers. Some operators have reported that their best performing outlets are situated near major shopping centres. In the US, many warehouse club outlets are locating in strip plazas and power centres. The Price Club and other chains are developing their own centres, using the warehouse club as an anchor tenant.

The warehouse club phenomenon has created issues that municipal officials must address. Although they are effective retailers, they hope to sidestep many of the land use regulations governing traditional commercial uses by classifying themselves as "warehouse" or "wholesaler." In response, some US municipalities have adopted "high-volume retail" zones to accommodate uses generating significant traffic volumes, such as home improvement centres, superstores, large furniture stores, and warehouse clubs. Other municipalities have recognized the unique nature of warehouse clubs by establishing special site designations, located in either industrial or commercial districts. Due to the potential for widespread impacts on the existing retail structure, planning for warehouse clubs in Canada should be addressed by both local and regional governments.

Warehouse clubs represent a substantial traffic generator. Local truck traffic can be significantly increased. Furthermore, as most customers travel by private vehicle, the parking ratio for warehouse clubs is about seven to eight parking spaces per 1000 square feet of gross leasable area, about 50 percent higher than that for a regional shopping centre. Consequently, careful traffic planning must be undertaken in conjunction with warehouse club development.

Finally, property and business tax revenues generated by warehouse clubs may represent a substantial economic development opportunity for a municipality. However, to be successful, warehouse clubs may require advantageous conditions not always available to other local retailers—for example, industrial sites, nonunionized labour, and direct purchasing from manufacturers. As a result, economic benefits generated by warehouse clubs may be offset by employment losses and store closings within the traditional retail sector.

In summary, warehouse clubs offer the consumer and small business owner a price advantage generally not available from conventional stores. While their place within the retail structure is becoming firmly established, municipalities must recognize their impacts to plan effectively. Clear guidelines are required to protect a desirable commercial structure, while still permitting healthy competition.

Category-Dominant Retailers and Power Centres

Similar to warehouse clubs, many specialty retailers are using large-scale outlets to offer both variety and low prices to customers. Although this trend is already well entrenched in the US, space-expansive retailers such as Toys "R" Us, Business Depot, and Aikenhead's Warehouse Store have become major players in Canadian communities.

Power centres are open plazas, anchored by these large space retailers. Generally, they contain a minimum of 200 000 to 400 000 square feet. This reverses the trend since the 1970s, when centres of this size were usually enclosed. In the US, some power centres are as large as 1 000 000 square feet.

Power centre tenants are typically retailers with a strong market presence and name recognition. Together, the anchors in a power centre comprise 60 to 85 percent of the total gross leasable area. Smaller tenants, such as restaurants, fast-food outlets, and banks, complement the store selection and enhance the overall attractiveness of the power centre. This contrasts with a regional centre, which typically has a 50:50 anchor to ancillary space ratio. Unlike regional centres, which rely to a large extent on the draw provided by large department stores, specialty outlets of 10 000 square feet could be considered power centre anchors.

These anchor tenants are generally quite distinct in terms of image, service, and quality from the specialty tenants that locate in regional shopping centres. For this reason, power centres often tend to complement rather than compete with regional centres. Although many power centre tenants would be viable as free-standing outlets, the power centre provides additional benefits of agglomeration, such as lower development and operating costs and a heightened market exposure.

Often, power centres comprise several distinct development blocks. In some cases, these blocks are organized according to specialty themes (home furnishings, fashion, and so on). A neighbourhood shopping centre, including a supermarket, could be one component of a power centre. A common development strategy is to phase the power centre on a block-by-block basis, as market conditions warrant. Power centres typically require high-traffic locations near major highway interchanges or arterial roads. In the US, sites are often sought in the immediate vicinity of regional malls. Canadian developers are adopting a similar locational strategy. As power centres are becoming more common throughout large metropolitan areas, regional centres are positioning themselves to capture upper-end and high-fashion shoppers.

In Canada, the range of potential tenants is much more limited, and for this reason, power centre development began later. There are two power centres in the GTA: Oakville Town Centre in Oakville and the Crossroads Business Centre in North York. Oakville Town Centre is about 460 000 square feet and contains a variety of category-dominant retailers, including Hy & Zel's, Business Depot, Winners, Valdi's, A&P, Toys "R" Us,

Chapter 11 / Land Use Issues

Jumbo Video, Pennington's Warehouse, Moore's the Suit People, Multitech Warehouse Direct, and a Famous Player's Theatre. Crossroads Centre accommodates some 400 000 square feet adjacent to a 200 000-square-foot Knob Hill Farms Food Terminal. Its anchors include Canadian Tire, The Brick, Giant Carpet, Toys "R" Us, Mark's Work Wearhouse, Fabricland, Liquor Control Board of Ontario, Future Shop, and Colour Your World. As new opportunities for enclosed malls are becoming scarce, developers must seek alternative ways of expanding their holdings. As a result, development applications for power centres in Canada have become more common.

From a planning perspective, power centres, which offer an attractive strip centre environment with landscaping, adequate parking, and provisions for optimal traffic movement, offer a solution to uncontrolled strip development. By designating power centre sites early in the planning process, municipalities have an opportunity to control such large space, high-traffic-generating retailers, which might otherwise locate sporadically along major arterial routes.

Outlet and Value Centres

Like power centres, outlet centres respond to the price-motivated shopping behaviour that has become a growing part of consumer behaviour since the late 1980s. In their purest sense, outlet centres provide units through which manufacturers can sell directly to the public. Manufacturers are able to benefit from marked-up prices, while consumers generally enjoy prices below those available from traditional retailers. In addition, outlet centres carry merchandise that is difficult to sell through the retail sector, such as out-of-season merchandise, previous year's models, factory defects and overruns.

A major source of cross-border retail competition is derived from outlet centres, where prices can be low enough to justify the extra travel time, duties and the risk of concealing undeclared purchases from customs officials.

In Canada, outlet centres have been only marginally successful due to the limited size of the manufacturing sector. As a result, Canadian outlet centres that have survived have been marketed as "value" centres and include a variety of other off-price stores, including retail clearance centres, dollar stores, discount drug and food stores, as well as a large number of independent operators that cannot afford the rents charged in traditional enclosed shopping centres.

A planning perspective should evaluate value or outlet centre proposals carefully. In many cases, centres planned according to this theme have had to be modified prior to construction due to the lack of potential tenants. In other cases, these types of centres have opened with large amounts of vacant space and have been subsequently remerchandised due to the failure of the original concept. Important to the success of these types of centres in Canada is a strong anchor component. Although not originally built as a value centre, Dixie Outlet Mall in Mississauga, for example, evolved into one of the most successful of these types of centres in Canada (Figure 11.6). It includes a 90 000-square-foot Sears outlet and a Hy & Zel's drug warehouse.

Shopping Centre Redevelopment

Many retail developments constructed during the shopping centre boom period in the 1970s no longer served their markets effectively by the early 1990s, due to such factors as outdated design features, changes in the local market, and changes in the local transportation system that affected accessibility. Also, communities with limited vacant land supplies are facing significant pressures for affordable housing, institutional facilities, and employment nodes. Suburban shopping centres, which generally range from about 25 to 30 percent coverage, are one of the least intensive of all major land uses. As a result, through the construction of underground and multilevel parking structures,

Figure 11.6

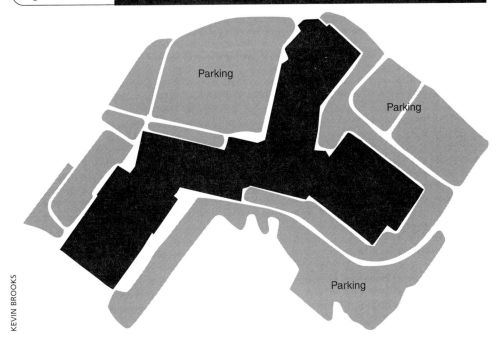

The Dixie Outlet Mall in Mississauga reveals the characteristics of suburban commercial uses: large parking areas surrounding a massive articulated structure.

substantial shopping centre lands can be freed for additional uses. Older shopping centres that have already developed into community focal points represent ideal sites for public facilities, such as community centres, libraries, and transit terminals. Shopping centres are also attractive for condominium, hotel, and office development, as they generally occupy highly-accessible locations, often with direct public transit service.

In some cases, while retail may be the most appropriate land use for a site, the existing shopping centre may no longer adequately serve its market. Such was the case with Edmonton's Centennial Village Mall, a 370 000-square-foot enclosed community centre, which saw a substantial portion of its market devoured by the mammoth West Edmonton Mall, which opened in 1981 and has since undergone major expansions. Using a strategy that some analysts have termed "de-malling," Centennial Village Mall was converted into a strip power centre, anchored originally by Woolco, Save-On-Foods, and Great Canadian Office Supplies. In this way, it shed its role as a traditional shopping centre to take advantage of the growing promotional retail sector.

The New Retail

In sum, municipalities must undertake a comprehensive review of their commercial structure, as the traditional hierarchy of shopping centres is becoming obscured in today's retail market. Official plan and zoning designations should be carefully evaluated in light of evolving trends. Uses such as membership warehouse clubs and power centres are quickly becoming a part of the new commercial environment. In addition, older centres are taking on new roles to better serve changing urban markets. Through careful planning, these new retail forms offer municipal policy makers realistic opportunities to accommodate the changing urban environment.

The Shape of the Information City: Understanding the Impacts of the Information Revolution on City Form

Pamela Blais

1998, Plan Canada 38(5): 8–11

The shape, organization, and evolution of cities are increasingly determined by a new dynamic with its own logic: the information revolution. The nature of urban change associated with this revolution goes well beyond teleworking. This article points to four key areas of impact that have important implications for cities and for planners: the changing composition and geography of economic activity, the two sides of a new live-work relationship, patterns of sprawl and concentration, and dematerialization.

The Changing Composition and Geography of Economic Activity

The information revolution is bringing about massive change in Canadian economic activities. Certain activities are expanding—particularly those that are knowledge and innovation intensive—while more routine functions are falling victim to international competition. In addition, information and telecommunications technology (ITT) is allowing whole classes of activities to become automated (e.g., bank tellers being replaced by ATMs), eliminated (e.g., "disintermediation," in which intermediary functions such as travel agents are eliminated by online travel services and electronic ticketing), or relocated (e.g., backoffice or off-shore routine data processing). Along with this economic restructuring comes a broad array of ITT-based organizational options, such as multinational corporations, network firms, and outsourcing. As a result, not only is the makeup of the economy being transformed, but also its organization and geography, from the global to the local scale.

The trends signal significant change in the structure, form, and economic makeup of cities and, of course, in their planning. While the trends are universal, their impacts on a given town or city are likely to vary depending on the existing economic profile, unique characteristics, and assets of the area, and how these fit in to the logic of the information revolution.

Planners need to begin to think about how these trends are affecting their own town or city. What kinds of economic activity can be expected, and how much? What locational requirements are these companies likely to have within the city? Are the old concepts and urban plans that segregate cities into residential areas, business parks, downtowns, and retail malls still relevant? Should projected employment land requirements be revised? What kind of urban form will best support the changes? Physical, long-range, and strategic city plans need to take these trends into account (Figure 11.7).

The Two Sides of a New Live-Work Relationship

From the planning perspective, one of the most important implications of the changes described is the transformation of the live-work relationship. This transformation has two important dimensions, both of which must be considered by planners: The first is a looser relationship between the home and the traditional workplace; and the second is a stronger relationship between work and the residential environment.

The first dimension has implications for residential location patterns as it provides residents with greater flexibility in where they may choose to live. Workers can now live farther from their central workplace, and, if they telecommute even part of the time, they rely less on the journey to work.

Figure 11.7

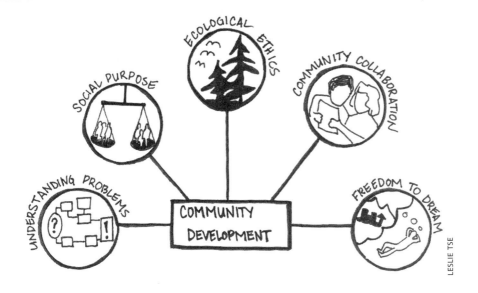

What does it take to achieve community development?

The shift of work to homes and neighbourhoods will also have important implications for the traditional workplaces left behind. Due to telework and other trends (e.g., mobile offices), a falling share of employment is likely to be accommodated in such traditional employment areas as business parks, office parks, industrial parks, and downtown office buildings.

Both dimensions of the new live-work relationship have implications for the kinds of amenities that people will look for in their neighbourhoods. These include access to ITT infrastructure (such as integrated services digital network, cable, or asymmetric digital subscriber line) and to business, financial, and personal services that support working at home. Since rollout of advanced ITT infrastructure often proceeds in a piecemeal pattern, different types of neighbourhoods and buildings may prove more connected, adaptive, and therefore more desirable than others. In addition, "softer" amenities such as sense of community, local facilities, and the design and quality of the residential environment become important location factors.

Planning new urban areas and retrofitting existing neighbourhoods, particularly the postwar communities, to support work at home is a key issue. Strategies for effectively integrating, supporting, and monitoring neighbourhood-based work are essential. Consideration of these trends must be integrated into local and secondary planning processes. Small-scale opportunities include redeveloping the corner convenience plaza to include mixed uses, such as telecentres and spaces for services and amenities that support work at home.

If these support services are not integrated into residential areas, teleworking could mean increased automobile trips rather than becoming the widely heralded solution to auto dependency. Compact, mixed-use, pedestrian-oriented centres allow many work-related and personal activities to be undertaken on foot. Conversely, work at home in a single-use, low-density environment may require separate and lengthy automobile trips for each business meeting, lunch date, or trip to the dry cleaners.

More or Less Sprawl?

Most planners assume that the information age heralds the "electronic cottage," the "footloose industry," and perhaps unprecedented levels of urban sprawl. The reality is more complex than this, with deconcentration and concentration happening simultaneously depending on the particular type of activity. The key is to understand which types of activities will have the ability or tendency to locate in lower-cost, peripheral areas, and which types will actually have a heightened need for concentration. Different kinds of economic activity will be drawn to different types of urban environments based on different locational requirements.

The term "footloose" is really a misnomer when used to describe the locational proclivities of certain industries. Instead of needing access to energy, water, or expressways, these firms are simply looking for a different set of production factors: skills, local amenities, and teleconnectivity.

Innovation- and knowledge-based activities, such as financial services or software development, often depend on physical concentration and the fast and informal movement of information. These industries, which rely on physical concentration, account for a growing share of the economy.

On the other hand, more routine activities, such as standardized production and data processing, can seek out lower-cost, peripheral locations. And telecommuting can mean that the geographical area of a city stretches out as residential locations become more weakly linked with a central workplace. Small towns and villages surrounding urban areas, which many people find attractive living environments, may become sought-after locations.

The overall result may be a heightened differentiation between urban, compact, mixed-use areas, and their surrounding low-density, sprawling, quasi-urban ring. These trends point to a renewed and stronger need for regional planning, as commutersheds and urban areas expand along with the potential costs of servicing and infrastructure. The geographic scope of these regional plans will have to increase to capture the larger, functional urban area.

Dematerialization

The information revolution signals a new relationship between economic growth and the demand for work space. Simply put, less floor space is required per unit of economic output than in the past. Given a stable rate of economic growth over time, we can expect the average growth rate for office, industrial, and retail floor space to be slower in comparison.

A number of factors come together to contribute to the "dematerialization" of industrial and commercial buildings. These factors include: increasing productivity as a result of ITT; automation; disintermediation; online shopping; just-in-time delivery; and new workspace options such as hotelling, teleworking, and mobile offices. Bank branch closures associated with ATMs, telephone banking, and electronic personal banking are just one example of these trends.

Dematerialization has important implications for long-term physical planning, municipal finance, and economic development. Certain kinds of establishments that used to be counted on to help create mixed-use environments may disappear: bank branches, the corner video store eliminated by video-on-demand, and online shopping replacing retail outlets. And, of course, there are direct implications for how planners estimate future urban area land requirements, particularly the amount of traditional land area set aside for employment uses.

The key areas briefly described here illustrate just some of the ways in which the information revolution is reshaping cities and towns according to a new logic. Successful towns and cities will be the ones that recognize, understand, and act on these transformations.

Study Questions

1. How have land uses shifted in the downtown of your community through the last century?

2. Based on your reading of the local newspaper, what are the key land use issues in your community in recent years? What do you see as the emerging land use issues over the next decade?

3. How are retail development trends in urban areas related to urban sprawl? How are they changing?

4. What measures should community planners be pursuing to ensure greater economic and energy efficiency in new development areas?

5. How are changing patterns in the economy affecting the development of the Canadian city?

6. Why has planning had such difficulty in addressing persistent land use questions like waste disposal, water management, and environmental conservation?

7. What strategies can community planners use to increase the supply of affordable housing and sustainable development opportunities?

8. How are information technologies changing the economy and land use patterns in Canadian communities?

Reference Notes

1. Hodge, G (2003) *Planning Canadian Communities: An Introduction to the Principles, Practices and Participants.* (4th ed) Toronto: Thomson Nelson.

    Leung, H-L (2003) *Land Use Planning Made Plain* (2nd edn) Toronto: University of Toronto Press.

2. Gilliard, G (2004) A new solution for stormwater management. *Plan Canada* 44(1): 29–31.

    Rowe, S (1992) Landfill planning in Ontario: Bringing in the public. *Plan Canada* 32(2): 22–5.

3. Caldwell, W & R Toombs (1999) Rural planning, the community and large livestock facilities. *Plan Canada* 29(5): 27–9.

4. Tunbridge, J (2003) Selling places: Heritage tourism and marketing your town. *Plan Canada* 43(2): 17–9.

5. Hulchanski, D & R Drdla (1993) And housing for all: Opening the doors to inclusive community planning. *Plan Canada* 33(3): 19–26.

    Thompson, S (2002) Meanings of home: Developing a humane and responsive planning practice. *Plan Canada* 42(1): 13–5.

6. Seasons, M (1994) Local economic development: Practice and prospects. *Plan Canada* 34(6): 10–5.

7. Jamieson, W (1996) Retailing in the 21st century: A planner's challenge. *Plan Canada* 36(6): 10.

    Toderian, B (1996) Big-box retailing: How are municipalities reacting? *Plan Canada* 36(6): 25–8.

8. Grant, J (2003) Is urban revitalization good for cities? Maybe not. *Plan Canada* 43(1): 23–5.

    Seasons, M (2003) Is urban revitalization good for cities? Yes, if properly planned. *Plan Canada* 43(1): 26–7.

9. Craig, K (2003) Siting wireless communication facilities: Issues and guidelines. *Plan Canada* 43(1): 17–9.

10. Gurstein, P (2001) *Wired to the World, Chained to the Home: Telework in Daily Life.* Vancouver: UBC Press.

11. Lang, R & A Armour (1982) *Planning Land to Conserve Energy.* Ottawa: Environment Canada, #25.

12. Dumont, R, M Lux, & H Orr (1982) *Hotcan: A Computer Programme for Estimating the Space Heating Requirement of Residences.* Saskatoon: Division of Building Research, National Research Council.

13. Anderson, B, W Place, & R Kammerud (1985) The impact of building orientation on residential heating and cooling. *Energy and Building* 8: 205–24.

14. Ibid.

15. Mazria, E (1979) *The Passive Solar Energy Book.* Emmaus: Rodale Press.

    Shaviv, E (1981) The influence of the orientation of the main solar glazing in the total energy consumption of a building. *Solar Energy* 25(5).

16. Lang, R & A Armour (1982) Op. cit.

17. Ibid.

18. Saskatchewan Government (1984) *Bill 106: An Act Respecting Planning and Development in Urban, Rural, and Northern Municipalities.* Regina.

19. Hamilton-Wentworth Regional Municipality, Planning and Development Department (1980) *Planning for Low Density—A Solar Approach.* Hamilton, Ontario.

    Hamilton-Wentworth Regional Municipality, Planning and Development Department (1982) *Design Criteria for Energy Efficient Neighbourhood Planning.* Hamilton, Ontario.

    Hamilton-Wentworth Regional Municipality, Planning and Development Department (1984) *Design Criteria for Energy Efficient Neighbourhood Planning,* Stage 3. Hamilton.

20. Matus, V (1984) Passive solar urban planning—a cellular technique. In F Curtis (ed) *Energy Developments: New Forms, Renewables, Conservation.* Toronto: Pergamon Press.

    Meehan, P (1981) Guidelines for climatic efficient residential planning. *Urban Land* 40(5).

    Ontario Ministry of Energy (1982) *Energy Conservation Through Land Use Planning.* City of Guelph, prepared by Landplan Collaborative Ltd and MM Dillon Ltd.

    Ontario Ministry of Municipal Affairs and Housing (1982) *Energy Conservation Through Official Plans—A Guideline.* Toronto.

21. Ontario Ministry of Housing (1980) *Residential Site Design and Energy Conservation*. Part 1 General Report, Toronto.

22. Ontario Municipal Affairs and Housing (2002) Oak Ridges Moraine Conservation Plan. Adopted 22 April 2002, http://www.mah.gov.on.ca/userfiles/HTML/nts_1_6846_1.html (accessed 21 April 2006).

23. Fitch, JM (1960) *Walter Gropius*. New York: George Braziler, 14–5.

24. Toronto Mail (1932) Why is Toronto so ugly? Editorial. *Toronto Mail*. June 20: 4.

25. James C (1943) Address to the Annual Dinner of RAIC. *Royal Architectural Institute of Canada Journal* May: 73.

26. United States Conference of Mayors (1966) *With Heritage So Rich*. Washington: United States Conference of Mayors.

27. Loos, A (1957) Ornament and crime. (Trans. Roger Banham). *Architectural Review* February: 121.

Chapter Twelve

Transportation Planning

The Dynamics of Urban Transportation

Jill Grant

Urban planners face two key questions every day in their practice: How do we provide adequate and appropriate housing for community members? And how do we effectively move people around the city? Neither question has proven easy to answer in Canada. In this chapter, we consider the second theme: transportation.

The volume of articles published annually on transportation planning indicates how important the topic is to Canadian planners. Through the years, authors have spilled a lot of ink in *Plan Canada* pondering the best way to design efficient and attractive street systems. They have regularly debated issues related to providing public versus private transportation. The six articles in this book offer an idea of some of the key questions from the last 15 years.

The discussion immediately reveals that the basic principles of transportation planning have changed dramatically over the past three decades. The consensus in the early postwar period—namely, that efficient highway systems and a hierarchy of urban roads would facilitate mobility in the modern city—has given way to skepticism about the effects of giving the automobile priority over other means of locomotion. Gordon Price challenges planners to avoid the trap of planning for more and bigger cars. He suggests that Vancouver's West Side shows that Canadian cities can create dense but livable environments that offer viable alternatives to sprawl. By contrast, Pierre Filion identifies the gaps between the compact urban form planners hope to see happen and the automobile-oriented development trends that dominate Toronto suburbs: He challenges those who believe that overcoming contemporary transportation patterns will be easy.

Most of the articles here reflect the prominent planning vision of the city today: one that accepts density, compactness, and connectivity as desirable and attractive attributes for Canadian cities. Wayne McEachern describes the environmental and economic benefits of transit-friendly land use planning. Most Canadian municipalities currently operate from the premise that good urban land use planning involves planning for access to public transportation.

Paul Mackey highlights another key issue in transportation: safety and traffic calming. Planners recognize that the design of streets affects the way that traffic behaves. Trying to find solutions to congestion and dangers to pedestrians has become an important urban issue.

The final paper by Andrew Curran comments on a growing phenomenon in Canadian cities: development on private streets. Reporting on a study of planning departments across the country, he identifies some factors that led to the popularity of the privatized residential environment, and raises some flags about the implication of reducing the public realm in the contemporary city.

The View from '56: Thoughts on the Short-term Future of Transportation Planning

Gordon Price

2002 Plan Canada 42(3): 21–2

A few years ago, the Ford Expedition assembling plant in Wayne, Michigan, made more money in after-tax profits than the combined budgets of all municipalities in British Columbia. The number of SUVs sold in North America roughly doubled between 1996 and 2002, to about four million a year. These vehicles are classified as light trucks (to drive through various legislative loopholes), and their percentage of the market approaches that of passenger cars.

If you want to know the future of transportation in North America, start here. This is where most of the money has gone, and where people's expectations reside—in big cars on big roads. The future, apparently, is like 1956, only more so.

I choose 1956 for a reason. That was the year US President Dwight Eisenhower signed the *Federal Aid Highway Act*, which funded the biggest public-works project in human history. The interstate freeway system—over 40,000 miles of superbly engineered roads crisscrossing the continent many times over—changed everything in its path, from cities and regions to popular culture. They were called "freeways" for a reason: no tolls, no stoplights, no limits.

Four Transportation Assumptions

Canada had a more modest program to build the Trans-Canada Highway. Yet, given the success of car culture, both countries have embedded in the collective consciousness a set of assumptions that are reinforced countless times a day through advertising. These assumptions continue to shape transportation policy and funding priorities.

First Assumption:

As we buy more cars, government will build more roads. It doesn't matter who builds the roads (even if they're tolled), as long as there's the expectation of more and more asphalt.

Second Assumption:

When it comes to the purchase and use of vehicles, there's always room for one more. No one goes into an auto showroom wondering if there's space out there for one more car, nor would it be acceptable for government to say, "Hold on, we're full up." With no upper limit, presumed capacity is effectively infinite. You'll rarely get a planner or engineer to tell you what the ultimate capacity of a road system should be; their job is to translate infinity into reality.

Third Assumption:

As every auto advertisement tells us, the car should never be constrained by other cars. The image of the open road is iconic; free-flowing traffic is assumed to be the natural state of affairs, if only our tax dollars were used effectively for their intended purpose (back to the first assumption).

Fourth Assumption:

The next trip is free. In other words, the marginal cost of the next trip is practically zero, at least as far as out-of-pocket expense is concerned. Save for the few places where parking is priced or roads are tolled, no loonies need be spent to drive somewhere, regardless of the amount owed on the car or expenses incurred. The next trip seems to be free, and we love free. Honest, apparent pricing of the car—what is often called transportation demand management—may work, but politicians call it suicide. It would be like putting the GST on each car trip, and it would not be well received.

The Not-So-Free Freeway

So important is the concept of "free"—again, as in "freeway"—that we do not even attempt to calculate the value of an increasingly scarce commodity that is vital to the economic functioning of our urban regions. That commodity is road space. We spend millions to build it and then dispose of it as though it had no price. The real cost is measured in time in congestion, but that is seen as the problem, not as the inevitable consequence of market failure and flawed assumptions.

Further, we are betting that we will have all the cheap fuel we need to power all those internal-combustion engines on all those free roads, despite current geopolitical uncertainties. Those who have predicted an imminent end to the Oil Age have not been treated kindly by history. Gas today remains cheaper in real dollars than it was in 1956—cheaper per litre than bottled water. So it's not surprising that we assume high-BTU, portable, ubiquitous, fluid fuel will remain abundant even if the Americans have to spend more on a military presence in the Middle East than the value of the oil exported.

In one of those delightful coincidences that mark real life, a man did indeed predict the end of the Oil Age, or at least the beginning of the end, in the same year as Eisenhower was launching the interstate freeway system. He was M King Hubbert, a petroleum geologist working for Shell Oil in Houston. Using science and good guesswork, Hubbert predicted domestic American oil production would peak in the mid-seventies: not a message Shell wanted to hear. Debate raged on this prediction until 1970, for that was the year in which US domestic oil production did indeed peak. Using similar techniques, Hubbert's disciples predict worldwide oil production will peak sometime this decade regardless of new discoveries. (The American government thinks it may come a few decades later: still overnight in historical terms.) Then things will get interesting.

The Beginning of the End?

Most of us are technological optimists at heart. If oil becomes too expensive or scarce, we expect to switch to fuel cells, or whatever. But the problem is not if but how—and, more important, how fast and at what price. Since we have been kidding ourselves for so long about the real price of the car, we are in no mood to accommodate a sudden shift in reality, nor are we ready to grasp the economic ripple effects of fluctuating oil prices.

But what are the odds, after all, that something catastrophic won't happen to the status quo of cheap roads, cheap fuel, and cheap car trips? Ignoring the obvious fact that history is full of surprises, we proceed as though nothing extraordinary will happen in the life of our transportation plans, save for the introduction of new funding mechanisms, variations on existing technologies, and, oh yes, a bikeway here or there.

From a planning (and political) point of view, one can never plan for apocalypse. Imagine: "Our plan calls for a catastrophic series of events during the life of the plan, the consequences of which will be ruinous for the status quo. Assume, therefore, that after this point, most of the assumptions on which the plan is based are wrong." Can't be done.

The best bet, then, is to look around for examples of what would work if conditions did indeed change rapidly and the automobile could not remain the centre of our transportation universe. Then, when leaders are desperately searching for options in the face of sudden change, you're ready to go. Fortunately, there are a few places that look like they could handle not only the disruptions of the future but also the conditions of the present. One of them began—guess when—in 1956.

Desirable Density

Urban critic Lewis Mumford once said the US Congress had no idea what it was doing when it approved the interstates. (Even Eisenhower was shocked when he saw the actual construction of a freeway through Washington, DC.) The same, I expect, was true of Vancouver city council in 1956, when it passed its first zoning and development bylaw and unleashed the forces of technology, modernism, and money to transform the decaying streetcar neighbourhoods that surrounded the downtown core. If anyone had showed them what the West End would look like at the end of the high-rise boom in the 1960s, they would have been stunned (Figure 12.1).

About 40,000 people now live in a single square mile, in a high-density neighbourhood that many have confused with an overcrowded one. In fact, it works pretty well for the dominant income group—lower-middle-income renters—who can afford higher-than-average rents because their transportation costs are proportionately lower. The West End still functions rather like the turn-of-the-century community it was: a grid of narrow streets with trolley lines and limited parking, where services are never more than three blocks away, and where feet function as the dominant mode of transportation.

This combination of density and transportation choice is not that unusual. Most urban populations have lived this way for most of human history. We stopped building

GORDON PRICE

High-rise towers now dominate West End Vancouver.

dense, mixed-use communities around 1956, when planning and engineering tried to accommodate the infinite needs of the car, which itself facilitated the sprawl that the automobile needed. Vancouver, with its confined geography, absence of freeways, reasonable transit, limited parking, and 30 years of traffic calming, has made a policy of constraining the car and has coincidentally turned out to be one of the most livable cities in the world. Actually, this is not a coincidence at all.

High-density communities aren't for everyone. And, no, they can't be built overnight. But it turns out that people will switch from car dependence to transportation choice faster than we reasonably expected. Recent figures show that as people substitute walking trips for car trips, there is now less vehicle movement downtown than there was five years ago, even though the population has increased by thousands. In other words, congestion can decrease as density increases, but only if there are constraints on the car, alternatives that work, and good land use planning and urban design.

There may even be a density level that must be reached before the benefits of dense development become apparent. And people will still drive their SUVs, even in the West End. They love their cars, even though they're going to have a difficult time answering their grandchildren's questions. ("Traffic congestion was awful, you were hostages to oil, the world was getting warmer, and you went out and bought the biggest gas-guzzler you could afford!? What were you thinking?")

I wouldn't stop people from buying SUVs; but I wouldn't be planning for them.

Planning Proposals and Urban Development Trends: Can the Gap Be Bridged?

Pierre Filion

1995 Plan Canada 35(5): 17–8

One can draw a parallel between planning documents produced in the 1950s and early 1960s and the recent crop of plans and reports. These two periods witnessed a consensus within planning documents over the need to redirect prevailing urban development trends and the means to reach this goal. This degree of agreement within documents is exceptional in recent Canadian urban planning history. Both periods are marked by calls for a profound transformation of prevailing transportation and land use patterns, even if the actual proposals voiced by their respective plans adhere to opposing urban planning principles and put forth antithetical measures. The planning context discussed here is that of the Greater Toronto Area (GTA), but the same sequence of events was repeated with minor variations in most other large Canadian metropolitan regions.

Pierre Filion's Update
Pierre Filion wrote this article toward the end of the Ontario New Democratic Party administration. He updates the view:
The first half of the 1990s had been a period of high ambition regarding public transit, urban intensification, and affordable housing development. Most projects were frustrated, however, by difficult economic circumstances and skyrocketing deficits, which severely curtailed governments' intervention capacity. NIMBY and local governments' resistance to affordable housing and intensification projects presented further obstacles to provincial planning goals. More than 10 years later, public transit and intensification objectives still seem as difficult to reach. The article describes the last years of Metro Toronto, before the amalgamation of its municipalities into the new City of Toronto.

Planning for the Car

In the 1950s and early 1960s, the emphasis was decidedly on updating transportation systems. Large-scale expressways were projected throughout the urbanized perimeter, including across dense inner-city neighbourhoods. The tone of the period is perhaps best captured by the 1964 *Metropolitan Toronto Plan—Recommended Transportation Plan*'s ambitious urban expressway proposals. Virtually all plans written over these years shared the vision of a metropolitan region where the car would assume growing importance, and where traffic would be channelled through a hierarchy of roads, with a well-developed expressway network at its summit. This transformation of the transportation system was deemed essential to obviate congestion, increase mobility and accessibility (and thus, it was believed, personal choice), and prevent the economic stagnation that would ensue from congestion and insufficient accessible locations for activities with a hearty appetite for land (shopping malls, industries, low-density residential).

As we now well know, this form of planning fostered a radical transformation of the urban structure. Urban expressways and associated rises in car use marked the passage from a monocentric to a dispersed urban form with scattered employment and retail activities. Transportation and land use planning also authorized significant density reductions at the metropolitan scale. Some of the consequences of this period's approach to urban planning were anticipated and even welcomed in planning documents. This was the case with decongestion of high density neighbourhoods and the availability of additional indoor and outdoor space for households (Figure 12.2). Others were unexpected. For example, the view was occasionally voiced that expressways could serve to intensify downtown office employment and retail concentration, a perspective amply contradicted by the experience of car-oriented metropolitan regions.

Much of the vision came to fruition. The financial climate of the time, the modernist ideology then at its peak, secured support for expert-led proposals, and enthusiasm for technology-driven change assured the implementation of such proposals. But from the

Figure 12.2

Toronto's suburbs reflect car-oriented sprawl.

JILL GRANT

mid-1960s, political and economic obstacles began to rise. By the mid-1970s, popular support and financial resources were no longer sufficient to proceed with important urban expressway projects.

Rethinking the Plan

Like these earlier plans, present documents (planning reports and official plans) call for a profound transformation of current urban development patterns. Now, however, proposals advocate a departure from postwar urbanization trends. These documents adopt a strong environmental stand, calling for a more compact form of urbanization, which would abate farmland and natural area absorption rates while lessening car transportation needs and thus emission levels. Compactness is to be achieved through reurbanization initiatives (redevelopment within built-up sectors) and more consolidated, nodal forms of suburban development. These documents, committed to higher density and reduced car dependence, also promote greater reliance on transit, walking, and cycling.

The difference between these two generations of planning documents does not end with the nature of their proposals. Another major distinction concerns the implementation potential of their recommendations. If the proposals voiced in the late 1950s and early 1960s were largely actualized thanks to the availability of essential preconditions, the situation appears quite different for proposals contained in recent documents. Both cases are marked by a profound gap between proposals and the prevalent urban reality, but such a gap is now more unlikely to be breached than it was 25 years ago. There are two reasons to expect difficulties in implementing the proposals of recent planning documents: Urbanization trends in Toronto are taking a direction that is increasingly contrary to the vision embedded in recent planning proposals; and the instruments needed to reverse these trends are unlikely to be available.

Challenging Change

The regions surrounding the city, which all register low-density levels, account for the brunt of the Toronto agglomeration growth. In York Region, the fastest growing region in the GTA, 80 percent of housing is single-detached; in the city, the equivalent is 34 percent. Not only is development taking place at a low density, but transit use, which had increased steadily until 1988, has since undergone precipitous decline. For instance, from 1988 to 1993, Toronto Transit Commission (TTC) ridership fell by nearly 16 percent. Several factors accounted for this trend: This was a period of fare increases and reduced services; the recession severely affected the service sector and caused downtown employment losses (in the TTC's privileged market); and car use dominates virtually all newly urbanized sectors, which register density levels too low to support anything beyond minimal public transit services.

This yawning gap between environmentally-minded proposals and the urban development reality begs the question of whether it will be possible in the near future to enact measures of a scope sufficient to reverse present urban development trends. Doubt can be thrown on this possibility, given the absence of the conditions necessary to support such measures. This differentiates present planning proposals from those embedded within plans dating from the mid-1950s and early 1960s.

For a start, the public sector is in the midst of a serious fiscal crisis, which has forestalled the investments required. Financial difficulties impeding transit development are severely felt by the TTC administration. It has been reluctant to endorse the more audacious provincial government subway extension commitments (with a 75/25 provincial/

metro financing formula). The provincial government's financial difficulties also translate into lower transit operational subsidies, which inescapably prompt fare hikes. In turn, these reduce passenger levels, which push transit properties into a spiral of decline: Lower fare-box revenues lead to service reductions or fare increases, which result in a further descent in ridership.

By contrast, car use is fairly impervious to public-sector financial restrictions. Their most serious effect is not a decline in use but growing congestion, as road investment fails to meet increasing demand. But here, privatization seems to provide a solution. The most important transportation investment in the area in the 1990s was Highway 407, a privately-funded 65-kilometre toll expressway that crosses the region to the north of Highway 401. Based on the impact of other expressways on urban land use, we can expect this highway to have major effects on Toronto's urban structure for years to come. It is unlikely that similar private investment schemes for public transit infrastructure funding will ever materialize due to this sector's need for both capital and operating subsidies.

Public-sector financial difficulties have an ambiguous effect on reurbanization. One could expect that reduced infrastructure funding would favour this form of development. But due to high site preparation expenses and clean-up costs in former industrial sites—the most likely candidates for reurbanization—such projects frequently require lavish government funding to proceed.

The potential of carrying out the agenda of recent planning documents is darkened by not only government's financial predicament. As well, residents' opposition to developments close to their home can seriously impede reurbanization and intensification (which consists of projects meant to elevate the density of urbanized sectors). Residents routinely object to the scale of proposed developments, the loss of existing buildings and natural sites, the environmental consequences of transportation and other infrastructure projects, an overuse of transportation and local services due to population increases, and perceived threats from newcomers. Three factors underlie this NIMBY attitude. One is an increased cultural distance between socioeconomic groups, which causes residents to perceive as a threat the arrival of newcomers, especially when they belong to a lower-income category than themselves. Another related concern is residential property values, and an attendant aversion to any development that may even remotely reduce this value. This is not surprising, given that the home is the foremost asset most households possess. The final underlying factor is the public-sector fiscal crisis alluded to earlier. In this stringent climate, the public sector is often unable to increase service in proportion to population growth resulting from intensification initiatives. Residents are thus justified in their apprehension that crowded schools, parks, and roads will result from additional housing in built-up areas.

Another likely obstacle to implementing recent planning proposals is the development industry's interest in contemporary forms of development. It has invested large sums to secure land and planning approvals and is unlikely to radically transform its development projects. At the present growth rate, sufficient approvals may have been awarded to secure development needs for the next 10 years. We can easily anticipate that any modification to the terms under which these approvals were granted would be ferociously contested by developers. This means that we will have to wait at least 10 years before witnessing significant planning-induced changes in the nature of urban development. Developers' commitment to present forms of urban development is largely tied to consumer preference. But we cannot anticipate major shifts in urban form originating from the developer/consumer relationship because consumer preference is largely shaped by the very options offered by the development industry.

The absence of a strong planning agency functioning at the scale of the GTA represents another impediment to the actualization of recent planning proposals. In a context of intense intermunicipal competition in the GTA, it is unlikely that peripheral municipalities would of their own accord forgo development to assist the City of Toronto's intensification pursuits. On the contrary, municipalities located outside Toronto are aggressively using their land availability and lower tax rates to lure residential and commercial development.

The final obstacle concerns the interaction between low-density urbanization, employment and retail dispersal, and car use. We are largely locked within this dynamic because it operates as a system. Tampering with one aspect can cause grave local and possibly systemic disruptions. For example, had the Toronto Main Street scheme (small apartment buildings with shops at the street level along commercial strips) gone ahead as intended, with minimal parking to encourage walking and transit use, it is likely that Main Street residents would have sought parking on surrounding neighbourhoods' streets. This is largely why residents from these neighbourhoods objected to the Main Street scheme. It is unrealistic to think that the provision of an island of intense and diversified urban development is in itself sufficient to enable residents to part with the car. In the increasingly dispersed contemporary agglomeration, some destinations are bound to be located in areas where transit accessibility is, at best, minimal. Unfortunately, the present financial context rules out one measure that could eventually alter the dispersal-car use dynamic. Considerable rail transit investments in anticipation of peripheral sector development could induce more concentrated suburban communities, reminiscent of prewar rail commuting towns and villages, which would result in higher transit use than in standard suburban areas.

Moving from Theory to Practice

The recent consensus in planning documents around intensification and higher transit use is clearly at odds with the prevailing sprawling and car-oriented reality. We have also seen that the wide gap between proposals and reality is not without precedent. The present situation is different, however, in that the implementation of ambitious proposals is confronted with formidable obstacles, which rule out, or at best severely constrict, the possibility that they will come to fruition. We therefore run the risk of planning becoming dichotomized into reports and certain sections of policy statements and official plans that express goals consistent with environmental ideals (transit-based transportation strategies and intensification, for example), and day-to-day planning practice, which would essentially reproduce present forms of urban development (mostly car dependent and sprawling). Statements of planning principles and objectives will soon lose relevance, causing them to be met with mounting cynicism.

Without a change in circumstances, we can expect to see present patterns of urban development continue with, at the most, a few transit improvements in a car-dominated transportation environment and occasional islands of intensification in a sea of sprawl. If we are serious about the objectives proclaimed by recent documents, and confident that they enjoy broad public support and are not just planners' most recent hobbyhorse, we must concentrate on measures to assure their attainment. In the present fiscal context, these measures will need to be primarily regulatory in nature. We must also give these objectives a high media profile to maintain public interest and thus sustain their political prominence. It is not that difficult to drum up support for intensification in Toronto and other large Canadian cities thanks to the lure of their more attractive inner-city neighbourhoods, which conform to the ideals put forth by proponents of intensification. We can also stress the link between environmental protection and a more compact urban form and lesser reliance on the car. Finally, new intensification initiatives and denser transit-oriented suburbs can act as demonstration projects and broaden the range of possibilities for consumers when making housing choices.

Transit-Friendly Land Use Planning: A Key Ingredient Supporting Urban Environmental Quality and Economic Development

Wayne L McEachern

1991 Plan Canada 31(5): 15–7

The contribution of transit in helping to make urban areas "work" has long been recognized. It is perhaps surprising, therefore, to discover that so little attention has been paid to the role of transit within planning documents.[1] Transit operators have often been left to provide whatever levels of service are possible to areas planned largely without their input. The resulting inefficiencies can be costly, in one way or another, to everyone. It is timely that urban area plans, and the process that creates them, now consciously incorporate strategies designed to support the operation of transit systems (Figure 12.3).

Urban places can contain a wide range of environments, from entirely built form to relatively untouched natural systems. It has become increasingly clear that the economic benefits of urban living must share the bottom line with quality of life (i.e., environmental) considerations. The viability of transit systems is affected by land use decisions, which in turn have a direct impact on quality of urban life and economic development.

Figure 12.3

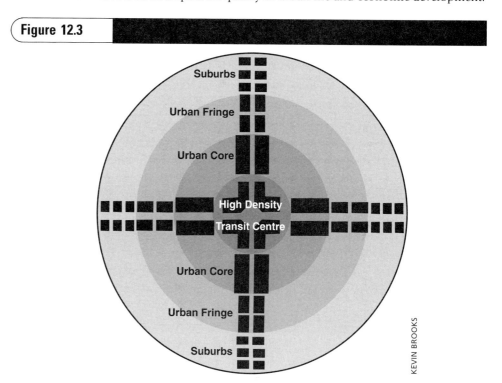

Transit-oriented development (TOD) focuses urban growth around transit stations, with high density and mixed uses nearest the station.

Many factors affect the viability of public transit service in urban and suburban areas. While not all these factors are related to land use planning, the form of planning and development is a key ingredient in support of transit. In turn, efficient and effective transit services contribute directly to the quality of the urban environment and the economic well-being of the community.

Environmental Benefits

The environmental benefits of public use of transit are clear. The average automobile emits 34.4 kilograms of hydrocarbons per year, 4029.3 kilograms of carbon dioxide, and 29.6 kilograms of nitrogen oxide. In 1988, there were over 12 million cars in Canada. Small wonder, then, that the largest single source of greenhouse emissions is the transportation sector. While buses are also a source of emissions, in the Greater Toronto Area (GTA), a full 12.2-metre bus equals about 50 cars. Even more impressive results are realized with rapid transit.

There are other benefits in transit use. As commuters switch from driving to transit, fewer vehicles contribute to rush hour congestion. Incentives such as exclusive bus lanes and transit-priority, high-occupancy vehicle lanes are encouraging drivers to switch in some communities. Reduced travel time has direct benefits, freeing more personal time for family and/or community activities. Such quality of life spinoffs are very much environmental benefits. Reduced vehicle emissions resulting from increased transit use will also help reduce the incidence of pollution-related health problems, such as respiratory diseases.

Economic Benefits

The economic benefits of transit use are often more difficult to quantify. The availability of efficient transit services can, however, be a significant factor for the developers of office, industrial and commercial buildings, since many blue-collar, office, and retail workers are transit captive. The importance of transit access is particularly important to prospective investors from outside the region or country seeking to reduce risk in as many areas as possible. Time spent trapped in traffic is a real cost to business. For example, traffic congestion in the GTA has been estimated to cost businesses about $2 billion per year. High transit ridership levels mean less traffic congestion and improved goods movement. This saves everybody money.

Another potential benefit occurs where several transportation modes (transit, commuter rail, intercity bus, car) can be planned to meet in a central facility: a transportation gateway. The economic opportunity for mixed use and other spinoff development, serving and served by a transit-based facility, can result in an important focal point for investment.

Transit operating costs may benefit from improved subdivision design. Based on an assessment of three case studies, Deluc consultants estimated that from $30,000 to $185,000 a year could be saved.[2] While the range varied considerably with the case studies (e.g., type of subdivision design improvements), significant potential cost savings were revealed in three categories: operating costs, municipal subsidy contributions, and passenger travel time.

In short, there are significant benefits to urban-suburban transit service, in the form of development opportunities, good efficiency of employee/goods movement, and improved environment/quality of life.

Transit-Friendly Land Use Planning

Five overlapping scales of municipal planning and development can be identified: regional, municipal, district, community, and site. Planning strategies that overlap among these five scales can be identified and brought into the plan preparation process. Each of these scales of planning presents opportunities and challenges to meet the needs of transit service. In particular, site planning considerations must focus on pedestrian (including disabled persons) access to transit facilities. This is true at both the residential end of the trip and the destination (e.g., workplace, shopping). For example, care facilities, apartments or large residential subdivisions should facilitate transit access. Road system design should meet maximum walking distance criteria to transit stops (about 400 metres). By the same token, office buildings, industrial areas, public buildings, and commercial developments (e.g., malls) should be designed with at least some portion of their structure near transit stops.

On a larger scale, transit-capable arterial roads should be spaced so that internal roads can be designed to meet the established maximum walking distance. An arterial grid or modified grid with arterial road spacing of about one kilometre appears adequate. Similarly, regional level plans should establish this broad skeleton of arterial roads to enable a healthy transit system to develop.

Beyond physical design considerations, municipal and upper-tier plans should consider the relationship of population and employment areas within the municipality in terms of transit accessibility. The presence of an efficient transit option is an attractive feature to many people who want to live and work in the same community.

The Challenges

Two main challenges face land use and transportation planners. The first is to incorporate transit-friendly policies and designs into plans for newly developing areas. Many suburban municipalities currently see little need to consider transit requirements for either present use or future needs. The second is retrofitting existing built-up areas during redevelopment planning to better support transit.

In Ontario, this will mean encouraging municipalities to use transit-supportive guidelines.[3] If the content of the guidelines is compelling enough, municipalities will incorporate appropriate strategies into their plans. Progress in this area can be made only through mutual support, cooperation, and action among provincial and municipal governments.

The Design of Streets

Paul Mackey

1990 Plan Canada 30(1): 2–10

Streets typically occupy more than 30 percent of urban land area. Yet planners focus little attention on the layout of the street. In practice, this topic is generally left to engineers, "who best know how to handle traffic." This attitude neglects the fact that streets serve several important functions, only one of which is moving automobiles (Figure 12.4). Planners have a definite role to play in highlighting the other aspects. Planning is needed to reconcile the interests of the different users of street space.

While little has been done in Canada to systematically rethink the design of streets, experiments have been carried out in Europe and incorporated into daily practice. These originated in the Netherlands,[4] where the poor soil conditions require relaying the brick pavements every 10 years or so, thus providing the opportunity for short-term experiments. The work was done primarily on low-volume residential streets. From there, the "revolution" in street design spread, most notably to West Germany and Denmark, but also to France, Switzerland, Australia, and the UK. The focus has also shifted from the local street to main roads.

The Opportunity For Reassessment

A great deal of street construction was undertaken in the 1950s and 1960s to accommodate the development of suburban areas and increased automobile ownership. Upkeep and repair of the network was curtailed in the high inflation 1970s and limited budget 1980s. As the Federation of Canadian Municipalities estimates the life span of streets and bridges to be 20 years, there is growing concern about the state of the infrastructure and greater willingness to invest in major road reconstruction. Streets and bridges are the prime infrastructure concern.

The discussion to date assumes that we will rebuild the streets according to existing standards, which are relatively unchanged from those 20 to 30 years ago. Is this really

---

Figure 12.4

In private communities like Fox Harb'r in Nova Scotia, streets are not open to public use.

advisable? The context today is very different. For example, cars are narrower now, opening the way to narrower local street widths, even if truck widths have increased.

Still more important are the demographic changes. For example, the number of elderly people is rising. Their visual perception and physical agility decrease, making walking more difficult. Yet studies show that the elderly walk more in their neighbourhoods than do younger adults. How is the street to respond to these changes? The increase in the 25 to 54 age group is likely to signal an increase in automobile traffic and a decrease in transit ridership. How is the street to cope?

Many standards are open to question. Up to 1977, Quebec law prescribed a minimum right-of-way of 66 feet; that was also conventional practice in Ontario.[5] The width was chosen in 1890 as an effective firebreak. It probably endured for so long because it was a convenient measure for land surveyors: exactly one chain. Such a standard pushed up land costs for housing and encouraged the construction of wide streets. Since 1977, Quebec municipalities have tended to use 50 feet, or 15 metres. Pavement widths have decreased when the developer has been given the option of building a private street. According to *Urban Development Standards*: "if there is one area meriting further detailed examination, it is the subject of road . . . width requirements."[6]

Since homeowners, and not motorists, pay for street expenditures, it is reasonable to plan the street to respond to the multiple needs of residents, especially in residential areas. Many options in street design are available. Street design could easily become an area where citizen participation might be encouraged.

The street is very much a part of quality of life for residents. It can act as a meeting place or as a barrier to social interaction.[7] It can provide play space for children, even when alternative areas are available. The street has always been a learning area where children discover space and the community around them. The street is irreplaceable.

Reinserting Streets into the Life of the City

In West Germany, planners got involved in overhauling the planning guidelines for street construction and design. In response to criticism about the neglect of the needs of cyclists and pedestrians, the rigidity, and the high cost of standards, new guidelines published in 1985 reflected a radically different and more interesting philosophy:

- *Street planning and road design must correspond to the urban environment, to land use and to architecture. A nationwide monotony of urban streets and their design is not acceptable at all . . .*
- *Urban streets have to be planned as a part of urban life. Their function is not only for car traffic but also for all other modes of transportation, for green open areas, for markets, for children's play, etc. . . .*
- *The chances for compromises in planning and design are dependent on the speed level. Only reduced speeds will allow effective compromises. It follows from this that street speeds have to be reduced efficiently on most urban streets through planning and design measures as well as through legislation.*[8]

In comparison, the *Geometric Design Standards* of the Roads and Transportation Association of Canada, the reference book most widely used in Canada, states that "every effort should be made to use as high a design speed as practicable to attain a desired degree of safety, mobility and efficiency."[9] If this is an acceptable practice when considering rural highways, it is totally inappropriate in the urban setting. In cities, several types of street users travel at slower speeds than cars: pedestrians (especially children and the elderly), people in wheelchairs, cyclists, transit patrons, etc. In cities, the design speed must account for these differences. In the 1999 edition of the *Geometric Design Guide for Canadian Roads*, the advice now reads: "Roads intended to provide high mobility, such as freeways and expressways, should be designed with the highest practical design speed to promote traffic mobility, efficiency and safety."[10] The guide does not mention appropriate design speeds for streets in urban areas. Urban streets designed between 1986 and 1999 were likely influenced by the earlier high design speed philosophy.

Safety, Speed, and Street Widths

The speed of traffic is governed by the presence of other vehicles, traffic control devices, and physical characteristics of the street. In residential areas, on local streets or even on arterials at off-peak hours, traffic volumes are low, and traffic control devices are rare or ignored; this leaves physical characteristics as the primary design tool for controlling speeds. Unfortunately, the Canadian standards consider only the safety of motorists; they neglect the safety needs of other street users despite major problems in this area.

Pomes-Barrere examined 1300 accidents involving children as pedestrians or cyclists over an 18-month period on the island of Montreal. Both the young and the elderly have special safety requirements.[11] For example, the young are easily distracted, and do not easily understand instructions, especially if they are abstract.[12] Canada, in fact, has a poor record for children's pedestrian safety.[13] The elderly fear the possibility of falling and may be more preoccupied with stepping off the curb than watching oncoming traffic. The elderly form an overrepresented group in traffic accident statistics.

The most efficient method of improving street safety is to reduce speeds of motorized traffic. On the one hand, there is a special need to discourage travel above the speed limit; on the other hand, even the normal speed limits need to be reexamined. Under unfavourable conditions (as when children dart unexpectedly across the street), it takes more than twice the distance for a car travelling at 50 kph to stop (up to 61 metres) than it does for a car at 30 kph.[14] Safe street design involves traffic calming, which encourages drivers to travel at low speeds and especially constrains speeders. Safety should be a prime objective over and above the concern with vehicle operation, simplicity, and convenience.

According to the Quebec highway safety code, the speed limit in cities, towns, and villages is 50 kph unless signs are placed along the road indicating otherwise. Municipalities have the right to set a different speed limit, but can be overruled by the Minister of Transport. Since 1984, municipalities in the Netherlands have had the power to fix a speed limit of 30 kph over a whole zone (rather than street by street), but only if they have taken measures to ensure that motorists do in fact travel at this speed.

The Gazette proposed that the Quebec highway safety code establish different speed limits: 30 kph on local streets, 50 kph on collector and arterial streets.[15] This move would accomplish little on existing streets if their designs were not modified. Many municipalities have set speed limit signs incompatible with the layout of the street; the main result is to encourage disrespect of the law. Compliance levels are low without costly police surveillance. The same can be said for stop signs that multiply and simply irritate motorists.

The most widely applicable way of limiting speeds is to narrow street lane widths. The Canadian standards specify a width of 3.0 metres for a local street lane (in the 1999 edition, the choice is given of between 3.0 and 3.7 metres for a local residential street) with 2.4 metres for the parking lane and larger widths for collectors and arterials where truck traffic is more important. Small cars are 1.5 metres wide, while large cars can reach 1.9 metres. Unfortunately, the local street lane width (3 metres) could easily allow small cars to travel at 90 kph.[16]

Reducing street widths is becoming more frequent in Europe with greater concern with speeding. Such a measure has been used often in residential streets, where it represents one of many techniques available (Figure 12.5). It is now being implemented on arterial roads, including sections of highways crossing urban areas in Switzerland, Germany, Denmark, and France.

Chapter 12/Transportation Planning

Figure 12.5

Narrow residential streets in Upton Grange, Northampton, UK, naturally calm traffic.

As an example of a limiting case, the Highway Research Board admits the possibility of a street width of 5.2 metres with two-way traffic and parking on one side.[17] It is normally impossible for two cars to meet beside a parked car. This arrangement is clearly not feasible for collectors or arterials, but can serve for local streets. In such cases, when traffic is low and houses have off-street parking, reduced widths also represent substantial savings in space and costs of construction, maintenance, and snow removal. They may, at times, impose a slight delay to the motorist. Narrow streets function already in older Canadian neighbourhoods without causing problems.

In deciding on street widths, planners must consider two other aspects. The first is bicycle traffic. On local streets with no traffic, it is possible to mix bicycles and motor vehicles. Planning for bicycle routes should be done early in subdivision design, and extra width allowed only on those collectors or arterials selected for bike lanes. For existing streets, narrowing motor traffic lanes may create sufficient room to establish a bike lane (Figure 12.6).

The other aspect, equally absent from the standards,[18] involves the requirements of public transit. The use of collector streets for transit may favour wider lanes than would otherwise have been suitable, even at low design speeds. Even with wide traffic lanes, planners can restrict overall street width by cutting back on parking lane width, since buses generally travel more slowly. On major bus routes, bus bays offer an alternative to adding street lanes.

Street Layout

When planners talk about street layout, it is usually in connection with subdivision design; they make a choice between grid streets, for example, and loop roads, crescents, and cul-de-sacs. The latter, besides their usual short length, which precludes long vehicle accelerations, also generally block the long-distance view of the driver, thus contributing to control of traffic speeds. However, these types of streets cause major inconvenience

Figure 12.6

Streets busy with cars offer little safe space for bicycles.

with respect to access to transit; service is often poor, since buses have to make many turns and stops along local streets, unless provision for adequate transit service has been planned beforehand on nearby collectors.

Another meaning can be given to the term "street layout," that is "the layout of the street" itself. A wide range of measures is available, both to reduce motor traffic speeds and to contribute directly to the enjoyment of the street.[19] The Transport and Road Research Laboratory in the UK has done extensive testing of one type of road hump or "sleeping policeman" (not to be confused with road bumps), which consists of a

Figure 12.7

PAUL MACKEY

A jog in Elkas Boulevard in Kirkland helps to slow traffic.

circular arc rising four inches (10 centimetres) over 12 feet (3.65 metres). Retesting in the US has proven these humps effective in reducing speeds to the 20 to 25 mph range.[20] No problems were encountered with snow removal. The French have adopted this design and a trapezoidal shape, while the Dutch also accepted a sinusoidal shape. The circular shape, with a rise greater than four inches, has been used on Rue du Campanile in Ste.-Foy, near Quebec City. Based on the Dutch idea, the measure was introduced to allow shoppers to cross the street easily to get to the stores on both sides.

Humps are appropriate for local streets and collectors without public transit service. For effective speed reduction, the humps should be less than 100 metres apart. The humps need to be clearly marked, and well-lit at night. The level part at the top of the hump may extend different lengths to prevent habituation and to keep drivers alert; however, if it is too wide, the speed reduction effect will be lost.

The goal is to keep the driver aware of the surroundings. The visual aspects of the street are a key element in alerting the driver to take care. One technique available is to shift the axis of the street, to offset the street, or to create a jog. This restricts the sight-line of drivers and keeps them vigilant. Rue St Charles in Longueuil has a very slight change in its axis, which creates an optical effect; the effect is more pronounced on Elkas Boulevard in Kirkland (Figure 12.7). As the change in axis becomes greater, the driver must pay more attention to negotiating the turns involved. Rue du Campanile in Ste.-Foy goes as far as to incorporate an elbow design, which creates a major discontinuity. The same principle is at work when roundabouts are installed.

Long, straight streets with long perspectives should be avoided, since they encourage speeding. On existing streets, it is sometimes possible to create a vegetated island in the centre. Where the overall width of the street is insufficient, it may be possible to widen boulevards or planting strips (between the sidewalk and the pavement) on one side of the street alternatively block by block and use the extra space to plant trees. Deciduous trees are an excellent way of blocking long-distance vision while permitting a view at ground level. Another possible measure is a series of chokers, a narrow section along a wider street: This creates a "ragged" arrangement. Care must be taken to not force cyclists to turn into the vehicle stream; this can be accomplished by cutting a passage for cyclists allowing them to continue straight through.

A different method of attracting the driver's attention is to vary the materials and colours of the street. The use of paving blocks in crosswalk construction is increasing in Quebec; in most cases red bricks are used to improve the respect of the pedestrian's priority by motorists. Many materials can be used: asphalt, brick, concrete paving blocks, poured concrete, stone panels. Problems involving maintenance of these materials and the borders between them are being resolved. Colour can also be incorporated into the asphalt: red asphalt bike lanes are common in the Netherlands, while yellow was used on a crosswalk in Quebec City where many amblyopic people cross. Besides improving safety, these measures also make the street more interesting visually.

Another aspect of street layout to investigate is cross-sectional design. Our streets generally have a convex shape, where drainage is to the side of the pavement. This creates two problems. First, snow is ploughed to the side of the road, and what remains, even after snow removal operations, can clog the gutters. Second, rain runoff and winter slush accumulate there, creating the risk of cars splashing passers-by. Bylaws prescribing reduced speeds for motorists to avoid this phenomenon are not completely effective.

One innovative alternative, which could be implemented when sewer lines are being improved or when building new streets, is a concave shape, where drainage is accomplished in the middle of the street. This arrangement is probably most suitable on streets where salt is applied in winter by spreader and where traffic flow prevents ice buildup. Duluth Street in Montreal, Saint-Jean-Baptiste Street in Montmagny, and Saint-Jean Street and Place de la Rivière in Quebec City all have concave shapes. However, more research is needed to test this type of street in winter conditions.

Another element of cross-sectional design involves the access to the driveway. Typical standards allow a transverse slope of five percent for the sidewalk at this point. However, above a two percent slope, it is nearly impossible to maintain traction on the wheels of a wheelchair, causing instability.[21] The cross-slope also constitutes a danger for the elderly, especially in winter. When a boulevard is provided, the sidewalk should remain level. If there is no boulevard, semi-mountable curbs should be used for residential driveways. On busy streets, to allow faster entry and exit, the rise of the curb can be smoothed with a little asphalt on the street surface. It would also be in order to study the appropriate height of the sidewalk with respect to the pavement.

Intersection Design

The classic design for intersections involves carriageways that connect on a level and sidewalks that stop abruptly at the curb. This arrangement causes problems in winter because the snow on the side of the street is usually poorly cleared. Thus pedestrians often pass from a clean sidewalk to a slush zone before getting to the wet pavement.

Two developments have modified this traditional structure. First, many safe-crossings have been built, especially on commercial streets. Quebec's Downtown Revitalization Program has subsidized this improvement in many cities. By physically eliminating the possibility of illegal parking too close to intersections, safe-crossings improve the reciprocal visibility of pedestrians and motorists. They provide space for beautifying the streetscape. They should, however, not be placed at street corners that serve as bus stops, because they force buses to swing out more sharply into traffic.

Second, sidewalks are now often ramped at intersections to allow wheelchairs to cross the street. Two problems arise: The blind no longer have a way to determine where the safe zone ends and the street begins; and the inclined plane increases the risk of slipping, especially in winter ice conditions, making the sidewalks less practical, especially for the elderly. As such, intersection ramps do not meet the standards for walkways set by CMHC, which require surfaces free of level changes that also remain nonslip under all weather conditions.[22]

In addressing the objectives of speed reduction, pedestrian crosswalk safety, and traffic control, while improving pedestrian comfort, "raised" crosswalks offer undeniable benefits.[23] In practice, the crosswalk is raised in relation to the pavement, but remains level with the sidewalk. This type of crosswalk allows optimal snow clearing of the walkway system, which, in conjunction with the level surface, decreases the risk of sliding. Also, walking is made easier and barrier free, and slush is directed away from pedestrians. Since this crosswalk also slows traffic, it may help replace stop signs by yield signs where visibility is sufficient and traffic light. An alternative of comparable efficiency is the intersection plateau or platform, implemented on Greene Avenue in Westmount and Decarie Boulevard in Ville Saint-Laurent, where the car rises on one side of the intersection and descends on the other. Another promising design is the roundabout (not to be confused with traffic circles). They function at low speeds, creating better safety for motorists and pedestrians, while providing fluid traffic movements. From an urban perspective, they offer a chance to create a sense of place, thanks to the landscape treatment they require in the central island.[24]

Safety Results

Physical and legal measures have significantly reduced accidents involving injury in the Netherlands. A large-scale experiment was conducted in the cities of Rijswijk and Eindhoven to measure their effectiveness.[25] In this case, the greatest safety benefits accrued to children under 15 years old and adults; the elderly do not seem to have improved their safety record. Accidents involving only material damage have increased, since the Dutch place obstacles in the street to protect pedestrians. Besides their safety problems, such obstacles are unsuited to Canadian climatic conditions. However, an economic evaluation that includes health costs still shows that benefits far outweigh the costs. The subjective feeling of safety was also enhanced, although this was not the case in all cities.[26]

Planners have an interest in the multiple use of facilities and urban space. But they have neglected streets, allowing them to serve as mere conduits for motor vehicles. A broader perspective is necessary to see streets as vital places for urban life. Streets constitute the major part of public urban space.

Pressure for change continues, as many residents request street closures or the installation of stop signs or traffic lights, especially when they fear for their children's safety. Residents are expressing a need, but do not have the resources to explore more appropriate solutions. This confers a professional responsibility on planners to rethink the design of the street. With the tools available, planners can feel empowered to question existing practices and to innovate. As can be seen, street design is not as staid a subject as some would think. There is room for more creative thinking.

Private Streets and Double Standards: The Canadian Planning Response

Andrew Curran

2005 Plan Canada 45(4): 42–5

The street has historically been one of the most important pieces of public infrastructure and most significant public spaces in Canadian cities. Over the past two decades, however, this traditionally public good has been increasingly planned, designed, and

Figure 12.8

Private roads, like those in Village by the Arboretum in Guelph, Ontario, fragment the urban street system.

governed in the private realm (Figure 12.8). With relatively little published on this trend, we set out to document the extent of private residential streets and the Canadian planning response to them. In the summer of 2005, we sent an e-mail survey to planners in the 172 largest Canadian municipalities and received 61 completed surveys (36 percent) covering every province.[27] The results of the survey point to a need to reform the sometimes excessive public standards that regulate development in Canada.

The Lure of Private Streets

While most respondents did not formally track such information, the estimates received indicate that some municipalities have a significant amount of residential development on private streets (Table 12.1).

These numbers are not surprising, as the private street offers benefits to residents, municipalities, and developers alike. The resident might be attracted by the potential cost savings, the protection of property values through neighbourhood preservation-oriented restrictive covenants, the promise of a potentially tight-knit community, and the enhanced sense of security and privacy. Although private streets allow for cheaper construction and higher densities, in many parts of Canada (especially in high-growth areas), private streets make a project more prestigious and exclusive and tend to increase property values and decrease housing affordability. More affluent residents are likely attracted to the exclusivity offered by this urban form.

Municipal councils approve private streets to accommodate development on unusually configured sites or difficult topography, to satisfy developer requests and market demand for condominium living, and to save money. Indeed, since residents living on private streets pay for most of their own services, while still contributing property

Table 12.1	Residential Development on Private Streets in Selected Canadian Municipalities		
Municipality	# Residential Units on Private Streets	# Residential Units (Total)	% Residential Units on Private Streets
City of Cambridge ON	11000	41400	26.6%
Township of Langley BC	8000	33000	24.2%
City of Burlington ON	12495	52000	24.0%
City of Abbotsford BC	7500	44000	17.0%
City of Chilliwack BC	4000	27280	14.7%
City of Pickering ON	3463	28261	12.3%
Municipality of East Hants NS	1007	8400	12.0%
City of Brantford ON	3000	28000	10.7%
City of Brandon MB	1000	11000	9.1%
City of Red Deer AB	2135	27500	7.8%
City of Fredericton NB	1350	22000	6.1%
Municipal District of Rocky View AB	800	17500	4.6%
Ville de Saint-Eustache QC	693	16617	4.2%

taxes to the municipal coffers, local governments can add valuable tax payers with little impact on service delivery costs.

Developers' interest in private streets suggests improved marketing opportunities. One overriding advantage attracts developers: the ability to circumvent rigid public street design standards in order to build potentially more innovative projects, usually at higher densities, while generating higher rates of return from their properties.

In many places, private streets can be narrower, take advantage of alternative materials for paving, are not required to include curbs or sidewalks, devise their own speed limits and parking rules, and limit public access through gates or signage. These alternative standards are clearly a major force in the spread of private streets, and so their origins and their logic merit some consideration.

With the tremendous growth of car ownership and rapid suburban expansion in the period following World War II, the Transportation Association of Canada (TAC) produced its *Manual of Geometric Design Standards for Canadian Roads and Streets*. Looking to gain some control over the shape of the rapid development, Canadian municipalities typically adopted standards from the readily available TAC Manual. Indeed, some provinces, such as Alberta, require that public roads and streets be built according to TAC's design guidelines.

Observers note that such standards were devised to accommodate the "worst possible case" scenario: parked cars on both sides of the street with enough space left for two fire engines to comfortably pass each other. As a result, we have thousands of kilometres of residential streets that are significantly wider than needed for typical traffic.

Of the 42 Canadian municipalities that responded to this question in our survey, 32 (76 percent) allowed alternative design standards on private streets often permitting roadway widths of 6 to 7 metres compared with the 9- to 10-metre widths typically required for public streets.

Unconventional public street designs face significant barriers to approval from engineers concerned about street geometry, lawyers concerned about liability, financial institutions concerned about marketability, and emergency services concerned about emergency vehicle access. A typical developer interested in building unconventional streets could avoid the bureaucratic hurdles and delays associated with getting municipal approval by using private streets, which come with less stringent design requirements.

Municipal planners offered several reasons to explain the lower standards applied to private streets: the privately-borne maintenance and liability costs; no onstreet parking; the difficulty in securing financing for innovative public road developments; and the lack of municipal powers as set out in provincial enabling legislation. Indeed, except for Nova Scotia and urban Newfoundland, enabling legislation does not explicitly permit municipalities to enforce design and construction requirements for private roads.

For all of these reasons, private streets are held to more lenient standards than are public streets in a majority of Canadian municipalities. The double standard contributes to the growth of private streets in Canada.

The Challenge of Private Streets

Conflicts between the municipality and residents of the private street over who should provide street maintenance and service delivery are routine and often bitter, especially when residents find themselves unable to pay for long-term maintenance costs. Poorly constructed and undermaintained roads can then present problems for traffic safety.

Private streets can be more easily gated and could contribute to a rise in unplanned gated communities. Even when roads are not gated, signage and other visual cues on private streets tend to impede street connectivity, with important implications for travel choices, emergency access, and quality of life.

A planner in Chilliwack noted that private streets tend to polarize communities along income lines and to diminish public engagement and civic thinking. Increasing privatism and the corresponding loss of public space—where freedom of speech can be practised, electioneering can occur, leaflets can be distributed, and civil liberties freely exercised—may pose a challenge to the healthy civic life envisioned in a good society.

The Planning Response

While the actions available to municipalities to address private streets are limited to what is permitted in their municipal enabling legislation, responses to the survey indicate that municipal planners use an array of tools to shape and manage private streets. Using zoning bylaws, planning policies, and recommended good design practice lets municipalities exert some influence over private street layouts, including pavement widths, curve radii, access to highways, turnaround facilities, and drainage.

Fire chief approvals and parking policies can also indirectly shape private streets. Private streets are often narrow, yet are designated fire routes. Planners in Stratford, Ontario, insist on sufficient visitor parking to compensate for the lack of onstreet parking on private streets.

Except for British Columbia, Manitoba, and Saskatchewan, which have legislation requiring residential community associations to establish reserve funds to maintain private roads, the long-term maintenance of private streets throughout the rest of Canada is not secure. A recent change in Nova Scotia's *Municipal Government Act* permits municipalities to help coordinate residents of private streets to collect fees on a regular basis. The District of Lunenburg recently adopted a private road maintenance and improvement bylaw, which enables it to levy lot charges on private roads for maintenance by a street association.

Some municipalities, such as St. John's and Kitchener, have placed a moratorium on new private streets. In other cases, municipalities have banned private streets from certain areas or restricted them to designated zones. In the Nova Scotia communities of Colchester, East Hants, and Cape Breton Regional Municipality, private roads are allowed only in rural settings beyond the serviced area or beyond reasonable commuting distance to an urban centre. In Halifax Regional Municipality, requirements for private streets have been raised to match public street standards, thereby eliminating one of the major incentives for developers to build private streets.

In a few places, such as Toronto and East Hants, reviews are under way examining the possibility of reducing standards for public streets. These changes are being considered partly to encourage the design of more context-sensitive public streets that can compete with the attractive design features of private streets. This strategy aims to reduce the appeal of private streets by permitting public streets to employ those same appealing features.

Regulatory Reform: Toward Better Public Neighbourhoods

Precise rules governing the planning, design, and construction of public streets help to assure a level of quality and predictability in new developments and serve to shield local governments from liability. At the same time, however, the widespread uniform application of TAC guidelines on public streets across Canada has resulted in public-sector planning unresponsive to local context and incapable of innovation. To address this problem, reform of public development regulations is required.

Oregon's state government is leading the way in North America, having concluded that there is no need for state and national street standards to apply uniformly in every instance, authorizing local municipalities to adopt narrower street standards and dispense with the Uniform Fire Code. As a result, Portland now allows streets 6 metres wide with parking on one side. The narrow mixed traffic public streets of many European cities, such as the Dutch *woonerf*, offer exciting examples of the livable public environments possible with some reform and flexibility in the rules governing street construction and design.

While private streets certainly provide several benefits to residents, municipalities, and developers, they also generate negative consequences. Private streets fundamentally pose a challenge to the practice of community planning and to the vision of an open, inclusive, and democratic society toward which many planners strive. While alternative street standards can only partially explain the growth of private streets, attempting to remedy the situation of double standards may contribute to reducing the appeal of the privatized urban form. And should we accomplish this task by changing the way we regulate street design, allowing for more innovation and context-sensitive solutions, we might build ourselves more livable communities along the way.

1. Contrast the road layouts for communities planned in the colonial period (e.g., Figure 1.1) with those designed in the immediate postwar period (e.g., Figures 2.3 and 2.6), and with plans you find in new suburbs. What trends and patterns do you find? How do you explain them?

2. What key planning principles should guide transportation planning in Canada? How should we accommodate bicycling in new neighbourhoods?

3. Compare road dimensions and characteristics in older parts of your community with road dimensions and characteristics in new developments. Describe and account for the differences. Consider whether recent standards are appropriate.

4. Why has walking and the use of public transportation remained a more significant proportion of travel route mode in Canadian cities than in American cities? What can cities do to encourage walking and public transportation use?

5. What concerns may planners have about permitting development on private roads?

6. How are Canadian cities implementing transit-oriented development? Which cities are proving most successful in the strategy, and why?

7. Examine the transportation policies in your community plan or local transportation plan. What values, visions, and premises do you find articulated there?

8. Document the history of the development (and removal) of major transportation arteries in your community, and examine how urban development patterns result from their implementation.

Reference Notes

1. Frisken, F (1989) *Relating Municipal Land Use Practices to Public Transit Operations in the Greater Toronto Area: Constraints and Opportunities.* Toronto: Ministry of Transportation of Ontario.

    Bowes, W, M Gravel, and G Noxon (1991) *Guide to Transit Consideration in the Subdivision Design and Approval Process.* Delcan Corporation. Ottawa: Transportation Association of Canada.

2. Deluc Inc (1990) *Rationalization du service de transport collectif dans les quartiers résidentiels.* Commission de transport de la Communauté régionale de l'Outaouais.

3. Ontario Minisistry of Municipal Affairs (1992) *Transit Supportive Land Use Planning Guide.* Available online at www.mah.gov.on.ca/userfiles/HTML/nts_1_3173_1.html (Accessed 4 February 2006).

4. Mackey, P (1988) Quelques innovations européennes en aménagement des rues. *Routes et Transports* 18(1): 32–5.

5. Barnard Associates, JG Williams Associates, Cumming Cockburn & Associates (1976) *Urban Development Standards.* Toronto: Ontario Ministry of Housing.

    SRQ (1964) *Loi des rues publiques* (Statutes of Québec) c. 179.

6. Barnard Associates, *et al.* (1976) : 29.

7. Appleyard, D and M Lintell (1972) Environmental quality of city streets: The residents' viewpoint. *Journal of the American Institute of Planners* 38(2): 84–101.

8. OECD (1985) *Innovations in Urban Transportation Planning–Germany.* Group on Urban Affairs. Paris: OECD: 15.

9. RTAC (1986) *Geometric Design Standards for Canadian Roads.* Ottawa: Roads and Transportation Association of Canada.

10. TAC (1999) *Geometric Design Guide for Canadian Roads.* Ottawa: Transportation Association of Canada.

11. Pomes-Barrere, MF (1985) Géographie des accidents de la route. Doctoral thesis, Université de Montréal.

12. Appleyard, D and M Lintell (1972) Environmental quality of city streets: The residents' viewpoint. *Journal of the American Institute of Planners* 38(2): 84–101.

13. OECD (1983) *Sécurité des enfants dans la circulation.* Paris: Organization for Economic Cooperation and Development.

14. Baass, K (1987) Quelques réflexions sur les distances intervéhiculaires. *Routes et Transports* 17(4): 46–9.

15. *The Gazette* (1985) September 9.

16. Couraud, R (1986) Rétrécissement de chaussée et ralentissement. *TEC.* 75.

17. Highway Research Board (1971) *Parking Principles,* Special Report 125, Washington.

18. RTAC (1986) Op. cit.

    TAC (1999) Op. cit.

19. Jenks, M (1986) Pedestrian priority: Shared surface residential roads. *Plan Canada* 26(6): 156–69.

    Smith, GP (1986) Calming the traffic and sharing the street. *Plan Canada* 26(4): 108–10.

20. Jr Smith, DT and S Appleyard (1981) *Improving the Residential Street Environment.* Executive Summary/Final Report. Washington: Federal Highway Administration.

21. Atkinson, WG (1984) *Pedestrian Crosswalk Systems for the Elderly and the Handicapped.* Montreal: Transportation Development Centre.

    Untermann, RK (1984) *Accommodating the Pedestrian.* New York: Van Nostrand Reinhold.

22. Associated Planning Consultants Inc (1982) *Accessible Residential Communities—Issues and Solutions.* Ottawa: Canada Mortgage and Housing Corporation.

23. Untermann, RK (1984) Op. cit.

24. Mackey, P (2003) Building better communities with roundabouts. Paper presented at the Conference of the Canadian Institute of Planners, Halifax, 7 July.

25. Institute for Road Safety Research (1985) *Reclassification and Reconstruction of Urban Roads in the Netherlands*. Leidshcendam: IRSR.

26. Smith, GP (1986) Op. cit.

27. The research was supported through the Social Sciences and Humanities Research Council of Canada.

Chapter Thirteen

Planning for Small and Remote Communities

The Other Twenty Percent

Jill Grant

A century ago, the average Canadian lived in a rural area. Today, most Canadians live in urban settlements. Some 20 percent of us, though, still live and work in the rural context. Small towns and villages remain idealized residential environments in our popular culture, and serve as models for planned new urbanism developments. The dream of country living continues to inspire urban residents, even as they drive home to their suburban bungalows. We may live in the city suburbs, but we still value the rural way of life.

The twentieth century witnessed a significant decline in the population and prospects of rural Canada. The pages of *Plan Canada* reveal planners' concerns about that reality, for instance, with headlines on the "crisis of agricultural land" in Ontario and the "crisis in rural Manitoba" interspersed with articles about the need for special approaches to suit the rural context.[1]

Planners have long recognized the threat that urban uses posed to agriculture. Early experts like Thomas Adams wrote extensively about the issue and the need for good planning for rural development.[2] The Town Planning Institute of Canada sought to manage unruly growth on the urban edge. Only the intercession of the Depression interrupted the mantra about containing cities within reasonable boundaries.

Despite planners' concerns, however, the loss of land to urban uses continued unabated.[3] Canada has a limited supply of good agricultural land: Only seven percent of our land base is suitable for farming. As Hofman notes, urban uses have consumed over 12 000 square kilometres of agricultural land since 1971.[4] Land more than twice the size of Prince Edward Island has shifted from food-producing fields to largely low-density suburbs. Some 18 percent of Class 1 farmland in Ontario now sprouts houses and streets. Some of the best land in rapidly urbanizing regions, such as Southern Ontario and the Lower Mainland of British Columbia, faces threats. The search for developable land could affect the ability of Canada to sustain specialty fruit crops in areas like the Niagara Peninsula and the Okanagan Valley.

We start the chapter with Wayne Caldwell's report on a strategy used by Huron County in Ontario to promote economic development in a region dependent on farming incomes. Like many agricultural communities, townships in Huron are trying to find ways to cope with rapid change, which potentially threatens livelihoods and lifestyles. Canadian agriculture has experienced technological and organizational shifts during the last century, with widespread mechanization and the rise of agribusiness. Large livestock operations are changing the rural landscape in some regions, replacing idyllic scenes of pastoral bliss with vast yards piled high with manure; such businesses require new techniques of rural planning and environmental management.[5]

With many ex-urbanites inhabiting large-lot developments in the rural fringe, the conflict over land use practices and activities intensifies. Authors have written extensively about such problems as the loss of rural character and concerns about increasing rural sprawl.[6] In their paper in this chapter, Barry Smith and Susan Haid describe programs in the Greater Vancouver area to preserve agricultural land in the face of extraordinary development pressures.

With resource exports driving our economy, Canada has many small and remote communities that accommodate the mining, forestry, and fishing industries. Minerals and forest products are subject to unpredictable commodity fluctuations and trade regimes, which throw communities into pinnacles of success and troughs of despair.[7] Early resource towns were either built by industry, as in the case of Grand Falls described by Jeff Ward in Chapter 2, or erected by workers who arrived to take advantage of job opportunities. By the mid-twentieth century, though, industry looked to government for help with planning and financing mining communities, like Kitimat and Tumbler Ridge in British Columbia.[8] Good design could not save either community from industries that moved on: In those cases, the settlements needed vision and good planning to find other employers to give continued usefulness. As planners, we have a reasonable idea of how to plan to build a new resource town, but how do we plan for the possible demise of one? How do we ensure resilience and diversity in the economy of these small and remote communities?

Atlantic Canada has seen many of its coastal communities suffer as the fish stocks collapsed. For instance, with the mines closed, the fisheries in decline, and many industries pulling out, rural Cape Breton has little chance of retaining its young people or attracting new residents. Between 1996 and 2001, the population of Cape Breton declined by seven percent. A rural exodus of this order threatens the ability of the community to plan services. Rapid aging of the population will leave local governments struggling to provide appropriate facilities. Many remote areas face similar struggles.

Gordon Fulton's paper describes the efforts of some small towns to keep their downtown areas strong and attractive. In the 1980s, many towns developed Main Street programs to fight back against the shopping malls. While some communities like Niagara-on-the-Lake in Ontario and Lunenburg in Nova Scotia (Figure 13.1) capitalized effectively on heritage features to attract tourism as an alternative economy, not every rural area can turn to visitors to save a way of life.[9] Thousands of communities across the country have thousands of historic homes and buildings crying out for adaptive reuse: Unfortunately, too many of the settlements have yet to find appropriate new uses for the structures. Millions of dollars invested in paving streets and sidewalks with alternative materials and installing attractive light standards did not prove an adequate planning strategy to solve the principal problems of rural Canada. Banks are closing, and shops on main street struggle to survive. Is government addressing the special needs of small communities?[10] What will it take to turn things around?

While the population of much of rural Canada is declining, Aboriginal and northern communities are growing.[11] Planners became increasingly concerned about these settlements in the 1980s,[12] but two decades of attention has not solved the problems that Wolfe identified (Table 13.1).

Land claims settlements are giving First Nations peoples new options and opportunities in some regions of Canada. The last decade has seen major changes in the north,

Figure 13.1

Lunenburg, Nova Scotia, capitalized on its history and designation as a UNESCO world heritage site to stimulate tourism.

with the formation of a new territory: Nunavut.[13] Some regions with significant Aboriginal populations are booming with petrochemical exploration and mining revenues. But continued social and economic problems in many First Nations communities remain a high priority for band councils and for government. Fears of catastrophic climate change add to the uncertainty about the future of northern communities.

Many reserves beside or inside cities are also growing. First Nations communities increasingly seek to express their rights to make decisions about the use of their land in ways that may compete with the land use planning agendas of municipalities. Hence, negotiation and collaboration between First Nations and local governments is becoming increasingly important for planning, as Kasia Tota explains in her paper.

Don Aubrey offers useful advice for planners working in Aboriginal northern communities. Planners who come to small and remote communities have to understand and work with the local culture and conditions. People in the settlements have unique relationships with the land and their own concerns, which must direct appropriate planning activity. The principles Aubrey suggests are good advice in almost any circumstance.

What is the future of rural and northern Canada, of our small and remote communities? As is true in our cities, we also look for sustainable options for the other 20 percent of our homes. Finding those strategies that will protect choices for future generations will require that we treat more of our resources as renewable. We must remain cautious in alienating agricultural land to urban uses: Some day, we may need that acreage for growing food. We have to treat our forests and fisheries as parts of ecosystems that will not survive and thrive unless we manage them responsibly.

We do find the occasional beacon of hope for small communities. Ibbitson describes the case of Craik, Saskatchewan. A small town facing the loss of its young people

Table 13.1	Some Problems in Aboriginal Communities in Canada[14]
High and increasing costs of pursuing the traditional economy, and continuing uncertainty of profitable returns	Lack of opportunity for or access to appropriate job training or higher education
Lack of skills and low level of interest in the traditional economy, especially among young people	Low level of school attendance and formal academic achievement
Lack of land for expansion of community infrastructure	Low incomes, high cost of living (store food, transportation, household items), and high incidence of financial poverty
High cost of installing, generating, and maintaining community physical infrastructure	Continuing high birth rates and a youthful and growing population
High demand for housing, high cost, inadequate existing stock, and inappropriate design for the climate and lifestyle	High incidence and increasing complexity of health problems
High under- and unemployment in the formal wage sector, with rates highest in remote and more traditionally-based communities	High incidence of social problems, including externally directed violence (vandalism, break and enter) and internally directed violence (alcohol and substance abuse, family member battering, suicide)
Few opportunities for wage employment outside of the public sector (federal, territorial, local)	

established an "eco-centre" and plan to build an ecovillage around it. By focusing aggressively on energy efficiency and associated technologies the community has established an identity and an economic generator.

> Individual rural communities often succumb to, or defy, their fate based on one intangible, but implacable, factor: the quality and collegiality of the local elites. If the business, professional and political classes of a small town work together, if they are prepared to take risks, and if they can convince the rest of the citizenry to take risks with them, then that community can tap into emerging technologies and alternative markets to rebrand and revitalize their town.[15]

Committed leadership and good planning can offer communities opportunities to retain their vitality so that they retain the other 20 percent of the population.

Rural Canada: Designing a Desirable Future

Wayne J Caldwell

1992 Plan Canada 32(5): 24–9

As in the past, the future of rural communities will be determined by prevailing economic and environmental trends. Exactly what the future holds, however, is nebulous and a matter of varying opinion. In this context, an appropriate response demands that planners put less emphasis on attempting to understand and predict the future of rural communities and concentrate instead on developing a vision of what the desired future should be and the means by which to achieve it.

From a policy perspective, we need to plan in two not always opposing directions: where our communities are likely to go, and where they would like to go. The planner can help a community to identify and attain a desired alternative future, but not within the framework of traditional regulatory approaches to land use planning. Land use planning tools, while important, tend to be reactionary. Fortunately, they can be complemented by planning approaches and processes that help coalesce community involvement and enhance the probability of achieving a desired outcome.

An Agricultural Perspective

Agriculture is a major activity with a fundamental influence on many rural communities. An understanding of this relationship—as well as anticipated agricultural trends and their impact on the rural community—are essential for community planning. Although rural communities are subject to a much broader set of external and internal trends and issues, here we focus on the relationship between agriculture and rural communities. (Many of the issues that dominate agricultural communities—economic stagnation or environmental degradation, for example—are often present in other types of rural communities.)

Economic and Environmental Considerations

The cost-price squeeze, low commodity prices, oversupply, future of supply management, and massive government subsidy programs justifiably dominate the thinking of many Canadian farmers (Figure 13.2). Moreover, uncertainty about trade agreements and the potential loss of world markets complicate day-to-day farming decisions. These

WAYNE CALDWELL

Figure 13.2

Harvesting the crops in Huron County, Ontario.

economic issues have a fundamental impact on the future of communities, producing several corresponding community issues. They include, among others, the probability of reduced employment and population, farm abandonment and intensification, and a depressed agricultural sector and rural economy. Largely driven by changes in agriculture, these community issues are compounded by equally threatening changes in other sectors of the rural economy, including the manufacturing and business sectors. The fear that many of these changes may be permanent rather than cyclical makes it even more critical that we anticipate the future of our rural communities.

Environmental issues play an equal part in determining the future of agriculturally-based communities. In fact, predictions indicate the real possibility of environmental catastrophe for much of Canada's agricultural lands. Evidence of soil erosion, soil compaction, and salinization support the arguments of those who anticipate serious problems for Canada's agricultural industry. Moreover, large-scale environmental issues, like climate change, also mean continued uncertainty for Canadian agriculture.

A relationship links the economic and environmental issues affecting agriculture. Economic pressures force many farmers to assume a mode of production that threatens their very livelihood and the long-term future of Canada's agriculturally-based communities. Over the short term and in response to narrow or nonexistent profit margins, farmers are forced to maximize their output by using fertilizers, pesticides, herbicides, monocultures, and inappropriate soil management practices. The result: environmental degradation. In some situations the outcome will be bleak.

Whether a rural community survives will depend on the ability of farmers and the community as a whole to manage continuous economic and environmental change. Hence, rural planners must not only anticipate change but also help communities work toward a desired future. In many cases, residents in these communities will support the trends or embrace the type of changes likely to occur. This is especially true if we consider the trends affecting other aspects of the rural economy, such as the manufacturing and business sectors.

How do communities and planners formulate a new vision for the future? Policy and action are implemented through various tools and mechanisms. Their success is ultimately a function of the willingness of community members to support not only the vision itself but also the means of achieving it. Ergo, the role of the planner is to devise an appropriate methodology to secure public involvement, with a goal of defining the people's aspirations about the future of their community.

The Huron County Experience

Huron County, in southwestern Ontario, possesses a strong and diverse agricultural industry well-recognized in the land use planning process. Extensive public participation defines the county's approach to planning. This philosophy is evident in work completed by the Huron County Department of Planning and Development to identify relevant issues and bring the nature of the county's official plan up to date. A desire to clarify and focus on the way people felt their communities should develop involved attitudinal studies to determine what issues were important.

The county conducted interviews and distributed a questionnaire to obtain a preliminary understanding of the goals and aspirations of its residents. One hundred twenty-five individuals were interviewed during the summer of 1991. The results were used to formulate a more detailed questionnaire mailed to a sample of 1000 households (with a 51 percent response rate). The questionnaires included both closed ordinal-scale attitudinal questions and open questions, thereby providing the public with an opportunity to identify additional issues and perspectives. Collectively, the responses provided the opportunity for residents to identify their wishes for the future of Huron County. The

Table 13.2	Community Priorities, Huron County Department of Planning and Development, 1992

Make economic development a top priority

- have an economic plan
- have a long-term commitment
- involve business, labour, industry, and education
- be competitive in pursuing new business
- lobby government
- promote the county

Strengthen agriculture

- promote agriculture
- protect prime agricultural land
- allow marginal land to be used for nonfarm purposes

Diversify the economic base of Huron County

- strengthen agriculture and related businesses
- diversify with complementary industry and services
- expand job opportunities
- provide a future for young people
- increase the tax base

Make job training part of education

- develop more skill, less academic courses
- develop more county-based training courses
- have industry, business, and education work together
- make education a part of the county's future

County leadership

- encourage less but better government
- encourage more decisions and leadership from the county, instead of Toronto and Ottawa
- promote more public awareness of county government
- think like a county rather than a collection of small communities

Protect the environment

- encourage fewer regulations, more know-how
- develop more practical, common-sense protection
- encourage more individual initiatives.
- provide more information

Promote towns and villages

- promote and develop as urban centres
- attract new industry, businesses, and services
- coordinate development on a countywide scale

comments helped to define, at the local level, the public's interest in the future state of their communities (Table 13.2).

Interestingly, a review of the individual statements indicated that traditional approaches to land use planning would not suffice. Only some aspirations relating to the strengthening of agriculture could be achieved through land use planning. The question that naturally arises is: "Are planners prepared to respond to these kinds of issues by developing appropriate processes and responses?"

Planning and Community Development: Toward an Alternative Future

The approach to community development in Huron County has provided the framework for a local, more direct response to the types of issues identified by the official plan review. Beginning in the early 1980s, the Department of Planning and Development began to pursue a more integrated approach to planning and economic development; by the late 1980s, while retaining expertise and involvement in land use planning, the department engaged in many community development initiatives.

The approach was a function of both opportunity and need. In the early 1980s, traditional approaches to economic development no longer seemed appropriate for a rural economy that relied heavily on the agricultural, service, and small-business sectors. In response to the types of issues, pressures, and changes occurring within rural communities, new models and approaches needed to be identified.

In response to concerns related to economic stagnation or decline in some parts of the county, the department began working with groups of municipalities in 1988. The county's 26 municipalities were divided into North, West, Central, and South Community Development Areas (CDAs). An informal network of municipalities already in place (Central and South CDAs) was formalized with the creation of a steering committee, which included the municipal clerk and one councillor from each municipality. The North and West CDAs were initiated through public meetings organized by the department. At these meetings, participants reviewed concepts, opportunities, and organizational approaches. Because of the public's willingness to seize the initiative and become actively involved, leadership of the organization quickly transferred to the local community.

Table 13.3, which describes the characteristics of the four development areas, illustrates why the community development approach is an appropriate model for helping rural communities secure an alternate future.

Organization

The four community development areas share similarities in organization, overall philosophy, mandate, and staffing, but are fundamentally different. Because community development must be community based and responsive, there was no single approach or organizational structure prescribed to each of the four areas. The intention was to facilitate the development of organizations that were both responsive to and supported by the local community. Each organization was encouraged to develop a structure suited to local circumstances. Each area appointed a representative to sit on a countywide steering committee responsible for overall project direction.

To reinforce the goal of local autonomy, the CDA steering committees were responsible for identifying issues, approaches, and projects to pursue within their individual areas. Staff resources assisted in this process by providing strategic planning assistance and helping to develop and implement projects. The steering committees were also given funding, which, although limited, provided the resources to pursue individual projects. Three CDAs developed volunteer subcommittees, which, in turn and often without the benefit of project staff assistance, identified individual projects.

The basic goal of community development is to encourage people to identify their problems collectively and to develop and work towards appropriate solutions. The intent is to maximize and coordinate resources toward achieving community betterment. The involvement of subcommittees broadened the base of community development initiatives in three of the four areas. These subcommittees have been established

	Central CDA	South CDA	North CDA	West CDA
Table 13.3		Characteristics of Huron County Community Development Areas		
Impetus for the organization	Concern over stagnant economy and depressed agricultural sector	Concern over local plant and business closings	County initiative to promote community development activity	County initiative to promote community development activity
Steering committee composition	Municipal	Municipal	Municipal/public	Municipal/public
Primary focus	Community economic development	Community economic development and information dissemination	Broad-based community development	Tourism
Subcommittees	Agriculture Government services Manufacturing Tourism		Environment Economic development Education Agriculture Health/social services	Environment Agriculture Tourism
Sample projects	Promote ethanol usage Organize and promote farm vacations Industrial property listing service Advertise economic opportunities	Industrial property listing service Area promotion Small business resource centre Information kiosks Research and forum for businesses	Counselling for farm families Directory of training programs Assistance to local entrepreneurs Recycling programs	Tourism night and brochure swap Support rural economy conference Promote tour packages Countywide tourism promotion

to pursue a range of interests, including agriculture, tourism, environment, education, and personal development. The subcommittees normally include several members of the public and at least one representative from the CDA steering committee. The participation of volunteers (about 100 on an ongoing basis), the variety of subcommittees, and extensive coverage by the local media revealed a broad base of support for community development initiatives.

And what of the planner? Traditionally, planners have assumed the role of the professional expert providing apolitical advice to elected decision makers. Clearly, however, the role of the planner in working with Huron County's four community development areas is more in keeping with that of the community development worker: that of facilitator or enabler. To paraphrase Jim Lotz: The planner doesn't solve problems but increases people's capacity to solve them.[16]

The CDA approach reflects this definition. The goal was to create an ever-widening circle of involved participants. The resulting diversity of interest and the total number of projects identified by the areas reinforced the role of the planner as an objective and informed facilitator.

Process and Product

Ultimately, the success of the community development approach in dealing with the issues identified in the Huron County official plan review relied on two things: the process used to implement the community development initiative and the resulting product or types of approaches. The results clearly indicated that the CDA approach offers a reasonable planning tool to assist local communities in pursuing an alternative future.

Process: An important component of the Huron County approach was the emphasis placed on developing an appropriate process. From the community perspective, a successful process has lasting benefits, including spinoffs from ongoing community-based initiatives and organizations. The adopted process stressed community involvement and ownership of the process; public education and capacity building within the community; cooperation and coordination among communities; and strategic planning as an overall framework for locally-based action and planning.

Product: The diversity and number of projects pursued reveals that the community development project initiated considerable local action. A comparison of the activities pursued by the CDAs with the issues identified by county residents during the official plan review indicates a high degree of correlation. The individual projects also share a common directive to disperse information.

While traditional approaches to land use planning remain important, they cannot significantly address many of the economic and environmental issues that threaten rural Canada. In this context, the door is open for the planning profession to work in a more active way toward influencing the future of rural communities. To seize this opportunity, however, planners must rethink traditional planning methods and adopt a more integrated community development approach.

The significance of the Huron County approach lies in the attempt made to integrate planning and development based on a community development model. While similarities exist between the Huron County example and approaches pursued elsewhere (such as the rural development corporations in Saskatchewan), few of the other approaches have been institutionalized, built upon an existing municipal structure, and integrated as part of an overall planning process.

The challenge of this opportunity, however, suggests that planners must be prepared to accept new roles and to develop new attitudes, definitions, and approaches toward planning practice. Planners must accept a broad-based definition of planning; function as informed facilitators, community enablers, and educators; value community involvement and participation as an essential component of the planning process; empower the local community with additional responsibility for its own future; develop a holistic view of the rural economy and the local community; include community development concepts as a basic part of the planner's knowledge base; articulate strategic planning concepts as an appropriate planning tool; be flexible in the approach to organization and process; and retain traditional skills in research, forecasting, analysis, and policy formulation. If planners are prepared to accept such ideas as relevant to planning practice and are ready to accept new issues and challenges, they will be in a better position to work with rural communities to plan for a brighter future.

Wayne Caldwell's Update
Planning in Huron: Reflections on the Evolution of Rural Planning

Wayne Caldwell

They say that nothing is as certain as change itself. Reflecting on the years since I wrote this article, I find it instructive to consider the evolution of rural planning in Huron County.

In 1992, the county organized four geographic community development areas, which pursued a range of initiatives. Over the years, these structures developed into responses to sectoral issues. Recent countywide initiatives involved proactive community development planning for tourism, manufacturing, the environment, and agriculture. The county identified five key actions.

1. One issue county residents targeted in the early 1990s related to economic development, employment, and training. In 1992, the county secured federal "Community Futures" designation leading to the formation of a Community Futures Development Corporation (providing loans and business counselling). Over the years, the offices of the Huron Business Centre delivered county, provincial, and federal initiatives.

2. The countywide Huron Tourism Association grew directly out of the West CDA. This group has an active board of directors and a broad membership base. The group promotes and coordinates tourism and works to develop capacity to enhance the tourism industry.

3. The Huron Manufacturing Association builds on the county commitment to enhance and develop industry. Even today, with the province forecast to grow by four million people over 30 years, the county struggles to maintain its population. Manufacturing is critical to providing employment, assessment, and related opportunities. The manufacturing association has an active membership, conducts strategic planning, and works toward common goals.

4. The Huron Farm Environmental Coalition addresses the common goal of farmers to enhance environmental quality while pursuing production agriculture. While farmers lead the coalition, the county has played an important role assisting with organization and the provision of a secretariat service.

5. The Huron County Water Protection Steering Committee, sponsored by the county, has broad community representation. Active since 2004, the group follows a community-based strategy toward water quality concerns. With the assistance of the planning department, this committee has raised more than $1 million for initiatives, such as incentives to adopt best management practices and to prepare a lakeshore stewardship manual.

The Rural–Urban Connection: Growing Together in Greater Vancouver

Barry E Smith and Susan Haid

2004 Plan Canada 44(1): 36–9

For several decades, suburban development in Canada has pushed the boundaries of metropolitan areas outward and converted large areas of farmland and natural areas into an often sprawling mix of urban residential, industrial, and commercial uses along with their supporting energy, transportation, and related infrastructure. The negative consequences of this growth pattern not only affect the agri-food industry, farming, and the natural environment, but also alter the livability of the resulting settlement patterns and adjacent urbanized areas (Figure 13.3). Tens of thousands of hectares of prime farmland and natural habitat have been lost in such metropolitan regions as the Greater Toronto Area and the Calgary-Edmonton corridor, with the process continuing largely unabated.[17] Beyond the immediate loss of land, metropolitan regions influence land use patterns up to 100 kilometres beyond their formal boundaries.[18] Recent studies confirm that low-density suburban sprawl has expanded significantly in Canada since the 1990s.[19]

Accelerated expansion of Canadian urban areas reflects locational and housing preferences that result in more land per urban dwelling with declining average densities: dropping from 1030 persons per square kilometre in 1971 to 796 in 1996.[20] The negative consequences of this land-consumptive form of urban growth are significant not only to the viability of the agri-food industry and ecological integrity of the natural environment, but also to the quality of life of residents.[21] British Columbia responded to these intense development pressures with strong mechanisms aimed at managing

Figure 13.3

Farming in Burnaby Big Bend, with the city in the distance.

growth and preserving agricultural land and natural assets through an integrated policy approach founded on a long history of regional planning.

British Columbia's Agricultural Land Reserve: *A de facto* Urban Growth Boundary

The largely mountainous terrain of British Columbia has resulted in keen historic competition for a limited developable land base. Rapid post–World War II growth in the province witnessed extensive suburbanization. The annual loss of an estimated 6000 hectares of prime agricultural land in the late 1960s and early 1970s began setting off public and political alarm bells. For instance, the clearly visible loss of high-quality farmland and natural habitat ran counter to the dominant public concern encapsulated in the 1966 Lower Mainland official regional plan, which reflected a vision of "cities in a sea of green."[22]

With the passage of the *Land Commission Act* in 1973, a commission was appointed to oversee the preservation of agricultural land and designate the provincewide Agricultural Land Reserve (ALR). After a consultative process, and based largely on biophysical attributes, about five percent of the province's land base was found suitable for designation in the ALR.

The province's agricultural land preservation program facilitated land use planning to help balance the forces of urbanization operating in the high growth areas of the province. A provincially inspired zone within which agriculture takes priority provided clarity and strength as a land use tool.

While the commission's duties over the years have been altered to provide a sharper focus on its agricultural land preservation mandate, the original legislation saw a need to take a comprehensive approach. Originally, the commission was charged with managing "greenbelt land" in and around urban areas, "land bank land" for urban and industrial purposes, and "park land reserves." Although these responsibilities were eventually removed (1978) from the mandate, they served to foreshadow the importance of functional integration and a regional perspective, which formed the hallmarks of the emerging regional growth strategy in the Greater Vancouver Regional District (GVRD).[23] Protecting the food land resource generated consequential benefits. Besides the more obvious contributions to the health and economy of the region, agricultural lands may provide ecological functions (e.g., habitat, soil protection, water infiltration) and define a "sense of place" for many communities across the province. Moreover, the agricultural land preservation program has had a positive influence on urban growth patterns in the province over the last 30 years.

Building upon the ALR

The agricultural land reserve provided a strong foundation for the development of the green zone, a cornerstone of the Livable Region Strategic Plan, approved by the GVRD board with the support of its member municipalities in 1996. The plan is the region's official growth strategy and is, in essence, a contract among member municipalities to achieve regionwide objectives. The green zone comprises about 205 520 hectares, or two-thirds of the region's area: It delineates lands protected from intensive urban development. The green zone includes four types of regionally significant lands: community health lands (drinking watersheds, flood plains), ecologically important areas (wetlands, forests), renewable resource lands (agriculture, forestry areas), and outdoor recreation and scenic lands. The protected areas offer a reservoir of ecological capital and other benefits for the region.

Recognizing the need to protect what is most important first, establishing the green zone was the first piece in preparing the Livable Region Strategic Plan. It defined the framework for the plan and supported other key policies of building complete communities, achieving a compact metropolitan region, and increasing transportation choice. Integrating agricultural lands within the network of "green" lands is a unique, but effective, smart growth tool for land conservation and growth management. The region's ALR, less a small portion, comprises about 26 percent of the green zone. Municipalities have designated their green zone lands: Substantial changes to green zone lands trigger a plan revision that ultimately requires the approval of the GVRD board of directors. Since the Livable Region Strategic Plan was adopted, the area of the ALR in the region has decreased only marginally (0.3%).

Integrating the "browner" working agricultural lands (largely private) with green lands (mostly public) in this framework also highlights sometimes competing values. An implementation agreement between the GVRD and the Provincial Agricultural Land Commission recognizes these values and strives for a sustainable balance. The agreement specifies how the organizations are jointly committed to preserving the ALR, enhancing agriculture in Greater Vancouver, and achieving the goals of the Livable Region Strategy. For ALR lands within the green zone, ensuring that farming remains a viable business undertaking is an essential implementation action. Similarly, protecting conservation features and wildlife corridors and providing parks and outdoor recreation opportunities are recognized as important activities in the green zone.

The ALR and GVRD's green zones have acted as springboards for a series of supporting initiatives. The provincial Strengthening Farming Program fosters partnerships between local governments, the farm community, and the province. In turn, it helped facilitate the appointment of local agricultural advisory committees and completion of agricultural land use inventories, geographic information systems initiatives, agricultural area plans, and "edge planning" to help lessen farm/nonfarm conflicts. A farmland and wildlife trust is addressing farm and wildlife issues in a spirit of cooperation and mutual benefit.

Municipalities play a critical role in the sustainability of agriculture: They function as the primary "gatekeepers" of the ALR. Applications to remove land from the reserve, subdivide lands, or carry out a nonfarm use are first received by municipalities. Aspects concerning rural-urban interfaces, compatibility of adjacent land uses, and infrastructure are under municipal purview. Many municipalities with significant agricultural areas have developed supportive agricultural policies and plans as expressed within their official community plans and agricultural area plans.

Collectively, these tools provide "on-the-ground" connectedness between municipal planning processes, regional policy directions, and provincial objectives focused on the region's rural, agricultural, and natural areas. Ultimately, the philosophy of responsible regional growth management in the GVRD has embraced the agri-food and environmental interests within the planning mainstream in a largely harmonizing rather than confrontational manner. As a result, agriculture and habitat issues are no longer planning afterthoughts. Policy development has moved beyond the question of land use preservation.

But challenges remain. Ensuring an appropriate urban-rural fit for the long term is still being addressed. Balancing habitat conservation and the economics of farming continues to be an issue. Concerns about greenhouse operations located in areas of wildlife significance, particularly the Pacific flyway, and on prime agricultural soils are under consideration. Regulatory requirements on agricultural lands are numerous, variable, and somewhat uncoordinated, which can be a disincentive to farming. Issues relating to air quality include decreased crop productivity owing to poor air quality and contributions of air contaminants from some agricultural operations. Establishing local markets, processing agricultural products, and realizing synergies with other activities will serve to enhance local economies, improve efficiencies, and advance the goal of sustainable agriculture in the region.

Managing growth in a manner that bridges economic prosperity, community well-being, and environmental integrity is a challenge front-and-centre in GVRD's Sustainable Region Initiative.[24] As challenges are met, its approach recognizes that the "green essentials" of the region not only need protecting but also make crucial, complementary, and integrated contributions to evolving regional strategies and municipal community plan policies.

Future Designs for Small Town Canada

Gordon W Fulton

1992 Plan Canada 32(2): 29–30

The town council in Gravelbourg, Saskatchewan (pop. 1300) faced an important decision in 1988: Let the town's commercial heart continue its slow economic decline or attempt to help the business community inject some new life into main street. It wasn't a very good time to be talking about committing town finances: Grain prices were down, farm bankruptcies were up, and the town's claim to fame, the immense College Mathieu, the only French-language college west of Winnipeg, had just burned to the ground.

Council made the decision to jump-start revitalization. They chose the Main Street Canada program, a self-help process developed by the nonprofit Heritage Canada Foundation. Part of the appeal of this program was its holistic approach. Main Street Canada also had the benefit of a successful record right across the country. If it could be done in Nelson, British Columbia, whose mayor credited the approach with saving downtown Nelson, then it could be done in Gravelbourg.

The process these and dozens of other communities of under 25 000 population bought into wasn't a big-city solution writ small; it was a process developed, tested, and refined in Canada's smaller cities and towns. Briefly, the process encourages a broad cross-section of the community to commit themselves to revitalization. A Main Street coordinator is hired to facilitate the town's attack on the problems of downtown. There is no standard solution. There is, however, a common process, based on the "four-point approach." Each issue is addressed in terms of its organizational, design,

Figure 13.4

Small towns offer neighbourhood retail but little in the way of specialized services.

marketing, or economic development shortcomings. Each point is addressed equally, without detriment to the other three. In other words, a solution to an economic development problem that runs counter to the town's marketing or design values is rejected. This is the essence of the holistic approach to downtown revitalization (Figure 13.4).

In functional terms, the overlap one finds in the roles in a small town—where the mayor is also a downtown business person, or the town clerk heads the Rotary Club's public improvement committee—allows an efficiency of effort not typically found in larger cities. With a couple of dozen people around a table, one has most of the town's organizations, service clubs, and special interest groups represented. The intricate social and professional overlap frequently makes reaching a broad consensus possible, and in months rather than years. In small town Canada, the pacts are made between friends, neighbours, and colleagues in the coffee shop and on the golf course.

This collaborative approach requires a clear and widely-accepted set of community values and objectives. A large part of a Main Street coordinator's time in the first 18 months of a project is spent bringing out and nailing down these values and objectives. The surprise to outsiders (and many insiders) is that it is possible to do this, given the reputation independent business people have for disagreeing on everything. But it is rare that common ground cannot be found. The great effort put into encouraging participation, finding a common vision, and reaching consensus pays off when the time comes to tackle the problems of downtown.

Larger downtown design issues are handled in a participatory fashion. In Seaforth, Ontario, a communitywide canvas in 1988 determined that public area improvements were a high priority in this town of 2200 people. The townspeople wanted the public areas to complement the downtown's historic buildings. The Main Street coordinator helped set up a streetscape committee of stakeholders—business owners, the general public, town council—to drive the process. It held open houses and visioning sessions to find out what people wanted downtown.

Public involvement continued even after the draft plan was prepared. Finally, the committee recommended a final plan, which the council adopted as a long-term commitment. Town council immediately undertook the first physical step by building a civic court downtown in front of the town hall. The total elapsed time from striking the committee to cutting the ribbon at the new civic court was less than one year.

The design story in Fort Macleod, Alberta, has a similar ring. Citizens in this town of 3200 began their concerted attack on downtown's stagnation in 1982. The local main street office emphasized community sensitization and education. They ran a "Main Street" column in the weekly newspaper; they took streetscape drawings to the schools to show the students what the main street buildings used to look like; they did before-and-after slide shows for the public to show the potential resource the buildings represented. Their storefront office became the focus of action. By 1986, it was clear the town was not only aware of main street, but it also cared what was happening to it. When the owners of the Village Greenery put three colours on their sign panel to see which looked best, citizens began to filter into the main street office to offer their opinion. Before long, Louise Heric, the Main Street coordinator, found she had an unofficial contest on her hands: She logged the votes for colours 1, 2, and 3 and the comments offered by dozens of concerned bystanders. To Heric's delight, the citizenry chose number 3, a colour with a long tradition in Fort Macleod. So did the owners. As Heric concluded, "They all knew what looked right for Fort Macleod."

And how is Gravelbourg doing? Pretty good, all things considered. A number of locally-relevant businesses have opened, including an expanded farm vacation/B&B network and an implement dealership. Best of all, money was raised to rebuild the college. The physical face of the town is beginning to reflect the town's brighter outlook on the future. Expectations are realistic for a town of 1300: Global forces have put a cramp on some of the best-laid plans for Gravelbourg—you can't make money growing wheat nowadays—but the town is not quite so close to the economic precipice. The Main Street legacy has been a widely accepted set of values and objectives for downtown. With these, the citizens know they can take control and make the changes necessary to maximize their town's future prospects.

Editor's Update

Did Main Street Revitalization Save the Small Towns?

Main Street programs across Canada helped to conserve heritage resources and made many small towns more attractive by investing in urban infrastructure, but they did not stanch the general trend of population loss from rural to urban areas. Gravelbourg declined to 1187 people by the 2001 census. Fort Macleod's website says it is a town of "over 3000." Of the three communities profiled by Fulton, only Seaforth appears to have grown: reaching 2692 by 2001. Many small towns continue to struggle to retain local businesses and to keep youth from moving away to find work.

The Old/New Neighbours: Breaking Ground in Collaborative Land Use Planning between First Nations and Local Governments

Kasia Tota

2003 Plan Canada 43(4): 31–3

Land, the source of many cultural and economic values, is the foundation of any self-governing society. What we take from the land, what we put on it, how we delineate lines of ownership and responsibility all express our particular worldview, our strategy to thrive in a particular place. If we want to understand land use planning in Canada, we must understand British and French cultures and their ideas of land ownership. If we want to understand the changing nature of land use planning in Canada, we must also understand the source of Aboriginal rights and the nature of Aboriginal title to land. Increasingly, we may need to be on a first-name basis with the chief and councillors of our neighbouring First Nations.

Uneasy Relations

We may get puzzled, perhaps even bewildered, when the Mohawk People of Kanesatake turn a "simple" expansion of a golf course into a standoff, when the Peoples of Six Nations block a municipal sewer expansion across the bed of the Grand River, when the Oujé-Bougamou in Quebec refuse to relocate quietly for the eighth time but instead declare jurisdiction over their territory and demand a traditional Cree village on the site. We share the territory but may not share values and a common version of the history of the land.

When a neighbouring First Nation decides to invest its land claim settlement monies in a new residential community just outside the municipal growth boundary, a big-box commercial mall minutes outside the fragile historic downtown, or in converting a surplus parcel of federal land in the centre of the city into a reserve, as land use planners we may face some interesting questions. We have a limited power to interfere, yet some proposals can affect municipal long-range plans, open space, servicing and tax revenue (Figure 13.5). We may wholeheartedly applaud the recent advancement of Aboriginal rights in Canada. We would like to support Aboriginal self-government and the growth and development of First Nation communities, yet we also hope that

Figure 13.5

Early settlements, like the Habitation at Part Royal in Nova Scotia, revealed uneasy relationships between newcomers and First Nations Communities.

the empowerment of First Nation communities will coincide with a governance of land that transcends isolation, distrust, potential conflict, and further ecological destruction. Recent developments suggest that this may indeed prove possible.

Separate Jurisdictions

Control over land use is of central interest to both local and First Nations governments, yet the two, until now, largely operated under separate legal frameworks: While section 92(8) of *Constitution Act* of 1985 delegates municipalities as statutory creatures of the province, s.91(24) identifies "Indians and lands reserved for the Indians" as exclusive federal jurisdiction. This legal separation—compounded by different governance systems, electoral cycles, priorities, access to resources, and geographical separation—partially explains the lack of formal relations between local governments and First Nations.

We must also remember that it has been at least 30 years since Aboriginal communities began to forcefully assert greater self-governing powers. Why has it taken us this long to notice our neighbours? Changes generated through land claims and modern treaty agreements increasingly affect densely populated urban areas, creating uncertainty and highlighting historical tensions. As communities grow and interact, they discover that they have common interests related to the health of regional ecological systems, the regional economy, and the quality of life of their citizens.

As part of a recent research project, I searched for models of collaborative agreements and processes of resolving potential land use conflicts between local governments and neighbouring First Nations. I looked at the local context, the process of developing specific agreements, challenges, opportunities, and lessons that local officials in Canada can learn from the experience of others. Some of the major findings follow.

On the Same Land: Learning from Other Places

In 1998, the Centre for Municipal Aboriginal Relations in Ottawa conducted a survey of agreements between First Nations, Aboriginal organizations, and local governments in Canada. The study demonstrated that a wide range of relationships is developing. This included service agreements, political accords and protocols, economic development partnerships, and efforts to facilitate urban Aboriginal involvement in municipal affairs.[25] While western provinces are leading the way, municipalities in other parts of the country often have agreements with more than one First Nation partner. Forty-eight municipal governments had economic development initiatives or partnerships with 96 First Nations or Aboriginal organizations. This suggests that, despite the lack of a clear mandate from higher levels of government and a fragmented and highly complex legal framework, local communities are finding a way to work together to resolve local issues.

One example of a collaborative arrangement is the Grand River Notification Agreement, signed between the Six Nations of the Grand River, the Mississaugas of the New Credit, the Grand River Conservation Authority, four municipal governments in Brant and Haldimand-Norfolk, the Province of Ontario, and the federal government. This relatively simple and legally nonbinding agreement commits the parties to exchange information on developments and land transfers within the Lower Grand River watershed.

The agreement builds on the long tradition of watershed planning in the region to include all parties in a seamless regional flow of information. Regular meetings between representatives of all the parties provide a forum to discuss common concerns and resolve issues before they have a chance to escalate. While this does not resolve outstanding land claims, the ongoing involvement of senior levels of government ensures that political pressure to resolve land claims is not diffused. The agreement provides First Nations with necessary information to react in a timely manner on proposals and land transfers that may affect their long-term interests. Municipalities also benefit from improved communication and smoother project implementation. The relatively modest agreement represents three years of formal and informal meetings and painstaking negotiations.[26]

Common Interest

Alongside the benefits of establishing regional mechanisms of collaboration, come significant barriers, such as the length of the process, required time and resources, access to negotiation skills, and unease with the potential of losing independence or current privilege. In most cases, either conflict or common interest must be sufficiently potent to warrant the initial engagement. Parties must appreciate that legal remedies are either insufficient or too risky, or that common goals can only be achieved jointly.

Understanding local history (particularly regarding settlement, government policy, and First Nation loss of land) is essential in initiating discussions. The first meetings may benefit from the guidance of a neutral facilitator. Once historic relations are understood and properly acknowledged, the parties can proceed. Collaboration may be facilitated, but cannot be forced or manufactured.

The legal basis of rights, authority, and jurisdiction are vital to structuring intergovernmental and institutional relations. Collaboration cannot commence without acknowledging the bases of Aboriginal self-government and local government jurisdiction. Furthermore, this understanding must recognize the values and rights of various communities while bridging the differences. Initial memoranda of understanding that set aside the question of authority and jurisdiction and establish the framework of interaction can formalize the process.

Reciprocity is implicit in collaborative agreements. Both parties give up something, yet gain in the exchange. This simple principle, the basis of all negotiations, is the most difficult to implement. It is all too easy to exaggerate the threat represented by the other side, and too easy to forget their vulnerability. The challenge is to move parties beyond the stalemate of narrow self-interest, to increase the level of trust.

Building relationships is critical to collaborative processes. In some cases, that may mean months or even years of informal meetings to bring political leaders, technical staff, and members of the public together. Once both sides can appreciate each other's culture and issues, the ground is prepared for formal negotiations, yet the process cannot be rushed. Sustaining collaborative processes requires entrenching new networks in institutional culture.

Local Approach

Communities need local approaches to resolving potential land use conflicts. Local geography will often dictate the nature of the concerns, and local culture the resolutions at hand. First Nations and local governments need the opportunity to determine how they want to interact. As a respondent said:

> We can develop all kinds of agreements, plans and regulation and we can point to court cases that are in our favour, but in the end we all live together here and we need to be able to live as good neighbours and respect each other and I think that if we do that this will be a better place to live.

Negotiations between First Nations and local governments can express commitment to the ideal of local governance, harmony between neighbouring communities, and quality of life in our communities.

Agreements are meaningful only if they are respected and implemented. Despite the careful wording and the extensive involvement of legal staff in crafting agreements, some agreements have no clauses related to breach of contract. Instead, they refer to "good faith commitment," "spirit of cooperation," "mutual benefits," "sustainable development," and mutual intentions to pursue "lasting relationships." Despite the soft language, the agreements are rarely breached because they build on a solid ground of trust and the need for cooperation. It may not be necessary, or even desirable, to make cooperative agreements into legally binding documents. Perhaps, here the First Nation dual ethic of sharing and respectful noninterference finds expression. In the end, well-negotiated collaborative agreements are not about creating more reasons to sue, but rather about developing trust and building strong communities.

The Planner's Job

We find a lot of flexibility inherent in the way agreements between First Nations and local governments are developed, from the issues addressed to the intensity of engagement. Interaction may vary from frequent to rare; structured or casual; limited to notification and consultation or involving joint planning and management. Agreements must be renewed periodically to reflect changing relationships and relevancy.

As planners, we may not be able to drive the process of developing political accords between local governments and First Nation communities. This is clearly the job of political representatives. But we can become informed about Aboriginal land issues in our communities, and be vigilant about identifying opportunities for dialogue and collaboration on important regional issues. If approached as an opportunity to break through long-entrenched patterns of prejudice and isolation, the planning process can be creative and transformative. Better relations with our neighbours will expand our notion of "community" and improve our capacity to make good places. The full potential of regional collaboration between First Nations and local governments is still to be realized.

Principles for Successful Community Planning in Northern Communities

Donald Aubrey

1999 Plan Canada 39(3): 12–5

Planning in northern Aboriginal Canadian communities still faces many of the challenges it did a decade ago, despite the political, social, and economic development taking place. Some of these issues—such as small communities with barriers to expansion, substandard and overcrowded housing, limited private-sector housing and employment—are systemic in nature and beyond the scope of planning alone to resolve. Yet, as Jackie Wolfe argued, a more holistic perspective can deal with many of the interconnected challenges of community development by means of a distinctive planning approach in which community priorities predominate.[27] This community-based approach, which pays as much attention to the environment and process of planning and capacity building as it does to attaining community goals, is especially applicable to northern communities and underlies the principles described here. Before discussing these principles in detail, however, this paper describes the context in which community planning is practised in the Western Arctic.

The Northern Context

In an area of Canada where spending by federal and territorial governments remains the mainstay of the economy, community planning is primarily a responsibility of the territorial government, exercised through the regional offices of the Department of

Figure 13.6

Small communities in the north face different issues than those in the south.

Municipal and Community Affairs. The regional offices provide a free collective subdivision development service (engineering, municipal administration, planning, subdivision design, and capital development) to small communities that do not have the resources to provide these services independently due to their minimal tax base.

Planning legislation is basic and geared toward ensuring that each community has a zoning bylaw and an approved land use or community plan to guide and control local development. Such planning meets the needs of most settlements, where the rate of expansion is generally slow and on the periphery of the community (Figure 13.6). Commercial development is significant only in the larger tax-based communities with populations exceeding 3500. As a result, one planner often manages the planning and development needs of a region comprising six or seven small communities.

These development needs, however, are a multidisciplinary mix that includes not only planning but also subdivision design and summertime lot development, as well as workshops for community councillors and hamlet staff on all aspects of the community planning and development process. The latter function is particularly important in helping empower community councils by making them more knowledgeable in and responsible for the key development decisions that affect their community.

Of the wide array of technical services organized by community planners (land use planning, subdivision planning and design, capital program management, development and site plan review, as well as training and mentoring), many activities are of necessity delegated to consultants who work under the direction of the planner or community council in helping move proposals forward in a timely fashion.

The land tenure pattern varies from community to community. Except for tax-based communities, which have a significant amount of fee-simple land and a developed market for the sale and purchase of property, much of the land within small community boundaries is leased or purchased from the territorial and federal governments. Some private land exists in these communities, but the market is still extremely small, consisting for the most part of people who work for the territorial and municipal governments or who have moved to the community on contract.

All community planning in northern Aboriginal communities has to start with the basic principle that the people best able to design or plan an environment or a community are the people who will use that environment or inhabit that community.[28] Of course, this principle is as applicable to any community in the south as in the north. But beyond that, other principles apply more specifically to Aboriginal communities: These lessons may prevent grief or frustration when a planner shares skills in preparing a community land use plan or subdivision design "north of 60."

Ten Principles for Practice

Principle 1. Recognize and respect the Aboriginal context from the start: "This is our land as long as the sun shines and the river flows."[29] Many Aboriginal groups and bands believe that others working for the federal or territorial government are part of a process that has taken control of their land. A land use planning process therefore offers an opportunity for people to reassert control over their space and remind all concerned that First Nations communities have the final say in what happens on their traditional landscape. Great reverence is still attached to treaty commitments and the "Honour of the Crown." The feeling of many Aboriginal leaders that these have been either broken or not respected by governments has hardened their resolve to press forward with land claims. A land use plan thus becomes a significant political event. Any planner contemplating work in a northern community would therefore be wise to do some basic research on political context. Is the community in a region where a treaty was signed? Are land claims settled or still being negotiated? What other policies affect the leasing and control of land within the community?

Principle 2. Patience, understanding, and a positive interest in the local culture/situation are as essential as listening skills. In combination, these elements form a crucial yardstick by which to measure whether what the community said has been sensitively interpreted by the community planner. Did the planner listen, for example, when the community said that it wanted more housing not at the back of the settlement but beside the river, where the cool summer breeze keeps the bugs down and householders can watch their boats?

The relationship between people, water, and land is still crucial in the north where the prices of imported foods can be very high. The summer fishing season provides human sustenance and feed for dogs; in winter, easy access to the land via skidoo is equally important for hunting caribou and for travelling. The planner will need patience, because it takes time to get to know the community and meet the people who will help interpret significant and sensitive issues. Allow plenty of time to socialize when visiting a community for the first time—people want to get to know newcomers. Patiently deal with criticism of past failures or unfulfilled promises of the planning process. A community that depends on government largesse and has seen promises evaporate may find it difficult to renew their faith in what planning has to offer.

Principle 3. Help people realize the potential of long-term vision as a catalyst for pragmatic action. Vision has a potent quality. Fundamentally oral, it speaks of where the community has come from and where it would like to go in the future. It can embrace the new while staying connected to the roots of the past.

What do residents want their community to look like 15 years from now? A community plan can help unfold that vision and give life to goals. It can also help the community believe in its own power to bring about such change and, in so doing, shape development according to local ideals. A successful community plan can thus be a symbol of renewal, hope, and, above all, determination to ensure that development takes place on the community's terms and according to the community's values as articulated by elders, parents, and leaders.

Principle 4. Maximize participation by involving the whole community. Every planner knows that the best plans are the ones in which the whole community is involved. And yet for planners working in the south, the idea of involving the whole community in anything more comprehensive than a neighbourhood plan is daunting. Not so in the north: Because many communities have fewer than 100 households, involving each one is a real possibility. Doing so requires creativity, of course: workshops, one-on-one meetings with Elders, and formal presentations. Involving children, especially teenagers who can take on the concept of planning their own community as a school project, will spread the word. An active and inclusive approach is generally much more amenable to the northern Aboriginal culture than a conventional technocratic approach in which a consultant advises a council or select group as it overlooks what ordinary people really want to see in their community in the future. It is also great fun.

Principle 5. Timing is everything when it comes to starting a community plan in a northern community. While a small community has intrinsic advantages in planning, it can also have disadvantages. Internal problems, divisive community issues, and competing political priorities can make it difficult, if not impossible, to discuss a land use plan in any detail. Many of these problems become magnified in the north because of the small size of settlements, the oral character of Aboriginal politics, and the perpetual conflict between immediate social issues and long-term development imperatives.

Often the best land use planning processes can start when the community requests assistance and the band council wants help, not when a government planner decides or finds it convenient to start. Sometimes, planners do not have a choice but need to work hard on selling the community on the idea of a land use plan by talking to the mayor and councillors informally. Even then, if the council is too busy with other meetings, and significant leaders or elders are away from the community on business, finding space in the community's calendar for serious discussions on a land use plan may prove elusive.

Principle 6. Be willing to let go. Try not to control the outcome. It is not uncommon for planners to start working on a land use plan with a "control" mentality, based on a fixed (and often tight) budget, the imperative to finish as soon as possible, and the need to simplify and rationalize differences over land use and space. This mentality is magnified when the community is not the other side of town but rather an hour and a half away by air or three hours away by road. And by focusing more on the outcomes than the process, the planner can easily overlook the need to slow down to allow local residents the freedom to come up with their own suggestions, solutions, and goals. For people whose surroundings have been developed and to a great extent controlled by the imperatives of outsiders, the opportunity to consider and directly influence where and when development takes place can be intoxicating. Thus, planners need to prepare for surprises: Residents may want to relocate a particular use. That's fine. It's the community's plan after all, and if that is the local consensus, then it becomes a future development objective written into the land use plan. How to fund the proposal is a debate for another day.

Principle 7. Informal land use planning in a poster format is something that everyone can understand. In the 1960s, town planning in the Northwest Territories resulted in thick book-style reports by consultants. Later, in the 1980s, an imaginative period produced photo-illustrated book plans. By the late 1990s, the format for plans for small communities evolved into colourful display posters, with existing and proposed land uses along with aerial photographs on one side, and on the other side the texts of land use policies combined with photographs of significant landmarks. Young and old like this visual style: They can see what the community is like and better appreciate where (for example) new housing may be developed in the future.

Principle 8. Life in the north has a tempo set by nature. This can make any significant planning activity a seasonal process with windows of opportunity to get things done.

Typically, December and August are holiday months to avoid, and early fall is moose-hunting season. For a few less predictable months in winter, a scheduled meeting might have to be postponed for a week or two because the caribou are near the community. All this can make the periods between September and November, and January and May, the time to get things done and move ahead. Once the snow has vanished, however, and the ice on rivers and lakes has melted away, the thoughts of the community turn to the land and water, and people can become less keen to attend evening community meetings to engage in extensive debate on serious long-term issues. Such seasonal delays are best viewed philosophically.

Principle 9. Do not study the community too much: "Experts" and curious outsiders have studied some of them repeatedly, leaving residents tired of surveys the results of which they rarely hear. Aboriginal leaders often face a fundamental conflict when they have to make big decisions using the results of scientific inquiry (made up of theory, survey data, and analysis), while respecting traditional knowledge based on the collective experience and wisdom of their peers and elders.

Review what is known in advance about the community to understand what has happened in recent times and what surveys, if any, have been done. On arriving in the community, avoid making premature judgments or expressing strong opinions; at the same time, resist pressures to produce quick results. Once the community understands that the planner is there to help them develop "their" ideas, the planning process will stand a better chance of success in producing a local product—one that instills pride and self-esteem amongst its authors.

Principle 10. Prepare for suspicion and cynicism: The community has seen many experts come and go. Gaining the trust of any small Aboriginal community takes time and commitment. They know they cannot afford to have a planner and engineer on staff and must depend on outside expertise to deal with the technology of growth and development. But this dependency can make people uneasy: They know that job turnover is high for professionals in the North. The reality is that it requires a certain amount of luck and determination for a planner to see a land use plan through from start to finish. The golden rule, therefore, is that planners should never promise more than they can personally deliver. Community leaders are savvy politically and know that the expenditure of any new significant development in a plan will require lobbying. What they will expect from the planner is an honest explanation of the technical advantages and disadvantages of certain options: straight answers to empower them to make the final decision themselves.

Planning with Communities

These principles may seem confusing to some planners as they are less about the technical aspects of planning than about an empathetic and philosophical approach to working with rural communities in a distant and remote part of Canada. They have less to do with planning methodology than with aspects of dealing with people from different cultures. The quality of these relationships can, however, make for a happy and productive experience for both planner and community. It can also contribute to the planner's reputation, as an interpreter of Aboriginal community needs: as a friend who understands and is remembered long after the plan he or she helped shape has been completed.

Planners and community development specialists, whether working for territorial or regional governments or as planning consultants in the private sector, will be needed for years to come in the North especially with the growth spurt in the NWT from the diamond mine boom. They should not, therefore, be put off by thinking that they are in for tough and frustrating working conditions in an unstable political environment. The work can involve a lot of fun, unforgettable landscapes, dynamic people and durable relationships, all of which can open up new vistas and opportunities that the planner will never regret.

1. Look at the demographic changes (in census records through Statistics Canada) in two rural communities in your province or territory over the last century. Pick one that is within 50 kilometres of a major urban centre, and one that is over 70 kilometres from a major urban centre. Describe and explain the trends you find.

2. What are the special issues and challenges that remote and northern communities face, and how can planning help to address them?

3. Investigate to determine what kinds of government programs and financial assistance are currently available for small towns and rural communities that want to use their heritage to enhance local economic development.

4. How significant is the threat of agricultural land loss in the parts of Canada that have the best soil for farming? What strategies can local governments use to try to protect farmland for future agricultural use? What tools may be effective?

5. What are the arguments for and against government playing a role in planning and building new towns for resource industries in remote regions of Canada?

6. Look at the legacy of the Main Street program(s) in your region. What effect did such programs have on the towns or villages? Evaluate successes (or failures) in achieving goals.

7. What are the key land use conflicts in the urban-rural fringe, and how do they affect the rural economy?

8. Contrast population trends among Aboriginal and northern communities with those in rural and remote areas farther south in Canada.

Reference Notes

1. Rodd, RS (1976) The crisis of agricultural land in the Ontario countryside. *Plan Canada* 16(3–4): 160–70.

   Mah, P (1992) The crisis in rural Manitoba. *Plan Canada* 32(6): 38.

   Qadeer, M (1979) Issues and approaches of rural community planning in Canada. *Plan Canada* 19(2): 106–21.

2. Adams, T (1917) *Rural Planning and Development: A Study of Rural Conditions and Problems in Canada*. Ottawa: Commission of Conservation.

3. Hofman, N (2001) Urban consumption of agricultural land. *Rural and Small Town Canada Analysis Bulletin* 3(2). Statistics Canada, http://www.crrf.ca/news/news0502.pdf (accessed 14 April 2006).

4. Ibid.

5. Caldwell, W & M Toombs (1999) Rural planning, the community and large livestock facilities: A cross-Canada survey. *Plan Canada* 39(5): 27–9.

6. Bryant, CR & LH Russwurm (1979) The impact of non-farm development on agriculture: A synthesis. *Plan Canada* 19(2): 122–39.

   Buchan, G (2004) The costs and impacts of rural sprawl: Not all sprawl is equal. *Plan Canada* 44(3): 38–40.

   Forbes, A & G Forrest (1997) Case study: Frustrated in Fredericton. *Plan Canada* 37(5): 34–41.

7. McCann, L (1978) The changing internal structure of Canadian resource towns. *Plan Canada* 18(1): 46–59.

8. Gill, A & W Shera (1990) Using social criteria to guide the design of a new community: The case of Tumbler Ridge. *Plan Canada* 30(1): 33–42.

   Richardson, N (1963) A tale of two cities. *Plan Canada* 4(3): 111–25.

   Tunbridge, J (2003) Selling places: Heritage tourism and marketing your town. *Plan Canada* 43(2): 17–9.

9. Reid, D (1995) Tourism: Savior or false hope for the rural economy? *Plan Canada* 35(3): 22–6.

10. Hodge, G (1981) The citification of small towns: A challenge to planning. *Plan Canada* 21(2): 43–7.

11. Bollman, R (2000) Rural and small town Canada: An overview. Statistics Canada, http://www.statcan.ca/english/freepub/21F0018XIE/21F0018XIE2001001.htm (Part 1), and http://www.statcan.ca/english/freepub/21F0018XIE/21F0018XIb.htm (Part 2) (accessed 14 April 2006).

12. Richardson, N (1989) Land use planning and sustainable development in the Canadian north. *Plan Canada* 29(2): 56–62.

13. Winter, W (1999) Community planning in Nunavut: The creation of Nunavut. *Plan Canada* 39(3): 19–21.

14. Wolfe, J (1989) Approaches to planning in native Canadian communities: A review and commentary on settlement problems and the effectiveness of planning practice. *Plan Canada* 29(2): 66.

15. Ibbitson, J (2005) Saving rural Canada: It takes a town. *Globe and Mail*, 10 August: A13.

16. Lotz, J (1977) *Understanding Canada*. Toronto: NC Press Limited.

17. Alberta Agriculture, Food and Rural Development (2002) *Loss and Fragmentation of Farmland*, http://www1.agric.gov.ab.ca/$department/deptdocs.nsf/all/psc4786 (accessed 14 April 2006).

    GTA Federations of Agriculture Project Management Committee (1999) *Greater Toronto Area – Agricultural Economic Impact Study*. Walton & Hunter Planning Associates, http://www.greater.toronto.on.ca/new-sectors/agribus/pdfs/intro1.pdf (accessed 14 April 2006).

18. Rambeau, S & K Todd (2000) *Census Metropolitan Area and Census Agglomeration Influenced Zones (MIZ) with Census Data*. Ottawa: Statistics Canada.

19. United Nations Environment Programme (UNEP) (2002) *North America's Environment*. Nairobi: United Nations.

20. Ibid.

21. Pim, L & JA Ornoy (2002) *A Smart Future for Ontario: How to Protect Nature and Curb Urban Sprawl in Your Community*. Toronto: Federation of Ontario Naturalists.

Richmond, City of (2003) *Agricultural Viability Strategy Report*, http://www.richmond.ca/__shared/assets/viability_strategy6314.pdf (accessed 14 April 2006).

22. Lower Mainland Regional Planning Board (1963) *Chance and Challenge: A Concept and Plan for the Development of the Lower Mainland Region*. New Westminster: 6.

23. Greater Vancouver Regional District (GVRD) (1999) *Livable Region Strategic Plan*, http://www.gvrd.bc.ca/growth/lrsp.htm (accessed 14 April 2006).

24. Greater Vancouver Regional District (GVRD) (2004) *The Sustainable Region Initiative: Turning Ideas into Action*, http://www.gvrd.bc.ca/sustainability/ (accessed 14 April 2006).

25. Larbi, P (1999) *A National Portrait of Municipal–Aboriginal Relations in Canada*. Ottawa: Centre for Municipal Aboriginal Relations.

26. The agreement did not prevent a Six Nation protest in 2006 to oppose the development of Douglas Creek subdivision on a parcel of land in Caledonia. In May 2006, the Ontario government appointed David Peterson, former Ontario premier, to help resolve the dispute (*The Hamilton Spectator*, 1 May 2006).

27. Wolfe, J (1989) Op. cit.: 63–79.

28. Simon, JC (1984) *A Culturally Sensitive Approach to Planning and Design with Native Canadians*. Ottawa: Canada Mortgage and Housing Corporation.

29. Fumoleau, R (1973) *As Long as This Land Shall Last: A History of Treaty 8 and Treaty 11, 1870–1939*. Toronto: McClelland and Stewart: 97.

Chapter Fourteen

Tools of the Trade

14

Why We Regulate Land

Jill Grant

In its early years, Canadian town planning focused primarily on the intent of government to shape its future; however, by the 1920s, the profession had committed to zoning as a tool of the trade. While plans might reflect visionary thinking, zoning offered practical mechanisms to determine land use.

Land use or zoning bylaws set the stage for contemporary planning activities. In Canadian provinces, municipalities enact such documents as a way of implementing the intent of policies set out in the plan. Planning and zoning are inextricably linked: concept and action; theory and practice. With municipalities in many regions depending largely on property taxes for their revenues, managing the use and value of land has become a significant focus of local government. Zoning is a key technique in that process.

Under the division of responsibilities between levels of government in Canada, the federal government regulates trade, defence, access to minerals and resources, and coastal waterways. Some areas of jurisdiction, like the environment and transportation, involve shared federal and provincial mandates. As sovereign governments, provinces have jurisdiction over health and education, and own the principal responsibility for regulating land use and property. The territories, by contrast, are not sovereign and have only the powers delegated to them by Parliament.

Municipalities are "creatures of the provinces": They are created as governmental units by provincial laws that define their powers and enable them to make policies and regulations. While they enjoy a measure of independence in adopting plans and approving bylaws, they remain subject to oversight by the provincial government. When the provinces identify an interest in amalgamating municipalities or creating a second tier of regional government over municipalities, they have the power to do so.

The basis of policy and regulations that govern land reflect the concept implicit in the Canadian legal system that the Crown holds the land. Therefore, private property rights are limited by the state in the public interest. Because the use of land potentially affects health, safety, and public order, the state asserts its right to regulate and control activities that occur on it. While private property rights are guaranteed by the constitution in the US, no such protection obtains in Canada.

Each province has planning legislation or municipal acts that identify what municipalities can control. The legislation is usually "enabling": It permits municipalities to adopt plans and sets out the conditions under which they may do so. Most commonly, the planning legislation has allowed

Figure 14.1

Suburban neighbourhoods often reflect rules that homes be set at least a minimum distance from the city's right-of-way to ensure a spacious feeling.

local governments to set minimums or maximums for defined conditions. For instance, it may permit municipalities to determine a value for the minimum distance a building must be set back from the public right of way, or to establish maximum allowable densities in multifamily housing districts (Figure 14.1). In theory, provinces could create quite diverse practices in regulating land; however, in practice, we see that conditions governing the development of land are generally quite similar across the country.

The Structure of Regulation

Under the planning systems generally operating in Canada, the local plan—which, depending on the jurisdiction, may be known as a community plan, an official plan, or a municipal planning strategy—sets out the vision of municipal government. Plans establish a land use planning framework for decision making. Policies in the plan usually cover such topics as housing, transportation, industrial development, and infrastructure. Some cities establish special plans to deal with thematic areas (like transportation) or with local districts or neighbourhoods. In recent years, cities have been writing special plans that reveal their new interest in such themes as culture and immigration.

The land use regulations or zoning bylaws establish specific policies to regulate districts and thus implement the more general policies in the plans. Each zone sets out the uses and activities permitted in the zone. Most communities have zones designated for residential, commercial, industrial, institutional, and mixed uses, for instance. Some uses are tightly regulated, like the adult entertainment activities David Farley describes in his paper on "erogenous zones" in this chapter.

The fundamental premise underlying zoning is that municipalities should separate particular kinds of land uses from each other. While industrial, commercial, and high-density residential uses are attractive to local governments for the tax revenue and economic spinoff they generate, residential uses are typically seen as the most highly valued to protect from "negative externalities." Thus, zoning operates to keep residential districts apart from other uses. In recent years, critics of zoning have taken to calling zoning that strictly segregates uses "Euclidean," after an early American court case that established the legality of zoning in Euclid, Ohio.

How Do Regulations Change?

Planning legislation generally provides for a process for altering plans, zones, and other agreements. In most provinces, plans are reviewed on a regular basis to ensure that they remain current and appropriate. The process of amending a plan typically involves extensive public consultation and discussion. Plans are changed by votes of municipal council, subject to the approval of provincial authorities.

Members of the community—including land developers—may apply to change the zoning if the alteration furthers the intent of the plan. Areas that municipalities designate as "holding," for instance, are typically intended to become another use when circumstances warrant. Zoning changes are often among the most contentious land use disputes.

Maps and schedules indicate where the zones apply. In most cases the bylaws indicate that the existing uses are the permitted ones. For this reason, critics suggest that zoning reinforces the status quo. In some cases, though, existing uses that are no longer desired may have begun before the zoning was applied: In these instances, the uses are called "nonconforming" but are permitted under a "grandfathering" provision.

Robert Lehman's urban fable in this chapter illustrates the challenge of accommodating a mix of uses in residential zones, given the limiting character of zoning. Many Canadian cities permit home businesses, small daycares, and residential group homes in residential areas, but such uses sometimes generate controversy and even NIMBYism.[1] Zoning reflects our cultural values, as well as concerns about property values.[2] Practice shows that people want to keep residential neighbourhoods protected and "safe" and hence resist permitting other uses—and even people who may be different in some ways from the residents—in the neighbourhood.[3]

To regulate creating lots and issuing building permits, municipalities apply subdivision regulations. These specify the expectations that must be met by development: separation distances, lot coverage maximums, parking requirements, and so on. Along with national building codes and any provincial standards that may apply, the subdivision regulations influence the built form that development takes.

Plans may identify some areas in particular zones as appropriate candidates for special negotiated conditions. Areas designated for comprehensive development districts or planned unit developments may be governed by development agreements negotiated between a municipal government and a developer. While elements of the permitted uses in these zones are set by the plan intent and zoning conditions, the rules of subdivision often do not apply. Hence, the development agreement offers planners design flexibility. By operating outside the formally stipulated rules, planners have found strategies for applying alternative standards that implement new urbanism principles, such as narrower roads.

Critics like Jane Jacobs began challenging zoning as inflexible, rigid, and inappropriate in the 1960s. By the 1980s, planners had renewed interest in the quality of the built environment. They recognized that, in many urban areas, design is as important as use. Through the 1980s, municipalities often changed their zoning codes to permit and even encourage mixed use in central districts. Urban design and heritage conservation guidelines became increasingly popular tools for shaping more sympathetic building forms and patterns.

Some communities also began to consider alternative standards that would allow narrower streets, smaller setbacks from the street, back alleys, or lanes. In its 1995 *Sustainable Suburbs Study*, for instance, the City of Calgary promoted municipal regulations

Chapter 14 / Tools of the Trade

that might transform the character of suburban development. The City of Toronto began to discuss "reurbanization."[4] The national and provincial governments advocated alternative standards by sponsoring design competitions and publishing reports on new community forms.[5] Recognizing that standard zoning conventions induced conformity and promoted sprawl, planners began to argue for greater flexibility in zoning.[6] Andrea Gabor and Frank Lewinburg, among the most ardent advocates of a new approach to zoning, argue in this chapter that zoning practices have to change to permit more attractive and sustainable urban environments.

In addition to government criteria that shape urban form, developers increasingly apply design-based and use-related codes, covenants, or restrictions to the properties that they market. Such codes remain tied to property deeds through time and cannot easily be changed by residents or communities.[7] Early covenants sometimes tried to exclude particular ethnic or religious groups from neighbourhoods: They are now illegal. Contemporary restrictions more typically limit design choices (like prescribing paint palettes), yard activities (no hanging laundry to dry or working on the car in the driveway, for instance), or even pet sizes and numbers. Such codes arguably have greater power to induce conformity than do zoning regulations.

With the ascendance of new urbanism and smart growth as planning paradigms, planners are taking a strong interest in form-based codes (Figure 14.2). These represent a kind of fusion between zoning codes and urban design guidelines. They may, for instance, mandate a vertical mix of uses in town centre districts while also managing the height and appearance of buildings. Where, for example, commercial zoning might indicate a maximum building height, a form-based code might specify both a

---

Figure 14.2

JILL GRANT

New urbanism communities more commonly employ "build to" lines or codes, requiring that structures be placed no more than a set distance from the public right-of-way to create a strong urban character.

minimum and a maximum height to establish a design identity along a street. Several Canadian municipalities are considering form-based codes to shape the public realm.

Practice shows that planners and designers are continually looking for new techniques to achieve their objectives within the current regulations. In the final paper in this chapter, Avi Friedman describes his innovative approach to promoting affordable housing. The Grow Home, a narrow-front rowhouse, has proven wildly successful in the starter home market. The model led the movement to encourage municipalities to reduce their standards for lot frontage.

Today, we find that townhouse development is one of the fastest growing segments of the Canadian housing market. The popularity of the townhouse form is contributing to increasing suburban densities in many parts of the country and enhancing the opportunity of households to purchase a home. Narrow rowhouses are used extensively in planned unit developments with high design standards and attractive private amenities.

Although regulations and policies may resist change in the short run, we see that, through time, the techniques favoured in planning do respond to new needs and opportunities. The continued debate about the tools used to manage land and land use is good for practice.

Erogenous Zones and Public Policy

David Farley

1990 Plan Canada 30(2): 19–21

At the beginning of the 1960s, American cities were overwhelmed by federal redevelopment funds to replace economically depressed neighbourhoods and their residents. Scollay Square in Boston, a sailor's delight, had been demolished for the new city hall and government centre. The West End next door was already bulldozed for new apartments, and Jane Jacobs was writing her book on the death and life of American cities. Across America, inner-city zones were razed in the name of civic improvement. Montreal caught the redevelopment bug, and Mayor Drapeau, a righteous reformer at the time, knocked down most of Montreal's transvestite bars and some other interesting facilities to make space for Place des Arts.

By the late 1960s, wholesale demolition had gone out of fashion in the United States and Canada. In fact, it had become political suicide, and other means to control, if not stamp out, obscenity were needed. Detroit planners can take the credit for starting the crusade to control smut without the bulldozer. It was a bit of an accident. Detroit adopted a regulation in 1962 that identified certain uses such as bars, pawnshops, and flophouses as contributing, when concentrated, to a "skid row" effect, the sleazy look. Adult theatres, adult bookstores, and porn shops were added to the list in the mid-1960s. Deteriorating property values, higher crime rates, traffic congestion, and depressed neighbourhood conditions were the harmful effects identified when these uses were concentrated.

Here was a demonstration that government could regulate sex businesses within the confines of the first and fourteenth amendments to the American constitution, freedom of speech and equal protection, respectively. By sidestepping the morality of the services and products offered to the public and concentrating on the relationship between a series of uses, cities were able to control their location.

The method used in the ordinance was to force the dispersal of listed uses and to ban them from residential districts. No listed use was permitted within 1000 feet of any two others, and none were permitted within 500 feet of a residential zone. In 1976, the US

Supreme Court upheld the Detroit ordinance on the basis that protecting a community from the skid row effect was a legitimate function of zoning.[8] The standard was set, and this kind of ordinance can now be found from Santa Maria, California, to New York City.

Some cities, like Boston, chose to concentrate "adult uses" in one zone, denying them any other. Boston authorities believe that the advantage of a "combat zone," as it is called, is that a strict age restriction can apply to all uses inside the zone. The police can better control criminal activity, and the skid-row effect from the community's point of view, is diminished. Concentrated or dispersed as the uses may be, the underlying objectives remain the same.

On the skids as downtown Detroit was, one can sympathize with municipal efforts to disperse the dregs of activity in what was essentially a very large parking lot interspersed with poor black ghettos and rundown retail streets: not the kind of circumstances to attract head offices and shopping malls. What is harder to sympathize with is the hypocrisy and sanctimonious nature of the policy. Sex businesses do not flourish in rundown parts of the city because they appeal to the poor and the disadvantaged. Quite the contrary: Their economic outlook is bright for the reason that they attract clientele from all sectors of society. Their location close to the working population on downtown retail streets reflects demand.

Repugnant as these activities may be to some, the facilities are not necessarily dumps. Nor do they attract more traffic or criminals than other retail uses. Depressed neighbourhood conditions come from poverty and public indifference and from governments catering to special interests, not from the libido.

Canadian municipalities do not have the power to regulate morality through licensing or zoning. The constitutional argument is that, in regulating morality, the municipality (a provincially-created body) is legislating in the field of criminal law, which is outside its jurisdiction. Public policy is a strictly federal concern.

What the municipality can do is define types of massage parlours, for example, and set the terms and conditions under which they may operate. What the municipality cannot do is subject all or any of such businesses to such stringent conditions as to put them out of business. The power to regulate implies the continued existence of what is regulated.

A few excerpts from Vancouver's puritanical Licence Bylaw 4450 and its amendments,[9] a typical Canadian bylaw, illustrate how the city council defined the body rub and regulated it for ordinary, or YMCA, types and sexy types. On the body rub:

> "Body-rub" includes the manipulating, touching or stimulating, by any means, of a person's body or part thereof, but does not include medical, therapeutic or cosmetic massage treatment given by a person duly licensed or registered under any statute of the Province of British Columbia governing such activities other than the Vancouver Charter.

On where the body rub occurs:
All rooms used for body-rub, bodypainting or nude photography shall comply with the following conditions:

(a) shall not be less than 8 feet by 8 feet;

(b) shall not be equipped with any locking device on any door there to;

(c) other than a door providing entrance thereto, shall not have means by which any person may view the interior thereof;

(d) shall be equipped with lighting of at least 50 candle power which shall remain "on" when the door is closed.

On the masseuse or masseur:
No person carrying on the business of a body-rub parlour shall permit any person engaged in providing a bodyrub in the licensed premises to perform the same unless he is wearing clean, washable, non-transparent outer garments covering his

Figure 14.3

STEPHANIE BOHDANOW

Adult entertainment uses create the character of parts of Montreal, but they engender debates about appropriate zoning in many communities.

or her body between the neck and the top of the knee, the sleeves of which do not reach below the elbows.

Appellants challenged the validity of this bylaw in the courts on the grounds that the effect was to prohibit sexy massages; it was discriminatory; and it purported to regulate public and private morality. They lost. Sexy massages, like their YMCA counterparts, must take place in large, well-lit, and unlocked rooms by opaquely clothed, if not unbuttoned, attendants. This could be fun.

Montreal does not single out sex businesses as a special use. They are treated in zoning like other retail functions. Concentrated and scattered, they have gone largely unnoticed except by the crowds in attendance. The city has received complaints about signs, and community groups have complained about sex businesses locating next door to arcades full of minors. Debatable as these objections may seem, the city is now studying the possibility of control by zoning.

Monsieur Lave-Auto, 2009 rue Montgomery in Montreal, illustrates the kind of definitional and classification problems that effective zoning faces.

CARWASH Open 24 hours a day. Nude girls, cars supplied. Monsieur Lave Auto. *Montreal Gazette* Monday, 2 October 1989

Similarly, Lave-Auto Erotic, located in a commercial zone at the end of a quiet residential street in East End Montreal not only attracts cars, but the establishment provides a car for libidinous patrons who prefer to arrive by Metro. On ladies' day (escorted males only), the washers are well-built young men in rubber boots and an earring or two. The soap, the hot water, the rubber, the bloated dingdongs—it's all clearly entertainment, but the boys do an excellent job of washing the car, too. Fifty dollars for your basic exterior clean. Prices for work inside the vehicle are negotiated. Cars circulate around the block for "seconds." Not surprisingly, one can see some very clean cars in the vicinity. The main nuisance effect of this business on the community, besides the traffic, is the constant sloshing of water over cars. This district is not recommended to people with weak kidneys.

Sex businesses can be considered a special type of retailing or "adult use" by municipalities for the purpose of zoning regulation. These special types of retailing, however, require clear definitions and a system of classification. Ambiguity must be avoided. Once all types of massage parlours, XXX-rated movie theatres, strip bars, and jelly-wrestling emporia have been sorted out, the more difficult task of defining sexual activities and detailing the anatomical areas that might be observed by patrons must be tackled. The standard American ordinance, as exemplified in New York, offers definitions that are probably as good as any.

Specified Sexual Activities.

1. Human genitals in a state of sexual stimulation or arousal;
2. Acts of human masturbation, sexual intercourse, or sodomy;
3. Fondling or other erotic touching of human genitals, pubic region, buttock, or female breast.

Specified Anatomical Areas.

1. Less than completely and opaquely covered:

   (a) human genitals, pubic region;
   (b) buttock, and
   (c) female breast below a point immediately above the top of the areola; and,

2. Human male genitals in a discernibly turgid state, even if completely and opaquely covered.[10]

Obviously a Canadian ordinance would eliminate "less than completely and opaquely covered" and "below a point immediately above the top of the areola," wherever that is, and would have to say something about the vulva and the anus, which are so evident at any show nowadays.

William Toner identifies the weaknesses of this sort of specific approach.[11] "Administrative cost is high because of the case by case evaluation which the approach demands. Furthermore, the costs of adding new uses to the list and new standards to the process are excessive. Each new use and each new standard must be evaluated separately."[12] Enforcing compliance and identifying nonconforming uses is also a problem.

A classification of adult uses for the purpose of a zoning list will require constant updating as new sex businesses emerge. The erotic car wash in Montreal has been followed by a topless *dépanneur* in Laval. These are not "mixed uses" in the ordinary sense of the word. In practice, they could be called "inextricable uses" indicating the intricate and perplexing nature of the combination. Just when the rituals of community purification through regulation, so characteristic of our Canadian towns and cities, seemed to have the situation in hand, sex businesses have found new horizons for the industry.

Notwithstanding the difficulties, sex businesses may benefit from a policy with clear zoning guidelines for their location. Controversy will be lessened. And the advantage to planners is that they will not have to explain to the municipal council the seeming unending craving for titillation before doing something about it. Considering the popularity of these facilities, is it possible to imagine an approach that supports, even encourages, the industry? Would tolerance not be a better source for public policy than prudery?

A professional stance on the rightness or wrongness of lewd behaviour is, fortunately, not required. The effect of sex businesses, unique as they are, on other land uses and on people—the effect on the community—allows municipalities to control these activities like any other use in the zoning code. They can either be encouraged or muzzled. They cannot be eliminated. Provided the planner is able to classify, to define, and to be precise about each local enterprise, and provided the Canadian courts take a hands-on position to shape this basket of problems, zoning may be an effective tool for regulating erogenous zones.

The Case of the Erroneous Zone

Robert Lehman

1997 Plan Canada 37(4): 24–7

I was sitting with my feet on the desk and my brain in the drawer when she came in. She walked in the office without knocking and stood there, all six feet of her, looking down at me. My feet and my brain both went south. My hangover disappeared.

"I need some information and I need it fast. I'm willing to pay for it." That was music to my ears. I was only two years out of the planning department, and being paid for information still sounded too good to be true. But her next words washed over me like a bathtub of iced vodka. "My problem is zoning."

Now I hadn't been a planning consultant longer than a Las Vegas wedding ceremony, but I already knew that in this town the only question when you were dealing with zoning was how long the problem would last. I finally asked her to sit down. As she gradually folded herself into my 50-year-old red leather companion, I realized that I was staring straight into her eyes, which held me as tightly as a pair of size-five shoes on size-ten feet.

"So tell me more," I volunteered. Seems she wanted to run a small business out of her house, and a visit to city hall had convinced her that the red tape wasn't worth the trouble (Figure 14.4).

"This zoning seems counterproductive to me," she explained, "particularly in a free-market postindustrial society committed to maximizing choice and individual freedoms." Her baby blues winked on and off like semaphore flags.

"Uh, right," I replied, gathering my wits like a pile of dropped laundry. "Zoning is our touchstone, the one constant in a sea of change. Without zoning, planners have no base, no structure, and our communities no certainty."

Figure 14.4

JILL GRANT

Many Canadians run businesses out of their homes.

Her ship-launching face twisted into an attractive sneer. "Bull. You planners are, as Peter Hall says in *Cities of Tomorrow*, the 'handmaidens of capital.'" Our relationship was clearly progressing.

I leaned as close to my desk as I could, stared into those custom headlights, and growled, "If you mean that anyone with a stake in the community is served by planning controls, I couldn't agree with you more. Why invest, why buy a home, why live anywhere without some certainty that your neighbour won't open a mixed use, community-based, blood-boiling Quiches-R-Us outlet?"

Her eyebrows shot up faster than twin space shuttles. I leaned back as she reached into her purse. Out came a single sheet of paper, obviously torn from some two-bit pulp rag. "You know what Robert Fulford said, you out-of-date bureaucrat. He claimed that planners aren't visionaries but nay-sayers, telling us what we can't do, and robbing us of creative options."

"Robert Fulford would probably be the first to complain if his neighbour put on an addition and blocked his morning sunlight," I offered. "And not only that, one person's creativity is another's headache."

My head was starting to hurt again. Who made me God? Why should I have to defend the status quo? The day was turning into a goddamn public meeting!

I stood up and moved to the zoning schedule on my wall. Her eyes followed me like tin cans tied to a bumper. "Look," I said, in what I hoped was a conciliatory tone, "zoning is just one way of giving certainty. If you want change, you have to go through a process; that's the democratic way. It just makes sure everyone can get involved." Involvement is what I had been looking for ever since my third wife took off with a local architect.

All of a sudden, she was on her feet. "But you've taken it too far," she hissed. "What started as a reasonable limit on obnoxious uses has turned into the most conservative and retrograde planning control imaginable."

I moved closer. "Don't blame me," I said, falling for her like a blind roofer. "Blame a society obsessed with mediocrity, obsessed with protecting itself from itself. Canadians don't want surprises. Mediocrity is king. Change is suspect: Go to any public meeting anywhere. Have you ever seen a petition asking for development? Zoning is the Canadian planning bible."

"But why?" she asked. "Why do we have to sacrifice creativity for conformity? Aren't we better off as a country and as a people if change is encouraged, new ideas tried? Look at my problem. I want to contribute to my community, but my own city hall and my own neighbours are stopping me."

I pushed up the brim of my hat. "I don't know much, but I do know that the problems of two people like you and me don't amount to a hill of beans in this crazy world. Why do you think this country has no heroes, why we envy success rather than celebrating it? We're driven by a climate that cocoons us for most of the year, a geography that makes us communicate over wires, and a history of being pleased that we were good enough to come second!"

My heart was pounding as loudly as a car stereo in a high-school parking lot. I wondered if she could hear it. "Don't stop," she said, nearly knocking me flat with her smile. "You're starting to make sense."

As I gasped for air, her perfume hit me like a 100-year storm. I was as happy as a new urbanist on a front porch. I started to talk faster. "Zoning is the quintessential Canadian control. It assumes that nobody can be trusted. It requires documentation on paper: specificity, codification. It's the institutionalization of the form of our neighbourhoods. It doesn't allow discretion. What could be more banal, less creative? Drive down any street built since 1950. We made sure that everyone and everything was as similar as possible. We created a cult that worshipped conformity."

The word "cult" made her eyes moist as the vegetables trapped under the mist generators in the grocery store. I decided we could spend the rest of our lives living in sin. "What can I . . . we . . . do?" she sobbed. "How can we fight a bylaw?"

I tossed my hat on the desk. "We can start taking some chances," I said, "although we've got a big demographic problem. Until the boomers are gone, the whole society will reflect their need to protect their equity. If you've got it made in the shade, why take a chance?"

Her lower lip trembled. "But you, you planners, it's your job. Why aren't you leading? We're ready to follow."

It wasn't even lunch yet, and I was ready to follow her into a not-yet-decommissioned toxic waste site to change the essential fabric of Canadian society. "We need two things. First, we have to value difference over sameness. Leave mediocrity to the mediocre. Second, we need to let our people go. We need to trust ourselves. Our zoning bylaws are like training bras. Nothing's happening, but we have them just in case something tries to change."

Her eyes narrowed. "You planners talk a good line, but where are you when it matters? Where are you when I want to run my business from my house? I'll tell you where you are, you're in the way." She was right; I had no answer. My brain was as empty as a New Year's Day agenda.

I recalled a Margaret Atwood poem:

This is where the City Planners with the insane faces of political conspirators are scattered over unsurveyed territories, concealed from each other, each in his own private blizzard;

guessing directions, they sketch transitory lines rigid as wooden borders on a wall in the white vanishing air

tracing the panic of suburban order in a bland madness of snows.[13]

Was I one of those "insane faces" working inside my "private blizzard"? Planners have completely failed in convincing the public of our value. People see us as the agents of bland, as the keepers of an arcane language, as processors. Processing: not leading, not creating. We need an attitude adjustment as severe as a Yellowknife blizzard. If we don't change, if we don't start leading, if we don't stop hiding behind our bylaws, then we will become increasingly marginalized.

Our 50-year experiment in standardization is over. We know what neighbourhoods with identical homes in identical locations look like. We know that we can change streets into "traffic sewers" with reverse frontage lots. We have learned a great deal; it's time to put it to use. Change the legislation that limits discretion in zoning. Give the planners some authority to exercise their knowledge and experience. Take a chance. Nothing happens without risk.

She coughed politely. She was the best excuse this planner ever had to be creative. I snapped back to attention. "Look, kid. How about lunch? I know a place just around the corner." We left arm in arm to drown our tears.

New Urbanism: New Zoning

Andrea Gabor and Frank Lewinberg

1997 Plan Canada 37(4): 12–7

Zoning seems like a strange field to be interested in: It is dry, technical, legalistic, and obtuse. Yet, zoning is the set of rules that really fixes how our culture has decided to arrange its patterns of living. As such, zoning can tell us something about our values as a society.

Most new communities developed since the end of World War II bear a striking resemblance to one another. This is particularly true of those areas known as the suburbs, which have been created on the edges of existing urban centres. The principles and community form of these communities are embodied in the zoning bylaws that describe them. The mid-twentieth century was a period of prosperity. The North American dream of a single-family home on a large lot was universally understood as the optimum in community living and a symbol of success. At the same time, society's love affair with the automobile, rendered requisite by the new community form, was in its first full blush.

The juxtaposition of these trends resulted in a pattern of living reflected in the zoning bylaws of the time. Densities are generally low, usually too low to support transit, even by bus. Homogeneity is mandated through a strict segregation of community by income group and household type: Higher-density apartments are carefully separated from single-detached homes, and nonresidential uses are segregated from low-density residential enclaves. Stores, community facilities (other than schools), and workplaces are located outside residential enclaves, resulting in the need to drive, even for a trip to the convenience store.

The importance we place on movement by car is also reflected in the community built form. The public street is considered to be primarily automobile territory. Sidewalks are often omitted or found only on one side of the street, and the garage is frequently the dominant aspect of the streetscape. Larger collector and arterial roads have been designed to siphon cars from local streets. To minimize impacts from traffic, houses built on these roads have been sited to turn their backs on the public realm.

This describes a different pattern of living from that reflected in older towns and villages across Canada. Today, we are beginning to question some of what has become the conventional way of building communities. The pressure to change zoning rules represents one of the last steps in a process of change sweeping the country. As with every aspect of our lives, our cities and how we shape their future growth are coming under pressure to adapt.

Figure 14.5

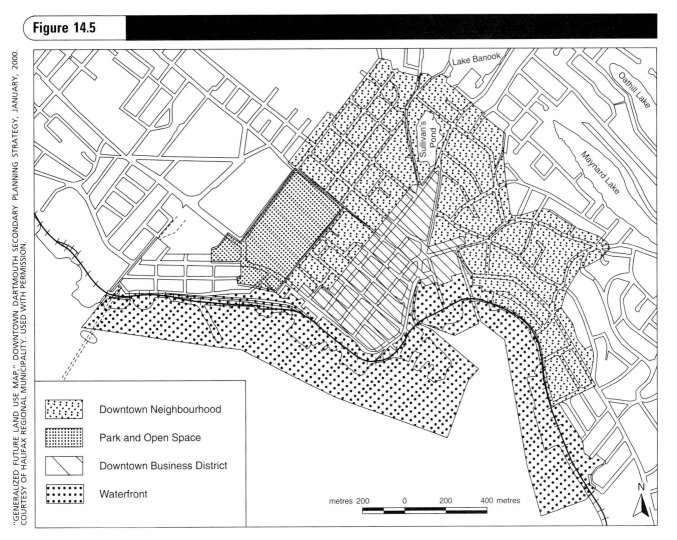

"GENERALIZED FUTURE LAND USE MAP," DOWNTOWN DARTMOUTH SECONDARY PLANNING STRATEGY, JANUARY, 2000. COURTESY OF HALIFAX REGIONAL MUNICIPALITY. USED WITH PERMISSION.

Land use maps, as in this one of Dartmouth, Nova Scotia, identify the areas designated for particular uses.

What Is New Urbanism?

Change in the process of urban growth and development has been under way across Canada for more than a decade. It appears in a new approach to environmental issues captured in such concepts as ecosystem planning and sustainable development. We have learned that we need to find ways to accommodate more people on less land, to intensify development. We are learning that we must reduce our reliance on the automobile by encouraging public transit, walking, and cycling. There is much discussion about defining limits to the extent of urban sprawl. The list of issues is long and controversial, frequently discussed and debated, and it ultimately reflects a gradual shift in our values.

The process of change in the field of urban development is also signalled in several important reports and studies, and a few significantly different developments undertaken over the past decades. This work has begun to change our understanding of planning new communities and to establish a new set of issues that planning is beginning to address. One important part of this process of change is known as new urbanism, an approach to suburban development making inroads in several provinces.

The term "new urbanism" is perhaps most succinctly described in the charter developed by the Congress for the New Urbanism, a group comprising architects, urban designers, planners, and landscape architects from across North America. The charter suggests that:

> neighborhoods should be diverse in use and population; communities should be designed for the pedestrian and transit as well as the car; cities and towns should be shaped by physically defined and universally accessible public spaces and community institutions; urban places should be framed by architecture and landscape design that celebrate local history, climate, ecology, and building practice.[14]

Before launching into a discourse on the creation of zoning regulations for new urbanist communities, we must be clear that the principles inherent in this "new" approach to community building cannot be implemented by zoning bylaws alone. A quick review of the principles illustrates the multiplicity of factors we must take into account. Zoning cannot regulate all of these factors.

New urbanism means:

- Designing communities with a connected and permeable public framework of streets and open spaces as the main structuring element of the community:
- Facilitating easy movement through all parts of the community by foot, bicycle, public transit, and automobile, without favouring any particular mode;
- Fostering community activity through ensuring that buildings enhance pedestrian comfort in the way that they relate to the public streets, and thereby providing an attractive, safe, and inviting public realm;
- Accommodating and integrating a diverse and wide range of land uses, densities, and building types within each neighbourhood to include the full range of activities found in any healthy community and to facilitate public transit;
- Integrating the natural environment into the new community; and
- Creating universally accessible public open spaces and community institutions that provide a sense of place and act as landmarks of community identity.

How Are These Plans Implemented?

The new urbanism approach entails a new way of planning communities in two important aspects. First, it requires changes to long-cherished policies (in official community plans) and development standards. This fact caused the first new urbanism developers to expend considerable time and energy working with municipal staff, politicians, and members of the public to assist them in accepting all the necessary changes. Second, it requires an integrated approach in which planners, landscape architects, environmental scientists, engineers, and architects work together to elaborate a physical concept into a master plan.

These changes in standards and approach shape the steps required in implementing a new urbanism development. Just as preparing the plan requires an integrated approach, implementing it requires a layered approach. The process starts with a comprehensive plan, which in Ontario would be the official plan, and advances through a plan of subdivision and finally a zoning bylaw.

The comprehensive plan sets out the structure of the new community by establishing the overall policy that implements the principles of new urbanism. In many cases in Ontario, urban design guidelines are appended to official plan policy to ensure that the design orientation of the new urbanism philosophy is carried through to final build out.

The subdivision plan sets in place other essential elements of the new urbanist approach. These include the street framework (which looks quite different from a

Figure 14.6

JILL GRANT

Rear lanes keep cars from dominating the streets of residential neighbourhoods, but when lined with garages can take on a monolithic character.

conventional form and is often an open grid that uses alternative development standards for streets and utilities); the creation of public rear lanes (a preferred but not essential feature); and the flexible delineation of development.

Because it is normally inflexible, zoning is the final and most difficult arena in which to effect change. The zoning rules hardwire detailed and intricate directions for land development. Bylaws are often deliberately written to create certainty, to offer only one way of doing things. But a new kind of zoning bylaw is beginning to emerge. The revised rules reflect new aspirations for community building. Although still detailed and prescriptive, these bylaws offer freedom regarding land use and intensity of development. Conversely, they retain rigidity regarding physical design issues to ensure the desired built form arrangements and public realm environment. Such zoning bylaws have generally been developed to implement a preconceived design concept, as in the case of Oak Park and Morrison Common in Oakville, and Montgomery Village in Orangeville. The Town of Markham adopted a generic zoning bylaw for its urban expansion area, which reflects and facilitates development along new urbanism principles. A review of some newer bylaws indicates the departures from previous zoning provisions necessary to implement the new approach. Table 14.1 identifies a few of the more significant of these and provides some examples.

With the emphasis shifting from land use and density to built form control, some municipalities will likely consider changing the form of their bylaws to one that is more visually illustrated and easy to understand. This was attempted in both Oakville and Markham, but was ultimately rejected for traditional bylaw language, presumably more understandable and enforceable by building inspectors, plan examiners, and lawyers.

Table 14.1	Examples of Conventional Versus New Urbanism Approaches

Principle: Integration of a mix of land uses

Conventional Approach	New Urbanism Approach
• Single-use zones, each clearly separated • Home occupation strictly regulated	• Mixed-use zones in which retail, office, and residential uses are permitted on one lot and within one building • Convenience stores within low-rise residential zones with no parking • Home occupation in all house types and accessory building

Example: Corner convenience store means a retail store that serves the daily needs of a local neighbourhood, with a floor area that shall not exceed 100 m²; which shall be located on a corner lot, and which may be combined with residential uses within the same building provided that the convenience store use is located at grade level at the corner of the structure closest to the intersection; in which access to the residential dwelling will be independent of access to the convenience store; and for which no offstreet parking is required. (Uptown Core, Oakville)

Accessory building means an attached or detached building located on the same lot as the main building, the use of which is incidental to the main building, and which may be used for human habitation, a dwelling unit, residential floor space accessory to a dwelling unit, a private garage, a tool shed, a greenhouse, a storage building, or combinations of these uses. (Montgomery Village, Orangeville)

Principle: Intensification and housing diversity

Conventional Approach	New Urbanism Approach
• Low-density zones, each encompassing a very narrow range of house types • Medium- and high-density zones isolated from low density areas	• Accessory units generally permitted in all dwelling types and in some accessory buildings • Broad range of housing types within all residential zones • Medium- and higher-density areas integrated with lower-density areas • General increase in permitted densities in all zones

Example: Residential zones: R3 permitted uses, semidetached dwellings, duplex dwellings, triplex dwellings, fourplex dwellings, townhouse dwellings, multiple dwellings, apartment dwellings, and home occupation. (Markham Bylaw 185–96)

Principle: Pedestrian-oriented streetscape

Conventional Approach	New Urbanism Approach
• Requirements for garage access to be from the street; car storage usually at front of building • Large frontyard setback for house assumes car parked in driveway • Onstreet parking usually prohibited	• Minimal frontyard setback or minimum and maximum frontyard setback • No parking permitted in front yard • Onstreet parking permitted for visitors • Accessory buildings, including garages, restricted to rear yard and fronting on rear lane

Example: Rear garages: Vehicular ingress and egress to lots shall only be provided and accessed through the laneway... For dwellings other than apartment houses, parking shall only be permitted within a rear yard, and within 6.0 metres of the rear lot line abutting the lane. (Morrison Common, Oakville)

Accessory use and building... any accessory building or other structure which is not part of the main building shall be erected within a maximum distance of 7.0 metres from the rear lot line, shall not exceed a coverage of 42 square metres in area, 6.0 metres in height.... (Montgomery Village, Orangeville)

Zoning in the Future

The changes in Ontario in Markham, Oakville, and Orangeville are happening in other communities across Canada. This is the leading edge of what we can anticipate in many communities over the coming years. We believe that it is one of the first steps in making our communities more responsive to the needs of the future. We believe new urbanism to be a form of community development that will find strong acceptance across suburban Canada.

This new form may reflect the fact that we are not as prosperous as we once were. More women work, and work opportunities within the local community make sense for both women and men. Many families find two cars beyond their means and may have to rely on public transit. A much wider mix of available housing types also reflects and accommodates the changing family structure.

As a community gains experience with a new community form, it could include such zoning provisions in its general zoning bylaw as an option for future development. Ideally, the next step will be to have municipal zoning bylaws that provide flexibility. The objective is to encourage creativity through flexibility while maintaining some certainty as to the final result.

What is clear from a review of changing regulations is how easily we become complacent about existing provisions, continuing to impose standards that are perhaps no longer relevant. The same could become true of new urbanism bylaws; we must continue to be vigilant. New urbanism offers flexibility and an alternative form of community development, but it should never be confused with a need to keep the process alive and vital by continually questioning how we do things and finding new and better ways to make our communities an appropriate reflection of our evolving society.

Narrow-Front Rowhousing for Affordability and Flexibility

Avi Friedman

1994 Plan Canada 34(5): 9–16

Economic constraints, sociodemographic changes, and attention to environmental issues have led to an increased interest in the narrow-front rowhouse as the elemental building block in the design and construction of affordable, sustainable communities. Since land and infrastructure costs are an increasing share of the total price of a new home, the housing industry and policy makers have reevaluated the current housing market to ensure that affordable housing is made available to future home owners near the city, especially to low- to moderate-income families and first-time home buyers. These vulnerable purchasing groups are subject to an "affordability gap," whereby the rate of increase of median new house prices has, since 1972, surpassed the rate of increase of median family incomes. Higher real interest rates, a scarcity of serviced land, higher infrastructure and construction costs, and increased speculation in real estate are causes commonly advanced to explain the widening gulf in home ownership affordability.[15]

Most of the housing stock in Canada is composed of single-detached dwelling units, the least dense of housing options and the most consumptive in terms of land, energy, and water. Detached houses consume from 15 to 67 percent more energy than other common ground-oriented housing options and accommodate 60 percent fewer people per net hectare than rowhouses.[16] Reduced house size and increased density achieve savings in the cost of land and infrastructure, building materials, and energy consumption.

With such economic advantages as these, home builders are beginning to redefine their expectations in their choice of narrow-front rowhousing as an increasingly efficient type of affordable accommodation.[17]

Recent demographic trends have also influenced the types of housing responsive to the new configuration of the market. Several significant changes in the socioeconomic composition of society have contributed to the need for diversity and flexibility in available housing types—housing designed to adapt to users' life cycle and lifestyle requirements and that provides the necessary amenities. The traditional image of the family of two married parents with the father working and the mother at home with the children has dropped to a fraction of households. Later marriages, the tendency of divorced or separated people to remain in separate households, and a steady rise in the number of elderly people continuing to reside in their homes has increased the proportion of single-person households. Heavy time pressures combined with reduced available time for home maintenance have created the need for multiple-use spaces such as kitchen/activity centres and home offices. Consequently, the demand for smaller, easily-maintained houses is stronger now than ever before.

As society becomes more aware of the depletion of the earth's natural resources and becomes increasingly willing to pay for its restoration, housing that uses resources efficiently both in the construction and operational phases and that creates pleasant and environmentally-sound living spaces can become an essential concept at the initial design phases. Environmental, social, and economic factors all contribute to the viability of the solution of increased development density using the narrow-front rowhouse as the basic, flexible housing unit.

The Narrow-Front Rowhouse

As a housing forms that offers affordability and sustainability, the narrow-front rowhouse (also called a townhouse or terraced housing) is the option closest to providing a prospective owner with the commonly preferred characteristics of home ownership (a single-family home with a private entrance and direct access to a yard) while, at the same time, extending the benefits of affordability and sustainability resulting from increased density. The various forms of tenure suited to the narrow-front rowhouse community include freehold, co-ownership, and condominium. In freehold tenure (where individual residents own the unit and lot) and co-ownership tenure (where a group of residents share ownership of the units and lots), the public space accessed by residents is owned by the city. In condominium tenure, however, residents own only the structure of their respective units while the lots and common open spaces are owned jointly.

Where the access routes of a rowhouse development are narrower than the standard required by municipal zoning, they are designated as private roads and owned conjointly by the residents, an arrangement suited to condominium tenure. Strong community identity and an equitable shared use of common open space are frequent results of condominium tenure in a rowhouse development.

The narrow-front rowhouse is built on a narrow plot (14 to 20 feet wide). Each unit shares side walls with neighbouring structures. The lack of interior load-bearing walls allows for flexibility in the partitioning of available space. The rowhouse possesses many of the advantages of the detached house: a private front door, easy access to the ground, a clear definition of a public street side, and a private rear garden. Its chief constraint is the narrow width between the shared walls. Since only two facades are available for windows, its width governs its depth as well as the number of rooms that can be positioned against the exterior, windowed walls.

LeBreton Flats, a 300-unit development (32 units/acre) initiated by Canada Mortgage and Housing Corporation and undertaken in the early 1970s in Ottawa on a site originally settled as a lumbering community, is a narrow-front development designed by Ian Johns. Land parcels were sold to private builders and nonprofit cooperatives, with co-ops allowed input into the design process. Three-bedroom units, some with living rooms one and a half storeys tall, sold initially for about $65 000. Every unit had a garage in front, a large outdoor area, and street frontage. The multilevel style gave rise to a townhouse plan that became popular among Ottawa, Calgary, and Vancouver developers. Cathcart Mews in Ottawa's Lowertown, designed by Johns and built in 1979–81, has 63 16-foot-wide units. Residents were satisfied with the openness of the design. Screens, terraces, and gardens provided the necessary privacy.[18]

The Grow Home, a 14-foot-wide rowhouse designed at McGill University's School of Architecture, was created with cost and resource reduction in mind. Intended as an afford-able and adaptable urban dwelling with 1000 square feet of space, the Grow Home has a kitchen, bathroom, and living room on the ground floor and an unpartitioned second floor that can be modified to include two bedrooms and a second bathroom. It was aimed at sensitizing the public to an alternative form of housing more suited to the chang-ing demographic profile of the household and more attainable for the average first-time buyer. Within one year following its introduction on McGill's campus as a demonstration model in 1990, over 1000 units were built in Quebec.[19] Labour and material costs are reduced by simplifying construction tasks and by standardizing the dimensions of the structural and cladding elements.[20] Floor area and architectural complexity were reduced to lower costs, but a high quality of materials and finishes was maintained.

The implications of the Grow Home on land use and on housing and operating costs are significant. Compared with a one-storey bungalow on a 60- by 100-foot lot (gross density of about five homes per acre), the two-storey rowhouse on a 14- by 100-foot lot (gross density of 24 homes per acre) can accommodate over four times as many people. An acre of land can house about 20 people in bungalows, but the same amount of land with the same number of roads, sewers, waterlines, and storm drains can accommodate over 80 people in narrow-front rowhouses. The grouping of units into clusters of two or more provides significant construction and energy savings: Grouping four detached units as semi-detached reduces the exposed wall area by 36 percent, and grouping all four units as rowhouses reduces exterior wall surfaces by a further 28 percent. Heat-loss reductions of 21 percent are achieved when two dwellings are attached, and a further 26 percent in savings result for the middle unit when three or more units are combined as rowhouses.[21]

The design challenge for affordable narrow-front rowhouse developments is to make these communities, with "squeezed space" by North American standards, pleasant and livable environments for all inhabitants. The social stigma attached to this type of hous-ing, especially in established communities where the single-detached home predomi-nates, may be overcome if the denser communities (often associated with barren and sterile surroundings) are designed with forethought, care, and attention paid to parking and vehicular circulation, private and public open spaces, and unit and community identity—important factors in achieving pleasant environments. Patterns for planning and designing rowhouse communities to address these three crucial factors were devel-oped by the McGill team. The next section reviews some techniques for dealing with one of these factors: accommodating cars.

One Key Factor: Parking and Vehicular Circulation

The extensive ownership and use of the passenger car along with a vast network of public roads has promoted the phenomenon of "leapfrogging," a pattern whereby builders develop land farther from supportive facilities.[22] New affordable communities are almost always located on or beyond the urban fringe: The potential benefits entail lower home prices due to reduced land costs and the relocation of the labour force closer to employment centres. The disadvantages, however, include urban sprawl, higher transportation costs resulting from increased commuting distances, and a greater dependence on the car, which aggravates the associated problems of automobile emissions, traffic congestion, and parking. Whether in an urban or suburban setting, the car is an inescapable reality in affordable communities. Parking in a project of 45 to 60 units per hectare can account for nearly half of the total site area. The higher the density of development, the greater the impact that parking and vehicular circulation can have. In high-density developments it is crucial to treat parking efficiently and unobtrusively (Figure 14.7).

The car's visual impact (wide roads, expanses of asphalt in large parking lots, long series of repetitive garage doors) can be reduced when parking is integrated into the landscaping. Several smaller screened parking areas result in a reduced visual presence than one large parking lot. Depressing the parking areas or creating earthen berms around their perimeters, combined with appropriate landscaping, are effective methods of concealment. When sites for affordable communities are marginally located, parking areas can be used to separate housing from unattractive adjacent elements. Vehicular circulation in high-density communities often creates conflicts with pedestrian circulation and play areas for children. Narrowing street width and establishing a clear hierarchy of priorities reduces costs and improves safety by slowing down automobile speed.

Designing parking areas on the periphery of the developments leaves the core of the site vehicle free.[23] The use of speed bumps, cobblestone segments, and highly textured driving surfaces such as stamped concrete, as well as emphasizing entryways by the placement of gateways, are useful strategies for controlling vehicular speed. Paving with textured blocks instead of asphalt increases the visual effect and absorbs stormwater, thereby reducing the infrastructure required for runoff.

In the Quartier du Parc Vinet project, the City of Montreal allowed narrower street widths, which contributed to the level of safety and to lower unit prices. The shared surface parking at Parc Vinet, concentrated in small areas screened with fences and landscaping, was located within short walking distance of the housing units.

Design for Affordability

Changes to Canada's economic, sociodemographic, and environmental landscapes have raised issues of housing affordability, which can be answered only by cost-effective, energy-efficient solutions that satisfy the requirements of designers, planners, decision makers, regulators, builders, and a diverse range of potential home buyers. The narrow-front rowhouse offers the flexible building block for affordable communities by rising to the challenge of accommodating the primary issues to be addressed in the design of any high-density development. Balancing these vital elements ensures the provision of pleasant and desirable housing as opposed to the type of neighbourhood homeowners avoid. The future of successful and affordable rowhouse communities resides in the thoughtful treatment of all the design factors that contribute to creating environments where people happily choose to live.

Calculating Development Charges

Cam Watson
1996 Plan Canada 36(1): 28–9

Development charges are used, in one form or another, throughout Canada. They represent one means by which municipalities finance the cost of growth-related net capital

Figure 14.7

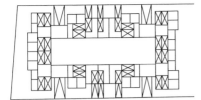

L'Îlot de Marseille

In an infill city block, interior shared and private parking was provided in order to reduce the number of garage doors

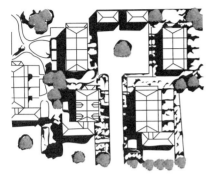

Parc Madaire

Covered parking structures were placed off the main road and in the rear

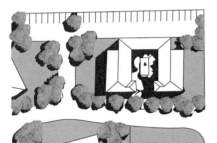

Gatineau, Quebec

Shared surface parking was placed at the edge of the property, bordering a busy highway

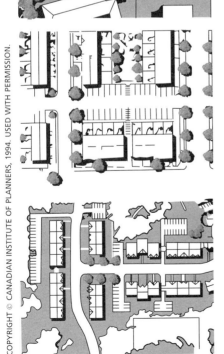

Parc Vinet

Shared surface parking was placed within a short distance of the units

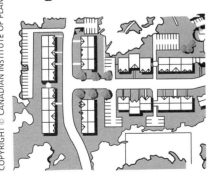

Nashua, N.H.

Parking was pushed to the rear of the units in order to reduce visibility from the main streets

With good design, narrow-lot housing can accommodate

costs attributable to specific development and to growth generally. They reflect the user-pay principle that has increasingly influenced public policy making. In some cases, development charges are used to fund a broad and unspecified range of growth-related works (in Ontario and the Yukon, for example). Some provinces (such as British Columbia, Alberta, and Saskatchewan) provide for the recovery of offsite growth-related costs in the case of sewage, water, drainage, highway and recreational facilities, and parkland. In the Maritimes, development charges are not widely used, except for parkland dedications and offsite contributions as part of planning approvals. Newfoundland & Labrador assesses service levies to recover the cost of public works necessary for property to be developed. In Quebec, municipalities can require a developer to construct or finance the cost of infrastructure made necessary by development, with some flexibility in defining such projects.

Development charges represent an important component of the capital funding program of many Canadian municipalities. Generally, they permit growth-related capital projects to be undertaken in a timely fashion and without creating additional burden on the primary capital funding sources of a municipality, especially property taxes and user rates. This is particularly important in the face of declining federal/provincial grants and subsidies, ratepayer resistance to tax increases, and the project cost implications of more stringent environmental standards. At the same time, with variable rates of economic growth in many parts of the country, it is also necessary to consider the "tax incidence" of development charges and the economic impact of using supplementary capital funding sources. Municipalities can consider dramatically reducing service standards or using different service delivery mechanisms.

The important issues involved in calculating a development charge are briefly discussed here. Even with the comparatively detailed development charge legislation and regulations found in Ontario, for example, questions have to be addressed and choices made in establishing a charge. This article addresses some of these questions.

What Are Growth-Related Municipal Capital Costs?

Growth-related municipal capital costs include a portion of the capital cost of all services for which a municipality is responsible. Questions often arise about the types of expenditures that should be included as a capital cost. Some items—including buildings, pipes, plants, drainage works—are clearly capital costs. Planning, design, and financing costs are normally deemed to be part of the cost of a capital work, provided that financing involves a formal long-term debt arrangement rather than simply the interim bank financing cost of construction.

More difficult to assess are the assets needed to make the facility functional (such as office furniture and equipment, library books, trucks and equipment for a firehall). In jurisdictions such as Ontario, these items are explicitly included as part of the definition of capital cost, although the line between capital and operating is generally not clear-cut.

Generally, local works within a subdivision plan are deemed the sole cost responsibility of the subdivider and are therefore not financed by a development charge.

Hard Services versus Soft Services

One perspective on the question of what is growth related involves identifying costs directly related to developing land: those physically and immediately required for the development to obtain planning approvals and to function at an adequate level in terms of essential services. These include road access (turning lanes, streetlights, traffic signals, and sidewalks, for example), as well as connections to sanitary and storm sewer and water systems, supported by adequate capacity in terms of treatment storage, pumping, and related facilities. These are hard services. However, one would think that electrical service, police and fire protection, waste collection and disposal, and road maintenance vehicles are equally essential to community life. Other municipal assets, such as parks, recreational spaces, and library facilities, may be widely used and important but are perhaps not essential. The requirements for these urban services are, however, growth related in many cases.

Oversizing

Where there is a clear and significant oversizing component to the cost of a growth-related work—that is where the municipality requires excess capacity beyond the amount required for the development—an additional level of cost sharing is required in financing. Normally, this involves the municipality or the first development front-ending the cost, with the municipality undertaking to collect cost shares from subsequent development.

Service Standards

Once directly-related costs have been considered, the second step in establishing growth-related capital costs involves identifying those related to growth generally, although only indirectly. These are works for which growth produces a gradually cumulating requirement eventually reflected in the need for an additional (or relocated) fire or town hall, indoor recreation complex, library, sports park addition, works equipment, waste disposal site, and so on. Some refer to these requirements as soft services.

The need for this type of growth-related capital cost can frequently be determined on the basis of the maintenance of service standards. These generally take the form of average per capita facility standards, coupled with cost standards. This could involve an indoor recreational facility standard of, for instance, two square feet of gross floor area per capita and an all-in cost of $200/square foot (in 2006 dollars, inclusive of design, site purchase/work, construction, equipping, furnishing). This approach is workable where:

- two square feet per capita reflects existing municipal service level, not an enriched level;
- the monetary amount is a reasonable cost and reflects recent municipal experience;
- the municipality is planning to construct facilities of this size and type in response to growth;
- other probable funding sources, such as subsidies and fund raising, have been netted out of the calculation;
- the charge is calculated fairly and reasonably for different types of development;
- the municipality is required to spend the funds collected in accordance with the plan underlying the calculation of the charge, and to report publicly and regularly on the continuity of the reserve fund; and
- the development community and the community at large have an opportunity to provide input into the calculation and to appeal the policy to an impartial reviewer if it is considered to be unfair or incorrectly applied.

These are all requirements of Ontario's *Development Charges Act.*

Broad Cost Attributions

Calculating fair and reasonable charges for different types of development requires policy analysis. For several hard services, the calculation should focus on the amount of potential or proposed development within the service or catchment area for the works involved. This calculation can be assigned to a specific area for a storm drainage pond or a local road improvement connecting a subdivision to the existing road network. However, in the case of an arterial road or a significant water main addition to the municipal system, the area that will benefit becomes broader and thus subject to various points of view.

Let's consider an arterial road improvement connecting an outlying "dormitory" community with a downtown employment centre. If the road is primarily to enable residents to travel to and from work, then its cost can be fully attributable to the residential development. If the road is primarily to improve employers' access to their workforce, then its cost can be attributed to commercial/industrial development.

More likely, however, the cost is attributable to both purposes and should be equitably shared. But what of those who use the improved facility at times other than morning and evening peak periods? Their use is not normally considered in the calculation, since peak period use is the prime determinant of road capacity design.

Time Considerations

If the calculation of a charge is based on a 10- or 20-year planning horizon to correspond with municipal capital planning initiatives, planners should consider the extent to which the capacity of the works project matches the capacity requirements of the growth expected during the planning period. Where significant unused capacity is expected to remain at the end of this period, it may be necessary to net it out of the calculation of the charge to arrive at a fair cost attribution. By the same token, where the municipal system contains significant capacity oversizing at the beginning of the period, it may be appropriate to use this cost to offset end-of-period excess capacity.

Average versus Marginal Costs

There is a continuing debate between "average-costers" and "area-specific costers." Advocates of average costing apply this approach across the municipality as a whole to arrive at a uniform set of charges for all development. Certainty, ease of administration, encouragement of development throughout the municipality, and general practice are several of the arguments used by those who favour this costing approach.

Advocates of area-specific costing, particularly for directly attributable services, are generally landowners (who can obtain cost savings) or policy analysts (who favour this more precise but complicated method). Calculations can be made with varying levels of complexity on a subdivision, community, or catchment area. In this case, property purchasers pay specifically for the costs their development generates.

Charges by Use

When these broad cost allocation issues have been resolved, municipalities must determine how the charge should be differentiated on a land use basis. Should all types of residential units make the same financial contribution, for example? The answer is usually in the negative. One reason is the wide range of average unit occupancies. These may range from 1.2 persons per unit (ppu) for small (senior citizen) apartments to 3.5 ppu or more for new single-detached subdivisions. The population-related component of the charge should vary accordingly.

Higher-density development offers potential efficiencies in terms of the length of trunks or arterials. Per capita standards for trip generation and water/sewer usage may be lower as well. In some cases, density-related efficiencies are offset by other factors, such as higher stormwater runoff coefficients. Thus, the setting of a properly differentiated charge is a complex matter that involves numerous assumptions.

Frequently, development charges do not distinguish between commercial and industrial development. Considerable variability exists in terms of municipal service standards, particularly among industrial uses. In addition, commercial and industrial uses may be located on similarly-zoned lands; the nature of a use can vary over time within the same structures. There are significant differences in employee floor area density, traffic generation, and average water/sewer usage between commercial and industrial uses. Despite the complexities, these differences are increasingly reflected in a more use-specific schedule of development charges.

How Does It Work?

Seven years after enacting its *Development Charges Act*, Ontario examined the types of services for which charges could be imposed and the means used to establish growth-related costs. The legislation is generally acknowledged as highly successful in mandating and achieving a fair and competent level of municipal development financing.

Study Questions

1. Find a land use or zoning bylaw for a Canadian community and compare the sections regulating low density residential zones with those regulating multifamily ground-oriented (townhouse or rowhouse) zones. What are the differences in requirements such as density, setback from street, and lot sizes, and how do they affect urban form?

2. How do zoning regulations induce conformity in the development of new residential areas?

3. Attend a planning meeting in your community. Describe and evaluate the process. How did planning rules, regulations, and tools feature in the discussion and the decisions reached?

4. Examine a provincial enabling act for local planning. What powers and tools does the legislation give municipalities for regulating the mix of land uses?

5. What arguments do the critics of zoning make against it? Do you accept the allegation that zoning facilitates sprawl? Why, or why not?

6. What role are narrow townhouse developments playing in new development in your community? Where are they located, and how significant is their contribution to the housing mix?

7. Some property lawyers in the US say that form-based codes will fail legal challenges because the state has no mandate to regulate taste. What are the arguments for and against regulating the form of development with design standards?

8. Discuss the ways in which zoning reflects deeply-held cultural values related to institutions like the family and work. Why do some land uses, like strip clubs or landfill sites, generate such controversy?

Reference Notes

1. Pinard, A (2002) An approach to home-based business. *Plan Canada* 42(1): 16–8.

   Smart Growth BC (2006) Strategies for overcoming community opposition to new residential development, http://www.smartgrowth.bc.ca/downloads/matt-ok.pdf (accessed 16 April 2006).

2. Goodale, T & S Wickwire (1979) Group homes and property values in residential areas. *Plan Canada* 19(2): 154–63.

   Moore, PW (1979) Zoning and planning: The Toronto experience, 1904–1970. In A Artibise & GA Stelter (eds) *The Usable Urban Past*. Toronto: Macmillan Canada.

3. Grant, J (1991) Contradictions in the neighbourhood: Planning residential spaces. *Plan Canada* 31(1): 16–20.

   White, J & B Ashton (1992) *Meeting Housing Needs and the NIMBY Syndrome*. Rural and Small Town Studies Program, Mount Allison University, with CMHC.

4. Berridge Greenberg Lewinburg (1991) *Guidelines for the Reurbanisation of Metropolitan Toronto*. Toronto: Municipality of Metropolitan Toronto.

5. Berridge Lewinberg Greenberg Dark Gabor with Cosburn Patterson Wardman Glatting Jackson Kercher Anglin Lopez Rinehart Consultants (1996) *The Integrated Community: A Study of Alternative Land Development Standards*. Ottawa: Canada Mortgage and Housing Corporation.

   Ontario, Government of (1997) *Breaking Ground: An Illustration of Alternative Development Standards in Ontario's New Communities*. Toronto: Queen's Printer.

   Ontario, Government of (1995) *Alternative Development Standards: Making Choices*. Toronto: Queen's Printer.

6. Friedman, A (1996) Flexible planning strategies: The La Prairie experiment. *Plan Canada* 36(2): 33–42.

7. Filion, P & M Alexander (1995) Restrictive covenants: Hidden obstacles. *Plan Canada* 35(1): 33–7.

8. Young, Mayor CA (1976) The City of Detroit *et al.* vs. American Mini Theaters Inc. *et al.* 427 US 50,96 SCt 2440, 49L Ed. 2D 310.

9. The current version of Vancouver's bylaw is available online at http://www.city.vancouver.bc.ca/bylaws/76166v8.pdf (accessed 15 April 2006).

10. Cities copy each other once the Supreme Court has approved. Example is extracted from New York City's ordinance, Comprehensive City Planning Calendar of the City of New York, City Planning Commission, Wednesday, May 18, 1977, page 16.

11. A more recent version of this pamphlet is now available by Cooper, CB & ED Kelly (2001) *Everything You Always Wanted to Know about Regulating Sex Businesses*. PAS 495/496. Chicago: APA Planners Press.

12. Toner, W (1977) *Regulating Sex Businesses*. Planning Advisory Service, Report no. 327. Chicago: American Society of Planning Officials.

13. Except from "The City Planners" from *The Circle Game*, copyright © 1996 by Margaret Atwood. Reprinted with the permission of House of Anansi Press.

14. CNU (1996) *Charter of the New Urbanism*. Congress for the New Urbanism, http://www.cnu.org/aboutcnu/index.cfm?formAction=charter (accessed 15 April 2006).

15. Rybczynski, W, A Friedman, & S Ross (1990) The Grow Home. Affordable Homes Program Project Paper No. 3. Montreal: McGill University School of Architecture.

16. Canada Mortgage and Housing Corporation (CMHC) (1991) *CMHC's Healthy Housing Design Competition, Guide and Technical Requirements*. Ottawa: Canada Mortgage and Housing.

17. Friedman, A, V Cammalleri, & J Archer (1993) *Sustainable Residential Developments: Planning, Design and Construction Principles ("Greening" the Grow Home)*. Ottawa: Canada Mortgage and Housing Corporation.

18. King, A (1990) Narrow minded: Montreal takes a second look at impressive housing idea. Montreal: *Montreal Gazette*, 21 June.

19. Friedman, A (2001) *The Grow Home*. Montreal: McGill-Queen's University Press.

20. Friedman, A & V Cammalleri (1992) Evaluation of affordable housing projects based on the Grow Home concept. *Affordable Homes Program Project Paper No. 10*. Montreal: McGill University School of Architecture.

21. Friedman, A, V Cammalleri, & J Archer (1993) Op. cit.

22. Brower, D (1976) *Urban Growth Management through Development Timing*. New York: Praeger Publishers.

23. Cooper Marcus, C & W Sarkissian (1986) *Housing as if People Mattered: Site Design Guidelines for Medium-Density Family Housing*. Berkeley: University of California Press.

Chapter Fifteen

Debates about Growth

Our Relationship with Growth

Jill Grant

Planning has something of a love/hate relationship with growth. A "healthy" Canadian economy needs a modest level of growth. Land use planners, though, have to deal with managing that growth in the context of community development. The public loathes the negative implications of rapid growth and some of the changes it generates. While planners have always seen managing sprawl as a vital responsibility, in recent years, that task has taken on new urgency.

Because our capitalist economy is predicated on growth, we worry about recession or even depression in the absence of growth. Regions like Cape Breton that face significant job loss and emigration create real dilemmas for planners: We resist the idea of planning for decline. Planners see value in the places we inhabit: They don't want communities to become redundant. Accordingly, Skaburskis and Brunner say, planning has tended to be pro-growth.[1] Municipal governments rely on growth to increase revenues from taxes. Many planning decisions involve bringing land "into use." Identifying the "best and highest use" drives decisions. The attachment to growth has long meant that conservation took a back seat in planning, because "progress" necessitated converting land from habitat or farmland to housing or malls (Figure 15.1).

Is growth inevitable? Is it desirable? In the last few decades, we have been more careful about differentiating growth from development, and in establishing arguments about what kinds of growth might be appropriate and "good." In the aftermath of World War II, planners tended to see growth as evidence of progress and success: The responsibility of planning in that context was to assist the process of community transformation and adaptation. Today, planners are more likely to suggest that growth is okay only if we get it right, if we do it in a "smart" or "sustainable" way.

During the 1960s and 1970s, many governments pushed for economic and industrial development. By the 1990s, governments more commonly focused on local economic and community development, trying to find locally appropriate strategies to encourage growth.[2] A new interest in sustainable development suggested that communities could grow without undermining the quality of the environment (as Stanley Yip suggested in Chapter 11).

The big media stories of the late twentieth century, though, featured public concerns about growth. Sprawl, traffic congestion, unaffordable housing, and inadequate infrastructure made headlines as community residents increasingly came to resist growth. NIMBYism—efforts by residents to prevent new development in their neighbourhoods—became increasingly problematic to

Figure 15.1

The irony of new development: A St. Thomas, Ontario, suburb promises "nature."

governments trying to approve projects. In this context, the smart growth movement developed. Incorporating new urbanism ideas and the language of sustainable development, smart growth advocates suggested that communities could manage growth to get the best from it while minimizing its negative impacts. Strategies for growth management and growth control became increasingly popular.[3] Some governments applied growth boundaries, like the Agricultural Land Reserve that Smith and Haid discussed in Chapter 13.

Cities also became interested in increasing urban densities. Urban infill and intensification projects in rehabilitated industrial, or brownfield sites, took off. "Reurbanization" became a new watchword for the larger cities.[4] The first paper in this chapter, by Robert Young, describes the St. Lawrence neighbourhood in Toronto, an early example of successful redevelopment in the city. Compact projects with high design quality and a mix of uses and housing types have become a common form of urban growth in many Canadian city cores.

Pierre Filion and Heidi Hoernig examine trends in the downtown areas of midsized cities to try to understand why some have declined while others have thrived. They tell a tale of alternate futures, arguing that many communities will need good planning if they hope to avoid continued population loss.

Three papers in the chapter ask the reader to critically examine the presumptions that underlie contemporary approaches to planning. Jill Grant asks why people keep choosing the suburbs and suggests that cultural values play a key role in making suburban living the popular choice for home buyers. Larry Bourne argues that, rather than blaming residential uses for sprawl, we should look more closely at commercial uses to see how they reduce suburban densities. Ray Young challenges the smart growth movement for its faith that a simple solution can resolve a complex set of problems.

Larry Beasley ends the chapter and the book on an optimistic note. Vancouver has shown what it takes to create a livable city. Its strategy of accommodating growth by building up has led to dramatic changes in the skyline over the last two decades. Throughout the process, though, the city has remained attractive (if not always affordable). Not only is Vancouver a national success story of how we can grow on our own terms, but it also represents an international beacon of hope that planners can find sustainable options to accommodate those who want to make our communities home.

Urban Design for Intensification: The St. Lawrence Test Case

Robert Young

1995 Plan Canada 35(4): 35–7

In 1975, Toronto's official plan was amended, at least in part, to encourage the development of new neighbourhoods in the city core. The St. Lawrence project was one of these urban neighbourhoods. Built in the late 1970s on 44 acres of underutilized industrial land, St. Lawrence is an intensified development that continues to draw praise for its livable combination of diverse land use, high density (80 units/gross acre), and broad mix of residential tenures and income groups. To a large extent, the success of St. Lawrence stems from its urban design: a sympathetic relationship to nearby historic buildings; short, well-connected blocks; and clear definition of space. These characteristics resulted as much from the municipal initiative and democratic process behind St. Lawrence as from the expertise of the professionals who worked on the project.[5]

Since much of St. Lawrence's construction was completed by the 1980s, the project stands as a test case in the current debate over intensification. St. Lawrence was planned and implemented by a municipality, not by a private-sector developer. Furthermore, the planners of St. Lawrence included more than the traditional planning and design professionals. Members of Toronto City Council and community-based organizations actively participated and had real power in determining the form of the neighbourhood. As David Hulchanski has written, this democratic partnership permitted the development of a unique large project that violated many of the traditional approaches that professional planners were using at the time to plan large-scale residential projects.[6] Indeed, with a less democratic planning process, many of the design features incorporated might have been dismissed as too radical or restrictive.

Place, Linkage, and Space

To visualize St. Lawrence's overall form, picture an east-west street spine flanked on either side by six- to eight-storey apartment buildings. This spine contains a promenade (The Esplanade) and Crombie Park, the central public space in the neighbourhood. Behind the apartment buildings, buffered from activity on The Esplanade, are blocks of three-storey rowhouses, arranged intentionally by the planning team to mimic Toronto's nineteenth-century neighbourhoods. To understand St. Lawrence's urban design, however, go beyond this preliminary sketch and focus on place, block pattern, and spatial definition.

Place: Sensitivity to Local Buildings and Streetscape

On each side of Crombie Park, apartment buildings echo the materials, scale, and ornamentation of nearby nineteenth-century industrial and commercial buildings. This visual compatibility is especially important, given the potential stigmatization of the neighbourhood as a lower-income area: Close to 66 percent of the dwellings involve nonprofit, nonmarket housing.

Several strategies help achieve a visual fit with the neighbourhood's historic architectural flavour. The facades of the apartment buildings facing Crombie Park and The Esplanade are made of red or brown brick to echo those of nearby historic buildings. Building heights, ranging from six to eight storeys, reflect the heights of bordering historic structures. Building structure and ornament echo Toronto's industrial architecture without slavishly copying it. For example, apartment buildings along Crombie Park reinterpret bay windows, Roman arches, and brick corbelling.

Linkage: Compact and Connected Blocks

St. Lawrence's block pattern (reflecting Toronto's traditional street network) is a compact grid, a pattern that not only supports transportation by car and bus but also makes walking and cycling to local businesses and institutions a convenient option. The abundance of street corners gives pedestrians convenient access to small neighbourhood businesses, thereby encouraging sustainable local ventures. Furthermore, the neighbourhood is well linked by streets to the surrounding area. St. Lawrence thus avoids the spatial isolation of so many high-density projects planned on the superblock pattern. Blocks are short, with roughly 70 percent of the block faces in the neighbourhood no more than 100 metres long. St. Lawrence connects to neighbouring areas by 11 streets.

Space: Distinct Boundaries between Public and Private

St. Lawrence exhibits well-defined streets, parks, and landmarks, which enable residents and visitors to orient themselves easily within the neighbourhood. Distinct boundaries between private and public space help to discourage crime and encourage social interaction. As well, appropriately oriented courtyards that serve to trap heat from the sun and reduce winter wind velocities create a pleasant pedestrian environment.

Urban solids, such as monuments, city blocks, and edge-defining buildings, form landmarks and spatially define important streets and parks. St. Lawrence's urban voids like courtyards and entryways, and transitional spaces such as front yards, have been designed to encourage a safe and positive social environment. They are also pedestrian friendly, a characteristic achieved in several ways. Townhouses and apartment buildings share courtyards, providing opportunities for casual chats between neighbours and play among local children. In winter, these courtyards also provide wind protection and sun traps for pedestrians.

Many family units have direct onstreet access. Because the windows and front doors of these dwellings face the street, residents can casually survey street activity. This is no guarantee that crime will not occur, but it is a deterrent. Townhouses and ground-floor apartments feature several territorial markers: short stairways, private gardens, recessed entrance doors, and high-quality paving stones. This arrangement gives residents control over and pride in their front yards and entryways. The entrances of most shops, restaurants, and offices open directly onto the sidewalk. There are no amorphous parking lots in front of buildings; parking is available on the street and behind buildings. This design encourages residents to walk to do their shopping and makes streets more animated and safe (Figure 15.2).

Lessons for Planners

For practising planners, three chief lessons emerge from an examination of St. Lawrence's urban design characteristics.

Figure 15.2

The streets in the St. Lawrence neighbourhood in Toronto pick up on nineteenth-century designs.

- *Use urban design guidelines to help developers and architects.* Architects may need guidance to fulfill the urban design intent for a particular development. Many municipalities have produced urban design guidelines to help developers at the site plan approval stage. St. Lawrence shows how effective such guidelines can be.
- *Beware of cookie-cutter solutions.* An intensified residential development has a better chance of fitting in with its surroundings if the streetscape and block pattern reflect successful local examples. In looking to St. Lawrence as an example of a contextually appropriate development, planners should be cautious: Some aspects of St. Lawrence's urban design may be inappropriate for other districts, cities, or smaller towns.
- *Educate the public about alternatives.* High-density infill does not necessarily require 30-storey, isolated buildings. By maximizing site coverage and having buildings front onto the streets, St. Lawrence demonstrates the possibility of achieving high-density infill growth with buildings of moderate height and well-defined streets that attract people. Planners should emphasize tested projects like St. Lawrence as alternatives to conventional high-density development.

Successful Infill

In the intensification debate, St. Lawrence represents a successful high-density infill development. Its diversity of tenure and land use is clearly related to its success, as is its municipally-driven and democratic process. In addition, St. Lawrence's urban design characteristics—quality of place, street linkages, and spatial definition—contribute greatly to its attractiveness and liveability. Given an increasing emphasis on intensification at both the municipal and provincial levels, St. Lawrence offers a valuable prototype of a well-designed, high-density redevelopment project.

Downtown Past, Downtown Present, Downtown Yet to Come: Decline and Revival in Middle-Size Urban Areas

Pierre Filion and Heidi Hoernig

2003 Plan Canada 43(1): 31–4

The downtowns of most middle-size Canadian urban areas with populations between 50 000 and 500 000 show signs of advanced decline. Once the unchallenged retail, service, and office centres of their urban regions, they are now relegated to a marginal role. In this article, we concentrate on middle-size urban areas, because the devastation wrought on their downtowns by suburbanization generally exceeds that experienced in larger metropolitan regions. Without the benefit of rail transit, the downtowns of middle-size urban areas are deprived of the accessibility enjoyed by the cores of larger cities. In addition, with weaker interfirm linkage networks and a smaller retail critical mass, the downtowns of middle-size urban areas have been less capable of resisting the onslaught of suburban business parks and shopping malls.[7]

Like Dickens's *A Christmas Carol*, we visit a downtown of the past, present, and future. As in the story, the visits have a transformative purpose: They are meant to inspire the changes needed to forestall a dark future.

Downtown Past

On a Saturday afternoon 50 years ago, the sidewalks of our generic middle-size urban area downtown bustled. People visited downtown as much to be seen and socialize as to shop, eat out, watch a movie, or access medical, legal, or financial services. Not only was downtown the most accessible place within the metropolitan region, the magnitude of its retail concentration exceeded that of the neighbourhood commercial street. These unique characteristics existed because downtown was located in the geographic centre of the built-up area and relied heavily on a transit network that radiated from the core. Only downtown could one find high-order shopping. The department stores, which comfortably dominated the retail scene in the 1950s, located in the core, as did most specialty stores. With socially diversified neighbourhoods nearby and virtually all office employment clustered downtown, this district could count on plentiful daily visitors.[8]

The discerning observer could already perceive threats to this downtown bliss, however. Adapting the core to rising car use was not easy. Walking conditions deteriorated as authorities widened streets at the expense of sidewalks in an effort to accommodate growing automobile circulation. Meanwhile, parking lots nibbled away at housing, retail establishments, and services, thereby reducing downtown land use diversity.

Downtown Present

Walking downtown on a Saturday afternoon has become a lonely experience. Few people walk the sidewalks; those who do are there because they have nowhere else to go. Indeed, a large proportion of the people found in our generic contemporary downtown are unemployed and homeless, or young people "hanging out." The appearance of the downtown area, which bears the scars of an emptying-out trend that has lasted half a century, also sends a message of desolation. Over time, most of its activities either relocated to the suburbs or closed down. Early on, downtown lost retail chains; later department stores and smaller locally-owned premises; and most recently, cinemas. Meanwhile, the proportion of the metropolitan region's jobs found downtown fell dramatically despite stabilizing office employment in many such districts. Monuments to failed attempts at competing head on with suburbs pockmark the landscape of core areas: half-empty parking lots and, most dramatically, failed indoor shopping malls.

The downward trajectory of downtowns reflects several interrelated factors. Retail decline follows the middle-class exodus to the suburbs and the suburban proliferation of regional malls and, more recently, big-box stores. These retail formulas proved remarkably successful in reaping economies of scale and agglomeration in a context of generalized car use.[9] Such suburban developments harm downtowns in two ways. First, downtown outlets are poorly positioned to compete with the prices and range of products offered by suburban malls and big-box stores. Second, the inferior automobile accessibility of downtown areas, their difficulty in attracting shoppers, and the scarcity therein of large assembled sites make them ill-suited to establishing such retail facilities.

While transit dominance created a hub pattern favourable to downtown, reliance on the automobile promotes a diffused form of accessibility with numerous crests at expressway interchanges and at the meeting of arterial roads. In the best of circumstances, downtowns are relegated to the status of one among many centres of activity within a metropolitan region. Most often, however, their economic activity is inferior to that of important suburban nodes.[10]

The health of a downtown rests on a synergistic relation between its different categories of activities. Synergy connotes an interactive process that benefits all involved. A typical downtown example is the relationship between restaurants and hotels: Restaurants derive advantages from their proximity to hotels, and hotels enjoy concomitant benefits from their presence in a lively urban environment where restaurants abound. Interactivity connections in a downtown generally take place on foot: hence the importance of proximity and a pleasant walking environment. A downside of these relationships is the sensitivity of the entire downtown to the faltering of any one of its sectors, as such decline is readily transmitted to other activities.

The impact of these factors of downtown decline is compounded by negative perceptions, which are frequently exaggerated. For example, because they cannot park their car right in front of their destination, drivers complain about automobile accessibility problems, even though they readily walk longer distances to reach a store in a suburban shopping mall. Also, a limited middle-class presence accentuates the visibility of poverty and fear of crime.

Yet, had we spent our Saturday afternoon in the core areas of Halifax, Kingston, or Victoria (Figure 15.3), the experience would have been very different. In these three downtowns, the sidewalks are busy and their continuous facades filled with stores, boutiques, restaurants, cafés, and bars. What factors distinguish these healthy cores from the faltering downtowns of other Canadian midsize urban areas? The answer lies in the capacity of the lively downtowns to secure markets that cannot easily be usurped by suburban facilities.[11] All three cities can rely heavily on tourism, thanks to their historical character and appealing waterfront. The preservation of their traditional street-oriented layout (none seriously disfigured by redevelopment) and the plentiful availability of hospitality services and specialty shopping further enhance their appeal to tourists and local residents looking for an alternative to the suburb. These downtowns are also adjacent to neighbourhoods that have retained or attracted middle-class households. Two of the successful downtowns, Halifax and Kingston, enjoy the presence of a university within walking distance and, as expected, host numerous establishments catering to the student population. Again, two of these cores, Halifax and Victoria, host a provincial legislature and a large share of the provincial civil service. In sum, these downtowns owe their success to the distinctiveness of their environment, activities, and markets compared to the suburbs.

Figure 15.3

HEIDI HOERNIG

Downtown Victoria enjoys a lively ambience and historic character.

Downtown Yet to Come

"Business as usual" that continues present trends causing further downtown decline seems the most likely scenario. On a Saturday afternoon 30 years in the future, little reason is left to come downtown. Most facades are boarded up, and, since numerous structures have fallen victim over time to fire or neglect, empty lots dominate the landscape. The repelling effect of the downtown has provoked a decline in both the number of core housing units and the socioeconomic status of their residents. The limited revival induced by the public sector focuses mostly on cultural activities and employment centres, efforts that have resulted in little more than a smattering of points of activity in a skid row or deserted environment.

Subscribing to the moral of *A Christmas Carol*, we paint an alternative future resulting from changes in attitudes and behaviour prompted by this sinister vision. The downtown utopia we sketch combines and amplifies the most compelling aspects of the three Canadian middle-size urban areas identified as successful in 2003.

Our ideal generic downtown of the future has preserved its street facades and offers a broad range of activities. On a Saturday afternoon, it fills with people: some shopping, some patronizing bars and restaurants, and some attracted by people-watching opportunities in a pedestrian-oriented environment—a unique opportunity in automobile-reliant metropolitan regions. The presence of large numbers of people contributes to its animation and fuels the development of hospitality establishments and specialized boutiques.

As the downtown becomes more appealing to visitors, residential areas within and around its boundaries experience new housing developments and the arrival of middle-class residents. The growing number of residents with increasingly substantial incomes reverberates through the downtown. To cater to its population, it accommodates stores and services: supermarkets, specialty food stores, convenience stores, medical services, and so on.[12] The same goes for downtown employment.

The activity level of the downtown is further stimulated by the niche markets it has captured.[13] By offering shopping and service options that are unavailable in the suburbs, niche activities bring a metropolitan-wide clientele downtown. Each category of niche activities—for example, agglomerations of night clubs, second-hand and antique stores, ethnic restaurants and grocery stores—concentrates in its respective sector of the downtown area.

Downtown Revitalization

Actualizing the positive vision hinges on successfully launching several interconnected cycles. These cycles first require activities attracting different categories of people, who then stimulate additional activity and enliven downtown, thus enhancing its appeal and bringing in more people. But downtown revitalization can be a slow and uncertain process. The market for tourism-oriented downtowns of middle-size cities is easily saturated; a region can support only so many such centres. Likewise, residential development in or near downtown confronts a typical "chicken-and-egg" predicament. New housing development is unlikely to proceed if the downtown is in decline, and, without new residential units, the district lacks a key revitalization instrument. Finally, for a niche market strategy to succeed, a downtown must contain a critical mass of establishments aimed at each targeted market.

It follows that public- and private-sector interests involved in revival strategies must demonstrate leadership, commitment, and patience. Downtown revitalization requires the investment of resources with limited expectations for short-term returns. Moreover, the experience of the last 50 years teaches us that the success of core areas hinges on their uniqueness relative to the suburbs. The few downtowns that have remained healthy owe their success to the differences that set their activities, markets, buildings, and layout apart from those of the remainder of the metropolitan areas.

Can Planning Save the Suburbs?

Jill Grant

1999 Plan Canada 39(4): 16–8

Planning has many critics who force the profession to reflect on the problems of the urban environment and to develop new planning approaches. The most vocal critics have drawn public attention to issues of sprawl, affordability, land use segregation, transportation, environmental degradation, and aesthetics. They argue that planning needs to renew its commitment to good design to solve the problems of the cities and especially those of the suburbs. By enhancing flexibility and allowing the private sector the means to explore new design practices, the critics suggest that they can create vibrant urban areas that better meet the needs of residents. The suburbs, in this view, seem anachronistic, doomed to disappear, as renewed planning changes regulations and offers compact urban models with mixed use and "traditional" design elements. Despite the efforts of many to spread the new gospel of planning, however, millions of suburban Canadians have little interest in "being saved" and show considerable resistance to forced conversion.

The persuasive appeal of improved urban design won many adherents in the planning profession and resulted in some changes in the built environment in Canadian cities in recent years. The new urbanism, as espoused by authorities like Peter Calthorpe, Andres Duany, and Elizabeth Plater-Zyberk, and by Canadian planner/designers such as Andrea Gabor and Frank Lewinberg (in Chapter 14), has had an impact on design standards and planning practices.[14] For example, the Municipality of Metropolitan Toronto prepared a draft plan incorporating new urbanist principles.[15] Edmonton imbued its downtown plans with extensive doses of the philosophy.[16] However, the reaction to some new urbanist plans have shown that, while community members appreciate high-quality design, they may be less ready to accept what they perceive as crowding. They generally do not favour changing the character of their communities, and may find the "cutesiness" of front porches and picket fences cloying. As one of the summer movie hits of 1998, *The Truman Show*, illustrated, the artificial ambiance of the neotraditional town as embodied in "Seahaven" (shot on location in the new urbanist model community of Seaside, Florida) has a disturbing subtext: Everything seems carefully designed and controlled by central planners.

Nonetheless, the new urbanism has become pervasive in Canadian planning in recent years: It has featured prominently in professional conferences, journals (such as *Plan Canada*), and books.[17] From Newfoundland to British Columbia, planners are supporting developers' proposals for suburban "villages" and "town centres" and adjusting bylaws to fit new urbanist models: narrow streets and lots (often in a modified grid), back lanes for parking, limited setbacks, mixed uses, civic squares, green spaces, nostalgic designs for houses.

Cities like Calgary and Markham have adopted new planning regulations to facilitate new urbanist development. Even small cities like Mount Pearl, Newfoundland, and Saint John, New Brunswick, are reviewing their regulations. Some proposed communities using new urbanist ideas, like Bamberton, British Columbia, had trouble securing financing. Others, like McKenzie Towne in Calgary gained prominence. Most common in regions with the strongest housing demand, new urbanist projects fill small niche markets differentiated by price range and housing philosophy: The costs associated with these projects place homes in new urbanist communities out of the reach of many households.[18]

Developers are taking a "wait-and-see" attitude toward the experiments: If they can market the projects successfully, they will continue to build them. Given the interests and means of the average home buyer, builders may find it harder to sell a new urbanist townhome than a sidesplit on a cul-de-sac. As was the case with the popularization of the Don Mills suburban type in the 1960s, developers pick and choose the elements they believe cost effective and buyer friendly. It seems likely that the retro house designs, elegant road layouts, and reduced front setback requirements may prove more popular than transit-oriented infill or significant increases in urban densities. Instead of eliminating the suburbs that so many contemporary critics find distasteful and sterile, new urbanism seems destined to generate "prettier" suburbs for those with the means to make a statement through their housing.[19]

Will New Urbanist Suburbs Solve the Problems of the City for Planners?

While new urbanism may create visually appealing urban landscapes, it cannot deliver its social promises.[20] Good design cannot recreate the social environment of the small community, solve the problems of affordability, reduce environmental exploitation, or tempt people to abandon their cars. Although new urbanism may limit sprawl and enhance opportunities for transit, it runs smack into cultural practices and values. When society defines privacy in spatial terms, spells out success in square feet and number of bathrooms, and links automobile use with personal identity, it is no trivial matter to propose significant changes to the urban landscape. Many of the "planning problems" of contemporary Canadian cities result from significant lifestyle choices that Canadians have made: The problems cannot be "solved" without dramatic cultural transformation, which seems unlikely to come anytime soon.

While planners and designers seem increasingly committed to new urbanist principles, the most notable trends affecting the built environment reflect the appeal of the values that contributed to suburbia. Whereas new urbanism draws on the historic design models of City Beautiful and baroque colonial town plans, the other two common contemporary development forms in North America offer allusions to other built traditions. The rapid spread of gated communities reveals the power of the concept of the medieval fortified town, while the growth in exurban (rural-urban fringe) development demonstrates the continued lure of the "frontier" in mass consciousness.

In the US and in some areas of Western and Central Canada, developers are enclosing new suburbs in walls or fences, and finding that they thereby enhance the attractiveness and marketability of their product.[21] The built form within the gated suburb is typically the traditional suburban layout of loops and cul-de-sacs, reminiscent of the organic street pattern of the medieval town and embodied in the garden city tradition. Large lots and houses, privatized amenities, and limited commercial functions appear within the compound. An intense cultural concern about security feeds this phenomenon of the gated community: People seek safe built environments with neighbours much like themselves, protected from "hostile" elements.

The other popular built form that exacerbates the problem of sprawl is "exurban" growth.[22] Outside the suburbs on the rural fringe of the city, large-lot residential development consumes land swiftly. North Americans idealize the rural environment, and urbanites often indicate a preference for living in the countryside. Developers cater to this search for rural lifestyles by providing up to five-acre lots within commuting distance of the city. Such large-lot developments are available near many Canadian cities. Could it be that Frank Lloyd Wright's concept of Broadacre City, with each residence on a one-acre lot, may be achieved in our lifetime?

Affluent Canadian cities like Toronto, Calgary, and Vancouver are most likely to show the hot trends in urban planning: the best urban design, upscale new neighbourhoods, and the most attractive homes. Leading planning and design approaches have always catered to the affluent, offering them a variety of lifestyle choices. Today, home buyers can select from among new urbanist retro-village, gentrified central neighbourhood, gated golfing park, rural estate with horse stables, or the "traditional" postwar suburb (Figure 15.4).

Although most North Americans came to define themselves as "middle class" in the postwar period, class-segregated neighbourhoods did not disappear. Economic segregation and its nasty twin, racial segregation, are a function of two processes: the financial

Figure 15.4

Designers love to hate conventional suburbs, but consumers love the concept.

link between income levels and housing costs, and social mores that make people feel most comfortable being around others like themselves. None of the popular planning and design approaches currently in use by planners or developers address these issues. While new urbanists claim they can provide affordable, integrated housing by offering varied housing types, the results of their projects show otherwise: Attractive units accommodate the wealthy. Those building gated communities and rural estates make no pretence about the market they serve: They cater happily to the upper and middle classes.

Despite the critiques of new urbanist designers and planners, suburbia still appeals to many Canadians. Realtors confirm that the average middle-class buyer is happy to find a home in a typical suburb. Homes on cul-de-sacs (a street form disdained by new urbanists) remain the easiest ones to sell. While progressive planning departments may be rewriting rules to enhance design flexibility and to accommodate new urbanism principles, traditional suburbs are still built in cities across Canada by developers catering to the mass market. Suburbia may seem formless to its critics, but it can and does provide a sense of place for many of its residents by offering the locus of a web of social relations around family, neighbours, schools, churches, and sports activities.[23] Suburbia provides a landscape that acknowledges and reifies the cultural values of the "middle class."

Clearly, however, neither the upscale villages for the affluent nor the mass suburbs for the middle classes provide a place for the growing numbers of economically disadvantaged households that face decreased choice in the urban and suburban environment. Nor do any of these approaches adequately address the need to reduce the environmental impacts of urban development. Unfortunately, the Canadian government's commitment to planning to improve the urban environment and to reduce inequity has weakened considerably in recent decades. Whereas planning played an important role in enhancing public health, efficiency, and amenity through this century, its ability to advocate for equity and environmental quality has become severely compromised. In the contemporary context, the values of equity and environmental protection are promoted as general planning goals but do not always come with sufficient tools and mechanisms for implementation. Instead, the dominant force in the cultural context within which planning is practised remains that of economic growth and prosperity. New urbanism has done nothing to change that reality.

Imagining a Good City

Has our society lost the ability to imagine a good habitat, as Kunstler asserts?[24] By facilitating suburban growth, have planners forgotten how to plan good communities, as the critics allege? Or do the critics espouse an elitist antisuburban ethic that denies the values and the urban reality of the masses?

These debates about how to plan and build cities reflect the tension inherent in planning theory and practice: What is the role of planning in a democratic society? Is the function of planning to create and implement a vision of the good community, or is the purpose of the profession to help fashion an urban environment in which people can achieve a good life on their own terms?

Certainly any profession worth its salt should be able to articulate a vision and espouse clear values to its clientele. However, the history of planning shows that the clearest vision comes from powerful regimes ready to implement a political and social agenda through built form. The planned towns of Europe, the colonial settlements of the New World, the renewal of major European cities by kings and emperors, the factory towns of the late nineteenth century, and the Disney Corporation "new town" of Celebration each exemplify in some way the power of planning to impose the values of those in control. Most planners today are understandably reluctant to wield their expertise with such authority, and few have sufficient power to do more than recommend options. Planning that seeks to offer alternate visions (e.g., egalitarian, ecological) of society has little hope of being more than a utopian scheme without the ability to influence and alter cultural values and practices.

Many would argue that planning in a democratic society should work to realize and affirm the cultural values of ordinary citizens. They believe that planners should work with community members to enable the community to develop and prosper through active participation. They believe that planning has to be pragmatic, understanding what people can accept and accommodate. Critics of such an approach suggest that accepting popular values means ignoring significant urban problems like affordability and environmental degradation, and that responding to people's concerns can result in planning by polling.[25] While some may argue that planning that supports contemporary mass values is mere "trending," others point to the arrogance of public servants who might seek to substitute their own personal predilections for those of the people they serve (based not on persuasive empirical documentation as much as on the aesthetic lure of a new development model).

Can Planning Solve All the Problems of Suburbia?

No, many suburban problems reflect deeply embedded economic and social problems far beyond the ability of planners to rectify; they will not disappear because planning policies and regulations change. Do we still need planning? Yes, planning continues to offer a useful set of tools for governments committed to allocating resources according to community ends. As long as our cities and towns thrive in a changing economy, governments will still face difficult choices. While the signs are clear that governments seem more willing in recent years to leave many decisions to the market, they cannot avoid the need to set some of the rules of the game. Governments have institutionalized planning as part of a cultural apparatus for dealing with the urban environment. While they may constrain its mandate in response to development pressures and changing community values, it seems unlikely that governments will completely abandon a process that has so many political, economic, and cultural functions.

Can planning save the suburbs? The answer to that question is for the communities for which planners work to explore. As professionals, planners can weigh in with our opinions and advice, but as facilitators of a democratic process we must hear what our communities tell us. We should offer residents new models of the "good city" and draw attention to the inequities and problems of contemporary built environments. At the same time, however, we should be cautious about proselytizing newly introduced professional models that are as yet poorly tested in practice. If suburban living remains the people's choice, we can expect that planners will still be facilitating the development of suburbs for years to come, albeit in a variety of forms to reflect the tastes and the issues of the times.

The Urban Sprawl Debate: Myths, Realities, and Hidden Agendas

Larry S Bourne

2001 Plan Canada 41(4): 26–8

Everyone is against urban sprawl. Judging by recent attention in professional journals and the popular media, the issue is high on political agendas. Unfortunately, few agree on what the term means, and thus discussions of its causes, consequences, and potential solutions are at best confused and at worst counterproductive.

To some observers, sprawl applies to any extension of the suburban margin; to others, it is synonymous with the spread of development onto sensitive green lands and agricultural soils, increases in highway congestion, or the proliferation of new subdivisions of homogeneous and low-density, single-family housing. The traditional definition of sprawl, however, is much more specific: It refers to suburban development that is haphazard, disorganized, poorly serviced, and largely unplanned. By this rather strict standard, urban Canada has relatively little sprawl. Instead, the larger urban regions—notably Toronto, Calgary, and Vancouver—exhibit extremely rapid growth, most of which inevitably occurs on the outer suburban margin, typically at lower densities. Does such growth constitute sprawl? Does suburbia's negative image reflect poor planning or media hype?

In an attempt to clarify the underlying elements of this debate, I pay particular attention to the current expression of that debate in the Greater Toronto Area (GTA), to the merits of tighter regulation of residential uses and densities, and to the implicit agendas that have shaped the debate.

On Density, Suburbanization, and Intensification

What is myth and what is reality with respect to urban densities and suburbanization? It may surprise some readers to learn that the densities of new residential developments in Toronto's outer suburbs are, on average, the highest on the continent (Figure 15.5). Despite higher standards for public space and servicing, these densities have also been increasing over the last two decades, primarily because of market demand, a wider mix of housing types, and the rising price of land. With a few exceptions, most new suburban single-family housing features 30- to 40-foot lot frontages, contrasting sharply with the 50- to 100-foot frontages typical of the 1950s and 1960s.

The media also frequently give the impression that all new housing is built in new suburbs. In fact, many cities, particularly Toronto and Vancouver, have been remarkably

Figure 15.5

Very narrow lots in the suburbs of the GTA generate high-density detached housing.

successful at encouraging high proportions of new construction as residential infill within the existing urban envelope. That proportion is now estimated at between 20 and 30 percent of all housing starts in the GTA, compared to less than 10 percent in most American metropolitan areas.

Would further residential intensification significantly reduce the extent and impact of suburban expansion? Of course, we could do more to increase residential densities by facilitating infill and reusing older brownfield sites. Providing physical infrastructure for housing on streets with 30-foot lots is less expensive per dwelling unit than it is for streets with 60-foot lots.[26] Yet, these costs are a relatively small proportion of the costs of new housing and services, particularly in rapidly-growing regions. Other local costs, such as those for schools, open space, soft services, and community facilities, are essentially fixed. The largest and most variable costs are on the regional scale: in the arrangement of uses, the rapid growth of nonresidential uses, and specifically in the disjuncture between residential and commercial-industrial activities.

An additional source of confusion, over and above the question of spatial scale, involves the measurement of density. Typically, densities are calculated using simple population numbers as the numerator in the density ratio. This ignores, among other factors, the impact of demographic change, as well as revisions in living arrangements, on suburban forms in general and density ratios in reducing densities in particular. Average household size has declined by over 35 percent since 1961, which translates into a requirement for 35 percent more dwelling units to house the same total population. Smaller households usually result in a thinning of the population of all neighbourhoods, old and new, at least those with a fixed housing stock. Nevertheless, smaller lot sizes and a wider mix of dwelling types have combined to reverse past declines in population density. In parallel, densities of the residential built environment (e.g., measured in terms of dwelling units and capital investment) have increased even faster in most new suburban areas.

Even so, antisprawl advocates argue that we could shift many of these new units to brownfield, or industrial redevelopment sites. Is this realistic? There is certainly considerable potential for further residential intensification, but there are also real limits to the capacity of the infill process and existing built-up areas to absorb new growth in the volume required. The infill process is administratively complicated, politically sensitive, subject to liability risks, regulatory barriers, and widespread NIMBYism, and is constrained in the longer term by limited effective demand and high costs.

Even in an ideal world, where all of the stakeholders, including conservative ratepayer groups, agreed with the objective of intensification, it would be a major achievement to maintain the existing proportion of brownfield construction, let alone increase that proportion to 40 or 50 percent over the next decade, as is widely proposed. This suggests that most units will have to be built in the new suburbs on formerly rural lands. This is not sprawl, by conventional definition, but rather demand-driven suburbanization. It can be improved, but it cannot be wished away.

What, Then, Is the Problem?

Given that low-density unplanned residential sprawl is not widespread, if suburban growth is as inevitable as expected population growth suggests, what is the primary problem? Three issues seem more important. One is the challenge, indeed the obligation, to provide sufficient space to accommodate anticipated growth while minimizing its negative side effects. Rapid growth does tend to overwhelm the ability of municipalities to plan and deliver appropriate social services (schools, for example) and to finance new infrastructure (such as sewers, roads, and transit). It also adds to feelings of unease among existing residents that their current lifestyles and living conditions are at risk.

One common response to this sense of risk, and to the negative images of sprawl, is to recommend slower population growth. But how? Growth in the GTA is driven overwhelmingly by immigration (75 percent), and secondarily by natural increase, not by domestic in-migrants. Thus, reducing the overall growth rate is largely a question of changing immigration policies, which is beyond local control. In the absence of lower immigration levels, governments must plan for anticipated levels of growth in ways that are efficient, equitable, and sensitive to social and environmental issues. The paranoia regarding sprawl tends to divert attention from addressing these genuine concerns.

Second, the main contributors to low-density suburban development are not residential uses but nonresidential activities: commercial, industrial, storage, and distributional uses, hobby farms, golf courses, and so forth (Figure 15.6). While suburban residential (net) densities have been increasing in most areas, measured in both population and dwelling units, the densities of other users of urban space, including public-sector uses, have been decreasing. Surprisingly, no one seems to notice. Why, we might ask, is so little attention paid to the increasing rates of land consumption by

Figure 15.6

Low-density commercial uses are consuming vast areas of suburban land.

nonresidential uses? Is it because these uses provide play space for the well-to-do, or generate substantial tax revenues for cash-starved local governments?

The third problem is the lack of regional coordination. The overwhelming source of our suburban problems is not residential sprawl but the weakness of regional integration of transportation, infrastructure provision, and land use, and specifically of housing and extensive nonresidential uses. There are, for instance, few examples in Toronto's outer suburbs of employment and living spaces being carefully coordinated or of new developments being closely linked either to the GO-system or to local transit.

Frequent calls to increase residential densities still further, as reflected (incorrectly it seems) in the design of "new urbanism" communities, serve no useful purpose if the contribution of commercial-industrial uses and the issue of coordinating land use and transportation are not addressed. Indeed, such policies may aggravate certain problems (affordability and access to jobs, for example), especially if these policies are implemented in stark isolation from other actions.

Why the Antisprawl Rhetoric? Hidden Agendas?

Why is the confusion over density and the nature of sprawl so entrenched in the media and in the public mind? One explanation is that the current antisprawl rhetoric serves as a protective "all-reason" umbrella under which special interest groups and politicians can cluster to advance their own political agendas and, in so doing, shield themselves from potential criticism. Such agendas, however rational for individuals, are often unrelated to broader issues of the form and quality of suburban development. Since no one openly advocates sprawl as such, taking a position against sprawl is safe. Residential uses are also the largest consumer of suburban land and thus represent an easy target. For politicians, an antisprawl posture often offers the benefit of appearing concerned for the quality of urban life while not having to make hard choices on other problems.

For special interest groups on the urban fringe, the antisprawl umbrella serves other purposes. For some, it is a means of preserving semirural habitats. For individuals, such a stance may be understandable; in a collective sense, however, it is inequitable and socially exclusionary. Those residents generally do not pay the full costs of their choice of location, and their actions implicitly limit the rights of others, including the next generation, to live there. For others, sprawl represents an environmental crusade with undeniably valid objectives, but one that is often one dimensional and whose remedial costs are seldom specified. Typically, those costs are also unevenly distributed across communities and social classes. Antisprawl rhetoric may also reflect concerns over the increasing social and ethnocultural diversity of the suburbs.

What Might Be Done?

An initial step in clarifying the issues would be to separate myth from reality. First, as a precondition for action, we must accept the simple fact that suburban growth is likely to continue as long as populations grow and a significant proportion of households express a desire for single-family ground-access housing. This is not an excuse for suburbanization, but rather a statement that lamenting sprawl is not a recipe for effective action.

Our challenge is to design policy objectives that more accurately reflect the development trajectory of large and growing urban regions. These should not be pie-in-the-sky objectives or pious statements against sprawl, which are comforting to some but largely useless as guidelines for policy decisions. Nor should they be objectives that benefit one special interest use or user in isolation from, or at the expense of, the needs of others. Instead, they should provide concrete goals and targets that recognize the difficult tradeoffs involved in satisfying the often conflicting demands for economic spaces, mobility, and environmental conservation. They should also recognize the uneven costs and benefits that flow from those decisions and identify the needs of the next generation for affordable housing and living space. The fourth challenge is to address the excessive use of space by nonresidential uses and to insist that such activities pay the true spillover costs of their developments.

Misleading Positions

Residential density, then, is not the crucial issue (although it is obviously relevant) in planning new suburban areas. Rather, the issues are the mix of uses, declining nonresidential densities, and the lack of strategic coordination between housing and other land uses in ways that facilitate service provision, conservation, and transit use. Despite the antisprawl rhetoric, tighter restrictions on residential uses alone are not the answer. These will only force up the price of land and housing and thus increase the affordability problems facing current renters and the next generation of homeowners, as Portland's experience has demonstrated.

The argument here is simple: Much of the antisprawl rhetoric focused on residential uses and densities in isolation is misdirected, counterproductive, and socially inequitable. It is underpinned by political and social agendas that often have little or nothing to do with the density or quality of suburban spaces. Politicians in power owe it to the next generation to avoid increasing prices by restricting suburban housing based on some fuzzy concept of sprawl, while ignoring nonresidential uses and public infrastructure standards.

What we can do is to address directly the social, intergenerational, and environmental costs of the current form and density of development, particularly those imposed by commercial-industrial and other nonresidential uses. Planners should insist that those uses be linked, wherever possible, to both regional and local transit systems. Further, governments should remove tax inequities and reduce or eliminate subsidies that discourage the efficient use of land—especially for low-density commercial, industrial and transportation uses. Specifically, these initiatives require the creation of a regional authority that has, first, the resources and responsibility to influence all forms of suburban uses, and second, the mandate to shape the linkages between such uses, especially those that cross municipal boundaries.

Some might argue that the battle for a more rational, functionally integrated, eco- and transit-friendly suburban form was lost decades ago; that the mould is cast, and everyone must live with the results and their social costs: I disagree. Given the massive growth anticipated in the GTA over the next 20 years, we still have the opportunity to remake the suburban landscape and to better integrate the new with the old. It will, however, take effective leadership, clear visions, and strategic investments.

The Tao of Smart Growth (The way that can be named is not the way)

Raymond Young

2001 Plan Canada 41(4): 29–30

> "Smart Growth is about... taking positive action... more livable communities... advance planning... healthy eco-systems... cooperative relationships between developers and local government... avoiding adversarial public hearings... [and appeals to those who want] to cut costs and taxes... safer and more natural communities for children... secure agricultural land base... social justice... public transit... housing options for all... to protect nature... preserve wildlife habitat... to reduce air and water pollution and to use resources more equitably and efficiently."
> *West Coast Environmental Law News* (15 December 2000)

Amazing—all that sizzle and no sprawl too! No wonder "smart growth" is North America's fastest selling remedy for all that ails our urban areas. The vision is more than appealing: It's just about perfect.

But wait. Isn't this vision identical to the foundations of the planning profession: the establishment of clean, healthy, safe, and natural places to live; the efficient, equitable provision of public services, housing, and social and economic opportunities; the preservation and protection of nature; and the maintenance of open, principled, and participatory decision making? It says a lot about the quality of the planning profession's core vision that it has remained so consistent and so appealing over generations. But it's not new. So why the current stampede?

Our concern about the smart growth movement should start with recognition that it is not based on a reasoned, widespread conversion to this worthy planning vision. The core of the planning vision has always been a good one, and, at the level of abstraction at which it is expressed—even hyped—in the smart growth pitch, it is as irresistible as mom and apple pie on Mother's Day. A stampede is basically "mindless" (to borrow a word from the smart growth lexicon). In this case, it is caused by a trendy commitment to a formalistic, almost ritualistic set of policies for achieving the planning vision.

While smart growth dresses itself well and promises all, it is in substance not about the vision at all: It is about marketing. And what is being marketed is a prepackaged prescription. From the perspective of smart growth, the planning vision is simply attractive, highly-recognizable packaging that is guaranteed to elicit a positive response. Having appropriated the packaging, smart growth is also "branding" the vision. What brand could be better than "smart growth," especially when the competition can be dismissed as "mindless sprawl"?

But what about the content? The answer involves perhaps the oldest marketing ploy of all: the suggestion of a potion that cures all ills, a formula that leads to the vision depicted on the package. The idea that a single remedy sounds good, looks good, and can do everything, has long been a dangerous one, capable of disarming critical faculties.

Perhaps the most dangerous aspect of the marketing efforts of the smart growth movement has been the commodification of the planning vision, coupled with the seduction of the planning profession itself. Once we accept a specific formula as the way to the vision, there is little room for the free play of ideas, for competition between concepts, or for vigorous debate that should be as diverse, broad, and complex as the problems that face us. Smart growth does not promote debate; it prescribes a set of solutions laid out in step-by-step instruction manuals that reduce planning to a checklist of "best practices" designed to implement a formula. Once we commodify the practice by relying on a series of checklists, we can't truly call ourselves professionals at all. We are no more practising planning than the average consumer who follows IKEA instructions is designing and building furniture.

In June 2000, one national organization posted a smart growth density calculator on the Internet (since removed). This tool, it was claimed, would automatically reveal the true environmental impacts of sprawl at different urban densities. All the assumptions and calculations were built in and invisible. You pushed the button and got the answer, and your thinking days were over. "Smart" urban densities were posted at 100 households per acre. Critics reacted with dismay, since those densities would allow the entire population of the world to reside in Virginia, and the entire US population in Los Angeles. Equally suspect was the "smart" analysis of automobile use at those densities. The calculator reported that, per household, "smart density" automobile travel would be reduced about 4.5 times, but of course the calculator missed the point that, at 100 households per acre, the miles travelled per day in each square mile would be over 30 times greater than that in the present average urban area, and 10 times greater than that in Los Angeles. The density calculator was quietly removed after its prescription proved unreasonable.

In the quote in the text box, the author extols the virtue of "avoiding adversarial public hearings." The implication is that smart growth is so smart and its solutions so obviously correct that debate will be unnecessary. Why in the world would planners embrace a formula for planning that promotes such a goal? Public debate reflects healthy competition between legitimate and varied public interests. We should recognize that adversarial debate is a thousand times more valuable than an endless series of "cooperative hearings" devoid of difference and "managed" to minimize competing ideas and interests. Any formalistic set of solutions that results in the flatlining of public debate on planning issues should be cause for panic, not praise, in our profession.

As planners, we serve the public and the profession by maintaining the purposive, independent, creative, critical, reforming, and even radical and irreverent nature of our profession. Be smart: Explore the concepts of smart growth and use what works, modify what may work, and reject what doesn't. If you want to put a name to it, just call it "planning."

Moving Forward in Canadian Communities: Soliloquy of an Urbanist

Larry Beasley

2004, Plan Canada 44(4): 16–9

Toronto is on a roll. The excitement is tangible. Strong political leadership, new ideas, and a groundswell of activity all illustrate what is happening throughout our great country. Across Canada, people are awakening to urbanism, quality of life, the value of our cities, and the imperative to make them flourish. It is as though we have come back from a long sleep. There is a sense of extraordinary expectations: the revival of urbanism and of planning as the influential profession for urbanism.

I have felt this energy only a few times in my 30 years as a planner. I remember the energy when I first started out. We have a solid history of workable, caring cities. When I came to Canada in the late 1960s, Canadian cities were pretty special. But when I started out as a planner in the early 1970s, we were already beginning to worry about the demise of neighbourhoods. So the call went out, and senior governments responded with exciting partnerships to revitalize inner-city communities and their housing; and we did. That was a time of optimism.

However, we have also gone through a long time when our cities have lost ground. Cities started to be shaped primarily by laissez-faire attitudes, or unshaped by special interests. Government was in a state of confusion about the public interest and blinded by management dilemmas like cutting budgets and red tape. Modernist architecture was brutal and blithely antiurban. Civic budgets became overwhelmed because of our outdated funding sources. That was a time of pessimism.

As planners, we were often seen as a part of the problem rather than the solution. Our profession was associated with what was going wrong. We lost our credibility and the trust of the public. Everywhere we were open to attack, and most of us felt it. At one point in British Columbia, the province was on the verge of outlawing planning, although saner heads prevailed. Fortunately, cities are robust, planning is robust, the concept of urbanism is reviving, and citizens are declaring everywhere that they want their cities to be great. Even politicians are beginning to use the right words and to sponsor the right ideas. We face big problems, however, and people want real, effective answers.

A Vision of Good Cities

Our cities are often ugly. We have to teach ourselves to see again and to use that vision to reshape the built form. Our cities are often inhumane: Look at our growing homelessness problem. We have to teach ourselves to care again and to use that compassion to reshape supports for people. Our cities are not sustainable: Look at the impact of the car and pollution. We have to teach ourselves to honour nature above all else and to tap natural forces to fix cities. So, this is a time of opportunity for planning and for planners—if we get it right, if we join hands with many others.

After all these years, I am now confident about some key qualities we must bring to the table. Most important, planners have to have vision. We have to have good ideas: new, strong, and simple ideas that come from a clear view of the world and a sure sense of urbanism. They cannot just be ideas on process. They must be substantive ideas like those we have learned from Jane Jacobs and Alan Jacobs.[27]

The Livable City

In Vancouver, three strong ideas have made all the difference: using the concept of "neighbourhood" as the basic building block of our city; having a "living-first" strategy for transforming our downtown; and creating a "city by design." Led by our young people, we are pursuing several newer ideas that are going to make all the difference.

Designing "sustainability" and developing "social equity" are two central tenets of Vancouver's future. We need fast and sustained action to pursue these ideas. Planners must show real leadership and not just be factotums for politicians or merely do background studies. We must inspire, mentor, and guide. We must tap interests, not just take positions. We must find solidarity with our citizens. We have to bring a strong process of engagement with all those around us. We know the public must be involved, so we need to be convenors—and good ones. But we cannot get bogged down. We must really solve problems and bring forward exciting new propositions if we want credibility and a place at the table. In Vancouver, we had to create a whole new way to do business with the cooperative planning model, and a new way to think about the future with *CityPlan*.

The Planner's Role

We have to really communicate. We need to say what we say well, demonstrate through examples, and communicate the whole package in a language people can understand.

Of course, we have to tap into common thinking; but we also need to connect with the humanity of those with whom we work, and not objectify people as we all too often have done in the past. We have to match process and communications with strong analysis, giving solid facts and projections, not just opinions. We need to use solid methodology, not just surf the Internet. We need to be critical and take nothing as given. We need to change the laws and processes, to do what is right. We need to bring technology to the heart of our work.

I have learned that planning is part philosophy and part craft. It is a dialectical reality. Theory is vital, and the public interest is our guide. Common sense is likewise as vital, and here practicality is our guide. A strong, critical attitude binds it together. The task at hand is to apply theory and practice to rescue and recreate our endangered cities and to illustrate for a new generation that Canadians are true experts at city building. Through this work as planners, we will also rebuild our stature as the profession that society will assign to undertake, even lead, this great endeavour. This will undoubtedly bring the old urban themes echoing back yet again. Maybe they have to be rediscovered with every generation; or maybe it is especially important to articulate them at this time, because politicians are ready to hear them and adopt them and make them happen through the world of politics.

What makes it tough—a continuing challenge—is that the barriers are huge and the forces against urbanism strong. The societal dysfunction hitting our cities is vast. Vancouver's Downtown Eastside is festering, and I could find the same conditions in every downtown in every city in this country.

Internal bureaucratic barriers are the Achilles' heel of the profession: unrealistic and antiurban standards from the past, competing interests, and bureaucratic inclination to conservatism hold us back. The selfishness of some and ignorance of others trample too much that we treasure. Just think of the negative effects on our cities of insensitive retail formats or fixed attitudes on parking: These are only some of many examples of self-interested pressures distorting urbanism. Our own lack of guts can be our greatest handicap. Sometimes, we just have to draw a line, say no, and be sanguine with that.

We know it is complicated out there. But in a fluid, messy world, this profession can always depend on its bedrock: our values, philosophy, ethics, and sense of justice and fair play. That is what brought most of us into this profession. We have a spiritual force.

Furthermore, one tether to that bedrock will serve us well as individual planners: our sense of self. We must face ourselves and know ourselves, because what we intend is often just as influential as what we do in how our work unfolds. That is important because each of us in our work holds a collective responsibility to this profession, not just to ourselves or our organization. Every time you act on something for today's crisis, you add to the opus of your own work that can or cannot sustain inspection. But you also add to the practice of the whole profession that does or does not facilitate the efforts of every other planner to plan.

Larry Beasley says that we know planning is working when:

- We match intuition and passion with logical thinking and technical prowess to tackle the hard issues of cities.
- We achieve equity and align our energy behind those most in need.
- We engage communities on their terms.
- We are addressing today's problems but also building carefully for the future.
- We balance critique and flexibility, but foster excellence and innovation.
- We have influence that has come from consistently good, useful advice.
- We take action backed up with contingencies; producing products; making change and owning that change.
- We are feeling stress but having fun.
- We reach out to constituencies but have personal relationships with people as individuals.
- We reinforce our ethics with our practice.

City by Design

Let us commit ourselves to rebuilding a strong sense of community and neighbourhood. Through this lens, *CityPlan* in Vancouver is uncovering clues of how to transform NIMBYism from a conservative barrier of fear to an engine of joy for revitalization. Let us commit to rebuilding inclusiveness. The initiatives under former Mayor Larry Campbell in Vancouver illustrate that a formula of social responsibility is still possible. Let us commit to rebuilding culture. Globalization cannot be allowed to steal away the soul of our towns and cities. Who really wants a geography of nowhere?

Let us commit to rebuilding the "city by design." Design need not be forgotten. Beauty is okay. We must harness the scale that is exploding our cities. Finally, let us commit to rebuilding the healthy organism of the city. This includes being sustainable and keeping the principles of balance, intensity, mix, and amenity high in our minds as we invent tomorrow's cities. It means cherishing and protecting the sense of mystery that remains in so many wonderful urban places.

We know that planning is working when our citizens are happy about the cities we create with and for them. This is the acid test. In the final analysis, planning has to touch the hearts of everyone—not just their minds, not just their pocketbooks.

Study Questions

1. How does economic growth differ from sustainable community development?

2. What are the relative contributions to urban sprawl from residential, commercial, and industrial development?

3. Analyze suburban development in your community to identify the patterns of density and urban form in new growth. How do contemporary suburbs differ from the older urban neighbourhoods?

4. By using census information for your community, track population growth, number of dwelling units, and household size over the last five decades. Prepare tables and graphs to show the change in population density and in housing unit density in the community through time. Explain the patterns you find.

5. The St. Lawrence neighbourhood in Toronto is often cited as a good example of the success of urban infill development. How easy or difficult is it to translate its success to other urban neighbourhoods? When does intensification become a good growth strategy?

6. What do you see as good strategies for managing growth? Are growth boundaries feasible?

7. What are the key principles of smart growth, and how are they influencing urban planning in the major Canadian cities?

8. What are the patterns in housing growth in Canada over the last two decades? How and why are the trends changing? (Canada Mortgage and Housing Corporation's Web site is a good resource. Look at the *Canadian Housing Observer* for trends.)

Reference Notes

1. Skaburskis, A & B Brunner (1999) The views of Canadian planners on growth problems and growth management strategies. *Plan Canada* 39(3): 26–31.

2. Seasons, M (1994) Local economic development: Practice and prospects. *Plan Canada* 34(6): 10–5.

3. Skaburskis, A & B Brunner (1999) Op. cit.

4. Lewinberg, F (1993) Reurbanization: The context for planning growth. *Plan Canada* 33(3): 10–3.

5. Toronto Housing Department (1979) *St. Lawrence: 1974–1979*. City of Toronto.

6. Hulchanski, JD (1990) *Planning New Urban Neighbourhoods: Lessons from Toronto's St. Lawrence Neighbourhood*. Vancouver: UBC Planning Papers in Canadian Planning Issues, School of Community and Regional Planning.

7. Robertson, KA (1999) Can small-city downtowns remain viable? A national study of development issues and strategies. *Journal of the American Planning Association* 65: 270–83.

8. Fogelson, RM (2001) *Downtown: Its Rise and Fall, 1880–1950*. New Haven: Yale University Press.

9. Gillette, H (1985) The evolution of the planned shopping center in suburb and city. *Journal of the American Planning Association* 51: 449–60.

    Jones, KG & J Simmons (1993) *Location, Location, Location: Analyzing the Retail Environment*. (2nd ed) Toronto: Nelson Canada.

10. Filion, P, T Bunting, & K Warriner (1999) The entrenchment of urban dispersion: Residential preferences and location patterns in the dispersed city. *Urban Studies* 36: 1317–47.

    Lewis, PF (1983) The galactic metropolis. In RH Platt & G Macinko (eds) *Beyond the Urban Fringe*. Minneapolis: University of Minnesota Press: 23–49.

11. Dane, SG (1997) *Main Street Success Stories*. Washington: National Main Street Center.

12. Knack, RE (1998) Downtown where the living is easy. *Planning* 64(12): 4–9.

    Sohmer R (1999) Downtown housing as an urban redevelopment tool: Hype or hope. *Housing Policy Debate* 10: 477–505.

13. Milder, D (1997) *Niche Strategies for Downtown Revitalization: A Hands-on Guide to Developing, Strengthening and Marketing Niches*. New York: Downtown Research and Development Center.

14. Calthorpe, P (1993) *The Next American Metropolis*. New York: Princeton Architectural Press.

    Duany, A & E Plater-Zyberk (1992) The second coming of the American small town. *Plan Canada* 32(3): 6–13.

    Duany, A & E Plater-Zyberk (1996) Neighborhoods and suburbs. *Design Quarterly* 164: 10–23.

15. Toronto, Municipality of Metropolitan (1992) *The Liveable Metropolis*. Draft Plan, Municipality of Metropolitan Toronto.

16. Edmonton, City of (1997) *Capital City Downtown Plan*. Edmonton, Planning and Development.

17. Grant, J (2003) Exploring the influence of new urbanism in community planning practice. *Journal of Architectural and Planning Research* 20 (3): 234–53.

18. Chidley, J (1997) The new burbs. *Maclean's*. 21 July: 16–21.

19. Grant, J (2002) From 'sugar cookies' to 'gingerbread men': Conformity in suburban design. *Planners Network Journal*, 151 (Spring): 10–3, http://www.plannersnetwork.org/publications/2002_152_spring/grant.htm (accessed 16 April 2006).

20. Audirac, I & AH Shermyen (1994) An evaluation of neotraditional design's social prescription: Postmodern placebo or remedy for suburban malaise? *Journal of Planning Education and Research* 13: 161–73.

21. Anthony, L (1997) Safe and sound behind the gate. *Maclean's*. 21 July: 25.

Blakely, EJ & MG Snyder (1997) *Fortress America: Gated Communities in the United States.* Washington: Brookings Institution Press.

22. Davis, JS, AC Nelson, & KJ Dueker (1994) The new 'burbs: The exurbs and their implications for planning policy. *Journal of the American Planning Association* 60(1): 45–9.

23. Altman, I & S Low (eds) (1992) Place attachment. *Human Behavior and Environment and Research* 12. New York: Plenum Press.

24. Kunstler, JH (1993) *The Geography of Nowhere: The Rise and Decline of America's Man-Made Landscape.* New York: Simon & Schuster.

25. Seelig, MY (1995) Citizen participation as a political cop-out. *Globe and Mail.* 27 February: A15.

26. Blais, P (2000) *Inching toward Sustainability: The Evolving Structure of the GTA* Toronto: University of Toronto and Metropole Consultants.

27. Jacobs, AB (1991) *Great Streets.* Cambridge: MIT Press.

Jacobs, J (1961) *The Death and Life of Great American Cities.* New York: Vintage Books.

1. Examine a plan or planning strategy from a Canadian community. (Many are available online or at the local planning department.) Identify the values that underpin it. What theories do you find represented in the policies? What issues are most important in the community, and what are the "problems" the plan defines? What approach does the plan take to public participation in the planning process? Do the policies adequately address the goals and objectives of the plan? Are the strategies likely to resolve the identified problems? What do you see as the strengths and weaknesses of the plan?

2. The authors included in this text suggest a variety of roles for the planner. Describe the range of approaches that planners may take to their work and the conditions under which particular roles become appropriate.

3. Local economic development has become an increasingly important strategy for smaller communities and disadvantaged neighbourhoods in Canada. Identify the prime approaches used and evaluate their successes (and failures) in achieving the objectives of social and economic improvement.

4. Evaluate the impact of the urbanization of high-quality agricultural land on the sustainability of long-term food production. What strategies and policies prove most effective at conserving agricultural land?

5. Characterize and explain the shifting population patterns in Canadian settlements during the last century. What dominant trends does your analysis reveal?

6. Describe and explain the relationship between the development of settlements and the role played by railway transportation. How did settlements along railroads grow in the early twentieth century? What is now happening to settlements along railroads that have closed?

7. What are the strengths and weaknesses of community planning in meeting the key needs of Canadians? How can planning remain responsive to changing population dynamics?

8. Compare and contrast the visions in the plans of several small to mid-sized (10 000 to 500 000 population) Canadian cities. (Most are available online with a search linking the city's name with "vision.") What visions do the plans offer of the future? Are the visions specific? Are they realistic? What values and theories underlie the visions?

9. Identify and assess the key issues and challenges facing Canadian cities that planners will need to address over the next decade. What approaches should we be using to prepare for an uncertain future?

10. Discuss the role of heritage conservation in community planning in Canada, focusing on either urban town centres or small-town revitalization projects. What role does heritage play in community development activities?

11. Words like "sustainable" and "smart" often appear in contemporary community plans in Canada. Using examples from some of Canada's larger cities, evaluate how successful the cities are in achieving sustainable development or smart growth.

12. Discuss the ways in which Canadian settlements reveal the pervasive influence of the automobile as a mode of transportation. What are the barriers to making cities better suited to pedestrians and cyclists?

13. Observe and document a neighbourhood in your community. Describe the land use and spatial patterns that you find there. Explain how its history and the regulations and financial conditions that obtained when it was built (or renovated) account for its form and function.

14. Compare and contrast land use or zoning bylaws or subdivision regulations from cities of similar size but in different regions of Canada. How can you account for the similarities and differences? What principles seem to lie behind the regulations?

15. Review population projections for small to mid-sized (10 000 to 500 000 population) Canadian municipalities. What predictions are made about growth (or decline)? What premises guide the projections? Do the projections provide options for the range of possibilities that futurists advise planners to

consider? (If not, which scenarios are ignored, and why?)

16. Some of the articles in this book suggest that the "public interest" is a problematic concept for guiding planning, while others argue that planners have to serve the public interest. What makes the concept of the public interest so appealing to planning, even as the idea has come under greater scrutiny?

17. Why is it fair to suggest that community planning in Canada involves a constant tug of war between utopianism and pragmatism?

18. What are the implications of the privatization of space in Canadian communities? What evidence do you find of this trend in your community?

19. What can communities facing population decline do to promote local economic development? What lessons can be learned from Canadian success stories?

20. Why has new urbanism had such a large impact on planning in Canada? How is new urbanism being adapted in practice in Canadian suburbs?

Further Readings on Canadian Planning

Bourne, LS (1982) *Internal Structure of the City: Readings on Urban Form, Growth and Policy.* New York: Oxford University Press.

Bourne, LS and D Ley (eds) (1993) *The Changing Social Geography of Canadian Cities.* Montreal: McGill-Queen's Press.

Bunting, T & P Filion(eds) (2006) *Canadian Cities in Transition* (3rd ed). Toronto: Oxford University Press.

Calthorpe, P (1993) *The Next American Metropolis.* New York: Princeton Architectural Press.

Cullingworth, JB (1987) *Urban and Regional Planning in Canada.* New Brunswick: Transaction Books.

Denhez, M (1984) *The Canadian Home: From Cave to Electronic Cocoon.* Toronto: Dundurn Press.

Gertler, LO & RW Crowley (1977) *Canadian Cities: The Next 25 Years.* Toronto: McClelland and Stewart.

Grant, J (1994) *The Drama of Democracy: Contention and Dispute in Community Planning.* Toronto: University of Toronto Press.

—— (2006) *Planning the Good Community: New Urbanism in Theory and Practice.* New York: Routledge.

Harris, R (1999) *Unplanned Suburbs: Toronto's American Tragedy 1900 to 1950.* Baltimore: Johns Hopkins Press.

—— (2004) *Creeping Conformity: How Canada Became Suburban 1900–1960.* Toronto: University of Toronto Press.

Higgins, D (1986) *Local and Urban Politics in Canada.* Toronto: Gage Educational Publishing.

Hygeia Consulting Services and REIC Ltd (1995) *Changing Values, Changing Communities: A Guide to the Development of Healthy, Sustainable Communities.* Ottawa: Canada Mortgage and Housing Corporation.

Isin, E & R Tomalty (1993) *Resettling Cities: Canadian Residential Intensification Initiatives.* Ottawa: Canada Mortgage and Housing Corporation.

Kemble, R (1989) *The Canadian City, St. John's to Victoria: A Critical Commentary.* Montreal: Harvest House.

Krieger, A (ed) (1991) *Andres Duany and Elizabeth Plater-Zyberk: Towns and Town-Making Principles.* Harvard University Graduate School of Design. New York: Rizzoli.

Leung, H-L (2003) *Land Use Planning Made Plain.* 2nd ed. Toronto: University of Toronto Press.

Palermo, F, P Cuttell, & B Dera (2000) *First Nations Community Planning Model.* Halifax: Cities and Environment Unit, Dalhousie University.

Peck and Associates (2000) *Implementing Sustainable Community Development: Charting a Federal Role for the 21st Century.* Ottawa: Canada Mortgage and Housing Corporation.

Punter, J (2003) *The Vancouver Achievement: Urban Planning and Design.* Vancouver: UBC Press.

Sewell, J (1993) *The Shape of the City: Toronto Struggles with Modern Planning.* Toronto: University of Toronto Press.

Wackernagel, M & W Rees (1995) *Our Ecological Footprint: Reducing Human Impact on the Earth.* Gabriola Island: New Society Publishers.

Witty, DR (2004) *Professional Practice Manual.* Ottawa: Canadian Institute of Planners.

Jill Grant PhD MCIP is professor and director of the School of Planning, Dalhousie University in Halifax. She is the author of *The Drama of Democracy: Contention and Dispute in Community Planning* and *Planning the Good Community: New Urbanism in Theory and Practice*. She coedited *Towards Sustainable Communities: East Asian, North American and European Perspectives on Managing Urban Regions* with André Sorensen and Peter Marcotullio. From January 2001 to December 2004, she was the chair of the editorial board of *Plan Canada*.

Planning consultant and adjunct professor at the UBC School of Community and Regional Planning, **Doug Aberley** PhD MCIP edited *Boundaries of Home: Mapping for Local Empowerment* and *Futures by Design: The Practice of Ecological Planning*.

Donald Aubrey MCIP AACIP is a senior policy advisor for Parks Canada at Wood Buffalo National Park in Fort Smith. He was a community planner for the NWT Department of Municipal and Community Affairs from 1991 to 1998.

Larry Beasley FCIP was codirector of planning for the City of Vancouver until 2006, and adjunct professor in the School of Community and Regional Planning at the University of British Columbia. In 2004, he became a member of the Order of Canada.

Susan Berlin was the coordinator of the Canadian Healthy Communities Project, which operated from 1988 to 1991. She now lives on Saltspring Island, British Columbia, and works as an independent social policy consultant and writer.

Joe Berridge FCIP RPP is a partner with Urban Strategies in Toronto. He is currently working on waterfront and downtown projects in Toronto, London, Manchester, and New York.

John Bianchin, former project manager for Sustainable Systems, an Oshawa-based consulting firm which developed and administered water efficiency initiatives for Durham Region, is a market analyst for the Liquor Control Board of Ontario.

Pamela Blais MCIP RPP is principal of Metropole Consultants, a Toronto-based planning company. Her work assists public- and private-sector clients to identify and understand urban change and to develop effective response strategies.

Formerly vice-chair of the PEI Regulatory and Appeals Commission, **John L Blakney** became the executive director of the Maritime Provinces Racing Commission in 2001; in 2004, was appointed CEO of the Ontario Racing Commission.

Larry S Bourne FRSC MCIP RPP is professor of geography and planning, and director of the graduate planning program, at the University of Toronto. His research focuses on growth in the Canadian urban system.

Kevin Brooks graduated with a master of planning from Dalhousie University and is a planner/urban designer with Terrain Group in Bedford, Nova Scotia.

Meyer Burstein, former executive head of the Metropolis Project, an international project to provide policy makers with research-based advice on managing migration and diversity issues in cities, works as an international policy consultant.

Wayne Caldwell MCIP RPP is associate professor in the School of Environmental Design and Rural Development, University of Guelph, and also works with Huron County's Department of Planning and Development in Goderich, Ontario.

Andrew Curran graduated with a master of planning from Dalhousie University, Halifax. A longer version of his article won the Association of Canadian University Planning Programs student paper prize at the 2005 CIP conference in Calgary.

Michael Dear MCIP is professor of geography and planning at the University of Southern California and honorary professor at the Bartlett School, University College London. *The Postmodern Condition* further develops his ideas.

Marc Denhez, author of *The Canadian Home, Heritage Strategy Planning Handbook*, and *Capitalizing on Heritage, Arts & Culture*, is an Ottawa-based lawyer and policy advisor, who was appointed to the Ontario Municipal Board in 2004.

As a graduate student at the University of Calgary, **Mayja Embleton** examined community safety audits in Calgary. She later worked as the safety audit coordinator for the Action Committee Against Violence.

Rowan Faludi MCIP RPP is the principal of Urbanmetrics, a Toronto consulting firm. He specializes in urban economic analysis, market analysis, economic impact, and financial impact studies.

David Farley, a designer and retired professor of the schools of Urban Planning and Architecture at McGill University, has a keen interest in "erogenous zoning."

Pierre Filion MCIP RPP is a professor at the School of Planning, University of Waterloo. He is the coeditor of *Canadian Cities in Transition* (3rd ed) with Trudi Bunting.

In 1986, **John Forester** was visiting professor in planning at MIT, and a research fellow at the Lincoln Institute. He is now professor of city and regional planning at Cornell University, working on a book on ways that planners handle public disputes.

Avi Friedman is the director of the Affordable Homes Architecture program at McGill, and codesigner of the Grow Home. He is the author of several books, including *The Grow Home* and *The Adaptable House*.

In 1992, **Gordon W Fulton** was an Ottawa-based consultant with international experience in downtown revitalization. In 2002, he served as project manager for Parks Canada's *Standards and Guidelines for the Conservation of Historic Places in Canada*.

Andrea Gabor MCIP is an urban planner with a practical understanding of the forces that shape the context for planning and development in our cities. She is a founding partner of Urban Strategies in Toronto.

Annick Germain is professor at the Institut national de la recherche scientifique-urbanisation, culture et société in Montreal. With Damaris Rose, she wrote *Montreal: The Quest for a Metropolis*.

Thomas Gunton is professor in the School of Resource and Environmental Management at Simon Fraser University, and former deputy minister for two government departments in British Columbia (Cabinet Policy Development; Environment, Lands and Parks).

Macklin Hancock MCIP RPP studied at Guelph and then Harvard before designing the famous new community of Don Mills. He worked as a planning consultant with Project Planning. In 2003, he received an honorary degree from the University of Guelph.

Lynda Hayward completed her PhD in planning at the University of Waterloo, focusing on planning for an aging population. She has since become the senior program coordinator for the Community Care Research Centre at McMaster University.

Susan Haid MCIP CSLA is manager of sustainable community development with the District of North Vancouver. She was previously senior environmental planner with the Greater Vancouver Regional District, Policy and Planning Department.

Sue Hendler MCIP RPP teaches in the School of Urban and Regional Planning at Queen's University. She has studied planning and ethics and feminist approaches to planning, and was active in the healthy communities movement in Kingston in the 1990s.

Fern Hietkamp MCIP has worked as a land use planner and integrated coastal management planner (Fisheries and Oceans Canada) and a strategic planner (Indian and Northern Affairs). She currently works in operational planning (National Energy Board).

Heidi Hoernig is a doctoral candidate in the School of Planning, University of Waterloo. Her current research interests include planning for diversity, urban geographies of immigration and religion, downtown revitalization, and social issues in planning.

Sandy James MCIP is the greenways planner for the City of Vancouver and works to develop streets for pedestrians and cyclists, where cars have low priority. She is also a master gardener and works on special projects between the city and the community.

Reg Lang FCIP RPP was a professor in the Faculty of Environmental Studies at York University and frequent contributor to *Plan Canada*. Now professor emeritus and life/work coach, he can be reached via his website http://www.reglang.ca.

Glenda Laws taught geography at McMaster before becoming associate professor of geography at Penn State University. She died suddenly in 1996, leaving a legacy of work on social justice and planning to inspire others.

Michael Lazarowich is associate professor emeritus in the School of Planning at the University of Waterloo. His expertise is in community and economic development, elderly housing and support services, and granny-flat implementation.

Robert Lehman MCIP RPP is the president of Meridian Planning consultants and lives in Barrie, Ontario. In winter 2007, he is planner in residence at the University of Waterloo.

Hok-Lin Leung MCIP RPP is professor and director of the School of Urban and Regional Planning, Queen's University, Kingston, Ontario. His research interests include land use and infrastructure, and planning in China.

A founder of Urban Strategies in Toronto, **Frank Lewinberg** FCIP focuses on the integration of design and regulation. He helped to create a zoning bylaw for the Oak Park Community in Oakville, designed along new urbanism principles.

David Ley holds the Canada Research Chair of Geography at the University of British Columbia. He is writing *Millionaire Migrants,* a study of wealthy East Asian immigrants to Canada.

Doug MacDonald MCIP is a planner with the City of Calgary's Planning and Building Department.

Paul Mackey OUQ MCIP, former safety research officer for the Ministère des transports du Québec, now works with Safestreet (Ruesécure) Inc.

In 1985, **Stanley Makuch** was associate dean, Faculty of Law, University of Toronto and Professor of Law and Planning. A partner with Cassels Brock Lawyers in Toronto, he is the author of *Canadian Municipal and Planning Law.*

Nancy Marshall MCIP MPIA worked in government and in the private sector in Alberta before pursuing a PhD in

Australia. She now teaches planning and urban development, at the University of New South Wales in Sydney.

Judith Maxwell retired in 2006 as President of Canadian Policy Research Networks, a think tank based on networks of policy advisors she founded in 1995. A member of the Order of Canada, she was chair of the Economic Council of Canada from 1985 to 1992.

Ann McAfee FCIP was codirector of planning for the City of Vancouver until 2006. She received a PhD in planning from the University of British Columbia in 1975 and has since lectured and practised planning in Vancouver.

Wayne McEachern MCIP RPP has been a planner for local, regional, and provincial governments and is manager of policy planning/urban design for the City of Vaughan, Ontario.

Constable **Tom McKay** is attached to the Peel Regional Police Crime Prevention Services, where he implements CPTED concepts. He is the founding chair of CPTED Ontario.

Grant Moore is a graduate of the University of Western Ontario and holds a master of urban and regional planning degree from Queen's University, Kingston, Ontario.

Keith Nicol is associate professor of environmental studies and geography at Sir Wilfred Grenfell College, Memorial University, Corner Brook, Newfoundland & Labrador. His current research focuses on adventure tourism and outdoor recreation.

Andrei Nicolai MCIP is an urban designer and a partner in Sandalack & Nicolai Landscape Architecture, Urban Design and Planning in Calgary.

Judy Oberlander is the former director of the City Program at Simon Fraser University and currently director of development at the Jewish Family Service Agency in Vancouver.

Gary Paget continues to try to resolve complex policy issues and intergovernmental relations in a turbulent environment as executive director for governance and structure, Ministry of Community Services in British Columbia.

Norman Pressman MCIP RPP is professor emeritus of planning and urban design at the University of Waterloo. He is the author of *Northern Cityscape: Linking Design to Climate.*

Serving six terms on Vancouver city council, **Gordon Price** also sat on the board of the Greater Vancouver Regional District and the Greater Vancouver Transportation Authority. He is currently the director of the City Program at Simon Fraser University.

Mohammad Qadeer FCIP RPP is professor emeritus of urban and regional planning at Queen's University. His current research on urban policies for multicultural cities drew him to "retire" in Toronto, where he is adjunct professor of planning at Ryerson University.

Dr William E Rees, human ecologist, ecological economist, and originator of the globally-recognized ecological footprint concept, has taught ecological planning at UBC's School of Community and Regional Planning since 1969.

Until he retired, **Nigel Richardson** FCIP RPP was a consultant in land use policy, with particular interests in sustainable development and environmental policy. A former editor of *Plan Canada*, he frequently contributed to discussions about Canadian planning.

Richard Roberts is an adjunct professor in the Faculty of Environmental Design at the University of Calgary and the president of Praxis Inc. in Calgary.

Beverly A Sandalack CSLA MCIP is associate professor in the Faculty of Environmental Design at the University of Calgary, where she is coordinator of urban design. She is partner in the consulting firm Sandalack & Nicolai.

Leonie Sandercock's research emphasizes sociocultural issues. In 2001, she joined the faculty of the School of Community and Regional Planning at the University of British Columbia. Her latest book is *Cosmopolis 2: Mongrel Cities of the 21st Century*.

Louis Sauer, FAIA Emeritus, is an American architect who worked as the director of urban design for Daniel Arbour and Associates in Montreal. He designed Bois Franc, while Daniel Arbour and Associates devised the master plan.

Mark Seasons MCIP RPP is associate professor of planning at the University of Waterloo and a past president of the Canadian Institute of Planners.

Julie Seelig MCIP AICP is a writer and planning consultant in Vancouver and in the UK.

Michael Y Seelig MCIP AICP is professor emeritus in the School of Community and Regional Planning at the University of British Columbia.

Barry Smith worked for the BC Provincial Agricultural Land Commission, where he coordinated the Strengthening Farming Program. He then worked as a planner with the BC Ministry of Agriculture, Food and Fisheries prior to retirement.

In 1994, **David Lewis Stein** was a *Toronto Star* urban affairs columnist, often writing about planning issues.

Sinisa (Sonny) Tomic MCIP is a senior urban designer with the City of Calgary and a coauthor of the Hamilton Urban Braille System. A keen promoter of urban design, he is a member of the CIP National Urban Design Initiative.

Kasia Tota is a planner with the Halifax Regional Municipality. The paper summarizes the findings of her master's thesis at Dalhousie University.

A recent graduate of Dalhousie University, **Leslie Tse** is an accomplished cartoonist and an emergency management specialist with SAIC Canada in Halifax.

Glenn Tunnock MCIP RPP MPA is president of Tunnock Consulting Ltd. in Perth, which provides community planning and municipal restructuring services to municipalities and planning boards in Ontario.

Jeffrey P Ward BDEP is a consulting land use and transportation planner with Delphi-MRC in Halifax. He works throughout Atlantic Canada.

Cam Watson CMC is principal of the land economics firm CN Watson and Associates Ltd. in Mississauga, which carries out most consulting studies on development charges, building permit fees, water and sewer rates, and fiscal impacts in Ontario.

Gerda R Wekerle MCIP RPP is a professor of environmental studies, York University. Her current research is on sprawl, growth, and nature. Her article in this book is based on *Safe Cities: Guidelines for Planning, Design and Management*.

Mark N Wexler PhD is professor of applied ethics in the Faculty of Business Administration at Simon Fraser University and author of *Leadership in Context*.

Ian Wight MCIP is associate professor and head of city planning at the University of Manitoba. His research interests include the development of integral planning praxis and such applications as spiral dynamics.

Jeanne M Wolfe FClP worked as a planner for CMHC, the City of Montreal, the Quebec Department of Municipal Affairs, and the private sector before serving as director of the School of Urban Planning, McGill University. She is now professor emerita.

Mary Ellen Wood is a recent graduate of the master of planning program at Dalhousie University. She is a land use planner for Rudy and Associates in Orillia, Ontario.

In 1994, **Stanley Yip** was a planner and urban designer with the planning division of Marshall Macklin Monaghan Limited in Thornhill, Ontario.

Raymond Young LLB MCIP is a partner with Lidstone Young Anderson in Vancouver and an adjunct professor with the Faculty of Law at the University of British Columbia. In 2003, he was a Fulbright senior scholar.

Robert Young BArch MES is a Web user-interface designer and developer with Blue North Strategies, based in Guelph, Ontario.

List of Acronyms

ALR	Agricultural land reserve
ATM	Automated teller machine
BTU	British thermal units
CBC	Canadian Broadcasting Corporation
CDA	Community development area
CIP	Canadian Institute of Planners
CMA	Census metropolitan area
CMHC	Canada Mortgage and Housing Corporation
CPTED	Crime prevention through environmental design
DFO	Department of Fisheries and Oceans
ESA	Environmentally sensitive areas
GIS	Geographic or geospatial information systems
GST	Goods and Services Tax
GTA	Greater Toronto Area
GVRD	Greater Vancouver Regional District
IBM	International Business Machines (IBM Corporation)
ITT	Information and telecommunications technology
NIMBY	Not in my backyard syndrome (residents protesting unwanted land uses)
NIP	Neighbourhood improvement program
RRAP	Residential Rehabilitation Assistance Program
SUV	Sport utility vehicle
TAC	Transportation Association of Canada
TTC	Toronto Transit Commission
UBC	University of British Columbia
UK	United Kingdom
UN	United Nations
US	United States of America

Index

E

F

Lucy, W., 84
Lunenburg, Nova Scotia, 314, 315
Lutsel K'e, Northwest Territories, 333
Lynch, Kevin, 191

M

Maclaren, V. W., 237
Macro level of neotraditional movement, 195
Mad Max (film), 137
Main Street Canada program, 326–328
Major pathways, 204, 205
Manitoba:
    gated communities in, 228, 229
    private roads legislation in, 309
Manual for Setting Speed Limits on Municipal Road Networks, 299
Manual of Geometric Design Standards for Canadian Roads and Streets, 308
Marginal costs, average *vs.*, 362
Maritime provinces, 22, 23
Market principles, 51
Markham, Ontario, 173, 246–248
    new urbanism in, 376
    zoning bylaws in, 353
Marsh, Leonard, 33
Martin, L., 9
Marxian theory, 56
Massage parlours, 344, 345
Master plans, 24, 38, 51
Mawson, Thomas, 30, 193
McGill University, 357
McKenzie Towne (Calgary), 194–195
    and Duany Plater-Zyberk Associates, 186
    new urbanism in, 9, 17
    problems in, 187
    prominence of, 376
McMaster University, 203
Media sensationalism, 222
Mediation, 80, 122
Megacities, 236
Megalopolis unbound, 189
Membership warehouse clubs, 277–279
Metro Action Committee on Public Violence Against Women and Children, 223, 225
Metro Toronto, 35
Metropolis Project, 168
Metropolitan Toronto Corporation, 46–47, 84, 86
Metropolitan Toronto Plan–Recommended Transportation Plan, 292
Metropolitan Vancouver, 65–66
Michael, D. N., 146, 147
Micro level of neotraditional movement, 195
Microclimatic planning, 202
Middle-size downtowns, 372–375

Migration:
    of aging population, 163
    and politics of multicultural citizenship, 93
    of workers in Depression Era, 32
Mill Woods (Edmonton), 34
Millet, Alberta, 263
Ministry of Natural Resources, 271, 272
Ministry of State for Urban Affairs, 35, 64
Minor pathways, 205
Mintzberg, H., 145
Mississaugas of the New Credit, 330
Mitlin, D., 237
Mobility Street Master Plan, 205
Modernist paradigm, 91
Mohr, P., 247–249
Montgomery, L. M., 150
Montgomery Village (Orangeville), 353
Montmagny, Quebec, 305
Montreal, Quebec:
    as economic hub, 22
    immigrants in, 168, 170–172
    redevelopment in, 343
    regional planning in, 55
    sex businesses in, 346
    street design in, 305
    working class conditions in, 22
Moore, P. W., 24
Morell and Nichols, 30
Morley, D., 144
Morocco, 171
Morris, William, 137
Morrison Common (Oakville, Ontario), 353
Mosques, 173
Mount Pearl (Newfoundland), 376
Multicultural literacy, 94–95
Multiculturalism, 172–175
    defined, 172–173
    as government policy, 8
    issues in, 175–178
    and pluralistic planning, 174–175
    and reconstructing common institutions, 175
    and urban development, 173–174
Multiculturalism Act, 173
Multiethnic neighbourhoods, 171–172
Multiple futures, 149
Multiple-use modules, 246, 247
Mumford, Lewis, 290
Municipal government:
    powers of, 339–340
    reform of, 23
Municipal Government Act (Nova Scotia), 309
Municipal planner's approach to planning, 13
Munro, Alice, 68
Mutual learning, 59, 70
Mutualistic community, 85
Myles, J., 241